ANTHROPOLOGY

THE
EXPLORATION
OF HUMAN DIVERSITY

GREENLAND
(Den)

ICELAND

CANADA

NORWAY SWEDEN FINLAND
ES
LAT
LITH
DENMARK
IRELAND UNITED POLAND BELA
UNITED STATES KINGDOM GERMANY
OF AMERICA NETH CZECH
BEL AUS HUNG ROM
FRANCE S YUG
ITALY M B-H BULG
VATICAN ALB
PORTUGAL SPAIN GREECE
MEXICO GIBRALTAR MALTA
TUNISIA
MOROCCO
BERMUDA
WESTERN SAHARA ALGERIA LIBYA
BAHAMAS
CUBA DOMINICAN
REPUBLIC MAURITANIA MALI NIGER CHAD
BELIZE St. KITTS ANTIGUA
GUATEMALA HONDURAS NEVIS & BARBUDA CAPE
EL SALVADOR JAMAICA HAITI PUERTO GUADELOUPE (Fr) VERDE SENEGAL BURKINA NIGERIA
NICARAGUA RICO (U.S.) DOMINICA GAMBIA FASO
COSTA RICA MARTINIQUE (Fr) GUINEA-BISSAU GUINEA BENIN CAR
VENEZUELA ST. LUCIA SIERRA LEONE COTE D'
PANAMA GUYANA ST. VINCENT & BARBADOS IVOIRE GHANA
COLOMBIA SURINAME GRENADINES LIBERIA TOGO CAMEROON
FRENCH GRENADA EQUATORIAL GUINEA GABON
GUIANA (Fr) TRINIDAD SAO TOME & PRINCIPE CONGO ZAIRE
ECUADOR & TOBAGO

PACIFIC
OCEAN
PERU BRAZIL ANGOLA

BOLIVIA NAMIBIA BOTSWANA

CHILE PARAGUAY SOUTH
AFRICA

URUGUAY

CURRENTLY RECOGNIZED ARGENTINA
SOVEREIGN STATES *1995*
uninterrupted independence since:

	1990–1993
	1960–1989
	1940–1959
	1915–1939
	1800–1914
	pre–1800
	occupied and dependent territories or other anomalies
	privileged zone: extended economic zone or exclusive fishing zone *schematic*

FALKLAND
ISLANDS (UK)

Sources: *Statesman's Year-Book 1993–94;*
U.S. State Department; press reports.

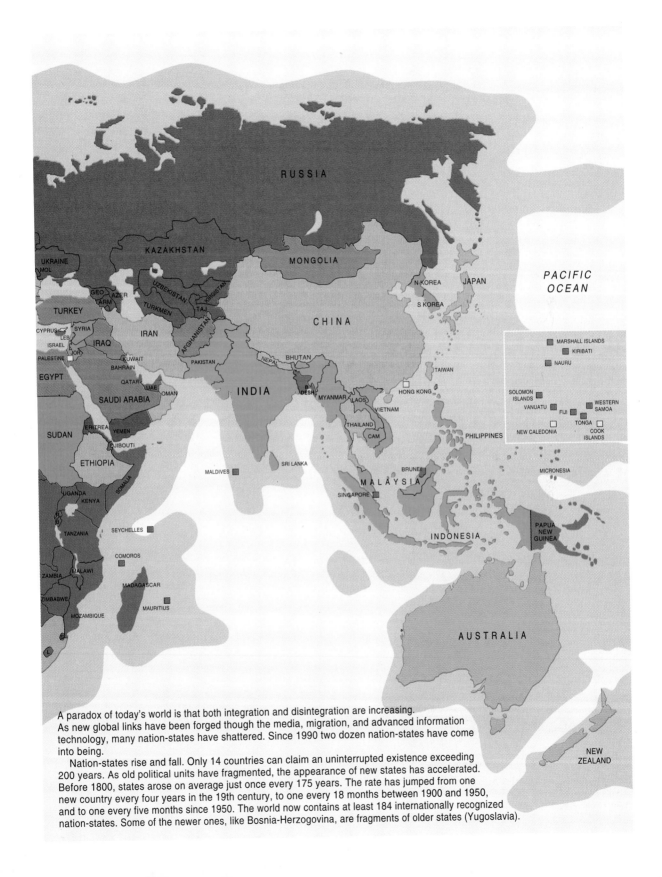

A paradox of today's world is that both integration and disintegration are increasing.
As new global links have been forged though the media, migration, and advanced information technology, many nation-states have shattered. Since 1990 two dozen nation-states have come into being.

Nation-states rise and fall. Only 14 countries can claim an uninterrupted existence exceeding 200 years. As old political units have fragmented, the appearance of new states has accelerated. Before 1800, states arose on average just once every 175 years. The rate has jumped from one new country every four years in the 19th century, to one every 18 months between 1900 and 1950, and to one every five months since 1950. The world now contains at least 184 internationally recognized nation-states. Some of the newer ones, like Bosnia-Herzogovina, are fragments of older states (Yugoslavia).

SEVENTH EDITION

ANTHROPOLOGY
THE
EXPLORATION
OF HUMAN DIVERSITY

SEVENTH EDITION

ANTHROPOLOGY
THE
EXPLORATION
OF HUMAN DIVERSITY

Conrad Phillip Kottak
The University of Michigan

THE McGRAW-HILL COMPANIES, INC.
New York   St. Louis   San Francisco   Auckland   Bogotá
Caracas   Lisbon   London   Madrid   Mexico City   Milan   Montreal
New Delhi   San Juan   Singapore   Sydney   Tokyo   Toronto

McGraw-Hill

A Division of The **McGraw·Hill** *Companies*

CULTURAL ANTHROPOLOGY:
THE EXPLORATION OF HUMAN DIVERSITY

Acknowledgments appear on pp. 513-517, and on this page by
reference.

This book is printed on acid-free paper.

1 2 3 4 5 6 7 8 9 0 DOW DOW 9 0 9 8 7 6

ISBN 0-07-036938-0

This book was set in Palatino by GTS Graphics.
The editors were Nancy Blaine, Jill Gordon, and Ira C. Roberts;
the design manager was Joseph A. Piliero;
the production supervisor was Kathryn Porzio.
The photo editor was Barbara Salz.
The cover was designed by Joan Greenfield.
R.R. Donnelley & Sons Company was printer and binder.

ABOUT THE AUTHOR

Conrad Phillip Kottak (A.B. Columbia College, 1963; Ph.D. Columbia University, 1966) is Professor and Chair of the Department of Anthropology at the University of Michigan, where he has taught since 1968. In 1991 he was honored for his teaching by the University and the state of Michigan. In 1992 he received an excellence in teaching award from the College of Literature, Sciences, and the Arts of the University of Michigan.

Professor Kottak has done field work in cultural anthropology in Brazil (since 1962), Madagascar (since 1966), and the United States. His general interests are in the processes by which local cultures are incorporated-and resist incorporation-into larger systems. This interest links his earlier work on ecology and state formation in Africa and Madagascar to his more recent research on global change, national and international culture, and the mass media.

The second edition of Kottak's case study *Assault on Paradise: Social Change in a Brazilian Village,* based on his field work in Arembepe, Bahia, Brazil, from 1962 through 1992, was published in 1992 by McGraw-Hill. In a project during the 1980s, collaborating with Brazilian and North American researchers, Kottak blended ethnography and survey research in studying "Television's Behavioral Effects in Brazil." That research is the basis of Kottak's book *Prime-Time Society: An Anthropological Analysis of Television and Culture* (Wadsworth 1990)-a comparative study of the nature and impact of television in Brazil and the United States.

Kottak's other books include *The Past in the Present: History, Ecology and Cultural Variation in Highland Madagascar* (1980), *Researching American Culture: A Guide for Student Anthropologists* (1982) (both University of Michigan Press), and *Madagascar: Society and History* (1986) (Carolina Academic Press). His *Mirror for Humanity: A Concise Introduction to Cultural Anthropology* was published by McGraw-Hill Overture Books in 1996.

Conrad Kottak's articles have appeared in academic journals including *American Anthropologist, Journal of Anthropological Research, American Ethnologist, Ethnology, Human Organization,* and *Luso-Brazilian Review.* He has also written for more popular journals, including *Transaction/SOCIETY, Natural History, Psychology Today,* and *General Anthropology.*

In current and recent research projects, Kottak and his colleagues have investigated the emergence of ecological awareness in Brazil, the social context of deforestation in Madagascar, and popular participation in economic development planning in northeastern Brazil.

Conrad Kottak appreciates comments about his textbook from professors and students. He can be readily reached by E-mail at the following Internet address:

ckottak@umich.edu

To my mother,
Mariana Kottak Roberts

CONTENTS IN BRIEF

List of Boxes   *xxiii*

Preface   *xxv*

1   THE SCOPE OF ANTHROPOLOGY   1
2   FIELD METHODS   19
3   CULTURE   35
4   ETHNICITY AND ETHNIC RELATIONS   49
5   HUMAN BIOLOGICAL DIVERSITY AND THE RACE CONCEPT   69
11 ADAPTIVE STRATEGIES AND ECONOMIC SYSTEMS   215
12 THE POLITICAL SYSTEMS OF BANDS AND TRIBES   237
13 CHIEFDOMS AND STATES   257
14 KINSHIP AND DESCENT   279
15 MARRIAGE   297
16 GENDER   315
17 RELIGION   335
18 PERSONALITY AND WORLDVIEW   353
19 LANGUAGE AND COMMUNICATION   371
20 THE WORLD SYSTEM, INDUSTRIALISM, AND
    STRATIFICATION   393
21 APPLIED ANTHROPOLOGY   409
22 DEVELOPMENT AND INNOVATION   425
23 CULTURAL EXCHANGE AND SURVIVAL   443

APPENDIX: AMERICAN POPULAR CULTURE   465

Bibliography   481

Internet Resources: Selected Reference Sites in Anthropology
   from the World Wide Web   507

Acknowledgments   513

Indexes   519
   Author Index   521
   Subject Index   525

CONTENTS

	List of Boxes	*xxiii*
	Preface	*xxv*
CHAPTER 1	**THE SCOPE OF ANTHROPOLOGY**	1
	ADAPTATION, VARIATION, AND CHANGE	2
	GENERAL ANTHROPOLOGY	3
	BOX: Even Anthropologists Get Culture Shock	4
	THE SUBDISCIPLINES OF ANTHROPOLOGY	5
	Cultural Anthropology	5
	Archaeological Anthropology	7
	Biological, or Physical, Anthropology	8
	Linguistic Anthropology	9
	Applied Anthropology	10
	ANTHROPOLOGY AND OTHER ACADEMIC FIELDS	11
	BOX: Margaret Mead: Public Anthropologist	12
	Cultural Anthropology and Sociology	12
	Anthropology, Political Science, and Economics	13
	Anthropology and the Humanities	14
	Anthropology and Psychology	14
	Anthropology and History	15
CHAPTER 2	**FIELD METHODS**	19
	ETHNOGRAPHY: ANTHROPOLOGY'S DISTINCTIVE STRATEGY	20
	ETHNOGRAPHIC TECHNIQUES	20
	Observation	20
	Participant Observation	21
	Conversation, Interviewing, and Interview Schedules	21
	The Genealogical Method	23
	Well-Informed Informants	24
	Life Histories	24

Emic and Etic Research Strategies   24
Problem-Orientated Ethnography   24
Longitudinal Research   25

BOX: The Evolution of Ethnography   26

SURVEY RESEARCH   27

DIFFERENCES BETWEEN SURVEY RESEARCH AND
ETHNOGRAPHY   29

ANTHROPOLOGICAL RESEARCH IN COMPLEX SOCIETIES   29
Urban Anthropology   30
Anthropology in Complex Societies   31

CHAPTER 3   CULTURE   35

WHAT IS CULTURE?   36
Culture Is Learned   36
Culture Is Symbolic   36
Culture Seizes Nature   37
Culture Is General and Specific   37
Culture Is All-Encompassing   37

BOX: Touching, Affection, Love, and Sex   38

Culture Is Shared   38
Culture Is Patterned   40
People Use Culture Creatively   41
Culture Is Adaptive and Maladaptive   41
Levels of Culture   41
Ethnocentrism and Cultural Relativism   42

UNIVERSALITY, PARTICULARITY, AND GENERALITY   43
Universality   43
Particularity   43
Generality   44

MECHANISMS OF CULTURAL CHANGE   45

CHAPTER 4   ETHNCITY AND ETHNIC RELATIONS   49

ETHNIC GROUPS AND ETHNICITY   50
Status Shifting   51

ETHNIC GROUPS, NATIONS, AND NATIONALITIES   52
Nationalities and Imagined Communities   52

ETHNIC TOLERANCE AND ACCOMMODATION 52
Assimilation 53
The Plural Society 54
Multiculturalism and the Ethnic Identity 54

BOX: Ethnic Nationalism Run Wild 56

ROOTS OF ETHNIC CONFLICT 59
Prejudice and Discrimination 59
Chips in the Mosaic 60
Aftermaths of Oppression 62

CHAPTER 5   HUMAN BIOLOGICAL DIVERSITY AND
THE RACE CONCEPT 69

SOCIAL RACE 71
Hypodescent: Race in the United States 71
Not Us: Race in Japan 72
Phenotype and Fluidity: Race in Brazil 75

RACE: A DISCREDITED CONCEPT IN BIOLOGY 77
Explaining Skin Color 79

STRATIFICATION AND "INTELLIGENCE" 80

BOX: Culture, Biology, and Sports 82

CHAPTER 11   ADAPTIVE STRATEGIES AND ECONOMIC SYSTEMS 215

ADAPTIVE STRATEGIES 216

FORAGING 216
Correlates of Foraging 217

CULTIVATION 218
Horticulture 219
Agriculture 219
The Cultivation Continuum 221
Implications of Intensification 222

PASTORALISM 222

MODES OF PRODUCTION 223
Organization of Production in Nonindustrial Societies 223
Means of Production 223
Alienation and Impersonality in Industrial Economies 225

ECONOMIZING AND MAXIMIZATION 226

Alternative Ends   226

BOX: Scarcity and the Betsileo   227

DISTRIBUTION, EXCHANGE   228
The Market Principle   228
Redistribution   228
Reciprocity   228
Coexistence of Exchange Principles   230

POTLATCHING   230

CHAPTER 12   THE POLITICAL SYSTEMS OF BANDS AND TRIBES   237

TYPES AND TRENDS   238

FORAGING BANDS   239

TRIBAL CULTIVATORS   241
Descent-Group Organization   241

BOX: The Great Forager Debate   242

The Village Head   243
Village Raiding   244
The "Big Man"   245
Segmentary Lineage Organization   246
Pantribal Sodalities, Associations, and Age Grades   248

PASTORALISTS   251

CHAPTER 13   CHIEFDOMS AND STATES   257

POLITICAL AND ECONOMIC SYSTEMS IN CHIEFDOMS   258

SOCIAL STATUS IN CHIEFDOMS   259

STATUS SYSTEMS IN CHIEFDOMS AND STATES   260

STATES   261
Population Control   261
Judiciary   262
Enforcement   263
Fiscal Systems   263

THE ORIGIN OF THE STATE   264
Hydraulic Systems   264
Ecological Diversity   264

Long-Distance Trade Routes 264
Population Growth, Warfare, and Environmental Circumscription 265

THE CHALLENGE OF THE STATE 266
The Role of Globalization, Transnationalism, and the Media 267
The Collapse of Mass Culture as a Challenge to the State 268
The New World Disorder 269
NGOs and Rights Movements 272
From State Formation to Government Decline 274

CHAPTER 14 KINSHIP AND DESCENT 279

KIN GROUPS AND KINSHIP CALCULATION 280
Biological Kin Types and Kinship Calculation 280

KIN GROUPS 281

THE NUCLEAR FAMILY 282
Industrialism, Stratification, and Family Organization 282
Recent Changes in North American Kinship Patterns 284
The Nuclear Family among Foragers 286

BOX: *Brady Bunch* Nirvana 287

TRIBAL SOCIAL ORGANIZATION 288
Lineages and Clans 288
Unilineal Descent Groups and Unilocal Residence 288
Flexibility in Descent-Group Organization 288

KINSHIP TERMINOLOGY 288
Kinship Terminology on the Parental Generation 289
Relevance of Kinship Terminology 292

CHAPTER 15 MARRIAGE 297

THE INCEST TABOO AND EXOGAMY 299

EXPLANATIONS FOR THE INCEST TABOO 301
Instinctive Horror 301
Biological Degeneration 302
Marry Out or Die Out 302

ENDOGAMY 302
Caste 303
Royal Incest 303

MARRIAGE IN TRIBAL SOCIETIES 303

IN THE NEWS: Anthropology Goes Looking for Love in All the
Old Places 304

Bridewealth 306
Durable Alliances 308

PLURAL MARRIAGES 308
Polygyny 309
Polyandry 310

CHAPTER 16 GENDER 315

GENDER ISSUES AMONG FORAGERS 317

IN THE NEWS: Masai Gender Roles 319

GENDER ISSUES AMONG HORTICULTURALISTS 320
Reduced Gender Stratification-Matrilineal, Uxorilocal Societies 320
Reduced Gender Stratification-Matrifocal Societies 322
Increased Gender Stratification - Patrilineal-Virilocal Societies 322
Etoro Homosexuality 323

GENDER ISSUES AMONG AGRICULTURALISTS 324

BOX: Hidden Women, Public Men-Public Women, Hidden Men 326

GENDER ISSUES AND INDUSTRIALISM 327
The Feminization of Poverty 329

WHAT DETERMINES VARIATION IN GENDER ISSUES? 330

CHAPTER 17 RELIGION 335

ORIGINS, FUNCTIONS, AND EXPRESSIONS OF RELIGION 336
Animism 336
Mana and Taboo 336
Magic and Religion 337
Anxiety, Control, Solace 338
The Social Functions of Ritual Acts 338
Rites of Passage 338
Totems: Symbols of Society 340
The Nature of Ritual 341

ANALYSIS OF MYTH 341
Structural Analysis 341
Fairy Tales 342

BOX: Halloween: An American Ritual of Rebellion 343

IN THE NEWS: A Japanese Ritual of Rebellion   344

Secular Rituals   344

RELIGION AND CULTURE   345

RELGION AND CHANGE   346
Revitalization Movements   346

RELIGION AND CULTURAL ECOLOGY   347
The Adaptive Significance of Sacred Cattle in India   347
The Cultural Ecology of Ceremonial Feasts   348

CHAPTER 18   PERSONALITY AND WORLDVIEW   353

THE INDIVIDUAL AND CULTURE   354

PERSONALITY   356

EARLY CULTURE AND PERSONALITY RESEARCH   356
Margaret Mead: Child Training and Gender Roles   356
Ruth Benedict: Cultures as Individuals   357
National Character   357

BOX: Varieties of Human Sexuality   358

CROSS-CULTURAL STUDIES   359

IN THE NEWS: Making Room on the Couch for Culture   361

WORLDVIEW   364
Peasants and Limited Good   364
The (Sub)Culture of Poverty   365
The Protestant Ethic and Capitalism   366

CHAPTER 19   LANGUAGE AND COMMUNICATION   371

THE STRUCTURE OF LANGUAGE   372
Phonemes and Phones   372

TRANSFORMATIONAL-GENERATIVE GRAMMAR   373

LANGUAGE, THOUGHT, AND CULTURE   375
The Sapir-Whorf Hypothesis   375
Focal Vocabulary   375
Meaning   376

SOCIOLINGUISTICS 377
Linguistic Diversity in Nation-State 377

BOX: Jocks, Burnouts, and Runts 378

Gender Speech Contrasts 379
Stratification and Symbolic Domination 379

IN THE NEWS: Japan's Feminine Falsetto Falls Right Out of Favor 380

HISTORICAL LINGUISTICS 382

CYBERSPACE: A NEW REALM OF COMMUNICATION 383
Inequality in Cyberspace 383

IN THE NEWS: Using Modern Technology to Preserve Linguistic
Diversity 384

Elitism and Gatekeeping 387
Cyberspace and Social Reality 388

CHAPTER 20 **THE WORLD SYSTEM, INDUSTRIALISM, AND
STRATIFICATION** 393

THE EMERGENCE OF THE WORLD SYSTEM 394

INDUSTRIALIZATION 396
Causes of the Industrial Revolution 396

STRATIFICATION 397

BOX: The American Periphery 398

Open and Closed Class Systems 400

INDUSTRIAL AND NONINDUSTRIAL SOCIETIES
IN THE WORLD SYSTEM TODAY 402
The Effects of Industrialization on the World Systems 404

CHAPTER 21 **APPLIED ANTHROPOLOGY** 409

THEORY AND PRACTICE 410
Applied Anthropology and the Subdisciplines 410

ANTHROPOLOGY AND EDUCATION 411

URBAN ANTHROPOLOGY 412
Urban versus Rural 412

Urban Poverty and Homelessness   413

MEDICAL ANTHROPOLOGY   414

IN THE NEWS: AIDS and Gender in Africa   416

BOX: Spirit Possession in Malaysian Factories   418

CAREERS IN ANTHROPOLOGY   419

CHAPTER 22   DEVELOPMENT AND INNOVATION   425

DEVELOPMENT   426
The Brazilian Sisal Scheme   427
The Greening of Java   429
Equity   431
The Third World Talks Back   432
The Code of Ethics   433

STRATEGIES FOR INNOVATION   433
Overinnovation   434
Underdifferentiation   435
Third World Models and Culturally Appropriate Development   436

BOX: Culturally Appropriate Marketing   438

CHAPTER 23   CULTURAL EXCHANGE, CREATIVITY, AND SURVIVAL   443

PEOPLE IN MOTION   444
Postmodern Moments in the World System   445
Cultural Contact in Larger Systems   446

DOMINATION   447
Development and Environmentalism   447

BOX: Voices of the Rainforest   448

Religious Domination   449

RESISTANCE AND SURVIVAL   450
Weapons of the Weak   451

IN THE NEWS: "Things Have Happened to Me as in a Movie"   452

SYNCRETISMS, BLENDS, AND ACCOMMODATION   453
Cargo Cults   454
Cultural Imperialism, Stimulus Diffusion, and Creative Opposition   455

MAKING AND REMAKING CULTURE 457
Popular Culture 457
Indigenizing Popular Culture 457
A World System of Images 458
A Transnational Culture of Consumption 459

THE CONTINUANCE OF DIVERSITY 460

APPENDIX   **AMERCIAN POPULAR CULTURE** 465

ANTHROPOLOGISTS AND AMERICAN CULTURE 465

FOOTBALL 467

STAR TREK AS A SUMMATION OF DOMINANT CULTURAL THEMES 468

FANTASY FILMS AS MYTH 470

DISNEY MYTH AND RITUAL 472
A Pilgrimage to Walt Disney World 473
Within the Magic Kingdom 474

RECOGNIZING RELIGION 475

RITUALS AT McDONALD'S 476

ANTHROPOLOGY AND AMERICAN "POP" CULUTRE 478

Bibliography 481

Internet Resources: Selected Reference Sites in Anthropology from the World Wide Web 507

Acknowledgments 513

Indexes 519
Author Index 521
Subject Index 525

LIST OF BOXES

ISSUES BOXES

EVEN ANTHROPOLOGISTS GET CULTURE SHOCK	4
MARGARET MEAD: PUBLIC ANTHROPOLOGIST	12
THE EVOLUTION OF ETHNOGRAPHY	26
TOUCHING, AFFECTION, LOVE, AND SEX	38
ETHNIC NATIONALISM RUN WILD	56
CULTURE, BIOLOGY, AND SPORTS	82
SCARCITY AND THE BETSILEO	227
THE GREAT FORAGER DEBATE	242
BRADY BUNCH NIRVANA 287	
HIDDEN WOMEN, PUBLIC MEN-PUBLIC WOMEN, HIDDEN MEN	326
HALLOWEEN: AN AMERICAN RITUAL OF REBELLION	343
VARIETIES OF HUMAN SEXUALITY	358
JOCKS, BURNOUTS, AND RUNTS	378
THE AMERICAN PERIPHERY	398
SPIRIT POSSESSION IN MALAYSIAN FACTORIES	418
CULTURALLY APPROPRIATE MARKETING	438
VOICES OF THE RAINFOREST	448

IN THE NEWS BOXES

ANTHROPOLOGY GOES LOOKING FOR LOVE IN ALL THE OLD PLACES	304
MASAI GENDER ROLES	319
A JAPANESE RITUAL OF REBELLION	344
MAKING ROOM ON THE COUCH FOR CULTURE	361
JAPAN'S FEMININE FALSETTO FALLS RIGHT OUT OF FAVOR	380
USING MODERN TECHNOLOGY TO PRESERVE LINGUISTIC DIVERSITY	384
AIDS AND GENDER IN AFRICA	416
"THINGS HAVE HAPPENED TO ME AS IN A MOVIE"	452

PREFACE

Because anthropology, reflecting the world itself, seems to change at an increasing rate, the introductory text should not restrict itself to subject matter defined decades ago, ignoring the pervasive changes affecting the peoples, places, and topics traditionally studied by anthropologists. Accordingly, the seventh edition of *Anthropology: The Exploration of Human Diversity,* pays particular attention to the demise of the Soviet Union and its relevance to issues of ethnicity and nationalism, the growing significance of multiculturalism in North America, and anthropology's increasingly transnational, multilocal, and longitudinal perspectives.

On the other hand, rapid change notwithstanding, **anthropology has a core** that any competent introductory text must expose: anthropology's nature, scope, and roles as a science and as a humanities field. As a *science*, anthropology is a "systematic field of study or body of knowledge that aims, through experiment, observation, and deduction, to produce reliable explanations of phenomena, with reference to the material and physical world" (*Websters's New World Encyclopedia*, 1993, p. 937). Clyde Kluckhorn (1944) called anthropology "the science of human similarities and differences" (p. 9), and his statement of the need for such a field still stands: "Anthropology provides a scientific basis for dealing with the crucial dilemma of the world today: how can peoples of different appearance, mutually unintelligible languages, and dissimilar ways of life get along peaceably together?" (p. 9). Anthropology has complied an impressive body of knowledge, which this textbook attempts to introduce.

Anthropology is also a *humanities* field. Indeed, it is among the most humanistic of academic fields because of its fundamental respect for human diversity. Anthropologists listen to, record, and attempt to represent voices from a multitude of times, places, nations, and cultures. We hope to convince our students of the value of local knowledge, of diverse worldviews and perspectives. Bringing a comparative, cross-cultural, and nonelitist perspective to forms of creative expression, anthropology influences and is influenced by the humanities.

Because **no single or monolithic theoretical perspective** orients this book, instructors with a wide range of views and approaches may use it effectively. This edition deemphasizes the cultural evolutionary perspective that characterized certain chapters of past editions, especially the chapters on economic and political organization (Chapters 11-13). We know from history that states rise and fall, and we are currently seeing more weakness and failure than vitality and growth in government institutions. Anthropologists have tended to regard the strengthening of political institutions as a general process, but nation-states are increasingly challenged by information flows, nongovernmental organizations, identity politics, and economic features of a globalizing world. Contemporary events and processes have led me to reevaluate some of my previous assumptions about the evolution of political organization.

This new edition incorporates many suggestions from users of previous editions and prepublication reviewers of this one. The seventh edition contains new writing, updating in all chapters, and a few organizational changes. The entire book has been scanned into a computer, allowing me to scrutinize every word, sentence, paragraph, and caption, so as to attend closely to style, content, and organization. I've also checked the writing level and comprehensibility of each chapter using the computer program Grammatik. The final result, I hope, is a well organized, interesting, and user-friendly introduction to anthropology.

One change in the seventh edition is a **shortening** of virtually every chapter. I've noticed that, with past editions, as I considered new issues and followed suggestions, I tended to add without subtracting an equivalent amount of text. Every few editions I have to focus on evaluating and deleting material that is less central now than it used to be. I don't want the book to get so big that is becomes unwieldy or intimidates students. This edition is shorter than the last one.

Here are some specific changes made for the seventh edition: I shortened and combined material from chapters formerly called "Cultural Change and Adaptation" (Chapter 11 in the sixth edition) and "Economic Systems" (formerly 15) to make a single new chapter (11) entitled "Adaptive Strategies and Economic Systems." I moved the chapter on "The World System, Industrialism, and Stratification" (formerly 14) to a more logical position toward the end of the book (20). **The organization of this text is intended to cover core concepts and basics, while also discussing prominent current issues.** This edition concludes with four chapters especially relevant to anthropology today: "The World System, Industrialism, and Stratification" (20), "Applied Anthropology" (21), "Development and Innovation" (22), and "Cultural Exchange and Survival" (23).

Anthropology: The Exploration of Human Diversity, seventh edition, has four important chapters not consistently found in anthropology texts: "Ethnicity and Ethnic Relations" (4), "Human Biological Diversity and the Race Concept" (5), "Gender" (16), and "Cultural Exchange and Survival" (23). These and other chapters explore the nature, role, and preservation of biological, cultural, and linguistic diversity in the face of globalization.

One of my goals is to show how linkages in the modern world system have both strengthened and weakened old boundaries and distinctions. A sociopolitical paradox of today's world is that both integration and disintegration are increasing. New sections that address this phenomenon are those on "The Challenge to the State" in Chapter 13 ("Chiefdoms and States") and "Cyberspace: A New Realm of Communication" in Chapter 19 ("Language and Communication"). "The Challenge to the State" focuses on a apparent decline in the power and role of government, as news bases for union and division form throughout the world. One such basis is **identity politics,** involving shared culture, language, religion, or "race," rather than citizenship in a nation-state. A key feature of the state is its territorial basis, and territory is declining as a basis of identity, with the rise of multilocality and transnationalism.

The new section on cyberspace discusses the role of advanced information technology (AIT) in creating both unity and division, in that people are linked in both wider and narrower communication networks. Also discussed are issues of inequality in access to AIT, elitism and gatekeeping, and the relation between cyberspace and social reality.

I am pleased to have been one of the textbook authors chosen to participate in the Gender in the Curriculum Project of the American Anthropological Association. In that project I was paired with Yolanda Moses (current President of the Association), who commented extensively on, and met with me to discuss, the treatment of gender (in writing and in the photo program) in my texts *Anthropology: The Exploration of Human Diversity* and *Cultural Anthropology.* I continue to draw on the lessons I learned: gender issues are the focus of a separate chapter (16), but they are also considered throughout the text.

The following **annotated outline** summarizes, by chapter, the main changes in the seventh edition of *Anthropology: The Exploration of Human Diversity:*

Chapter
1. The Scope of Anthropology: **New** discussion of anthropology as a humanistic science, describing links between anthropology and the sciences, and humanities. Revised introductory section; the chapter has been shortened and simplified.
2. Field Methods: This chapter has been shortened and simplified
3. Culture: This chapter has been reorganized, with a **new** section (at the end) on "Mechanisms of Cultural Change." There is greater attention to the role of the individual in culture.
4. Ethnicity and Ethnic Relations: The chapter has been shortened, simplified, and updated, with **new** information on immigration to and immigrants in North America. There is an up-to-date Bosnia box.
5. Human Biological Diversity and the Race Concept: The section on skin color has been rewritten. Updating includes a discussion of arguments against those of Herrnstein and Murray in *The Bell Curve.*

6. Evolution, Genetics, and Biological Adaptation: This chapter has been updated.

7. The Primates: This chapter has been updated and shortened slightly, with a **new** In-the-News box on chimpanzee hunting and meat eating.

8. Early Hominids: This chapter has been updated, shortened, and thoroughly revised, with a **new** In-the-News box on bipedalism.

9. The Emergence of Modern Humans: This chapter has been updated and shortened, with a **new** In-the-News box on recent (1994) discovery of a spectacular cave painting site in southern France.

10. The Origin and Spread of Food Production: This chapter has been updated and shortened.

11. Adaptive Strategies and Economic Systems: This chapter is **new**; it combines material from Chapters 11 and 15 in the sixth edition.

12. The Political Systems of Bands and Tribes: This chapter has been updated and shortened.

13. Chiefdoms and States: This chapter has had a major revision. A substantial **new** section has been added (at the end), called **"The Challenge to the State."**

14. Kinship and Descent: This chapter has been updated and shortened.

15. Marriage: This chapter has been updated, shortened, and reorganized.

16. Gender: This chapter has been updated and shortened.

17. Religion: This chapter has been updated and shortened.

18. Personality and Worldview: This chapter has been updated and shortened, with a **new** In-the-News box on culture-bound psychological syndromes.

19. Language and Communication: This chapter has had a major revision. A substantial **new** section has been added called **"Cyberspace: A New Realm of Communication."**

20. The World System, Industrialism, and Stratification: This chapter has been updated and shortened.

21. Applied Anthropology: This chapter has been updated and shortened.

22. Development and Innovation: This chapter has been updated and shortened.

23. Cultural Exchange and Survival: This chapter has been updated and shortened.

Appendix

American Popular Culture: This chapter has been updated and shortened.

WHAT ABOUT DESIGN, PEDAGOGY, AND STUDY AIDS?

The McGraw-Hill staff and I pay careful attention to suggestions offered by users and reviewers for making this text visually clear and appealing. We've added new and up-to-date photos, charts, and other illustrations.

We've retained the pedagogical devices at the end of each chapter: **summary, study questions, a glossary** defining terms boldfaced in that chapter, and an up-to-date list of **suggested reading.** In addition, a complete **bibliography** and a new section on internet resources and World Wide Web sites appear at the end of the book.

The new **instructor's manual** contains a list of **free films** for adopters, organized by topic. (Order forms for the films are available from McGraw-Hill sales representatives.) The instructor's manual also contains a huge selection of multiple-choice, true-or-false, and essay questions. These are also available on diskette for use with the **computerized testmaker,** making it possible for instructors to generate entirely new tests from questions included on the diskette.

This seventh edition contains both **issues boxes** and several new **In-the-News boxes.** The latter describe recent discoveries (e.g., a cave painting site in southern France, new findings on chimpanzee hunting, new theories about the origin of bipedalism) or topics of anthropological relevance that are drawing increased public attention. Some boxes examine current events or debates; others are personal accounts of field experience, which add human feelings to the presentation of anthropology's subject matter. Many boxes illustrate a point by bringing in an example familiar to students from their enculturation or everyday experience.

Available for use with *Anthropology: The Exploration of Human Diversity,* seventh edition, is an **ethnographic case studies** book, *Culture Sketches,* by Professor Holly Peters-Golden. This supplement profiles several of the cultures discussed in this text. Dr. Peters-Golden has taught introductory anthropology at the University of Michigan, using my textbook, for several years.

ACKNOWLEDGEMENTS

I am grateful to my present and past colleagues at McGraw-Hill. I always enjoy working closely with Phil Butcher, McGraw-Hill's social science publisher, as I did on this edition. I thank Jill Gordon and Nancy Blaine, McGraw-Hill's recent and current anthropology editors, respectively, for their help. Sylvia Shepard, my former developmental editor, will also recognize her input from past editions.

I thank Ira C. Roberts for his efficient work as editing manager and for keeping everything moving on schedule. It's been a pleasure to work again with Barbara Salz, photo researcher, and Nancy Dyer, photo manager. I also thank Carole Berglie and Gretlyn Cline for copyediting and proofreading; Joseph Piliero for conceiving and executing the design; Kathryn Porzio for shepherding the manuscript through production; and Carl Leonard, marketing project manager.

I am grateful to the prepublication reviewers of *Anthropology: The Exploration of Human Diversity,* seventh edition: John W. Fox, Baylor University, Kathy T. Molohon, Laurentian University; and Susan J. Rasmussen, University of Houston. I was delighted by the enthusiasm expressed in their reviews.

I thank my colleagues and the many students who have read this text and who have sent me their comments, corrections, and suggestion - personally, through McGraw-Hill sales representatives, and, increasingly, via E-mail. Anyone-student or instructor-with access to the internet can contact me at the following address: **ckottak@umich.edu.**

As usual, my wife, Isabel Wagley Kottak, has offered me understanding, support, and inspiration during the preparation of this edition. I renew my dedication of this book to my mother, Mariana Kottak Roberts, for kindling my interest in the human condition, for reading and commenting on what I write, and for the insights about people and society she continues to provide.

After some 30 years of teaching, I have benefited from the knowledge, help, and advice of so many friends, colleagues, teaching assistants, and students that I can no longer fit their names into a short preface. I hope they know who they are and accept my thanks.

Since 1968 I've regularly taught Anthropology 101 ("Introduction to Anthropology") to a class of 500-600 students, with the help of 7 to 12 teaching assistants each time. Feedback from students, teaching assistants, and my fellow "Introductory Anthropology" instructors at Michigan (Holly Peters-Golden, David Brawn, and William Meltzer) keeps me up-to-date on the interests, needs, and views of the people for whom this text is written. I continue to believe that effective textbooks are rooted in enthusiasm and in practice - in the enjoyment of one's own teaching experience. I hope that this product of my experience will continue to be helpful to others.

Conrad Phillip Kottak

ANTHROPOLOGY
THE
EXPLORATION
OF HUMAN DIVERSITY

C H A P T E R 1

THE SCOPE OF ANTHROPOLOGY

ADAPTATION, VARIATION, AND CHANGE

GENERAL ANTHROPOLOGY

Box: Even Anthropologists Get Culture Shock

THE SUBDISCIPLINES OF ANTHROPOLOGY
Cultural Anthropology
Archaeological Anthropology
Biological, or Physical, Anthropology
Linguistic Anthropology

Applied Anthropology

ANTHROPOLOGY AND OTHER ACADEMIC FIELDS

Box: Margaret Mead: Public Anthropologist

Cultural Anthropology and Sociology
Anthropology, Political Science, and Economics
Anthropology and the Humanities
Anthropology and Psychology
Anthropology and History

Humans are among the world's most adaptable animals. In the Andes of South America, people awaken in villages 17,500 feet above sea level and then trek 1,500 feet higher to work in tin mines. Tribes in the Australian desert worship animals and discuss philosophy. People survive malaria in the tropics. Men have walked on the moon. The model of the *Starship Enterprise* in Washington's Smithsonian Institution symbolizes the desire to "seek out new life and civilizations, to boldly go where no one has gone before." Wishes to know the unknown, control the uncontrollable, and bring order to chaos find expression among all peoples. Adaptability and flexibility are basic human attributes, and human diversity is the subject matter of anthropology.

Students are often surprised by the breadth of anthropology, which is a uniquely comparative and **holistic** science. It studies the whole of the human condition: past, present, and future; biology, society, language, and culture. Most people think anthropologists study fossils and nonindustrial cultures, and many of them do. But anthropology is much more than the study of nonindustrial peoples. It is a comparative science that examines all societies, ancient and modern, simple and complex. Most of the other social sciences tend to focus on a single society, usually an industrial nation such as the United States or Canada. Anthropology, however, offers a unique cross-cultural perspective, constantly comparing the customs of one society with those of others.

People share **society**—organized life in groups—with other animals. Culture, however, is distinctly human. **Cultures** are traditions and customs, transmitted through learning, that govern the beliefs and behavior of the people exposed to them. Children *learn* these traditions by growing up in a particular society. Cultural traditions include customs and opinions, developed over the generations, about proper and improper behavior. These traditions answer such questions as: How should we do things? How do we make sense of the world? How do we tell right from wrong? A culture produces a degree of consistency in behavior and thought among the individuals who make up a given society.

The most critical element of cultural traditions is their transmission through learning rather than biological inheritance. Culture is not itself biological, but it rests on certain features of hominid biology.

(**Hominids** are members of the zoological family that includes fossil and living humans.) For more than a million years, hominids have had at least some of the biological capacities on which culture depends. These abilities are to learn, to think symbolically, to use language, and to employ tools and other cultural products in organizing their lives and adapting to their environments.

Bound neither by time nor by space, anthropology ponders and confronts major questions of human existence. By examining ancient bones and tools, anthropologists explore the mysteries of hominid origins. When did our own ancestors separate from those remote great-aunts and great-uncles whose descendants are the apes? Where and when did *Homo sapiens* originate? How has our species changed? What are we now and where are we going? How have changes in culture and society influenced biological change? Our genus, *Homo*, has been changing for more than 1 million years. Humans continue to adapt and change both biologically and culturally.

ADAPTATION, VARIATION, AND CHANGE

Human **adaptation** (the process by which organisms cope with environmental stresses) involves an interplay between culture and biology. As an illustration, consider four different ways in which humans may cope with low oxygen pressure. Pressurized airplane cabins equipped with oxygen masks illustrate *cultural* (technological) adaptation. Natives of highland Peru seem to have certain *genetic* advantages for life at very high altitudes, where air pressure is low. However, human adaptation to high altitudes is not limited to culture and genes.

People who have grown up at a high altitude are physiologically more efficient there than are genetically similar people who have not. Human biological plasticity (the ability to change) permits such *long-term physiological* adaptation during growth and development. We also have the capacity for *immediate physiological* adaptation. Thus, lowlanders arriving in the highlands immediately increase their breathing rate, often doubling their usual rate at sea level. Hyperventilation increases the oxygen in their arteries and lungs, and, as the pulse also increases, blood reaches their tissues more rapidly. All these varied adaptive responses—cultural and biological, voluntary and involuntary, conscious and unconscious—are directed at a single goal: increasing the supply of oxygen to the human organism.

Much of the diversity we see in cultures, as in nature, reflects adaptation to varied environments and circumstances. People creatively manipulate their environment; they are not just determined by it. Recognizing this, John Bennett (1969, p. 19) has defined cultural adaptation as "the problem-solving, creative or coping element in human behavior." People get and use resources and solve the immediate problems confronting them. A second, and equally important, dimension of cultural adaptation is conservation of resources. "An economy that realizes economic gain but does so at the cost of exhausting or abusing its resources may be adapting in one dimension (the first) but can be said to be *maladaptive* [emphasis added] along the other." In other words, behavior that benefits *individuals* may harm the environment and threaten the *group*'s continuity. Societies "must attempt to balance conservation of resources against economic success to ensure survival in their environment" (Bennett 1969, p. 13).

As hominid history has unfolded, social and cultural means of adaptation have become increasingly important. In this process, humans have devised diverse ways of coping with the range of environments and social systems they have occupied in time and space. The rate of cultural change has accelerated, particularly during the past 10,000 years. For millions of years, hunting and gathering of nature's bounty—*foraging*—was the sole basis of hominid subsistence. However, it took only a few thousand years for **food production** (cultivation of plants and domestication of animals), which originated in the Middle East 10,000 to 12,000 years ago, to replace foraging in most areas. People started producing their own food, planting crops and stockbreeding animals, rather than simply taking what nature had to offer.

Between 6000 and 5000 B.P. (before the present), the first civilizations arose in the Middle East. (**Civilizations, nation-states,** or, most simply, **states** are complex societies with a formal government and social classes.) Much more recently, industrial production has profoundly influenced people throughout the world. Today's global economy and communications link all contemporary people, directly or indirectly, in the modern world system.

People must cope with forces generated by progressively larger systems—region, nation, and world. The study of such contemporary adaptations generates new challenges for anthropology: "The cultures of world peoples need to be constantly *re*discovered as these people reinvent them in changing historical circumstances" (Marcus and Fischer 1986, p. 24).

Over the course of human history, major innovations have spread at the expense of earlier ones. Each economic revolution has had social and cultural repercussions. This book will examine behavior and institutions, beliefs, customs, and practices associated with several economic systems: foraging, food production, industrialism, and the modern world system.

GENERAL ANTHROPOLOGY

The academic discipline of anthropology, which is also known as **general anthropology,** includes four main subdisciplines: sociocultural, archaeological, biological, and linguistic anthropology. (From here on, I will use the shorter term *cultural anthropology* as a synonym for "sociocultural anthropology.") Most American anthropologists, myself included, specialize in cultural anthropology. However, most are also familiar with the basics of the other subdisciplines. Major departments of anthropology usually include representatives of each.

There are historical reasons for the inclusion of four subdisciplines in a single field. American anthropology arose a century ago out of concern for the history and cultures of the native populations of North America ("American Indians"). Interest in the origins and diversity of Native Americans brought together studies of customs, social life, language, and physical traits. Such a unified anthropology did not develop in Europe, where the subdisciplines tend to exist separately.

There are also logical reasons for the unity of American anthropology. Each subdiscipline considers variations in time and space (that is, in different geographic areas). Cultural and archaeological anthropologists study (among many other topics) changes in social life and customs. Biological anthropologists examine changes in physical form. Linguistic anthropologists may reconstruct the basics of ancient languages by studying modern ones. This concern with variation in time may be stated

EVEN ANTHROPOLOGISTS GET CULTURE SHOCK

I first lived in Arembepe (Brazil) during the (North American) summer of 1962. That was between my junior and senior years at New York City's Columbia College, where I was majoring in anthropology. I went to Arembepe as a participant in a now-defunct program designed to provide undergraduates with experience doing ethnography—firsthand study of an alien society's culture and social life.

Brought up in one culture, intensely curious about others, anthropologists nevertheless experience culture shock, particularly on their first field trip. *Culture shock* refers to the whole set of feelings about being in an alien setting, and the ensuing reactions. It is a chilly, creepy feeling of alienation, of being without some of the most ordinary, trivial (and therefore basic) cues of one's culture of origin.

As I planned my departure for Brazil in 1962, I could not know just how naked I would feel without the cloak of my own language and culture. My sojourn in Arembepe would be my first trip outside the United States. I was an urban boy who had grown up in Atlanta, Geor-

gia, and New York City. I had little experience with rural life in my own country, none with Latin America, and I had received only minimal training in the Portuguese language.

New York City direct to Salvador, Bahia, Brazil. Just a brief stopover in Rio de Janeiro; a longer visit would be a reward at the end of field work. As our prop jet approached tropical Salvador, I couldn't believe the whiteness of the sand. "That's not snow, is it?" I remarked to a fellow field team member. . . .

My first impressions of Bahia were of smells—alien odors of ripe and decaying mangoes, bananas, and passion fruit—and of swatting the ubiquitous fruit flies I had never seen before, although I had read extensively about their reproductive behavior in genetics classes. There were strange concoctions of rice, black beans, and gelatinous gobs of unidentifiable meats and floating pieces of skin. Coffee was strong and sugar crude, and every tabletop had containers for toothpicks and for manioc (cassava) flour to sprinkle, like Parmesan cheese, on anything one might eat. I remember oatmeal soup and a slimy stew of beef

tongue in tomatoes. At one meal a disintegrating fish head, eyes still attached, but barely, stared up at me as the rest of its body floated in a bowl of bright orange palm oil. . . .

I only vaguely remember my first day in Arembepe. Unlike ethnographers who have studied remote tribes in the tropical forests of interior South America or the highlands of Papua–New Guinea, I did not have to hike or ride a canoe for days to arrive at my field site. Arembepe was not isolated relative to such places, only relative to every other place *I* had ever been. . . .

I do recall what happened when we arrived. There was no formal road into the village. Entering through southern Arembepe, vehicles simply threaded their way around coconut trees, following tracks left by automobiles that had passed previously. A crowd of children had heard us coming, and they pursued our car through the village streets until we parked in front of our house, near the central square. Our first few days in Arembepe were spent with children following us everywhere. For weeks we had few moments of privacy. Children

---

differently: An interest in **evolution** unifies anthropology's subdisciplines. Defined simply, evolution is change in form over generations. Charles Darwin called it "descent with modification."

The subdisiplines influence each other as anthropologists talk, read books and journals, and associate in professional organizations. General anthropology explores the basics of human biology, psychology, society, and culture and considers their interrelations. Anthropologists share certain key assumptions. One is that sound conclusions about "human nature" can't be drawn from a single cultural tradition.

We often hear the "nature-nurture" and "genetics-environment" questions. Consider gender differences. Do male and female capacities, attitudes, and behavior reflect biological or cultural variation? Are there universal emotional and intellectual contrasts between the sexes? Are females less aggressive than males? Is male dominance a human universal? By examining diverse cultures, anthropology shows that many contrasts between men and women reflect cultural training rather than biology.

Anthropologists also use their knowledge of biological and cultural diversity to evaluate assertions about intellectual differences. They have found no

An ethnographer at work. During a 1980 visit, the author, Conrad Kottak, catches up on the news in Arembepe, a coastal community in Bahia state, northeastern Brazil, which he has been studying since 1962.

watched our every move through our living room window. Occasionally one made an incomprehensible remark. Usually they just stood there. Sometimes they would groom one another's hair, eating the lice they found. . . .

The sounds, sensations, sights, smells, and tastes of life in northeastern Brazil, and in Arembepe, slowly grew familiar. I gradually accepted the fact that the only toilet tissue available at a reasonable price had almost the texture of sandpaper.

I grew accustomed to this world without Kleenex, in which globs of mucus habitually drooped from the noses of village children whenever a cold passed through Arembepe. A world where, seemingly without effort, women with gracefully swaying hips carried 18-liter kerosene cans of water on their heads, where boys sailed kites and sported at catching houseflies in their bare hands, where old women smoked pipes, storekeepers offered *cachaça* (common rum) at nine in the morn-

ing, and men played dominoes on lazy afternoons when there was no fishing. I was visiting a world where human life was oriented toward water—the sea, where men fished, and the lagoon, where women communally washed clothing, dishes, and their own bodies.

This description is adapted from my ethnographic study *Assault on Paradise: Social Change in a Brazilian Village,* 2nd ed. (New York: McGraw-Hill, 1992).

evidence for biologically determined contrasts in intelligence between rich and poor, black and white, or men and women.

Anthropology is not a science of the exotic carried on by quaint scholars in ivory towers but a discipline with a lot to tell the public. One of its contributions is its broadening, liberating role in a college education. Anthropology's foremost professional organization, the American Anthropological Association, has formally acknowledged a public service role by recognizing a fifth subdiscipline. This is **applied anthropology**—the application of anthropological data, perspectives, theory, and methods to

identify, assess, and solve contemporary social problems. More and more anthropologists from the four main subdisciplines now work in such "applied" areas as public health, family planning, and economic development.

THE SUBDISCIPLINES OF ANTHROPOLOGY

Cultural Anthropology

Cultural anthropologists study society and culture, describing, analyzing, and explaining social and

Cross-cultural comparison shows that many differences between the sexes arise from cultural training rather than biology. As shown here, men in Kenya do the laundry in the river.

cultural similarities and differences. In considering diversity in time and space, anthropologists perceive the universal, the generalized, and the particular. Certain biological, psychological, social, and cultural features are *universal*—shared by all human populations. Others are merely *generalized*—common to several but not all human groups. Still others are *particular*—not shared at all.

Cultural anthropology has two aspects: ethnography (based on field work) and ethnology (based on cross-cultural comparison). **Ethnography** provides an "ethnopicture" of a particular group, society, or culture. During ethnographic field work the ethnographer gathers data, which he or she organizes, describes, analyzes, and interprets to build and present the *ethnopicture* (e.g., a book, article, or film). Traditionally, ethnographers have lived in small communities and studied local behavior, beliefs, customs, social life, economic activities, politics, and religion.

The resulting anthropological perspective often differs radically from that of economics or political science. Those disciplines focus on national and official organizations and policies and often on elites. However, the groups that anthropologists have traditionally studied have usually been relatively poor and powerless. Ethnographers often observe discriminatory practices directed toward such people, who experience food shortages, dietary deficiencies, and other aspects of poverty. The anthropological

perspective is different—not necessarily better. Political scientists study programs that national planners develop. Anthropologists see how these programs work on the local level. Both perspectives are necessary to understand human life in the late twentieth century.

Cultures are not isolated. As noted by Franz Boas (1940/1966) many years ago, contact between neighboring tribes has always existed and has extended over enormous areas. A *world-system perspective* recognizes that many local cultural features reflect the economic and political position a society occupies in a larger system. "Human populations construct their cultures in interaction with one another, and not in isolation" (Wolf 1982, p. ix). Villagers increasingly participate in regional, national, and world events.

Exposure to external forces comes through the mass media, migration, and modern transportation. City and nation increasingly invade local communities in the guise of tourists, development agents, government and religious officials, and political candidates. Such **linkages,** or interconnections, are prominent components of regional, national, and international systems of politics, economics, and information. These larger systems increasingly affect the people and places anthropology has traditionally studied. The study of such linkages and systems is part of the subject matter of modern anthropology.

Ethnology examines, interprets, and compares the results of ethnography—the data gathered in different societies. Ethnologists try to identify and explain cultural differences and similarities, to distinguish between universality, generality, and particularity (see the chapter "Culture"). Ethnology gets data for comparison not just from ethnography but also from the other subdisciplines, particularly from archaeological anthropology, which reconstructs social systems of the past.

Archaeological Anthropology

Archaeological anthropology (more simply, "archaeology") reconstructs, describes, and interprets human behavior and cultural patterns through material remains. Although archaeologists are best known for studying **prehistory** (the period before the invention of writing), they also study historical and even living cultures. Through a research project begun in 1973 in Tucson, Arizona, for example, archaeologist William Rathje has learned about contemporary life by studying modern garbage. The value of "garbology," as Rathje calls it, is that it provides "evidence of what people did, not what they think they did, what they think they should have done, or what the interviewer thinks they should have done" (Harrison, Rathje, and Hughes 1994, p. 108). What people report may contrast strongly with their real behavior as revealed by garbology.

For example, the garbologists discovered that the three Tucson neighborhoods that reported the lowest beer consumption had the highest number of discarded beer cans per household (Podolefsky and Brown, eds. 1992, p. 100).

Using material remains as primary data, and informed by ethnographic knowledge and ethnological theory, archaeologists analyze cultural processes and patterns. Several kinds of remains interest archaeologists. Garbage tells stories about consumption and activities. Wild and domesticated grains have different characteristics, which allow archaeologists to distinguish between gathering and cultivation. Examination of animal bones reveals the ages of slaughtered animals and provides other information useful in determining whether species were wild or domesticated.

Analyzing such data, archaeologists answer several questions about ancient economies. Did the group being studied get its meat from hunting, or did it domesticate and breed animals, killing only those of a certain age and sex? Did plant food come from wild plants or from sowing, tending, and harvesting crops? At sites where people live or have lived, archaeologists find **artifacts,** material items that humans have manufactured or modified. Did the residents make, trade for, or buy particular items? Were raw materials available locally? If not, where did they come from? From such information, archaeologists reconstruct patterns of production, trade, and consumption.

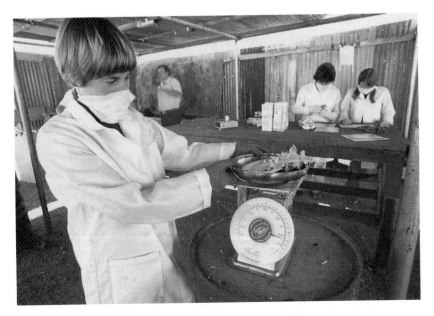

Archaeological anthropology reconstructs, describes, and interprets human behavior through material remains. Besides prehistory, archaeologists also study living cultures. In Tucson, University of Arizona archaeologists learn about contemporary life by analyzing recent garbage.

Archaeologists have spent much time studying **potsherds,** fragments of earthenware. Potsherds are more durable than many other artifacts, such as textiles and wood. The pottery types at a site can suggest its technological complexity. The quantity of pottery fragments allows estimates of population size and density. The discovery that potters used materials that were not locally available suggests systems of trade. Similarities in manufacture and decoration at different sites may be proof of cultural connections. Groups with similar pots may be historically related. Perhaps they shared common cultural ancestors, traded with each other, or belonged to the same political system.

Many archaeologists examine paleoecology. **Ecology** is the study of interrelations among living things in an environment. The organisms and environment together constitute an **ecosystem,** a patterned arrangement of energy flows and exchanges. Human ecology, or **cultural ecology,** studies ecosystems that include people, focusing on the ways in which human use "of nature influences and is influenced by social organization and cultural values" (Bennett 1969, pp. 10–11). **Paleoecology** looks at the ecosystems of the past.

In addition to reconstructing ecological patterns, archaeologists infer cultural transformations, for example, from changes in the size and type of sites and the distance between them. A city develops in a region where only towns, villages, and hamlets existed a century earlier. The number of settlement levels (city, town, village, hamlet) is a measure of social complexity. Buildings offer clues about political and religious features. Special-purpose structures such as temples and pyramids suggest that an ancient society had a central authority capable of marshaling team labor. The presence or absence of certain structures reveals differences in function between settlements. For example, some towns were ceremonial centers with prominent architecture. Others were burial sites; still others were farming communities.

Archaeologists also document cultural patterns and processes by *excavating* (digging through a succession of levels) at particular sites. In a given area, through time, settlements may change in form and purpose, as may the connections between settlements. Excavation can document changes in economic, social, and political activities.

To learn about prehistoric populations—those without written records—archaeology is essential. Comparison of sequences in different areas allows archaeologists to observe generalized processes. For example, certain environments or economies correlate with particular types of social groups or political systems. Comparative archaeology and ethnography both contribute to the understanding of social processes.

Biological, or Physical, Anthropology

The subject matter of **biological, or physical, anthropology** is human biological diversity in time and space. A combination of genetic and environmental features produces this variation. Relevant environmental factors include heat and cold, moisture, sunlight, altitude, and disease. The focus on human variation unites five special interests within biological anthropology:

1. Hominid evolution as revealed by the fossil record (**paleoanthropology**)
2. Human genetics
3. Human growth and development
4. Human biological plasticity (the body's ability to cope with stresses, such as heat, cold, and altitude)
5. The biology, evolution, behavior, and social life of monkeys, apes, and other nonhuman primates

These interests link physical anthropology to other fields: biology, zoology, geology, anatomy, physiology, medicine, and public health. **Osteology**—the study of bones—helps paleoanthropologists, who examine skulls, teeth, and bones, to identify hominid ancestors and chart changes in anatomy. Biological anthropologists collaborate with archaeologists in reconstructing biological and cultural aspects of human evolution. Fossils and tools are often found together. Different types of tools provide information about the habits, customs, and life styles of the hominids who used them.

More than a century ago, Charles Darwin noticed that the variety that exists within any population permits some individuals (those with the favored, or adaptive, characteristics) to do better than others at surviving and reproducing. Genetics, which developed later, enlightens us about the causes and

Near Olduvai Gorge, Tanzania, several paleoanthropologists, including Louis S. B. Leakey (deceased), Mary Leakey, and Richard Leakey, admire an early hominid skull. The Leakey family, along with many Kenyan colleagues, have substantially increased our knowledge of hominid evolution.

transmission of this variety. However, it isn't just genes that cause variety. During any individual's lifetime, the environment works along with heredity to determine biological features. For example, people with a genetic tendency to be tall will be shorter if they are poorly nourished during childhood. Thus biological anthropology investigates the influence of environment (nutrition, altitude, temperature, and disease) on the body as it develops. As noted earlier, human biological and cultural changes have been interrelated and complementary, and humans continue to adapt both biologically and culturally. This is why both subdisciplines are studied within general anthropology.

Biological anthropology (along with zoology) also includes **primatology.** The **primates** include our closest biological relatives—apes and monkeys. Primatologists study their biology, evolution, behavior, and social life, often in their natural environments. Primatology assists paleoanthropology, because primate behavior may shed light on early hominid behavior and on issues of human nature and human universals.

Linguistic Anthropology

We don't know (and probably never will) when hominids began to speak. We do know that the well-developed, grammatically complex languages have existed for thousands of years. **Linguistic anthropology** offers further illustration of anthropology's interest in comparison, variation, and change. Linguistic anthropologists study language in its social and cultural context, in space and through time. Some make inferences about universal features of language, linked perhaps to uniformities in the human brain. Others reconstruct ancient languages by comparing their contemporary descendants and in so doing make discoveries about history. Still others study linguistic differences to discover varied perceptions and patterns of thought in a multitude of cultures. *Sociolinguists* examine diversity in a single language to show how speech reflects social differences.

Descriptive linguistics studies sounds, grammar, and meaning in particular languages. *Historical* linguistics considers variation in time, such as the changes in sounds, grammar, and vocabulary between Middle English (spoken from approximately 1050 to 1550 A.D.) and modern English. There is also variation among the speakers of any language at any given time. One reason for variation is geography, as in regional dialects and accents. Linguistic variation is also associated with social divisions. Examples include the bilingualism of ethnic groups and speech patterns associated with particular social classes. Linguistic and cultural anthropologists collaborate in studying links between language and other aspects of culture.

Applied Anthropology

In its most general sense, applied anthropology includes any use of the knowledge and/or techniques of the four subdisciplines to identify, assess, and solve practical problems. Because of anthropology's breadth, it has many applications. For example, the growing field of **medical anthropology** considers the sociocultural context and implications of disease and illness. Perceptions of good and bad health, along with actual health threats and problems, differ among cultures. Various societies and ethnic groups recognize different illnesses, symptoms, and causes and have developed different health-care systems and treatment strategies. Medical anthropologists are both biological and cultural, and both theoretical and applied. Applied medical anthropologists have, for example, served as cultural interpreters in public health programs, which must fit into local culture and be accepted by local people.

Other applied anthropologists work for development agencies, assessing the social and cultural features that influence economic development and change. Anthropologists are experts on local cultures. As such, they often can identify specific social conditions and local needs that must be addressed and that influence the failure or success of development schemes. Planners in Washington or Paris often know little about, say, the labor necessary for crop cultivation in rural Africa. Forecasts and estimates of project success are often unrealistic if no one consults an anthropologist familiar with the rural scene. Development funds are often wasted if an anthropologist is not asked to identify local needs, demands, priorities, and constraints. Such considerations have led development organizations to include anthropologists as well as agronomists, economists, veterinarians, geologists, engineers, and health specialists on planning teams. Anthropologists also apply their skills in studying the human dimension of environmental degradation (e.g., deforestation, pollution). Anthropologists examine how the environment influences humans and how human activities affect the biosphere and the earth itself.

Applied anthropologists also work in North America. Garbologists help the Environmental Protection Agency, the paper industry, and packaging and trade associations. Many archaeologists now work in cultural resource management—applying their knowledge and skills to interpret, inventory, and preserve historic resources for local, state (provincial), and federal governments. Forensic (physical) anthropologists work with the police, medical examiners, and the courts to identify victims of crimes and accidents. From skeletal remains they determine age, sex, size, race, and number of victims. Applied physical anthropologists link injury patterns to design flaws in aircraft and vehicles.

Ethnographers have influenced social policy by showing that strong kin ties exist in city neighborhoods whose social organization was previously

Both biological and cultural anthropologists contribute to the growing field of medical anthropology. Here, Richard Wrangham and Robert Bailey watch Elizabeth Ross measure an Efe "pygmy" man in the Ituri forest of Zaire, Central Africa. This team research investigated Efe health and nutrition, along with social, cultural, economic, and ecological dimensions of Efe life.

Applied anthropology is the use of anthropological data, perspectives, theory, and methods to identify, assess, and solve contemporary problems affecting humans, such as deforestation. One threat to forests is fuelwood production to supply rapidly growing Third World cities. Here, firewood is sold along the road at Gitarama, Rwanda in 1991.

considered "fragmented" or "pathological." Suggestions for improvements in the education system emerge from ethnographic studies of classrooms and surrounding communities. Linguistic anthropologists show the influence of dialect differences on classroom learning. In general, applied anthropology aims to find humane and effective ways of helping the people whom anthropologists have traditionally studied.

ANTHROPOLOGY AND OTHER ACADEMIC FIELDS

As a discipline that is both scientific and humanistic, anthropology has links with many other academic fields. Anthropology is a **science**—a "systematic field of study or body of knowledge that aims, through experiment, observation, and deduction, to produce reliable explanations of phenomena, with reference to the material and physical world" (*Webster's New World Encyclopedia* 1993, p. 937). Clyde Kluckhohn (1944, p. 9) called anthropology "the science of human similarities and differences." His statement of the need for such a science still stands: "Anthropology provides a scientific basis for dealing with the crucial dilemma of the world today: how can peoples of different appearance, mutually unintelligible languages, and dis-

similar ways of life get along peaceably together?" (p. 9). Anthropology has compiled an impressive body of knowledge that this textbook attempts to encapsulate.

Anthropology is also a **humanities** field. The humanities are academic fields like English, classics, art history, and philosophy that study languages, texts, philosophies, arts, music, performances, and other forms of creative expression. Actually, anthropology may well be the most humanistic of academic fields because of its fundamental respect for human diversity. Anthropologists listen to, record, and represent voices from a multitude of nations and cultures. Anthropology values local knowledge, diverse worldviews, and alternative philosophies. Cultural and linguistic anthropology in particular bring a comparative and nonelitist perspective to forms of creative expression, including language, art, narratives, music, and dance, viewed in their social and cultural context.

As mentioned above, one of the main differences between anthropology and the other fields that study people is *holism*, anthropology's unique blend of biological, social, cultural, linguistic, historical, and contemporary perspectives. Paradoxically, while distinguishing anthropology, this breadth is what also links it to many other disciplines. Techniques used to date fossils and artifacts have come to anthropology from physics, chemistry, and

MARGARET MEAD: PUBLIC ANTHROPOLOGIST

Margaret Mead (1901–1978), the most famous anthropologist who ever lived, was for many years a full-time staff member at the American Museum of Natural History in New York City. Mead also taught as an adjunct professor at Columbia University.

During her entire professional life Mead was a public anthropologist. She wrote for social scientists, the educated public, and the popular press. She had a column in *Redbook* and often appeared on *The Tonight Show*. Mead wrote several popular books about culture and personality (now usually called *psychological anthropology*). She was heavily influenced by Franz Boas (1858–1942), her mentor at Columbia and a "father" of American anthropology. Mead eventually did ethnography in the South Pacific, including Samoa and New Guinea. From her first field work emerged the popular book *Coming of Age in Samoa* (1928/1961).

Mead embarked for Samoa with a research topic that Boas had suggested: contrasts between female adolescence in Samoa and the United States. She shared Boas's assumption that different cultures train children and adolescents to have different personalities and behavior. Suspicious of biologically determined universals, she assumed that Samoan adolescence would differ from the same period in the United States and that this would affect adult personality. Using her Samoan ethnographic findings, Mead contrasted apparent sexual freedom and experimentation there with repression of adolescent sexuality in the United States.

Her findings supported the Boasian view that culture, not biology or race, determines variation in human behavior and personality. Derek Freeman (1983) has offered a severe critique of Mead's Samoan work. Freeman's critique has, in turn, been criticized (Brady, ed. 1983). Holmes (1987) attempts to offer a balanced view based on his own field work in Samoa.

Mead's later field work among the Arapesh, Mundugumor, and Tchambuli of New Guinea resulted in *Sex and Temperament in Three Primitive Societies* (1935/1950). That book documented variation in male and female personality traits and behavior across cultures. She offered it as further support for cultural determinism.

Mead's reputation rested on her adventurous spirit, intellect, insight, forceful personality, writing ability, and productivity, along with the topics she chose to address. She made primitive life relevant to her time and her own society. Thus, *Coming of Age in Samoa* was subtitled *A Psychological Study of Primitive Youth* for Western Civilization [emphasis added]. *Growing Up in New Guinea* (1930) was subtitled

---

geology. Because plant and animal remains often are found with human bones and artifacts, anthropologists collaborate with botanists, zoologists, and paleontologists.

Cultural anthropology has clear ties to the other social sciences and the humanities. Thus contemporary sociology is experiencing an "opening to culture." Interpretive anthropology (Geertz 1973, 1983), which approaches cultures as texts whose meaning the anthropologist must decipher, links anthropology to the humanities and to history. More and more historians are interpreting historical narratives as texts, paying attention to their cultural meaning and the social context of their creation. Interdisciplinary collaboration is a hallmark of contemporary academic life, with ready borrowing of ideas and methods between disciplines (Geertz 1980). This is especially true for anthropology.

Cultural Anthropology and Sociology

Cultural anthropology and sociology share an interest in social relations, organization, and behavior. However, important differences between these disciplines arose from the kinds of societies each traditionally studied. Initially sociologists focused on the industrial West; anthropologists, on nonindustrial societies. Different methods of data collection and analysis emerged to deal with those different kinds of societies. To study large-scale, complex nations, sociologists came to rely on questionnaires and other means of gathering masses of quantifiable data. For many years sampling and statistical techniques have been basic to sociology, whereas statistical training has been less common in anthropology (although this is changing as anthropologists increasingly work in modern nations).

Traditional ethnographers studied small and

A Comparative Study of Primitive Education.

The public viewed Margaret Mead as a romantic, exotic, and controversial figure. She lived an unorthodox life for her time and gender. She was an early feminist. She married three times. Her last two husbands, Reo Fortune and Gregory Bateson, were anthropologists. She was a small, lone, daring, and determined woman who journeyed to remote areas, lived with the natives, and survived to tell of it. Accounts of Mead's life include her autobiography, *Blackberry Winter* (1972), and biography by her only daughter, Mary Catherine Bateson (1984).

Mead's clear, forceful, and vivid writing captures prominent themes of the Depression era. Her books fueled a revolution in the discussion of human sexuality spurred by Freudian psychology. The preoccupations of Depression-era society included issues that Americans still discuss: family breakdown, teenage

Margaret Mead, then Associate Curator of Ethnology at the American Museum of Natural History, holds two samples of Manus art brought back from a seven-month visit to the Manus of the Admiralty Islands. Mead helped anthropology flourish, using her research in the South Sea islands as lessons in alternative life styles.

sex, the "New Woman," birth control, an increasing divorce rate, and extramarital affairs. Anthropology flourished as South Sea islands offered lessons in romance, sexuality, and alternative life styles. "Free love" in Samoa and the Trobriand Islands (as described by Bronislaw Malinowski [1927, 1929*b*]) provided models for a new sexual order (Stocking 1986).

non-literate (without writing) populations and relied on methods appropriate to that context. "Ethnography is a research process in which the anthropologist closely observes, records, and engages in the daily life of another culture—an experience labeled as the fieldwork method—and then writes accounts of this culture, emphasizing descriptive detail" (Marcus and Fischer 1986, p. 18). One key method described in this quote is **participant observation**—taking part in the events one is observing, describing, and analyzing.

With increasing interdisciplinary communication, anthropology and sociology are converging. As the modern world system grows, sociologists pursue research topics in Third World countries and in places that were once almost exclusively within the anthropological orbit. As industrialization spreads, many anthropologists work in industrial societies, where they study diverse topics, including rural decline, inner-city life, and the role of the mass media in creating national cultural patterns. Anthropologists and sociologists also share an interest in issues of race, ethnicity, social class, gender, and popular or mass culture in modern nations, including the United States and Canada.

Anthropology, Political Science, and Economics

Political science and economics developed to investigate particular domains of human behavior—as with sociology—mainly in modern nations. In the small-scale societies where ethnography grew up, politics and economics usually don't stand out as distinct activities amenable to separate analysis, as they do in a modern society. Rather, they are submerged, or *embedded*, in the general social order. Anthropologists have expanded our comparative understanding of political systems by showing, for example, that law and crime are not cultural universals and by examining such matters as the expression and resolution of conflict in societies without governments.

The subject matter of economics has been defined as economizing—the *rational* allocation of scarce means (resources) to alternative ends (uses). The goal of maximizing profit is assumed to be the force behind such rational allocation. However, the social theorist Max Weber (1904/1958) drew an important distinction between formal rationality and substantive rationality. *Formal rationality* refers to abstract standards of rational procedure based purely on the profit motive. *Substantive rationality* refers to standards of efficient procedure adjusted to different cultural values. In other words, motivations vary cross-culturally and guide the kinds of decisions people make in different cultures. Following Weber's lead, anthropologists have contributed to *comparative* economics by showing that principles other than the profit motive propel the economy in other cultures. Through ethnography and cross-cultural comparison, the findings of economists and political scientists, usually based on research in Western nations, can be placed in a broader perspective.

Anthropology and the Humanities

The humanities study art, literature, music, dance, and other forms of creative expression. Traditionally (but this has changed—see below), they focused on highbrow "fine arts," knowledge of which was considered basic to a "cultured" person. Anthropology has always extended the definition of *cultured* beyond the elitist meaning of cultivated, sophisticated, college-educated, proper, and tasteful. For anthropologists, culture is not confined to elites or to any single social segment. Everyone acquires culture through **enculturation,** the social process by which culture is learned and transmitted across the generations. All creative expressions, therefore, are of potential interest as cultural products and documents. Growing acceptance of this view has helped broaden the study of the humanities from fine art and elite art to popular and folk art and the creative expressions of the masses.

Anthropology has influenced and is being influenced by the humanities—another example of *convergence*, the process of interdisciplinary communication and collaboration that was mentioned earlier.

Adopting a characteristic anthropological view of creativity in its social and cultural context, current "postmodern" (Jameson 1984, 1988) approaches in the humanities are shifting the focus toward "lowbrow," mass, and popular culture and local creative expressions. Another area of convergence between anthropology and the humanities is the view of cultural expressions as patterned texts (Ricoeur 1971; Geertz 1973). Thus "unwritten behavior, speech, beliefs, oral tradition, and ritual" (Clifford 1988, p. 39) are interpreted in relation to their meaning within a particular cultural context. A final link between anthropology and the humanities is the study of ethnographic accounts as a form of writing (Clifford 1988; Marcus and Fischer 1986).

Anthropology and Psychology

Like sociologists and economists, most psychologists do research in their own society. Anthropology again contributes by providing cross-cultural data. Statements about "human" psychology cannot be based solely on observations made in one society or in a single type of society. The area of cultural anthropology known as psychological anthropology, or **culture and personality** (the study of variation in psychological traits and personality characteristics among cultures), links up with psychology. Margaret Mead, in her many books (1928/1961, 1930), attempted to show that psychological traits vary widely among cultures. Societies instill different values by training children differently. Adult personalities reflect a culture's child-rearing practices.

An early contributor to the cross-cultural study of psychology was Bronislaw Malinowski, who did research among the Trobriand Islanders of the South Pacific. The Trobrianders reckon kinship matrilineally. They consider themselves related to the mother and her relatives, not to the father. The relative who disciplines the child is not the father but the mother's brother, the maternal uncle. One inherits from the uncle rather than the father. Trobrianders show a marked respect for the uncle, with whom a boy usually has a cool and distant relationship. In contrast, the Trobriand father-son relationship is friendly and affectionate.

Malinowski's work among the Trobrianders suggested modifications in Sigmund Freud's famous theory of the universality of the Oedipus complex (Malinowski 1927). According to Freud (1918/ 1950), boys around the age of five become sexually attracted to the mother. The Oedipus complex is resolved, in Freud's view, when the boy overcomes his sexual jealousy of, and identifies with, his father. Freud lived in patriarchal Austria during the late nineteenth and early twentieth centuries—a social milieu in which the father was a strong authoritarian figure. The Austrian father was the child's primary authority figure and the mother's sexual partner. In the Trobriands the father had only the sexual role.

If, as Freud contended, the Oedipus complex always creates social distance based on jealousy toward the mother's sexual partner, this would have shown up in Trobriand society. It *did not.* Malinowski concluded that the authority structure did more to influence the father-son relationship than did sexual jealousy. Like many later anthropologists, Malinowski showed that individual psychology depends on its cultural context. Anthropolo-

gists continue to provide cross-cultural perspectives on psychoanalytic propositions (Paul 1989) as well as on issues of developmental and cognitive psychology.

Anthropology and History

Convergence between history and anthropology was noted above in relation to the trend toward interdisciplinary communication. Historians increasingly interpret historical documents and accounts as texts requiring placement and interpretation within specific cultural contexts. Anthropologists and historians collaborate in the study of issues such as colonialism and the development of the modern world system (Cooper and Stoler 1989).

Despite this convergence, I think it is useful to maintain a distinction between history (change in personnel) and evolution (change in form) as two aspects of change that involve people. In this sense *history* focuses on individuals. In a stable social sys-

An early contributor to the comparative study of psychology was Bronislaw Malinowski, who did ethnographic research among the Trobriand Islanders of the South Pacific. Here, a Trobriand woman prepares dinner as her kin and neighbors watch.

tem, people enter at birth and leave through death and migration. If there is true stability, people come and go but the system stays the same. There are changes in the *personnel*—in individuals—but not in the system's basic form. The second aspect of change (*evolution*) requires a larger perspective. A stable social system can become unstable. *A social system can change its structure or form.* Evolution is the study of such changes in form. (Although individual action always propels such systemic change, the focus here is on the system.)

Although there are still historians who focus on individual names and dates without much concern for process or social context, the distinction between personnel change and formal change certainly doesn't pit all, or even most, historians against anthropologists. An increasing number of historians study changes in social form—social transformations. Indeed, the growing collaboration of historians and anthropologists has been institutionalized in joint programs in history and anthropology at several universities.

SUMMARY

Anthropology, a uniquely holistic discipline, studies human biological and cultural diversity. It attempts to explain similarities and differences in time and space. Culture, which is passed on through learning rather than through biological inheritance, is a major reason for human adaptability.

Anthropology is characterized by an interest in the origins of and changes in biology and culture. The four subdisciplines of general anthropology are (socio)cultural, archaeological, biological, and linguistic anthropology. All share an interest in variation in time and space and in adaptation—the process by which organisms cope with environmental stresses. All study evolution: change in form over the generations. Anthropology attempts to identify and explain universal, generalized, and particular aspects of the human condition.

Cultural anthropology examines the cultural diversity of the present and the recent past. Archaeology reconstructs social, economic, religious, and political patterns, usually of prehistoric populations. Biological anthropology relates biological diversity in time and space to variation in environment. It studies fossils, genetics, growth and development, bodily responses, and nonhuman primates. Linguistic anthropology documents diversity among contemporary languages. It studies ways in which speech changes in different social situations and over

time. Applied anthropology uses anthropological knowledge and methods to identify and solve social problems in North America and abroad.

Concerns with past and present and with biology, society, culture, and language link anthropology to many other fields—sciences and humanities. The main difference between cultural anthropology and sociology is that sociologists have traditionally studied urban and industrial populations whereas anthropologists have studied rural, nonindustrial peoples. Anthropologists bring a comparative perspective to economics and political science. Anthropologists also study art, music, and literature across cultures. However, their concern is more with the creative expressions of common people than with art commissioned and appreciated by elites. Anthropologists examine creators and products in their social context. Despite these traditional contrasts, interdisciplinary collaboration is a hallmark of contemporary academic life, with ready borrowing of ideas and methods between disciplines. This is especially true for anthropology because of its breadth and topical diversity.

Psychological anthropology, which relates human psychology to social and cultural variation, links anthropology and psychology. Anthropologists and historians collaborate increasingly in placing historical events in their social and cultural context.

GLOSSARY

adaptation: The process by which organisms cope with environmental stresses.

applied anthropology: The application of anthropological data, perspectives, theory, and methods to identify, assess, and solve contemporary social problems.

archaeological anthropology (prehistoric archaeology): The study of human behavior and cultural patterns and processes through the culture's material remains.

artifacts: Material items that humans have manufactured or modified.

biological anthropology: The study of human biological variation in time and space; includes evolution, genetics, growth and development, and primatology.

civilization: A complex society with a government and social classes; synonyms are *nation-state* and *state*.

cultural ecology: The study of ecosystems that include people, focusing on how human use of nature influences and is influenced by social organization and cultural values.

culture: Distinctly human; transmitted through learning; traditions and customs that govern behavior and beliefs.

culture and personality: A subfield of cultural anthropology; examines variation in psychological traits and personality characteristics among cultures.

ecology: The study of interrelationships among living things in an environment.

ecosystem: A patterned arrangement of energy flows and exchanges; includes organisms sharing a common environment and that environment.

enculturation: The social process by which culture is learned and transmitted across the generations.

ethnography: Field work in a particular culture.

ethnology: Cross-cultural comparison; the comparative study of ethnographic data, of society, and of culture.

evolution: Descent with modification; change in form over generations.

food production: Cultivation of plants and domestication (stockbreeding) of animals; first developed in the Middle East 10,000 to 12,000 years ago.

general anthropology: The field of anthropology as a whole, consisting of cultural, archaeological, biological, and linguistic anthropology.

holistic: Interested in the whole of the human condition: past, present, and future; biology, society, language, and culture.

hominids: Members of the zoological family (Hominidae) that includes fossil and living humans.

humanities: Academic fields that study languages, texts, philosophies, arts, music, performances, and other forms of creative expression.

linguistic anthropology: The descriptive, comparative, and historical study of language and of linguistic similarities and differences in time, space, and society.

linkages: Interconnections between small-scale and large-scale units and systems; political, economic, informational, and other cultural links among village, region, nation, and world.

medical anthropology: Field including biological and cultural, theoretical and applied, anthropologists concerned with the sociocultural context and implications of disease and illness.

nation-state: See *civilization*.

osteology: The study of bones; useful to biological anthropologists studying the fossil record.

paleoanthropology: The study of hominid evolution as revealed by the fossil record.

paleoecology: The study, often by archaeologists, of ecosystems of the past.

participant observation: A characteristic ethnographic technique; taking part in the events one is observing, describing, and analyzing.

physical anthropology: See *biological anthropology*.

potsherds: Fragments of earthenware; pottery studied by archaeologists in interpreting prehistoric life styles.

prehistory: The period before the invention of writing (less than 6,000 years ago).

primates: Monkeys, apes, and prosimians; members of the zoological order that includes humans.

primatology: The study of the biology, behavior, social life, and evolution of monkeys, apes, and other nonhuman primates.

science: A systematic field of study or body of knowledge that aims, through experiment, observation, and deduction, to produce reliable explanations of phenomena, with reference to the material and physical world.

society: Organized life in groups; typical of humans and other animals.

state: See *civilization*.

STUDY QUESTIONS

1. What does it mean to say that anthropology is comparative and holistic?
2. What are the subdisciplines of general anthropology? What unifies them into a single discipline?
3. How do cultural anthropology and sociology differ?
4. How is anthropology related to other human sciences, and what has it contributed to them?

SUGGESTED ADDITIONAL READING

CLIFFORD, J.
1988 *The Predicament of Culture: Twentieth-Century Ethnography, Literature, and Art.* Cambridge, MA: Harvard University Press. Literary evaluation of classic and modern anthropologists and discussion of issues of ethnographic authority.

FAGAN, B. M.
1991 *People of the Earth: An Introduction to World Prehistory,* 7th ed. New York: HarperCollins. Introduction to the archaeological study of prehistoric societies, using examples from all areas.
1994 *Archeology: A Brief Introduction,* 5th ed. New York: HarperCollins. Introduction to archaeological theory, techniques, and approaches, including field survey, excavation, and analysis of materials.

GEERTZ, C.
1995 *After the Fact: Two Countries, Four Decades, One Anthropologist.* Cambridge, MA: Harvard University Press. A prominent cultural anthropologist reflects on his work in Morocco and Indonesia.

HARRIS, M.
1989 *Our Kind: Who We Are, Where We Came From, Where We Are Going.* New York: Harper-Collins. Fascinating popular anthropology; origins of humans, culture, and major sociopolitical institutions.

MARCUS, G. E., AND M. M. J. FISCHER
1986 *Anthropology as Cultural Critique: An Experimental Moment in the Human Sciences.* Chicago: University of Chicago Press. Different types of ethnographic accounts as forms of writing, a vision of modern anthropology, and a consideration of anthropologists' public and professional roles.

NASH, D.
1993 *A Little Anthropology,* 2nd ed. Englewood Cliffs, NJ: Prentice-Hall. Short introduction to societies and cultures, with comments on developing nations and modern America.

PFEIFFER, J. E.
1985 *The Emergence of Humankind,* 4th ed. New York: HarperCollins. Introduction to human biological evolution and the primates.

PODOLEFSKY, A., AND P. J. BROWN, EDS.
1994 *Applying Anthropology: An Introductory Reader,* 3rd ed. Mountain View, CA: Mayfield. Fifty essays focusing on anthropology's relevance to contemporary life; a readable survey of the current range of activities in applied anthropology.

C H A P T E R 2

FIELD METHODS

**ETHNOGRAPHY: ANTHROPOLOGY'S
DISTINCTIVE STRATEGY**

ETHNOGRAPHIC TECHNIQUES
Observation
Participant Observation
Conversation, Interviewing, and Interview Schedules
The Genealogical Method
Well-Informed Informants
Life Histories
Emic and Etic Research Strategies
Problem-Oriented Ethnography
Longitudinal Research

Box: The Evolution of Ethnography

SURVEY RESEARCH

**DIFFERENCES BETWEEN SURVEY RESEARCH
AND ETHNOGRAPHY**

**ANTHROPOLOGICAL RESEARCH IN COMPLEX
SOCIETIES**
Urban Anthropology
Anthropology in Complex Societies

Anthropology differs from other fields that study human beings because it is comparative, holistic, and global. Anthropologists study biology, language, and culture, past and present, in ancient and modern societies. This chapter compares the field methods of cultural anthropology with those of the other social sciences.

Anthropology started to separate from sociology around the turn of the twentieth century. Early students of society, such as the French scholar Emile Durkheim, were among the founders of both sociology and anthropology. Comparing the organization of simple and complex societies, Durkheim studied the religions of Native Australia (Durkheim 1912/1961) as well as mass phenomena (such as suicide rates) in modern nations (Durkheim 1897/1951). Eventually anthropology would specialize in the former, sociology in the latter.

ETHNOGRAPHY: ANTHROPOLOGY'S DISTINCTIVE STRATEGY

Anthropology developed into a separate field as early scholars worked on Indian (Native American) reservations and traveled to distant lands to study small groups of foragers and cultivators. This type of firsthand personal study of local settings is called *ethnography*. Traditionally, the process of becoming a cultural anthropologist has required a field experience in another society. Early ethnographers lived in small-scale, relatively isolated societies, with simple technologies and economies.

Ethnography thus emerged as a research strategy in societies with greater cultural uniformity and less social differentiation than are found in large, modern, industrial nations. In such nonindustrial settings, ethnographers have needed to consider fewer paths of enculturation to understand social life. Traditionally, ethnographers have tried to understand the whole of an alien culture (or, more realistically, as much as they can, given limitations of time and perception). To pursue this holistic goal, ethnographers adopt a free-ranging strategy for gathering information. They move from setting to setting, place to place, and subject to subject to discover the totality and interconnectedness of social life.

Ethnography, by expanding our knowledge of the range of human diversity, provides a foundation for generalizations about human behavior and social life. Ethnographers draw on a variety of techniques to piece together a picture of otherwise alien life styles. Anthropologists usually employ several (but rarely all) of the techniques discussed here.

ETHNOGRAPHIC TECHNIQUES

The characteristic *field techniques* of the ethnographer include the following:

1. Direct, firsthand observation of daily behavior, including *participant observation*
2. Conversation with varying degrees of formality, from the daily chitchat that helps maintain rapport and provides knowledge about what is going on to prolonged *interviews*, which can be unstructured or structured
3. *Interview schedules* to ensure that complete, comparable information is available for everyone of interest to the study
4. The *genealogical method*
5. Detailed work with *well-informed informants* about particular areas of community life
6. In-depth interviewing, often leading to the collection of *life histories* of particular people
7. **Emic** (actor-oriented) research strategies that focus on local (native) beliefs and perceptions and **etic** (observer-oriented) approaches that give priority to the ethnographer's perceptions and conclusions
8. Problem-oriented research of many sorts
9. Longitudinal research—the continuous long-term study of an area or site

Observation

Ethnographers must pay attention to hundreds of details of daily life, seasonal events, and unusual happenings. They must observe individual and collective behavior in varied settings. They should record what they see as they see it. Things will never seem quite as strange as they do during the first few days and weeks in the field. The ethnographer eventually gets used to, and accepts as normal, cultural patterns that were initially alien.

Many ethnographers record their impressions in a personal *diary*, which is kept separate from more formal *field notes*. Later, this record of early impressions will help point out some of the most basic aspects of cultural diversity. Such aspects include distinctive smells, noises people make, how they cover their mouths when they eat, and how they gaze at others. These patterns, which are so basic as to seem almost trivial, are part of what Bronislaw Malinowski called "the imponderabilia of native life and of typical behavior" (Malinowski 1922/1961, p. 20). These features of culture are so fundamental that natives take them for granted. They are too basic even to talk about, but the unaccustomed eye of the fledgling anthropologist perceives them. Thereafter they are submerged in familiarity and fade to the edge of consciousness. This is why initial impressions are valuable and should be recorded. First and foremost, ethnographers should be accurate observers, recorders, and reporters of what they see in the field.

Participant Observation

Ethnographers don't study animals in laboratory cages. The experiments that psychologists do with pigeons, chickens, guinea pigs, and rats are very different from ethnographic procedure. Anthropologists don't systematically control subjects' rewards and punishments or their exposure to certain stimuli. Our subjects are not speechless animals but human beings. It is not part of ethnographic procedure to manipulate them, control their environments, or experimentally induce certain behaviors.

One of ethnography's characteristic procedures is *participant observation*, which means that we take part in community life as we study it. As human beings living among others, we cannot be totally impartial and detached observers. We must also take part in many of the events and processes we are observing and trying to comprehend. To exemplify participant observation, let me describe aspects of my own ethnographic field work in Madagascar, a large island off the southeastern coast of Africa, and in Brazil. During the fourteen months I lived in Madagascar in 1966–67, I simultaneously observed and participated in many occasions in Betsileo life. I helped out at harvest time, joining other people who climbed atop—in order to stamp down on and compact—accumulating stacks of rice stalks. One September, for a reburial ceremony, I bought a silk shroud for a village ancestor. I entered the village tomb and watched people lovingly rewrap the bones and decaying flesh of their ancestors. I ac-

companied Betsileo peasants to town and to market. I observed their dealings with outsiders and sometimes offered help when problems arose.

In Arembepe, a fishing community in Bahia state, on Brazil's northeast coast, I sailed on the Atlantic in simple boats with local fishermen. I gave Jeep rides into the capital to malnourished babies, to pregnant mothers, and once to a teenage girl possessed by a spirit. All those people needed to consult specialists outside the village. I danced on Arembepe's festive occasions, drank libations commemorating new births, and became a godfather to a village girl. Most anthropologists have similar field experiences. The common humanity of the student and the studied, the ethnographer and the researched community, makes participant observation inevitable.

Conversation, Interviewing, and Interview Schedules

Participating in local life means that ethnographers constantly talk to people and ask questions about what they observe. As their knowledge of the native language increases, they understand more. There are several stages in learning a field language. First is the naming phase—asking name after name of the objects around us. Later we are able to pose more complex questions and understand the replies. We begin to understand simple conversations between two villagers. If our language expertise proceeds far enough, we eventually become able to comprehend rapid-fire public discussions and group conversations. The special oratory of political events and ceremonial or ritual occasions often contains **liturgies,** set formal sequences of words and actions that we can record for later analysis with a local expert.

One data-gathering technique I have used in both Arembepe and Madagascar involves an ethnographic survey that includes an interview schedule. In 1964, my fellow field workers and I attempted to complete an interview schedule in each of Arembepe's 160 households. We entered almost every household (fewer than 5 percent refused to participate) to ask a set of questions on a printed form.

Our results provided us with a census and basic information about the village. We wrote down the name, age, and sex of each household member. We gathered data on family type, political party, religion, present and previous jobs, income,

Ethnographers strive to establish rapport—a good, friendly relationship based on personal contact—with informants. These women in Guatemala are pleased with this anthropologist's gift—photos of themselves.

expenditures, diet, possessions, and many other items on our eight-page form.

Although we were doing a survey, our approach differed from the survey research design routinely used by sociologists and other social scientists working in large, industrial nations. That survey research, discussed below, involves sampling (choosing a small, manageable study group from a larger population) and impersonal data collection. We did not select a partial sample from the total population. Instead, we tried to interview in all households in the community we were studying (that is, to have a total sample). We used an interview schedule rather than a questionnaire. With the **interview schedule,** the ethnographer talks face to face with informants, asks the questions, and writes down the answers. **Questionnaire** procedures tend to be more indirect and impersonal; the respondent often fills in the form.

Our goal of getting a total sample allowed us to meet almost everyone in the village and helped us establish rapport. Arembepeiros still talk warmly about how, three decades ago, we were interested enough in them to visit their homes and ask them questions. We stood in sharp contrast to the other outsiders the Arembepeiros had known who considered them too poor and backward to be taken seriously.

Like other survey research, however, our interview-schedule survey did gather comparable quantifiable information. It gave us a basis for assessing patterns and exceptions in village life. Our home visits also provided opportunities to do informal and follow-up interviewing. Our schedules included a core set of questions that were posed to everyone. However, some interesting side issues often came up during the interview.

We would pursue these leads into many dimensions of village life. One woman, for instance, a midwife, became the "well-informed informant" we consulted later, when we wanted detailed information about local childbirth. Another woman had done an internship at an Afro-Brazilian cult (*candomblé*) house in the city. She still went there regu-

Working in natural communities, anthropologists form personal relationships with informants as they study their lives. Sometimes ethnographers become fictive or "adoptive" relatives of informants to whom they are especially close. Here, David Maybury-Lewis—host of the "Millennium" TV series shown on PBS in 1992—sits with his Xavante brother, Sipuba.

Kinship and descent are important social building blocks in nonindustrial cultures. Without writing, genealogical information may be preserved in art. Here, carvings on a tomb built by the Tanosy people of Ampanihy, Madagascar, depict their ancestors.

larly to study, dance, and get possessed. She became our *candomblé* expert.

Thus, our interview-schedule survey provided a structure that *directed but did not confine* us as researchers. It enabled our ethnography to be both quantitative and qualitative. The quantitative part consisted of the basic information we gathered and later analyzed statistically. The qualitative dimension came from our follow-up questions, open-ended discussions, pauses for gossip, and work with well-informed informants.

The Genealogical Method

Another ethnographic technique is the **genealogical method.** Early ethnographers developed genealogical notation to deal with principles of kinship, de-

scent, and marriage, which are the social building blocks of nonindustrial cultures. In contemporary North America most of our contacts outside the home are with nonrelatives. However, people in nonindustrial cultures spend their lives almost exclusively with relatives. Anthropologists must record genealogical data to reconstruct history and understand current relationships. In societies without a central government, these links are basic to social life and to political organization. Anthropologists even classify such societies as **kin-based.** Everyone is related to, and spends most of his or her time with, everyone else, and rules of behavior attached to particular kin relationships are basic to everyday life. Marriage is also crucial in organizing nonindustrial societies because strategic marriages between villages, tribes, and clans create political alliances.

Well-Informed Informants

Every community has people who by accident, experience, talent, or training can provide the most complete or useful information about particular aspects of life. These people are **well-informed informants.** In Ivato, the Betsileo village where I spent most of my time, a man named Rakoto was a particularly good informant about village history. However, when I asked him to work with me on a genealogy of the fifty to sixty people buried in the village tomb, he called in his cousin Tuesdaysfather, who knew more about this subject. Tuesdaysfather had survived an epidemic of Spanish influenza that ravaged Madagascar, along with much of the world, around 1919. Immune to the disease himself, Tuesdaysfather had the grim job of burying his kin as they died. He kept track of everyone buried in the tomb. Tuesdaysfather helped me with the tomb genealogy. Rakoto joined him in telling me personal details about the deceased villagers.

Life Histories

In nonindustrial societies as in our own, individual personalities, interests, and abilities vary. Some villagers prove to be more interested in the ethnographer's work and are more helpful, interesting, and pleasant than others. Anthropologists develop likes and dislikes in the field as we do at home. Often, when we find someone unusually interesting, we collect his or her **life history.** This recollection of a lifetime of experiences provides a more intimate and personal cultural portrait than would be possible otherwise. Life histories reveal how specific people perceive, react to, and contribute to changes that affect their lives. Such accounts can illustrate diversity, which exists within any community, since the focus is on how different people interpret and deal with some of the same problems.

Emic and Etic Research Strategies

To study cultures, anthropologists have used two approaches, the emic (actor-oriented) and the etic (observer-oriented). An **emic** approach investigates how natives (or one native, in the case of a life history) think. How do they perceive and categorize the world? What are their rules for behavior and thought? What has meaning for them? How do they

imagine and explain things? The anthropologist seeks the "native viewpoint" and relies on the culture bearers—the actors in a culture—to determine whether something they do, say, or think is significant.

However, natives aren't scientists. They may think that spirits cause illnesses that come from germs. Also, they may believe political leaders who tell them that missiles are peacemakers. The **etic** (observer-oriented) approach shifts the focus of research from native categories, expressions, explanations, and interpretations to those of the anthropologist. The etic approach realizes that culture bearers are often too involved in what they are doing to interpret their cultures impartially. The etic ethnographer gives more weight to what he or she (the observer) notices and considers important. As a trained scientist, the anthropologist should try to bring an objective and comprehensive viewpoint to the study of other cultures. Of course, the anthropologist, like any other scientist, is also a human being with cultural blinders that prevent complete objectivity. As in other sciences, proper training can reduce but not totally eliminate the observer's bias. But anthropologists do have special training to compare behavior between different societies.

In practice, most anthropologists combine emic and etic strategies in their field work. Native statements, perceptions, and opinions help ethnographers understand how cultures work. Native beliefs are also interesting and valuable in themselves and broaden the anthropologist's view of the world. However, natives often fail to admit, or even recognize, certain causes and consequences of their behavior. This is as true of North Americans as it is of people in any other society. To describe and interpret culture, ethnographers should recognize the biases that come from their own culture as well as those of the people being studied.

Problem-Oriented Ethnography

Although anthropologists are interested in the whole context of human behavior, it is impossible to study everything, and field research usually addresses specific questions. Most ethnographers enter the field with a specific problem to investigate, and they collect data about variables deemed relevant to that problem. And informants' answers to questions are not the only data source. Anthropolo-

Ethnographers typically enter the field with a specific topic to investigate. Using varied research methods, including interviews with well-informed informants, they collect data about variables deemed relevant to that topic—such as rice production, the mainstay of the economy in West Java, Indonesia.

gists also gather information on factors like population density, environmental quality, climate, physical geography, diet, and land use. Sometimes this involves direct measurement—of rainfall, temperature, fields, yields, dietary quantities, or time allocation (Bailey 1990; Johnson 1978). Often it means that we consult government records or archives.

The information of interest to ethnographers is not limited to what informants can and do tell us. For much that is significant we can rely on neither participant observation nor intensive local interviews. In an increasingly interconnected world, local informants lack knowledge about many factors (regional, national, and international) that affect their lives. Our informants may be as mystified as we are by the exercise of power from regional, national, and international centers.

Longitudinal Research

Geography limits anthropologists less now than in the past, when it could take months to reach a field site, and return visits were rare. New systems of transportation allow anthropologists to widen the area of their research and to return repeatedly. Ethnographic reports now routinely include data from two or more field stays. **Longitudinal research** is the long-term study of a community, region, society, culture, or other unit, usually based on repeated visits. One example of such research is the longitudinal study of the interplay of social and economic forces in Gwembe District, Zambia. This study, planned in 1956 as a longitudinal project by Elizabeth Colson and Thayer Scudder, continues with Colson, Scudder, and their associates of various

THE EVOLUTION OF ETHNOGRAPHY

The Polish anthropologist Bronislaw Malinowski (1884–1942), who spent most of his professional life in England, is generally considered the father of ethnography. Like most anthropologists of his time, Malinowski did *salvage ethnography,* in the belief that the ethnographer's job is to study and record cultural diversity threatened by westernization. Early ethnographic accounts (*ethnographies*), including Malinowski's classic *Argonauts of the Western Pacific* (1922/1961), were similar to earlier traveler and explorer accounts in describing the writer's discovery of unknown people and places. However, the *scientific* aims of ethnographies set them apart from books by explorers and amateurs.

The style that dominated "classic" ethnographies was *ethnographic realism.* The writer's goal was to present an accurate, objective, scientific account of a different way of life, written by someone who knew it firsthand. This knowledge came from an "ethnographic adventure" involving immersion in an alien language and culture. Ethnographers derived

their authority—both as scientists and as voices of "the native" or "the other"—from this personal research experience.

Malinowski drafted *functionalist* ethnographies, guided by the assumption that all aspects of culture are linked (functions of each other). A functionalist ethnography begins with *any* aspect of a culture, such as a Trobriand Islands sailing expedition. The ethnographer then follows the links between that entry point and other areas of the culture, such as magic, religion, myths, kinship, and trade. Contemporary ethnographies tend to be less inclusive, focusing on particular topics, such as kinship or religion.

According to Malinowski, a primary task of the ethnographer is "to grasp the native's point of view, his relation to life, to realize *his* vision of *his* world (1922/1961, p. 25—Malinowski's italics). Since the 1970s *interpretive anthropology* has considered the task of describing and interpreting that which is meaningful to natives. Interpretivists such as Clifford Geertz (1973) view cultures as meaningful texts which natives

constantly "read" and which ethnographers must decipher. According to Geertz, anthropologists may choose anything in a culture that interests them, fill in details, and elaborate to inform their readers about meanings in that culture. Meanings are carried by public symbolic forms, including words, rituals, and customs. In the interpretive view, cross-cultural understanding emerges through "dialogues" among natives, anthropologist, and reader, who are all parties to a conversation.

A current trend in ethnographic writing is to question traditional goals, methods, and styles, including salvage ethnography and ethnographic realism (Marcus and Cushman 1982; Clifford 1982, 1988). Marcus and Fischer argue that anthropology has reached "an experimental moment." Experimentation is needed because all people and cultures have already been "discovered" and must now be "*rediscovered* . . . in changing historical circumstances" (1986, p. 24).

These experimental anthropologists recognize that ethnographies

nationalities. The Gwembe research project is both longitudinal (multitime) and multisite (considering several local field sites) (Colson and Scudder 1975; Scudder and Colson 1980). Four villages, in different areas, have been followed for four decades. Periodic village censuses provide basic data on population, economy, and other variables chosen to monitor changes in kinship and religious behavior. Censused people who have moved are traced and interviewed (if possible) to see how their lives compare with those of people who have stayed in the village. Information on labor migration, visits between town and country, and other linkages show the extent to which rural and urban belong to a single system.

Zambian assistants have kept records of local events and diaries of food bought and eaten. From field notes it is possible to reconstruct prices for different periods. Shifts in preferences for products are documented by shopping lists provided by villagers. Field notes also contain observations from attendance at courts, village and district meetings, church services, funerals, and ceremonies.

This information is supplemented by interviews with traders and officials, technical workers, political leaders, and foreigners who work for religious missions and *nongovernmental organizations* (NGOs). The anthropologists have also consulted government and other records, both published and unpublished. Zambian social scientists who have worked

are works of art as well as works of science. Ethnographic texts are literary creations in which the ethnographer, as mediator, communicates information from the "natives" to readers. Some recent experimental ethnographies are "dialogic," presenting ethnography as a dialogue between the anthropologist and one or more native informants (e.g., Dwyer 1982). These works draw attention to ways in which ethnographers, and by extension their readers, communicate with other cultures.

Ethnographers interpret and mediate between cultures in two ways. During field work they must interpret from native categories to their own, and in writing they must interpret for their readers. However, some dialogic ethnographies have been criticized as being too confessional, spending too much time on the anthropologist and too little on the natives and their culture.

The dialogic ethnography is one genre within a larger experimental category—that is, *reflexive ethnography*. Here the ethnographer-writer puts his or her personal feelings and reactions to the field situation right in the text. An experimental writing strategy is prominent in reflexive accounts. The ethnographer may adopt some of the conventions of the novel, including first-person narration, conversations, dialogues, and humor.

Marcus and Fischer (1986) caution that the desire to be personal can be overplayed to the point of exhibitionism. Nevertheless, experimental ethnographies, using new ways of showing what it means to be a Samoan or a Brazilian, may convey to the reader a richer and more complex understanding of human experience. The result may be to convince readers that culture matters more than they might otherwise have thought.

Recent ethnographic writers have also attempted to correct the deficiency of *romanticized timelessness*, which is obvious in the classics. Linked to salvage ethnography was the idea of the *ethnographic present*—the period before westernization, when the "true" native culture flourished. This notion gives classic ethnographies an eternal, timeless quality. The cultures they describe seem frozen in the ethnographic pre-sent. Providing the only jarring note in this idealized picture are occasional comments by the author about traders or missionaries, suggesting that in actuality the natives were already part of the world system.

Anthropologists now recognize that the ethnographic present is a rather unrealistic and romantic construct. Cultures have been in contact—and have been changing—throughout history. Most native cultures had at least one major foreign encounter before any anthropologist ever came their way. Most of them had already been incorporated in some fashion into nation-states or colonial systems.

Classic ethnographies neglected history, politics, and the world system, but contemporary ethnographies usually recognize that cultures constantly change and that an ethnographic account applies to a particular moment. A current trend in ethnography is to focus on the ways in which cultural ideas serve political and economic interests. Another trend is to describe how various particular "natives" participate in broader historical, political, and economic processes (Shostak 1981).

in the district also provide their insights about the changes taking place.

Successively different questions have come to the fore, while basic data on communities and individuals continue to be collected. The first focus of study was the impact of a large hydroelectric dam, which flooded much of the Zambezi River plain and subjected the Gwembe people to forced resettlement. However, the dam also spurred road building and other activities that brought the people of Gwembe more closely in touch with the rest of Zambia (Colson 1971; Scudder 1982; Scudder and Habarad 1991).

By the late 1960s education had become a major concern at Gwembe and was playing an important role in the changes then taking place. Accordingly, Scudder and Colson (1980) designed research to examine the role of education in providing access to new opportunities and in increasing social differentiation within the district and nation. At the same time, it was evident that alcohol consumption was a growing problem. A third major study then examined the role of changing markets, transportation, and exposure to town values in the transformation of domestic brewing and a radical change in drinking patterns (Colson and Scudder 1988).

SURVEY RESEARCH

As anthropologists work increasingly in large-scale societies, they have developed innovative ways of blending ethnography and survey research (Fricke 1994). Before considering such combinations of field methods, I must describe survey research and the main differences between survey research and ethnography as traditionally practiced. Working mainly in large, populous nations, sociologists, social psychologists, political scientists, and economists have developed and refined the **survey research** design, which involves sampling, impersonal data collection, and statistical analysis. Survey research usually draws a **sample** (a manageable study group) from a much larger population. By studying a properly selected and representative sample, social scientists can make accurate inferences about the larger population.

In smaller-scale societies, ethnographers get to know most of the people, but given the greater size and complexity of nations, survey research cannot help being more impersonal. Survey researchers call the people they study **respondents.** (Ethnographers work with **informants.**) Respondents are people who respond to questions during a survey. Sometimes survey researchers personally interview them. Sometimes, after an initial meeting, they ask respondents to fill out a questionnaire. In other cases researchers mail printed questionnaires to randomly selected sample members or have graduate students interview or telephone them. (In a **random sample,** all members of the population have an equal statistical chance of being chosen for inclusion. A random sample is selected by randomizing procedures, such as tables of random numbers, which are found in many statistics textbooks.)

Anyone who has grown up recently in the United States or Canada has heard of sampling. Probably the most familiar example is the polling used to predict political races. The media hire agencies to estimate outcomes and do exit polls to find out what kinds of people voted for which candidates. During sampling, researchers gather information about age, gender, religion, occupation, income, and political party preference. These characteristics (**variables**— attributes that vary among members of a sample or population) are known to influence political decisions.

The number of variables influencing social identity and behavior increases with, and can be considered a measure of, social complexity. Many more variables affect social identities, experiences, and activities in a modern nation than is the case in the small communities and local settings where ethnography grew up. In the contemporary United States or Canada hundreds of factors influence social behavior and attitudes. These social predictors include our religion; the region of the country we grew up in; whether we come from a town, suburb, or inner city; and our parents' professions, ethnic origins, and income levels.

Sociologists, social psychologists, and political scientists typically do survey research, which is indispensable for the scientific study of large, populous nations. Social surveys involve sampling, structured interviews or questionnaires, and statistical analysis. Survey research is also used in political polling and market research. This photo shows polltakers working for the Gallup organization in Mexico City.

DIFFERENCES BETWEEN SURVEY RESEARCH AND ETHNOGRAPHY

There are several differences between survey research and ethnography:

1. In survey research, the object of study is usually a sample chosen (randomly or otherwise) by the researcher. Ethnographers normally study whole, functioning communities.
2. Ethnographers do firsthand field work, establishing a direct relationship with the people they study. Ethnographers strive to establish **rapport,** a good, friendly working relationship based on personal contact, with informants. Often, survey researchers have no personal contact with respondents. They may hire assistants to interview by phone or ask respondents to fill out a printed form or write answers to a questionnaire.
3. Ethnographers get to know their informants and usually take an interest in the totality of their lives. Often, a social survey focuses on a small number of variables, such as the ones that influence voting, rather than on the totality of people's lives.
4. Survey researchers normally work in modern nations, where most people are literate, permitting respondents to fill in their own questionnaires. Ethnographers are more likely to study people who do not read and write.
5. Because survey research deals with large and diverse groups and with samples and probability, its results must be analyzed statistically. Because the societies that anthropologists traditionally study are smaller and less diverse, many ethnographers have not acquired detailed knowledge of statistics.

ANTHROPOLOGICAL RESEARCH IN COMPLEX SOCIETIES

During World War I, Malinowski spent several years studying the Trobriand Islanders. In his classic ethnographic *monograph* (a report based on ethnographic field work) *Argonauts of the Western Pacific,* Malinowski describes how an ethnographer "sets up shop" in another society. Like Malinowski's research in the Trobriands, my field work

"OH, YEAH! THE ANTHROPOLOGIST WHO IS STUDYING OUR TRIBE CAN WRITE RINGS AROUND THE ANTHROPOLOGIST WHO IS STUDYING YOUR TRIBE!"

in Arembepe, Brazil, focused on a single community as the object of intensive study. I could get to know everyone in Arembepe because its population was small and its social system was uncomplicated. However, unlike the Trobriands, Arembepe was not a tribal society but part of a large, populous, and diverse nation. The Trobriand Islands are small enough for an ethnographer to visit every village. Malinowski might well have managed to talk with every Trobriander. I could never hope to visit every Brazilian community or meet every Brazilian.

Malinowski used his field site as a basis for describing Trobriand society as a whole. Anthropologists have been criticized for generalizing about an entire culture on the basis of research in just one community, a practice which is somewhat more defensible for small-scale, homogeneous societies than for complex nations. My study of Arembepe, a rural community in a particular region of an urbanized nation, could never encapsulate Brazil as a whole. Thus I viewed my Arembepe field study as part of a larger research program. I was just one ethnographer among many, each working separately in

Particularly since the 1950s, anthropologists have investigated contemporary life styles, including urban problems and social contrasts in North America. Here the rich meet the poor—tourists and homeless people exchange an awkward glance on the palm-lined waterfront of Santa Barbara, California.

different Brazilian communities. Eventual comparison of those studies would help reveal the range of diversity in Brazil.

One way of using ethnography in modern nations is to do such a series of **community studies.** Field sites in different regions can be used to sample different economic adaptations, degrees of participation in the modern world, and historical trends. However, even a thousand rural communities cannot constitute an adequate sample of national diversity. We must also consider urban life and social contrasts that are absent in small communities. The range of variation encountered in any nation makes the social survey an obligatory research procedure.

Nevertheless, ethnography can be used to supplement and fine-tune survey research. Anthropologists can transfer the personal, direct, observation-based techniques of ethnography to social groups and social networks in *any setting*. A combination of survey research and ethnography can provide new perspectives on life in **complex societies** (large and populous societies with social stratification and central governments). Preliminary ethnography can also help develop relevant and culturally appropriate questions for inclusion in national surveys.

Urban Anthropology

A series of community studies in a nation reveals variation in its small-town and rural life. However, there is much more to national life than small communities. One response to this problem has been **urban anthropology**—the anthropological study of cities. Particularly since the 1950s, anthropologists have systematically investigated urban problems and life styles in the United States, Canada, and abroad. A common illustration of urban anthropology is the practice of having students do local field work for an anthropology course (assuming the college is in an urban setting).

In my own courses in Ann Arbor, Michigan, undergraduates have done research on sororities, fraternities, teams, campus organizations, and the local homeless population. Other students have systematically observed behavior in public places. These include racquetball courts, restaurants, bars, football stadiums, markets, malls, and classrooms. Other "modern anthropology" projects use anthropological techniques to interpret and analyze mass media. Anthropologists have been studying their own cultures for decades, and anthropological research in the United States and Canada is booming today. (The appendix, "American Popular Culture," provides several examples.) Wherever there is patterned human behavior, there is grist for the anthropological mill.

Anthropology in Complex Societies

Anthropologists can use field techniques such as participant observation and firsthand data collection in any social setting. However, for contemporary societies, anthropologists increasingly supplement traditional techniques with new procedures, many borrowed from survey research. During studies of urban life, modern anthropologists routinely gather statistical data. In any complex society, many predictor variables (*social indicators*) influence behavior and opinions. Because we must be able to detect, measure, and compare the influence of social indicators, many contemporary anthropological studies have a statistical foundation. Even in rural field work, more anthropologists now draw samples, gather quantitative data, and use statistics to interpret them (see Bernard 1994). Quantifiable information may permit a more precise assessment of similarities and differences between communities. Statistical analysis can support and round out an ethnographic account of local social life.

However, in the best studies, the hallmark of ethnography remains: Anthropologists enter the community and get to know the people. They participate in local activities, networks, and associations, in the city or in the countryside. They observe and experience social conditions and problems. They watch the effects of national policies and programs on local life. I believe that the ethnographic method and the emphasis on personal relationships in social research are valuable gifts that anthropology brings to the study of a complex society.

In rural as well as urban settings, contemporary anthropologists increasingly use formal methods and/or rely on advanced technology to store, process, and analyze information. Although research techniques are changing, the hallmark of ethnography remains: the anthropologist enters the community and gets to know the people. Shown here—in Kitari, Kenya—an anthropologist intrigues local children with her notebook computer, hooked up to a car battery.

SUMMARY

Ethnography has several characteristic field procedures, including observation, establishing rapport, participant observation, conversation, listening to native accounts, formal and informal interviewing, the genealogical method, work with well-informed informants, life histories, emic and etic research strategies, problem-oriented ethnography, and longitudinal research. Recording the imponderabilia of daily life is particularly useful early in field work. That is when the most basic, distinctive, and alien features of another culture are most noticeable. Ethnographers do not systematically manipulate their subjects or conduct experiments. Rather, they work in natural communities and form personal relationships with informants as they study their lives.

Interview schedules are forms that ethnographers fill in by visiting many households. The schedules guide formal interviews, ensuring that the ethnographer collects comparable information from everyone. These interviews also introduce the researcher to many people. The schedule organizes the interview. However, ethnographers may also pursue additional topics in accordance with the particular interests and attributes of the interviewee.

Ethnographers work closely with well-informed informants to learn about particular areas of native life. Many ethnographers work long hours with particular informants. Life histories dramatize the fact that culture bearers are also individuals and document personal experiences with culture and culture change. The collection and analysis of genealogical information is particularly important in societies in which principles of kinship, descent, and marriage organize and integrate social and political life. Emic approaches focus on native perceptions and explanations of behavior. Etic approaches give priority to the ethnographer's own observations and conclu-sions. Anthropologists conduct many kinds of problem-oriented ethnography, and people are not our only data source. Measurements are made as well. Longitudinal research is the systematic study of an area or site over time.

Traditionally, anthropologists worked in small-scale societies; sociologists, in modern nations. Different field techniques emerged for the study of different types of societies. Sociologists and other social scientists who work in complex societies use survey research to sample variation.

There are several contrasts between survey research and ethnography. With more literate respondents, sociologists employ questionnaires, which the research subjects fill out. Anthropologists are more likely to use interview schedules, which the ethnographer fills in during a personal interview. Anthropologists do their field work in communities and study the totality of social life. Sociologists study samples to make inferences about a larger population. Sociologists are often interested in causal relationships between a limited number of variables. Anthropologists are more typically concerned with the interconnectedness of all aspects of social life.

Anthropologists use modified ethnographic techniques to study complex societies. The diversity of social life and subcultural variation in modern nations and cities requires social survey procedures. However, anthropologists add the intimacy and firsthand investigation characteristic of ethnography. Community studies in regions of modern nations provide firsthand, in-depth accounts of cultural variation and of regional historical and economic forces and trends. Anthropologists may use ethnographic procedures to study urban life, but they also make greater use of statistical techniques and analysis of the mass media in their research in complex societies.

GLOSSARY

community study: Anthropological method for studying complex societies. Small communities are studied ethnographically as being (partially) representative of regional culture or particular contrasts in national life.

complex societies: Nations; large and populous, with social stratification and central governments.

emic: The research strategy that focuses on native explanations and criteria of significance.

etic: The research strategy that emphasizes the observer's rather than the natives' explanations, categories, and criteria of significance.

genealogical method: Procedures by which ethnographers discover and record connections of kinship, descent, and marriage, using diagrams and symbols.

informants: Subjects in ethnographic research; people the ethnographer gets to know in the field, who teach him or her about their culture.

interview schedule: Ethnographic tool for structuring a formal interview. A prepared form (usually printed or mimeographed) that guides interviews with households or individuals being compared systematically. Contrasts with a *questionnaire* because the researcher has personal contact with the informants and records their answers.

kin-based: Characteristic of many nonindustrial societies. People spend their lives almost exclusively with their relatives; principles of kinship, descent, and marriage organize social life.

life history: Of an informant; provides a personal cultural portrait of existence or change in a culture.

liturgies: Set formal sequences of words and actions; common in political events and rituals or ceremonies.

longitudinal research: Long-term study of a community, region, society, culture, or other unit, usually based on repeated visits.

questionnaire: Form (usually printed) used by sociologists to obtain comparable information from respondents. Often mailed to and filled in by research subjects rather than by the researcher.

random sample: A sample in which all members of the population have an equal statistical chance of being included.

rapport: A good, friendly working relationship between people, for example, ethnographers and their informants.

respondents: Subjects in sociological research; the people who answer questions in questionnaires and other social surveys.

sample: A smaller study group chosen to represent a larger population.

survey research: Characteristic research procedure among social scientists other than anthropologists. Studies society through sampling, statistical analysis, and impersonal data collection.

urban anthropology: The anthropological study of cities.

variables: Attributes (e.g., sex, age, height, weight) that differ from one person or case to the next.

well-informed informant: Person who is an expert on a particular aspect of native life.

STUDY QUESTIONS

1. What are the characteristic field techniques of the ethnographer?
2. What are the imponderabilia of daily life, and when are they most obvious to the ethnographer?
3. What is participant observation?
4. What is the genealogical method, and why did it develop in anthropology?
5. What are the advantages for ethnography of life histories and working with well-informed informants?
6. What is the difference between emic and etic research strategies? Must anthropologists choose one of these approaches and reject the other?
7. Do all ethnographic data come from informants?
8. What is longitudinal research, and why is it of increasing importance in anthropology?
9. What is survey research design, and how does it differ from ethnography?
10. What are the differences between questionnaires and interview schedules?
11. What are the problems and advantages of community study research?
12. What techniques do anthropologists use to study urban life?

SUGGESTED ADDITIONAL READING

AGAR, M. H.
  1980 *The Professional Stranger: An Informal Introduction to Ethnography.* New York: Academic Press. Basics of ethnography, illustrated by the author's field experiences in India and among heroin addicts in the United States.

BERNARD, H. R.
  1994 *Research Methods in Anthropology,* 2nd ed. Thousand Oaks, CA: Sage. The most complete and up-to-date survey of methods of data collection, organization, and analysis in cultural anthropology.

BRIM, J. A., AND D. H. SPAIN
  1974 *Research Design in Anthropology.* New York: Harcourt Brace Jovanovich. Discusses hypotheses testing and anthropological research design.

KOTTAK, C. P., ED.
  1982 *Researching American Culture: A Guide for Student Anthropologists.* Ann Arbor: University of Michigan Press. Advice for college students doing field work in the United States. Includes papers by undergraduates and anthropologists on contemporary American culture.

PELTO, P. J., AND G. H. PELTO

1978   *Anthropological Research: The Structure of Inquiry*, 2nd ed. New York: Cambridge University Press. Discusses data collection and analysis, including the relationship between theory and field work, hypothesis construction, sampling, and statistics.

SPRADLEY, J. P.

1979   *The Ethnographic Interview.* New York: Harcourt Brace Jovanovich. Discussion of the ethnographic method, with emphasis on discovering native viewpoints.

CHAPTER 3

CULTURE

WHAT IS CULTURE?
Culture Is Learned
Culture Is Symbolic
Culture Seizes Nature
Culture Is General and Specific
Culture Is All-Encompassing

Box: Touching, Affection, Love, and Sex

Culture Is Shared
Culture Is Patterned
People Use Culture Creatively

Culture Is Adaptive and Maladaptive
Levels of Culture
Ethnocentrism and Cultural Relativism

UNIVERSALITY, PARTICULARITY, AND GENERALITY
Universality
Particularity
Generality

MECHANISMS OF CULTURAL CHANGE

The concept of culture has long been basic to anthropology. More than a century ago, in his classic book *Primitive Culture,* British anthropologist Edward Tylor proposed that systems of human behavior and thought are not random. Rather, they obey natural laws and therefore can be studied scientifically. Tylor's definition of culture still offers a good overview of the subject matter of anthropology and is widely quoted.

"Culture . . . is that complex whole which includes knowledge, belief, arts, morals, law, custom, and any other capabilities and habits acquired by man as a member of society" (Tylor 1871/1958, p. 1). The crucial phrase here is "acquired by man as a member of society." Tylor's definition focuses on beliefs and behavior that people acquire not through biological heredity but by growing up in a particular society where they are exposed to a specific cultural tradition. **Enculturation** is the process by which a child *learns* his or her culture.

WHAT IS CULTURE?

Culture Is Learned

The ease with which children absorb any cultural tradition reflects the uniquely elaborated hominid capacity to learn. There are different kinds of learning, some of which we share with other animals. One kind is **individual situational learning,** which occurs when an animal learns from, and bases its future behavior on, its own experience, for example, avoiding fire after discovering that it hurts. Animals also exhibit **social situational learning,** in which they learn from other members of the social group, not necessarily through language. Wolves, for example, learn hunting strategies from other pack members. Social situational learning is particularly important among monkeys and apes, our closest biological relatives. Finally there is **cultural learning.** This depends on the uniquely developed human capacity to use *symbols,* signs that have no necessary or natural connection with the things for which they stand.

A critical feature in hominid evolution is dependence on cultural learning. Through culture people create, remember, and deal with ideas. They grasp and apply specific systems of symbolic meaning. Anthropologist Clifford Geertz defines culture as ideas based on cultural learning and symbols. Cultures have been characterized as sets of "control mechanisms—plans, recipes, rules, constructions, what computer engineers call programs for the governing of behavior" (Geertz 1973, p. 44). These programs are absorbed by people through enculturation in particular traditions. People gradually internalize a previously established system of meanings and symbols which they use to define their world, express their feelings, and make their judgments. Thereafter, this system helps guide their behavior and perceptions throughout their lives.

Every person begins immediately, through a process of conscious and unconscious learning and interaction with others, to internalize, or incorporate, a cultural tradition through the process of enculturation. Sometimes culture is taught directly, as when parents tell their children to say "thank you" when someone gives them something or does them a favor.

Culture is also transmitted through observation. Children pay attention to the things that go on around them. They modify their behavior not just because other people tell them to but as a result of their own observations and growing awareness of what their culture considers right and wrong. Culture is also absorbed unconsciously. North Americans acquire their culture's notions about how far apart people should stand when they talk not by being directly told to maintain a certain distance but through a gradual process of observation, experience, and conscious and unconscious behavior modification. No one tells Latins to stand closer together than North Americans do, but they learn to do so anyway as part of their cultural tradition.

Culture Is Symbolic

Symbolic thought is unique and crucial to humans and to culture. Anthropologist Leslie White defined culture as

> dependent upon symbolling. . . . Culture consists of tools, implements, utensils, clothing, ornaments, customs, institutions, beliefs, rituals, games, works of art, language, etc. (White 1959, p. 3)

For White, culture originated when our ancestors acquired the ability to symbol, or freely and arbitrarily to originate and bestow meaning upon a thing or event, and, correspondingly, . . . to grasp and appreciate such meaning. (White 1959, p. 3)

A symbol is something verbal or nonverbal, within a particular language or culture, that comes to stand for something else. There is no obvious, natural, or necessary connection between the symbol and what it symbolizes. A pet that barks is no more naturally a *dog* than a *chien*, *Hund*, or *mbwa*, to use the words for the animal we call "dog" in French, German, and Swahili. Language is one of the distinctive possessions of *Homo sapiens*. No other animal has developed anything approaching the complexity of language.

Symbols are usually linguistic. However, there are also nonverbal symbols, such as flags, which stand for countries, as arches do for hamburger chains. Holy water is a potent symbol in Roman Catholicism. As is true of all symbols, the association between a symbol (water) and what is symbolized (holiness) is arbitrary and conventional. Water is not intrinsically holier than milk, blood, or other liquids. Holy water is not chemically different from ordinary water. Holy water is a symbol within Roman Catholicism, which is part of an international cultural system. A natural thing has been arbitrarily associated with a particular meaning for Catholics, who share common beliefs and experiences that are based on learning and are transmitted across the generations.

For hundreds of thousands of years, people have shared the abilities on which culture rests. These abilities are to learn, to think symbolically, to manipulate language, and to use tools and other cultural products in organizing their lives and coping with their environments. Every contemporary human population has the ability to symbol and thus to create and maintain culture. Our nearest relatives—chimpanzees and gorillas—have rudimentary cultural abilities. However, no other animal has elaborated cultural abilities—to learn, to communicate, and to store, process, and use information—to the same extent as *Homo*.

Culture Seizes Nature

Culture imposes itself on nature. I once arrived at a summer camp at 5 P.M. I was hot and wanted to swim in the lake. However, I read the camp rules and learned that no swimming was permitted after five. A cultural system had seized the lake, which is part of nature. Natural lakes don't close at five, but cultural lakes do.

Culture takes the natural biological urges we share with other animals and teaches us how to express them in particular ways. People have to eat, but culture teaches us what, when, and how. In many cultures people have their main meal at noon, but North Americans prefer a large dinner. English people eat fish for breakfast, but North Americans prefer hot cakes and cold cereals. Brazilians put hot milk into strong coffee, whereas North Americans pour cold milk into a weaker brew. Midwesterners dine at five or six, Spaniards at ten.

Like the lake at summer camp, human nature is appropriated by cultural systems and molded in hundreds of directions. All people must eliminate wastes from their bodies. However, some cultures teach people to defecate standing, while others tell them to do it sitting down. Frenchmen aren't embarrassed to urinate in public, routinely stepping into barely shielded *pissoirs* in Paris streets. Peasant women in the Andean highlands squat in the streets and urinate into gutters. They get all the privacy they need from their massive skirts. All these habits are parts of cultural traditions that have converted natural acts into cultural customs.

Culture Is General and Specific

All human populations have culture, which is therefore a generalized possession of the genus *Homo*. This is Culture (capital C) in the general sense, a capacity and possession shared by hominids. However, anthropologists also use the word *culture* to describe the different and varied cultural traditions of specific societies. This is culture in the specific sense (small c). Humanity shares a capacity for Culture, but people live in particular cultures, where they are enculturated along different lines. All people grow up in the presence of a particular set of cultural rules transmitted over the generations. These are the specific cultures or cultural traditions that anthropologists study.

Culture Is All-Encompassing

For anthropologists, Culture includes much more than refinement, taste, sophistication, education,

TOUCHING, AFFECTION, LOVE, AND SEX

Comparing the United States to Brazil—or virtually any Latin nation—we can see a striking cultural contrast between a culture that discourages physical contact and demonstrations of affection and one in which the contrary is true. We can also see the rampant confusion in North American culture about love, sex, and affection. This stands in sharp contrast to the more realistic Brazilian separation of the three.

"Don't touch me." "Take your hands off me." These are normal statements in North American culture that are virtually never heard in Brazil, the Western Hemisphere's second most populous country. North Americans don't like to be touched. The world's cultures have strikingly different opinions about matters of personal space. When North Americans talk, walk, and dance, they maintain a certain distance from others—their personal space. Brazilians, who maintain less physical distance, interpret this as a sign of coldness. When conversing with a North American, the Brazilian characteristically moves in as the North American "instinctively" retreats. In these body movements, neither Brazilian nor North American is trying consciously to be especially friendly or unfriendly. Each

The world's cultures have strikingly different opinions about personal space—how far apart people should be in normal encounters and interactions. Contrast the gap between these Japanese people with the closeness (including touching) of these Saudi Arabian men.

and appreciation of the fine arts. Not only college graduates but all people are "cultured." The most interesting and significant cultural forces are those that affect people every day of their lives, particularly those which influence children during enculturation. *Culture*, as defined anthropologically, encompasses features that are sometimes regarded as trivial or unworthy of serious study, such as "popular" culture. To understand contemporary North American culture, we must consider television, fast-

food restaurants, sports, and games. As a cultural manifestation, a rock star may be as interesting as a symphony conductor, a comic book as significant as a book-award winner.

Culture Is Shared

Culture is an attribute not of individuals per se but of individuals as members of *groups*. Culture is transmitted in society. We learn our culture by obis merely executing a program written on the self by years of exposure to a particular cultural tradition. Because of different ideas about proper social space, cocktail parties in international meeting places such as the United Nations can resemble an elaborate insect mating ritual as diplomats from different cultures advance, withdraw, and sidestep.

One of the most obvious differences between Brazil and the United States involves kissing, hugging, and touching. Middle-class Brazilians teach their children—both boys and girls—to kiss (on the cheek, two or three times, coming and going) every adult relative they ever see. Given the size of Brazilian extended families, this can mean hundreds of people. Females continue kissing throughout their lives. They kiss male and female kin, friends, relatives of friends, friends of relatives, friends of friends, and, when it seems appropriate, more casual acquaintances. Males go on kissing their female relatives and friends. Until they are adolescents, boys also kiss adult male relatives. Thereafter, Brazilian men greet each other with hearty handshakes and a traditional male hug (abraço). The closer the relationship, the tighter and longer-lasting the embrace. These comments apply to brothers, cousins, uncles, and friends. Many Brazilian men keep on kissing their fathers and uncles throughout their lives.

Like other North Americans who spend time in a Latin culture, I miss these kisses and handshakes when I get back to the United States. After several months in Brazil, I find North Americans rather cold and impersonal. Many Brazilians share this opinion. I have heard similar feelings expressed by Italian-Americans as they describe North Americans with different ethnic backgrounds.

Many North Americans fear physical contact and confuse love and affection with sex. According to clinical psychologist David E. Klimek, who has written about intimacy and marriage, "in American society, if we go much beyond simple touching, our behavior takes on a minor sexual twist" (Slade 1984). North Americans define demonstrations of affection with reference to marriage. Love and affection are supposed to unite the married pair, and they blend into sex. When a wife asks her husband for "a little affection," she may mean, or he may think she means, sex. Listening as North Americans discuss love and sex on talk shows and in other public forums, it is obvious that North American culture confuses these needs and feelings.

This confusion between love, affection, and sex is clear on Valentine's Day, which used to be just for lovers. Valentines used to be sent to wives, husbands, girlfriends, and boyfriends. Now, after years of promotion by the greeting card industry, they also go to mothers, fathers, sons, daughters, aunts, and uncles. Valentine's Day "personals" in the local newspaper also illustrate this blurring of sexual and nonsexual affection, which is a source of so much confusion in contemporary North American culture. In Brazil, Lovers' Day retains its autonomy. Mother, father, and children each have their own separate days of recognition.

It is true, of course, that in a good marriage love and affection exist alongside sex. Nevertheless, affection does not necessarily imply sex. The Brazilian culture shows that there can be rampant kissing, hugging, and touching without sex— or fears of improper sexuality. In Brazilian culture, many physical demonstrations help cement several kinds of close personal relationships that have no sexual component.

serving, listening, talking, and interacting with other people. Shared cultural beliefs, values, memories, expectations, and ways of thinking and acting override differences between people. Enculturation unifies people by providing us with common experiences.

People in the United States sometimes have trouble understanding the power of Culture because of the value that American culture places on the idea of the individual. Americans are fond of saying that everyone is unique and special in some way. However, in American culture individualism itself is a distinctive shared value that is transmitted through hundreds of statements and settings in our daily lives. From daytime TV's Mr. Rogers to "real-life" parents, grandparents, and teachers, our enculturative agents insist that we are all "someone special."

Today's parents were yesterday's children. If they grew up in American culture, they absorbed certain values and beliefs transmitted over the generations. People become agents in the enculturation of their children, just as their parents were for them. Although a culture constantly changes, certain fundamental beliefs, values, worldviews, and child-rearing practices endure. Consider a simple American example of enduring shared enculturation. As children, when we didn't finish a meal, our parents reminded us of starving children in some foreign country, just as our grandparents had done a generation earlier. The specific country changes (China, India, Bangladesh, Ethiopia, Somalia, Rwanda). Still, American culture goes on transmitting the idea that by eating all our brussels sprouts or broccoli, we can justify our own good fortune, compared to a hungry Third World child.

Culture Is Patterned

Cultures are not haphazard collections of customs and beliefs but integrated, patterned systems. Customs, institutions, beliefs, and values are interrelated; if one changes, others change as well. During the 1950s, for example, most American women expected to have domestic careers as homemakers and mothers. Most of today's college women expect to get jobs when they graduate.

As women enter the work force in increasing numbers, attitudes toward marriage, family, and children change. Outside work places strains on marriage and the family. Late marriage, "living together," and divorce become more common. Economic changes have produced changes in attitudes and behavior in regard to work, gender roles, marriage, and the family.

Cultures are integrated not simply by their dominant economic activities and social patterns but also by sets of values, ideas, and judgments. Cultures train their individual members to share certain personality traits. Separate elements of a culture can be integrated by key symbols, such as fertility or militarism. A set of characteristic central or **core values** (key, basic, or central values) integrates each culture and helps distinguish it from others. For instance, the work ethic, individualism, achievement, and self-reliance are core values that have integrated American culture for generations. Different value sets pattern other cultures.

Cultures are integrated, patterned systems: when one custom, belief, or value changes, others change as well. During the 1950s most American women expected to have domestic careers. With women entering the work force in increasing numbers over the past three decades, attitudes toward work and family have changed. Most of today's college graduates plan to balance jobs and family responsibilities. Contrast the "fifties Mom" with a modern career woman—Illinoisan Carol Moseley Braun, the first African-American woman to be elected to the United States Senate.

People Use Culture Creatively

Although cultural rules tell us what to do and how to do it, we don't always do what the rules dictate. People can learn, interpret, and manipulate the same rule in different ways. People use their culture creatively, rather than blindly following its dictates. Even if they agree about what should and shouldn't be done, people don't always do as their culture directs or as other people expect. Many rules are violated, some very often (for example, automobile speed limits). Some anthropologists find it useful to distinguish between ideal and real culture. The *ideal culture* consists of what people say they should do and what they say they do. *Real culture* refers to their actual behavior as observed by the anthropologist. This contrast is like the emic-etic contrast discussion in the previous chapter.

Culture is both public and individual, both in the world and in people's minds. Anthropologists are interested not only in public and collective behavior but also in how *individuals* think, feel, and act. The individual and culture are linked because human social life is a process in which individuals internalize the meanings of *public* (i.e., cultural) messages. Then, alone and in groups, people influence culture by converting their private understandings into public expressions (D'Andrade 1984). We may study this process by focusing on shared, public aspects of culture or by focusing on individuals. Anthropology and psychology intersect in **psychological anthropology,** the ethnographic and cross-cultural study of differences and similarities in human psychology. Focusing on the individual, psychological anthropology exists because a complete account of cultural process requires both perspectives—private and public.

Culture Is Adaptive and Maladaptive

To cope with or adapt to environmental stresses, humans can draw on both biological traits and learned, symbol-based behavior patterns. Besides biological means of adaptation, human groups also employ "cultural adaptive kits" containing customary patterns, activities, and tools. Although humans continue to adapt biologically as well as culturally, reliance on social and cultural means of adaptation has increased during hominid evolution.

Sometimes, adaptive behavior that offers short-term benefits to particular individuals may also harm the environment and threaten the group's long-term survival. Creative manipulation of culture and the environment by men and women can foster a more secure economy, but it can also deplete strategic resources (Bennett 1969, p. 19). Thus, despite the crucial role of cultural adaptation in human evolution, cultural traits and patterns can also be **maladaptive,** threatening the group's continued existence (survival and reproduction). Many modern cultural patterns, such as policies that encourage overpopulation, inadequate food distribution systems, overconsumption, and pollution, appear to be maladaptive in the long run.

Levels of Culture

Of increasing importance in today's world are the distinctions between different levels of culture: national, international, and subcultural. **National culture** refers to the experiences, beliefs, learned behavior patterns, and values shared by citizens of the same nation. **International culture** is the term for cultural traditions that extend beyond national boundaries. Because Culture is transmitted through learning rather than genetically, cultural traits can spread through borrowing or *diffusion* from one group to another.

Through diffusion, migration, and multinational organizations, many cultural traits and patterns have international scope. Roman Catholics in different countries share experiences, symbols, beliefs, and values transmitted by their church. Contemporary United States, Canada, Great Britain, and Australia share cultural traits they have inherited from their common linguistic and cultural ancestors in Great Britain.

Cultures can also be smaller than nations. Although people in the same society or nation share a cultural tradition, all cultures also contain diversity. Individuals, families, villages, regions, classes, and other subgroups within a culture have different learning experiences as well as shared ones. **Subcultures** are different symbol-based patterns and traditions associated with subgroups in the same complex society. In a complex nation such as the contemporary United States or Canada, subcultures originate in ethnicity, class, region, and religion.

Through varied mechanisms—including diffusion, migration, the spread of multinational organizations, marketing, and religious proselytizing—many cultural traits and patterns have international scope. Illustrating the international level of culture, Roman Catholics in different nations—including these worshippers in Canton, China—share knowledge, symbols, beliefs, and values transmitted by their church.

The religious backgrounds of Jews, Baptists, and Roman Catholics create subcultural differences between them. Although they share the same national culture, U.S. northerners and southerners exhibit differences in beliefs and customary behavior as a result of regional subcultural variation. French-speaking Canadians contrast on the subcultural level with English-speaking people in the same country. Italian-Americans have ethnic traditions different from those of Irish-, Polish-, and African-Americans.

Despite characteristic American notions that people should "make up their own minds" and "have a right to their opinion," little of what we think is original or unique. We share our opinions and beliefs with many other people. Illustrating the power of shared cultural background, we are most likely to agree with and feel comfortable with people who are socially, economically, and culturally similar to ourselves. This is one reason why Americans abroad tend to socialize with each other, just as French and British colonials did in their overseas empires. Birds of a feather flock together, but for people the familiar plumage is culture.

Ethnocentrism and Cultural Relativism

One of anthropology's main goals is to combat ethnocentrism, the tendency to view one's own culture as superior and to apply one's own cultural values in judging the behavior and beliefs of people raised in other cultures. Ethnocentrism is a cultural universal. People everywhere think that the familiar explanations, opinions, and customs are true, right, proper, and moral. They regard different behavior as strange, immoral, or savage. The tribal names that appear in anthropology books often come from the native word for *people*. "What are you called?" asks the anthropologist. "Mugmug," reply informants. *Mugmug* may turn out to be synonymous with *people*, but it also may be the only word the natives have for themselves. Other tribes are not considered fully human. The not-quite-people in neighboring groups are not classified as *Mugmug*. They are given different names that symbolize their inferior humanity.

The opposite of ethnocentrism is **cultural relativism,** the argument that behavior in a particular culture should not be judged by the standards of another. This position can also present problems. At its most extreme, cultural relativism argues that there is no superior, international, or universal morality, that the moral and ethical rules of all cultures deserve equal respect. In the extreme relativist view, Nazi Germany is evaluated as nonjudgmentally as Athenian Greece.

How should anthropologists deal with ethnocentrism and cultural relativism? I believe that anthropology's main job is to present accurate accounts and explanations of cultural phenomena. The anthropologist doesn't have to approve customs such as infanticide, cannibalism, and torture to record their existence and determine their causes. However, each anthropologist has a choice about where to do field work. Some anthropologists choose not to study a particular culture because they discover in advance or early in field work that behavior they consider morally repugnant is practiced there. Anthropologists respect human diversity. Most ethnographers try to be objective, accurate, and sensitive in their accounts of other cultures. However, objectivity, sensitivity, and a cross-cultural perspective don't mean that anthropologists have to ignore international standards of justice and morality.

UNIVERSALITY, PARTICULARITY, AND GENERALITY

Anthropologists agree that cultural learning is uniquely elaborated among hominids, that Culture is the major reason for human adaptability, and that the capacity for Culture is shared by all humans. Anthropologists also unanimously accept a doctrine originally proposed in the nineteenth century: "the psychic unity of man." Anthropology assumes **biopsychological equality** among human groups. This means that although *individuals* differ in emotional and intellectual tendencies and capacities, all human *populations* have equivalent capacities for Culture. Regardless of physical appearance and genetic composition, humans can learn *any* cultural tradition.

To understand this point, consider that contemporary Americans and Canadians are the genetically mixed descendants of people from all over the world. Our ancestors were biologically varied, lived in different countries and continents, and participated in hundreds of cultural traditions. However, the earliest colonists, later immigrants, and their descendants have all become active participants in American and Canadian life. All now share a common national culture.

To recognize biopsychological equality is not to deny differences between populations. In studying human diversity in time and space, anthropologists distinguish among the universal, the generalized, and the particular. Certain biological, psychological, social, and cultural features are **universal,** shared by all human populations in every culture.

Others are merely **generalities,** common to several but not all human groups. Still other traits are **particularities,** unique to certain cultural traditions.

Universality

Universal traits are the ones that more or less distinguish *Homo sapiens* from other species (see Brown 1991). Biologically based universals include a long period of infant dependency, year-round (rather than seasonal) sexuality, and a complex brain that enables us to use symbols, languages, and tools. Psychological universals arise from human biology and from experiences common to human development in all cases. These include growth in the womb, birth itself, and interaction with parents and parent substitutes.

Among the social universals is life in groups and in some kind of family. In all human societies Culture organizes social life and depends on social interactions for its expression and continuation. Family living and food sharing are universals. Among the most significant cultural universals are exogamy and the incest taboo (prohibition against marrying or mating with a close relative). Humans everywhere consider some people (various cultures differ about *which* people) too closely related to mate or marry. The violation of this taboo is *incest*, which is discouraged and punished in a variety of ways in different cultures. If incest is prohibited, exogamy—marriage outside one's group—is inevitable. Because it links human groups together into larger networks, exogamy has been crucial in hominid evolution. Exogamy elaborates on tendencies observed among other primates. Recent studies of monkeys and apes show that these animals also avoid mating with close kin and often mate outside their native groups.

Particularity

Many cultural traits are widely shared because of diffusion and independent invention and as cultural universals. Nevertheless, different cultures emphasize different things. Cultures are patterned and integrated differently and display tremendous variation and diversity. Uniqueness and particularity stand at the opposite extreme from universality.

Unusual and exotic beliefs and practices lend distinctiveness to particular cultural traditions. Many

Although many cultures use rituals to mark such universal life cycle events as birth, puberty, marriage, parenthood, and death, particular cultures differ as to which event merits special celebration. Compare the lavish traditional wedding party of these Bai Chinese with the colorful and well-attended funeral at Quetzaltenango in the western highlands of Guatemala.

and lifetime achievement, and it may attract a thousand people. Why use money on a house, the Betsileo say, when one can use it on the tomb where one will spend eternity in the company of dead relatives? How different from contemporary Americans' growing preference for quick and inexpensive funerals and cremation, which would horrify the Betsileo, whose ancestral bones and relics are important ritual objects.

Cultures vary tremendously in their beliefs and practices. By focusing on and trying to explain alternative customs, anthropology forces us to reappraise our familiar ways of thinking. In a world full of cultural diversity, contemporary American culture is just one cultural variant, no more natural than the others.

Generality

Between universals and uniqueness is a middle ground that consists of cultural generalities: regularities that occur in different times and places but not in all cultures. One reason for generalities is diffusion. Societies can share the same beliefs and customs because of borrowing or through (cultural) inheritance from a common cultural ancestor. Other generalities originate in independent invention of the same cultural trait or pattern in two or more different cultures. Similar needs and circumstances have led people in different lands to innovate in parallel ways. They have independently come up with the same cultural solution or arrangement.

One cultural generality that is present in many but not all societies is the nuclear family, a kinship group consisting of parents and children. Although many middle-class Americans ethnocentrically view the nuclear family as a proper and "natural" group, it is not universal. It is totally absent, for example, among the Nayars, who live on the Malabar Coast of India. The Nayars live in female-headed households, and husbands and wives do not live together. In many other societies, the nuclear family is submerged in larger kin groups, such as extended families, lineages, and clans. However, the nuclear family is prominent in many of the technologically simple societies that live by hunting and gathering. It is also a significant kin group among contempo-

cultures ritually observe such universal life-cycle events as birth, puberty, marriage, parenthood, and death. However, cultures vary in just which event merits special celebration. Americans regard expensive weddings as more socially appropriate than lavish funerals. However, the Betsileo of Madagascar take the opposite view. The marriage ceremony is a minor event that brings together just the couple and a few close relatives. However, a funeral is a measure of the deceased person's social position

rary middle-class North Americans and Western Europeans. Later, an explanation of the nuclear family as a basic kinship unit in specific types of society will be given.

MECHANISMS OF CULTURAL CHANGE

In biology, different species cannot share their genes, but cultures in contact can get traits from each other through borrowing, or **diffusion.** Diffusion, an important mechanism of cultural change, has gone on throughout human history because cultures have never been truly isolated. Contact between neighboring groups has always existed and has extended over vast areas (Boas 1940/1966). Diffusion is *direct* when two cultures trade, intermarry, or wage war on one another. Diffusion is *forced* when one culture subjugates another and imposes its customs on the dominated group. Diffusion is *indirect* when products and patterns move from group A to group C via group B without any firsthand contact between A and C. In the modern world, much international diffusion is due to the spread of the mass media and advanced information technology.

Acculturation, another mechanism of cultural change, is the exchange of cultural features that results when groups have continuous firsthand contact. The original cultural patterns of either or both groups may be changed by this contact (Redfield, Linton, and Herskovits 1936). We usually speak of acculturation when the contact is *between* nations or cultures. Parts of the cultures change, but each group remains distinct. One example of acculturation is a **pidgin,** a mixed language that develops to ease communication between members of different cultures in contact. This usually happens in situations of trade or colonialism. Pidgin English, for example, is a simplified form of English. It blends English grammar with the grammar of a native language. Pidgin English was first used for commerce in Chinese ports. Similar pidgins developed later in Papua–New Guinea and West Africa. In situations of continuous contact, cultures have also exchanged and blended foods, recipes, music, dances, clothing, tools, and technologies.

Independent invention—the process by which humans innovate, creatively finding new solutions to old and new problems—is another important mechanism of cultural change. Faced with comparable problems and challenges, people in different cultures have innovated in similar or parallel ways, which is one reason cultural generalities exist. One example is the independent invention of agriculture in the Middle East and Mexico. In both areas people who faced food scarcity began to domesticate crops. Over the course of human history, major innovations have spread at the expense of earlier ones. Often a major invention, such as agriculture, triggers a series of subsequent interrelated changes. These economic revolutions have social and cultural repercussions. Thus in both Mexico and the Middle East, agriculture led to many social, political, and legal changes, including notions of property and distinctions in wealth, class, and power.

Cultural convergence, or convergent cultural evolution, refers to the development of similar traits, institutions, and behavior patterns by separate groups as a result of adaptation to similar environments. Given long-term adaptation by different cultures to similar environments, the same institutions tend to develop, in the same order. Julian Steward (1955), an influential advocate of the position that scientific laws govern human behavior and cultural change, sought to explain convergent cultural evolution. He showed that parallel cultural changes have occurred repeatedly and independently in different places, mainly for economic or environmental reasons.

Another reason for cultural change is **globalization**—the process that links modern nations and people economically, politically, and through modern media and transportation. Local people must increasingly cope with forces generated by progressively larger systems—region, nation, and world. Different degrees of destruction, domination, resistance, survival, adaptation, and modification of native cultures have followed contact between cultures and ethnic groups. Indigenous peoples and traditional cultures have devised various strategies to resist attacks on their autonomy, identity, and livelihood. New forms of political mobilization and cultural expression are emerging from the interplay of local, regional, national, and international cultural forces.

SUMMARY

Culture, a distinctive possession of humanity, is acquired by all humans through enculturation. Culture encompasses rule-governed, shared, symbol-based learned behavior and beliefs transmitted across the generations. Culture rests on the hominid capacity for cultural learning. *Culture* refers to customary beliefs and behavior and to the rules for conduct internalized in human beings through enculturation. These rules lead people to think and act in certain consistent, distinctive, and characteristic ways.

Other animals learn, but only humans have cultural learning, which depends on symbols. Cultural learning rests on the universal human capacity to think symbolically, arbitrarily bestowing meaning on a thing or event. By convention, a symbol, which may be linguistic or nonverbal, stands for something else with which it has no necessary or natural relation. Symbols have a particular meaning and value for people in the same culture. People share experiences, memories, values, and beliefs as a result of common enculturation. People absorb cultural lessons consciously and unconsciously.

Cultural traditions seize natural phenomena, including biologically based desires and needs, and channel them in particular directions. Everyone is cultured, not just people with elite educations. The genus *Homo* has the capacity for Culture (in a general sense), but people live in specific cultures where they are raised according to different traditions. Cultures are patterned and integrated through their dominant economic forces, social patterns, key symbols, and core values. Cultural rules do not always dictate behavior. There is room for creativity, flexibility, and diversity within cultures. Anthropologists distinguish between what people say they do and what they actually do. Cultural means of adaptation have been crucial in hominid evolution, although aspects of Culture can also be maladaptive.

There are different levels of cultural systems. Diffusion and migration carry the same cultural traits and patterns to different areas. These traits are shared across national boundaries. Nations include subcultural differences associated with ethnicity, region, and social class.

Anthropology finds no evidence that genetic differences explain cultural variation. Adopting a comparative perspective, anthropology examines biological, psychological, social, and cultural universals and generalities. It also considers unique and distinctive aspects of the human condition. In examining cultural elaborations on the fundamental biological plasticity of *Homo sapiens*, anthropology shows that American cultural traditions are no more natural than any others. Mechanisms of cultural change include diffusion, acculturation, independent invention, cultural convergence, and globalization.

GLOSSARY

acculturation: The exchange of cultural features that results when groups come into continuous firsthand contact; the original cultural patterns of either or both groups may be altered, but the groups remain distinct.

biopsychological equality: The premise that although individuals differ in emotional and intellectual capacities, all human populations have equivalent capacities for Culture.

core values: Key, basic, or central values that integrate a culture and help distinguish it from others.

cultural convergence (or convergent cultural evolution): Development of similar traits, institutions, or behavior patterns as a result of adaptation to similar environments; parallel development without contact or mutual influence.

cultural learning: Learning based on the human capacity to think symbolically.

cultural relativism: The position that the values and standards of cultures differ and deserve respect. Extreme relativism argues that cultures should be judged solely by their own standards.

Culture, general: Spelled with a capital C; Culture in the general sense as a capacity and possession shared by hominids.

culture, specific: Spelled with a small c; a culture in the specific sense, any one of the different and varied cultural traditions of specific societies.

diffusion: Borrowing of cultural traits between societies, either directly or through intermediaries.

enculturation: The social process by which Culture is learned and transmitted across the generations.

ethnocentrism: The tendency to view one's own culture as best and to judge the behavior and beliefs of culturally different people by one's own standards.

exogamy: Mating or marriage outside one's kin group; a cultural universal.

generality: Culture pattern or trait that exists in some but not all societies.

globalization: The accelerating interdependence of nations in a world system linked economically and through mass media and modern transportation systems.

incest taboo: Universal prohibition against marrying or mating with a close relative.

independent invention: Development of the same cultural trait or pattern in separate cultures as a result of comparable needs and circumstances.

individual situational learning: Type of learning in which animals learn from and base their future behavior on personal experience.

international culture: Cultural traditions that extend beyond national boundaries.

maladaptive: Harmful to survival and reproduction.

national culture: Cultural experiences, beliefs, learned behavior patterns, and values shared by citizens of the same nation.

nuclear family: Kinship group consisting of parents and children.

particularity: Distinctive or unique culture trait, pattern, or integration.

pidgin: A mixed language that develops to ease communication between members of different cultures in contact, usually in situations of trade or colonial domination.

psychological anthropology: The ethnographic and cross-cultural study of differences and similarities in human psychology.

social situational learning: Learning from other members of the social group, not necessarily through language.

subcultures: Different cultural traditions associated with subgroups in the same complex society.

symbol: Something, verbal or nonverbal, that arbitrarily and by convention stands for something else, with which it has no necessary or natural connection.

universal: Something that exists in every culture.

STUDY QUESTIONS

1. What are the different kinds of learning? On which is culture based?
2. What does it mean to say culture is symbolic?
3. What is the difference between Culture in the general sense and culture in the specific sense?
4. What does it mean to say culture is all-encompassing?
5. What does it mean to say culture is shared?
6. What does it mean to say culture is patterned or integrated?
7. How is culture adaptive?
8. How are human adaptability and culture related?
9. What does it mean to say there are levels of culture?
10. What is ethnocentrism?
11. What is cultural relativism, and what are its potential problems?
12. What is meant by cultural universals, generalities, and particularities?
13. How is the idea of cultural particularity related to the notion of cultural patterning or integration?
14. What are the main mechanisms that influence cultural change?

SUGGESTED ADDITIONAL READING

BOHANNAN, P.
1995   *How Culture Works.* New York: Free Press. A recent consideration of the nature of culture.
BROWN, D.
1991   *Human Universals.* New York: McGraw-Hill. Surveys the evidence for "human nature" and explores the roles of culture and biology in human variation.
GAMST, F. C., AND E. NORBECK, EDS.
1976   *Ideas of Culture: Sources and Uses.* New York: Harcourt Brace Jovanovich. Surveys various aspects and definitions of culture. Contains both classic and original essays.

GEERTZ, C.
1973   *The Interpretation of Cultures.* New York: Basic Books. Essays about culture viewed as a system of symbols and meaning.
HALL, E. T.
1990   *Understanding Cultural Differences.* Yarmouth, ME: Intercultural Press. Focusing on business and industrial management, this book examines the role of national cultural contrasts among France, Germany, and the United States.
1992   *An Anthropology of Everyday Life: An Autobiography.* New York: Doubleday. A prominent

student of language and culture examines his own life in the context of intercultural communication.

HESS, D. J., AND R. A. DAMATTA, EDS.
1995   *The Brazilian Puzzle: Culture on the Borderlands of the Western World.* New York: Columbia University Press. Readable essays on the culture of the Western Hemisphere's second most populous country, with some comparative comments about North America.

KROEBER, A. L., AND C. KLUCKHOHN
1963   *Culture: A Critical Review of Concepts and Definitions.* New York: Vintage. Discusses and categorizes more than a hundred definitions of culture.

WAGNER, R.
1981   *The Invention of Culture,* rev. ed. Chicago: University of Chicago Press. Culture, creativity, society, and the self.

ETHNICITY AND ETHNIC RELATIONS

ETHNIC GROUPS AND ETHNICITY
Status Shifting

ETHNIC GROUPS, NATIONS, AND NATIONALITIES
Nationalities and Imagined Communities

ETHNIC TOLERANCE AND ACCOMMODATION
Assimilation

The Plural Society

Multiculturalism and Ethnic Identity

Box: Ethnic Nationalism Run Wild

ROOTS OF ETHNIC CONFLICT
Prejudice and Discrimination
Chips in the Mosaic
Aftermaths of Oppression

We know from the last chapter that culture is learned, symbolic, shared, patterned, all-encompassing, adaptive, and maladaptive. Now we consider the relation between culture and ethnicity. Ethnicity is based on cultural similarities and differences in a society or nation. The similarities are with members of the same ethnic group; the differences are between that group and others.

ETHNIC GROUPS AND ETHNICITY

As with any culture, members of an **ethnic group** *share* certain beliefs, values, habits, customs, and norms because of their common background. They define themselves as different and special because of cultural features. This distinction may arise from language, religion, historical experience, geographic isolation, kinship, or race (see the next chapter). Markers of an ethnic group may include a collective name, belief in common descent, a sense of solidarity, and an association with a specific territory, which the group may or may not hold (Ryan 1990, pp. xiii, xiv).

Ethnicity means identification with, and feeling part of, an ethnic group, and exclusion from certain other groups because of this affiliation. Ethnic feeling and associated behavior vary in intensity within ethnic groups and countries and over time. A change in the degree of importance attached to an ethnic identity may reflect political changes (Soviet rule ends—ethnic feeling rises) or individual life-cycle changes (young people relinquish, or old people reclaim, an ethnic background).

We saw in the last chapter that people participate in various levels of culture. Subgroups within a culture (including ethnic groups in a nation) have different learning experiences as well as shared ones. Subcultures originate in ethnicity, class, region, and religion. Individuals often have more than one group identity. People may be loyal (depending on circumstances) to their neighborhood, school, town, state or province, region, nation, continent, religion, ethnic group, or interest group (Ryan 1990, p. xxii). In a complex society like the United States or Canada people constantly negotiate their social identities. All of us "wear different hats," presenting ourselves sometimes as one thing, sometimes as another.

The term **status** can be used to refer to such "hats"—to any position that determines where someone fits in society (Light, Keller, and Calhoun 1994). Social statuses include parent, professor, student, factory worker, Democrat, shoe salesperson, labor leader, ethnic group member, and thousands of others. People always occupy multiple statuses (e.g., Hispanic, Catholic, infant, brother). Among the statuses we occupy, particular ones dominate in particular settings, such as son or daughter at home and student in the classroom.

Some statuses are **ascribed:** people have little or no choice about occupying them. Age is an ascribed status; people can't choose not to age. Race and ethnicity are usually ascribed; people are born members of a certain group and remain so all their lives. **Achieved statuses,** by contrast, aren't automatic but come through traits, talents, actions, efforts, activities, and accomplishments (Figure 4.1).

In many societies an ascribed status is associated with a position in the social-political hierarchy. Certain groups, called **minority groups,** are subordinate. They have inferior power and less secure ac-

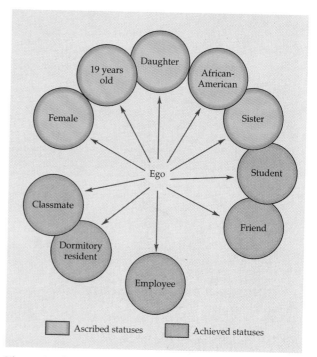

Figure 4.1 *Social statuses. The person in this figure—"ego," or "I"—occupies many social statuses. The green circles indicate ascribed statuses; the orange circles represent achieved statuses.*

cess to resources than do **majority groups** (which are superordinate, dominant, or controlling). Minorities need not have fewer members than the majority group does. Women in the United States and blacks in South Africa have been numerical majorities but minorities in terms of income, authority, and power. Often ethnic groups are minorities. When an ethnic group is assumed to have a biological basis, it is called a **race.** Discrimination against such a group is called **racism.** The next chapter considers race in social and biological perspective.

Status Shifting

Sometimes statuses, particularly ascribed ones, are mutually exclusive. It's hard to bridge the gap between black and white, or male and female (although some rock stars seem to be trying to do so). Sometimes, taking a status or joining a group requires a conversion experience, acquiring a new and overwhelming primary identity, such as becoming a "born again" Christian.

Some statuses aren't mutually exclusive, but contextual. People can be both black and Hispanic, or both a mother and a senator. One identity is used in certain settings, another in different ones. We call this the *situational negotiation of social identity.* When ethnic identity is flexible and situational (Moerman 1965), it can become an achieved status.

Hispanics, for example, may move through levels of culture (shifting ethnic affiliations) as they negotiate their identities. "Hispanic" is an ethnic category based mainly on language. It includes whites, blacks, and "racially" mixed Spanish speakers and their ethnically conscious descendants. (There are also "Native American," and even "Asian," Hispanics). "Hispanic" lumps together millions of people of diverse geographic origin—Puerto Rico, Mexico, Cuba, El Salvador, Guatemala, the Dominican Republic, and other Spanish-speaking countries of Central and South America and the Caribbean. "Latino" is a broader category, which can also include Brazilians (who speak Portuguese).

Mexican-Americans (Chicanos), Cuban-Americans, and Puerto Ricans may mobilize to promote general Hispanic issues (e.g., opposition to "English-only" laws), but act as three separate interest groups in other contexts. Cuban-Americans are richer on average than Chicanos and Puerto Ricans are, and their class interests and voting patterns differ. Cubans often vote Republican, but Puerto Ricans and Chicanos generally favor Democrats. Some Mexican-Americans whose families have lived in the United States for generations have little in common with new Hispanic immigrants, such as those from Central America. Many Americans (especially those fluent in English) claim Hispanic ethnicity in some contexts but shift to a general "American" identity in others.

The ethnic label "Hispanic" lumps together millions of people of diverse geographic origin—Puerto Rico, Mexico, Cuba, El Salvador, Guatemala, the Dominican Republic, and other Spanish-speaking countries of Central and South America and the Caribbean. Hispanics of diverse national backgrounds, like these Cuban-Americans in Miami, may mobilize to promote general Hispanic issues (such as opposition to "English-only" laws), but act as separate interest groups in other contexts. Images of Cuba decorate this restaurant in Miami's "Little Havana."

ETHNIC GROUPS, NATIONS, AND NATIONALITIES

What is the relation between an ethnic group and a nation? The term **nation** was once synonymous with "tribe" or "ethnic group." All three of these terms referred to a single culture sharing a single language, religion, history, territory, ancestry, and kinship. Thus one could speak interchangeably of the Seneca (American Indian) nation, tribe, or ethnic group. Now *nation* has come to mean a **state**—an independent, centrally organized political unit, or a government. *Nation* and *state* have become synonymous. Combined in **nation-state** they refer to an autonomous political entity, a "country"—like the United States, "one nation, indivisible."

Because of migration, conquest, and colonialism (see below), most nation-states are not ethnically homogeneous. Of 132 nation-states existing in 1971, Connor (1972) found just 12 (9 percent) to be ethnically homogeneous. In another 25 (19 percent) a single ethnic group accounted for more than 90 percent of the population. Forty percent of the countries contained more than five significant ethnic groups. In a later study, Nielsson (1985) classified only 45 (27 percent) of 164 states as "single nation-group" (i.e., ethnic group) states (with one ethnic group accounting for more than 95 percent of the population).

Nationalities and Imagined Communities

Ethnic groups that once had, or wish to have or regain, autonomous political status (their own country) are called **nationalities.** In the words of Benedict Anderson (1991), nationalities are "imagined communities." Even when they become nation-states, they remain imagined communities, because most of their members, though feeling deep comradeship, will never meet (Anderson 1991, pp. 6–10). They can only imagine that they all participate in the same social group.

Anderson traces Western European nationalism, which arose in imperial powers like England, France, and Spain, back to the eighteenth century. He stresses that language and print played a crucial role in the growth of European national consciousness. The novel and the newspaper were "two forms of imagining" communities (consisting of all the people who read the same sources and thus wit-

nessed the same events) that flowered in the eighteenth century (Anderson 1991, pp. 24–25).

Making a similar point, Terry Eagleton (1983, p. 25) describes the vital role of the novel in promoting English national consciousness and identity. The novel gave the English "a pride in their national language and literature; if scanty education and extensive hours of labor prevented them personally from producing a literary masterpiece, they could take pleasure in the thought that others of their kind—English people—had done so."

Over time, political upheavals and wars have divided many imagined national communities that arose in the eighteenth and nineteenth centuries. The German and Korean homelands were artificially divided after wars, and according to Communist and capitalist ideologies. World War I split the Kurds, who remain an imagined community, forming a majority in no state. Kurds are a minority group in Turkey, Iran, Iraq, and Syria. Similarly, Azerbaijanis, who are related to Turks, were a minority in the former Soviet Union, as they still are in Iran.

Migration is another reason certain ethnic groups live in different nation-states. Massive migration in the decades before and after 1900 brought Germans, Poles, and Italians to Brazil, Canada, and the United States. Through migration Chinese, Senegalese, Lebanese, and Jews have spread all over the world. Some of these (e.g., descendants of Germans in Brazil and the United States) have assimilated to their host nations and no longer feel attached to the imagined community of their origin.

ETHNIC TOLERANCE AND ACCOMMODATION

Ethnic diversity may be associated with positive group interaction and coexistence or with conflict—discussed in another section. There are nation-states in which multiple cultural groups live together in reasonable harmony, including some less-developed countries. In Indonesia, for example, a common language and school system have promoted ethnic harmony, national identity, and integration, as Anderson (1991, pp. 120–123, 132) describes. Indonesia, a large and populous nation, spans about 3,000 islands. Its national consciousness straddles religious, ethnic, and linguistic di-

In Indonesia a common language (lingua franca) and school system have promoted national consciousness, identity, and integration despite ethnic and religious diversity. This Chinese merchant family has assimilated to Indonesian culture by converting to Islam.

versity. For example, Indonesia contains such religious groups as Muslims, Buddhists, Catholics, Protestants, Hindu-Balinese, and animists. Despite these contrasts, more than 100 distinct ethnolinguistic groups have come to view themselves as fellow Indonesians.

Under Dutch rule (which ended in 1949), the school system extended over the islands. Advanced study brought youths from different areas to Batavia, the colonial capital. The colonial educational system offered Indonesian youths uniform textbooks, standardized diplomas, and teaching certificates. It created a "self-contained, coherent universe of experience" (Anderson 1991, p. 121). Literacy acquired through the school system also paved the way for a single national print language. Indonesian developed as the national language out of an ancient lingua franca (common language) used in trade between the islands.

In creating multitribal and multiethnic states, colonialism often erected boundaries that corresponded poorly with preexisting cultural divisions. But colonial institutions also helped create new "imagined communities" beyond nations. A good example is the idea of *négritude* ("African identity") developed by African intellectuals in Francophone (French-speaking) West Africa. *Négritude* can be traced to the association and common experience of youths from Guinea, Mali, the Ivory Coast, and Senegal at the William Ponty school in Dakar, Senegal (Anderson 1991, pp. 123–124).

Assimilation

Assimilation describes the process of change that a minority ethnic group may experience when it moves to a country where another culture dominates. By assimilating, the minority adopts the patterns and norms of its host culture. It is incorporated into the dominant culture to the point that it no longer exists as a separate cultural unit. Some countries, like Brazil, are more assimilationist than others are. Germans, Italians, Japanese, Middle Easterners, and East Europeans started migrating to Brazil late in the nineteenth century. These immigrants have assimilated to a common Brazilian culture, which has Portuguese, African, and Native American roots. The descendants of these immigrants speak the national language (Portuguese) and participate in national culture. (During World War II, Brazil, which was on the Allied side, forced assimilation by banning instruction in any language other than Portuguese—especially in German.)

Brazil has been more of a "melting pot" than have the United States and Canada, in which ethnic groups retain more distinctiveness and self-identity. I remember my first visit to the southern Brazilian city of Porto Alegre, the site of mass migration by Germans, Poles, and Italians. Transferring an expectation derived from my North American culture to Porto Alegre, I asked my tour guide to show me his city's ethnic neighborhoods. He couldn't understand what I was talking about. Except for a

Germans, Italians, Japanese, Mid-Easterners, and East Europeans started migrating to Brazil late in the nineteenth century. All have assimilated to a common Brazilian culture, which has Portuguese, African, and Native American roots. The descendants of the immigrants speak the national language (Portuguese) and participate in national culture. Here, a Japanese-Brazilian woman reminds her grandson of his heritage by teaching him Japanese script. Except for certain Japanese-Brazilian areas of São Paulo, the idea of an ethnic neighborhood is alien to Brazil

Japanese-Brazilian neighborhood in the city of São Paulo, the idea of an ethnic neighborhood is alien to Brazil.

The Plural Society

Assimilation isn't inevitable, and there can be ethnic harmony without it. Ethnic distinctions can persist despite generations of interethnic contact. Through a study of three ethnic groups in Swat, Pakistan, Fredrik Barth (1958/1968) challenged an old idea that interaction always leads to assimilation. He showed that ethnic groups can be in contact for generations without assimilating and can live in peaceful coexistence.

Barth (1958/1968, p. 324) defines **plural society** as a society combining ethnic contrasts, ecological specialization (that is, use of different environmental resources by each ethnic group), and the economic interdependence of those groups. Consider his description of the Middle East (in the 1950s): "The 'environment' of any one ethnic group is not only defined by natural conditions, but also by the presence and activities of the other ethnic groups on which it depends. Each group exploits only part of the total environment, and leaves large parts of it open for other groups to exploit." The ecological interdependence (or, at least, the lack of competition) between ethnic groups may be based on different activities in the same region, or on longtime occupation of different regions in the same nation-state.

In Barth's view, ethnic boundaries are most stable and enduring when the groups occupy different ecological niches. That is, they make their living in different ways and don't compete. Ideally, they should depend on each other's activities and exchange with one another. When different ethnic groups exploit the *same* ecological niche, the militarily more powerful group will normally replace the weaker one. If they exploit more or less the same niche, but the weaker group is better able to use marginal environments, they may also coexist (Barth 1968/1958, p. 331). Given niche specialization, ethnic boundaries, distinctions, and interdependence can be maintained although the specific cultural features of each group may change. By shifting the analytic focus from individual cultures or ethnic groups to *relationships* between cultures or ethnic groups, Barth (1958/1968 and 1969) has made important contributions to ethnic studies.

Multiculturalism and Ethnic Identity

The view of cultural diversity in a country as something good and desirable is called **multiculturalism.** The multicultural model is the opposite of the assimilationist model, in which minorities are expected to abandon their cultural traditions and values, replacing them with those of the majority population. The multicultural view encourages the practice of cultural-ethnic traditions. A multicultural society socializes individuals not only into the dominant (national) culture but also into an ethnic culture. Thus in the United States millions of people speak both English and another language, eat both "American" (apple pie, steak, hamburgers) and "ethnic" foods, celebrate both national (July 4, Thanksgiving) and ethnic-religious holidays, and study both national and ethnic group histories. Multiculturalism succeeds best in a society whose political system promotes freedom of expression and in which there are many and diverse ethnic groups.

In the United States and Canada multiculturalism is of growing importance. This reflects an awareness that the number and size of ethnic groups have grown dramatically in recent years. If this trend continues, the ethnic composition of the United States will change dramatically (Figure 4.2).

Because of immigration and differential population growth, whites are now outnumbered by minorities in many urban areas. For example, of the 7,323,000 people living in New York City in 1990,

28.7 percent were black, 24.4 percent Hispanic, 7.0 percent Asian, 0.4 percent Native American, and 39.5 percent other—including non-Hispanic whites. The comparable figures for Los Angeles (3,485,000 people) were 14.0 percent black, 39.9 percent Hispanic, 9.8 percent Asian, 0.5 percent Native American, and 35.8 percent non-Hispanic whites (*American Almanac* 1994, p. 45).

One response to ethnic diversification and awareness has been for many whites to reclaim ethnic identities (Italian, Albanian, Serbian, Lithuanian, etc.) and to join ethnic associations (clubs, gangs). Some such groups are new. Others have existed for decades, although they lost members during the assimilationist years of the 1920s and through the 1950s.

Multiculturalism seeks ways for people to understand and interact that don't depend on sameness but on respect for differences. Multiculturalism stresses the interaction of ethnic groups and their contribution to the country. It assumes that each

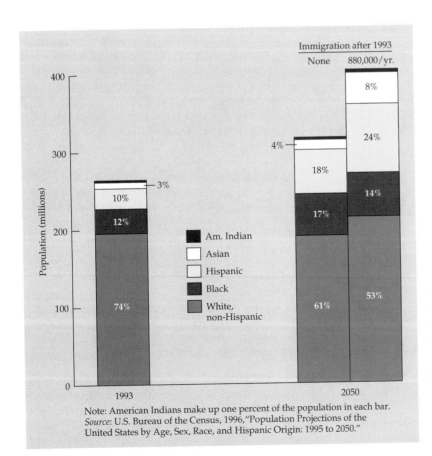

Note: American Indians make up one percent of the population in each bar.
Source: U.S. Bureau of the Census, 1996,"Population Projections of the United States by Age, Sex, Race, and Hispanic Origin: 1995 to 2050."

Figure 4.2 *The proportion of the American population that is white and non-Hispanic is declining. Consider two projections of the ethnic composition of the United States in* A.D. *2050. The first assumes an annual immigration rate of zero; the second assumes continuation of the current level of immigration—about 880,000 immigrants per year. With either projection, the non-Hispanic white proportion of the population declines dramatically. (Martin and Midgley 1994, p. 9)*

ETHNIC NATIONALISM RUN WILD

The Socialist Federal Republic of Yugoslavia, although Communist, was a nonaligned country outside the Soviet Union. But like the U.S.S.R., Yugoslavia fell apart, mainly along ethnic and religious lines, in the early 1990s. Among Yugoslavia's nationalities were Roman Catholic Croats, Eastern Orthodox Serbs, Muslim Slavs, and ethnic Albanians. Citing ethnic and religious differences, several republics broke away from Yugoslavia in 1991–92. These included Slovenia, Croatia, and Bosnia-Herzegovina (see map). Of Yugoslavia, with Belgrade as its capital, only Serbia, Montenegro, and Kosovo remain.

The ethnic differentiation in Yugoslavia was based on religion, culture, and political and military history, rather than race or language. Serbo-Croatian is a South Slavic language spoken (with dialect variation) by Serbs, Croats, and Muslim Slavs. But Croats and Serbs use different alphabets. The Croats have adopted our Roman alphabet, but the Serbs use the Cyrillic alphabet, which they share with Russia and Bulgaria. The two alphabets help promote ethnic differentiation and nationalism. Serbs and Croats, who share speech, are divided by writing—by literature, newsprint, and political manifestos. With print (like religion) uniting some people while separating them from others, literate Serbs and Croats belong to different imagined communities (Anderson 1991).

The Yugoslav Serbs reacted violently—with military intervention—

The former Yugoslavia, although Communist, was a nonaligned country outside the Soviet Union, but like the U.S.S.R. Yugoslavia disintegrated in the early 1990s. The breakaway portions included Slovenia, Croatia, and Bosnia-Herzegovina. Of Yugoslavia, with Belgrade as its capital, only Serbia, Montenegro, and Kosovo remain.

after a February 1992 vote for the independence of Muslim-led Bosnia-Herzegovina, whose population is one-third Serbian. Nationalist Serbs (from both Bosnia and Yugoslavia) initiated a policy, in the secessionist Bosnia-Herzegovina, of forced expulsion—"ethnic purification"—against Croats, but mainly against Muslim Slavs. Serbs in Yugoslavia, who controlled the National Army, lent their support to the Bosnian Serbs in their "ethnic-cleansing" campaign, which recalled the policies of Adolf Hitler.

Backed by the Yugoslav army, Serbian militias rounded up Muslims, killed groups of them, and burned and looted their homes. Thousands of Slavs fled. Hundreds of thousands of Muslims became involuntary refugees in tent camps,

group has something to offer and learn from the others.

We see evidence of multiculturalism all around us. Seated near you in the classroom are students whose parents were born in other countries. Islamic mosques have joined Jewish synagogues and Christian churches in American cities. To help in exam scheduling, colleges inform professors about the

school gyms, and parks. The Serbian campaign in Bosnia created Europe's worst refugee crisis since World War II.

The Serbs sought to end the inter-ethnic coexistence that Yugoslav socialism had encouraged. They also wanted to avenge historic affronts by Muslims and Croats. In the fifteenth century Muslim Turks (from the Ottoman Empire) had overthrown the medieval Serbian ruler, persecuted the Serbs, and—eventually—converted many local people to Islam during their centuries of rule in this area. Bosnian Serbs still resent all Muslims—including the converts, the ancestors of the Muslim Slavs—for the Turkish conquest.

Bosnian Serbs claimed to be fighting to resist the Muslim-dominated government of Bosnia-Herzegovina. They feared that a policy of Islamic fundamentalism (like that in Iran) might threaten the Serbian Orthodox Church and other expressions of Serbian identity. The Serbs' goal was to carve up Bosnia-Herzegovina along ethnic lines, and they wanted two-thirds of it for themselves.

The Serbs also sought vengeance against the Croats for arrests, deportations, and executions of Serbs by Croatian fascists during World War II. A stated aim of ethnic purification was to ensure that the Serbs would never again be dominated by another ethnic group (Burns 1992a).

In other breakaway areas of Yugoslavia, Muslim Slavs and Croats also forced deportations, but the Serbian campaign in Bosnia was the widest and the most systematic.

Bosnian Croats (following the example of the Serbs) also declared their own separate minirepublic next to Croatia, which in 1995 forced the deportation of thousands of Serbs from its own Krajina region. With the Muslim Slavs caught in the middle and with Bosnia's capital, the multi-ethnic city of Sarajevo, under siege, the conflict was suspended following a December 1995 peace settlement. The future of Bosnia seemed brighter but remained uncertain as of this writing. More than 200,000 people were killed during the Bosnian conflict (Cohen 1995).

How can we explain Bosnia's ethnic conflict and its nationalism run wild? According to Fredrik Barth (1969), ethnic differences are most secure and enduring where the groups occupy different ecological niches: They make their livings in different ways or places and don't compete. In Barth's view, peaceful coexistence is most likely when the ethnic groups are mutually dependent. In Bosnia-Herzegovina, the Serbs, the Croats, and the Muslim Slavs were more mixed than in any other former Yugoslav Republic (Burns 1992b). The boundaries between the three groups may not have been sharp enough to keep them together by keeping them apart.

The "ethnic cleansing" campaign waged against Muslim Slavs and Croats by Bosnian Serbs led to Europe's most severe refugee crisis since World War II. Shown here, some 5,000 Muslims of Srebrénica—who had taken refuge in the mountains—begin surrendering to Serbian forces.

main holidays of many religions. You can attend ethnic fairs and festivals, watch ethnically costumed dancers on television, eat ethnic foods, even outside ethnic restaurants, and buy ethnic foods at your supermarket. Some such foods (e.g., bagels, pasta, tacos) have become so familiar that their ethnic origin is fading from our memories. There is even a popular shrine celebrating the union of diversity

In the United States and Canada, multiculturalism is of growing importance. Especially in large cities like Montreal (shown here), people of diverse backgrounds attend ethnic fairs and festivals and feast on ethnic foods.

and globalization: At Disneyland and Walt Disney World we can see and hear a chorus of ethnically correct dolls drone on that "it's a small world after all." All these exemplify growing tolerance and support of ethnic communities in the United States and Canada.

Several forces have propelled North America away from the assimilationist model toward multiculturalism. First, multiculturalism reflects the fact of recent large-scale migration, particularly from the "less-developed countries" to the "developed" nations of North America and Western Europe. The global scale of modern migration introduces unparalleled ethnic variety to host nations. Multiculturalism is related to globalization: People use modern means of transportation to migrate to nations whose life styles they learn about through the media and from tourists who increasingly visit their countries.

Migration is also fueled by rapid population growth, coupled with insufficient jobs (both for educated and uneducated people), in the less-developed countries. As traditional rural economies decline or mechanize, displaced farmers move to cities, where they and their children are often unable to find jobs. As people in the less-developed countries get better educations, they seek more skilled employment. They hope to partake in an international culture of consumption that includes such modern amenities as refrigerators, televisions, and automobiles.

Contrary to popular belief, the typical migrant to the United States or Canada isn't poor and unskilled but middle-class and fairly well educated. Educated people migrate for several reasons. Often they can't find jobs to match their skills in their countries of origin (Grasmuck and Pessar 1991; Margolis 1994). Also, they are knowledgeable enough to manipulate international regulations. Many migrants have been raised to expect a life style that their own nations can offer to just a few. On arrival in North America or Western Europe, immigrants find themselves in democracies where citizens are allowed (or even encouraged) to organize for economic gain and a "fair share" of resources, political influence, and cultural respect. Educated immigrants often become political organizers and particularly effective advocates of multiculturalism.

In a world with growing rural-urban and transnational migration, ethnic identities are used increasingly to form self-help organizations focused mainly on enhancing the group's economic competitiveness (Williams 1989). People claim and express ethnic identities for political and economic reasons. Michel Laguerre's (1984) study of Haitian immigrants in New York City shows that they make no conscious decision to form an ethnic group. Rather, they have to mobilize to deal with the discriminatory structure (racist in this case, since Haitians tend to be black) of American society. Ethnicity (their common Haitian creole language and cultural background) is an evident basis for their mobilization. Haitian ethnicity then helps distinguish them from African-Americans and other ethnic groups who may be competing for the same resources and recognition. In studying ethnic relations, it is not enough to look at the cultural content of the ethnic group. Equally important are the structural constraints and the political-economic context in which ethnic differentiation develops.

In the face of globalization, much of the world, including the entire "democratic West," is experiencing an "ethnic revival." The new assertiveness of long-resident ethnic groups extends to the Basques and Catalans in Spain, the Bretons and Corsicans in France, and the Welsh and Scots in the United Kingdom. The United States and Canada are becoming increasingly multicultural, focusing on their internal diversity. "Melting pots" no longer, they are better described as ethnic "salads" (each ingredient remains distinct, although in the same bowl, with the same dressing). In 1992, then New York mayor David Dinkins called his city a "gorgeous mosaic."

A document of the University of Michigan American Culture Program published in 1992 offers a good exposition of the multicultural model. It recognizes "the multiplicity of American cultures." It presents multiculturalism as a new approach to the central question in American studies: What does it mean to be an American? The document suggests a shift from the study of core myths and values, and people's relationships to them as generalized Americans, to "recognizing that 'America' includes people of differing community, ethnic, and cultural histories, different points of view and degrees of empowerment." Such a perspective spurs studies of specific ethnic groups rather than the country as a whole (Internal Review document of the Program in American Culture of the University of Michigan—3/12/92).

ROOTS OF ETHNIC CONFLICT

Ethnicity, based on perceived cultural similarities and differences in a society or nation, can be expressed in peaceful multiculturalism, or in discrimination or violent interethnic confrontation. Culture is both adaptive and maladaptive. The perception of cultural differences can have disastrous effects on social interaction.

The roots of ethnic differentiation—and therefore, potentially, of ethnic conflict—can be political, economic, religious, linguistic, cultural, or "racial." Why do ethnic differences often lead to conflict and violence? The causes include a sense of injustice because of resource distribution, economic and/or political competition, and reaction to discrimination, prejudice, and other expressions of threatened or devalued identity (Ryan 1990, p. xxvii).

Prejudice and Discrimination

Ethnic conflict often arises in reaction to prejudice (attitudes and judgments) or discrimination (action). **Prejudice** means devaluing (looking down on) a group because of its assumed behavior, values, capabilities, or attributes. People are prejudiced when they hold stereotypes about groups and apply them to individuals. (**Stereotypes** are fixed ideas—often unfavorable—about what the members of a group are like.) Prejudiced people assume that members of the group will act as they are "supposed to act" (according to the stereotype) and interpret a wide range of individual behaviors as evidence of the stereotype. They use this behavior to confirm their stereotype (and low opinion) of the group.

Discrimination refers to policies and practices that harm a group and its members. Discrimination may be *de facto* (practiced, but not legally sanctioned) or *de jure* (part of the law). An example of *de facto* discrimination is the harsher treatment that American minorities (compared with other Americans) tend to get from the police and the judicial system. This unequal treatment isn't legal, but it happens anyway. Segregation in the southern United States and *apartheid* in South Africa provide two examples of *de jure* discrimination, which are no longer in existence. In the United States *de jure* segregation has been illegal since the 1950s, and the South African *apartheid* system was abandoned in 1991. In both systems, by law, blacks and whites had different rights and privileges. Their social interaction ("mixing") was legally curtailed. Slavery, of course, is the most extreme and coercive form of legalized inequality; people are treated as property.

We can also distinguish between attitudinal and institutional discrimination. With **attitudinal discrimination,** people discriminate against members of a group because they are prejudiced toward that group. For example, in the United States members of the Ku Klux Klan have expressed their prejudice against blacks, Jews, and Catholics through verbal, physical, and psychological harassment.

The most extreme form of anti-ethnic (attitudinal) discrimination is **genocide,** the deliberate elimination of a group through mass murder. The United Nations defines *genocide* as acts "committed with intent to destroy, in whole or in part, a national, ethnical, racial, or religious group, as such" (Ryan 1990, p. 11). Strongly prejudicial attitudes (hate) and resulting genocide have been directed against people viewed as "standing in the way of progress" (e.g., Native Americans) and people with jobs that the dominant group wants (e.g., Jews in Hitler's Germany).

Institutional discrimination refers to programs, policies, and institutional arrangements that deny equal rights and opportunities to, or differentially harm, members of particular groups. This form of discrimination is usually less personal and intentional than attitudinal discrimination is, but it may be based on a long history of inequality that also includes attitudinal bias. One example of institutional discrimination is what Bunyan Bryant and Paul Mohai (1991, p. 4) call **environmental racism**—"the systematic use of institutionally based power by whites to formulate policy decisions that will lead to the disproportionate burden of environmental hazards in minority communities." Thus, toxic waste dumps tend to be located in areas with nonwhite populations.

Environmental racism is discriminatory but not always intentional. Sometimes toxic wastes *are* deliberately dumped in areas whose residents are considered unlikely to protest (because they are poor, powerless, "disorganized," or "uneducated"). In other cases property values fall after toxic waste sites are located in an area. The wealthier people move out, and poorer people, often minorities, move in, to suffer the consequences of living in a hazardous environment.

Chips in the Mosaic

Although the multicultural model is increasingly prominent in contemporary North America, ethnic competition and conflict are just as evident. We hear increasingly of conflict between new arrivals, like Central Americans and Koreans, and long-established ethnic groups, like African-Americans. Ethnic antagonism flared in South-Central Los Angeles in spring 1992, in rioting that followed the acquittal of the four white police officers who were tried for the videotaped beating of Rodney King.

Angry blacks attacked whites, Koreans, and Hispanics. This violence expressed the frustration of African-Americans about their prospects in an increasingly multicultural society. A *New York Times*/CBS News poll conducted May 8, 1992, just after the Los Angeles riots, found that blacks had a bleaker outlook than whites did about the effects of immigration on their lives. Only 23 percent of the blacks felt they had more opportunities than recent immigrants, compared with twice that many whites (Toner 1992).

South-Central Los Angeles, where most of the 1992 rioting took place, is an ethnically mixed area, which used to be mainly African-American. As blacks have moved out, there has been an influx of Latin Americans (Mexicans and Central Americans—mainly recent and illegal immigrants). The Hispanic population of South-Central Los Angeles increased by 119 percent in a decade, as the number of blacks declined by 17 percent. By 1992 the neighborhood had become 45 percent Hispanic and 48 percent black. Many store owners in South-Central Los Angeles are Korean immigrants (see Abelmann and Lie 1995).

Korean stores were hard hit during the 1992 riots, and more than a third of the businesses destroyed were Hispanic-owned. A third of those who died in the riots were Hispanics. These mainly recent migrants lacked deep roots to the neighborhood and, as Spanish speakers, faced language barriers (Newman 1992). Many Koreans also had trouble with English.

Koreans interviewed on ABC's *Nightline* on May 6, 1992, recognized that blacks resented them and considered them unfriendly. One man explained, "It's not part of our culture to smile." African-Americans interviewed on the same program did complain about Korean unfriendliness. "They come into our neighborhoods and treat us like dirt." These comments suggest a shortcoming of the multicultural perspective: Ethnic groups (blacks here) expect other ethnic groups in the same nation-state to assimilate to some extent to a shared (national) culture. The African-Americans' comments invoked a general American value system that includes friendliness, openness, mutual respect, community participation, and "fair play." Los Angeles blacks wanted their Korean neighbors to act more like generalized Americans—and good neighbors.

Korean-American culture promotes family-run business and encourages children to study and work hard with professional careers in mind. These values fit general American ideals about work and achievement. But during the Los Angeles riots of 1992, African-Americans blamed their Korean neighbors for neglecting other American values—friendliness, openness, and community participation. Los Angeles blacks wanted their Korean neighbors to be less family-oriented and to act more like good neighbors.

Whatever their ethnic background, people can't hope to live in social isolation from the communities from which they derive their livelihoods. They have to take steps to adapt. Some African-Americans jointly interviewed with a few Koreans by ABC told the store owners they could improve relations in the neighborhood by hiring one or two local people. The Koreans said they couldn't afford to hire nonrelatives.

One way in which Koreans in cities like New York and Los Angeles have succeeded economically is through family enterprise. Family members work together in small grocery stores, like those in South-Central Los Angeles, pooling their labor and their wealth. Korean culture also stresses the value of education; children, supervised and encouraged by their parents, study hard to do well in school. In a society whose economy is shifting from manufacturing toward specialized services and information processing, good jobs demand education beyond high school. Asian family values and support systems encourage children to plan, study, and work hard, with such careers in mind.

These values also fit certain general American ideals. Work and achievement are American values that the Korean-Americans being interviewed invoked to explain their behavior. (Family solidarity is also a general American value, but the specific meaning of "family" varies between groups.) The Koreans also felt that they couldn't succeed financially if they had to hire nonrelatives.

The key question is whether such groups can prosper in impoverished multiethnic areas like South-Central Los Angeles if they don't extend their social ties to their host communities. Providing an economic service is not enough. Without efforts designed to gain social acceptance, storekeepers (of whatever ethnic group) will continue to face looting, boycotts, and other **leveling mechanisms.** This term refers to customs or social actions that operate to reduce differences in wealth and bring standouts in line with community norms. Leveling mechanisms surface when there is an expectation of community solidarity and economic similarity—especially that of shared poverty—and some people are profiting more than, or at the expense of, others.

Leveling mechanisms tend to discourage people from surpassing their peers—punishing those who do, pushing them back to the common level. Such mechanisms, according to Max Weber (1904/1958), were common in European peasant communities before the rise of capitalism. Peasants, Weber believed, worked just hard enough to satisfy their immediate needs. Then they quit, mistrusting people who needlessly worked more than others. The individualism associated with capitalism had to surmount the collectivism of the peasant community, in which gossip and other social pressures brought overachievers back in line.

Anthropologist George Foster (1965) stresses the importance of leveling mechanisms in "classic" peasant societies throughout the world. According to Foster, peasants have an "image of limited good," according to which all valued things are finite. They regard the total amount of health, wealth, honor, or success available to community members as limited. Thus, one person can excel only at the expense of others. Unless good fortune clearly comes from outside (for example, external wage work or a lottery) and unless the fruits of success are shared with others, successful people face ostracism through leveling mechanisms including gossip, avoidance, insults, and physical attack.

Leveling mechanisms are found not only in peasant communities but also in many other societies anthropologists have studied. The 1992 Los Angeles riots show that leveling mechanisms continue to operate in urban, stratified, multiethnic America.

Aftermaths of Oppression

Also fueling ethnic conflict are such forms of discrimination as forced assimilation, ethnocide, and cultural colonialism. A dominant group may try to destroy the cultures of certain ethnic groups (**ethnocide**) or force them to adopt the dominant culture (**forced assimilation**). Many countries have penalized or banned the language and customs of an ethnic group (including its religious observances). One example of forced assimilation is the anti-Basque campaign that the dictator Francisco Franco (who ruled between 1939 and 1975) waged in Spain. Franco banned Basque books, journals, newspapers, signs, sermons, and tombstones and imposed fines for using the Basque language in schools. His policies led to the formation of a Basque terrorist group and spurred strong nationalist sentiment in the Basque region (Ryan 1995).

A policy of **ethnic expulsion** aims at removing groups who are culturally different from a country. There are many examples, including Bosnia-Herzegovina in the 1990s. Uganda expelled 74,000 Asians in 1972. The neofascist parties of contemporary Western Europe advocate repatriation (expulsion) of immigrant workers (West Indians in England, Algerians in France, and Turks in Germany) (Ryan 1995).

A policy of expulsion may create **refugees**—people who have been forced (involuntary refugees) or who have chosen (voluntary refugees) to flee a country, to escape persecution or war. For example, Palestinian refugees moved to camps in Egypt, Jordan, and Lebanon after the Arab-Israeli wars of 1948 and 1967 (Ryan 1995).

Colonialism, another form of oppression, refers to the political, social, economic, and cultural domination of a territory and its people by a foreign power for an extended time (Bell 1981). The British and French colonial empires are familiar examples of colonialism, but we can extend the term to the former Soviet empire, formerly known as "the Second World."

Using the labels "First World," "Second World," and "Third World" is a common, although clearly ethnocentric, way of categorizing nations that may be defined here. The **First World** refers to the "democratic West"—traditionally conceived in opposition to a "Second World" ruled by "communism." The First World includes Canada, the United States, Western Europe, Japan, Australia, and New Zealand. The **Second World** refers to the Warsaw Pact nations, including the former Soviet Union and the Socialist and once-Socialist countries of Eastern Europe, and Asia. Proceeding with this classification, the "less-developed countries" (LDCs) make up the **Third World.** Some even assign the poorest nations to a **Fourth World.** This usage would, for example, distinguish Bangladesh (Fourth World) from India (Third World).

The frontiers imposed by colonialism weren't usually based on, and often didn't reflect, preexisting cultural units. In many countries, colonial nation-building left ethnic strife in its wake. Thus, over a million Hindus and Moslems were killed in the violence that accompanied the division of the Indian subcontinent into India and Pakistan. Problems between Arabs and Jews in Palestine began during the British mandate period. Ethnic conflicts in the less-developed countries have proliferated since the early 1960s, when decolonization reached its height. There have been bitter ethnic conflicts in Zaire, Nigeria, Bangladesh, Sudan, India, Sri Lanka, Iraq, Ethiopia, Uganda, Lebanon, and Cyprus. Few of these have been resolved.

Like other colonial powers, the Soviet Union politically suppressed ethnic expression, including potential and actual conflict, for decades. Multiculturalism may be growing in the United States and Canada, but the opposite is happening in the disintegrating Second World, where ethnic groups (nationalities) want their own nation-states. The flowering of ethnic feeling and conflict as the Soviet

The flowering of ethnic/nationalist feeling and conflict as the Soviet Union disintegrated illustrates that years of political repression and ideology provide insufficient common ground for lasting unity. Shown here, nationalists in Chechnya rebel against Russian rule, with separation as their goal.

empire disintegrated illustrates that years of political repression and ideology provide insufficient "common ground" for lasting unity.

Cultural colonialism refers to internal domination—by one group and its culture/ideology over others. One example is the domination over the former Soviet empire by Russian people, language, and culture, and by Communist ideology. The dominant culture makes itself the official culture. This is reflected in schools, the media, and public interaction. Under Soviet rule ethnic minorities had very limited self-rule in republics and regions controlled by Moscow. All the republics and their peoples were to be united by the oneness of "socialist internationalism."

One common technique in cultural colonialism is to flood ethnic areas with members of the dominant ethnic group. Thus, in the former Soviet Union, ethnic Russian colonists were sent to many areas, like Tajikistan (Figure 4.3), to diminish the cohesion and clout of the local people. Tajikistan is a small, poor state (and former Soviet republic) in central Asia, near Afghanistan, with 5.1 million people. In Tajikistan, as in central Asia generally, most people are Muslims. Today Islam, as an alternative way of ordering spiritual and social life, is replacing the ideology of Soviet Communism. This comes after more than seventy years of official atheism and suppression of religion. The Soviet empire limited Islamic teaching and worship, converting and destroying

mosques, discouraging religious practice by the young, but allowing it for old people. Still, Islam was taught at home, around the kitchen table, so it has been called "kitchen Islam."

Now, as the Russians leave Tajikistan, the force of Russian culture and language is receding. Islamic influence is growing. Women have started covering their arms, legs, and hair. More and more people

One example of cultural colonialism is the domination of the former Soviet empire by Russian people, language, and culture, and by communist ideology. This domination was felt in schools, media, and public interaction. Under Soviet rule ethnic minorities had very limited self-rule in republics and regions controlled by Moscow. These Siberian children are trained to be model Soviet (Russian) citizens.

Figure 4.3 *Former Soviet Socialist Republics of Central Asia, including Tajikistan.*

speak and pray in Tajik, a language related to Persian (which is spoken in Iran) (Erlanger 1992).

"The Commonwealth of Independent States" is all that remains of the Soviet Union. In this group of new nations, ethnic groups (nationalities) like the Tajiks and Chechens are seeking to establish separate and viable nation-states based on cultural boundaries. This celebration of ethnic autonomy is an understandable reaction to the Soviet Union's years of suppressing diversity: historic, national, linguistic, ethnic, cultural, and religious. It is part of an ethnic florescence that—as surely as globalization and transnationalism—is a trend of the late twentieth century.

SUMMARY

Ethnicity is based on cultural similarities (among members of the same ethnic group) and differences (between that group and others). Ethnic distinctions can arise from language, religion, history, geography, kinship, or "race." A race is an ethnic group assumed to have a biological basis. Usually race and ethnicity are ascribed statuses; people are born members of a group and remain so all their lives.

The term *nation* was once synonymous with "ethnic group." Now *nation* has come to mean a state—a centrally organized political unit, a government. *Nation* and *state* have become synonymous. Combined in *nation-state*, they refer to such an autonomous political entity, a "country." Because of migration, conquest, and colonialism, most nation-states are not ethnically homogeneous. States sometimes encourage ethnic divisions for political and economic ends.

Ethnic groups that once had, or wish to have or regain, autonomous political status (their own country) are called *nationalities.* Language and print have played a crucial role in the growth of national consciousness. But over time, political upheavals, wars, and migrations have divided many imagined national communities.

Ethnic diversity may be associated with positive group interaction and coexistence (harmony) or with conflict. In creating multitribal and multiethnic states, colonial regimes often erected boundaries that corresponded poorly with preexisting cultural divisions. But certain colonial policies and institutions also helped create new "imagined communities."

Assimilation describes the process of change that an ethnic group may experience when it moves to a country where another culture dominates. By assimilating, the minority adopts the patterns and norms of its host culture.

Assimilation isn't inevitable, and there can be ethnic harmony without it.

A plural society combines ethnic contrasts and economic interdependence. Such interdependence (or, at least, the lack of competition) between ethnic groups may be based on different activities in the same region, or on longtime occupation of different regions in the same country.

The view of cultural diversity in a nation-state as good and desirable is multiculturalism. The multicultural model is the opposite of the assimilationist model, in which minorities are expected to abandon their cultural traditions and values, replacing them with those of the majority population. A multicultural society socializes individuals not only into the dominant (national) culture but also into an ethnic culture. Multiculturalism succeeds best in a society whose political system promotes freedom of expression and in which there are many and diverse ethnic groups.

Ethnicity can be expressed in peaceful multiculturalism, or in discrimination or violent interethnic confrontation. Ethnic conflict often arises in reaction to prejudice (attitudes and judgments) or discrimination (action). *Prejudice* means devaluing (looking down on) a group because of its assumed behavior, values, capabilities, or attributes. *Discrimination* refers to policies and practices that harm a group and its members. Discrimination may be *de facto* (practiced, but not legally sanctioned) or *de jure* (part of the law). With *attitudinal discrimination*, people discriminate because they are prejudiced toward a group. The most extreme form of anti-ethnic discrimination is genocide, the deliberate elimination of a group through mass murder. *Institutional discrimination* refers to programs, policies, and arrangements that deny equal rights and opportunities to, or differentially harm, particular groups.

Although the multicultural model is increasingly prominent in North America, ethnic competition and conflict are also evident. One shortcoming of the multicultural perspective is that ethnic groups may expect other ethnic groups who live in the same country to assimilate to some extent to a more general, supposedly shared, national culture and value system.

A dominant group may try to destroy the cultures of certain ethnic groups (ethnocide), or force them to adopt the dominant culture (forced assimilation). A policy of ethnic expulsion may create refugees—people who have been forced (involuntary refugees) or who have chosen (voluntary refugees) to flee a country. *Colonialism* refers to the political, social, economic, and cultural domination of a territory and its people by a foreign power for an extended time. In many countries, colonial nation-building left ethnic strife in its wake. *Cultural colonialism* refers to internal domination—by one group and its culture and/or ideology over others. One example is the domination of the former Soviet empire by the Russian people, language, and culture. The flowering of ethnic feeling and conflict as the Soviet empire disintegrated illustrates that years of political repression provide insufficient common ground for lasting unity. Celebration of ethnic autonomy is an understandable reaction to years of suppressing diversity: historic, national, linguistic, ethnic, cultural, and religious. It is part of an ethnic florescence that is a trend of the late twentieth century.

GLOSSARY

achieved status: Social status that comes through talents, actions, efforts, activities, and accomplishments, rather than ascription.

ascribed status: Social status (e.g., race or gender) that people have little or no choice about occupying.

assimilation: The process of change that a minority group may experience when it moves to a country where another culture dominates; the minority is incorporated into the dominant culture to the point that it no longer exists as a separate cultural unit.

attitudinal discrimination: Discrimination against members of a group because of prejudice toward that group.

colonialism: The political, social, economic, and cultural domination of a territory and its people by a foreign power for an extended time.

cultural colonialism: Internal domination—by one group and its culture/ideology over others; for example, Russian domination of the former Soviet Union.

discrimination: Policies and practices that harm a group and its members.

environmental racism: The systematic use of institutionally based power by a majority group to make policy decisions that create disproportionate environmental hazards in minority communities.

ethnic expulsion: A policy aimed at removing groups who are culturally different from a country.

ethnic group: Group distinguished by cultural similarities (shared among members of that group) and differences (between that group and others); ethnic group members share beliefs, values, habits, customs, and norms, and a common language, religion, history, geography, kinship, and/or race.

ethnicity: Identification with, and feeling part of, an ethnic group, and exclusion from certain other groups because of this affiliation.

ethnocide: Destruction by a dominant group of the cultures of an ethnic group.

First World: The "democratic West"—traditionally conceived in opposition to a "Second World" ruled by "communism."

forced assimilation: Use of force by a dominant group to compel a minority to adopt the dominant culture—for example, penalizing or banning the language and customs of an ethnic group.

Fourth World: The very poorest of the less-developed countries—for example, Madagascar, Bangladesh.

genocide: The deliberate elimination of a group through mass murder.

institutional discrimination: Programs, policies, and arrangements that deny equal rights and opportunities to, or differentially harm, members of particular groups.

leveling mechanisms: Customs and social actions that operate to reduce differences in wealth and thus to bring standouts in line with community norms.

majority groups: Superordinate, dominant, or controlling groups in a social-political hierarchy.

minority groups: Subordinate groups in a social-political hierarchy, with inferior power and less secure access to resources than majority groups.

multiculturalism: The view of cultural diversity in a country as something good and desirable; a multicultural society socializes individuals not only into the dominant (national) culture but also into an ethnic culture.

nation: Once a synonym for "ethnic group," designating a single culture sharing a language, religion, history, territory, ancestry, and kinship; now usually a synonym for "state" or "nation-state."

nationalities: Ethnic groups that once had, or wish to have or regain, autonomous political status (their own country).

nation-state: An autonomous political entity; a country like the United States or Canada.

négritude: African identity—developed by African intellectuals in Francophone (French-speaking) West Africa.

plural society: A society that combines ethnic contrasts and economic interdependence of the ethnic groups.

prejudice: Devaluing (looking down on) a group because of its assumed behavior, values, capabilities, or attitudes.

race: An ethnic group assumed to have a biological basis.

racism: Discrimination against an ethnic group assumed to have a biological basis.

refugees: People who have been forced (involuntary refugees) or who have chosen (voluntary refugees) to flee a country, to escape persecution or war.

Second World: The Warsaw Pact nations, including the former Soviet Union, the Socialist and once-Socialist countries of Eastern Europe and Asia.

state: An independent, centrally organized political unit; a government.

status: Any position that determines where someone fits in society; may be ascribed or achieved.

stereotypes: Fixed ideas—often unfavorable—about what the members of a group are like.

Third World: The less-developed countries (LDCs); used in combination with "Fourth World," "Third World" refers to the better-off LDCs (e.g., Brazil, India) compared with poorer LDCs (Bangladesh, Madagascar).

STUDY QUESTIONS

1. How is ethnicity based on cultural similarities and differences?
2. What does it mean to say that we "wear different hats" and negotiate our social identities?
3. What is the difference between ascribed and achieved status?
4. Is ethnicity ever an achieved status?
5. What is a minority group? Must it be a numerical minority?
6. What is the relation between an ethnic group, a nation, and a nation-state?
7. Are most nation-states ethnically homogeneous, and why or why not?
8. What is an imagined community, and how does it relate to ethnicity and nationality?
9. What role have print and language played in the rise of national consciousness?
10. How may linguistic and cultural similarities contribute to ethnic harmony, national identity, and integration?
11. What roles did colonialism play with respect to nationalism and ethnic unity and diversity?
12. What role does globalization play in ethnic relations?
13. What is the difference between acculturation and assimilation?
14. What is a plural society?
15. What is multiculturalism, and how does it differ from the assimilationist model?
16. What does it mean to say that ethnic relations in-

volve not just cultural content but also the political-economic context in which ethnic differentiation occurs?

17. How does prejudice differ from discrimination? Give examples of each.

18. Do you see any problems with the multicultural perspective?

19. What are various forms of ethnic discrimination? What is the difference between ethnocide and genocide?

20. What role did the former Soviet Union play in ethnic differentiation?

21. What are the main forms of "ethnic florescence" in the modern world?

SUGGESTED ADDITIONAL READING

ABELMANN, N., AND J. LIE
  1995   *Blue Dreams: Korean Americans and the Los Angeles Riots.* Cambridge, MA: Harvard University Press. Some of the roots of ethnic conflict in Los Angeles today.

ANDERSON, B.
  1991   *Imagined Communities: Reflections on the Origin and Spread of Nationalism,* rev. ed. London: Verso. The origins of nationalism in Europe and its colonies, with special attention to the role of print, language, and schools.

BARTH, F.
  1969   *Ethnic Groups and Boundaries: The Social Organization of Cultural Difference.* London: Allyn and Unwin. Classic discussion of the prominence of differentiation and boundaries (versus cultural features per se) in interethnic relations.

DELAMONT, S.
  1995   *Appetites and Identities: An Introduction to the Social Anthropology of Western Europe.* London: Routledge. An anthropological account of national cultures and ethnic variation in Western Europe.

FOX, R. G., ED.
  1990   *Nationalist Ideologies and the Production of National Cultures.* American Ethnological Society Monograph Series, no. 2. Washington, DC: American Anthropological Association. A series of papers about ethnicity and nationalism in Israel, Romania, India, Guatemala, Guyana, Burundi, and Tanzania.

FRIEDMAN, J.
  1994   *Cultural Identity and Global Process.* Thousand Oaks, CA: Sage. Issues of ethnic and cultural identity in the face of globalization.

GELLNER, E.
  1983   *Nations and Nationalism.* Ithaca, NY: Cornell University Press. Industrialism and nation-building.

HOBSBAWM, E. J.
  1992   *Nations and Nationalism since 1780: Programme, Myth, Reality,* 2nd ed. New York: Cambridge University Press. The making of modern nation-states.

LAGUERRE, M.
  1984   *American Odyssey: Haitians in New York.* Ithaca, NY: Cornell University Press. Interesting case study of the role of "race" and competition in ethnic differentiation in contemporary urban America.

RYAN, S.
  1995   *Ethnic Conflict and International Relations,* 2nd ed. Brookfield, MA: Dartmouth. Cross-national review of the roots of ethnic conflict.

YETMAN, N.
  1991   *Majority and Minority: The Dynamics of Race and Ethnicity in American Life,* 5th ed. Boston: Allyn and Bacon. A wide-ranging anthology focusing on the United States.

HUMAN BIOLOGICAL DIVERSITY AND THE RACE CONCEPT

SOCIAL RACE
Hypodescent: Race in the United States
Not Us: Race in Japan
Phenotype and Fluidity: Race in Brazil

RACE: A DISCREDITED CONCEPT IN BIOLOGY
Explaining Skin Color

STRATIFICATION AND "INTELLIGENCE"

Box: Culture, Biology, and Sports

Members of an ethnic group may define themselves—and/or be defined by others—as different and special because of their language, religion, geography, history, ancestry, or physical traits. When an ethnic group is assumed to have a biological basis (shared "blood" or genetic material), it is called a *race*. This chapter will examine "race" both as a cultural construct and as a discredited biological term. Examples from different cultures will be used to show that race, like ethnicity in general, is a cultural category rather than a biological reality. That is, ethnic groups, including "races," derive from contrasts perceived and perpetuated in particular societies, rather than from scientific classifications based on common genes.

It is not possible at this time to define races biologically. Only cultural constructions of race are possible—even though the average citizen conceptualizes "race" in biological terms. The belief that races exist and are important is much more common among the public than it is among scientists. Most Americans, for example, believe that their population includes biologically based "races" to which various labels have been applied. These labels include "white," "black," "yellow," "red," "Caucasoid," "Negroid," "Mongoloid," "Amerindian," "Asian-American," "African-American," "Euro-American," and "Native American."

We hear the words *ethnicity* and *race* frequently, but American culture doesn't draw a very clear line between them. As illustration, consider two articles in *The New York Times* of May 29, 1992. One, discussing the changing ethnic composition of the United States, states (correctly) that Hispanics "can be of any race" (Barringer 1992, p. A12). In other words, "Hispanic" is an ethnic category that crosscuts "racial" contrasts such as that between "black" and "white." The other article reports that during the Los Angeles riots of spring 1992, "hundreds of Hispanic residents were interrogated about their immigration status on the basis of their *race* alone [emphasis added]" (Mydans 1992a, p. A8). Use of "race" here seems inappropriate because "Hispanic" is usually perceived as referring to a linguistically based (Spanish-speaking) ethnic group, rather than a biologically based race. Since these Los Angeles residents were being interrogated because they were Hispanic, the article is actually reporting on ethnic, not racial, discrimination. However, given the lack of a precise distinction between race and ethnicity, it is probably better to use the "ethnic group" instead of "race" to describe *any* such social group, for example, African-Americans, Asian-Americans, Irish-Americans, Anglo-Americans, or Hispanics. (Table 5.1 lists the main ethnic groups in the United States.)

"Hispanic" and "Latino" are ethnic categories that crosscut "racial" contrasts such as that between "black" and "white." Note the physical diversity exemplified by these Puerto Rican university students.

Table 5.1 *Ethnic Groups in the United States,*
1990 Census Data

Claimed Identity	Millions of People
Whites, German ancestry	57.9
Whites, Irish ancestry	38.7
Whites, English ancestry	32.6
Blacks	30.0
Asians and Pacific Islanders	7.3
American Indians, Eskimos, and Aleuts	1.9
Hispanics (any "race")	22.3
Others	58.0
Total population	248.7

Source: Barringer 1992, p. A12.

SOCIAL RACE

Races are ethnic groups assumed (by members of a particular culture) to have a biological basis, but actually race is socially constructed. The "races" we hear about every day are cultural, or social, rather than biological categories. In Charles Wagley's terms (Wagley 1959/1968), they are **social races** (groups assumed to have a biological basis but actually defined in a culturally arbitrary, rather than a scientific, manner). Many Americans mistakenly assume that "whites" and "blacks," for example, are biologically distinct and that these terms stand for discrete races. But these labels, like racial terms used in other societies, really designate culturally perceived rather than biologically based groups.

Hypodescent: Race in the United States

How is race culturally constructed in the United States? In American culture, one acquires his or her racial identity at birth, as an ascribed status, but race isn't based on biology or on simple ancestry. Take the case of the child of a "racially mixed" marriage involving one black and one white parent. We know that 50 percent of the child's genes come from one parent and 50 percent from the other. Still, American culture overlooks heredity and classifies this child as black. This rule is arbitrary. From genotype (genetic composition), it would be just as logical to classify the child as white.

American rules for assigning racial status can be even more arbitrary. In some states, anyone known to have any black ancestor, no matter how remote, is classified as a member of the black race. This is a rule of **descent** (it assigns social identity on the basis of ancestry), but of a sort that is rare outside the contemporary United States. It is called **hypodescent** (Harris and Kottak 1963) (*hypo* means "lower") because it automatically places the children of a union or mating between members of different groups in the minority group. Hypodescent divides American society into groups that have been unequal in their access to wealth, power, and prestige.

The following case from Louisiana is an excellent illustration of the arbitrariness of the hypodescent rule and of the role that governments (federal, or state in this case) play in legalizing, inventing, or eradicating "race" and ethnicity (Williams 1989). Susie Guillory Phipps, a light-skinned woman with "Caucasian" features and straight black hair, discovered as an adult that she was "black." When Phipps ordered a copy of her birth certificate, she found her race listed as "colored." Since she had been "brought up white and married white twice," Phipps challenged a 1970 Louisiana law declaring anyone with at least one-thirty-second "Negro blood" to be legally black. Although the state's lawyer admitted that Phipps "looks like a white person," the state of Louisiana insisted that her racial classification was proper (Yetman, ed. 1991, pp. 3–4).

Cases like Phipps's are rare because "racial" identity is usually ascribed at birth and doesn't change. The rule of hypodescent affects blacks, Asians, Native Americans, and Hispanics differently. It's easier to negotiate Indian or Hispanic identity than black identity. The ascription rule isn't as definite, and the assumption of a biological basis isn't as strong.

To be considered "Native American," one ancestor out of eight (great-grandparents) or four (grandparents) may suffice. This depends on whether the assignment is by federal or state law, or an Indian tribal council. The child of a Hispanic may (or may not, depending on context) claim Hispanic identity. Many Americans with an Indian or Latino grandparent consider themselves "white" and lay no claim to minority-group status.

Something like hypodescent even works with the classification of sexual orientation in the United States. Bisexuals are lumped with gays and lesbians, rather than with heterosexuals. These statuses (sexual orientations) are viewed by many people as ascribed (no choice) rather than achieved (ambivalent or changing sexual preference possible).

The controversy that erupted in 1990–91 over the casting of the Broadway production of the musical *Miss Saigon* offers a final illustration of the cultural construction of race in the United States. The musical had opened a few years earlier in London, where the Filipina actress Lea Salonga played Kim, a young Vietnamese woman. Another major role is that of the Eurasian (half-French, half-Vietnamese) pimp known as the "Engineer." For the New York production the producer, Cameron Mackintosh, wanted Salonga to play Kim and the English actor Jonathan Pryce, who had originated the part in London, to play the Engineer. Actors' Equity must approve the casting of foreign stars in New York productions. The union voted that Mackintosh couldn't cast Pryce, a "Caucasian," in the role of a Eurasian. The part should go to an Asian.

In this case the American hypodescent rule was being extended from the offspring of black-white unions to "Eurasians" (in this case French-Vietnamese). Again, the cultural construction of ethnicity is that children get their social identity from the minority parent—Asian rather than European. This cultural construction of ethnicity also assumes that all Asians (e.g., Vietnamese, Chinese, and Filipinos) are the same. Thus it's okay for Filipinos to play Vietnamese (or even Eurasians), but an English actor can't play a half-French Eurasian.

In fact, Vietnamese and Filipinos are further apart in language, culture, and ancestry than French and English are. It would be "more logical" (based on language, culture, and common ancestry) to give the Engineer's part to an English actor than to a Filipino one. But Actors' Equity didn't see it that way. (The most "correct" choices for the part would have been a French man, a Vietnamese man, or a Eurasian of appropriate background.)

When Actors' Equity vetoed Pryce, Mackintosh canceled the New York production of *Miss Saigon*. Negotiations continued, and *Miss Saigon* eventually opened on Broadway, with a well-integrated cast, starring Pryce and Salonga (whose demanding part was shared, for two performances per week, with a Chinese-American actress). A year after the opening, Pryce and Salonga had left the production, and the three main "Asian" (Vietnamese) parts (including the Eurasian Engineer) were being played by Filipinos.

The culturally arbitrary hypodescent rule—not logic—is behind the notion that an Asian is more appropriate to play a Eurasian than a "Cuucasian" is. But, the protest over the casting of Miss Saigon *illustrates that what has been used against a group can also be used to promote the interests of that group. There has been a shortage of parts for Asian and Asian-American actors. In this case they used the hypodescent rule as a basis for political action—to stake their claim to "Eurasian" as well as "Asian" parts.*

The culturally arbitrary hypodescent rule—not logic—is behind the motion that an Asian is more appropriate to play a Eurasian than a "Caucasian" is. Hypodescent governs ethnic ascription in the United States and channels discrimination against offspring of mixed unions, who are assigned minority status. But, as the case of *Miss Saigon* illustrates, what has been used against a group can also be used to promote the interests of that group. There has been a shortage of parts for Asian and Asian-American actors. In this case they used the hypodescent rule as a basis for political action—to stake their claim to "Eurasian" as well as "Asian" parts.

Not Us: Race in Japan

American culture ignores considerable diversity in biology, language, and geographic origin as it socially constructs race within the United States. North Americans also overlook diversity by seeing Japan as a nation that is homogeneous in race, ethnicity, language, and culture—an image the Japanese themselves cultivate. Thus in 1986 former Prime Minister Nakasone created an international furor by contrasting his country's supposed homogeneity (responsible, he suggested, for Japan's success in international business) with the ethnically mixed

United States. To describe Japanese society, Nakasone used *tan'itsu minzoku*, an expression connoting a single ethnic-racial group (Robertson 1992).

Japan is hardly the uniform entity Nakasone described. Some dialects of Japanese are mutually unintelligible, and scholars estimate that 10 percent of the national population of 124 million are minorities of various sorts. These include aboriginal Ainu, annexed Okinawans, outcast *burakumin*, children of mixed marriages, and immigrant nationalities, especially Koreans, who number more than 700,000 (De Vos et al. 1983).

Americans tend to see Japanese and Koreans as alike, but the Japanese stress the difference between themselves and Koreans. To describe racial attitudes in Japan, Jennifer Robertson (1992) uses Kwame Anthony Appiah's (1990) term "intrinsic racism"—the belief that a (perceived) racial difference is a sufficient reason to value one person less than another.

In Japan the valued group is majority ("pure") Japanese, who are believed to share "the same blood." Thus, the caption to a printed photo of a Japanese-American model reads: "She was born in Japan but raised in Hawaii. Her nationality is American but no foreign blood flows in her veins" (Robertson 1992, p. 5). Something like hypodescent also operates in Japan, but less precisely than in the United States, where mixed offspring automatically become members of the minority group. The children of mixed marriages between majority Japanese and others (including Euro-Americans) may not get the same "racial" label as their minority parent, but they are still stigmatized for their non-Japanese ancestry (De Vos and Wagatsuma 1966).

How is race culturally constructed in Japan? The (majority) Japanese define themselves by opposition to others, whether minority groups in their own nation or outsiders—anyone who is "not us." Aspects of phenotype (detectable physical traits, such as perceived body odor) are considered part of being *racially different by opposition*. Other races don't smell as "we" do. The Japanese stigmatize Koreans by saying they smell different (as Europeans also do). The Japanese contend that Koreans have a pungent smell, which they mainly attribute to diet— Koreans eat garlicky foods and spicy kimchee. Japanese also stereotype their minorities with behavioral and psychological traits. Koreans are seen as underachievers, crime-prone, and working class,

in opposition to dominant Japanese, who are positively stereotyped as harmonious, hard-working, and middle class (Robertson 1992).

The "not us" should stay that way; assimilation is generally discouraged. Cultural mechanisms, especially residential segregation and taboos on "interracial" marriage, work to keep minorities "in their place." (Still, many marriages between minorities and majority Japanese do occur.) However, perhaps to give the appearance of homogeneity, people (e.g., Koreans) who become naturalized Japanese citizens are expected to take Japanese-sounding names (Robertson 1992; De Vos et al. 1983).

In its construction of race, Japanese culture regards certain ethnic groups as having a biological basis, when there is no evidence that they do. The best example is the *burakumin*, a stigmatized group of at least 4 million outcasts, sometimes compared to India's untouchables. The *burakumin* are physically and genetically indistinguishable from other Japanese. Many of them "pass" as (and marry) majority Japanese, but a deceptive marriage can end in divorce if *burakumin* identity is discovered (Aoki and Dardess, eds. 1981).

Burakumin are perceived as standing apart from the majority Japanese lineage. Through ancestry, descent (and thus, it is assumed, "blood," or genetics) *burakumin* are "not us." Majority Japanese try to keep their lineage pure by discouraging mixing. The *burakumin* are residentially segregated in neighborhoods (rural or urban) called *buraku*, from which the racial label is derived. Compared with majority Japanese, the *burakumin* are less likely to attend high school and college. When *burakumin* attend the same schools, they face discrimination. Majority children and teachers may refuse to eat with them because *burakumin* are considered unclean.

In applying for university admission or a job, and in dealing with the government, Japanese must list their address, which becomes part of a household or family registry. This list makes residence in a *buraku*, and likely *burakumin* social status, evident. Schools and companies use this information to discriminate. (The best way to pass is to move so often that the *buraku* address eventually disappears from the registry.) Majority Japanese also limit "race" mixture by hiring marriage mediators to check out the family histories of prospective spouses. They are especially careful to check for *burakumin* ancestry (De Vos et al. 1983).

The origin of the *burakumin* lies in a historic tiered system of stratification (from the Tokugawa period—1603–1868). The top four ranked categories were warrior-administrators (*samurai*), farmers, artisans, and merchants. The ancestors of the *burakumin* were below this hierarchy, an outcast group who did unclean jobs, like animal slaughter and disposal of the dead. *Burakumin* still do related jobs, including work with animal products, like leather. The *burakumin* are more likely than majority Japanese are to do manual labor (including farm work) and to belong to the national lower class. *Burakumin* and other Japanese minorities are also more likely to have careers in crime, prostitution, entertainment, and sports (De Vos et al. 1983).

Like blacks in the United States, the *burakumin* are class-stratified. Because certain jobs are reserved for the *burakumin*, people who are successful in those occupations (e.g., shoe factory owners) can be wealthy. *Burakumin* have also found jobs as government bureaucrats. Financially successful *burakumin* can temporarily escape their stigmatized status by travel, including foreign travel.

Today most discrimination against the *burakumin* is *de facto* rather than *de jure*. It is strikingly like the discrimination—attitudinal and institutional—that blacks have experienced in the United States. The *burakumin* often live in villages and neighborhoods with poor housing and sanitation. They have limited access to education, jobs, amenities, and health facilities. In response to *burakumin* political mobilization, Japan has dismantled the legal structure of discrimination against *burakumin* and has worked to improve conditions in the *buraku*. Still, Japan has yet to institute American-style affirmative action programs for education and jobs. Discrimination against nonmajority Japanese is still the rule in companies. Some employers say that hiring *burakumin* would give their company an unclean image and thus create a disadvantage in competing with other businesses (De Vos et al. 1983).

By contrast with the *burakumin*, who are citizens of Japan, most Japanese Koreans, who form one of the nation's largest minorities (about 750,000 people), are not. Koreans in Japan continue, as resident aliens, to face discrimination in education and jobs. They lack citizens' health-care and social-service benefits, and government and company jobs don't usually go to non-Japanese.

Koreans started arriving in Japan, mainly as manual laborers, after Japan conquered Korea in 1910 and ruled it through 1945. During World War II, there were more than 2 million Koreans in Japan. They were recruited to replace Japanese farm workers who left the fields for the imperial army. Some Koreans were women (numbering from 70,000 to 200,000) forced to serve as prostitutes ("comfort women") for Japanese troops. By 1952 most Japanese Koreans had been repatriated to a divided Korea. Those who stayed in Japan were denied citizenship. They became "resident aliens," forced, like Japanese criminals, to carry an ID card, which re-

Japan's stigmatized burakumin *are physically and genetically indistinguishable from other Japanese. In response to* burakumin *political mobilization, Japan has dismantled the legal structure of discrimination against* burakumin *and has worked to improve conditions in their neighborhoods, which are called* buraku. *This Sports Day for* burakumin *children is one kind of mobilization.*

sentful Koreans call a "dog tag." Unlike most nations, Japan doesn't grant automatic citizenship to people born in the country. One can become Japanese by having one parent born in Japan and living there three successive years (Robertson 1992).

Like the *burakumin*, many Koreans (who by now include third and fourth generations) fit physically and linguistically into the Japanese population. Most Koreans speak Japanese as their primary language, and many pass as majority Japanese. Still, they tend to be segregated residentially, often in the same neighborhoods as *burakumin*, with whom they sometimes intermarry. Koreans maintain strong kin ties and a sense of ethnic identity with other Koreans, especially in their neighborhoods. Most Japanese Koreans qualify for citizenship but choose not to take it because of Japan's policy of forced assimilation. Anyone who naturalizes is strongly encouraged to take a Japanese name. Many Koreans feel that to do so would cut them off from their kin and ethnic identity. Knowing they can never become majority Japanese, they choose not to become "not us" twice.

Phenotype and Fluidity: Race in Brazil

There are more flexible, less exclusionary ways of constructing social race than those used in the United States and Japan. Along with the rest of Latin America, Brazil has less exclusionary categories, which permit individuals to change their racial classification. Brazil shares a history of slavery with the United States, but it lacks the hypodescent rule. Nor does Brazil have racial aversion of the sort found in Japan. The history of Brazilian slavery dates back to the sixteenth century, when Africans were brought as slaves to work on sugar plantations in northeastern Brazil. Later, Brazilians used slave labor in mines and on coffee plantations. The contributions of Africans to Brazilian culture have been as great as they have been to North American culture. Today, especially in areas of Brazil where slaves were most numerous, African ancestry is evident.

The system that Brazilians use to classify biological differences contrasts with those used in the United States and Japan. First, Brazilians use many more racial labels (over 500 have been reported—Harris [1970]) than North Americans or Japanese do. In northeastern Brazil I found forty different racial terms in use in Arembepe, a village of only 750 people (Kottak 1992). Through their classification system Brazilians recognize and attempt to describe the physical variation that exists in their population. The system used in the United States, by recognizing only three or four races, blinds North Americans to an equivalent range of evident physical contrasts. Japanese races, remember, don't even originate in physical contrasts. *Burakumin* are physically indistinguishable from other Japanese but are considered to be biologically different.

The system that Brazilians use to construct social race has other special features. In the United States one's race is an ascribed status; it is assigned automatically by hypodescent and doesn't usually change. In Japan race is also ascribed at birth, but it can change when, say, a *burakumin* or a naturalized Korean passes as a majority Japanese. In Brazil racial identity is more flexible, more of an achieved status. Brazilian racial classification pays attention to phenotype. **Phenotype** refers to an organism's evident traits, its "manifest biology"—anatomy and physiology. There are thousands of evident (detectable) physical traits, ranging from skin color, hair form, and eye color (which are visible), to blood type, colorblindness, and enzyme production (which become evident through testing). A Brazilian's phenotype, and racial label, may change due to environmental factors, such as the tanning rays of the sun.

For historical reasons, darker-skinned Brazilians tend to be poorer than lighter-skinned Brazilians are. When Brazil's Princess Isabel abolished slavery in 1889, the freed men and women received no land or other reparations. They took what jobs were available. For example, the freed slaves who founded the village of Arembepe, which I have been studying since 1962, turned to fishing. Many Brazilians (including slave descendants) are poor because they lack a family history of access to land or commercial wealth and because upward social mobility is difficult. Continuing today, especially in cities, it is poor, dark-skinned Brazilians, on average, who face the most intense discrimination.

Given the correlation between poverty and dark skin, the class structure affects Brazilian racial classification, so that someone who has light skin and is poor will be perceived and classified as darker than a comparably colored person who is rich. The racial term applied to a wealthy person who has dark skin will tend to "lighten" the skin color, which gives rise to the Brazilian expression "money whitens." In the United States, by contrast, race and class are correlated, but racial classification isn't changed by class. Because of hypodescent, racial identity in the United States is an ascribed status—fixed and lifelong—regardless of phenotype or economic status. One illustration of the absence of hypodescent in Brazil is the fact that (unlike the United States) full siblings there may belong to different races (if they are phenotypically different).

Arembepe has a mixed and physically diverse population, reflecting generations of immigration and intermarriage between its founders and outsiders. Some villagers have dark, others, light, skin color. Facial features, eye and hair color, and hair type also vary. Although physically heterogeneous, Arembepe is economically homogeneous—local residents have not risen out of the national lower class. Given such economic uniformity, wealth contrasts don't affect racial classification, which Arembepeiros base on the physical differences they perceive between individuals. As physical characteristics change (sunlight alters skin color, humidity affects hair form), so do racial terms. Furthermore, racial differences are so insignificant in structuring community life that people often forget the terms they have applied to others. Sometimes they even forget the ones they've used for themselves. To reach this conclusion, I made it a habit to ask the same person on different days to tell me the races of others in the village (and my own). In the United States I am always "white" or "Euro-American," but in Arembepe I got lots of terms besides *branco* ("white"). I could be *claro* ("light"), *louro* ("blond"), *sarará* ("light-skinned redhead"), *mulato claro* ("light mulatto"), or *mulato* ("mulatto"). The racial term used to describe me or anyone else varied from person to person, week to week, even day to day. My best informant, a man with very dark skin color, changed the term he used for himself all the time—from *escuro* ("dark") to *preto* ("black") to *moreno escuro* ("dark brunet").

The North American and Japanese racial systems are creations of particular cultures, rather than scientific—or even accurate—descriptions of human biological differences. Brazilian racial classification is also a cultural construction, but Brazilians have developed a way of describing human biological diversity that is more detailed, fluid, and flexible than the systems used in most cultures. Brazil lacks

Japan's racial aversion, and it also lacks a rule of descent like that which ascribes racial status in the United States (Harris 1964; Degler 1970).

The operation of the hypodescent rule helps us understand why the populations labeled "black" and "Indian" (Native American) are growing in the United States but shrinking in Brazil. North American culture places all "mixed" children in the minority category, which therefore gets all the resultant population increase. Brazil, by contrast, assigns the offspring of mixed marriages to intermediate categories, using a larger set of ethnic and racial labels. A Brazilian with a "white" (*branco*) parent and a "black" (*preto*) parent will almost never be called *branco* or *preto* but instead by some intermediate term (of which dozens are available). The United States lacks intermediate categories, but it is those categories that are swelling in Brazil. Brazil's assimilated Indians are called *cabôclos* (rather than *indíos*, or a specific tribal name, like Kayapó or Yanomami). With hypodescent, by contrast, someone may have just one of four or eight Indian grandparents or great-grandparents and still "feel Indian," be so classified, and even have a tribal identity.

For centuries the United States and Brazil each have had mixed populations, with ancestors from Native America, Europe, Africa, and Asia. Although "races" have mixed in both countries, Brazilian and North American cultures have constructed the results differently. The historic reasons for this contrast lie mainly in the different characteristics of the settlers of the two countries. The mainly English early settlers of the United States came as women, men, and families, but Brazil's Portuguese colonizers were mainly men—merchants and adventurers. Many of these Portuguese men married Native American women and recognized their "racially mixed" children as their heirs. Like their North American counterparts, Brazilian plantation owners had sexual relations with their slaves. But the Brazilian landlords more often freed the children that resulted—for demographic and economic reasons. (Sometimes these were their only children.) Freed offspring of master and slave became plantation overseers and foremen and filled many intermediate positions in the emerging Brazilian economy. They were not classed with the slaves, but allowed to join a new intermediate category. No hypodescent rule ever developed in Brazil to ensure that whites and blacks remained separate (see Harris 1964; Degler 1970).

RACE: A DISCREDITED CONCEPT IN BIOLOGY

Races are culturally constructed categories that may have little to do with actual biological differences. Historically, scientists have approached the study of human biological diversity from two main directions: (1) racial classification, an approach that has been rejected; and (2) the current explanatory approach, which focuses on understanding specific differences. I'll briefly review each approach, first considering the problems with racial classification, then providing an example of the explanatory approach to human biological diversity.

Racial classification has fallen out of favor in biology for several reasons. The main reason is that scientists have trouble grouping people into distinct racial units. A race is supposed to reflect shared *genetic* material, but early scholars used *phenotypical* traits (usually skin color) for racial classification. There are several problems with a phenotypical approach to race. First, which traits should be primary in assigning people who look different to different races? Should races be defined by height, weight, body shape, facial features, teeth, skull form, or skin color? Like their fellow citizens, early European and American scientists gave priority to skin color. The phenotypic features, for example, skin color, that were most apparent to those early scientists were also the very characteristics that had been assigned arbitrary cultural value for purposes of discrimination. Genetic variations (e.g., differences in blood types) that were not directly observable were not used in early racial classification.

Many school textbooks and encyclopedias still proclaim the existence of three great races: the white, the black, and the yellow. This simplistic classification was compatible with the political use of race during the colonialist period of the late nineteenth and early twentieth centuries. The tripartite scheme kept white Europeans neatly separate from their African and Asian subjects. Colonial empires began to break up, and scientists began to question established racial categories, after World War II.

Politics aside, one obvious problem with "color-based" racial labels is that the terms don't accurately describe skin color. "White" people are more pink, beige, or tan than white. "Black" people are various shades of brown, and "yellow" people are tan or beige. But these terms have also been digni-

The photos in this chapter illustrate just a small part of the range of human biological diversity. Traditional racial classification, now discredited, would classify this young woman from Beijing, China as "Mongoloid."

fied by more scientific-*sounding* synonyms: Caucasoid, Negroid, and Mongoloid.

Another problem with the tripartite scheme is that many populations don't neatly fit into any one of the three "great races." For example, where would one put the Polynesians? **Polynesia** is a triangle of South Pacific islands formed by Hawaii to the north, Easter Island to the east, and New Zealand to the southwest. Does the "bronze" skin color of Polynesians connect them to the Caucasoids or to the Mongoloids? Some scientists, recognizing this problem, enlarged the original tripartite scheme to include the Polynesian "race." Native Americans presented a similar problem. Were they red or yellow? Some scientists added a fifth race—the "red," or Amerindian—to the major racial groups.

Many people in southern India have dark skins, but scientists have been reluctant to classify them with "black" Africans because of their "Caucasoid" facial features and hair form. Some, therefore, have created a separate race for these people. What about the Australian aborigines, hunters and gatherers native to what has been, throughout human history, the most isolated continent? By skin color, one might place some Native Australians in the same race as tropical Africans. However, similarities to Europeans in hair color (light or reddish) and facial features have led some scientists to classify them as Caucasoids. But there is no evidence that Australians are closer genetically or historically to either

This Native Australian boy has brown skin, light hair, large front teeth, and a broad nose. There is no evidence that Native Australians are genetically closer to either Europeans or Africans than to Asians.

of these groups than they are to Asians. Recognizing this problem, scientists often regard Native Australians as a separate race.

Finally, consider the San ("Bushmen") of the Kalahari Desert in southern Africa. Scientists have perceived their skin color as varying from brown to yellow. Some who regard San skin as "yellow" have placed them in the same category as Asians. In theory, people of the same race share more recent common ancestry with each other than they do with any others. But there is no evidence for recent common ancestry between San and Asians. Somewhat more reasonably, some scholars assign the San to the Capoid (from the Cape of Good Hope) race, which is seen as being different from other groups inhabiting tropical Africa.

Similar problems arise when any single trait is used as a basis for racial classification. An attempt to use facial features, height, weight, or any other phenotypical trait is fraught with difficulties. For example, consider the Nilotes, natives of the upper Nile region of Uganda and Sudan. Nilotes tend to be tall and to have long, narrow noses. Certain Scandinavians are also tall, with similar noses. Given the distance between their homelands, to classify them as members of the same race makes little sense. There is no reason to assume that Nilotes and Scandinavians are more closely related to each other than either is to shorter and nearer populations with different kinds of noses.

Would it be better to base racial classifications on a combination of physical traits? This would avoid some of the problems mentioned above, but others would arise. First, skin color, stature, skull form, and facial features (nose form, eye shape, lip thickness) don't go together as a unit. For example, people with dark skin may be tall or short and have hair ranging from straight to very curly. Dark-haired populations may have light or dark skin, along with various skull forms, facial features, and body sizes and shapes. The number of combinations is very large, and the amount that heredity (versus environment) contributes to such phenotypical traits is often unclear.

There is a final objection to racial classification based on phenotype. The phenotypical characteristics on which races are based supposedly reflect genetic material that is shared and that has stayed the same for long time periods. But phenotypical similarities and differences don't necessarily have a genetic basis. Because of changes in the environment that affect individuals during growth and development, the range of phenotypes characteristic of a population may change without any genetic change. There are several examples. In the early twentieth century, the anthropologist Franz Boas (1940/1966) described changes in skull form among the children of Europeans who had migrated to North America. The reason for this was not a change in genes, for the European immigrants tended to marry among themselves, and some of their children had been born in Europe and merely raised in the United States. Something in the environment, probably in the diet, was producing this change. We know now that changes in average height and weight produced by dietary differences in a few generations are common and may have nothing to do with race or genetics.

Explaining Skin Color

Traditional racial classification assumed that biological characteristics were determined by heredity and stable (immutable) over long periods of time. We now know that a biological similarity doesn't necessarily indicate recent common ancestry. Dark skin color, for example, can be shared by tropical Africans and Native Australians for reasons other than common ancestry. It is not possible at this time to *define races* biologically. Still, scientists have made much progress in *explaining* variation in human skin color, along with many other expressions of human biological diversity. We shift now from classification to *explanation*, in which natural selection plays a key role.

First recognized by Charles Darwin and Alfred Russell Wallace, **natural selection** is the process by which nature selects the forms most fit to survive and reproduce in a given environment—such as the tropics. Over the years, the less fit organisms die out and the favored types survive by producing more offspring. The role of natural selection in producing variation in skin color will illustrate the explanatory approach to human biological diversity. Comparable explanations have been provided for many other aspects of human biological variation, some of which are discussed in the next chapter.

Skin color is a complex biological trait, influenced by several genes—just how many isn't known. **Melanin,** the primary determinant of human skin color, is a chemical substance manufactured in the epidermis, or outer skin layer. The melanin cells of darker-skinned people produce more and larger granules of melanin than do those of lighter-skinned people. By screening out ultraviolet radiation from the sun, melanin offers protection against a variety of maladies, including sunburn and skin cancer.

Before the sixteenth century, most of the world's very dark-skinned populations lived in the **tropics,** a belt extending about 23 degrees north and south of the equator, between the Tropic of Cancer and the Tropic of Capricorn. The association between dark skin color and a tropical habitat existed throughout the Old World, where hominids have lived for millions of years. The darkest populations of Africa evolved not in shady equatorial forests but in sunny open grassland, or savanna, country.

Outside the tropics, skin color tends to be lighter. Moving north in Africa, for example, there is a gradual transition from dark brown to medium brown. Average skin color continues to lighten as one moves through the Middle East, into southern Europe, through central Europe, and to the north. South of the tropics skin color is also lighter (Figure 5.1). In the Americas, by contrast, tropical populations do not have very dark skin. This is because the settlement of the New World, by light-skinned Asian ancestors of Native Americans, was relatively recent, probably dating back no more than 30,000 years.

How, aside from migrations, can we explain the geographic distribution of skin color? Natural selection provides an answer. In the tropics, with intense ultraviolet radiation from the sun, unprotected humans face the threat of severe sunburn, which can increase susceptibility to disease. This confers a selective *dis*advantage (i.e., less success in surviving and reproducing) on lighter-skinned people in the tropics (unless they stay indoors or use cultural products, like umbrellas or lotions, to screen sunlight). Sunburn also impairs the body's ability to sweat. This is a second reason why light skin color, given tropical heat, can diminish the human ability to live and work in equatorial climates. A third disadvantage of having light skin color in the tropics is that exposure to ultraviolet radiation can cause skin cancer (Blum 1961). A fourth factor affecting the geographic distribution of skin color is vitamin D production by the body. W. F. Loomis (1967) focuses on the role of ultraviolet radiation in stimulating the manufacture of vitamin D by the human body. The unclothed human body can produce its own vitamin D when exposed to sufficient sunlight. But in a cloudy environment that is also so cold that people have to dress themselves much of the year (such as northern Europe, where very light skin color evolved), clothing interferes with the body's manufacture of vitamin D. The ensuing shortage of vitamin D diminishes the absorption of calcium in the intestines. A nutritional disease known as **rickets,** which softens and deforms the bones, may develop. In women, deformation of the pelvic bones from rickets can interfere with childbirth. During northern winters, light skin color maximizes the absorption of ultraviolet radiation and the manufacture of vitamin D by the few parts of the body that are exposed to direct sunlight. On the other hand, there

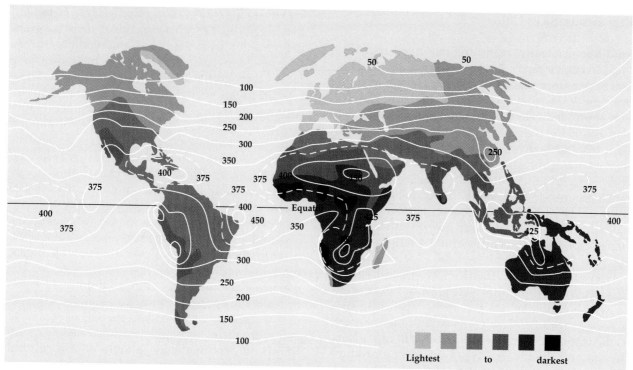

Figure 5.1 *The distribution of human skin color before* A.D. *1400. Also shown is the average amount of ultraviolet radiation in watt-seconds per square centimeter. (Figure from* Evolution and Human Origins *by B. J. Williams. Copyright © 1979 by B. J. Williams. Reprinted by permission of HarperCollins, Publishers, Inc.)*

has been selection against dark skin color in northern areas because melanin screens out ultraviolet radiation.

Considering vitamin D production, light skin is an advantage in the cloudy north, but a disadvantage in the sunny tropics. Loomis has suggested that in the tropics, dark skin color protects the body against an *overproduction* of vitamin D by screening out ultraviolet radiation. Too much vitamin D can lead to a potentially fatal condition (**hypervitaminosis D**), in which calcium deposits build up in the body's soft tissues. The kidneys may eventually fail. Gallstones, joint problems, and circulation problems are other symptoms of hypervitaminosis D.

This discussion of skin color shows that common ancestry, the presumed basis of race, is not the only reason for biological similarities. Here natural selection has made a major contribution to this example of human diversity.

STRATIFICATION AND "INTELLIGENCE"

We see that scientists have shifted from racial *classification* to the *explanation* of human biological diversity. No longer is race considered a valid biological concept. Race has meaning only in social, cultural, and political terms. Over the centuries groups with power have used racial ideology to justify, explain, and preserve their privileged social positions. Dominant groups have declared minorities to be *innately*, that is, biologically, inferior. Racial ideas are used to suggest that social inferiority and presumed shortcomings (in intelligence, ability, character, or attractiveness) are immutable and passed across the generations. This ideology defends stratification as inevitable, enduring, and "natural"—based in biology rather than society. Thus the Nazis argued for the superiority of the "Aryan race," and European colonialists asserted the "white man's burden."

Before the sixteenth century, almost all the very dark-skinned populations of the world lived in the tropics, as does this Samburu woman from Kenya.

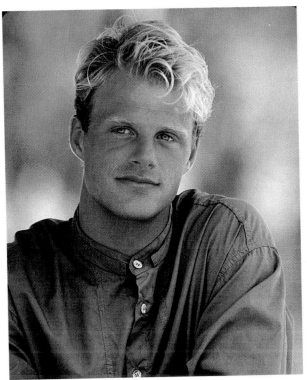

The northward trend toward lighter skin color continues around the Mediterranean into Europe. Very light skin color, illustrated in this photo, maximizes absorption of ultraviolet radiation by those few parts of the body exposed to direct sunlight during northern winters. This helps prevent rickets.

South Africa institutionalized *apartheid*. Again and again, to justify exploitation of minorities and native peoples, those in control have proclaimed the innate inferiority of the oppressed. In the United States the supposed superiority of whites was once standard segregationist doctrine. Belief in the biologically based inferiority of Native Americans has been an argument for their slaughter, confinement, and neglect.

However, anthropologists know that most of the behavioral variation among contemporary human groups rests on culture rather than biology. The cultural similarities revealed through thousands of ethnographic studies leave no doubt that capacities for cultural evolution are equal in all human populations. There is also excellent evidence that within any **stratified** (class-based) society, differences in performance between economic, social, and ethnic groups reflect different experiences and opportunities rather than genetic makeup. (Stratified societies

are those with marked differences in wealth, prestige, and power between social classes.)

Stratification, political domination, prejudice, and ignorance continue to exist. They propagate the mistaken belief that misfortune and poverty result from lack of ability. Occasionally doctrines of innate superiority are even set forth by scientists, who, after all, tend to come from the favored stratum of society. Among recent examples, the best known is Jensenism, named for the educational psychologist Arthur Jensen (Jensen 1969; Herrnstein 1971), its leading proponent. Jensenism is a highly questionable interpretation of the observation that African-Americans, on average, perform less well on intelligence tests than Euro-Americans do. Jensenism asserts that blacks are hereditarily incapable of performing as well as whites do. Writing with Charles Murray, Richard Herrnstein makes a similar argument in the 1994 book *The Bell Curve*, to which the following critique also applies (see also Jacoby and Glauberman, eds. 1995).

CULTURE, BIOLOGY, AND SPORTS

Culture constantly molds human biology. Culture promotes certain activities, discourages others, and sets standards of physical well-being and attractiveness. Sports activity, which is influenced by culture, helps build phenotype. North American girls are encouraged to pursue—and they therefore do well in—competitive track and field, swimming, and diving. Brazilian girls, in contrast, haven't fared nearly as well in international athletic competition. Why are girls encouraged to become athletes in some nations but discouraged from physical activities in others? Why don't Brazilian women, and Latin women generally, do better in athletics?

Cultural standards of attractiveness affect athletic activities. North Americans run or swim not just to compete but to keep trim and fit. Brazil's beauty standards accept

Years of swimming have sculpted the physique of this Chinese swimmer, illustrated by her enlarged upper torso, massive neck, and powerful shoulders. The countries that produce the most successful female competitive swimmers are China, the United States, Germany, and the former Soviet Union, where this phenotype is not as stigmatized for women as it is in Latin countries.

more fat, especially in female buttocks and hips. Brazilian men have had some international success in swimming and running, but Brazil rarely sends female swimmers or runners to the Olympics. One rea-

---

Environmental explanations for test scores are much more convincing than are the genetic arguments of Jensen, Herrnstein, and Murray. An environmental explanation does not deny that some people may be smarter than others. In any society, for many reasons, genetic and environmental, the talents of individuals vary. An environmental explanation does deny, however, that these differences can be generalized to whole groups. Even when talking about individual intelligence, however, we have to decide which of several abilities is an accurate measure of intelligence.

Psychologists have devised several kinds of tests to measure intelligence, but there are problems with all of them. Early intelligence tests demanded skill in manipulating words. Such tests do not accurately measure learning ability for several reasons. For example, individuals who have learned two languages as children—bilinguals—don't do as well, on average, on verbal intelligence tests as do people who have learned a single language. It would be absurd to

suppose that children who master two languages have inferior intelligence. One explanation seems to be that because bilinguals have vocabularies, concepts, and verbal skills in both languages, their ability to manipulate either one suffers a bit. Still, this is offset by the advantage of being fluent in two languages.

Most tests are written by educated people in Europe and North America. They reflect the experiences of the people who devise them. It is not surprising that middle- and upper-class children do better because they are more likely to share the test makers' educational background and standards. Numerous studies have shown that performance on Scholastic Achievement Tests (SATs) can be improved by coaching and preparation. Parents who can afford $500 for an SAT preparation course enhance their kids' chances of getting high scores. Standardized college entrance exams are similar to IQ tests in that they purportedly measure intellectual aptitude. They may do this, but they also measure type and quality of high school education, linson Brazilian women avoid competitive swimming in particular is that sport's effects on phenotype. Years of swimming sculpt a distinctive physique—an enlarged upper torso, a massive neck, and powerful shoulders and back. Successful female swimmers tend to be big, strong, and bulky. The countries that produce them include the United States, Canada, Germany, China, and the former Soviet Union, where this phenotype isn't as stigmatized as it is in Latin countries. Swimmers develop hard bodies, but Brazilian culture says that women should be soft, with big hips and buttocks, not big shoulders.

Cultural factors also help explain why blacks excel in certain sports and whites in others. In North American schools, parks, sandlots, and city playgrounds, African-Americans have access to baseball diamonds, basketball courts, football fields, and tracks. However, because of restricted economic opportunities, many black families can't afford to buy hockey gear or ski equipment, take ski vacations, pay for tennis lessons, or belong to clubs with tennis courts and pools. In the United States mainly light-skinned boys (often in private schools) play soccer, the most popular sport in the world. In Brazil, however, soccer is the national pastime of all males—black and white, rich and poor. There is wide public access. Brazilians play soccer on the beach and in streets, squares, parks, and playgrounds. Many of Brazil's best soccer players, including the world-famous Pelé, have dark skins. When blacks have opportunities to do well in soccer, tennis, or any other sport, they are physically capable of doing as well as whites.

Why does the United States have so many black football and basketball players and so few black swimmers and hockey players? The answer lies mainly in cultural factors, such as variable access and social stratification. Many Brazilians practice soccer, hoping to play for money with a professional club. Similarly, North American blacks are aware that certain sports do provide good career opportunities for African-Americans. They start developing skills in those sports in childhood. The better they do, the more likely they are to persist, and the pattern continues. Countering a claim made by TV sports commentator Jimmy the Greek Snyder a few years ago, culture—specifically differential access to sports resources—has more to do with sports success than does "race."

guistic and cultural background, and parental wealth. No test is free of class, ethnic, and cultural biases.

Tests invariably measure particular learning histories, not the potential for learning. They use middle-class performance as a standard for determining what should be known at a given chronological age. Furthermore, tests are usually administered by middle-class white people who give instructions in a dialect or language that may not be totally familiar to the child being tested. Test performance improves when the subcultural, socioeconomic, and linguistic backgrounds of subjects and test personnel are similar (Watson 1972).

Recognizing the difficulties in devising a culture-free test, psychologists have developed several nonverbal tests, hoping to find an objective measure that is not bound to a single culture. In one such test, individuals score higher by adding body parts to a stick figure. In a maze test, subjects trace their way out of various mazes. The score increases with the speed of completion. Other tests also base scores on speed, for example, in fitting geometric objects into appropriately shaped holes. All these tests are culture-bound because American culture emphasizes speed and competition whereas most nonindustrial cultures do not.

Examples of cultural biases in intelligence testing abound. Biases affect performance by people in other cultures and by different groups within the same culture, such as Native Americans in the United States. Many Native Americans have grown up on reservations or under conditions of urban or rural poverty. They have suffered social, economic, political, and cultural discrimination. In one study, Native Americans scored the lowest (a mean of 81, compared with a standard of 100) of any minority group in the United States (Klineberg 1951). But when the environment offers opportunities similar to those available to middle-class Americans, test performance tends to equalize. Consider the Osage Indians, on whose reservation oil was discovered.

*No test measures innate intelligence that is free of class, ethnic, and cultural bias.
Entrance exams are similar to IQ tests in that success on them is correlated with type
and quality of prior education, linguistic and cultural background, and parental
wealth. An elite education, such as is available at this prep school in Christchurch,
New Zealand, produces higher average test scores.*

Profiting from oil sales, the Osage did not experience the stresses of poverty. They developed a good school system, and their average IQ was 104. Here the relationship between test performance and environment is particularly clear. The Osage did not settle on the reservation because they knew that oil was there. There is no reason to believe that these people were innately more intelligent than were the Indians on different reservations. They were just luckier.

Similar relationships between social, economic, and educational environment and test performance show up in comparisons of American blacks and whites. At the beginning of World War I, intelligence tests were given to approximately 1 million American army recruits. Blacks from some northern states had higher average scores than did whites from some southern states. This was caused by the fact that early in this century northern blacks got a better public education than did many southern whites. Thus, their superior performance is not surprising. On the other hand, southern whites did better than southern blacks. This is also expectable, given the unequal school systems then open to whites and blacks in the South.

Some people tried to get around the environmental explanation for the superior performance of northern blacks over southern whites by suggesting selective migration—smarter blacks had moved north. However, it was possible to test this hypothesis, which turned out to be false. If smarter blacks had moved north, their superior intelligence should have been obvious in their school records while they were still living in the South. It was not. Furthermore, studies in New York, Washington, and Philadelphia showed that as length of residence increased, test scores also rose.

Studies of identical twins raised apart also illustrate the impact of environment on identical heredity. In a study of nineteen pairs of twins, IQ scores varied directly with years in school. The average difference in IQ was only 1.5 points for the eight twin pairs with the same amount of schooling. It was 10 points for the eleven pairs with an average of five years' difference. One subject, with fourteen years more education than his twin, scored 24 points higher (Bronfenbrenner 1975).

These and similar studies provide overwhelming evidence that test performance measures education and social, economic, and cultural background rather than genetically determined intelligence. During the past 500 years Europeans and their descendants extended their political and economic control over most of the world. They colonized and occupied environments that they reached in their ships and conquered with their weapons. Most people in the most powerful contemporary nations—located in North America, Europe, and Asia—have light skin color. Some people in these currently powerful countries may incorrectly assert and believe that their world position has resulted from innate biological superiority. However, all contemporary human populations seem to have comparable learning abilities.

We are living in and interpreting the world at a particular time. In the past there were far different associations between centers of power and human physical characteristics. When Europeans were barbarians, advanced civilizations thrived in the Middle East. When Europe was in the Dark Ages, there were civilizations in West Africa, on the East African coast, in Mexico, and in Asia. Before the Industrial Revolution, the ancestors of many white Europeans and Americans were living much more like precolonial Africans than like current members of the American middle class. Their average performance on twentieth-century IQ tests would have been abominable.

SUMMARY

An ethnic group assumed (by a particular culture) to have a biological basis is called a *race*. Race, like ethnicity in general, is a cultural category rather than a biological reality. That is, ethnic groups, including "races," derive from contrasts perceived and perpetuated in particular societies, rather than from scientific classifications based on common genes. In the United States "racial" labels like "white" and "black" designate social races—categories defined by American culture. Given the lack of a precise distinction between race and ethnicity, it is better to use the "ethnic group" instead of "race" to describe any such social group.

In American culture, one acquires his or her racial identity at birth, as an ascribed status, but American racial classification, governed by the rule of hypodescent, is based neither on phenotype nor genetics. Children of mixed unions, no matter what their appearance, are automatically classified with the minority-group parent.

Japan is not the uniform society that many imagine. Ten percent of the Japanese population consists of minorities: Ainu, Okinawans, outcast *burakumin*, the children of mixed marriages, and immigrant nationalities, especially Koreans. Racial attitudes in Japan illustrate "intrinsic racism"—the belief that a perceived racial difference is a sufficient reason to value one person less than another. The valued group is majority ("pure") Japanese, who are believed to share "the same blood." Majority Japanese define themselves by opposition to others, whether minority groups in their own nation or outsiders—anyone who is "not us." Assimilation is discouraged; residential segregation and taboos on "interracial" marriage work to keep minorities "in their place." Japanese culture regards certain ethnic groups as having a biological basis, when there is no evidence that they do. The *burakumin*, for example, are physically and genetically indistinguishable from other Japanese but still face discrimination as a social race.

Racial classification in Brazil shows that the exclusionary American and Japanese systems are not inevitable. Brazil shares a history of slavery with the United States, but it lacks the hypodescent rule. One illustration of the absence of hypodescent is the fact that (unlike the United States) full siblings may belong to different races if they are phenotypically different. Nor does Brazil have racial aversion of the sort found in Japan. Brazilians recognize more than 500 races. Brazilian racial identity is more of an achieved status; it can change during a person's lifetime, reflecting phenotypical changes. It also varies depending on who is doing the classifying. But given the correlation between poverty and dark skin, the class structure affects Brazilian racial classification, so that someone who has light skin and is poor will be perceived and classified as darker than a comparably colored person who is rich.

Historically, scientists have approached the study of human biological diversity from two main directions: racial classification, an approach that has been rejected, and the current explanatory approach. It is not possible at this time to define races biologically. Because of a range of problems involved in classifying humans into racial categories, contemporary biologists focus on specific biological differences and try to explain them. Skin color and other biological similarities between geographically separate groups may reflect—rather than common ancestry—similar but independent evolution in response to similar natural selective forces.

Some people assert that there are genetically determined differences in the learning abilities of "races," classes, and ethnic groups. However, environmental variables (particularly educational, economic, and social background) provide much better explanations for performance on intelligence tests by such groups. Intelligence tests reflect the cultural biases and life experiences of the people who develop and administer them. All tests are to some extent culture-bound. Equalized environmental opportunities show up in test scores.

GLOSSARY

descent: Rule assigning social identity on the basis of some aspect of one's ancestry.

hypervitaminosis D: Condition caused by an excess of vitamin D; calcium deposits build up on the body's soft tissues and the kidneys may fail; symptoms include gallstones, and joint and circulation problems; may affect unprotected light-skinned individuals in the tropics.

hypodescent: Rule that automatically places the children of a union or mating between members of different socioeconomic groups in the less-privileged group.

melanin: Substance manufactured in specialized cells in the lower layers of the epidermis (outer skin layer); melanin cells in dark skin produce more melanin than do those in light skin.

natural selection: Originally formulated by Charles Darwin and Alfred Russell Wallace, the process by which nature selects the forms most fit to survive and reproduce in a given environment—such as the tropics.

phenotype: An organism's evident traits, its "manifest biology"—anatomy and physiology.

Polynesia: Triangle of South Pacific islands formed by Hawaii to the north, Easter Island to the east, and New Zealand to the southwest.

rickets: Nutritional disease caused by a shortage of vitamin D; interferes with the absorption of calcium and causes softening and deformation of the bones.

social race: A group assumed to have a biological basis but actually perceived and defined in a social context—by a particular culture rather than by scientific criteria.

stratified: Class-structured; stratified societies have marked differences in wealth, prestige, and power between social classes.

tropics: Geographic belt extending about 23 degrees north and south of the equator, between the Tropic of Cancer (north) and the Tropic of Capricorn (south).

STUDY QUESTIONS

1. How do "races" differ from other kinds of ethnic groups?
2. Are races based on biology or culture?
3. Should categories like "African-American," "Anglo-American," and "Asian-American" be called "ethnic groups" or "races"? Why?
4. What is the hypodescent rule, and how does it affect American racial classification?
5. How may governments influence racial classification and discrimination?
6. How is race culturally constructed in Japan? What are the main physical differences between majority Japanese, on the one hand, and *burakumin* and Koreans in Japan, on the other?
7. What does it mean to say that the system of social race in Japan is based on opposition, intrinsic racism, aversion, and discrimination?
8. What kind of racial classification system operates in the community where you grew up or now live? Does it differ from the racial classification system described for American culture in this chapter?
9. What is the difference between race and skin color in contemporary American culture? Are the social identities of Americans and discrimination against some Americans based on one or both of these attributes?
10. What are the main contrasts involving race in Brazil, the United States, and Japan?
11. If you had to devise an ideal system of "race relations," would it be more like the North American, the Japanese, or the Brazilian system? Why?
12. Why is *race* a discredited term in biology? What has replaced it?
13. What are the main problems with racial classification based on phenotype?
14. What explanations have been proposed for the distribution of light and dark skin color?
15. What factors help us understand different average scores on "intelligence" tests by members of different stratified groups?
16. What is Jensenism, and what arguments and evidence may be offered for rejecting it?

SUGGESTED ADDITIONAL READING

CROSBY, A. W., JR.
  1972 *The Columbian Exchange: Biological and Cultural Consequences of 1492.* Westport, CT: Greenwood Press. Disease, migration, slavery, and other consequences of the age of discovery.

DE VOS, G. A., AND H. WAGATSUMA
1966   *Japan's Invisible Race: Caste in Culture and Personality.* Berkeley: University of California Press. Considers many aspects of the *burakumin* (and other minorities) and their place in Japanese society and culture, including psychological factors.

DEGLER, C.
1970   *Neither Black or White: Slavery and Race Relations in Brazil and the United States.* New York: Macmillan. The main contrasts between Brazilian and North American race relations and the historic, economic, and demographic reasons for them.

GOLDBERG, D. T., ED.
1990   *Anatomy of Racism.* Minneapolis: University of Minnesota Press. Collection of articles on race and racism.

HARRIS, M.
1964   *Patterns of Race in the Americas.* New York: Walker. Reasons for different racial and ethnic relations in North and South America and the Caribbean.

HERRNSTEIN, R. R., AND C. MURRAY
1994   *The Bell Curve: Intelligence and Class Structure in American Life.* New York: Free Press. Controversial treatise linking stratification and intelligence.

JACOBY, R., AND N. GLAUBERMAN, EDS.
1995   *The Bell Curve Debate: History, Documents, Opinions.* New York: Free Press. New York: Random House Times Books. A group of scholars critique arguments for a relation between race, class, and intelligence, particularly as set forth in the book *The Bell Curve,* by Herrnstein and Murray.

MONTAGU, A., ED.
1975   *Race and IQ.* New York: Oxford University Press. Scientists from several disciplines review and counter neoracist reasoning.

NELSON, H., AND R. JURMAIN
1991   *Introduction to Physical Anthropology,* 5th ed. St. Paul: West Publishing. This basic text discusses aspects of human biological diversity.

SHANKLIN, E.
1995   *Anthropology and Race.* Belmont, CA: Wadsworth. A concise introduction to the race concept from the perspective of anthropology.

WEISS, M. L., AND A. E. MANN
1992   *Human Biology and Behavior: An Anthropological Perspective,* 6th ed. Glenview, IL: Scott, Foresman. Basic biological anthropology textbook; includes discussions of evolutionary principles, genetics, and human variability.

CHAPTER 11

ADAPTIVE STRATEGIES AND ECONOMIC SYSTEMS

ADAPTIVE STRATEGIES

FORAGING
Correlates of Foraging

CULTIVATION
Horticulture
Agriculture
The Cultivation Continuum
Implications of Intensification

PASTORALISM

MODES OF PRODUCTION
Organization of Production in Nonindustrial Societies

Means of Production
Alienation and Impersonality in Industrial Economies

ECONOMIZING AND MAXIMIZATION
Alternative Ends

Box: Scarcity and the Betsileo

DISTRIBUTION, EXCHANGE
The Market Principle
Redistribution
Reciprocity
Coexistence of Exchange Principles

POTLATCHING

Cultures and communities are being incorporated, at an accelerating rate, into larger systems. The origin and spread of food production was an important impetus to the formation of regional social systems, and eventually of nation-states. Food production led to major changes in human life, as the pace of cultural transformation increased enormously. This chapter provides a framework for understanding a variety of human adaptive strategies and economic systems.

ADAPTIVE STRATEGIES

The anthropologist Yehudi Cohen (1974*b*) used the term *adaptive strategy* to describe a group's system of economic production. Cohen argued that the most important reason for similarities between two (or more) unrelated cultures is their possession of a similar adaptive strategy. In other words, similar economic causes produce similar cultural effects. For example, there are clear similarities among cultures that have a foraging strategy. Cohen developed a typology of cultures based on correlations between their economies and their social features. His typology includes six adaptive strategies: foraging, horticulture, agriculture, pastoralism, mercantilism (trade), and industrialism. The last two strategies are discussed in Chapter 20, "The World System, Industrialism, and Stratification." The present chapter focuses on the first four adaptive strategies.

FORAGING

Until 10,000 years ago all humans were foragers. However, environmental specifics created contrasts among foraging populations. Some were big game hunters; others hunted and collected a wider range of animals and plants. Nevertheless, ancient foraging economies shared one essential feature: People relied on nature for food and other necessities.

In the last chapter, we saw that domestication (initially of sheep and goats) and cultivation (of wheat and barley) began 10,000 to 12,000 years ago in the Middle East. Cultivation (of different crops, such as maize, manioc, and potatoes) arose independently 3,000 to 4,000 years later in the Western Hemisphere. In both hemispheres the new economy

spread rapidly. Most foragers eventually turned to food production. Today almost all foragers have at least some dependence on food production or food producers (Kent 1992).

The foraging way of life held on (and sometimes reemerged) in a few areas. In most of those places, foraging should be described as "recent" rather than "contemporary." All modern foragers live in nation-states, depend to some extent on government assistance, and have contacts with food-producing neighbors, missionaries, and other outsiders. We should not view contemporary foragers as isolated or pristine survivors of the Stone Age. Modern foragers are late-twentieth-century people who are influenced by regional forces (e.g., trade and war), national and international policies, and

All modern foragers live in nation-states, depend to some extent on government assistance, and have contact with outsiders. Contemporary hunter-gatherers are not isolated or pristine survivors of the Stone Age. Modern foragers—such as this rifle-wielding Australian hunter—are influenced by regional forces, national and international policies, and political and economic events in the world system.

political and economic events in the world system. (See the box in Chapter 12.)

Although foraging is on the wane, the outlines of Africa's two broad belts of recent foraging remain evident. One is the Kalahari Desert of southern Africa. This is the home of the **San** ("Bushmen"), who include the **!Kung** (The exclamation point stands for a distinctive sound made in their language, a click.) (See Lee 1984; Lee and DeVore, eds. 1977.) The other main African foraging area is the equatorial forest of central and eastern Africa, home of the Mbuti, Efe, and other "pygmies" (Turnbull 1965; Bailey et al. 1989).

People still do subsistence foraging in certain remote forests in Madagascar, Southeast Asia, Malaysia, the Philippines, and on certain islands off the Indian coast. Some of the best-known recent foragers are the aborigines of Australia. Those Native Australians lived on their island continent for more than 40,000 years without developing food production.

The Western Hemisphere also had recent foragers. The Eskimos, or Inuit, of Alaska and Canada are well-known hunters. These (and other) northern foragers now use modern technology, including rifles and snowmobiles, in their subsistence activities (Pelto 1973). The native populations of California, Oregon, Washington, and British Columbia were all foragers, as were those of inland subarctic Canada and the Great Lakes. For many Native Americans fishing, hunting, and gathering remain important subsistence (and sometimes commercial) activities.

Coastal foragers also lived near the southern tip of South America, in Patagonia. On the grassy plains of Argentina, southern Brazil, Uruguay, and Paraguay, there were other hunter-gatherers. The contemporary Aché of Paraguay are usually called "hunter-gatherers" even though they get just a third of their livelihood from foraging. The Aché also grow crops, have domesticated animals, and live in or near mission posts, where they receive food from missionaries (Hawkes et al. 1982; Hill et al. 1987).

Throughout the world, foraging survived mainly in environments that posed major obstacles to food production. (Some foragers took refuge in such areas after the rise of food production, the state, colonialism, or the modern world system.) The difficulties of cultivating at the North Pole are obvious. In southern Africa the Dobe !Kung San area studied by Richard Lee is surrounded by a waterless belt 70 to 200 kilometers in breadth. The Dobe area is hard to reach even today, and there is no archaeological evidence of occupation of this area by food producers before the twentieth century (Solway and Lee 1990). However, environmental limits to other adaptive strategies aren't the only reason foragers survived. Their niches have one thing in common—their marginality. Their environments haven't been of immediate interest to groups with other adaptive strategies.

Note, too, that foraging held on in a few areas that could be cultivated, even after contact with cultivators. Those tenacious foragers did not turn to food production because they were supporting themselves adequately by hunting and gathering. As the modern world system spreads, the number of foragers continues to decline.

Correlates of Foraging

Typologies, such as Cohen's adaptive strategies, are useful because they suggest **correlations**—that is, association or covariation between two or more variables. (Correlated variables are factors that are linked and interrelated, such as food intake and body weight, such that when one increases or decreases, the other tends to change, too.) Ethnographic studies in hundreds of cultures have revealed many correlations between the economy and social life. Associated (correlated) with each adaptive strategy is a bundle of particular cultural features. Correlations, however, are rarely perfect. Some foragers lack cultural features usually associated with foraging, and some of those features are found in groups with other adaptive strategies.

What, then, are the usual correlates of foraging? People who subsist by hunting, gathering, and fishing often live in band-organized societies. Their basic social unit, the **band**, is a small group of fewer than a hundred people, all related by kinship or marriage. Band size varies between cultures and often from one season to the next in a given culture. In some foraging societies, band size stays about the same year-round. In others, the band splits up for part of the year. Families leave to gather resources that are better exploited by just a few people. Later, they regroup for cooperative work and ceremonies. Several examples of seasonal splits and recongregation are known from archaeology and ethnography. In southern Africa, some San aggregate around

"WE TRIED HUNTING AND WE TRIED GATHERING, BUT NOW WE USUALLY EAT OUT."

water holes in the dry season and split up in the wet season, whereas other bands disperse in the dry season (Barnard 1979; Kent 1992). This reflects environmental variation. San who lack permanent water must disperse and forage widely for moisture-filled plants.

One typical characteristic of the foraging life is mobility. In many San groups, as among the Mbuti of Zaire, people shift band membership several times in a lifetime. One may be born, for example, in a band where one's mother has kin. Later, one's family may move to a band where the father has relatives. Because bands are exogamous (people marry outside their own band) one's parents come from two different bands, and one's grandparents may come from four. People may affiliate with any band to which they have kinship or marriage links. A couple may live in, or shift between, the husband's and the wife's band.

One may also affiliate with a band through **fictive kinship**—personal relationships modeled on kinship, such as that between godparents and godchil-

dren. San, for example, have a limited number of personal names. People with the same name have a special relationship; they treat each other like siblings. San expect the same hospitality in bands where they have **namesakes** as they do in a band in which a real sibling lives. Namesakes share a strong identity. They call everyone in a namesake's band by the kin terms the namesake uses. Those people reply as if they were addressing a real relative. Kinship, marriage, and fictive kinship permit San to join several bands, and nomadic (regularly on-the-move) foragers do change bands often. Band membership can therefore change tremendously from year to year.

All human societies have some kind of division of labor based on gender. Among foragers, men typically hunt and fish while women gather and collect, but the specific nature of the work varies among cultures. Sometimes women's work contributes most to the diet. Sometimes male hunting and fishing predominate. Among foragers in tropical and semitropical areas, gathering tends to contribute more to the diet than hunting and fishing do—even though the labor costs of gathering tend to be much higher than those of hunting and fishing.

All foragers make social distinctions based on age. Often old people receive great respect as guardians of myths, legends, stories, and traditions. Younger people value the elders' special knowledge of ritual and practical matters. Most foraging societies are *egalitarian*. This means that contrasts in prestige are minor and are based on age and gender.

When considering issues of "human nature," we should remember that the egalitarian band was a basic form of human social life for most of our history. Food production has existed less than 1 percent of the time *Homo* has spent on earth. However, it has produced huge social differences. We now consider the main economic features of food-producing strategies.

CULTIVATION

The three adaptive strategies based on food production in nonindustrial societies are horticulture, agriculture, and pastoralism. In non-Western cultures, as in the United States and Canada, people carry out a variety of economic activities. Each adaptive strategy refers to the main economic activity. Pastoralists (herders), for example, consume milk, butter, blood, and meat from their animals as mainstays of their diet. However, they also add grain to the diet by doing some cultivating or by trading with neighbors. Food producers may also hunt or gather to supplement a diet based on domesticated species.

Horticulture

Horticulture and agriculture are two types of cultivation found in nonindustrial societies. Both differ from the farming systems of industrial nations like the United States and Canada, which use large land areas, machinery, and petrochemicals. **Horticulture** makes intensive use of *none* of the factors of production: land, labor, capital, and machinery. Horticulturalists use simple tools such as hoes and digging sticks to grow their crops. Their fields are not permanent property and lie fallow for varying lengths of time.

Horticulture is also known as **slash-and-burn** cultivation. Each year horticulturalists clear land by cutting down (slashing) and burning forest or bush

In slash-and-burn cultivation, horticulturalists clear the land by cutting down (slashing) and burning trees and bush. For one or two years, and sometimes longer, crops thrive in the ash-enriched soil, like the maize in this plot in the Brazilian Amazon.

or by setting fire to the grass covering the plot. The vegetation is broken down, pests are killed, and the ashes remain to fertilize the soil. Crops are then sown, tended, and harvested. Use of the plot is not continuous. Often it is cultivated for only a year. This depends, however, on soil fertility and weeds, which compete with cultivated plants for nutrients.

When horticulturalists abandon a plot because of soil exhaustion or a thick weed cover, they clear another piece of land, and the original plot reverts to forest. After several years of fallowing (the duration varies in different societies), the cultivator returns to farm the original plot again. Because the relationship between people and land is not permanent, horticulture is also called *shifting cultivation.* Shifting cultivation does not mean that whole villages must move when plots are abandoned. Horticulture can support large permanent villages. Among the Kuikuru of the South American tropical forest, for example, one village of 150 people remained in the same place for ninety years (Carneiro 1956). Kuikuru houses are large and well made. Because the work involved in building them is great, the Kuikuru would rather walk farther to their fields than construct a new village. They shift their plots rather than their settlements. On the other hand, horticulturalists in the montaña (Andean foothills) of Peru live in small villages of about thirty people (Carneiro 1961/1968). Their houses are small and simple. After a few years in one place, these people build new villages near virgin land. Because their houses are so simple, they prefer rebuilding to walking even a half mile to their fields.

Agriculture

Agriculture is cultivation that requires more labor than horticulture does, because it uses land intensively and continuously. The greater labor demands associated with agriculture reflect its common use of domesticated animals, irrigation, or terracing.

Domesticated Animals

Many agriculturalists use animals as means of production—for transport, as cultivating machines, and for their manure. For example, the Betsileo of central Madagascar incorporate cattle into their agricultural economy based on rice production (Kottak 1980). First the Betsileo sow rice in nursery beds. Then, once the seedlings are big enough, women transplant them into flooded rice fields. Before transplanting, the men till and flood the fields. They bring cattle to trample the prepared fields just before transplanting. Young men yell at and beat the cattle, striving to drive them into a frenzy so that they will trample the fields properly. Trampling breaks up clumps of earth and mixes irrigation water with soil to form a smooth mud into which women transplant seedlings. Like many other agriculturalists, the Betsileo collect manure from their animals, using it to fertilize their plots, thus increasing the yield.

Irrigation

While horticulturalists must await the rainy season, agriculturalists can schedule their planting in advance, because they control water. The Betsileo irrigate their fields with canals from rivers, streams, springs, and ponds. Irrigation makes it possible to cultivate a plot year after year. Irrigation enriches the soil because the irrigated field is a unique ecosystem with several species of plants and animals, many of them minute organisms, whose wastes fertilize the land.

An irrigated field is a capital investment that usually increases in value. It takes time for a field to start yielding; it reaches full productivity only after several years of cultivation. The Betsileo, like other

irrigators, have farmed the same fields for generations. In some agricultural areas, including the Middle East, however, salts carried in the irrigation water can make fields unusable after fifty or sixty years.

Terracing

Terracing is another agricultural technique the Betsileo have mastered. Central Madagascar has small valleys separated by steep hillsides. Because the population is dense, people need to farm the hills. However, if they simply planted on the steep hillsides, fertile soil and crops would be washed away during the rainy season. To prevent this, the Betsileo, like the rice-farming Ifugao of the Philippines, cut into the hillside and build stage after stage of terraced fields rising above the valley floor. Springs located above the terraces supply their irrigation water. The labor necessary to build and maintain a system of terraces is great. Terrace walls crumble each year and must be partially rebuilt. The canals that bring water down through the terraces also demand attention.

Costs and Benefits of Agriculture

Agriculture requires human labor to build and maintain irrigation systems, terraces, and other works. People must feed, water, and care for their

In some areas of Irian Jaya, Indonesia (which is on the island of New Guinea), labor-intensive cultivation in valleys involves the construction of long drainage ditches. Here, members of the Dani tribe use their bare hands and feet to maintain such a canal.

Agriculture requires more labor than horticulture does and uses land intensively and continuously. Labor demands associated with agriculture reflect its use of domesticated animals, irrigation, and terracing. The rice farmers of Luzon in the Philippines are famous for their terraced fields.

animals. Given sufficient labor input and management, agricultural land can yield one or two crops annually for years or even generations. An agricultural field does not necessarily produce a higher single-year yield than does a horticultural plot. The first crop grown by horticulturalists on long-idle land may be larger than that from an agricultural plot of the same size. Furthermore, because agriculturalists work harder than horticulturalists do, agriculture's yield relative to labor is also lower. Agriculture's main advantage is that the long-term yield per area is far greater and more dependable. Because a single field sustains its owners year after year, there is no need to maintain a reserve of uncultivated land as horticulturalists do. This is why agricultural societies are more densely populated than are horticultural ones.

The Cultivation Continuum

Because nonindustrial economies can have features of both horticulture and agriculture, it is useful to discuss cultivators as being arranged along a **cultivation continuum.** Horticultural systems stand at one end—the "low-labor, shifting-plot" end. Agriculturalists are at the other—the "labor-intensive, permanent-plot" end.

We speak of a continuum because there are today intermediate economies, combining horticultural and agricultural features—more intensive than annually shifting horticulture but less intensive than agriculture. These recall the intermediate economies revealed by archaeological sequences leading from horticulture to agriculture in the Middle East, Mexico, and other areas of early food production. Unlike nonintensive horticulturalists, who farm a plot just once before fallowing it, the South American Kuikuru grow two or three crops of **manioc,** or cassava—an edible tuber—before abandoning their plots. Cultivation is even more intense in certain densely populated areas of Papua–New Guinea, where plots are planted for two or three years, allowed to rest for three to five, and then recultivated. After several of these cycles the plots are abandoned for a longer fallow period. Such a pattern is called **sectorial fallowing** (Wolf 1966). Besides Papua–New Guinea, such systems occur in places as distant as West Africa and highland Mexico. Sectorial fallowing is associated with denser populations than is simple horticulture. The simpler system is the norm in tropical forests, where weed invasion and delicate soils prevent more intensive cultivation.

The key difference between horticulture and agriculture is that horticulture always uses a fallow period whereas agriculture does not. The earliest cultivators in the Middle East and in Mexico were rainfall-dependent horticulturalists. Until recently, horticulture was the main form of cultivation in several areas, including parts of Africa, Southeast Asia, Indonesia, the Philippines, the Pacific islands, Mexico, Central America, and the South American tropical forest.

Implications of Intensification

The range of environments open to human use widens as people increase their control over nature. Agricultural populations exist in many areas that are too arid for nonirrigators or too hilly for non-terracers. Many ancient civilizations in arid lands arose on an agricultural base. Increasing labor intensity and permanent land use have major demographic, social, and political consequences.

Thus, because of their permanent fields, intensive cultivators are sedentary. People live in larger and more permanent communities located closer to other settlements. Growth in population size and density increases contact between individuals and groups. There is more need to regulate interpersonal relations, including conflicts of interest. Economies that support more people usually require more coordination in the use of land, labor, and other resources.

Agriculture poses many regulatory problems— which central governments have often arisen to solve. Most agriculturalists live in **states** (nation-states)—complex sociopolitical systems that administer a territory and populace with substantial contrasts in occupation, wealth, prestige, and power. In such societies, cultivators play their role as one part of a differentiated, functionally specialized, and tightly integrated sociopolitical system. The social and political implications of food production and intensification are examined more fully in the next two chapters.

PASTORALISM

Pastoralists live in North Africa, the Middle East, Europe, Asia, and sub-Saharan Africa. These herders are people whose activities focus on such domesticated animals as cattle, sheep, goats,

camels, and yak. East African pastoralists, like many others live in symbiosis with their herds. (**Symbiosis** is an obligatory interaction between groups—here humans and animals—that is beneficial to each.) Herders attempt to protect their animals and ensure their reproduction in return for food and other products, like leather. Herds provide dairy products and meat. East Africans also consume cooked cattle blood. Animals are killed at ceremonies, which occur throughout the year, and so beef is available regularly.

People use livestock in a variety of ways. Natives of North America's Great Plains, for example, didn't eat, but only rode, their horses. (Europeans reintroduced horses to the Western Hemisphere; the native American horse had become extinct thousands of years earlier.) For Plains Indians horses served as "tools of the trade," means of production used to hunt buffalo, a main target of their economies. So the Plains Indians were not true pastoralists but *hunters* who used horses—as many agriculturalists use animals—as means of production.

Unlike the use of animals merely as productive machines, pastoralists typically make direct use of their herds for food. They consume their meat, blood, and milk, from which they make yogurt, butter, and cheese. Although some pastoralists rely on their herds more completely than others do, it is impossible to base subsistence solely on animals. Most pastoralists therefore supplement their diet by hunting, gathering, fishing, cultivating, or trading. To get crops, pastoralists either trade with cultivators or do some cultivating or gathering themselves.

Unlike foraging and cultivation, which existed throughout the world before the Industrial Revolution, pastoralism was almost totally confined to the Old World. Before European conquest, the only pastoralists in the Americas lived in the Andean region of South America. They used their llamas and alpacas for food and wool and in agriculture and transport. Much more recently, Navajo of the southwestern United States developed a pastoral economy based on sheep, which were brought to North America by Europeans. The populous Navajo are now the major pastoral population in the western hemisphere.

Two patterns of movement occur with pastoralism: nomadism and transhumance. Both are based on the fact that herds must move to use pasture available in particular places in different seasons. In **pastoral nomadism,** the entire group—women, men, and children—moves with the animals throughout the year. With **transhumance,** only part of the group follows the herds while the rest remain in home villages. During their annual trek, nomads trade for crops and other products with more sedentary people. Transhumants don't have to trade for crops. Because only part of the population accompanies the herds, transhumants can maintain year-round villages and grow their own crops.

MODES OF PRODUCTION

An **economy** is a system of production, distribution, and consumption of resources; *economics* is the study of such systems. Economists tend to focus on modern nations and capitalist systems, while anthropologists have broadened understanding of economic principles by gathering data on nonindustrial economies. Economic anthropology studies economics in a comparative perspective.

A **mode of production** is a way of organizing production—"a set of social relations through which labor is deployed to wrest energy from nature by means of tools, skills, organization, and knowledge" (Wolf 1982, p. 75). In the capitalist mode of production, money buys labor power, and there is a social gap between the people (bosses and workers) involved in the production process. By contrast, in nonindustrial societies, labor is not usually bought but is given as a social obligation. In such a *kin-based* mode of production, mutual aid in production is one among many expressions of a larger web of social relations.

Societies representing each of the adaptive strategies just discussed (e.g., foraging societies) tend to have a similar mode of production. Differences in the mode of production within a given strategy may reflect the differences in environments, target resources, or cultural traditions. Thus a foraging mode of production may be based on individual hunters or teams, depending on whether the game is a solitary or a herd animal. Gathering is usually more individualistic than hunting. People may fish alone or in crews.

Organization of Production in Nonindustrial Societies

Although some kind of division of economic labor related to age and gender is a cultural universal, the specific tasks assigned to each sex and to people of different ages vary. Some horticulturalists assign a major productive role to women; others make men's work primary. Similarly, among pastoralists men generally tend large animals, but in some cultures women do the milking. Jobs accomplished through teamwork in some cultivating societies are done by smaller groups or individuals working over a longer period of time in others.

Among the Betsileo of Madagascar there are two stages of teamwork in rice cultivation: transplanting and harvesting. Team size varies with the size of the field. Both transplanting and harvesting feature a traditional division of labor by age and gender which is well known to all Betsileo and is repeated across the generations. The first job in transplanting is the trampling of a flooded field by young men driving cattle in order to mix earth and water. Once the tramplers leave the field, older men arrive. With their spades they break up the clumps that the cattle missed. Meanwhile, the owner and other adults uproot rice seedlings and bring them to the field. Women plant the seedlings.

At harvest time, four or five months later, young men cut the rice off the stalks. Young women carry it to the clearing above the field. Older women arrange and stack it. The oldest men and women then stand on the stack, stomping and compacting it. Three days later, young men thresh the rice, beating the stalks against a rock to remove the grain. Older men then attack the stalks with sticks to make sure all the grains have fallen off.

Most of the other tasks in Betsileo rice cultivation are done by individual owners and their immediate families. Men maintain and repair the irrigation and drainage systems and the earth walls that separate one plot from the next. Men also till with spade or plow. All members of the household help weed the rice field.

Means of Production

In nonindustrial societies there is a more intimate relationship between the worker and the means of

The cultivation of rice, one of the world's most important food crops, often features a division of task by age and gender. Women often transplant; men often thresh. These young women are transplanting rice seedlings in Sulawesi, Indonesia, and these men are threshing rice, to separate the grains from the stem, in Bangladesh.

production than there is in industrial nations. **Means, or factors, of production** include land (territory), labor, and technology.

Territory

Among foragers, ties between people and land are less permanent than they are among food producers. Although many bands have territories, the boundaries are not usually marked, and there is no way they can be enforced. The hunter's stake in an animal that is being stalked or has been hit with a poisoned arrow is more important than where the animal finally dies. A person acquires the rights to use a band's territory by being born in the band or by joining it through a tie of kinship, marriage, or fictive kinship. In Botswana in southern Africa, !Kung San women, whose work provides over half the food, habitually use specific tracts of berry-bearing trees. However, when a woman changes bands, she immediately acquires a new gathering area.

Among food producers, rights to the means of production also come through kinship and marriage. Descent groups (groups whose members claim common ancestry) are common among nonindustrial food producers, and those who descend from the founder share the group's territory and resources. If the adaptive strategy is horticulture, the estate includes garden and fallow land for shifting cultivation. As members of a descent group, pastoralists have access to animals to start their own herds, to grazing land, to garden land, and to other means of production.

Labor, Technology, Technical Knowledge, and Specialization

Like land, labor is a means of production. In nonindustrial societies, access to both land and labor comes through social links such as kinship, marriage, and descent. Mutual aid in production is merely one aspect of ongoing social relationships that are expressed on many other occasions.

Nonindustrial societies contrast with industrial nations in regard to another means of production—technology. In bands and tribes manufacturing is often linked to age and gender. Women may weave and men may make pottery or vice versa. Most people of a particular age and gender share the technical knowledge associated with that age and gender. If married women customarily make baskets, most married women know how to make baskets. Neither technology nor technical knowledge is as specialized as it is in states.

However, some tribal societies do promote specialization. Among the Yanomami of Venezuela and Brazil, for instance, certain villages manufacture clay pots and others make hammocks. They don't specialize, as one might suppose, because certain raw materials happen to be available near particular villages. Clay suitable for pots is widely available. Everyone knows how to make pots, but not everybody does so. Craft specialization reflects the social and political environment rather than the natural environment. Such specialization promotes trade, which is the first step in creating an alliance with enemy villages (Chagnon 1983/1992). Specialization contributes to keeping the peace, although it has not prevented intervillage warfare.

Alienation and Impersonality in Industrial Economies

What are the most significant contrasts between industrial and nonindustrial economies? When factory workers produce for sale and for the employer's profit rather than for their own use, they may be alienated from the items they make. Such alienation means they do not feel strong pride in or personal identification with their products. In nonindustrial societies people usually see their work

Manufacturing is often linked to age and gender. Men may make pottery and women, baskets (like these Malaysians)—or vice versa. In traditional societies most people of a particular age and gender share the technical knowledge associated with that age and gender. Thus, if married women customarily make baskets, most married women know how to make baskets.

through from start to finish and have a sense of accomplishment in the product.

In nonindustrial societies the economic relationship between coworkers is just one aspect of a more general social relationship. They aren't just coworkers but kin, in-laws, or celebrants in the same ritual. In industrial nations, people don't usually work with relatives and neighbors. If coworkers are friends, the personal relationship usually develops during their common employment rather than being based on a previous association.

Thus, industrial workers have impersonal relationships with their products, coworkers, and employers. People sell their labor for cash, and the economic domain stands apart from ordinary social life. In nonindustrial societies, however, the relations of production, distribution, and consumption are *social relations with economic aspects*. Economy is not a separate entity but is *embedded* in the society.

ECONOMIZING AND MAXIMIZATION

The economic anthropologists have been concerned with two main questions:

1. How are production, distribution, and consumption organized in different societies? This question focuses on *systems* of human behavior and their organization.
2. What motivates people in different cultures to produce, distribute or exchange, and consume? Here the focus is not on systems of behavior but on the *individuals* who participate in those systems.

Anthropologists view both economic systems and motivations in a cross-cultural perspective. Motivation is a concern of psychologists, but it has also been, implicitly or explicitly, a concern of economists and anthropologists. American economists assume that producers and distributors make decisions rationally using the *profit motive*, as do consumers when they shop around for the best value. Although anthropologists know that the profit motive is not universal, the assumption that individuals try to maximize profits is basic to the capitalist world economy and to Western economic theory. In fact, the subject matter of economics is of-

ten defined as economizing, or the rational allocation of scarce means (or resources) to alternative ends (or uses). What does that mean? Classical economic theory assumes that our wants are infinite and that our resources are limited. Since means are always scarce, people have to make choices. They must decide how they will use their scarce resources—their time, labor, money, and capital. Western economists assume that when confronted with alternatives, people tend to choose the one that maximizes profit. This is assumed to be the most rational (reasonable) choice.

The idea that individuals maximize profits was a basic assumption of the classical economists of the nineteenth century and one that is held by many contemporary economists. However, certain economists now recognize that individuals in Western cultures, as in others, may be motivated by many other goals. Depending on the society and the situation, people may try to maximize profit, wealth, prestige, pleasure, comfort, or social harmony. Individuals may want to realize their personal or family ambitions or those of another group to which they belong.

Alternative Ends

To what uses do people in various societies put their scarce resources? Throughout the world, people devote some of their time and energy to building up a **subsistence fund** (Wolf 1966). In other words, they have to work to eat, to replace the calories they use in their daily activity. People must also invest in a **replacement fund.** They must maintain their technology and other items essential to production. If a hoe or plow breaks, they must repair or replace it. They must also obtain and replace items that are essential not to production but to everyday life, such as clothing and shelter.

People everywhere also have to invest in a **social fund.** They have to help their friends, relatives, in-laws, and neighbors. It is useful to distinguish between a social fund and a **ceremonial fund.** The latter term refers to expenditures on ceremonies or rituals. To prepare a festival honoring one's ancestors, for example, requires time and the outlay of wealth.

Citizens of nonindustrial states must also allocate scarce resources to a **rent fund.** We think of rent as

SCARCITY AND THE BETSILEO

From October 1966 through December 1967 my wife and I lived among the Betsileo people of Madagascar, studying their economy and social life (Kottak 1980). Soon after our arrival we met two well-educated schoolteachers who were interested in our research. The woman's father was a congressman who became a cabinet minister during our stay. Our schoolteacher friends told us that their family came from a historically important and typical Betsileo village called Ivato, which they invited us to visit with them.

We had traveled to many other villages, where we were often displeased with our reception. As we drove up, children would run away screaming. Women would hurry inside. Men would retreat to doorways, where they lurked bashfully. Eventually someone would summon the courage to ask what we wanted. This behavior expressed the Betsileos' great fear of the *mpakafo*. Believed to cut out and devour his victim's heart and liver, the *mpakafo* is the Malagasy vampire. These cannibals are said to have fair skin and to be very tall. Because I have light skin and stand six feet four inches tall, I was a natural suspect. The fact that such creatures were not known to travel with their wives helped convince the Betsileo that I wasn't really a *mpakafo*.

When we visited Ivato, we found that its people were different. They were friendly and hospitable. Our very first day there we did a brief census and found out who lived in which households. We learned people's names and their relationships to our schoolteacher friends and to each other. We met an excellent informant who knew all about the local history. In a few afternoons I learned much more than I had in the other villages in several sessions.

Ivatans were willing to talk because I had powerful sponsors, village natives who had made it in the outside world, people the Ivatans knew would protect them. The schoolteachers vouched for us, but even more significant was the cabinet minister, who was like a grandfather and benefactor to everyone in town. The Ivatans had no reason to fear me because their more influential native son had asked them to answer my questions.

Once we moved to Ivato, the elders established a pattern of visiting us every evening. They came to talk, attracted by the inquisitive foreigners but also by the wine, cigarettes, and food we offered. I asked questions about their customs and beliefs. I eventually developed interview schedules about various subjects, including rice production. I mimeographed these forms to use in Ivato and in two other villages I was studying less intensively. Never have I interviewed as easily as I did in Ivato. So enthusiastic were the Ivatans about my questions that even people from neighboring villages came to join the study. Since these people knew nothing about the social scientist's techniques, I couldn't discourage them by saying that they weren't in my sample. Instead, I agreed to visit each village, where I filled out the interview schedule in just one house. Then I told the other villagers that the household head had done such a good job of teaching me about their village I wouldn't need to ask questions in the other households.

As our stay drew to an end, the elders of Ivato began to lament, saying, "We'll miss you. When you leave, there won't be any more cigarettes, any more wine, or any more questions." They wondered what it would be like for us back in the United States. Ivatans had heard of American plans to send a man to the moon. Did I think it would succeed? They knew that I had an automobile and that I regularly purchased things, including the wine, cigarettes, and food I shared with them. I could afford to buy products they would never have. They commented, "When you go back to your country, you'll need a lot of money for things like cars, clothes, and food. We don't need to buy those things. We make almost everything we use. We don't need as much money as you, because we produce for ourselves."

The Betsileo are not unusual among people whom anthropologists have studied. Strange as it may seem to an American consumer, who may believe that he or she can never have enough money, some rice farmers actually believe that *they have all they need*. The lesson from the Betsileo is that scarcity, which economists view as universal, is variable. Although shortages do arise in nonindustrial societies, the concept of scarcity (insufficient means) is much less developed in stable subsistence-oriented societies than in the societies characterized by industrialism, particularly as consumerism increases.

payment for the use of property. However, *rent fund* has a wider meaning. It refers to resources that people must render to an individual or agency that is superior politically or economically. Tenant farmers and sharecroppers, for example, either pay rent or give some of their produce to their landlords, as peasants did under feudalism.

Peasants are small-scale agriculturalists who live in nonindustrial states and have rent fund obligations. They produce to feed themselves, to sell their produce, and to pay rent. All peasants have two things in common:

1. They live in state-organized societies.
2. They produce food without the elaborate technology—chemical fertilizers, tractors, airplanes to spray crops, and so on—of modern farming or agribusiness.

In addition to paying rent to landlords, peasants must satisfy government obligations, paying taxes in the form of money, produce, or labor. The rent fund is not simply an *additional* obligation for peasants. Often it becomes their foremost and unavoidable duty. Sometimes, to meet the obligation to pay rent, their own diets suffer. The demands of social superiors may divert resources from subsistence, replacement, social, and ceremonial funds.

Motivations vary from society to society, and people often lack freedom of choice in allocating their resources. Because of obligations to pay rent, peasants may allocate their scarce means toward ends that are not their own but those of government officials. Thus, even in societies where there is a profit motive, people are often prevented from rationally maximizing self-interest by factors beyond their control.

DISTRIBUTION, EXCHANGE

The economist Karl Polanyi (1968) stimulated the comparative study of exchange, and several anthropologists followed his lead. To study exchange cross-culturally, Polanyi defined three principles orienting exchanges: the **market principle, redistribution,** and **reciprocity.** These principles can all be present in the same society, but in that case they govern different kinds of transactions. In any society, one of them usually dominates. The principle of exchange that dominates in a given society is the one that allocates the means of production.

The Market Principle

In today's world capitalist economy, the market principle dominates. It governs the distribution of the means of production—land, labor, natural resources, technology, and capital. "Market exchange refers to the organizational process of purchase and sale at money price" (Dalton 1967). With market exchange, items are bought and sold with an eye to maximizing profit, and value is determined by the **law of supply and demand** (things cost more the scarcer they are and the more people want them).

Bargaining is characteristic of market-principle exchanges. The buyer and seller strive to maximize—to get their "money's worth." Bargaining doesn't require that the buyer and seller meet. Consumers bargain whenever they shop around or use advertisements in the decision making.

Redistribution

Redistribution operates when goods, services, or their equivalent move from the local level to a center. The center may be a capital, a regional collection point, or a storehouse near a chief's residence. Products move through a hierarchy of officials for storage at the center. Along the way officials and their dependents consume some of them, but the exchange principle here is *re*distribution. The flow of goods eventually reverses direction—out from the center, down through the hierarchy, and back to the common people.

Reciprocity

Reciprocity is exchange between social equals, who are normally related by kinship, marriage, or another close personal tie. Because it occurs between social equals, it is dominant in the more egalitarian societies—among foragers, cultivators, and pastoralists. There are three degrees of reciprocity: generalized, balanced, and negative (Sahlins 1968, 1972; Service 1966). These may be imagined as areas of a continuum defined by these questions:

1. How closely related are the parties to the exchange?
2. How quickly are gifts reciprocated?

Generalized reciprocity, the purest form of reciprocity, is characteristic of exchanges between closely related people. In **balanced reciprocity,** social distance increases, as does the need to reciprocate. In **negative reciprocity,** social distance is greatest and reciprocation is most urgent.

With generalized reciprocity, someone gives to another person and expects nothing concrete or immediate in return. Such exchanges (including parental gift giving in contemporary North America) are not primarily economic transactions but expressions of personal relationships. Most parents don't keep accounts of every penny they spend on their children. They merely hope that the children will respect their culture's customs involving love, honor, loyalty, and other obligations to parents.

Among foragers, generalized reciprocity tends to govern exchanges. People routinely share with other band members (Bird-David 1992; Kent 1992). A study of the !Kung San found that 40 percent of the population contributed little to the food supply (Lee 1974). Children, teenagers, and people over sixty depended on other people for their food. Despite the high proportion of dependents, the average worker hunted or gathered less than half as much (twelve to nineteen hours a week) as the average American works. Nonetheless, there was always food because different people worked on different days.

So strong is the ethic of reciprocal sharing that most foragers lack an expression for "thank you." To offer thanks would be impolite because it would imply that a particular act of sharing, which is the keystone of egalitarian society, was unusual. Among the Semai, foragers of central Malaysia (Dentan 1979), to express gratitude would suggest surprise at the hunter's generosity or success (Harris 1974).

Balanced reciprocity applies to exchanges between people who are more distantly related than are members of the same band or household. In a horticultural society, for example, a man presents a gift to someone in another village. The recipient may be a cousin, a trading partner, or a brother's fictive kinsman. The giver expects something in return. This may not come immediately, but the social relationship will be strained if there is no reciprocation.

Many nonindustrial societies also feature negative reciprocity, which applies to people on the fringes of their social systems. To people who live in a world of close personal relations, exchanges with outsiders are full of ambiguity and distrust. Exchange is one way of establishing friendly relations with outsiders, but when trade begins, the relationship is still tentative. The initial exchange is close to being purely economic; people want something back immediately. Just as in market economies, they

Sharing the fruits of production, which is the keystone of egalitarian societies, has also been a goal of socialist nations, such as China. These workers in Yunnan province strive for an equal distribution of meat.

try to get the best possible immediate return for their investment.

One example of negative reciprocity is silent trade or barter between the Mbuti "pygmy" foragers of the African equatorial forest and neighboring horticultural villagers. There is no personal contact during the exchange. A Mbuti hunter leaves game, honey, or another forest product at a customary site. Villagers collect it and leave crops in exchange. The parties can bargain silently. If one feels that the return is insufficient, he or she simply leaves it at the trading site. If the other party wants to continue trade, it will be increased.

Coexistence of Exchange Principles

In contemporary North America, the market principle governs the means of production and most exchanges, for example, those involving consumer goods. We also have redistribution, but it is not highly developed. Much of our tax money goes to support the government, but some of it comes back as social services, education, Medicare, and road building. We also have reciprocal exchanges. Generalized reciprocity characterizes the relationship between parents and children. However, even here the dominant market mentality surfaces in comments about the high cost of raising children and in the stereotypical statement of the disappointed parent: "We gave you everything money could buy."

Exchanges of gifts, cards, and invitations exemplify reciprocity, usually balanced. Everyone has heard remarks like "They invited us to their daughter's wedding, so when ours gets married, we'll have to invite them" and "They've been here for dinner three times and haven't invited us yet. I don't think we should ask them back until they do." Such precise balancing of reciprocity would be out of place in a foraging band, where resources are communal (common to all) and daily sharing based on generalized reciprocity is an essential ingredient of social life and survival.

POTLATCHING

One of the most famous cultural practices studied by ethnographers is the **potlatch,** a festive event within a regional exchange system among tribes of the North Pacific Coast of North America, including the Salish and Kwakiutl of Washington and British Columbia. Some tribes still practice the potlatch, sometimes as a memorial to the dead (Kan 1986, 1989). At each such event, assisted by members of their communities, potlatch sponsors traditionally gave away food, blankets, pieces of copper, or other items. In return for this, they got prestige. To give a potlatch enhanced one's reputation. Prestige increased with the lavishness of the potlatch, the value of the goods given away in it.

The potlatching tribes were hunters and gatherers, but compared with other foragers, they were more like food producers. They lived in sedentary tribes and had chiefs. Unlike those of most recent foragers, their environments were not marginal. They had access to a wide variety of land and sea resources. Their most important foods were salmon, herring, candlefish, berries, mountain goats, seals, and porpoises (Piddocke 1969).

Within the spreading world capitalist economy of the nineteenth century, the potlatching tribes, particularly the Kwakiutl, began to trade with Europeans (fur for blankets, for example), and their wealth increased as a result. Simultaneously, a huge proportion of the population died from previously unknown diseases brought by the Europeans. The increased wealth from trade flowed into a drasti-

Piling up blankets in a Kwakiutl potlatch on Vancouver Island in British Columbia. As foreign trade goods poured in, Kwakiutl hosts received, then gave away or destroyed, increasing amounts of property. Sometimes, chiefs even burned down their wooden houses in impressive displays of the conversion of wealth into prestige.

cally reduced population. With many of the traditional sponsors dead, the Kwakiutl extended the right to give a potlatch to the entire population, and this stimulated intense competition for prestige. Given trade, increased wealth, and a decreased population, the Kwakiutl also started converting wealth into prestige by destroying wealth items such as blankets and pieces of copper (Vayda 1961/1968).

Scholars once regarded Kwakiutl potlatching as economically wasteful behavior, the result of an irrational drive for social status and prestige. They stressed the destructiveness of the Kwakiutl to support their contention that in some societies people strive irrationally to maximize prestige—even by destroying valuable resources.

However, a more recent interpretation views potlatching not as wasteful but as a useful cultural adaptive mechanism. This view not only helps us understand potlatching, it also has comparative value because it helps us understand similar patterns of feasting throughout the world. This is the new interpretation: *Customs such as the potlatch are adaptations to alternating periods of local abundance and shortage.*

How did this work? The overall natural environment of the North Pacific Coast is favorable, but resources fluctuate from year to year and place to place. Salmon and herring aren't equally abundant every year in a given locality. One village can have a good year while another is experiencing a bad one. Later their fortunes reverse. In this context, the potlatch cycle of the Kwakiutl and Salish had adaptive value, and the potlatch was not an irrational competitive display.

A village enjoying an especially good year had a surplus of subsistence items, which it could exchange for wealth, and wealth could be converted into prestige. The potlatches distributed food and wealth to other communities that needed such items. In return, the sponsors and their villages got prestige. The decision to potlatch was determined by the health of the local economy. If there had been a subsistence surplus, and thus a buildup of wealth over several good years, the village could afford a potlatch to convert food and wealth into prestige.

The adaptive value of intercommunity feasting becomes clear when we consider what happened when a formerly prosperous village had a bad year. Its people started accepting invitations to potlatches in villages that were doing better. The tables were turned as the temporarily rich became temporarily poor and vice versa. The newly needy accepted food and wealth items. They were willing to receive rather than bestow gifts and thus to relinquish some of their stored-up prestige. Later, if the village's fortunes continued to decline, its people could exchange wealth items for food, for example, slaves for herring or canoes for cherries (Vayda 1961/1968). They hoped that their luck would eventually improve so that resources could be recouped and prestige regained.

Note that potlatching also impeded the development of socioeconomic stratification. Wealth relinquished or destroyed was converted into a nonmaterial item—prestige. Under capitalism we reinvest our profits (rather than burning our cash), with the hope of making an additional profit. However, the potlatching tribes were content to destroy their surpluses rather than use them to widen the social distance between themselves and their fellow tribe members.

The potlatch linked local groups along the North Pacific Coast into a regional alliance and exchange network. Potlatching and intervillage exchange had adaptive functions, regardless of the motivations of the individual participants. The anthropologists who stressed rivalry for prestige were not wrong. They were merely emphasizing motivations at the expense of an analysis of economic and ecological systems.

The use of feasts to enhance individual and community reputations and to redistribute wealth is not peculiar to populations of the North Pacific Coast. Competitive but adaptive feasting is widely characteristic of nonindustrial food producers. But among most foragers, who live, remember, in marginal areas, resources are too meager to support feasting on such a level. In such societies, sharing rather than competition prevails.

SUMMARY

Yehudi Cohen's six adaptive strategies are foraging (hunting and gathering), horticulture, agriculture, pastoralism, mercantilism (trade), and industrialism. Foraging was the only human strategy until food production (cultivation and animal domestication) appeared around 10,000 years ago. Food production eventually replaced foraging in most areas. Almost all modern foragers have at least some dependence on food production or food producers.

Among most foragers, the band is a basic social unit. Often band members split up seasonally into microbands or families. Kinship, marriage, and other arrangements link band members. Foragers assign tasks by gender and age. Men usually hunt and fish, and women gather. Old people guard traditions.

Cultivation is often combined with other adaptive strategies, such as pastoralism or foraging. Horticulture and agriculture stand at different ends of a continuum based on labor intensity and continuity of land use. Horticulture does not use land or labor intensively. Horticulturalists cultivate a plot for one or two years and then abandon it. Further along the continuum, horticulture becomes more intensive, but there is always a fallow period. Horticulturalists can shift plots while living in permanent villages. The first cultivating economies were horticultural. Horticulture still occurs in many areas of both hemispheres.

Agriculturalists farm the same plot of land continuously and use labor intensively. They use one or more of the following practices: irrigation, terracing, domesticated animals as means of production, and manuring. Because of permanent land use, agricultural populations are denser than are those associated with other adaptive strategies. Agriculturalists often have complex regulatory systems, including state organization.

The mixed nature of the pastoral strategy is evident. Nomadic pastoralists trade with cultivators. Transhumants grow their own crops. Part of the transhumant population cultivates while another part takes the herds to pasture. Except for some Peruvians and the Navajo, who are recent herders, the New World lacks native pastoralists.

Economic anthropologists study systems of production, distribution, and consumption cross-culturally. In nonindustrial societies, a kin-based mode of production prevails, and production is personal. The relations of production are aspects of continuous social relationships. One acquires rights to resources through membership in bands, descent groups, villages, and other social units, not impersonally through purchase and sale. Labor is also recruited through personal ties. Work is merely one aspect of social relationships that are expressed in a variety of social and ceremonial contexts.

Manufacturing specialization can exist in nonindustrial societies, promoting trade and alliance between groups. In nonindustrial societies there is usually a personal relationship between producer and commodity, in contrast to the alienation of labor, product, and management in industrial economies.

Economics has been defined as the science of allocating scarce means to alternative ends. Western economists assume that the notion of scarcity is universal—which it isn't—and that in making choices, people strive to maximize personal profit. However, in nonindustrial societies, as in our own, people maximize values other than individual profit. Furthermore, people often lack free choice in allocating their resources.

In nonindustrial societies, people invest in subsistence, replacement, social, and ceremonial funds. States add a rent fund: People must share their output with government officials and other social superiors. In states, the obligation to pay rent often becomes primary, and family subsistence may suffer.

Besides production, economic anthropologists study and compare exchange systems. The three principles of exchange are the market principle, redistribution, and reciprocity. The market principle, based on supply and demand and the profit motive, is dominant in states. Its characteristics are impersonal purchase and sale and bargaining. With redistribution, goods are collected at a central place, and some of them are eventually given back, or redistributed, to the people. Reciprocity governs exchanges between social equals. It is the characteristic mode of exchange among foragers and nonintensive cultivators. There are different degrees of reciprocity. With generalized reciprocity, there is no immediate expectation of return. With balanced reciprocity, which is characteristic of exchanges between more distantly related people, donors expect their gifts to be returned, although not immediately. Exchanges on the fringes of the social system are governed by negative reciprocity. As with the market principle, there is concern about immediate return, as well as bargaining. Reciprocity, redistribution, and the market principle may coexist in a society, but the primary exchange mode is the one that allocates the means of production.

Patterns of feasting and exchanges of wealth between villages in a region are common among nonindustrial food producers, as among the potlatching cultures of North America's North Pacific Coast. Such systems have adaptive value because they help even out the availability of resources over time. The destruction of wealth characteristic of some such systems also impedes the emergence of socioeconomic stratification.

GLOSSARY

agriculture: Nonindustrial systems of plant cultivation characterized by continuous and intensive use of land and labor.

balanced reciprocity: See generalized reciprocity.

band: Basic unit of social organization among foragers. A band includes fewer than 100 people; it often splits up seasonally.

ceremonial fund: Resources invested in ceremonial or ritual expenses or activity.

correlation: An association between two or more variables such that when one changes (varies), the other(s) also change(s) (covaries); for example, temperature and sweating.

cultivation continuum: A continuum based on the comparative study of nonindustrial cultivating societies in which labor intensity increases and fallowing decreases.

economic typology: Classification of societies based on their adaptive strategies; e.g., foraging, horticulture, pastoralism, agriculture.

economizing: The rational allocation of scarce means (or resources) to alternative ends (or uses); often considered the subject matter of economics.

economy: A population's system of production, distribution, and consumption of resources.

fictive kinship: Personal relationships modeled on kinship, such as that between godparents and godchildren.

generalized reciprocity: Principle that characterizes exchanges between closely related individuals: As social distance increases, reciprocity becomes balanced and finally negative.

horticulture: Nonindustrial system of plant cultivation in which plots lie fallow for varying lengths of time.

!Kung: Group of San (Bushmen) foragers of southern Africa; the exclamation point indicates a click sound in the San language.

Kwakiutl: A potlatching society on the North Pacific Coast of North America.

market principle: Profit-oriented principle of exchange that dominates in states, particularly industrial states. Goods and services are bought and sold, and values are determined by supply and demand.

means (or factors) of production: Land, labor, technology, and capital—major productive resources.

mode of production: Way of organizing production—a set of social relations through which labor is deployed to wrest energy from nature by means of tools, skills, and knowledge.

namesakes: People who share the same name; a form of fictive kinship among the San, who have a limited number of personal names.

negative reciprocity: See generalized reciprocity.

nomadism, pastoral: Movement throughout the year by the whole pastoral group (men, women, and children) with their animals. More generally, such constant movement in pursuit of strategic resources.

pastoralists: People who use a food-producing strategy of adaptation based on care of herds of domesticated animals.

peasant: Small-scale agriculturalist living in a state with rent fund obligations.

potlatch: Competitive feast among Indians on the North Pacific Coast of North America.

reciprocity: One of the three principles of exchange; governs exchange between social equals; major exchange mode in band and tribal societies.

redistribution: Major exchange mode of chiefdoms, many archaic states, and some states with managed economies.

rent fund: Scarce resources that a social inferior is required to render to an individual or agency that is superior politically or economically.

replacement fund: Scarce resources invested in technology and other items essential to production.

San: Foragers of southern Africa, also known as Bushmen; speakers of San languages.

sectorial fallowing: Intensive horticulture; plots are cultivated for two to three years, then fallowed for three to five, with a longer rest after several of these shorter cycles.

slash and burn: Form of horticulture in which the forest cover of a plot is cut down and burned before planting to allow the ashes to fertilize the soil.

social fund: Scarce resources invested to assist friends, relatives, in-laws, and neighbors.

state (nation-state): Complex sociopolitical system that administers a territory and populace with substantial contrasts in occupation, wealth, prestige, and power. An independent, centrally organized political unit, a government.

subsistence fund: Scarce resources invested to provide food in order to replace the calories expended in daily activity.

supply and demand, law of: Economic rule that things cost more the scarcer they are and the more people want them.

symbiosis: An obligatory interaction between groups that is beneficial to each.

transhumance: One of two variants of pastoralism; part of

the population moves seasonally with the herds while the other part remains in home villages.

typology, economic: See *economic typology.*

STUDY QUESTIONS

1. What are Cohen's four nonindustrial adaptive strategies? What are the main characteristics of each?
2. How do social ties facilitate individual mobility between bands?
3. What are the main differences and similarities between ancient and modern foragers?
4. What are the main differences between agriculture and horticulture?
5. What are the advantages and disadvantages of irrigation?
6. What is the difference between pastoral nomadism and transhumance?
7. What are the two main definitions of economics?

How do they relate to individual motivations and systems of behavior?

8. What are the primary differences between the economies of bands and tribes and those of peasants?
9. What are the main contrasts between industrial and nonindustrial economies?
10. What are the differences among reciprocity, redistribution, and the market principle?
11. What examples can you give from your own culture to illustrate these three types of exchange?
12. What are the differences among the three degrees of reciprocity?
13. What explanations have been given for potlatching behavior? Which one seems best to you and why?

SUGGESTED ADDITIONAL READING

BOSERUP, E.
> 1965 *The Conditions of Agricultural Growth.* Chicago: Aldine. Influential book linking population increase, agricultural intensification, and level of sociopolitical development.

CHATTY, D.
> 1996 *Mobile Pastoralists: Development Planning and Social Change in Oman.* New York: Columbia University Press. Based on ten years of research in a nomadic Middle Eastern community, this study examines forces of "modernization," including a shift from herding to cash employment and the changing role of women.

CLAMMER, J., ED.
> 1976 *The New Economic Anthropology.* New York: St. Martin's Press. Essays link economic anthropology to problems affecting the less developed countries.

COHEN, Y.
> 1974a *Man in Adaptation: The Cultural Present,* 2nd ed. Chicago: Aldine. Presents Cohen's economic typology of adaptive strategies and uses it to organize a valuable set of essays on culture and adaptation.

GOODY, J.
> 1977 *Production and Reproduction: A Comparative Study of the Domestic Domain.* New York: Cambridge University Press. Relationships among agriculture, property transmission, and family relations in Africa, Asia, and Europe.

INGOLD, T., D. RICHES, AND J. WOODBURN
> 1991 *Hunters and Gatherers.* New York: Berg (St. Martin's). Volume I examines history and social change among foragers. Volume II looks at their property, ideology, and power relations. These broad regional surveys illuminate current issues and debates.

KEARNEY, M.
> 1996 *Reconceptualizing the Peasantry: Anthropology in Global Perspective.* Boulder, CO: Westview. How peasants live today, in post–Cold War nation-states.

LeCLAIR, E. E., AND H. K. SCHNEIDER, EDS.
> 1968 (orig. 1961). *Economic Anthropology: Readings in Theory and Analysis.* New York: Holt, Rinehart and Winston. A set of classic essays in economic anthropology.

LEE, R. B.
> 1984 *The Dobe !Kung.* Fort Worth: Harcourt Brace. Account of well-known San foragers, by one of their principal ethnographers.

LEE, R. B., AND I. DeVORE, EDS.
> 1977 *Kalahari Hunter-Gatherers: Studies of the !Kung San and Their Neighbors.* Cambridge, MA: Har-

vard University Press. Long-term interdisciplinary study.

PLATTNER, S., ED.

1989   *Economic Anthropology.* Stanford, CA: Stanford University Press. More up-to-date compilation of articles on economic features of foraging, tribal, peasant, state, and industrial societies.

SHIGERU, K.

1994   *Our Land Was a Forest: An Ainu Memoir.* Boulder, CO: Westview. An Ainu storyteller places his people, traditional foragers, in the context of development in modern Japan.

WILK, R. R.

1996   *Economies and Cultures: An Introduction to Economic Anthropology.* Boulder, CO: Westview. An up-to-date introduction to economic anthropology.

WILMSEN, R.

1989   *Land Filled with Flies: A Political Economy of the Kalahari.* Chicago: University of Chicago Press. A revisionist view of the San, in the context of colonialism and the world system.

YOUNG, W. C.

1996   *The Rashaayada Bedouin: Arab Pastoralists of Eastern Sudan.* Fort Worth: Harcourt Brace. This examination of a pastoral economy also weaves in information on gender and "race."

THE POLITICAL SYSTEMS OF BANDS AND TRIBES

TYPES AND TRENDS

FORAGING BANDS

TRIBAL CULTIVATORS
Descent-Group Organization

Box: The Great Forager Debate

The Village Head
Village Raiding
The "Big Man"
Segmentary Lineage Organization
Pantribal Sodalities, Associations, and Age Grades

PASTORALISTS

nthropologists and political scientists share an interest in political systems and organization, but the anthropological approach is global and comparative. Anthropological data reveal substantial variations in power, authority, and legal systems in different cultures. (*Power* is the ability to exercise one's will over others; *authority* is the socially approved use of power.)

Several years ago the anthropologist Elman Service (1962) listed four types, or levels, of political organization: band, tribe, chiefdom, and state. *Bands,* as we have seen, are small **kin-based** groups (all members of the group are related to each other by kinship or marriage ties) found among foragers. **Tribes,** which are associated with nonintensive food production (horticulture and pastoralism), have villages and/or descent groups but lack a formal government and social classes (socioeconomic stratification). In a tribe, there is no reliable means of enforcing political decisions. The **chiefdom,** a form of sociopolitical organization that is intermediate between the tribe and the state, is kin-based, but it has differential access to resources (some people have more wealth, prestige, and power than do others) and a permanent political structure. The **state** is a form of sociopolitical organization based on a formal government structure and socioeconomic stratification.

Many anthropologists have criticized Service's typology as being too simple. However, it does offer a handy set of labels for highlighting cross-cultural similarities and differences in social and political organization. For example, in bands and tribes, the political order, or **polity,** is not a separate entity but is submerged in the total social order. It is difficult to characterize an act or event as political rather than merely social.

Recognizing that political organization is sometimes just an aspect of social organization, Morton Fried offered this definition:

> Political organization comprises those portions of social organization that specifically relate to the individuals or groups that manage the affairs of *public policy* or seek to control the appointment or activities of those individuals or groups. (Fried 1967, pp. 20–21, emphasis added)

This definition certainly fits contemporary North America. Under "individuals or groups that manage the affairs of public policy" come federal, state (provincial), and local (municipal) governments. Those who "seek to control . . . appointment or activities" include such interest groups as political parties, unions, corporations, consumers, activists, action committees, and religious groups.

Fried's definition is much less applicable to bands and tribes, where it is often difficult to detect any "public policy." For this reason, I prefer to speak of *socio*political organization in discussing cross-cultural similarities and differences in the **regulation** or management of interrelations among groups and their representatives. In a general sense regulation is the process that ensures that variables stay within their normal ranges, corrects deviations from the norm, and thus maintains a system's integrity. In the case of political regulation this includes such things as the settling of conflicts between individuals and groups and methods of decision making within the group. The study of political regulation draws our attention to questions about who performs these tasks (are there formal leaders?) and how they are managed.

TYPES AND TRENDS

Ethnographic and archaeological studies in hundreds of places have revealed many correlations between economy and social and political organization. Band, tribe, chiefdom, and state are categories or types in a system of **sociopolitical typology.** These types are correlated with the adaptive strategies (**economic typology**) discussed in the last chapter. Thus, foragers (an economic type) tend to have band organization (a sociopolitical type). Similarly, many horticulturalists and pastoralists live in tribal societies (or, more simply, tribes). The economies of chiefdoms tend to be based on intensive horticulture or agriculture, but some pastoralists also participate in chiefdoms. Nonindustrial states usually have an agricultural base.

Food producers tend to have larger, denser populations and more complex economies than do foragers. These features create new regulatory problems, which give rise to more complex relations and linkages. Many sociopolitical trends reflect the increased regulatory demands associated with food production. Archaeologists have studied these trends through time, and cultural anthropologists have observed them among contemporary groups.

This chapter and the next one examine societies that differ in their economic and political systems. A common set of questions will be considered for different types of societies. What kinds of social groups do they have? How do people affiliate with those groups? How do the groups link up with larger ones? How do the groups represent themselves to each other? How are their internal and external relations regulated?

FORAGING BANDS

In most foraging societies only two kinds of groups are significant: the nuclear family and the band. Unlike sedentary villages (which appear in tribal societies), bands are impermanent. They form seasonally as component nuclear families assemble. The particular combination of families in a band may vary from year to year. In such settings the main social building blocks (linking principles) are the personal relationships of individuals. For example, marriage and kinship create ties between members of different bands. Because one's parents and grandparents come from different bands, a person has relatives in several of these groups. Trade and visiting also link local groups, as does fictive kinship, such as the San namesake system described in the last chapter. Similarly, Eskimo men traditionally had trade partners, whom they treated almost like brothers, in different bands.

In a foraging band, there is very little differential authority and no differential power, although particular talents lead to special respect. For example, someone can sing or dance well, is an especially good storyteller, or can go into a trance and communicate with spirits. Band leaders are leaders in name only. They are first among equals. Sometimes they give advice or make decisions, but they have no means of enforcing their decisions.

Although foragers lack formal law in the sense of a legal code that includes trial and enforcement, they do have methods of social control and dispute settlement. The absence of law does not mean total anarchy. The aboriginal Eskimos (Hoebel 1954, 1968), or Inuit, as they are called in Canada, provide a good example of methods of settling disputes in stateless societies. As described by E. A. Hoebel (1954) in a study of Eskimo conflict resolution, a sparse population of some 20,000 Eskimos spanned 9,500 kilometers (6,000 miles) of the Arctic region. The most significant Eskimo social groups were the nuclear family and the band. Personal relationships linked the families and bands. Some bands had headmen. There were also shamans (part-time religious specialists). However, these positions conferred little power on those who occupied them.

Unlike tropical foraging societies, in which gathering—usually a female task—is more important, hunting and fishing by men were the primary Eskimo subsistence activities. The diverse and abundant plant foods available in warmer areas were

Typically among foragers only two groups are significant: the nuclear family and the band. Bands, like this group in the Ituri forest of Zaire, form seasonally, as component families assemble. In most band-organized societies, there is little or no differential wealth, authority, or power, although special talents (such as singing or storytelling) are respected.

Among tropical foragers, gathering (for example, of edible roots like the ones shown here) contributes more to the diet than hunting or fishing do. Gathering is usually a female task, as among the San shown here in Botswana. Men usually hunt and do most of the fishing.

absent in the Arctic. Traveling on land and sea in a bitter environment, Eskimo men faced more dangers than women did. The traditional male role took its toll in lives. Adult women would have outnumbered men substantially without occasional female **infanticide** (killing of a baby), which Eskimo culture permitted.

Despite this crude (and to us unthinkable) means of population regulation, there were still more adult women than men. This permitted some men to have two or three wives. The ability to support more than one wife conferred a certain amount of **prestige,** but it also encouraged envy. (*Prestige* is esteem, respect, or approval for culturally valued acts or qualities.) If a man seemed to be taking additional wives just to enhance his reputation, a rival was likely to steal one of them. Most disputes were between men and originated over women, caused by wife stealing or adultery. If a man discovered that his wife had been having sexual relations without his permission, he considered himself wronged.

Although public opinion would not let the husband ignore the matter, he had several options. He could try to kill the wife stealer. However, if he succeeded, one of his rival's kinsmen would surely try to kill him in retaliation. One dispute could escalate into several deaths as relatives avenged a succession of murders. No government existed to intervene and stop such a **blood feud** (a feud between families). However, one could also challenge a rival to a

song battle. In a public setting, contestants made up insulting songs about each other. At the end of the match, the audience judged one of them the winner. However, if a man whose wife had been stolen won, there was no guarantee she would return. Often she would decide to stay with her abductor.

Several acts of killing that are crimes in contemporary North America were not considered criminal by the Eskimos. Infanticide has already been mentioned. Furthermore, people who felt that, because of age or infirmity, they were no longer useful might kill themselves or ask others to kill them. Old people or invalids who wished to die would ask a close relative, such as a son, to end their lives. It was necessary to ask a close relative in order to ensure that the kin of the deceased did not take revenge on the killer.

Thefts are common in state-organized societies, which have marked property differentials. However, thefts were not a problem for the Eskimos—or for most foragers. Each Eskimo had access to the resources needed to sustain life. Every man could hunt, fish, and make the tools necessary for subsistence. Every woman could obtain the implements and materials needed to make clothing, prepare food, and do domestic work. Eskimos could even hunt and fish in territories of other local groups. There was no notion of private ownership of territory or animals.

To describe certain property notions of people who live in societies without state organization, Elman Service (1966) coined the term **personalty** (note the spelling). Personalty refers to items other than strategic resources that are indelibly associated with a specific person. These items include things such as arrows, a tobacco pouch, clothing, and personal ornaments. The term points to the personal relationship between such items and their owner. Personalty is so tied to a specific person that theft is inconceivable (think of your toothbrush). The "grave goods" that are often found in archaeological sites dating to the period before food production probably represent personalty. These items were not passed on to heirs. Their association with the deceased was too definite.

One of the most basic Eskimo beliefs was that "all natural resources are free or common goods" (Hoebel 1968). Band-organized societies usually lack differential access to strategic resources. The only private property is personalty. If people want something from someone else, they ask for it, and it is usually given.

TRIBAL CULTIVATORS

Tribes usually have a horticultural or pastoral economy and are organized by village life and/or descent-group membership. Socioeconomic stratification (i.e., a class structure) and a formal government are absent. Many tribes have small-scale warfare, often in the form of intervillage raiding. Tribes have more effective regulatory mechanisms than do foragers, but tribalists have no sure means of enforcing political decisions. The main regulatory officials are village heads, "big men," descent-group leaders, village councils, and leaders of pantribal associations. All these figures and groups have limited authority.

Like foragers, horticulturalists tend to be egalitarian, although some have marked gender stratification—an unequal distribution of resources, power, prestige, and personal freedom between men and women. Horticultural villages are usually small, with low population density and open access to strategic resources. Age, gender, and personal traits determine how much respect people receive and how much support they get from others. Egalitarianism diminishes, however, as village size and population density increase. Horticultural villages usually have headmen—rarely, if ever, headwomen.

Descent-Group Organization

Kin-based bands are basic social units among foragers. An analogous group among food producers is the **descent group.** A descent group is a permanent social unit whose members claim common ancestry. The group endures even though its membership changes as members are born and die, move in and move out. Often, descent-group membership is determined at birth and is lifelong.

Descent groups frequently are exogamous (members must seek their mates from other descent groups). Two common rules serve to admit certain people as descent-group members while excluding others. With a rule of **matrilineal descent,** people join the mother's group automatically at birth and stay members throughout life. Matrilineal descent groups therefore include only the children of the group's women. With **patrilineal descent,** people automatically have lifetime membership in the father's group. The children of all the men join the group, but the children of the women are excluded. Matrilineal and patrilineal descent are types of **unilineal descent.** This means that the descent rule uses *one line only,* either the male or the female [Figures 12.1 (below) and 12.2 (on page 244)]. Patrilineal descent is much more common than is matrilineal descent. In a sample of 564 societies (Murdock 1957), about three times as many were found to be patrilineal (247 to 84).

Descent groups may be **lineages** or **clans.** Common to both is the belief that members descend

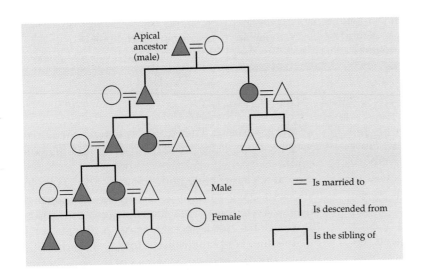

Figure 12.1 *A patrilineage five generations deep. Lineages are based on demonstrated descent from an apical ancestor. With patrilineal descent, children of men (blue) are included as descent-group members. Children of women are excluded; they belong to their father's patrilineage. Also notice lineage exogamy.*

THE GREAT FORAGER DEBATE

How representative are modern hunter-gatherers of Paleolithic (Stone Age) peoples, all of whom were foragers? G. P. Murdock (1934) described living hunter-gatherers as "our primitive contemporaries." This label gave an image of foragers as living fossils—frozen, primitive, unchanging social forms that had managed to hang on in remote areas (like the Hollywood natives on King Kong's island).

Later, many anthropologists followed the prolific ethnographer Richard Lee (1984) in using the San ("Bushmen") of the Kalahari Desert of southern Africa to represent the hunting-gathering way of life. But critics increasingly wonder about how much modern foragers can tell us about the economic and social relations that characterized humanity before food production. Modern foragers, after all, live in nation-states and an increasingly interlinked world. For generations, the pygmies of Zaire have traded with their neighbors who are cultivators. They exchange forest products (e.g., honey and meat) for crops (e.g., bananas and manioc). The San have been influenced by Bantu speakers for 2,000 years and by Europeans for centuries. All foragers now trade with food producers, and most rely on governments and on

missionaries for at least part of what they consume. The Aché of Paraguay get food from missionaries, grow crops, and have domesticated animals (Hawkes et al. 1982; Hill et al. 1987). They spend only a third of their subsistence time foraging.

A debate is now raging in hunter-gatherer studies between "traditionalists" (e.g., Richard Lee) and "revisionists" (e.g., Edwin Wilmsen). Reconsideration of the status of contemporary foragers is related to the reaction against the ethnographic present discussed in the box in Chapter 2. Anthropologists have rejected the old tendency to depict societies as uniform and frozen in time and space. Attempts to capture the ethnographic present often ignored internal variation, change, and the influence of the world system.

The debate over foragers has focused on the San, whom the traditionalists view as autonomous foragers with a cultural identity different from that of their neighbors who are herders and cultivators (Lee 1979; Silberbauer 1981; Tanaka 1980). These scholars depict most San as egalitarian band-organized people who until recently were nomadic or seminomadic. Traditionalists recognize contact between the

San and food producers, but they don't think this contact has destroyed San culture.

The revisionists claim the San tell us little about the ancient world in which all humans were foragers. They argue that the San have been linked to food producers for generations, and that this contact has changed the basis of their culture. For Edwin Wilmsen (1989) the San are far from being isolated survivors of a pristine era. They are a rural underclass in a larger political and economic system dominated by Europeans and Bantu food producers. Many San now tend cattle for wealthier Bantu, rather than foraging independently. Wilmsen also argues that many San descend from herders who were pushed into the desert by poverty or oppression.

The isolation and autonomy of foragers have also been questioned for African pygmies (Bailey et al. 1989) and for foragers in the Philippines (Headland and Reid 1989). The Mikea of southwest Madagascar may have moved into their remote forest habitat to escape the nearby Sakalava state. Eventually the Mikea became an economically specialized group of hunter-gatherers on the fringes of that state. The Tasaday of the Philippines maintain ties with food producers and proba-

from the same **apical ancestor.** This person stands at the apex, or top, of the common genealogy. How do lineages and clans differ? A lineage uses **demonstrated descent.** Members can recite the names of their forebears in each generation from the apical ancestor through the present. (This doesn't mean that their recitations are accurate, only that lineage members think they are.) Clans use **stipulated descent.** Clan members merely say they descend from

the apical ancestor. They don't try to trace the actual genealogical links between themselves and that ancestor.

Some societies have both lineages and clans. In this case, clans have more members and cover a larger geographical area than lineages do. Sometimes a clan's apical ancestor is not a human at all but an animal or plant (called a **totem**). Whether human or not, the ancestor symbolizes the social unity

bly descend from cultivating ancestors. This is true despite the initial "Lost Tribe" media accounts. The reports that followed the "discovery" of the Tasaday portrayed them as survivors of the Stone Age, hermetically sealed in a pristine world all their own. Many scholars now question the authenticity of the Tasaday as a separate cultural group (Headland, ed. 1992).

The debate about foragers raises a larger question: Why do the ethnographic accounts and interpretations vary? The reasons include variation in space and time in the society, and different assumptions by ethnographers. Susan Kent (1992) notes a tendency to stereotype foragers, to treat them as all alike. Foragers used to be stereotyped as isolated, primitive survivors of the Stone Age. A new stereotype sees them as culturally deprived people forced by states, colonialism, or world events into marginal environments. This view is probably more accurate, although often exaggerated. All modern foragers have links with external systems, including food producers and nation-states. Because of this they differ substantially from Paleolithic hunter-gatherers.

In challenging both stereotypes, Kent (1992) stresses the variation among foragers. She focuses on diversity in time and space among the San. The traditionalist-revisionist debate, suggests Kent, is largely based on failure to recognize the extent of diversity among the San. Researchers on both sides may be correct, depending on the group of San being described and the time period of the research.

San economic adaptations range from hunting and gathering to fishing, farming, herding, and wage work. Solway and Lee (1990) describe environmental degradation caused by herding and population increase. These factors are depleting game and forcing more and more San to give up foraging. Even traditionalists recognize that all San are being drawn inexorably into the modern world system. (Many of us remember the Coke bottle that fell from the sky into a San band in the movie *The Gods Must Be Crazy*—a film filled with many stereotypes.)

The nature of San life has changed appreciably since the 1950s and 1960s, when a series of anthropologists from Harvard University, including Richard Lee, embarked on a systematic study of life in the Kalahari. Lee and others have documented many of the changes in various publications. Such longitudinal research monitors variation in time, while field work in many San areas has revealed variation in space. One of the most important contrasts is between settled (sedentary) and nomadic groups (Kent and Vierich 1989). Sedentism is increasing, but some San groups (along rivers) have been sedentary, or have traded with outsiders, for generations. Others, including Lee's Dobe !Kung San and Kent's Kutse San, have been more cut off and have retained more of the hunter-gatherer life style.

Modern foragers are not Stone Age relics, living fossils, lost tribes, or noble savages. Still, to the extent that foraging is the basis of subsistence, modern hunter-gatherers can illustrate links between a foraging economy and other aspects of culture. For example, San groups that are still mobile, or that were so until recently, emphasize social, political, and gender equality. Social relations that stress kinship, reciprocity, and sharing work well in an economy with limited resources and few people. The nomadic pursuit of wild plants and animals tends to discourage permanent settlements, accumulation of wealth, and status distinctions. People have to share meat when they get it; otherwise it rots. Kent (1992) suggests that by studying diversity among the San, we can better understand foraging and how it is influenced by sedentism and other factors. Such study will enhance our knowledge of past, present, and future small-scale societies.

and identity of the members, distinguishing them from other groups.

A tribal society normally contains several descent groups. Any one of them may be confined to a single village, but they usually span more than one village. Any branch of a descent group that lives in one place is a **local descent group.** Two or more local branches of different descent groups may live in the same village. Descent groups in the same village or different villages may establish alliances through frequent intermarriage.

The Village Head

The Yanomami (Chagnon 1992) are Native Americans who live in southern Venezuela and adjacent Brazil. Their tribal society has about 20,000 people living in 200 to 250 widely scattered villages, each

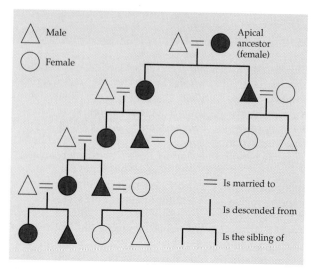

Figure 12.2 *A matrilineage five generations deep. Matrilineages are based on demonstrated descent from a female ancestor. Only the children of women (red) belong to the matrilineage. The children of men are excluded; they belong to their mother's matrilineage.*

with a population between 40 and 250. The Yanomami are horticulturalists who also hunt and gather. Their staple crops are bananas and plantains (a bananalike crop). There are more significant social groups among the Yanomami than exist in a foraging society. The Yanomami have nuclear families, villages, and descent groups. Their descent groups are patrilineal and exogamous. They span more than one village. However, local branches of two different descent groups may live in the same village and intermarry.

As in many village-based tribal societies, the only leadership position among the Yanomami is that of **village head** (always a man). His authority, like that of the foraging band leader, is severely limited. If a headman wants something done, he must lead by example and persuasion. The headman lacks the right to issue orders. He can only persuade, harangue, and try to influence public opinion. For example, if he wants people to clean up the central plaza in preparation for a feast, he must start sweeping it himself, hoping that his covillagers will take the hint and relieve him.

When conflict erupts, the headman may be called on as a mediator who listens to both sides. He will give an opinion and advice. If a disputant is unsatisfied, the headman can do nothing. He has no power

to back his decisions and no way to impose punishments. Like the band leader, he is first among equals.

A Yanomami village headman must also lead in generosity. Because he must be more generous than any other villager, he cultivates more land. His garden provides much of the food consumed when his village holds a feast for another village. The headman represents the village in its dealings with outsiders. Sometimes he visits other villages to invite people to a feast.

The way a person acts as headman depends on his personal traits and the number of supporters he can muster. One village headman, Kaobawa, intervened in a dispute between a husband and wife and kept him from killing her (Chagnon 1992). He also guaranteed safety to a delegation from a village with which a covillager of his wanted to start a war. Kaobawa was a particularly effective headman. He had demonstrated his fierceness in battle, but he also knew how to use diplomacy to avoid offending other villagers. No one in the village had a better personality for the headmanship. Nor (because Kaobawa had many brothers) did anyone have more supporters. Among the Yanomami, when a group is dissatisfied with a village headman, its members can leave and found a new village; this is done from time to time.

Village Raiding

Yanomami society, with its many villages and descent groups, is more complex than a band-organized society. The Yanomami also face more regulatory problems. A headman can sometimes prevent a specific violent act, but there is no government to maintain order. In fact, intervillage raiding in which men are killed and women are captured has been a feature of some areas of Yanomami territory, particularly those studied by Chagnon (1992).

We must also stress that the Yanomami are not isolated from outside events (although there are still uncontacted villages). The Yanomami live in two nation-states, Venezuela and Brazil, and external warfare waged by Brazilian ranchers and miners has increasingly threatened them (*Cultural Survival Quarterly* 1989; Chagnon 1992). During the recent Brazilian gold rush (1987–1991), one Yanomami died each day, on average, from external attacks (including biological warfare—introduced diseases to which the Indians lack resistance). By 1991 there were some 40,000 Brazilian miners in the Yanomami homeland. Some Indians were killed outright. The miners introduced new diseases, and the swollen population ensured that old diseases became epidemic. In 1991 a commission of the American Anthropological Association reported on the plight of the Yanomami (*Anthropology Newsletter*, September 1991). Brazilian Yanomami were dying at a rate of 10 percent annually, and their fertility rate had dropped to zero. Since then, both the Brazilian and the Venezuelan governments have intervened to protect the Yanomami. The former Brazilian president, Fernando Collor, declared a huge Yanomami territory off-limits to outsiders. Unfortunately, by mid-1992 local politicians, miners, and ranchers were increasingly evading the ban, and the future of the Yanomami remains uncertain. These external attacks pose a much more serious threat to Yanomami survival than does traditional intervillage raiding.

The "Big Man"

In many areas of the South Pacific, particularly the Melanesian Islands and Papua–New Guinea, native cultures have a kind of political leader that we call the **big man.** The big man (almost always a male) is an elaborate version of the village head, but there is one very significant difference. The village head's leadership is within one village; the big man has supporters in several villages. He is therefore a more effective (but still limited) regulator of *regional* political organization. Here we see the trend toward expansion in the scale of sociopolitical regulation—from village to region.

The Kapauku Papuans live in Irian Jaya, Indonesia (which is on the island of New Guinea). Anthropologist Leopold Pospisil (1963) studied the Kapauku (45,000 people), who grow crops (with the sweet potato as their staple) and raise pigs. Their economy is too complex to be described as simple horticulture. Beyond the household, the only political figure among the Kapauku is the big man, known as a *tonowi*. A *tonowi* achieves his status through hard work, amassing wealth in the form of pigs and other native riches. Characteristics that can distinguish a big man from his fellows include wealth, generosity, eloquence, physical fitness, bravery, and supernatural powers. Notice that big men are what they are because they have certain personalities and have amassed their resources during their lifetimes, not because they have inherited their wealth or position.

Any man who is determined enough can become a big man, because people create their own wealth through hard work and good judgment. Wealth depends on successful pig breeding and trading. As a man's pig herd and prestige grow, he attracts supporters. He sponsors ceremonial pig feasts in which pigs are slaughtered and their meat is distributed to guests.

The big man has some advantages that the Yanomami village headman lacks. His wealth exceeds that of his fellows. His primary supporters, in recognition of past favors and anticipation of future

The "big man" is an important regulator of regional events. He persuades people to organize feasts, which distribute pork and wealth. Shown here is such a regional event, drawing on several villages, in Papua–New Guinea. Big men owe their status to their individual personalities rather than to inherited wealth or position.

rewards, recognize him as a leader and accept his decisions as binding. He is an important regulator of regional events in Kapauku life. He helps determine the dates for feasts and markets. He persuades people to sponsor feasts, which distribute pork and wealth. He regulates intervillage contacts by sponsoring dance expeditions. He initiates economic projects that require the cooperation of a regional community.

The Kapauku big man again exemplifies a generalization about leadership in tribal societies: If people achieve wealth and widespread respect and support, they must be generous. The big man works hard not to hoard wealth but to be able to *give away* the fruits of his labor, to convert wealth into prestige and gratitude. If a big man is stingy, he loses his supporters, and his reputation plummets. The Kapauku take even more extreme measures against big men who hoard. Selfish and greedy rich men may be murdered by their fellows.

Political figures such as the big man emerge as regulators both of demographic growth and of economic complexity. Kapauku cultivation uses varied techniques for specific kinds of land. Labor-intensive cultivation in valleys involves mutual aid in turning the soil before planting. The digging of long drainage ditches is even more complex. Kapauku plant cultivation supports a larger and denser population than does the simpler horticulture of the Yanomami. Kapauku society could not survive in its present form without collective cultivation and political regulation of the more complex economic tasks.

Segmentary Lineage Organization

The big man is a *temporary* regional regulator. Big men can mobilize supporters in several villages to pool produce and labor on specific occasions. Another temporary form of regional political organization in tribal society is **segmentary lineage organization (SLO).** This means that the descent-group structure (usually patrilineal) has several levels—nested segments—that are like dolls nesting inside other dolls or boxes placed within boxes (Figure 12.3). The largest segments are maximal lineages, segments of which are known as major lineages. Major lineages are divided up into minor lineages. Minor lineages in turn are segmented into minimal lineages, whose common ancestor lived fairly re-

cently—no more than four generations ago. The larger segments have spread throughout a region, but members of the minimal lineage occupy the same village. New minimal lineages develop when people move away and establish new settlements. Over time, minimal lineages grow into minor ones, minor into major ones, and major into maximal ones.

Segmentary lineage organization exists in broad outline in many cultures, such as the traditional societies of North Africa and the Middle East, including prestate Arabs and biblical Jews. However, the classic examples of SLO are two African groups, the Tiv of Nigeria and the Nuer of the Sudan (Sahlins 1961). Segmentary lineage structure organized more than 1 million Tiv, who believe that they all share the same remote ancestor, a man named Tiv who settled in their homeland many generations ago. They trace the line of descent leading from Tiv to the present, listing his male descendants in each generation.

Although the Nuer cannot demonstrate patrilineal descent that far back, they believe that they have a common ancestry separate from that of their neighbors. One of several **Nilotic populations** (populations that inhabit the Upper Nile region of eastern Africa), the Nuer (Evans-Pritchard 1940), numbering more than 200,000, live in Sudan. Cattle pastoralism is fundamental to their mixed economy, which also includes horticulture. The Nuer have many institutions that are typical of tribal societies, including patrilineal descent groups arranged into a segmentary structure. Their political organization is based on descent rules and genealogical reckoning.

Brothers are very close in segmentary societies, especially when the father is alive. He manages their joint property and stops them from quarreling too much. He also arranges their marriages. When he dies, the brothers usually keep on living in the same village, but one may take his share of the herds and start a settlement of his own. However, his brothers are still his closest allies. He will live as close as he can to them. Even if the brothers all stay in the same village, some of the grandchildren will move away in search of new pastures. However, each will try to remain as close to the home village as possible, settling nearest his brothers and nearer to his first cousins than to more distant relatives.

With SLO, the basic principle of solidarity is that the closer the relationship of the descent-group, the

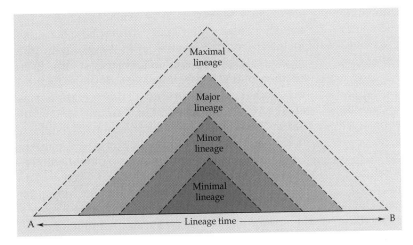

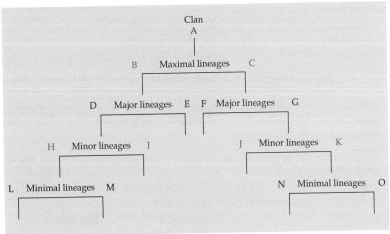

Figure 12.3 *Two views of segmentary lineage organization. (Reprinted by permission from E. E. Evans-Pritchard,* The Nuer: A Description of the Modes of Livelihood and Political Institutions of a Nilotic People *[Oxford: Clarendon Press, 1940].)*

(top) *Minimal lineages nest within minor lineages, which nest within major lineages, which nest within maximal lineages, which may in turn belong to a clan, as in the bottom figure. Common ancestry is most recent in the minimal lineage.*

(bottom) *Clan A is segmented into* maximal lineages *B and C. These have divided into* major lineages *D, E, F, and G. At the next level down,* minor lineages *H, I, J, and K are segments of major lineages D and G. L, M, N, and O are* minimal lineages *that are segments of H and K. For simplification, the minor lineages of E and F and the minimal lineages of I and J aren't shown.*

greater the mutual support. The more distant the shared ancestor, the greater the potential for hostility. This extends right up the genealogy; maximal lineages are more likely to fight each other than are major lineages.

Segmentary lineage organization seems to have been advantageous for the Tiv and the Nuer, allowing them to expand at their neighbors' expense. This sociopolitical organization confers a feeling of tribal identity. It provides an orderly way to mobilize temporarily against other societies. When the need arises, the Nuer or the Tiv can easily present a common front against outsiders—people who claim different genealogical and ethnic identity (Sahlins 1961).

Segmentary descent also regulates disputes and their resolution. If a fight breaks out between men who share a living patrilineal ancestor, he inter-venes to settle it. As head of the minimal descent group that includes the disputants, he backs his authority with the threat of banishment. However, when there is no common living ancestor, a blood feud may develop.

Disputes among the Nuer do not arise over land, which a person acquires as a member of a lineage. As a member of a minimal descent group, one has a right to its estate. A frequent cause of quarrels is adultery, and if a person injures or kills someone, a feud may develop. Conflicts also arise over divorce.

There is an alternative to a blood feud. The disputants may consult the leopard-skin man, so called because he customarily wears a leopard skin over his shoulders. Leopard-skin men conduct rituals, but their most important role is to mediate disputes. For instance, elders may ask a leopard-skin man to persuade a murder victim's kin to accept a certain number of cattle in recompense. While the mediator attempts to arrange a peaceful settlement, the murderer may take refuge in the leopard-skin man's village, which offers sanctuary until the mediator resolves the dispute or withdraws.

The leopard-skin man relies on persuasion and avoids blaming either side. He cannot enforce his decisions, but in theory he can use the threat of supernatural punishment. If one of the disputing groups is adamant, he may, in disgust, threaten to curse it. If, after seeking mediation, the disputants refuse to agree, the leopard-skin man may withdraw.

Negotiations involve the disputants, their elders, and other close kin. There is full and free discussion before a settlement is reached. The disputants may gradually come to accept the collective opinion of the mediator and the elders. However, although the peace-making abilities of the leopard-skin man are greater than anything found among the Yanomami and Eskimos, blood feuds still exist among the stateless Nuer.

With SLO, no one has a constant group of allies. One's allies change from one dispute to the next, depending on genealogical distance. Still, common descent does permit a temporary common front, as minimal lineages unite to form minor ones. Minor lineages form majors, and major lineages come together in a maximal lineage that, in the presence of an outside threat, unites all Nuer or Tiv society through its claim of common patrilineal descent.

Similarly, Arabs claim to demonstrate their segmentary descent patrilineally from the biblical Ishmael. There is an Arab adage, "I and my brother against my cousin [father's brother's son]. I, my brother, and my cousin against all other Arabs. I, my brother, my cousin, and all other Arabs against all the world" (Murphy and Kasdan 1959, p. 20). Jews believe themselves to be descended from Isaac, half-brother of Ishmael. The Jews and Arabs share a common ancestor, Abraham, the father of both Ishmael and Isaac. In the modern world, of course, political mechanisms other than SLO, including national governments and regional alliances, work to determine relations between Arabs and Jews.

Pantribal Sodalities, Associations, and Age Grades

We have seen that events initiated by big men temporarily unite people from different villages. Segmentary lineage organization permits short-term mobilization of an entire society against an outside threat. There are many other kinds of sociopolitical linkages between local groups in a region. Clans, for example, often span several villages.

Kinship and descent provide important social linkages in tribal societies. Principles other than kinship also may link local groups. In a modern nation, a labor union, national sorority or fraternity, political party, or religious denomination may provide

Some unigender groups (all male or all female) are confined to a single village. This is true of the Turkoman women's quarters in Central Asia shown here. Other unigender groups span several local groups. Only the latter, the pantribal groups, are important in regional political organization.

such a non-kin-based link. In tribes, nonkin groups called associations or **sodalities** may serve the same linking function. Often sodalities are based on common age or gender, with all-male sodalities more common than all-female ones.

Pantribal sodalities (those which extend across the whole tribe, spanning several villages) tend to be found in areas where two or more different cultures come into regular contact. They are especially likely to develop when there is warfare *between tribes* (as opposed to raiding between villages of the same tribe, as practiced by the Yanomami). Sodalities help organize the warfare that men wage against neighboring cultures. Since sodalities draw their members from different villages of the same tribe, they can mobilize men in many local groups for attack or retaliation against another tribe. Like SLO, pantribal sodalities have military value because they facilitate temporary regional mobilization. In particular, pantribal sodalities are common among pastoralists. One culture's sodality may organize raids to steal cattle or horses from another.

In the cross-cultural study of nonkin groups, we must distinguish between those which are confined to a single village and those which span several local groups. Only the latter, the *pantribal* groups, are important in general military mobilization and regional political organization. *Localized* men's houses and clubs, limited to particular villages, are found in many horticultural societies in tropical South America, Melanesia, and Papua–New Guinea. These groups may organize village activities and even intervillage raiding, but their leaders are similar to village heads and their political scope is mainly local. The following discussion, which continues our examination of the growth in scale of regional sociopolitical organization, concerns pantribal groups.

The best examples of pantribal sodalities come from the Central Plains of North America and from tropical Africa. During the eighteenth and nineteenth centuries, native populations of the Great Plains of the United States and Canada experienced a rapid growth of pantribal sodalities. This development reflected an economic change that followed the spread of horses, which had been brought to the New World by the Spanish, to the states between the Rocky Mountains and the Mississippi River. Many Plains Indian societies changed their adaptive

strategies because of the horse. At first they had been foragers who hunted bison (buffalo) on foot. Later they adopted a mixed economy based on hunting, gathering, and horticulture. Finally they changed to a much more specialized economy based on horseback hunting of bison (eventually with rifles).

As the Plains tribes were undergoing these changes, other Indians also adopted horseback hunting and moved into the Plains. Attempting to occupy the same ecological niche, groups came into conflict. A pattern of warfare developed in which the members of one tribe raided another, usually for horses, as was portrayed in the movie *Dances with Wolves*. The new economy demanded that people follow the movement of the bison herds. During the winter, when the bison dispersed, a tribe fragmented into small bands and families. In the summer, as huge herds assembled on the Plains, members of the tribe reunited. They camped together for social, political, and religious activities, but mainly for communal bison hunting.

Only two activities in the new adaptive strategy demanded strong leadership: organizing and carrying out raids on enemy camps (to capture horses) and managing the summer bison hunt. All the Plains cultures developed pantribal sodalities, and leadership roles within them, to police the summer hunt. Leaders coordinated hunting efforts, making sure that people did not cause a stampede with an early shot or an ill-advised action. Leaders imposed severe penalties, including seizure of a culprit's wealth, for disobedience.

Some of the Plains sodalities were **age sets** of increasing rank. Each set included all the men—from that tribe's component bands—born during a certain time span. Each set had its distinctive dance, songs, possessions, and privileges. Members of each set had to pool their wealth to buy admission to the next higher level as they moved up the age hierarchy. Most Plains societies had pantribal warrior associations whose rituals celebrated militarism. As noted previously, the leaders of these associations organized bison hunting and raiding. They also arbitrated disputes during the summer, when large numbers of people came together.

Many of the tribes that adopted this Plains strategy of adaptation had once been foragers for whom hunting and gathering had been individual or small-group affairs. They had never come together

Natives of the Great Plains of North America originally hunted bison (buffalo) on foot. The introduction of horses and rifles fueled a pattern of horse raiding and warfare. The Plains cultures developed pantribal sodalities based on age and gender, and leadership roles within them for warfare and to police the summer hunt. Plains groups often used rituals to inculcate strong solidarity between people of the same age and gender. Here, in a kind of initiation rite, young warriors sit in a circle smoking, while older riders whip them. At the end of the ceremony, each rider gave a horse to the man he had whipped.

previously as a single social unit. *Age and gender were available as social principles that could quickly and efficiently forge unrelated people into pantribal groups.*

Raiding of one tribe by another, this time for cattle rather than horses, was also common in eastern and southeastern Africa, where pantribal sodalities, including age sets, also developed. Among the pastoral Masai of Kenya, men born during the same

four-year period were circumcised together and belonged to the same named group, an age set, throughout their lives. The sets moved through grades, the most important of which was the warrior grade. Members of the set who wished to enter the warrior grade were at first discouraged by its current occupants, who eventually vacated the warrior grade and married. Members of a set felt a strong allegiance to one another and eventually had sexual rights to each other's wives. Masai women lacked comparable set organization, but they also passed through culturally recognized age grades: the initiate, the married woman, and the postmenopausal woman.

To understand the difference between an *age set* and an *age grade*, think of a college class, the Class of '99, for example, and its progress through the university. The age set would be the group of people constituting the Class of '99, while the first ("freshman"), sophomore, junior, and senior years would represent the age grades.

Not all cultures with age grades also have age sets. When there are no sets, men can enter or leave a particular grade individually or collectively, often by going through a predetermined ritual. The grades most commonly recognized in Africa are these:

1. Recently initiated youths
2. Warriors
3. One or more grades of mature men who play important roles in pantribal government
4. Elders, who may have special ritual responsibilities

In certain parts of West Africa and Central Africa, the pantribal sodalities are **secret societies,** made up exclusively of men or women. Like our college fraternities and sororities, these associations have secret initiation ceremonies. Among the Mende of Sierra Leone, men's and women's secret societies are very influential. The men's group, the Poro, trains boys in social conduct, ethics, and religion and supervises political and economic activities. Leadership roles in the Poro often overshadow village headship and play an important part in social control, dispute management, and tribal political regulation. Like descent, then, age, gender, and ritual can link members of different local groups into a single social collectivity in tribal society and thus create a sense of ethnic identity, of belonging to the same cultural tradition.

PASTORALISTS

Although many pastoralists live in tribes, a range of demographic and sociopolitical diversity occurs with pastoralism. A comparison of pastoralists shows that as regulatory problems increase, political hierarchies become more complex. Political organization becomes less personal, more formal, and less kinship-oriented. The pastoral strategy of adaptation does not dictate any particular political organization. A range of authority structures manage regulatory problems associated with specific envi-

Among the pastoral Masai of Kenya, men born during the same four-year period were circumcised together and belonged to the same named group, an age set, throughout their lives. The sets moved through grades, of which the most important was the warrior grade. Two Masai age sets are shown here.

ronments. Many pastoralists (such as the Nuer and other East African herders) live in tribal societies. Others have powerful chiefs and live in nation-states. This reflects pastoralists' need to interact with other populations—a need that is less characteristic of the other adaptive strategies.

The scope of political authority among pastoralists expands considerably as regulatory problems increase in densely populated regions. Consider two Iranian pastoral nomadic tribes—the Basseri and the Qashqai (Salzman 1974). These groups followed a nomadic route more than 480 kilometers (300 miles) long. Starting each year from a plateau near the coast, they took their animals to grazing land 5,400 meters (17,000 feet) above sea level. These tribes shared this route with one another and with several other ethnic groups.

Use of the same pasture land at different times was carefully scheduled. Ethnic-group movements were tightly coordinated. Expressing this schedule is *il-rah*, a concept common to all Iranian nomads. A group's *il-rah* is its customary path in time and space. It is the schedule, different for each group, of when specific areas can be used in the annual trek.

Each tribe had its own leader, known as the *khan* or *il-khan*. The Basseri *khan*, because he dealt with a smaller population, faced fewer problems in coordinating its movements than did the leaders of the

Qashqai. Correspondingly, his rights, privileges, duties, and authority were weaker. Nevertheless, his authority exceeded that of any political figure we have discussed so far. However, the *khan's* authority still came from his personal traits rather than from his office. That is, the Basseri followed a particular *khan* not because of a political position he happened to fill but because of their personal allegiance and loyalty to him as a man. The *khan* relied on the support of the heads of the descent groups into which Basseri society was divided, following a rough segmentary lineage model.

In Qashqai society, however, allegiance shifts from the person to the office. The Qashqai had multiple levels of authority and more powerful *khans*. Managing 400,000 people required a complex hierarchy. Heading it was the *il-khan*, helped by a deputy, under whom were the heads of constituent tribes, under each of whom were descent-group heads.

A case illustrates just how developed the Qashqai authority structure was. A hailstorm prevented some nomads from joining the annual migration at the appointed time. Although everyone recognized that they were not responsible for their delay, the *il-khan* assigned them less favorable grazing land, for that year only, in place of their usual pasture. The tardy herders and other Qashqai considered the

Political organization is well-developed among the Qashqai, who share their nomadic route and strategic resources with several other tribes. Here, Qashqai nomads cross a river in Iran's Fars province.

judgment fair and didn't question it. Thus Qashqai authorities regulated the annual migration. They also adjudicated disputes between people, tribes, and descent groups.

These Iranian cases illustrate the fact that pastoralism is often just one among many specialized economic activities within complex nation-states and regional systems. As part of a larger whole, pastoral tribes are constantly pitted against other ethnic groups. In these nations, the state becomes a final authority, a higher-level regulator that attempts to limit conflict between ethnic groups. State organization arose not just to manage agricultural economies but also to regulate the activities of ethnic groups within expanding social and economic systems. We turn in the next chapter to chiefdoms and states.

SUMMARY

Anthropologists may use a sociopolitical typology of bands, tribes, chiefdoms, and states along with an economic typology based on adaptive strategy. Through these classification schemes we can compare the scale and effectiveness of social linkages and political regulation and of variations in power, authority, and legal systems cross-culturally. There are important cross-cultural contrasts in the kinds of groups that are significant, determinants of leadership, reasons for disputes, and means for resolving them.

Foragers usually have egalitarian societies, with bands and families as characteristic groups. Personal networks link individuals, families, and bands. There is little differential power. Band leaders are first among equals and have no means of enforcing decisions. Disputes rarely arise over strategic resources, because the resources are available to everyone. Among the Eskimos, disputes traditionally originated in adultery or wife stealing. Aggrieved individuals might kill offenders, but this could trigger a blood feud. Although no government existed to halt blood feuds, there were certain customary means of resolving disputes.

The descent group is a basic kin group in tribal societies. Unlike families, descent groups have perpetuity—they last for generations. There are several types of descent groups. Lineages are based on demonstrated descent; clans, on stipulated descent. Patrilineal and matrilineal descent are unilineal descent rules.

Political authority increases as population size and density and the scale of regulatory problems grow. Egalitarianism diminishes as village size increases. With more people, there are more interpersonal relationships to regulate. Increasingly complex economies pose further regulatory problems.

Horticultural villages generally have heads with limited authority. The heads lead by example and persuasion and have no sure means of enforcing their decisions. The Yanomami are tribal horticulturalists. Their sociopolitical organization has more varied groups than does the foraging society. There are villages and patrilineal descent groups. Authority is more developed than it is among foragers. However, village heads, the main Yanomami political figures, have no sure power. The Yanomami also illustrate a pattern of warfare that is widespread among tribal cultivators.

Big men are temporary regional regulators. Their influence extends beyond the village; they mobilize the labor of supporters in several villages. Big men have prestige, commanding the loyalty of many, but they must be generous. Sponsorship of feasts leaves them with little wealth but with a reputation for generosity, which must be maintained if the big man is to retain his influence.

Another form of temporary regional sociopolitical organization is segmentary lineage organization (SLO). The Nuer, tribal pastoralists of the Upper Nile, have SLO, as do the horticultural Tiv of Nigeria. The closest allies of the Tiv and the Nuer are their patrilineal relatives. The term *segmentary* describes the organization of descent groups into segments at different genealogical levels. Nuer belong to minimal lineages, which are residential units. Groups of minimal lineages constitute minor lineages, and groups of minor lineages make up major lineages. Groups of major lineages make up maximal lineages, and groups of maximal lineages make up clans. Although Nuer clans do not trace descent from the same ancestor, they believe that they share a common ethnic origin separate from that of their neighbors.

Among populations with segmentary descent organization, alliance is relative, depending on genealogical distance. Social solidarity is proportional to the closeness of patrilineal ancestry and geographical proximity. The Nuer have disputes over murder, injuries, and adultery. People support the disputant with whom they share the closest ancestor. Despite mediators, there is no sure way of halting feuds. Disputes can mobilize the entire segmentary lineage—that is, the entire society—against outsiders.

Age and gender are obvious social variables that, like SLO, can be used in regional political integration. The Plains cultures of native North America developed pantribal sodalities during the eighteenth and nineteenth centuries as they changed from generalized foraging and horticulture to horseback hunting of bison. Men's associations organized raiding parties and communal hunting and maintained order in the summer camp.

Pantribal sodalities, often emphasizing the warrior grade, develop in areas where people from different cultures come into contact, particularly when there is intertribal raiding for domesticated animals. The differential authority among pastoralists reflects population size and density, interethnic relationships, and pressure on resources. Regulatory problems increase and political organization is well-developed among the Basseri and especially the Qashqai of Iran. Each group shares its nomadic route and its strategic resources with several others.

GLOSSARY

age set: Group uniting all men or women born during a certain time span; this group controls property and often has political and military functions.

apical ancestor: In a descent group, the individual who stands at the apex, or top, of the common genealogy.

big man: Figure often found among tribal horticulturalists and pastoralists. The big man occupies no office but creates his reputation through entrepreneurship and generosity to others. Neither his wealth nor his position passes to his heirs.

blood feud: Feud between families, usually in a nonstate society.

chiefdom: Form of sociopolitical organization intermediate between the tribe and the state; kin-based with differential access to resources and a permanent political structure.

clan: Unilineal descent group based on stipulated descent.

demonstrated descent: Basis of the lineage; descent-group members cite the names of their forebears in each generation from the apical ancestor through the present.

descent group: A permanent social unit whose members claim common ancestry; fundamental to tribal society.

head, village: A local leader in a tribal society who has limited authority, leads by example and persuasion, and must be generous.

infanticide: Killing a baby; a form of population control in some societies.

kin-based: Characteristic of many nonindustrial societies. People spend their lives almost exclusively with their relatives; principles of kinship, descent, and marriage organize social life.

law: A legal code, including trial and enforcement; characteristic of state-organized societies.

lineage: Unilineal descent group based on demonstrated descent.

local descent group: All the members of a particular descent group who live in the same place, such as the same village.

matrilineal descent: Unilineal descent rule in which people join the mother's group automatically at birth and stay members throughout life.

Nilotic populations: Populations, including the Nuer, that inhabit the Upper Nile region of eastern Africa.

pantribal sodality: A non-kin-based group that exists throughout a tribe, spanning several villages.

patrilineal descent: Unilineal descent rule in which people join the father's group automatically at birth and stay members throughout life.

personalty: Items other than strategic resources that are indelibly associated with a particular person; contrasts with property.

polity: The political order.

prestige: Esteem, respect, or approval for acts, deeds, or qualities considered exemplary.

regulation: Management of variables within a system of related and interacting variables. Regulation assures that variables stay within their normal ranges, corrects deviations from the norm, and thus maintains the system's integrity.

secret societies: Sodalities, usually all-male or all-female, with secret initiation ceremonies.

segmentary lineage organization (SLO): Political organization based on descent, usually patrilineal, with multiple descent segments that form at different genealogical levels and function in different contexts.

sociopolitical typology: Classification scheme based on the scale and complexity of social organization and the effectiveness of political regulation; includes band, tribe, chiefdom, and state.

sodality: See *pantribal sodality*.

state: Sociopolitical organization based on central government and socioeconomic stratification—a division of society into classes.

stipulated descent: Basis of the clan; members merely say they descend from their apical ancestor; they don't trace the actual genealogical links between themselves and that ancestor.

totem: An animal or plant apical ancestor of a clan.

tribe: Form of sociopolitical organization usually based on horticulture or pastoralism. Socioeconomic stratification and centralized rule are absent in tribes, and there is no means of enforcing political decisions.

typology, sociopolitical: See *sociopolitical typology.*

unilineal descent: Matrilineal or patrilineal descent.

STUDY QUESTIONS

1. What is the rationale for using the term *sociopolitical organization* rather than *political organization?*
2. How is the sociopolitical typology discussed in this chapter related to the previously discussed economic typology based on adaptive strategy?
3. How would you characterize the usual sociopolitical organization of foragers?
4. How would you characterize the legal system of the Eskimos/Inuit?
5. What are the main types of descent groups, and how do they differ?
6. What is the significance of Yanomami warfare?
7. How do the political roles of village head and big man differ?
8. What is segmentary lineage organization (SLO), and how does it work politically? How is it similar to a big man system?
9. What are sodalities, and how do they work politically? How are they similar to SLO?
10. What conclusions can be drawn from this chapter about the relationship between population density and political hierarchy?
11. List the local, regional, temporary, and permanent forms of sociopolitical organization discussed in this chapter.

SUGGESTED ADDITIONAL READING

CHAGNON, N.
  1992   *Yanomamö,* 4th ed. Fort Worth: Harcourt, Brace. Most recent revision of a classic account of the Yanomami, including their social organization, politics, warfare, cultural change, and the crisis they now confront.

EDER, JAMES
  1987   *On the Road to Tribal Extinction: Depopulation, Deculturation, and Adaptive Well-Being among the Batak of the Philippines.* Berkeley: University of California Press. Cultural devastation among hunter-gatherers in the Philippines.

FERGUSON, B., AND N. L. WHITEHEAD
  1991   *War in the Tribal Zone: Expanding States and Indigenous Warfare.* Santa Fe: School of American Research Press. The effects of colonialism and the world system on native warfare.

HARRIS, M.
  1989   *Our Kind: Who We Are, Where We Came From, Where We Are Going.* New York: Harper & Row. Popular anthropology; origins of humans, culture, and major sociopolitical institutions.

HEIDER, K. G.
  1991   *Grand Valley Dani: Peaceful Warriors,* 2nd ed. Fort Worth: Harcourt Brace. Comprehensive and readable account of a tribal group on the island of New Guinea, now under Indonesian rule.

INGOLD, T., D. RICHES, AND J. WOODBURN
  1991   *Hunters and Gatherers.* New York: Berg (St. Martin's). Volume I examines history, evolution, and social change among foragers. Volume II looks at their property, ideology, and power relations. These broad regional surveys illuminate current issues and debates.

KEISER, L.
  1991   *Friend by Day, Enemy by Night: Organized Vengeance in a Kohistani Community.* Fort Worth: Harcourt Brace. Blood feuding and its implications in Pakistan.

LIZOT, J.
  1985   *Tales of the Yanomami: Daily Life in the Venezuelan Forest.* New York: Cambridge University Press. Account of the Yanomami by a French anthropologist who has spent about two decades in the field with them.

MIDDLETON, J.
  1993   *The Lugbara of Uganda,* 2nd ed. Fort Worth: Harcourt Brace. Sociopolitical change over thirty years of anthropological study.

PODOLEFSKY, A.
1992   *Simbu Law: Conflict Management in the New Guinea Highlands.* Fort Worth: Harcourt Brace. How conflict is resolved in a society without leaders and formal judicial institutions.

ROBERTS, S.
1979   *Order and Dispute: An Introduction to Legal Anthropology.* New York: Penguin Books. Social control in Africa and New Guinea.

SAITOTI, T. O.
1988   *The Worlds of a Maasai Warrior: An Autobiography.* Berkeley: University of California Press. The autobiography of a former warrior from Kenya.

SCHEPER-HUGHES, N.
1992   *Death without Weeping: The Violence of Everyday Life in Brazil.* Berkeley: University of California Press. Reproductive strategies and mother love in the context of poverty in northeastern Brazil.

C H A P T E R 1 3

CHIEFDOMS AND STATES

**POLITICAL AND ECONOMIC SYSTEMS
IN CHIEFDOMS**

SOCIAL STATUS IN CHIEFDOMS

**STATUS SYSTEMS IN CHIEFDOMS
AND STATES**

STATES
Population Control
Judiciary
Enforcement
Fiscal Systems

THE ORIGIN OF THE STATE

Hydraulic Systems
Ecological Diversity
Long-Distance Trade Routes
Population Growth, Warfare, and Environmental
    Circumscription

THE CHALLENGE TO THE STATE
The Role of Globalization, Transnationalism,
    and the Media
The Collapse of Mass Culture as a Challenge
    to the State
The New World Disorder
NGOs and Rights Movements
From State Formation to Government Decline

Having looked at bands and tribes, we turn to more complex forms of sociopolitical organization—that of chiefdoms and states. The first states (or *civilizations,* a near synonym) emerged in the Old World about 5,500 years ago. The first chiefdoms developed perhaps a thousand years earlier, but few survive today. The chiefdom was a transitional form of sociopolitical organization that emerged during the evolution of tribes into states. State formation began in Mesopotamia (currently Iran and Iraq) and then occurred in Egypt, the Indus Valley of Pakistan and India, and northern China. A few thousand years later states also arose in two parts of the Western Hemisphere—Mesoamerica (Mexico, Guatemala, Belize) and the central Andes (Peru and Bolivia). Early states are known as **archaic,** or nonindustrial, **states,** in contrast to modern industrial nation-states. Robert Carneiro defines the state as

> an autonomous political unit encompassing many communities within its territory, having a centralized government with the power to collect taxes, draft men for work or war, and decree and enforce laws. (Carneiro 1970, p. 733)

The chiefdom and the state, like many categories used by social scientists, are **ideal types.** That is, they are labels that make social contrasts seem sharper than they really are. In reality there is a continuum from tribe to chiefdom to state. Some societies have many attributes of chiefdoms but retain tribal features. Some advanced chiefdoms have many attributes of archaic states and thus are difficult to assign to either category. Recognizing this "continuous change" (Johnson and Earle 1987), some anthropologists speak of "complex chiefdoms" (Earle 1987), which are almost states.

POLITICAL AND ECONOMIC SYSTEMS IN CHIEFDOMS

State formation remained incomplete and only chiefdoms emerged in several areas, including the circum-Caribbean (e.g., Caribbean islands, Panama, Colombia), lowland Amazonia, what is now the southeastern United States, and Polynesia. Chiefdoms created the megalithic cultures of Europe, such as the one that built Stonehenge. Indeed, between the emergence and spread of food production and the expansion of the Roman empire, much of Europe was organized at the chiefdom level, to which it reverted for centuries after the fall of Rome in the fifth century A.D.

Much of our ethnographic knowledge about chiefdoms comes from Polynesia, where they were common at the time of European exploration. In chiefdoms, social relations are mainly based on kinship, marriage, descent, age, generation, and gender—just as they are in bands and tribes. This is a fundamental difference between chiefdoms and states. States bring nonrelatives together and oblige them all to pledge allegiance to a government.

Chiefdoms created the megalithic cultures of Europe, such as the one that built Stonehenge—shown here. Between the emergence and spread of food production and the expansion of the Roman empire, much of Europe was organized at the chiefdom level, to which it reverted after the fall of Rome.

Chiefdoms were common in Polynesia at the time of European exploration. Some "complex" chiefdoms, such as ancient Hawaii, had many attributes of archaic states. Monument building begins in chiefdoms, where "ceremonies of place" are associated with the creation of a "sacred landscape" through temples and sculptures, such as the Hawaiian statues shown here.

Unlike bands and tribes, however, chiefdoms are characterized by *permanent political regulation* of the territory they administer, which includes thousands of people living in many villages and/or hamlets. Regulation is carried out by the chief and his or her assistants, who occupy political offices. An **office** is a permanent position, which must be refilled when it is vacated by death or retirement. Because offices are systematically refilled, the structure of a chiefdom endures across the generations, ensuring permanent political regulation.

In the Polynesian chiefdoms, the chiefs were full-time political specialists in charge of regulating production, distribution, and consumption. Polynesian chiefs relied on religion to buttress their authority. They regulated production by commanding or prohibiting (using religious taboos) the cultivation of certain lands and crops. Chiefs also regulated distribution and consumption. At certain seasons—often on a ritual occasion such as a first-fruit ceremony—

people would offer part of their harvest to the chief through his or her representatives. Products moved up the hierarchy, eventually reaching the chief. Conversely, illustrating obligatory sharing with kin, chiefs sponsored feasts at which they gave back much of what they had received.

Such a flow of resources to and then from a central office is known as *chiefly redistribution*. Redistribution offers economic advantages. If the different areas specialized in particular crops, goods, or services, chiefly redistribution made those products available to the whole society. Chiefly redistribution also played a role in risk management. It stimulated production beyond the immediate subsistence level and provided a central storehouse for goods that might become scarce at times of famine (Earle 1987, 1991). Chiefdoms and archaic states had similar economies, often based on intensive cultivation, and both administered systems of regional trade or exchange.

SOCIAL STATUS IN CHIEFDOMS

Social status in chiefdoms was based on seniority of descent. Because rank, power, prestige, and resources came through kinship and descent. Polynesian chiefs kept extremely long genealogies. Some chiefs (without writing) managed to trace their ancestry back fifty generations. All the people in the chiefdom were thought to be related to each other. Presumably, all were descended from a group of founding ancestors.

The chief (usually a man) had to demonstrate seniority in descent. Degrees of seniority were calculated so intricately on some islands that there were as many ranks as people. For example, the third son would rank below the second, who in turn would rank below the first. The children of an eldest brother, however, would all rank above the children of the next brother, whose children would in turn outrank those of younger brothers. However, even the lowest-ranking person in a chiefdom was still the chief's relative. In such a kin-based context, everyone, even a chief, had to share with his or her relatives.

Because everyone had a slightly different status, it was difficult to draw a line between elites and common people. Although other chiefdoms calculated seniority differently and had shorter genealogies

Social status in chiefdoms is based on seniority of descent. In the modern world system, seniority may still confer prestige, but the differences in wealth and power between chiefs and their juniors are often minor. Shown here is a contemporary chief (center) in the Marquesas Islands, Polynesia.

than did those in Polynesia, the concern for genealogy and seniority and the absence of sharp gaps between elites and commoners are features of all chiefdoms.

STATUS SYSTEMS IN CHIEFDOMS AND STATES

The status systems of chiefdoms and states are similar in that both are based on **differential access** to resources. This means that some men and women had privileged access to power, prestige, and wealth. They controlled strategic resources such as land, water, and other means of production. Earle characterizes chiefs as "an incipient aristocracy with advantages in wealth and lifestyle" (1987, p. 290). Nevertheless, differential access in chiefdoms was still very much tied to kinship. The people with privileged access were generally chiefs and their nearest relatives and assistants.

Compared with chiefdoms, archaic states drew a much firmer line between elites and masses, distinguishing at least between nobles and commoners. Kinship ties did not extend from the nobles to the commoners because of *stratum endogamy*—marriage within one's own group. Commoners married commoners; elites married elites. Such a division of society into socioeconomic strata contrasts strongly with the status systems of bands and tribes, which

are based on prestige, not resources. The prestige differentials that do exist in bands reflect special qualities, and abilities. Good hunters get respect from their fellows as long as they are generous. So does a skilled curer, dancer, storyteller—or anyone else with a talent or skill that others appreciate.

In tribes, some prestige goes to descent-group leaders, to village heads, and especially to the big man, a regional figure who commands the loyalty and labor of others. However, all these figures must be generous. If they accumulate more resources—i.e., property or food—than others in the village, they must share them with the others. Since strategic resources are available to everyone, social classes based on the possession of unequal amounts of resources can never exist.

In many tribes, particularly those with patrilineal descent, men have much greater prestige and power than women do. The gender contrast in rights may diminish in chiefdoms, where prestige and access to resources are based on seniority of descent, so that some women are senior to some men. Unlike big men, chiefs are exempt from ordinary work and have rights and privileges that are unavailable to the masses. However, like big men, they still return much of the wealth they take in.

The status system in chiefdoms, although based on differential access, differed from the status sytem in states because the privileged few were always relatives and assistants of the chief. However, this type of status system didn't last very long. Chiefs would start acting like kings and try to erode the kinship basis of the chiefdom. In Madagascar they would do this by demoting their more distant relatives to commoner status and banning marriage between nobles and commoners (Kottak 1980). Such moves, *if accepted by the society,* created separate social strata—*unrelated* groups that differ in their access to wealth, prestige, and power. (A **stratum** is one of two or more groups that contrast in regard to social status and access to strategic resources. Each stratum includes people of both sexes and all ages.) The creation of separate social strata is called **stratification,** and its emergence signified the transition from chiefdom to state. *The presence and acceptance of stratification is one of the key distinguishing features of a state.*

Influential sociologist Max Weber (1968/1922) defined three related dimensions of social stratification: (1) Economic status, or **wealth,** encompasses all a person's material assets, including income, land, and other types of property (Schaefer and Lamm 1992). (2) **Power,** the ability to exercise one's will over others—to do what one wants—is the basis of political status. (3) **Prestige**—the basis of social status—refers to esteem, respect, or approval for acts, deeds, or qualities considered exemplary. Prestige, or "cultural capital" (Bourdieu 1984), provides people with a sense of worth and respect, which they may often convert into economic advantage (Table 13.1).

Table 13.1 *Max Weber's Three Dimensions of Stratification*

wealth	→	economic status
power	→	political status
prestige	→	social status

These Weberian dimensions of stratification are present to varying degrees in chiefdoms. However, chiefdoms lack the sharp division into classes that characterized states. Wealth, power, and prestige in chiefdoms are all tied to kinship factors.

In archaic states—for the first time in human evolution—there were contrasts in wealth, power, and prestige between entire groups (social strata) of men and women. Each stratum included people of both sexes and all ages. The **superordinate** (the higher or elite) stratum had privileged access to wealth, power, and other valued resources. Access to resources by members of the **subordinate** (lower

or underprivileged) stratum was limited by the privileged group.

Socioeconomic stratification continues as a defining feature of all states, archaic or industrial. The elites control a significant part of the means of production, for example, land, herds, water, capital, farms, or factories. Those born at the bottom of the hierarchy have reduced chances of social mobility. Because of elite ownership rights, ordinary people lack free access to resources. Only in states do the elites get to keep their differential wealth. Unlike big men and chiefs, they don't have to give it back to the people whose labor has built and increased it.

STATES

States, remember, are autonomous political units with social classes and a formal government, based on law. States tend to be large and populous, as compared to bands, tribes, and chiefdoms. Certain statuses, systems, and subsystems with specialized functions are found in all states. They include the following:

1. *Population control:* fixing of boundaries, establishment of citizenship categories, and the taking of a census
2. *Judiciary:* laws, legal procedure, and judges
3. *Enforcement:* permanent military and police forces
4. *Fiscal:* taxation

In archaic states, these subsystems were integrated by a ruling system or government composed of civil, military, and religious officials (Fried 1960).

Population Control

To know whom they govern, all states conduct censuses. States demarcate boundaries that separate them from other societies. Customs agents, immigration officers, navies, and coast guards patrol frontiers, attempting to regulate passage from one state to another. Even nonindustrial states have boundary-maintenance forces. In Buganda, an archaic state on the shores of Lake Victoria in Uganda, the king rewarded military officers with estates in outlying provinces. They became his guardians against foreign intrusion.

States also control population through administrative subdivision: provinces, districts, "states," counties, subcounties, and parishes. Lower-level officials manage the populations and territories of the subdivisions.

In nonstates, people work and relax with their relatives, in-laws, fictive kin, and age mates—people with whom they have a personal relationship. Such a personal social life existed throughout most of human history, but food production spelled its eventual decline. After millions of years of human evolution, it took a mere 4,000 years for the population increase and regulatory problems spawned by food production to lead from tribe to chiefdom to state. With state organization, kinship's pervasive role diminished. Descent groups may continue as kin groups within archaic states, but their importance in political organization declines, and their exclusive control over their members ends.

States—archaic and modern—foster geographic mobility and resettlement, severing long-standing ties among people, land, and kin. Population displacements have increased in the modern world. War, famine, and job seeking across national boundaries churn up migratory currents. People in states come to identify themselves by new statuses, both ascribed and achieved, including ethnic background, place of birth or residence, occupation, party, religion, and team or club affiliation, rather than only as members of a descent group or extended family.

States also manage their populations by granting different rights and obligations to citizens and noncitizens. Status distinctions among citizens are also common. Many archaic states granted different rights to nobles, commoners, and slaves. Unequal rights within state-organized societies persist in today's world. In recent American history, before the Emancipation Proclamation, there were different laws for slaves and free people. In European colonies, separate courts judged cases involving only natives and those which involved Europeans. In contemporary America, a military code of justice and court system continue to coexist alongside the civil judiciary.

Judiciary

States have *laws* based on precedent and legislative proclamations. Without writing, laws may be preserved in oral tradition, with justices, elders, and other specialists responsible for remembering them. Oral traditions as repositories of legal wisdom have continued in some nations with writing, such as Great Britain. Laws regulate relations between individuals and groups.

Crimes are violations of the legal code, with specified types of punishment. However, a given act, such as killing someone, may be legally defined in different ways (e.g., as manslaughter, justifiable homicide, or first-degree murder). Furthermore, even in contemporary North America, where justice is supposed to be "blind" to social distinctions, the poor are prosecuted more often and more severely than are the rich.

To handle disputes and crimes, all states have courts and judges. Precolonial African states had subcounty, county, and district courts, plus a high court formed by the king or queen and his or her advisers. Most states allow appeals to higher courts, although people are encouraged to solve problems locally.

A striking contrast between states and nonstates is intervention in family affairs. In states, aspects of parenting and marriage enter the domain of public law. Governments step in to halt blood feuds and regulate previously private disputes. States attempt

States foster geographic mobility and resettlement, severing long-standing ties between people, land, and kin. War, famine, and job seeking across national boundaries churn up migratory currents. Many mine workers in South Africa come from neighboring countries, such as Mozambique.

to curb *internal* conflict, but they aren't always successful. About 85 percent of the world's armed conflicts since 1945 have begun within states—in efforts to overthrow a ruling regime or as disputes over tribal, religious, and ethnic minority issues. Only 15 percent have been fights across national borders (Barnaby, ed. 1984). Rebellion, resistance, repression, terrorism, and warfare continue. Indeed, recent states have perpetrated some of history's bloodiest deeds.

Enforcement

All states have agents to enforce judicial decisions. Confinement requires jailers, and a death penalty calls for executioners. Agents of the state collect fines and confiscate property. These officials wield power that is much more effective than the curse of the Nuer leopard-skin man.

A major concern of government is to defend hierarchy, property, and the power of the law. The government suppresses internal disorder (with police) and guards the nation against external threats (with the military). As a relatively new form of sociopolitical organization, states have competed successfully with less complex societies throughout the world. Military organization helps states subdue neighboring nonstates, but this is not the only reason for the spread of state organization. Although states impose hardships, they also offer advantages. More obviously, they provide protection from outsiders and preserve internal order. They curb the feuding that has plagued tribes such as the Yanomami and the Nuer. By promoting internal peace, states enhance production. Their economies support massive, dense populations, which supply armies and colonists to promote expansion.

Fiscal Systems

A financial or **fiscal** system is needed in states to support rulers, nobles, officials, judges, military personnel, and thousands of other specialists. As in the chiefdom, the state intervenes in production, distribution, and consumption. The state may decree that a certain area will produce certain things or forbid certain activities in particular places. Although, like chiefdoms, states also have redistribution (through taxation), generosity and sharing are

played down. A smaller proportion of what comes in flows back to the people.

In nonstates, people customarily share with relatives, but residents of states face added obligations to bureaucrats and officials. Citizens must turn over a substantial portion of what they produce to the state. Of the resources that the state collects, it reallocates part for the general good and uses another part (often larger) for the elite.

The state does not bring more freedom or leisure to the common people, who usually work harder than do the people in nonstates. They may be called on to build monumental public works. Some of these projects, such as dams and irrigation systems, may be economically necessary. However, people also build temples, palaces, and tombs for the elites.

Monument building began in chiefdoms, where "ceremonies of place" were associated with the creation of a "sacred landscape" through constructions such as (stone) henges of Europe, the mounds of the southeastern United States, and the temples of Hawaii (Earle 1987, 1991). Like chiefs, state officials may use religion to buttress their authority. Archaeology shows that temples abounded in early states. Even in mature states, rulers may link themselves to godhood through divine right or claim to be deities or their earthly representatives. Rulers convoke peons or slaves to build magnificent castles or tombs, cementing the ruler's place in history or status in the afterlife. Monumental architecture survives as an enduring reminder of the exalted prestige of priests and kings.

Markets and trade are usually under at least some state control, with officials overseeing distribution and exchange, standardizing weights and measures, and collecting taxes on goods passing into or through the state. Taxes support government and the ruling class, which is clearly separated from the common people in regard to activities, privileges, rights, and obligations. Elites take no part in subsistence activities. Taxes also support the many specialists—administrators, tax collectors, judges, lawmakers, generals, scholars, and priests. As the state matures, the segment of the population freed from direct concern with subsistence grows.

The elites of archaic states revel in the consumption of **sumptuary goods**—jewelry, exotic food and drink, and stylish clothing reserved for, or affordable only by, the rich. Peasants' diets suffer as they struggle to meet government demands. Commoners perish in territorial wars that have little relevance to their own needs.

THE ORIGIN OF THE STATE

Why were people willing to give up so many of the freedoms, pleasures, and personal bonds that their ancestors had enjoyed throughout human history? The answer is that people didn't choose but were *forced* to accept state organization. Because state formation may take centuries, people experiencing the process at any time rarely perceive the significance of the long-term changes. Later generations find themselves dependent on government institutions that took generations to develop.

The state develops to handle regulatory problems encountered as the population grows and/or the economy increases in scale and diversity. Anthropologists and historians have identified the causes of state formation and have reconstructed the rise of several states. Many factors always contribute to state formation, with the effects of one magnifying those of the others. Although some contributing factors appear again and again, no single one is always present. In other words, state formation has generalized rather than universal causes.

Hydraulic Systems

One suggested cause of state formation is the need to regulate **hydraulic** (water-based) agricultural economies (Wittfogel 1957). States have emerged in certain arid areas to manage systems of irrigation, drainage, and flood control. Nevertheless, hydraulic agriculture is neither a sufficient nor a necessary condition for the rise of the state. That is, many societies with irrigation never developed state structure, and many states developed without hydraulic systems.

However, hydraulic agriculture does have certain implications for state formation. Water control increases production in arid lands, such as ancient Mesopotamia and Egypt. Irrigated agriculture fuels population growth because of its labor demands and its ability to feed more people. This in turn leads to enlargement of the system. The expanding hydraulic system supports larger and denser concentrations of people. Interpersonal problems increase, and conflicts over access to water and irrigated land become more frequent. Political systems may arise to regulate interpersonal relations and the means of production.

Larger hydraulic works can sustain towns and cities and become essential to their subsistence. Given such urban dependence, regulators protect the economy by mobilizing crews to maintain and repair the hydraulic system. These life-and-death functions enhance the authority of state officials. Thus, growth in hydraulic systems is often, but not always, associated with state formation.

Ecological Diversity

Some anthropologists have suggested that states tend to arise in areas of ecological diversity in order to regulate the production and exchange of products between zones. What about this theory? Although ecological diversity and interzonal regulation do strengthen state organization, such diversity is neither necessary nor sufficient to cause state formation. Diversity is a matter of scale, and state formation has occurred in places without much environmental diversity—the Nile Valley, for example. Furthermore, in many areas with environmental diversity, no indigenous states developed. Finally, diversity is as much a result as a cause of state formation. As the states grow, they create diversity, promoting regional and local specialization in the production, manufacture, and supply of goods and services.

Long-Distance Trade Routes

Another theory is that states develop at strategic locations in regional trade networks. These sites include points of supply or exchange, such as crossroads of caravan routes, and places (e.g., mountain passes and river narrows) situated so as to threaten or halt trade between centers. Like ecological diversity, features of regional trade can certainly contribute to state formation. Here again, however, the cause is generalized but neither necessary nor sufficient. Although long-distance trade has been important in the evolution of many states and does eventually develop in all states, it can follow rather than precede state formation. Furthermore, long-distance trade also occurs in the tribal societies, such as those of Papua–New Guinea, where no states developed.

Population Growth, Warfare, and Environmental Circumscription

Carneiro (1970) proposed a theory that incorporates three factors working together instead of a single cause of state formation. (We call a theory involving multiple factors or variables a **multivariate** theory.) Wherever and whenever *environmental circumscription* (or *resource concentration*), *increasing population*, and *warfare* exist, says Carneiro, state formation will begin. Environmental circumscription may be physical or social. Physically circumscribed environments include small islands and, in arid areas, river plains, oases, and valleys with streams. Social circumscription exists when neighboring societies block expansion, emigration, or access to resources. When strategic resources are concentrated in limited areas—even when no obstacles to migration exists—the effects are similar to those of circumscription.

Coastal Peru, one of the world's most arid areas, illustrates the interaction of environmental circumscription, warfare, and population increase. Early cultivation was limited to valleys with springs. Each valley was circumscribed by the Andes mountains to the east, the Pacific Ocean to the west, and desert regions to the north and south. The transition from foraging to food production triggered population increase in these valleys (Figure 13.1). In each valley, villages got bigger. Colonists split off from the old villages and founded new ones. Rivalries and raiding developed between villages in the same valley. As villages proliferated and the valley population grew, a scarcity of land developed.

Population pressure and land shortages were developing in all the valleys. Because the valleys were circumscribed, when one village conquered another, the losers had to submit to the winners—they had nowhere else to go. Conquered villagers could keep their land only if they agreed to pay tribute to their conquerors. To do this, they had to intensify production, using new techniques to produce more food. By working harder, they managed to pay tribute while meeting their subsistence needs. Villagers brought new areas under cultivation by means of irrigation and terracing.

Those early Peruvians didn't work harder because they chose to. They were *forced* to pay tribute, accept political domination, and intensify production by factors beyond their control. Once estab-

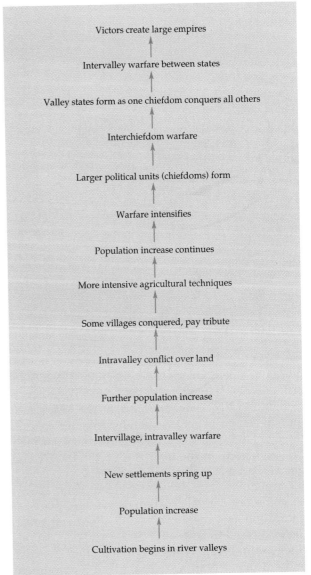

Figure 13.1 *Carneiro's multivariate approach to the origin of the state as applied to coastal Peru. In this very arid area, food production developed in narrow river valleys where water for cultivation was available (resource concentration). With cultivation, the population increased. Population pressure on land led to warfare, and some villages conquered others. Physical circumscription meant that the losers had no way to escape. The process accelerated as the population grew and as warfare and cultivation intensified. Chiefdoms, states, and empires eventually developed.*

lished, all these trends accelerated. Population grew, warfare intensified, and villages were eventually united in chiefdoms. The first states developed

Population increase, warfare, environmental circumscription, resource concentration, and agricultural intensification played key roles in ancient Peruvian state formation. The valleys in which early chiefdoms developed were circumscribed—surrounded by mountains, deserts, and the Pacific Ocean. When one village conquered another, the losers had to submit and pay tribute to the victors. They had nowhere else to go. They intensified production through irrigation and terracing. Shown here is an arid valley in the Arequipa region of Peru, where ancient agricultural terraces are still used, along with river waters for irrigation.

when one chiefdom in a valley conquered the others (Carneiro 1990). Eventually, different valleys began to fight, and the winners brought the losers into growing empires. States expanded from the coast to the highlands. By the sixteenth century, from their capital, Cuzco, in the high Andes, the Incas ruled one of the major empires of the tropics.

Carneiro's theory is very useful, but again, the association between population density and state organization is generalized rather than universal. States do tend to have large and dense populations (Stevenson 1968). However, population increase and warfare within a circumscribed environment were insufficient to trigger state formation in highland Papua–New Guinea. Certain valleys there are socially or physically circumscribed and have population densities similar to those of many states. Warfare was also present, but no states emerged. Again we are dealing with an important theory that explains many but not all cases of state formation.

States arose in different areas for many reasons. In each case, interacting causes (often comparable ones) magnified each other's effects. To explain any instance of state formation, we must search for the specific changes in the access to resources and in the regulation that fostered stratification and state machinery.

THE CHALLENGE TO THE STATE

We have seen that state organization—the presence of a central, effective government—can be traced back more than 5,500 years to the ancient Middle East–Mesopotamian civilization and its predecessors in what is now Iraq and Iran. Robert Carneiro calls the origin of the state "by all odds the most far-reaching political development in human history" (1970, p. 733). Ancient states rose and fell; some became empires, establishing control over large territories. After the collapse of the Roman empire in 476 A.D., a succession of petty kings and chiefs with limited power vied with each other and with the Roman Catholic Church in Europe for centuries. The period of weak government known as feudalism ended in 1648, the conclusion of the Thirty Years' War. To that date many historians trace the beginning of the era of the European nation-state—a model of political organization that was strengthened by industrialization, overseas expansion, colonialism, imperialism, state socialism, the Cold War, and the threat of nuclear conflagration.

Now, as a new millennium approaches, the power of government and other traditional institutions seems to be declining. Each day we can read or hear of some new challenge to the legitimacy of an existing nation-state. Simultaneously, new bases for union and division are forming. One such basis is **identity politics.** As Robert D. Kaplan (1994) notes, sociopolitical identities based on the perception of sharing a common culture, language, religion, or "race" are becoming the basis of allegiance, rather than citizenship in a nation-state, which may contain diverse social groups.

A key feature of the state is its territorial basis. Carneiro (1970, p. 733) sees the state as "an autonomous political unit, encompassing many communities within its territory." Elizabeth Brumfiel (1980, p. 459) characterizes states as "territorially extensive, administratively complex political systems in which governmental institutions monopolize the use of legal force." States bring unrelated people— members of different groups (of various sorts)—together and oblige them to pledge allegiance to a government. But in today's world more and more people are refusing to make that pledge, and territory is declining as a basis of identity.

The Role of Globalization, Transnationalism, and the Media

Globalization promotes intercultural communication, including travel and migration, which bring people from different cultures into direct contact. Long-distance communication is easier, faster, and cheaper than ever, and it extends to remote areas.

People travel more than ever, but migrants and other travelers maintain their ties with home (phoning, faxing, making visits, sending money), so that, in a sense, they live *multilocally*—in different places at once. More and more people live multilocal and transnational lives, rather than territorially confined ones.

The mass media assist in the formation and maintenance of transnational cultural, "racial," and religious identities. For example, Muslim identity and the spread of Islam across nations have been abetted by CNN's coverage of clashes between the United States and the Middle East, especially during the Persian Gulf War. For a younger world population, TV images have replaced remembrance of common colonial history or struggles for liberation in forming and maintaining identities, divisions, and oppositions. As people move, they stay linked to each other and to their homeland through the media and travel services targeted at specific ethnic, national, or religious audiences.

The mass media also propel a globally spreading culture of consumption, stimulating participation in the cash economy. Those who control the media have become key gatekeepers, regulating public access to information, a role played historically by political and religious leaders. The moguls, magnates, managers, and mouths of television and radio, including talk show hosts, have the power to direct public attention toward some issues and away from

The mass media play a role in the formation and maintenance of transnational cultural, "racial," and religious identities. Muslim identity has been abetted by CNN's coverage of clashes between the United States and the Middle East, especially during the Gulf War. As people move or study abroad, they stay linked to each other and to their homeland through the media.

others. Politicians and government officials also attempt to use radio and television for their own ends, and ordinary people increasingly use the media (e.g., talk radio) to bring their concerns to the attention of their fellow citizens and policy makers.

The media spread awareness of options and alternatives in products, services, "rights," institutions, and life styles, but they also fuel cynicism. Scandals spread through the media about corruption in government, business, religion, and sports have increased distrust of authorities, influencing electoral outcomes and policy. This process has encouraged people to clamor for "rights" and benefits and to demand more from familiar institutions.

Throughout the world, government control of the media appears to be weakening. The mass media, which bring information directly to the people, have the power both to encourage popular participation in democracy and to aid and abet the challenge to the state. One result of media exposure, in the United States, Canada, and many other countries, has been to encourage accountability by government agents. Democratization of tyrannical and authoritarian governments has been another result of exposure to media messages, as in South Africa and the Soviet Union, and potentially in China and Iran. One wonders whether slavery would have endured so long had TV sets brought daily information about external options and events to slaves.

Governments, as might be expected, are not eager to relinquish their gatekeeping authority. Many governments take steps to restrict the free flow of information. Laws are made to regulate access to pornography on the Internet. The Iranian parliament bans satellite dishes, as did China, to limit exposure to information about external events, Western culture, and alternative models of society and government.

The media have the capacity to liberate, opening people's minds, allowing for the expression of dissident and subaltern voices. (**Subaltern** means lower in rank, subordinate, traditionally lacking an influential role in decision making.) However, mass media can also reinforce stereotypes and unfounded opinions, and close people's minds to complexity, variety, and change. The promotion of excessive and unwarranted suspicion, mistrust, even hatred of public officials and institutions is a less desirable result of exposure to the media.

The challenge to the state is part of a more general pattern of uncertainty, suspicion, and disquiet concerning traditional institutions. American commentators lament the breakdown of society, the demise of "family values," and the rise of crime. Fundamentalists seek order based on strict adherence to purportedly traditional standards, beliefs, rules, and customs. Although Christian and Islamic fundamentalists recognize, decry, and attempt to redress change, they also contribute to change. In a worldwide process, new religions challenge established churches. In the United States, for example, conservative Christian TV hosts have become influential broadcasters and opinion shapers. In Latin America, evangelical Protestantism is winning millions of converts from Roman Catholicism.

Concern about lawlessness and institutional breakdown is another reflection of the decline of the state. Many states can no longer do the bare minimum that states are supposed to do: maintain law and order and keep their citizens safe. Fear of crime and the search for order and security are worldwide phenomena, found in places as different as Harlem, Guatemala, and Madagascar.

Some fears are justified, others are exaggerated. Here again the media play a role. Waves of internationally transmitted images and information reinforce the perception that the world is a dangerous place, with threats to security and order everywhere. For recipients of such messages, as for the people who face the real threats (e.g., residents of Rwanda and Burundi), the goal may become survival at the local level—getting through daily life. What seems to be collapsing is the level between the local and the global—that is, the national level.

The rise of cable TV and twenty-four-hour newscasting has blurred the distinctions among the international, the national, and the local, bringing all threats closer to home. Constant rebroadcasting magnifies risk perception. Geographical distance is obscured by the barrage of "bad news" received daily from so many places. Many viewers have no idea how far away the disasters and threats really are; Chicago, London, and Kinshasa may be just down the block.

The Collapse of Mass Culture as a Challenge to the State

Following the Second World War through the early 1960s, the United States was "one nation indivisible" ("under God" was added to the Pledge of Allegiance under President Eisenhower), a "melting pot" united by mass culture, abetted by the spread of television. The draft provided a common experience for millions of men who were called up for military service. A fairly uniform public school system taught kids nationwide to read the same stories about Dick, Jane, and their pets. With TV a novelty and just two or three networks, Americans shared common programming. Housewives watched, and bought, their soaps, which they used to wash clothes purchased in downtown department stores in their new mass-produced appliances.

Today's America is another world. Contributing to the transformation were the civil-rights and antiwar movements and the white backlash of the 1960s and 1970s. Unity and union eventually yielded to diversity and dissension—in the United States and, more recently, in the former U.S.S.R. In North America the trend toward diversification has been the result of many factors: political mobilization and identity politics, immigration, and resistance to homogenization through mass media and education.

One key development in North American culture since the 1970s, especially evident in the media, has been a general shift from "massification" to "segmental appeal." An increasingly differentiated nation celebrates diversity and fosters identity politics. The mass media—print and electronic—join the trend, measuring various "demographics" and aiming their products and messages at particular segments, rather than at an undifferentiated mass audience. Television, films, radio, music, magazines, and Internet news groups all gear their topics, formats, and styles toward particular homogeneous segments of the population (i.e., "interest groups" and target audiences). In particular, cable TV and the videocassette have helped direct television—the most important mass medium—away from the networks' cherished mass audiences toward particular viewing segments.

In North America, special-interest audiences are proliferating as part of a general pattern of increasing specialization and diversification, a key feature of contemporary lives. High technology has the capacity to tear all of us apart as it brings some of us together. The Internet, the fax machine, and satellite dishes establish virtual communities and instantaneous communication. National boundaries are permeable; new units form; people participate in multiple social systems and play various roles depending on the situation.

The New World Disorder

Different parts of the world are more connected now than ever before, but *dis*integration also surrounds us. Nations have dissolved, along with political blocks (the Warsaw Pact nations) and ideologies (communism). Kaplan (1994) suggests that internal diversity may doom many nation-states. Identity politics fractures countries into divisions based on "race," class, ethnicity, language, religion, age, gender, and sexual orientation. Kaplan speculates that regional and ethnic identities may disrupt the United States and Canada, but he foresees a successful future for a potentially independent Quebec, which he sees as a viable potential nation based on a single religion (Catholicism) and dominance of French language and culture.

With the end of the Cold War, the ideological, political, and military bases for international alliances have been largely replaced by a focus on trade and economic issues. NAFTA, GATT, and the EEC create economic unions that may come into conflict with national interests. A southern-cone economic union is forming in South America, and a similar movement is under way in southern Africa, with the end of war and repression in many nations there.

Regional and ethnic identities can challenge the unity of the United States and Canada. The movement for an independent Quebec aims to create a new nation-state based on a single religion (Catholicism) and dominance of French language and culture.

The great sociopolitical paradox of today's world is that both integration and disintegration are increasing. Economic interests and new technologies establish new linkages, even as those and other forces erode or destroy old associations and institutions. Contradicting the opinions expressed every day on American call-in radio, a global perspective makes it clear that government is not getting stronger. Rather, governments are weaker, less respected, and less relevant than they were fifty years ago. Established political structures are being challenged worldwide. West Africa and Eastern Europe are full of "failed states." The North American airwaves reveal and promote a lack of respect for government and "public servants" that is unprecedented in world history. Never have so many people said so many disparaging things to so many others about their leaders.

In nation after nation the media report actual and alleged corruption and scandals involving political figures. Distrust of government and its representatives increases. Potential public servants are reluctant to subject themselves and their families to a system of media scrutiny that seems to have run wild. Dozens of members of the U.S. Congress have declined to run for reelection. It becomes harder to attract outstanding people to government service.

The Bush presidency proudly proclaimed a New World Order in the making, with the fall of the Soviet Union and the end of the Cold War. But disorder is rampant. In many places (Bosnia, West Africa, Somalia, Rwanda) the world seems to have reverted to feudal times. Without state socialism and Soviet support, Yugoslavia disintegrated into ministates. With no "Communist threat," First World nations have cut their support for puppet regimes and loyal Third World allies. American foreign aid to African governments is decreasing at precisely the time when some of them (particularly in southern Africa) are becoming more democratic. Given the economic and ecological disruption caused by population increase and by the miniwars spawned by Cold War rivalries in places like Angola and Mozambique, it is questionable whether democratic institutions will be able to survive without continued external support.

Social chaos, political disintegration, and lawlessness are evident everywhere, despite the spread of democratization, even as communication channels, migration, and tourism increasingly link people and nations in a worldwide web. Kaplan describes the collapse of governmental authority in West Africa, which he presents as a preview of the "coming anarchy" of the twenty-first century.

Even states like Somalia that are not multiethnic or linguistically diverse are being challenged throughout the world, most notably perhaps in Africa. Hutu and Tutsi kill one another in Rwanda and Burundi as government control passes chaotically from one faction to the other. The difference

In Burundi and Rwanda (shown here), Hutu and Tutsi kill one another as government control passes from one faction to the other. The difference between Tutsi and Hutu is one of different social strata, rather than language, "race," or ethnicity. Rwanda's civil war has raged without evident racial difference and after generations of intermarriage that make any physical contrast between Tutsi (stereotyped as taller) and Hutu all but indistinguishable.

between Tutsi (the numeric minority, but socioeconomically favored stratum) and Hutu is one of different social strata, rather than language, "race," or ethnicity. This civil war has raged without evident racial difference and after generations of intermarriage that make any physical contrast between Tutsi (stereotyped as taller) and Hutu all but indistinguishable. And militant pro-Hutu and pro-Tutsi voices on the radio have helped keep the hate alive.

State control and intervention are sporadic and ineffective in large areas of East Africa and Madagascar, where crimes go unpunished and where rustlers raid cattle for international export. Business-savvy cattle raiders from Tanzania's Kuria tribe take their prey to Kenya to sell for a higher price than they can get in Tanzania. The export network is so wide that some of the cattle wind up in Saudi Arabia (Michael Fleisher, personal communication). In many parts of the world, people like the Kuria are easing trade barriers on their own, arranging their own informal economic unions long before governments get around to formal agreements. Routinely, people manage to market their products in neighboring nations where they fetch higher prices. In some parts of West Africa, foreign beers are easier to get and cheaper than local brews (Kaplan 1994). Many nation-states, after all, have been artificial, colonial creations. In West Africa, for example, by geographic logic, several adjacent countries could be one (Togo, Ghana, Ivory Coast, Guinea, Guinea-Bissau, Sierra Leone, Liberia). Instead, they are separated by linguistic, political, and economic contrasts promoted under colonialism. Small wonder they are unstable.

Increasingly, governments fail to maintain law and order. Neither in Rio de Janeiro, Brazil, nor in major West African cities can governments protect their citizens (New York City, Los Angeles, and Detroit are somewhat better in this respect). In Freetown, Sierra Leone, as Kaplan (1994) reports, the streets are unsafe at night. In Rio's shantytowns, drug lords wage war against one another and police, and their bullets ricochet through nearby middle-class apartments. Exclusive restaurants hire armed guards to escort their patrons to and from the parking lot.

Urban and rural citizens of Tanzania, Kenya, and Madagascar fear criminals, especially cattle rustlers, who may even be members of their own extended families. Madagascar's rice farmers now must sleep

In the shantytowns of Rio de Janeiro, drug lords wage war against one another and police. They hire armed guards, like this boy, to protect their turf. Skirmishes between rival gangs, and between drug lords and police, send bullets ricocheting through nearby middle-class apartments.

in their fields to fend off poachers at harvest time. In Somalia, clan leaders defy both state organization and the United Nations. There is almost no law enforcement in Papua–New Guinea. Thriving networks of illegal drug trafficking link South America, South Africa, Zambia, Europe, North America, and India.

In Madagascar, the national government, now weakened, can, however, be traced back two centuries to indigenous processes of state formation comparable to those that occurred in many parts of Africa. Before and after French colonial rule was imposed in 1896, Madagascar has experienced periods of strong and weak state authority. Other nations have witnessed similar cycles: To historians the current "Balkanization" of the Balkans is not surprising. Today, as in much of Africa, Madagascar's government is weak and economically dependent on outsiders. After independence in 1960, French influence eventually yielded to Soviet and Chinese assistance. During the 1980s, like many other Third World nations, Madagascar became increasingly dependent on international loans and grants. Currently, the national government has relinquished some of its regulatory authority to international nongovernmental organizations (NGOs) with substantial funding from USAID (the U.S. Agency for International Development).

NGOs and Rights Movements

The proliferation of nongovernmental organizations is another major trend of late-twentieth-century political organization that poses a challenge to the state. Over the past decade, the allocation of international aid for "development" has systematically challenged government authority in many countries by increasing the share of funds awarded to NGOs, which have gained prominence as social-change enablers. NGOs directly challenge government authority at various levels, sometimes militantly. In northeastern Brazil, for example, many NGOs see it as their business to confront traditional politicians and elites. In theory, such organizations should work with local NGOs; in fact, the larger national and international NGOs dominate. There are too few local organizations, and they are inadequately funded.

In the "development community" (e.g., the World Bank, USAID, UNDP or United Nations Development Programme), it is widely assumed that a strategy of channeling funds to NGOs, PVOs (private voluntary organizations), and GROs (grassroots organizations)—rather than government—will maximize immediate benefits to community residents. NGOs are generally viewed as more responsive to local wishes and more effective in encouraging community participation than are the authoritarian and totalitarian governments. However, this strategy is being increasingly criticized, especially in cases (e.g., Madagascar) in which powerful, expatriate-staffed international NGOs are allowed to encroach on the regulatory authority of existing governments. There is a real issue of neocolonialism when it is assumed that NGOs with headquarters in Europe or North America are better representatives of the people than are their own elected governments, although certainly they may be. (**Neocolonialism** is a revival or new form of colonialism—the political, social, economic, and cultural domination of a territory and its people by a foreign power, often justified by the assertion that foreigners are more enlightened at governing than are natives of the colonial area.) In a typical less-developed country (**LDC**), many well-educated people and prominent intellectuals are part of government (e.g., in universities, administration, or elective office). Such people often perceive a strategy that removes them from decisions about the allocation of benefits as a throwback to colonialism.

Posing yet another challenge to existing nation-states are the "rights" movements (human, cultural, animal), which have emerged within the arena of identity politics. Minority groups demand certain "rights"; political movements take up the cause, and media pressure becomes intense. The idea of **human rights** challenges the nation-state by invoking a realm of justice and morality beyond and superior to particular countries, cultures, and religions. Human rights, usually seen as vested in individuals, includes the right to speak freely, to hold religious beliefs without persecution, and to not be enslaved or imprisoned without charge. The domain of human rights condemns state-perpetrated injustices. These rights are not ordinary laws, which particular governments make and enforce. Human rights are seen as *inalienable* (nation-states cannot abridge or terminate them) and *metacultural* (larger than and superior to individual nations and cultures).

The doctrine of human rights challenges the state by appeal to a level *above and beyond* it; cultural rights apply to units *within* the state. **Cultural rights** are vested not in individuals but in identifiable *groups,* such as religious and ethnic minorities and indigenous societies. Cultural rights include a group's ability to preserve its culture, to raise its children in the ways of its forebears, to continue its language, and not to be deprived of its economic base by the nation-state in which it is located (Greaves 1995).

Certain rights are codified: Nation-states have agreed to them in writing. Four United Nations documents—the UN Charter; the Universal Declaration of Human Rights; the Covenant on Economic, Social and Cultural Rights; and the Covenant on Civil and Political Rights—describe nearly all the human rights that have been internationally recognized. However, almost all of them are seen as vested in *individuals* rather than groups. As Thomas Greaves (1995) notes, nation-states have been slow to recognize group rights, which may seriously challenge government sovereignty, by legitimating fundamental loyalties to groups *within* the state, thus offsetting the state's exclusive hegemony.

Many countries have signed pacts endorsing, for cultural minorities in nation-states, such group rights as self-determination; some degree of home rule; and the right to practice the group's religion, culture, and language. Greaves (1995) points out that because cultural rights are mainly uncodified, their realization must rely on the same mechanisms that create them—pressure, publicity, and politics. Such rights have been published by a wave of political assertiveness throughout the world, in which the media and NGOs have played a prominent part. This has been accomplished fairly peacefully, through the law and established political channels, in the Western Hemisphere. The process has been much more disruptive, involving warfare, ethnic conflict, separatism, and genocide in Eastern Europe and Africa.

The notion of indigenous intellectual property rights (**IPR**) has arisen in an attempt to conserve each society's cultural base—its core beliefs and principles. IPR is claimed as a group right—a cultural right, allowing indigenous groups to control who may know and use their collective knowledge and its applications. Much traditional cultural knowledge has commercial value; examples include ethnomedicine (traditional medical knowledge and techniques), cosmetics, cultivated plants, foods, folklore, arts, crafts, songs, dances, costumes, and rituals. According to the IPR concept, a particular group may determine how indigenous knowledge and its products may be used and distributed, and the level of compensation required.

As in the rights discussion, issues involving property and ownership are also debated at levels *within* the state (e.g., IPR of minorities) and *beyond* the state. Challenging the state from above (with an appeal to a more exalted—global—moral order), especially abetted by environmentalist NGOs, is the idea that resources within nations (e.g., biodiversity, rain forests) belong to the world. This claim disputes the notion of national sovereignty, and nations, not surprisingly, reject it. Brazilians, for example, are incensed when informed by Northerners that the Amazon is a global resource. Another example is a June 8, 1995, *New York Times* article about the pollution-related mass death of birds in Mexico. The article called the birds a "North American" rather than a Mexican resource, and certain environmental provisions of NAFTA (the North American Free Trade Agreement) were invoked to save future birds.

The notion of indigenous property rights has arisen in an attempt to conserve each society's cultural base, which may have substantial commercial value. One example is ethnomedicine—traditional medical knowledge and techniques, including the use of medicinal plants, such as this one from the forests of Papua–New Guinea.

From State Formation to Government Decline

Since the nineteenth century, tacitly accepting certain ideas about human progress, anthropologists have tended to regard the growth and strengthening of political institutions as a general process. Courses on "state formation" and "the evolution of political organization" have been standard in the anthropology curriculum. Today's world forces a reappraisal. We know from history that states rise and fall; we are currently seeing more weakness and failure than vitality and growth in government institutions. Nation-states are increasingly challenged by information flows, nongovernmental organizations, identity politics, and economic features of a globalizing world. If a world state is to form, it will not do so in the near future.

SUMMARY

The first states emerged in the Old World, in Mesopotamia, about 5,500 years ago. The first chiefdoms had developed a thousand years earlier, but few survive today. States also arose in two parts of the Western Hemisphere—Mesoamerica and the central Andes. The state is an autonomous political unit encompassing many communities; its central government has the power to collect taxes, draft people for work or war, and decree and enforce laws. The state is defined as a form of sociopolitical organization based on central government and socioeconomic stratification—a division of society into classes. Early states are known as archaic, or nonindustrial, states, in contrast to modern industrial nation-states.

The chiefdom is a form of sociopolitical organization intermediate and transitional between tribes and states. Like states and unlike tribes, chiefdoms are characterized by permanent regional regulation and differential access to strategic resources, but chiefdoms lack stratification. Unlike states but like bands and tribes, chiefdoms are organized by kinship, descent, and marriage.

State formation remained incomplete, and only chiefdoms emerged in several areas, including the circum-Caribbean, lowland Amazonia, the southeastern United States, and Polynesia. Between the rise of food production and the Roman empire, much of Europe was organized at the chiefdom level, to which it reverted after Rome's collapse. Much of our ethnographic knowledge of chiefdoms comes from Polynesia, where they were common at the time of European exploration. Although other chiefdoms calculated seniority differently and had shorter genealogies, the concern for genealogy and seniority and the absence of sharp gaps between elites and commoners are features of all chiefdoms. Chiefdoms have redistribution, a flow of resources to and then from a central office.

The sociologist Max Weber defined three related dimensions of social stratification: wealth, power, and prestige. In archaic states—for the first time in human evolution—contrasts in wealth, power, and prestige between entire groups (social strata) of men and women came into being. A socioeconomic stratum includes people of both sexes and all ages. The superordinate—higher or elite—stratum enjoys privileged access to wealth, power, and other valued resources. The lower stratum is subordinate. Its members' access to resources is limited by the privileged group.

Certain systems and subsystems with specialized functions are found in all states. They include population control, judiciary, enforcement, and fiscal. In archaic states, these subsystems were integrated by a ruling system or government composed of civil, military, and religious officials. To know whom they govern, all states conduct censuses and demarcate boundaries. States have laws based on precedent and legislative proclamations. To handle disputes and crimes, all states have courts and judges. Governments intervene to preserve internal peace, halt blood feuds, and regulate previously private disputes. All states have agents to enforce judicial decisions.

The major concern of government is to defend hierarchy, property, and the power of the law. The government suppresses internal disorder (with the police) and defends the nation against external threats (with the military). As a relatively new form of sociopolitical organization, states have competed successfully with less complex societies throughout the world.

A financial or fiscal subsystem is necessary to support rulers, nobles, officials, judges, military personnel, and other specialists. The state does not bring more freedom or leisure to the common people, who usually work harder than people do in nonstates.

People did not choose but were forced to accept state organization. Complex political organization develops to handle regulatory problems as the population grows and the economy increases in scale and diversity. Anthropologists and historians have reconstructed sequences of events and processes leading to formation of the state in several areas. Many factors always contribute to this process, with the effects of one magnifying those of the others. Although some contributing factors appear again and again, no single one is always present.

The most important contributing factors are hydraulic (water-based) agricultural economies, ecological diversity, long-distance trade, population growth, warfare, and environmental circumscription. Coastal Peru, one of the world's most arid areas, illustrates the interaction of environmental circumscription, warfare, and population increase.

Today, the power and role of government seem to be declining, as new bases for union and division form. One such basis is identity politics, involving shared culture, language, religion, or "race," rather than citizenship in a nation-state. A key feature of the state is its territorial basis, and territory is declining as a basis of identity, with the rise of multilocality and transnationalism.

One way the mass media challenge the nation-state is by promoting transnational identities. Those who control the media are key gatekeepers, like traditional political and religious leaders. The media have the capacity to liberate, opening people's minds and allowing the expression of many voices. But suspicion and hatred of public officials and institutions is another result of media exposure. Many states can no longer maintain law and order.

The collapse of mass culture has also posed a challenge to the state. In North America the trend toward diversification has been the result of many factors—political mobilization and identity politics, immigration, and resistance to homogenization through mass media and education. One key development in North America is the shift from massification to segmental appeal, with the spread of special-interest groups and audiences.

A sociopolitical paradox of today's world is that both integration and disintegration are increasing. The ideological, political, and military bases of international alliances have been largely replaced by a focus on trade and economic issues. Social chaos, political disintegration, and lawlessness are evident worldwide.

The spread of nongovernmental organizations is another relevant trend. The idea of human rights also challenges the nation-state by imagining a realm of justice and morality beyond and superior to particular countries, cultures, and religions. Cultural rights are seen as vested not in individuals but in groups, such as religious and ethnic minorities and indigenous societies within a nation-state. IPR, indigenous intellectual property rights, are being claimed as a group right—a cultural right, allowing indigenous groups to control who may know and use their collective knowledge and its applications.

Previously, anthropologists have tended to regard the growth and strengthening of political institutions as a general process, but today's world forces a reappraisal. Government weakness and failure are more apparent than vitality and growth.

GLOSSARY

archaic state: Nonindustrial state.

cultural rights: Doctrine that certain rights are vested not in individuals but in identifiable groups, such as religious and ethnic minorities and indigenous societies. Cultural rights include a group's ability to preserve its culture, to raise its children in the ways of its forebears, to continue its language, and not to be deprived of its economic base by the nation-state in which it is located.

differential access: Unequal access to resources; basic attribute of chiefdoms and states. Superordinates have favored access to such resources, while the access of subordinates is limited by superordinates.

fiscal: Pertaining to finances and taxation.

human rights: Doctrine that invokes a realm of justice and morality beyond and superior to particular countries, cultures, and religions. Human rights, usually seen as vested in individuals, would include the right to speak freely, to hold religious beliefs without persecution, and to not be enslaved, or imprisoned without charge.

hydraulic systems: Systems of water management, including irrigation, drainage, and flood control. Often associated with agricultural societies in arid and river environments.

ideal types: Labels that make contrasts seem more extreme than they really are (e.g., big and little). Instead of discrete categories, there is actually a continuum from one type to the next.

identity politics: Sociopolitical identities based on the perception of sharing a common culture, language, religion, or "race," rather than citizenship in a nation-state, which may contain diverse social groups.

IPR: Intellectual property rights, consisting of each society's cultural base—its core beliefs and principles. IPR is claimed as a group right—a cultural right, allowing indigenous groups to control who may know and use their collective knowledge and its applications.

LDC: A less-developed country; by contrast with an industrial nation.

multivariate: Involving multiple factors or variables.

neocolonialism: A revival or new form of colonialism—the political, social, economic, and cultural domination of a territory and its people by a foreign power, often justified by the assertion that foreigners are more enlightened at governing than are natives of the colonial area.

office: Permanent political position.

power: The ability to exercise one's will over others—to do what one wants; the basis of political status.

prestige: Esteem, respect, or approval for acts, deeds, or qualities considered exemplary.

stratification: Characteristic of a system with socioeconomic strata; see *stratum*.

stratum: One of two or more groups that contrast in regard to social status and access to strategic resources. Each stratum includes people of both sexes and all ages.

subaltern: Lower in rank, subordinate, traditionally lacking an influential role in decision making.

subordinate: The lower, or underprivileged, group in a stratified system.

sumptuary goods: Items whose consumption is limited to the elite.

superordinate: The upper, or privileged, group in a stratified system.

wealth: All a person's material assets, including income, land, and other types of property; the basis of economic status.

STUDY QUESTIONS

1. What are the similarities and differences between chiefdoms and tribes?
2. What are the similarities and differences between chiefdoms and states?
3. What is redistribution, and what are its economic advantages? How does it differ from taxation?
4. What are the four special-purpose subsystems found in all states?
5. What is the relationship among state organization, conflicts, and warfare?
6. What are the advantages and disadvantages of the state from the citizen's perspective? Why have people been willing to sacrifice personal freedom to live in states?
7. How have anthropologists attempted to explain state formation? Which do you think is the best explanation, and why?
8. What is identity politics, and how does it challenge the basis of state organization?
9. What are some of the ways in which the mass media challenge the nation-state?
10. What are some of the repercussions of the decline of mass culture? What is the difference between massification and segmental appeal? Give three examples of segmental appeal.
11. What does it mean to say that both integration and disintegration are increasing?
12. What factors have contributed to the spread of nongovernmental organizations, and how have those groups contributed to the decline of nation-states?
13. What is the doctrine of human rights and how does that doctrine relate to state organization?
14. What do the concepts cultural rights and IPR mean?

SUGGESTED ADDITIONAL READING

ARNOLD, B., AND B. GIBSON, EDS.
1995   *Celtic Chiefdom, Celtic State.* New York: Cambridge University Press. This collection of articles examines the structure and development of Europe's prehistoric Celtic societies and debates whether they were chiefdoms or states.

COHEN, R., AND E. R. SERVICE, EDS.
1978   *Origins of the State: The Anthropology of Political Evolution.* Philadelphia: Institute for the Study of Human Issues. Several articles on state formation in many areas.

DRENNAN, R. D., AND C. A. URIBE, EDS.
1987   *Chiefdoms in the Americas.* Landon, MD: University Press of America. Chiefdoms in the precolonial Western Hemisphere.

EARLE, T.
1991   *Chiefdoms: Power, Economy, and Ideology.* New York: Cambridge University Press. Ten case studies illustrate the dynamics of chiefdoms as political institutions.

FLANNERY, K. V.
1972   The Cultural Evolution of Civilizations. *Annual Review of Ecology and Systematics* 3: 399–426. Survey of theories of state origins.

FOX, J. W.
1987   *Maya Postclassic State Formation.* Cambridge: Cambridge University Press. The role of the "segmentary state" among the Mayas.

FRIEDMAN, J., AND M. J. ROWLANDS, EDS.
1978   *The Evolution of Social Systems.* Pittsburgh, PA:

University of Pittsburgh Press. Twenty studies of social change, including the rise of the state.

JOHNSON, A. W., AND T. EARLE, EDS.
1987   *The Evolution of Human Society: From Forager Group to Agrarian State.* Stanford, CA: Stanford University Press. Recent comprehensive look at sociocultural evolution.

JONES, G., AND R. KRAUTZ
1981   *The Transition to Statehood in the New World.* Cambridge: Cambridge University Press. Processes of state formation, including chiefdoms, in the Americas.

KIRCH, P. V.
1984   *The Evolution of the Polynesian Chiefdoms.* Cambridge: Cambridge University Press. Diversity and sociopolitical complexity in native Oceania.

KOTTAK, C. P.
1980   *The Past in the Present: History, Ecology, and Cultural Variation in Highland Madagascar.* Ann Arbor: University of Michigan Press. Examines the process of state formation using ethnohistorical and ethnographic data and relates this historical process to contemporary cultural variation.

PATTERSON, T. C.
1993   *Archaeology: The Historical Development of Civilizations,* 2nd ed. Englewood Cliffs, NJ: Prentice-Hall. The emergence of states and civilizations in several areas.

READE, J.
1991   *Mesopotamia.* Cambridge, MA: Harvard University Press. The origin of irrigation, writing, and mathematics; surveys the world's first civilization from prehistoric times to the rise of Babylon.

SAGGS, H.
1989   *Civilization before Greece and Rome.* New Haven, CT: Yale University Press. Overview of the earliest states.

SERVICE, E. R.
1975   *Origins of the State and Civilization: The Process of Cultural Evolution.* New York: W. W. Norton. State formation accessed through several case studies.

SIMONS, A.
1995   *Networks of Dissolution: Somalia Undone.* Boulder, CO: Westview. The dissolution of the Somali state, at national, regional, and local levels.

STEPONATIS, V.
1986   Prehistoric Archaeology in the Southeastern United States. *Annual Review of Anthropology* 15: 363–404. Overview of the archaeology of an area of chiefdoms.

TAINTER, J.
1987   *The Collapse of Complex Societies.* New York: Cambridge University Press. Why ancient states failed.

TRIGGER, B. G.
1995   *Early Civilizations: Ancient Egypt in Context.* New York: Columbia University Press. Considers the Incas (Inka); the Shang and western Chou of China; the Aztecs and Mayas of Mesoamerica; the Yoruba and Benin of West Africa; Mesopotamia; and ancient Egypt.

CHAPTER 14

KINSHIP AND DESCENT

KIN GROUPS AND KINSHIP CALCULATION
Biological Kin Types and Kinship Calculation

KIN GROUPS

THE NUCLEAR FAMILY
Industrialism, Stratification, and Family Organization
Recent Changes in North American Kinship Patterns
The Nuclear Family among Foragers

Box: *Brady Bunch* Nirvana

TRIBAL SOCIAL ORGANIZATION
Lineages and Clans
Unilineal Descent Groups and Unilocal Residence
Flexibility in Descent-Group Organization

KINSHIP TERMINOLOGY
Kinship Terminology on the Parental Generation
Relevance of Kinship Terminology

The kinds of societies that anthropologists have traditionally studied have stimulated a strong interest in systems of kinship and marriage. Kinship—as vitally important in daily life in nonindustrial societies as work outside the home is in our own—has become an essential part of anthropology because of its importance to the people we study. We are ready to take a closer look at the systems of kinship, descent, and marriage that have organized human life for much of our history.

KIN GROUPS AND KINSHIP CALCULATION

Anthropologists study the kin *groups* that are significant in a society as well as **kinship calculation**—the system by which people in a society reckon kin relationships. Ethnographers quickly recognize social divisions (groups) within any society they study. During field work, they learn about significant groups by observing their activities and composition. People often live in the same village or neighborhood or work, pray, or celebrate together because they are related in some way. To understand the social structure, an ethnographer must investigate such kin ties. For example, the most significant local groups may consist of descendants of the same grandfather. These people may live in neighboring houses, farm adjoining fields, and help each other in everyday tasks. Other groups, perhaps based on other kin links, get together less often.

To study kinship calculation, an ethnographer must first determine the word or words for different types of "relatives" used in a particular language and then ask questions such as, "Who are your relatives?" Kinship, like race and gender (discussed in other chapters), is culturally constructed. This means that some biological kin are considered to be relatives whereas others are not. Through questioning, the ethnographer discovers the specific genealogical relationships between "relatives" and the person who has named them—the **ego**. By posing the same questions to several informants, the ethnographer learns about the extent and direction of kinship calculation in that society. The ethnographer also begins to understand the relationship between kinship calculation and kin groups—how people use kinship to create and maintain personal ties and to join social groups. In some of the kinship charts that follow, the black square labeled "ego" (Latin for *I*) identifies the person whose kinship calculation is being examined.

Biological Kin Types and Kinship Calculation

At this point we may distinguish between **kin terms** (the words used for different relatives in a particular language) and **biological kin types.** We designate biological kin types with the letters and symbols shown in Figure 14.1. *Biological kin type* refers to an actual genealogical relationship (e.g., father's brother) as opposed to a kin term (e.g., *uncle*).

Kin terms reflect the social construction of kinship in a given culture. A kin term may (and usually does) lump together several genealogical relationships. In English, for instance, we use *father* primarily for one kin type—the genealogical father. How-

Figure 14.1 *Kinship symbols and biological kin type notation.*

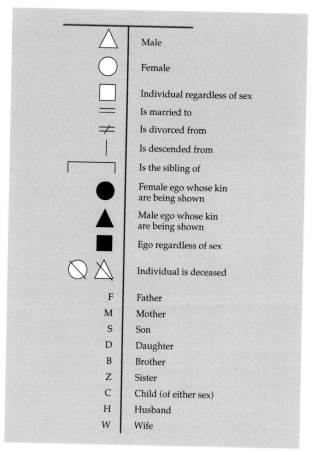

ever, *father* can be extended to an adoptive father or stepfather—and even to a priest. *Grandfather* includes mother's father and father's father. The term *cousin* lumps together several kin types. Even the more specific *first cousin* includes mother's brother's son (MBS), mother's brother's daughter (MBD), mother's sister's son (MZS), mother's sister's daughter (MZD), father's brother's son (FBS), father's brother's daughter (FBD), father's sister's son (FZS), father's sister's daughter (FZD). *First cousin* thus lumps together at least eight biological kin types.

Uncle encompasses mother's and father's brothers, and *aunt* includes mother's and father's sisters. We also use *uncle* and *aunt* for the spouses of our "blood" aunts and uncles. We use the same term for mother's brother and father's brother because we perceive them as being the same sort of relative. Calling them *uncles*, we distinguish between them and another kin type, F, whom we call *Father, Dad,* or *Pop*. In many societies, however, it is common to call a father and a father's brother by the same term. Later we'll see why.

In the United States and Canada, the *nuclear family* (a kin group composed of parents and children residing together) continues to be the most important group based on kinship. This is true despite an increased incidence of single parenthood, divorce, and remarriage. The nuclear family's relative isolation from other kin groups in modern nations reflects geographical mobility within an industrial economy with sale of labor for cash. (The nuclear family is also the most important kin group in many foraging societies for reasons that will be discussed later.)

It's reasonable for North Americans to distinguish between relatives who belong to their nuclear families and those who don't. We are more likely to grow up with our parents than with our aunts or uncles. We tend to see our parents more often than we see our uncles and aunts, who may live in different towns and cities. We often inherit from our parents, but our cousins have first claim to inherit from our aunts and uncles. If our marriage is stable, we see our children daily as long as they remain at home. They are our heirs. We feel closer to them than to our nieces and nephews.

American kinship calculation and kin terminology reflect these social features. Thus the term *uncle* distinguishes between the kin types MB and FB on

the one hand and the kin type F on the other. However, this term also lumps kin types together. We use the same term for MB and FB, two different kin types. We do this because American kinship calculation is **bilateral**—traced equally through males and females, for example, father and mother. Both kinds of uncle are brothers of one of our parents. We think of both as roughly the same kind of relative.

"No," you may object, "I'm closer to my mother's brother than to my father's brother." That may be. However, in a representative sample of American students, we would find a split, with some favoring one side and some favoring the other. We'd actually expect a bit of **matrilateral skewing**—a preference for relatives on the mother's side. This occurs because—for many reasons—when contemporary children are raised by just one parent, it's more likely to be the mother than the father. Thus, in the United States in 1993, 23 percent of all children lived in fatherless homes versus 3 percent residing in motherless homes and 71 percent living with both parents (*American Almanac* 1994–1995, p. 66).

Bilateral kinship means that people tend to perceive kin links through males and females as being similar or equivalent. This bilaterality is expressed in interaction with, living with or near, and rights to inherit from relatives. We don't usually inherit from uncles, but if we do, there's about as much chance that we'll inherit from the father's brother as from the mother's brother. We don't usually live with either aunt, but if we do, the chances are about the same that it will be the father's sister as the mother's sister.

KIN GROUPS

The nuclear family is one kind of kin group that is widespread in human societies. Other kin groups include extended families (families consisting of three or more generations) and descent groups—lineages and clans. *Descent groups*, which are composed of people claiming common ancestry, are basic units in the social organization of nonindustrial food producers.

There are important differences between nuclear families and descent groups. A descent group is *permanent;* a nuclear family lasts only as long as the parents and children remain together. Descent-group membership often is ascribed at birth (by a rule of patrilineal or matrilineal descent, as discussed in Chapter 12) and lifelong. In contrast, most people belong to at least two nuclear families at different times in their lives. They are born into a family consisting of their parents and siblings. When they reach adulthood, they may marry and establish a nuclear family that includes the spouse and eventually the children. Since most societies permit divorce, some people establish more than one family through marriage.

Anthropologists distinguish between the **family of orientation** (the family in which one is born and grows up) and the **family of procreation** (formed when one marries and has children). From the individual's point of view, the critical relationships are with parents and siblings in the family of orienta-

tion and with spouse and children in the family of procreation.

THE NUCLEAR FAMILY

Nuclear family organization is widespread but not universal. In certain societies, the nuclear family is rare or nonexistent. In other cultures, the nuclear family has no special role in social life. Other social units—most notably descent groups and extended families—can assume most or all of the functions otherwise associated with the nuclear family. In other words, there are many alternatives to nuclear family organization.

One example is provided by the Nayars, who live on the Malabar Coast of southern India. Their kinship system is matrilineal (descent is traced only through females). Traditional Nayar marriages were mere formalities. Adolescent females went through a marriage ceremony with a man, after which the girl returned home, usually without having had sex with her husband. The man returned to his own household. Thereafter, Nayar women had many sexual partners. Children became members of the mother's household and kin group; they were not considered to be relatives of the biological father. Indeed, many Nayar children didn't even know who their father was. However, for children to be legitimate, a man, often neither the genitor nor the mother's original "husband," had to go through a ritual acknowledging paternity. Nayar society therefore reproduced itself biologically without the nuclear family.

Industrialism, Stratification, and Family Organization

For many Americans and Canadians, the nuclear family is the only well-defined kin group. Family isolation arises from geographic mobility, which is associated with industrialism, so that a nuclear family focus is characteristic of many modern nations. Born into a family of orientation, North Americans leave home for work or college, and the break with parents is underway. Eventually most North Americans marry and start a family of procreation. Because less than 3 percent of the U.S. population now farms, most people aren't tied to the land. Selling our labor on the market, we often move to places where jobs are available.

In many cultures grandparents, uncles, aunts, and other nonnuclear kin play important roles in childrearing. Grandparents take an active role in child care in many parts of China. This extended family lives in China's Yunnan province.

One exception to reproduction through marriage and the nuclear family is provided by the Nayars of southern India. Their kinship system is matrilineal (descent is traced only through females), and Nayar marriages are mere formalities. Children become members of the mother's household and kin group; they are not considered to be relatives of their biological father.

Many married couples live hundreds of miles from their parents. Their jobs have determined where they live. Such a postmarital residence pattern is called **neolocality:** Married couples are expected to establish a new place of residence—a "home of their own." Among middle-class North Americans, neolocal residence is both a cultural preference and a statistical norm. Most middle-class Americans eventually establish households and nuclear families of their own.

Within stratified nations, value systems vary to some extent from class to class, and so does kinship. There are significant differences between middle-

class, poorer, and richer North Americans. For example, in the lower class the incidence of **expanded family households** (those which include nonnuclear relatives) is greater than it is in the middle class. When an expanded family household includes three or more generations, it is an **extended family.** Another type of expanded family is the **collateral household,** which includes siblings and their spouses and children.

The higher proportion of expanded family households in certain North American ethnic groups and

Compared with middle-class whites, certain ethnic groups in the United States and Canada—especially Native Americans—have a larger proportion of expanded family households. This reflects a combination of cultural values and economic necessity. Finding it difficult to survive economically as nuclear families, relatives may pool their resources in an expanded family household. Here, in Arizona, Hopi Indians assemble in such a household to celebrate an infant-naming ceremony.

classes has been explained as an adaptation to poverty (Stack 1975). Unable to survive economically as nuclear family units, relatives band together in an expanded household and pool their resources.

Poverty causes kinship values and attitudes to diverge from middle-class norms. Thus, when North Americans raised in poverty achieve financial success, they often feel obligated to provide considerable financial help to less fortunate relatives. Upper-class households, living in bigger homes supported by greater wealth, may also diverge from the nuclear family norm. Upper-class households can afford to lodge and feed extended family kin, guests, and servants.

Recent Changes in North American Kinship Patterns

Although the nuclear family remains a cultural ideal for many Americans, Figure 14.2 shows that nuclear families accounted for just 25.6 percent of American households in 1993. *Nonnuclear family arrangements now outnumber the "traditional" American household by almost four to one.* Table 14.1, which compares American and Canadian households of the 1960s with households in those countries in 1993 and 1986, demonstrates substantial change. There are several reasons for changing household composition. North Americans leave home to work, often in a different community. Women are increasingly joining men in the workforce. This often removes

them from the family of orientation while making it economically feasible to delay marriage. Furthermore, job demands compete with romantic attachments.

Single-parent families are increasing at a rapid rate. In 1960, 88 percent of American children lived with both parents versus 71 percent in 1993 (*American Almanac* 1994–1995, p. 66). The percentage of American children living in fatherless households rose from 8 percent in 1960 to 23 percent in 1993. The percentage living in motherless households increased from 1 percent in 1960 to 3 percent in 1993 (Table 14.2).

The numbers in Table 14.1 suggest that life is growing increasingly lonely for many North Americans. The disappearance of extended families and descent groups reflects the mobility of industrialism. However, even nuclear families are breaking up. In the United States the unmarried population aged eighteen and over (single, widowed, and divorced) rose from 38 million in 1970 (28 percent of all adults) to 73 million in 1993 (39 percent of all adults) (*American Almanac* 1994–1995, p. 56). To be sure, contemporary Americans maintain social lives through work, friendship, sports, clubs, religion, and organized social activities. However, the isolation from kin that these figures suggest is unprecedented in human history.

Our changing household organization has been reflected in the mass media. During the 1950s and early 1960s such television sitcoms as *Ozzie and Har-*

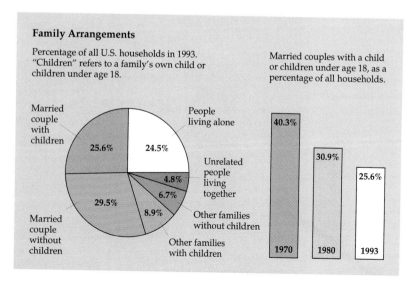

Family Arrangements

Percentage of all U.S. households in 1993. "Children" refers to a family's own child or children under age 18.

Married couple with children — 25.6%
People living alone — 24.5%
Unrelated people living together — 4.8%
Other families without children — 6.7%
Other families with children — 8.9%
Married couple without children — 29.5%

Married couples with a child or children under age 18, as a percentage of all households.

1970 — 40.3%
1980 — 30.9%
1993 — 25.6%

Figure 14.2 (*Source: American Almanac 1994–1995, pp. 59, 65.*)

Table 14.1 *Classification of North American Households, United States (1960 and 1993) and Canada (1961 and 1986)*

| | PERCENTAGE OF ALL HOUSEHOLDS | | | |
| | United States | | Canada | |
	1960	1993	1961	1986
Married with children	44	26	51	32
Married couple, no resident children	30	30	27	32
One adult	13	24	9	22
One parent and child(ren)	4	9	4	6
Other*	8	11	9	8

*Includes unrelated people living together, extended families, adult siblings, and so on.
Sources: *American Almanac* 1994–1995, p. 59; *Statistical Abstract*, 1991, p. 837.

riet and *Leave It to Beaver* portrayed "traditional" nuclear families. The incidence of **blended families** (kin units formed when parents remarry and bring their children into a new household) has risen, as represented in programs such as *The Brady Bunch*. Three-quarters of divorced Americans remarry (*Ann Arbor News* 1989). Television programs and other media presentations now routinely feature coresident "friends," "roommates," unmarried couples, "singles," single parents, unrelated retirees, hired male housekeepers, working mothers, and even "two dads." Changes in life styles are reflected by the media, which in turn help promote further modifications in our values concerning kinship, marriage, and living arrangements (Kottak 1990).

The entire range of kin attachments is narrower for North Americans, particularly those in the middle class, than it is for nonindustrial peoples. Although we recognize ties to grandparents, uncles, aunts, and cousins, we have less contact with, and depend less on, those relatives than people in other cultures do. We see this when we answer a few questions: Do we know exactly how we are related

to all our cousins? How much do we know about our ancestors, such as their full names and where they lived? How many of the people with whom we associate regularly are our relatives?

Differences in the answers to these questions by people from industrial and those from nonindustrial societies confirm the declining importance of kinship in contemporary nations. Most of the people whom middle-class North Americans see every day are either nonrelatives or members of the nuclear family. On the other hand, Stack's (1975) study of welfare-dependent families in a ghetto area of a midwestern city shows that sharing with nonnuclear relatives is an important strategy that the urban poor use to adapt to poverty.

One of the most striking contrasts between the United States and Brazil, the two most populous nations of the Western Hemisphere, is in the meaning and role of the family. Contemporary North American adults usually define their families as consisting of their husbands or wives and their children. However, when Brazilians talk about their families, they mean their parents, siblings, aunts, uncles, grandparents, and cousins. Later they add their children, but rarely the husband or wife, who has his or her own family. The children are shared by the two families. Because middle-class Americans lack an extended family support system, marriage assumes more importance. The husband-wife relationship is supposed to take precedence over either spouse's relationship with his or her own parents. This places a significant strain on North American marriages.

The cultural contrast runs even deeper. Family relationships themselves are more important in Brazil

Table 14.2 *Percentage of American Children Residing with One or Both Parents, 1960 and 1993*

	1960	1993
Both parents	88	71
Mother only	8	23
Father only	1	3
Neither parent	3	3

Source: *American Almanac* 1994–1995, p. 66.

In contemporary North America, single-parent families are increasing at a rapid rate. In 1960, 88 percent of American children lived with both parents, versus about 70 percent today. The percentage of American children living in fatherless households rose from 8 percent in 1960 to 23 percent in 1993, as the percentage of those living in motherless households also tripled, from 1 to 3 percent in 1993.

than they are in the United States. Living in a less mobile society, Brazilians stay in closer contact with their relatives, including members of the extended family. Residents of Rio de Janeiro and São Paulo, two of South America's largest cities, are reluctant to leave those urban centers to live away from family and friends. Brazilians find it hard to imagine, and unpleasant to live in, social worlds without relatives. Contrast this with a characteristic American theme—learning to live with strangers.

The Nuclear Family among Foragers

Populations with foraging economies are far removed from industrial societies in terms of social complexity. Here again, however, the nuclear family is often the most significant kin group, although in no foraging culture is the nuclear family the only group based on kinship. The two basic social units of traditional foraging societies are the nuclear family and the band.

Unlike middle-class couples in industrial nations, foragers don't usually reside neolocally. Instead, they join a band in which either the husband or the wife has relatives. However, couples and families may move from one band to another several times. Although nuclear families are ultimately as impermanent among foragers as they are in any other society, they are usually more stable than bands are.

The Brady Bunch, *a blended family, was created not through divorce, as happens so frequently in the media and in "real life" today, but through the deaths of former spouses.*

BRADY BUNCH NIRVANA

The first-year students I teach at the University of Michigan belong to a generation raised after the almost total diffusion of television into the American home. Young Americans have never known a world without TV. The tube is as familiar as Mom or Dad. Indeed, considering how common divorce has become, TV sets outlast the father in many homes. One habit I began about ten years ago, taking advantage of my students' familiarity with television, is to demonstrate changes in American kinship and marriage patterns by contrasting the programs of the fifties with more recent ones. Four decades ago, the usual TV family was a nuclear family made up of father (who often knew best), homemaker mother, and children. Examples include *Father Knows Best, Ozzie and Harriet,* and *Leave It to Beaver.* These programs were appropriate for the 1950s market, but they are out of sync with today's social and economic realities. Only 16 million American women worked outside the home in 1950, compared with three times that number today. Today less than 7 percent of American households fit the former ideal: breadwinner father, homemaker mother, and two children.

Virtually all my students have seen reruns of the more recent family series *The Brady Bunch.* The social organization of *The Brady Bunch* provides an instructive contrast with 1950s programs, because it illustrates what we call **blended family** organization. A new (blended) family forms when a widow with three daughters marries a widower with three sons. Blended families have been increasing in American society because of more frequent divorce and remarriage. During *The Brady Bunch*'s heyday, divorce remained controversial and could not give rise to a TV family. However, the first spouse's death may also lead to a blended family, as in *The Brady Bunch.*

The Brady husband-father was a successful architect. Even today, the average TV family tends to be more professional, successful, and rich than the average real-life family. The Bradys were wealthy enough to employ a housekeeper, Alice. Mirroring American culture when the program was produced, the wife's career was part-time and subsidiary. Women lucky enough to find wealthy husbands did not compete with other women—even professional housekeepers—in the work force. (It is noteworthy that when *The Bradys* was revived as a weekly series in 1990, Mrs. Brady had a full-time job.)

Students enjoy learning about anthropological techniques through culturally familiar examples. Each time I begin my kinship lecture, a few people in the class immediately recognize (from reruns) the nuclear families of the 1950s. However, as soon as I begin diagramming the Brady characters (without saying what I'm doing), students start shouting out their names: "Jan," "Bobby," "Greg," "Cindy," "Marsha," "Peter," "Mike," "Carol," "Alice." The response mounts. As the cast of characters nears completion, almost everyone has joined in. Whenever I give this kinship lecture, Anthropology 101 is guaranteed to resemble a revival meeting, as hundreds of TV-enculturated American natives shout out in unison names made almost as familiar as their parents' through exposure to television reruns.

Furthermore, as the natives participate in this chant, based on common knowledge acquired by growing up in the post-1950s United States, there is an enthusiasm, a warm glow, that my course will not recapture until the next semester's rerun of my *Brady Bunch* lecture. My students seem to find *nirvana* (a feeling of religious ecstasy) through their collective remembrance of the Bradys and in the ritual-like incantation of their names.

Some segments of our society stigmatize television as "trivial," yet the average American family owns 2.3 television sets (*World Almanac* 1992, p. 318). Given this massive penetration of the modern home (98 percent of all households), television's effects on our socialization and enculturation can hardly be trivial. Indeed, the common information and knowledge we acquire by watching the same TV programs is indisputably culture in the anthropological sense. Culture is collective, shared, meaningful. It is transmitted by conscious and unconscious learning experiences acquired by humans not through their genes but as a result of growing up in a particular society. Of the hundreds of culture bearers who have passed through the Anthropology 101 classroom over the past decade, many have been unable to recall the full names of their parents' first cousins. Some have forgotten their grandmother's maiden name. But most have absolutely no trouble identifying names and relationships in a family that exists only in television land.

Many foraging societies lacked year-round band organization. The Native American Shoshone of the Great Basin in Utah and Nevada provide an example. The resources available to the Shoshone were so meager that for most of the year families traveled alone through the countryside hunting and gathering. In certain seasons families assembled to hunt cooperatively as a band; after a few months together they dispersed.

Industrial and foraging economies do have something in common. In neither type are people tied permanently to the land. The mobility and the emphasis on small, economically self-sufficient family units promote the nuclear family as a basic kin group in both types of societies.

TRIBAL SOCIAL ORGANIZATION

Lineages and Clans

We have seen that the nuclear family is important among foragers and in industrial nations. The analogous group among nonindustrial food producers is the descent group (described in Chapter 12, where we distinguished between clans and lineages). Descent groups, unlike nuclear families, are permanent and enduring units, with new members added in every generation. Members have access to the lineage estate. Unlike the nuclear family, the descent group lives on even though specific members die.

Unilineal Descent Groups and Unilocal Residence

Most cultures have a prevailing opinion about where couples should live after they marry. Neolocality, which is the rule for most middle-class Americans, is not very common outside modern North America, Western Europe, and the European-derived cultures of Latin America. Much more common is **virilocality** (*vir* in Latin means "husband"): Married couples live with the husband's relatives. Often virilocality is associated with patrilineal descent. This makes sense. If the children of males are to become descent-group members, with rights in the father's estate, it's a good idea to raise them on that estate. This can be done if a woman moves to her husband's village rather than vice versa.

A less common postmarital residence rule that often is associated with matrilineal descent is **uxorilocality** (*uxor* in Latin means "wife"): Married couples live with the wife's relatives. Together, virilocality and uxorilocality are known as **unilocal** rules of postmarital residence.

Flexibility in Descent-Group Organization

Some descent rules admit certain people as members while excluding others. A unilineal rule uses one line only, either the female or the male. Besides the unilineal rules, there is another descent rule called nonunilineal or **ambilineal** descent. As in any descent group, membership comes through descent from a common ancestor. However, ambilineal groups differ from unilineal groups in that they do not *automatically* exclude either the children of sons or those of daughters. People can choose the group they join (for example, that of their FF, FM, MF, or MM), change their descent-group membership, or belong to two or more groups at the same time. With unilineal descent, membership is automatic—with no choice permitted. People are born members of the father's group in a patrilineal society or of the mother's group in a matrilineal society. They stay members of that group for the rest of their lives.

Before 1950, descent groups were generally described simply as patrilineal or matrilineal. If the society tended toward patrilineality, the anthropologist classified it as a patrilineal rather than an ambilineal group. The treatment of ambilineal descent as a separate category was a formal recognition that many descent systems are flexible—some more so than others.

KINSHIP TERMINOLOGY

People perceive and define kin relations differently in different cultures. In any culture, kinship terminology is a classification system, a taxonomy or typology. However, it is not a system developed by anthropologists. Rather, it is a **native taxonomy,** developed over generations by the people who live in a particular society. A native classification system is based on how people perceive similarities and differences in the things being classified.

However, anthropologists have discovered that

Most cultures have a prevailing opinion about where a couple should live after they marry; this is called a postmarital residence rule. A common rule is virilocality—the couple lives with the husband's relatives. On the top, in West Pakistan, the wedding party carries the bride from her home to her new husband's dwelling. On the bottom, in Lendak, Slovakia, women transport the bride's dowry (wedding gifts) to the groom's house.

there are a limited number of ways in which people classify their kin. People who speak very different languages may use exactly the same system of kinship terminology. This section examines the four main ways of classifying kin on the parental generation: lineal, bifurcate merging, generational, and bifurcate collateral. We also consider the social correlates of these classification systems.

Several factors influence the way people interact with, perceive, and classify relatives. For example, do certain kinds of relatives customarily live together or apart? How far apart? What benefits do they derive from each other, and what are their obligations? Are they members of the same descent group or of different descent groups? With these questions in mind, let's examine systems of kinship terminology.

Kinship Terminology on the Parental Generation

Figure 14.3 applies to kin types on the generation above ego, the first ascending generation. The letters at the top identify six biological kin types. Numbers and colors indicate the manner of classification. Where the same number and color is shown

	MB	MZ	M	F	FB	FZ
Lineal	3	4	1	2	3	4
Bifurcate merging	3	1	1	2	2	4
Generational	2	1	1	2	2	1
Bifurcate collateral	3	6	1	2	5	4

Figure 14.3 *Types of kinship classification on the first ascending generation.*

below two biological kin types, the kin types are called by the same term.

Lineal Terminology

Our system of kinship classification is called the *lineal system* (Figure 14.4). The number 3 and the color green, which appear below the kin types FB and MB in Figures 14.3 and 14.4, stand for the term *uncle*, which we apply both to FB and to MB. **Lineal kinship terminology** is found in societies such as the United States and Canada, in which the nuclear family is the most important group based on kinship.

Lineal kinship terminology distinguishes lineal relatives from collateral relatives. A **lineal relative** is an ancestor or decendant, anyone on the direct line of descent that leads to and from ego (Figure 14.5). Thus, lineal relatives are one's parents, grandparents, great-grandparents, and other direct forebears. Lineal relatives also include children, grandchildren, and great-grandchildren.

Collateral relatives are all other biological kin types. They include siblings, nieces and nephews, aunts and uncles, and cousins (Figure 14.5). **Affi-**

Figure 14.4 *Lineal kinship terminology.*

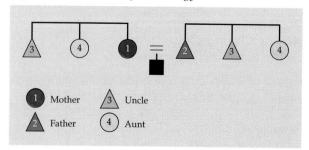

nals are relatives by marriage, whether of lineals (e.g., son's wife) or collaterals (sister's husband).

Bifurcate Merging Kinship Terminology

Bifurcate merging kinship terminology is another common way of classifying kin types (Figure 14.6). People use this system in societies with unilineal descent rules and unilocal postmarital residence. When the society is both unilocal and unilineal, the logic of bifurcate merging terminology is fairly clear. In a patrilineal society, for example, father and father's brother belong to the same descent group, gender, and generation. Since patrilineal societies usually have virilocal residence, the father and his brother live in the same local group. Because they share so many attributes that are socially relevant, ego regards them as social equivalents and calls them by the same kinship term—2. However, the mother's brother belongs to a different descent group, lives elsewhere, and has a different kin term—3.

What about mother and mother's sister in a patrilineal society? They belong to the same descent group, the same gender, and the same generation. Often they marry men from the same village and go to live there. These social similarities help explain the use of the same term—1—for both.

Similar observations apply to matrilineal societies. Consider a society with two matrilineal clans, the Ravens and the Wolves. Ego is a member of his mother's clan, the Raven clan. Ego's father is a member of the Wolf clan. His mother and her sister are female Ravens of the same generation. If there is uxorilocal residence, as there often is in matrilineal societies, they will live in the same village. Because they are so similar socially, ego calls them by the same kin term—1.

The father's sister, however, belongs to a different group, the Wolves, lives elsewhere, and has a different kin term—4. Ego's father and father's brother are male Wolves of the same generation. If they marry women of the same clan and live in the same village, this creates additional social similarities that reinforce this usage.

Generational Kinship Terminology

Like bifurcate merging kinship terminology, **generational kinship terminology** uses the same term for

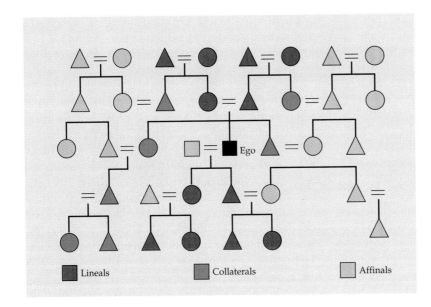

Lineals   Collaterals   Affinals

Figure 14.5 *The distinctions among lineals, collaterals, and affinals as perceived by ego.*

parents and their siblings, but the lumping is more complete (Figure 14.7). With generational terminology, there are only two terms for the parental generation. We may translate them as "father" and "mother," but more accurate translations would be "male member of the parental generation" and "female member of the parental generation."

Generational kinship terminology does not distinguish between the mother's and father's sides. It uses just one term for father, father's brother, and mother's brother. In matrilineal and patrilineal societies, these three kin types do not belong to the same descent group. Generational kinship terminology also uses a single term for mother, mother's sister, and father's sister. In a unilineal society, these three would never be members of the same group.

Nevertheless, generational terminology suggests closeness between ego and his or her aunts and un-

cles—much more closeness than exists between Americans and these kin types. We would therefore expect to find generational terminology in cultures in which kinship is much more important than it is in our own but in which there is no rigid distinction between the father's side and the mother's side.

It is no surprise, then, that generational kin terminology is typical of societies with ambilineal descent. In such contexts, descent-group membership is not automatic. People may choose the group they join, change their descent-group membership, or belong to two or more descent groups simultaneously. Generational terminology fits these conditions. The use of intimate kin terms allows people to maintain close personal relationships with all their relatives on the parental generation. People exhibit similar behavior toward aunts, uncles, and parents. Someday they will have to choose a descent group

Figure 14.6 *Bifurcate merging kinship terminology.*

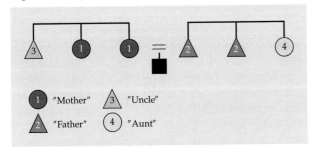

1 "Mother"   3 "Uncle"
2 "Father"   4 "Aunt"

Figure 14.7 *Generational kinship terminology.*

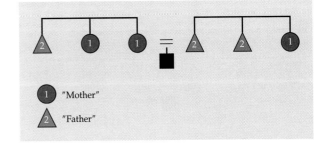

1 "Mother"
2 "Father"

to join. Furthermore, in ambilineal societies, post-marital residence is usually **ambilocal.** This means that the married couple can live with either the husband's or the wife's group.

Significantly, generational terminology also characterizes certain foraging bands, including Kalahari San groups and several native cultures of North America. Use of the same kinship terminology reflects certain similarities between foraging bands and ambilineal descent groups. In both societies, people have a choice about their kin-group affiliation. Foragers always live with kin, but they often shift band affiliation and so may be members of several different bands during their lifetimes. Just as in food-producing societies with ambilineal descent, generational kinship terminology among foragers helps maintain close personal relationships with several parental-generation relatives whom ego may eventually use as a point of entry into different groups.

Bifurcate Collateral Kinship Terminology

Of all the kinship classification systems, **bifurcate collateral kinship terminology** is the most specific. It has separate terms for each of the six kin types on the parental generation (Figure 14.8). Bifurcate collateral terminology isn't as common as the other types. Most of the societies that use it are in North Africa and the Middle East, and many of them are offshoots of the same ancestral group. They are also geographically close and have experienced many of the same historical events.

How can we explain bifurcate collateral terminology? Perhaps it arose accidentally in one society in this region and then diffused to others. Or perhaps bifurcate collateral terminology emerged in an ancient Middle Eastern society and now exists among descendant societies because of their common cultural heritage. Either explanation would be an example of a **historical explanation.** Similar customs often exist in different societies because those cultures have shared a period of common history or common sources of information.

Notice that the explanation being proposed for bifurcate collateral terminology is unlike the **functional explanations** that were offered for the other systems of kinship terminology. Functional explanations attempt to relate particular customs to other features of a society. Certain aspects of a culture are so closely related that when one of them changes, the others inevitably change too. For lineal, bifurcate merging, and generational terminologies, the social correlates (as discussed above) are very clear. However, because we lack a satisfactory functional explanation for bifurcate collateral terminology, a historical explanation was proposed instead. This discussion has a more general aim: It helps illustrate the kinds of explanations that anthropologists have proposed or considered for many other aspects of culture.

Relevance of Kinship Terminology

Anthropologists have to pay attention to kinship terminology because kinship is vitally important in bands, tribes, and chiefdoms. We saw in earlier chapters that kinship and descent play basic roles in regulating both interpersonal relations and political organization in such cultures. Kinship terms provide useful information about social patterns. If two relatives are designated by the same term, we can assume that they are perceived as sharing socially significant attributes.

Nevertheless, cross-cultural studies have found that kinship *terminology* is one of the slowest-changing aspects of social organization. Land ownership, inheritance patterns, residence rules, and descent rules all change more easily and quickly than terminology does. As a result, many societies have kinship terminology that doesn't fit their other social patterns. If we find generational terminology in a society with virilocal residence and patrilineal descent, for example, we may conclude that the kinship terminology has lagged behind the changes in residence and descent. We would expect that the kinship terminology will eventually become bifurcate merging.

Figure 14.8 *Bifurcate collateral kinship terminology.*

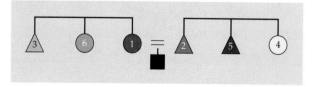

SUMMARY

In non-Western, nonindustrial cultures, kinship is very important. In fact, kinship, descent, and marriage form the basis of social life and political organization. We must distinguish between kin groups, whose composition and activities can be observed, and kinship calculation—the manner in which people identify and designate their relatives.

One widespread but nonuniversal kin group is the nuclear family, which consists of a married couple and their children. There are many functional alternatives to the nuclear family. These are social forms that assume functions that devolve on the nuclear family in other societies.

The nuclear family is most important in foraging and industrial societies. Food producers have kinship-based ties to estates, and other kinds of kinship and descent groups often overshadow the nuclear family.

In contemporary North America, the nuclear family is the characteristic kinship group for the middle class. Other kin groups assume somewhat greater importance in different social strata. Expanded households and sharing with extended family kin occur more frequently among disadvantaged minorities. The greater significance of expanded kinship in the lower class is an adaptation to poverty. It entails pooling of strategic resources by people with limited access to wealth and power. Today, however, even in the American middle class, nuclear family households are declining as single-person households and other domestic arrangements increase.

The descent group is the basic kin group among nonindustrial food producers. Unlike nuclear families, descent groups have perpetuity—they last for several genera-

tions. Descent-group members share and manage a common estate. Descent rules may be unilineal or ambilineal. Unilineal (patrilineal and matrilineal) descent is associated with unilocal (respectively, virilocal and uxorilocal) postmarital residence rules.

Kin terms, in contrast to biological kin types, are parts of native taxonomies. These are culturally specific ways of dividing up the world of kin relations on the basis of perceived differences and similarities. Although perceptions and classifications vary from culture to culture, comparative research has revealed a limited number of systems of kinship terminology. Because there are correlations between kinship terminology and other social practices, we can often predict kinship terminology from other aspects of culture.

Four basic classification systems, three of which are widely distributed throughout the world, categorize kin types on the parental generation. Many foraging and industrial societies have lineal terminology, which is correlated with nuclear family organization. Cultures with unilocal residence and unilineal descent tend to have bifurcate merging terminology. Generational terminology correlates with ambilineal descent and ambilocal residence. The more restricted bifurcate collateral terminology is concentrated among societies of the Middle East and North Africa. Its social functions and correlates are unclear. Kinship terminology changes more slowly than do patterns of inheritance, postmarital residence, and descent-group organization. Therefore, the correlation between kin terms and social structure is incomplete.

GLOSSARY

affinals: Relatives by marriage, whether of lineals (e.g., son's wife) or collaterals (e.g., sister's husband).

ambilineal: Principle of descent that does not automatically exclude the children of either sons or daughters.

ambilocal: Postmarital residence pattern in which the couple may reside with either the husband's or the wife's group.

bifurcate collateral kinship terminology: Kinship terminology employing separate terms for M, F, MB, MZ, FB, and FZ.

bifurcate merging kinship terminology: Kinship terminology in which M and MZ are called by the same term, F and FB are called by the same term, and MB and FZ are called by different terms.

bilateral kinship calculation: A system in which kinship ties are calculated equally through both sexes: mother and father, sister and brother, daughter and son, and so on.

biological kin types: Actual genealogical relationships, designated by letters and symbols (e.g., FB), as opposed to the kin terms (e.g., *uncle*) used in a particular society.

blended family: Kin unit formed when parents remarry and bring their children into a new household.

collateral household: Type of expanded family household including siblings and their spouses and children.

collateral relative: A biological relative who is not a lineal.

ego: Latin for *I*. In kinship charts, the point from which one views an egocentric genealogy.

expanded family household: Coresident group that can include siblings and their spouses and children (a *collateral* household) or three generations of kin and their spouses (an *extended family* household).

extended family: Expanded household including three or more generations.

family of orientation: Nuclear family in which one is born and grows up.

family of procreation: Nuclear family established when one marries and has children.

functional explanation: Explanation that establishes a correlation or interrelationship between social customs. When customs are functionally interrelated, if one changes, the others also change.

generational kinship terminology: Kinship terminology with only two terms for the parental generation, one designating M, MZ, and FZ and the other designating F, FB, and MB.

historical explanation: Demonstration that a social institution or practice exists among different populations because they share a period of common history or have been exposed to common sources of information; includes diffusion.

kin terms: The words used for different relatives in a particular language, as opposed to actual genealogical relationships (*biological kin types*).

kinship calculation: The system by which people in a particular society reckon kin relationships.

lineal kinship terminology: Parental generation kin terminology with four terms: one for M, one for F, one for FB and MB, and one for MZ and FZ.

lineal relative: Any of ego's ancestors or descendants (e.g., parents, grandparents, children, grandchildren); on the direct line of descent that leads to and from ego.

matrilateral skewing: A preference for relatives on the mother's side.

native taxonomy: Classification system invented and used by natives rather than anthropologists.

neolocality: Postmarital residence pattern in which a couple establishes a new place of residence rather than living with or near either set of parents.

unilocal: Either virilocal or uxorilocal postmarital residence; requires that a married couple reside with the relatives of either the husband (*vir*) or the wife (*uxor*), depending on the society.

uxorilocality: Customary residence with the wife's relatives after marriage.

virilocality: Customary residence with the husband's relatives after marriage.

STUDY QUESTIONS

1. Why has kinship been so important in ethnographic studies?
2. What is the nuclear family, and why is it significant?
3. What is the difference between the family of orientation and the family of procreation?
4. How did Nayar society reproduce itself biologically without the nuclear family?
5. What factors are linked with neolocal postmarital residence and household composition?
6. Nuclear families account for what percentage of North American households? What are the other household types?
7. How is the content of television programs related to changes in household organization in twentieth-century North America?
8. What is the key causal factor underlying the nuclear family's role in both foraging and industrial societies?
9. What is lineal kinship terminology, and how is it related to American culture?
10. What are the three most common systems of kinship terminology, and with what social structures are they associated?
11. What types of explanations do anthropologists use for systems of kinship terminology?

SUGGESTED ADDITIONAL READING

AMADIUME, I.
  1987   *Male Daughters, Female Husbands.* Atlantic Highlands, NJ: Zed. How women fill male roles, including husband, among the Igbo of Nigeria.

BRØGGER, J.
  1992   *Nazaré: Women and Men in a Prebureaucratic Portuguese Fishing Village.* Fort Worth: Harcourt Brace. Dynamics of the nuclear family in

a changing community, where women control the local economy and decision making.

BUCHLER, I. R., AND H. A. SELBY
1968   *Kinship and Social Organization: An Introduction to Theory and Method.* New York: Macmillan. Introduction to comparative social organization; includes several chapters on interpretations of kinship classification systems.

COLLIER, J. F., AND S. J. YANAGISAKO, EDS.
1987   *Gender and Kinship: Essays toward a Unified Analysis.* Stanford, CA: Stanford University Press. Consideration of kinship in the context of gender issues.

GRABURN, N., ED.
1971   *Readings in Kinship and Social Structure.* New York: Harper & Row. Several important articles on kinship terminology.

HOSTETLER, J., AND G. E. HUNTINGTON
1992   *Amish Children: Education in the Family,* 2nd ed. Fort Worth: Harcourt Brace. The reflection of Amish family values in their school system.

1996   *The Hutterites in North America,* 3rd ed. Fort Worth: Harcourt Brace. Life on the collective farms of a German-dialect speaking Christian sect on the Great Plains of the United States and Canada.

NETTING, R. M. C., R. R. WILK, AND E. J. ARNOULD, EDS.
1984   *Households: Comparative and Historical Studies of the Domestic Group.* Berkeley: University of California Press. Excellent collection of articles on household research.

RADCLIFFE-BROWN, A. R., AND D. FORDE, EDS.
1994   *African Systems of Kinship and Marriage.* New York: Columbia University Press. Reissue of a classic work, indispensable to understand kinship, descent, and marriage.

SIGNO, A.
1994   *Economics of the Family.* New York: Oxford University Press. How economists explain changes in birth rates and divorce rates and other features of family organization and functioning.

STACEY, J.
1990   *Brave New Families: Stories of Domestic Upheaval in Late Twentieth Century America.* New York: Basic Books. Contemporary family life in the United States, based on fieldwork in California's Silicon Valley.

STEPHENS, S., ED.
1996   *Children and the Politics of Culture.* Princeton, NJ: Princeton University Press. Children and childhood "at risk" in South Africa, Japan, Korea, Singapore, Western Europe, North America, and Brazil.

CHAPTER 15

MARRIAGE

THE INCEST TABOO AND EXOGAMY

EXPLANATIONS FOR THE INCEST TABOO
Instinctive Horror
Biological Degeneration
Marry Out or Die Out

ENDOGAMY
Caste
Royal Incest

MARRIAGE IN TRIBAL SOCIETIES

In the News: Anthropology Goes Looking for Love
    in All the Old Places

Bridewealth
Durable Alliances

PLURAL MARRIAGES
Polygyny
Polyandry

No definition of marriage is broad enough to apply easily to all societies. A commonly quoted definition comes from *Notes and Queries in Anthropology:*

> Marriage is a union between a man and a woman such that the children born to the woman are recognized as legitimate offspring of both partners. (Royal Anthropological Institute 1951, p. 111)

This definition may describe marriage in contemporary North America, but it isn't universally valid for several reasons. For example, some nations recognize homosexual marriages. Also, in many societies marriages unite more than two spouses. Here we speak of *plural marriages,* as when a woman weds a group of brothers—an arrangement called *fraternal polyandry* that is characteristic of certain Himalayan cultures. In certain societies (usually patrilineal), a woman may marry another woman, in a nonsexual union. This can happen in West Africa when a successful market woman (perhaps already married to a man) wants a wife of her own to take care of her home and children while she works outside (Amadiume 1987).

In the African Sudan a Nuer woman can marry a woman if her father has only daughters but no male

Marriage conveys certain rights, obligations, and benefits. This lesbian couple holds a mock wedding in front of the Internal Revenue Service in Washington, D.C., during a 1993 march for lesbian and gay rights, which protested the lack of income tax benefits for same-sex couples.

heirs, who are necessary if his patrilineage is to survive. He may ask his daughter to stand as a son in order to take a bride. This is a symbolic and social relationship rather than a sexual one. Indeed, the woman who serves as a man may already be living in another village as a man's wife!

The Nuer woman doesn't live with her "wife," who has sex with a man or men until she becomes pregnant. What's important here is *social* rather than *biological paternity;* we see again how kinship is socially constructed. The bride's children are considered the legitimate offspring of her "husband," who is biologically a woman but socially a man, and the descent line continues.

The British anthropologist Edmund Leach (1955) despaired of ever arriving at a universal definition of marriage. Instead, he suggested that depending on the society, several different kinds of rights are allocated by institutions classified as marriage. These rights vary from one culture to another, and no single one is widespread enough to provide a basis for defining marriage.

According to Leach, marriage can accomplish the following:

1. Establish the legal father of a woman's children and the legal mother of a man's
2. Give either or both spouses a monopoly in the sexuality of the other
3. Give either or both spouses rights to the labor of the other
4. Give either or both spouses rights over the other's property
5. Establish a joint fund of property—a partnership—for the benefit of the children
6. Establish a socially significant "relationship of affinity" between spouses and their relatives

This list highlights particular aspects of marriage in different cultural contexts. However, I believe that we need some definition—even a loose one—to identify an institution found in some form in all human societies. I suggest the following:

> **Marriage** is a socially approved relationship between a socially recognized male (the husband) and a socially recognized female (the wife) such that the children born to the wife are accepted as the offspring of both husband and wife. The husband may be the actual **genitor** (biological father) of the children or only the **pater** (socially recognized father).

THE INCEST TABOO AND EXOGAMY

In the stateless society a person's social world includes two main categories—friends and strangers. Strangers are potential or actual enemies. Marriage is one of the primary ways of converting strangers into friends, of creating and maintaining personal and political alliances. **Exogamy,** the practice of seeking a mate outside one's own group, has adaptive value because it links people into a wider social network that nurtures, helps, and protects them in times of need.

Incest refers to sexual relations with a close relative. All cultures have taboos against it. However, although the taboo is a cultural universal, cultures define incest differently. As an illustration, consider some implications of the distinction between two kinds of first cousins, cross cousins and parallel cousins.

The children of two brothers or two sisters are **parallel cousins.** The children of a brother and a sister are **cross cousins.** Your mother's sister's children and your father's brother's children are your parallel cousins. Your father's sister's children and your mother's brother's children are your cross cousins.

The American kin term *cousin* doesn't distinguish between cross and parallel cousins, but in many societies, especially those with unilineal descent, the distinction is essential. As an example, consider a community with only two descent groups. This exemplifies what is known as **moiety** organization—from the French *moitié,* which means "half." Descent bifurcates the community so that everyone belongs

to one half or the other. Some societies have patrilineal moieties; others have matrilineal moieties.

In Figures 15.1 and 15.2, notice that cross cousins are always members of the opposite moiety and parallel cousins always belong to your (ego's) own moiety. With patrilineal descent (Figure 15.1), people take the father's descent-group affiliation; in a matrilineal society (Figure 15.2), they take the mother's affiliation. You can see from these diagrams that your mother's sister's children (MZC) and your father's brother's children (FBC) belong to your group. Your cross cousins—that is, FZC and MBC—belong to the other moiety.

Parallel cousins therefore belong to the same generation and the same descent group as ego does, and they are like ego's brothers and sisters. They are called by the same kin terms as brother and sister are. Defined as close relatives, parallel cousins are tabooed as sex or marriage partners. They fall within the incest taboo, but cross cousins don't.

In societies with unilineal moieties, cross cousins belong to the opposite group. Sex with cross cousins isn't incestuous, because they aren't considered relatives. In fact, in many unilineal societies people must marry either a cross cousin or someone from the same descent group as a cross cousin. A unilineal descent rule ensures that the cross cousin's descent group is never one's own. With moiety exogamy, spouses must belong to different moieties.

Among the Yanomami of Venezuela and Brazil (Chagnon 1983/1992), men anticipate eventual marriage to a cross cousin by calling her "wife." They call their male cross cousins "brother-in-law."

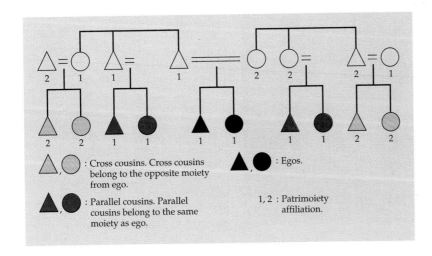

Figure 15.1 *Parallel and cross cousins and patrilineal moiety organization.*

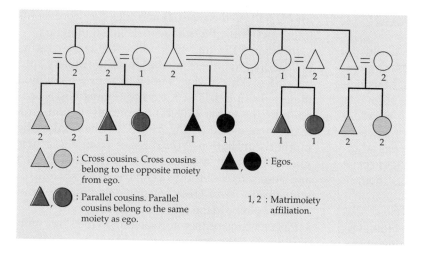

Figure 15.2 *Matrilineal moiety organization.*

Yanomami women call their male cross cousins "husband" and their female cross cousins "sister-in-law." Among the Yanomami, as in many societies with unilineal descent, sex with cross cousins is proper but sex with parallel cousins is considered incestuous.

A custom that is much rarer than cross-cousin marriage also illustrates that people define their kin, and thus incest, differently in different societies. When unilineal descent is very strongly developed, the parent who does not belong to one's own descent group isn't considered a relative. Thus, with strict patrilineality, the mother is not a relative but a kind of in-law who has married a member of ego's group—ego's father. With strict matrilineality, the father isn't a relative, because he belongs to a different descent group.

The Lakher of Southeast Asia are strictly patrilineal (Leach 1961). Using the male ego in Figure 15.3, let's suppose that ego's father and mother get divorced. Each remarries and has a daughter by a second marriage. A Lakher always belongs to his or her father's group, all the members of which (one's **agnates,** or patrikin) are considered too closely related

Among the Yanomami of Venezuela and Brazil, sex with (and marriage to) cross cousins is proper, but sex with parallel cousins is considered incestuous. With unilineal descent, sex with cross cousins isn't incestuous because cross cousins never belong to ego's descent group.

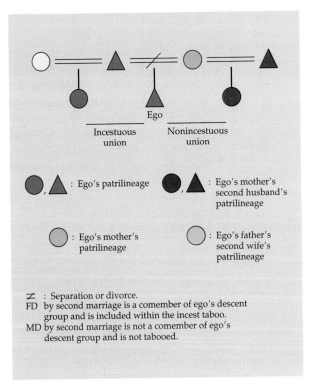

Figure 15.3 *Patrilineal descent-group identity and incest among the Lakher.*

to marry because they are members of the same patrilineal descent group. Therefore, ego can't marry his father's daughter by the second marriage, just as in contemporary North America it's illegal for half-siblings to marry.

However, in contrast to our society, where all half-siblings are tabooed, the Lakher permit ego to marry his mother's daughter by a different father. She is not ego's relative because she belongs to her own father's descent group rather than ego's. The Lakher illustrate very well that definitions of relatives, and therefore of incest, vary from culture to culture.

We can extend these observations to strict matrilineal societies. If a man's parents divorce and his father remarries, ego may marry his paternal half-sister. By contrast, if his mother remarries and has a daughter, the daughter is considered ego's sister, and sex between them is taboo. Cultures therefore have different definitions of relationships that are biologically or genetically equivalent.

EXPLANATIONS FOR THE INCEST TABOO

Instinctive Horror

There is no simple or universally accepted explanation for the fact that all cultures ban incest. Do primate studies offer any clues? Research with primates does show that adolescent males (among monkeys) or females (among apes) often move away from the group in which they were born (Rodseth et al. 1991). This emigration helps reduce the frequency of incestuous unions. The human avoidance of mating with close relatives may therefore express a generalized primate tendency.

One argument (Westermarck 1894; Hobhouse 1915; Lowie 1920/1961) is that the incest taboo is universal because incest horror is instinctive—*Homo sapiens* has a genetically programmed disgust toward incest. Because of this feeling, early humans banned it. However, cultural universality doesn't necessarily entail an instinctual basis. Fire making, for example, is a cultural universal, but it certainly is not an ability transmitted by the genes. Furthermore, if people really did have an instinctive horror of mating with blood relatives, a formal incest taboo would be unnecessary. No one would ever do it. However, as social workers, judges, psychiatrists, and psychologists know, incest isn't rare but happens all the time.

A final objection to the instinctive horror theory is that it can't explain why in some societies people can marry their cross cousins but not their parallel cousins. Nor does it tell us why the Lakher can marry their maternal, but not their paternal, half-siblings. No known instinct can distinguish between parallel and cross cousins.

The specific kin types included within the incest taboo—and the taboo itself—have a cultural rather than a biological basis. Even among nonhuman primates there is no evidence for an instinct against incest. Adolescent dispersal does not prevent—but merely limits the frequency of—incestuous unions. Among humans, cultural traditions determine the specific relatives with whom sex is considered incestuous. They also deal with the people who violate prohibited relationships in different ways. Banishment, imprisonment, death, and threats of supernatural retaliation are some of the punishments imposed.

Biological Degeneration

Another theory is that the taboo emerged because early *Homo* noticed that abnormal offspring were born from incestuous unions (Morgan 1877/1963). To prevent this, our ancestors banned incest. The human stock produced after the taboo originated was so successful that it spread everywhere.

What is the evidence for this theory? Laboratory experiments with animals that reproduce faster than humans do (such as mice and fruit flies) have been used to investigate the effects of inbreeding: A decline in survival and fertility does accompany

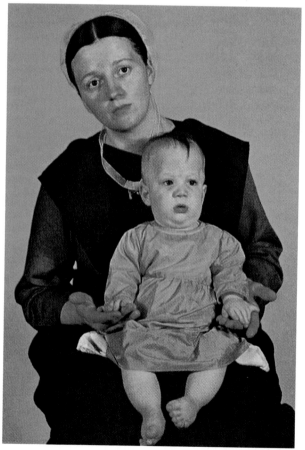

The Old Order Amish of Lancaster, Pennsylvania, have a high frequency of a gene that causes a combination of dwarfism and polydactylism (extra fingers). The Amish, who settled this area in the 1770s, have maintained a high incidence of endogamy. Despite the potentially harmful biological effects of systematic inbreeding, marriage preferences and prohibitions are based on specific cultural beliefs rather than universal concerns about future biological degeneration.

brother-sister mating across several generations. However, despite the potentially harmful biological results of systematic inbreeding, human marriage patterns are based on specific cultural beliefs rather than universal concerns about biological degeneration several generations in the future. Neither instinctive horror nor fear of biological degeneration explains the very widespread custom of marrying cross cousins. Nor can fears about degeneration explain why breeding with parallel cousins but not cross cousins is so often tabooed.

Marry Out or Die Out

One of the most accepted explanations for the incest taboo is that it arose in order to ensure exogamy, to force people to marry outside their kin groups (Tylor 1889; White 1959; Lévi-Strauss 1949/1969). In this view, the taboo originated early in human evolution because it was adaptively advantageous. Marrying a close relative, with whom one is already on peaceful terms, would be counterproductive. There is more to gain by extending peaceful relations to a wider network of groups.

This view emphasizes the role of marriage in creating and maintaining alliances. By forcing members to marry out, a group increases its allies. Marriage within the group, by contrast, would isolate that group from its neighbors and their resources and social networks, and might ultimately lead to the group's extinction. Exogamy and the incest taboo that propels it help explain human adaptive success. Besides the sociopolitical function, exogamy ensures genetic mixture between groups and thus maintains a successful human species.

ENDOGAMY

Exogamy pushes social organization outward, establishing and preserving alliances among groups. In contrast, rules of **endogamy** dictate mating or marriage within a group to which one belongs. Endogamic rules are less common but are still familiar to anthropologists. Indeed, most cultures *are* endogamous units, although they usually do not need a formal rule requiring people to marry someone from their own society. Members of the endogamic groups would never consider doing anything else.

Caste

An extreme example of endogamy is India's caste system. Castes are stratified groups in which membership is ascribed at birth and is lifelong. Indian castes are grouped into five major categories, or *varna*. Each is ranked relative to the other four, and these categories extend throughout India. Each *varna* includes a large number of castes (*jati*), each of which includes people within a region who may intermarry. All the *jati* in a single *varna* in a given region are ranked, just as the *varna* themselves are ranked.

Occupational specialization often sets off one caste from another. A community may include castes of agricultural workers, merchants, artisans, priests, and sweepers. The untouchable *varna*, found throughout India, includes castes whose ancestry, ritual status, and occupations are considered so impure that higher-caste people consider even casual contact with untouchables to be defiling.

The belief that intercaste sexual unions lead to ritual impurity for the higher-caste partner is important in maintaining endogamy. A man who has sex with a lower-caste woman can restore his purity with a bath and a prayer. However, a woman who has intercourse with a man of a lower caste has no such recourse. Her defilement cannot be undone. Because the women have the babies, these differences protect the purity of the caste line, ensuring the pure ancestry of high-caste children. Although Indian castes are endogamous groups, many of them are internally subdivided into exogamous lineages. This means that Indians must marry a member of another descent group from the same caste.

Royal Incest

Royal incest is similar to caste endogamy. The best-known examples come from Inca Peru, ancient Egypt, and traditional Hawaii. Those cultures allowed royal brother-sister marriages. Privileged endogamy, a violation of the incest taboo that applied to commoners in those cultures, was a means of differentiating between rulers and subjects.

Manifest and Latent Functions

To understand why royalty did not observe the incest taboo, it is useful to distinguish between the manifest and latent functions of behavior. The **man-ifest function** of a custom refers to the reasons natives give for it. Its **latent function** is an effect the custom has on the society that the native people don't mention or may not even recognize.

Royal incest illustrates this distinction. Hawaiians and other Polynesians believed in an impersonal force called *mana*. Mana could exist in things or people, in the latter case marking them off from other people and making them divine. The Hawaiians believed that no one had as much mana as the ruler. Mana depended on genealogy. The person whose own mana was exceeded only by the king's was his sibling. The most appropriate wife for a king was his own full sister. Notice that the brother-sister marriage also meant that royal heirs would be as manaful, or divine, as possible. The manifest function of royal incest in ancient Hawaii was part of that culture's beliefs about mana and divinity.

Royal incest also had latent functions—political repercussions. The ruler and his spouse had the same parents. Since mana was believed to be inherited, they were almost equally divine. When the king and his sister married, their children indisputably had the most mana in the land. No one could question their right to rule. However, if the king had taken a wife with less mana than his sister, his sister's children with someone else might eventually cause problems. Both sets of children could assert their divinity and right to rule. Royal sibling marriage therefore limited conflicts about succession because it reduced the number of people with claims to rule. Other kingdoms have solved this problem differently. Some succession rules, for instance, specify that only the oldest child (usually the son) of the reigning monarch can succeed; this custom is called **primogeniture.** Commonly, rulers have banished or killed claimants who rival the chosen heir.

Royal incest also had a latent economic function. If the king and his sister had rights to inherit the ancestral estate, their marriage to each other, again by limiting the number of heirs, kept it intact. Power often rests on wealth, and royal incest tended to ensure that royal wealth remained concentrated in the same line.

MARRIAGE IN TRIBAL SOCIETIES

Outside industrial societies, marriage is often more a relationship between groups than one between

IN THE NEWS: ANTHROPOLOGY GOES LOOKING FOR LOVE IN ALL THE OLD PLACES

Love and marriage, the song says, go together like a horse and carriage. But the link between love and marriage, like the horse-carriage combination, isn't a cultural universal. This news item describes a cross-cultural survey, published in the anthropological journal *Ethnology,* which found romantic ardor to be widespread, perhaps universal. Previously anthropologists had tended to ignore evidence for romantic love in other cultures, probably because arranged marriages were so common. Today, diffusion, mainly via the mass media, of Western ideas about the importance of love for marriage appears to be influencing marital decisions in other cultures.

Some influential Western social historians have argued that romance was a product of European medieval culture that spread only recently to other cultures. They dismissed romantic tales from other cultures as representing the behavior of just the elites. Under the sway of this view, Western anthropologists did not even look for romantic love among the peoples they studied. But they are now beginning to think that romantic love is universal.

The fact that it does not loom large in anthropology, they say, reflects the efforts most societies have made to quash the unruly inclination. In many countries, they suspect, what appears to be romance newly in bloom is rather the flowering of instincts that were always there, but held in check by tradition and custom. Romantic ardor has long been at odds with social institutions that knit peoples together in an orderly fashion: romantic choices rarely match the "proper" mates a family would select.

Romantic love may be muted or repressed by arranged marriages, which become political alliances between groups. Many cultures have arranged marriages between young children, as is shown in this wedding procession in Lombok, the Lesser Sunda Islands, Indonesia.

In that light, falling in love has been seen by many peoples throughout the world as a dangerous and subversive—though undeniably alluring—act, one warned against in folk tale and legend. "For decades anthropologists and other scholars have assumed romantic love was unique to the modern West," said Dr. Leonard Plotnicov, an anthropologist at the University of Pittsburgh and editor of the journal Ethnology. "Anthropologists came across it in their field work, but they rarely mentioned it because it wasn't supposed to happen."

Anthropologists distinguish between romantic passion and plain lust, as well as other kinds of love, like that between companions or parents and children. By "romantic love," anthropologists mean an intense attraction and longing to be with the loved one.

"Why has something so central to our culture been so ig-nored by anthropology?" asked Dr. William Jankowiak, an anthropologist at the University of Nevada.

The reason, in the view of Dr. Jankowiak and others, is a scholarly bias throughout the social sciences that viewed romantic love as a luxury in human life, one that could be indulged only by people in Westernized cultures or among the educated elites of other societies. For example it was assumed in societies where life is hard that romantic love has less chance to blossom, because higher economic standards and more leisure time create more opportunity for dalliance. That also contributed to the belief that romance was for the ruling class, not the peasants.

But, said Dr. Jankowiak, "There is romantic love in cultures around the world." Last year Dr. Jankowiak, with Dr. Edward Fischer, an anthropologist at Tulane University, published in *Ethnology* the first cross-cultural study, systematically comparing romantic love in many cultures.

In the survey of ethnographies from 166 cultures, they found what they considered clear evidence that romantic love was known in 147 of them—89 percent. And in the other 19 cultures, Dr. Jankowiak said, the absence of conclusive evidence seemed due more to anthropologists' oversight than to a lack of romance.

Some of the evidence came from tales about lovers, or folklore that offered love potions or other advice on making someone fall in love.

Another source was accounts by informants to anthropologists. For example, Nisa, a !Kung woman among the Bushmen of the Kalahari, made a clear distinction between the affection she felt for her husband, and that she felt for her lovers, which was "passionate and exciting," though fleeting. Of these extramarital affairs, she said: "When two people come together their hearts are on fire and their passion is very great. After a while the fire cools and that's how it stays."

Much of the evidence for romantic love came from cautionary tales. For example, a famous story in China during the Song Dynasty (960–1279) was that of the Jade Goddess. Similar in its description of romantic love to the European tale of Tristan and Isolde, it recounts how a young man falls in love with a woman who has been committed by her family to marry someone else, but who returns his love. The couple elope, but end in desperate straits and finally return home, in disgrace.

Still, given cultures may channel romantic feelings in different ways. Romantic love, Dr. Jankowiak said, may be muted or repressed by cultural mores like marriages arranged by families while the betrothed are still children.

"The proportion of members of a community who experience romantic love may well depend on that culture's social organization," Dr. Jankowiak said.

In an editorial note to the cross-cultural survey of romantic love, Dr. Plotnicov wrote that, in retrospect, it was an oversight to ignore the topic in his own field work. "I wish I had thought of looking at this 30 years ago in Nigeria," he said. "But it wasn't part of our tool kit."

The traditional pattern of marriage among the people Dr. Plotnicov studied was for a man to ask his relatives to find him a wife. But, if they could afford the expense, men there could have more than one wife—allowing romance to enter the picture.

"It's often the third wife who is married for romantic reasons," said Dr. Plotnicov. "I remember one man who told me he first saw his third wife walking through the market and, as he put it, 'she took my life away.' He was passionately in love, and pursued her until she married him."

While finding that romantic love appears to be a human universal, Dr. Jankowiak allows that it is still an alien idea in many cultures that such infatuation has anything to do with the choice of a spouse.

"What's new in many cultures is the idea that romantic love should be the reason to marry someone," said Dr. Jankowiak. "Some cultures see being in love as a state to be pitied. One tribe in the mountains of Iran ridicules people who marry for love."

Of course, even in arranged marriages, partners may grow to feel romantic love for each other. For example, among villagers in the Kangra valley of northern India, "people's romantic longings and yearnings ideally would become focused on the person they're matched with by their families," said Dr. Kirin Narayan, an anthropologist at the University of Wisconsin.

But that has begun to change, Dr. Narayan is finding, under the influence of popular songs and movies. "In these villages the elders are worried that the younger men and women are getting a different idea of romantic love, one where you choose a partner yourself," said Dr. Narayan. "There are starting to be elopements, which are absolutely scandalous."

The same trend toward love matches, rather than arranged marriages, is being noted by anthropologists in many other cultures. Among aborigines in Australia's Outback, for example, marriages had for centuries been arranged when children were very young.

That pattern was disrupted earlier in this century by missionaries, who urged that marriage not occur until children reached adolescence. Dr. Victoria Burbank, an anthropologist at the University of California at Davis, said that in pre-missionary days, the average age of a girl at marriage was always before menarche, sometimes as young as 9 years. Today the average age at marriage is 17; girls are more independent by the time their parents try to arrange a marriage for them.

"More and more adolescent girls are breaking away from arranged marriages," said Dr. Burbank. "They prefer to go off into the bush for a 'date' with someone they like, get pregnant, and use that pregnancy to get parental approval for the match."

Even so, parents sometimes are adamant that the young people should not get married. They prefer, instead, that the girls follow the traditional pattern of having their mothers choose a husband for them.

"Traditionally among these people, you can't choose just any son-in-law," said Dr. Burbank. "Ideally, the mother wants to find a boy who is her maternal grandmother's brother's son, a pattern that insures partners are in the proper kin group."

Dr. Burbank added: "These groups have critical ritual functions. A marriage based on romantic love, which ignores what's a proper partner, undermines the system of kinship, ritual, and obligation."

Nevertheless, the rules for marriage are weakening. "In the grandmothers' generation, all marriages were arranged. Romantic love had no place, though there were a few stories of a young man and woman in love running off together. But in the group I studied, in only one recent case did the girl marry the man selected for her. All the rest are love matches."

A similar pattern is going on in the village in northern Morocco studied by Dr. Susan Davis, an anthropologist and consultant in Haverford, Pa. "When I first went there in 1965, marriage was a strictly utilitarian economic ar-rangement," she said. "Your parents arranged your marriage."

But with the arrival of television and cinema in the village, bringing Egyptian soap operas and American movies, ideas of romance spread. "It's still taboo for a girl to say to her parents, 'I love a certain boy and want to marry him,'" said Dr. Davis. "But what's new is that a girl now expects to have a veto over the mate her parents propose, and that her parents will eventually approve of someone she likes."

Source: Daniel Goleman, "Anthropology Goes Looking in All the Old Places," *The New York Times,* November 24, 1992, B1.

individuals. We think of marriage as an individual matter. Although the bride and groom usually seek their parents' approval, the final choice (to live to-gether, to marry, to divorce) lies with the couple. The idea of romantic love symbolizes this individ-ual relationship.

In nonindustrial societies, marriage is a group concern. People don't just take a spouse; they as-sume obligations to a group of in-laws. When resi-dence is virilocal, for example, a woman must leave the community where she was born. She faces the prospect of spending the rest of her life in her hus-band's village, with his relatives. She may even have to transfer her major allegiance from her own group to her husband's.

Bridewealth

In societies with descent groups, people enter mar-riage not alone but with the help of the descent group. Descent-group members often have to con-tribute to the **bridewealth,** a customary gift before, at, or after the marriage from the husband and his kin to the wife and her kin. Another word for bridewealth is **brideprice,** but this term is inaccu-rate because people with the custom don't usually regard the exchange as a sale. They don't think of marriage as a commercial relationship between a man and an object that can be bought and sold.

Bridewealth compensates the bride's group for the loss of her companionship and labor. More im-

Gift-giving customs, including dowry and brideprice, are associated with marriage throughout the world. In this photo, guests bring presents in baskets to a wedding in Wenjiang, China.

In this more elaborate royal wedding photo, plates of money are presented at the marriage of an Indian maharajah.

portant, it makes the children born to the woman full members of her husband's descent group. For this reason, the institution is also called **progeny price.** Rather than the woman herself, it is her children who are permanently transferred to the husband's group. Whatever we call it, such a transfer of wealth at marriage is common in patrilineal tribes. In matrilineal societies, children are members of the mother's group, and there is no reason to pay a progeny price.

Dowry is a marital exchange in which the wife's group provides substantial gifts to the husband's family. Dowry, best known from India, correlates with low female status. Women are perceived as burdens. When husbands and their families take a wife, they expect to be compensated for the added responsibility.

Bridewealth exists in many more cultures than dowry does, but the nature and quantity of transferred items differ. In many African societies, cattle constitute bridewealth, but the number of cattle given varies from society to society. *As the value of bridewealth increases, marriages become more stable.* Bridewealth is insurance against divorce.

Imagine a patrilineal society in which a marriage requires the transfer of about twenty-five cattle from the groom's descent group to the bride's. Michael, a member of descent group A, marries Sarah from group B. His relatives help him assemble the bridewealth. He gets the most help from his close agnates—his older brother, father, father's brother, and closest patrilineal cousins.

The distribution of the cattle once they reach Sarah's group mirrors the manner in which they were assembled. Sarah's father, or her oldest brother if the father is dead, receives her bridewealth. He keeps most of the cattle to use as bridewealth for his sons' marriages. However, a share also goes to everyone who will be expected to help when Sarah's brothers marry.

When Sarah's brother David gets married, many of the cattle go to a third group—C, which is David's wife's group. Thereafter, they may serve as bridewealth to still other groups. Men constantly use their sisters' bridewealth cattle to acquire their own wives. In a decade, the cattle given when Michael married Sarah will have been exchanged widely.

In tribal societies, marriage entails an agreement between descent groups. If Sarah and Michael try to make their marriage succeed but fail to do so, both groups may conclude that the marriage can't last. Here it becomes especially obvious that tribal marriages are relationships between groups as well as between individuals. If Sarah has a younger sister or niece (her older brother's daughter, for example), the concerned parties may agree to Sarah's replacement by a kinswoman.

However, incompatibility isn't the main problem that threatens marriage in societies with bridewealth. Infertility is a more important concern. If Sarah has no children, she and her group have not fulfilled their part of the marriage agreement. If the relationship is to endure, Sarah's group must furnish another woman, perhaps her younger sister, who can have children. If this happens, Sarah may choose to stay in her husband's village. Perhaps she will someday have a child. If she does stay on, her husband will have established a plural marriage.

Most nonindustrial food-producing societies, unlike most foraging societies and industrial nations, allow **plural marriages, or polygamy.** There are two varieties, one is common and the other is very rare. The more common variant is **polygyny,** in which a man has more than one wife. The rare variant is **polyandry,** in which a woman has more than one husband. If the infertile wife remains married to her husband after he has taken a substitute wife provided by her descent group, this is polygyny. Reasons for polygyny other than infertility will be discussed shortly.

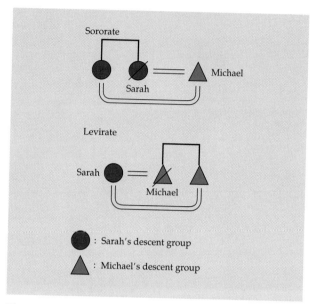

Figure 15.4 *Sororate and levirate.*

Durable Alliances

It is possible to exemplify the group-alliance nature of marriage in tribal societies by examining still another common practice—continuation of marital alliances when one spouse dies.

Sororate

What happens if Sarah dies young? Michael's group will ask Sarah's group for a substitute, often her sister. This custom is known as the **sororate** (Figure 15.4). If Sarah has no sister or if all her sisters are already married, another woman from her group may be available. Michael marries her, there is no need to return the bridewealth, and the alliance continues. The sororate exists in both matrilineal and patrilineal societies. In a matrilineal society with uxorilocal postmarital residence, a widower may remain with his wife's group by marrying her sister or another female member of her matrilineage (Figure 15.4).

Levirate

What happens if the husband dies? In many societies, the widow may marry his brother. This custom is known as the **levirate** (Figure 15.4). Like the sororate, it is a continuation marriage that main-

tains the alliance between descent groups, in this case by replacing the husband with another member of his group. The implications of the levirate vary with age. A recent study found that in African societies the levirate, though widely permitted, rarely involves cohabitation of the widow and her new husband. Furthermore, widows don't automatically marry the husband's brother just because they are allowed to. Often they prefer to make other arrangements (Potash 1986).

PLURAL MARRIAGES

In contemporary North America, where divorce is fairly easy and common, polygamy (marriage to more than one spouse at the same time) is against the law. Marriage in industrial nations joins individuals, and relationships between individuals can be severed more easily than can those between groups. As divorce grows more common, North Americans practice **serial monogamy:** Individuals have more than one spouse but never, legally, more than one at the same time. As stated earlier, the two forms of polygamy are polygyny and polyandry. Polyandry is practiced in only a few cultures, notably among certain groups in Tibet, Nepal, and India. Polygyny is much more common.

Polygyny

We must distinguish between the social approval of plural marriage and its actual frequency in a particular society. Many cultures approve of a man's having more than one wife. However, even when polygyny is encouraged, most people are monogamous, and polygyny characterizes only a fraction of the marriages. Why?

One reason is equal sex ratios. In the United States, about 105 males are born for every 100 females. In adulthood the ratio of men to women equalizes, and eventually it reverses. The average North American woman outlives the average man. In many nonindustrial societies as well, the male-biased sex ratio among children reverses in adulthood.

The custom of men marrying later than women also promotes polygyny. Among Nigeria's Kanuri people (Cohen 1967), men get married between the ages of eighteen and thirty; women, between twelve and fourteen. The age difference between spouses means that there are more widows than widowers. Most of the widows remarry, some in polygynous unions. Among the Kanuri and in other polygynous societies, widows make up a large number of the women involved in plural marriages (Hart, Pilling, and Goodale 1988). In many societies, including the Kanuri, the number of wives is an indicator of a man's household productivity, prestige, and social position. The more wives, the more workers. Increased productivity means more wealth. This wealth in turn attracts additional wives to the household. Wealth and wives bring greater prestige to the household and head.

In certain societies, the first wife requests a second wife to help with household chores. The second wife's status is lower than that of the first; they are

There is no single explanation for polygyny, illustrated by this Mormon man and his three wives and children. Some men are polygynous because they have inherited a widow from a brother. Others have plural wives because they want to increase household productivity.

In many societies polygyny is a measure of a man's prestige and social position. Shown here are a Masai chief, his two wives, and their children (in Kenya).

senior and junior wives. The senior wife sometimes chooses the junior one from among her close kinswomen. Among the Betsileo of Madagascar, the different wives always lived in different villages. A man's first and senior wife, called "Big Wife," lived in the village where he cultivated his best rice field and spent most of his time. High-status men with several rice fields and multiple wives had households near each field. They spent most of their time with the senior wife but visited the others occasionally throughout the year.

Plural wives can play important political roles in nonindustrial states. The king of the Merina, a society with more than 1 million people in the highlands of Madagascar, had palaces for each of his twelve wives in different provinces. He stayed with them when he traveled through the kingdom. They were his local agents, overseeing and reporting on provincial matters. The king of Buganda, the major precolonial state of Uganda, took hundreds of wives, representing all the clans in his nation. Everyone in the kingdom became the king's in-law, and all the clans had a chance to provide the next ruler. This was a way of giving the common people a stake in the government.

These examples show that there is no single explanation for polygyny. Its context and function vary from society to society and even within the same society. Some men are polygynous because they have inherited a widow from a brother. Others have plural wives because they seek prestige or want to increase household productivity. Still others use marriage as a political tool or a means of economic advancement. Men and women with political and economic ambitions cultivate marital alliances that serve their aims. In many societies, including the Betsileo of Madagascar and the Igbo of Nigeria, women arrange the marriages.

Polyandry

Polyandry is rare and is practiced under very specific conditions. Most of the world's polyandrous peoples live in South Asia—Tibet, Nepal, India, and Sri Lanka. India's polyandrous groups inhabit the lower ranges of the Himalayas, in northern India. They are known as Paharis, which means "people of the mountains." Gerald Berreman (1962, 1975) did a comparative study of two Pahari groups, one in the foothills of the western Himalayas and the other in the central foothills.

The western and central Paharis are historically and genetically related to each other and speak dialects of the same language. Polyandry exists among the western, but not the central, Paharis. Because there are so many other cultural and social similarities between the western and central Paharis, including caste stratification and patrilineal clans, Berreman wondered why one group practiced polyandry and the other did not.

Pahari marriage customs turned out to correlate with demographic contrasts. Sex ratios were different in the two areas. In the polyandrous west, there was a shortage of females (789 per 1,000 males). Although female infanticide was not documented in the area, neglect of girls (*covert* female infanticide) helped explain the shortage of women (Levine 1988). The polyandry was always **fraternal:** Husbands were brothers. The oldest brother arranged the marriage, which made all the brothers legal husbands of the wife. Subsequently, they could marry additional women. All these women were joint wives and sexual partners of the brothers. Children born to any wife called all the brothers "father."

Nevertheless, there was considerable variation in the actual marriage arrangements in western Pahari households (Berreman 1975). In one village only 9 percent of the households were polyandrous, 25 percent were polygynous, and 34 percent were monogamous. Variation in the marriage type and household composition reflected household wealth, the age of the brothers, and divorce. Household composition went through a developmental cycle. For example, one group of three brothers took their first wife in 1910. In 1915 they added a second wife. This changed simple fraternal polyandry into a polyandrous-polygynous household. A few years later they added a third wife, and later they added a fourth. By a decade later, one of the brothers had died and two of the wives had divorced and remarried elsewhere. By 1955 the household had become monogamous, as only one husband and one wife survived.

This flexible marriage system was adaptive because it allowed the western Paharis to spread people and labor out over the land. The number of working adults in a western Pahari household was proportional to the amount of farmland it owned. Because women did as much agricultural work as men, given the same amount of land, two brothers might require and support three or four wives whereas three or four brothers might have only one or two. Plural marriages were uncommon in landless households, whose resources and labor needs were lowest. Landless people were more monogamous (43 percent) than were landowners (26 percent).

Among the nonpolyandrous central Paharis, by contrast, there were more women than men. Most (85 percent) marriages were monogamous. Only 15 percent were plural—polygynous. Despite the absence of a formal polyandry here, it was customary for brothers to contribute to each other's bridewealth, and they could have sex with each other's wives. The major difference was that central Pahari children recognized only one father. However, because brothers had common sexual rights, socially recognized fathers were not necessarily the true genitors.

Polyandry in other parts of South Asia seems to be a cultural adaptation to mobility associated with customary male travel for trade, commerce, and military operations. Polyandry ensures that there will be at least one man at home to accomplish male

Polyandry in northwest Nepal. The seated young woman is Terribal, age 15. She holds her youngest husband, age 5. Left of Terribal is another husband, age 12. Standing directly behind her is her third husband, age 9. The two older standing men are brothers who are married to the same woman, standing to the right. These are Terribal's "fathers" and mother.

activities within a gender-based division of labor. Fraternal polyandry is also an effective strategy when resources are scarce. Brothers with limited resources (in land) pool their resources in expanded (polyandrous) households. They take just one wife. Polyandry restricts the number of wives and heirs. Less competition among heirs means that land can be transmitted with minimal fragmentation.

SUMMARY

Marriage is a socially sanctioned relationship between a socially recognized male (the husband) and a socially recognized female (the wife) such that the children born to the wife are accepted as the offspring of both husband and wife. Various sorts of rights may be transmitted by marriage.

All societies have incest taboos. However, different cultures taboo different biological kin types. Among the explanations that have been offered for the taboo's universality are the following: (1) It codifies instinctive human horror of incest, (2) it results from concern about the biological degeneration that can follow from incestuous unions, and (3) it has a selective advantage because it promotes exogamy and intergroup alliances, thereby increasing networks of friends and allies.

The main adaptive advantage of exogamy is the extension of social and political ties outward. This is confirmed by a consideration of endogamy—marriage within the group. Endogamic rules are common in stratified societies. One example is India, where castes are the endogamous units. Castes are subdivided into exogamous descent groups. The same culture can therefore have both endogamic and exogamic rules. Certain ancient kingdoms encouraged royal incest while condemning incest by commoners. The manifest functions of royal incest in ancient Hawaii were linked to the idea of mana. However, royal incest also served latent functions in the political and economic domains—limiting succession struggles and keeping royal wealth intact.

In societies with descent groups, marriages are relationships between groups as well as between spouses. With the custom of bridewealth, the groom and his relatives transmit wealth to the bride and her relatives. As the bridewealth's value increases, the divorce rate declines.

Bridewealth customs show that marriages among nonindustrial food producers create and maintain group alliances. So do the sororate, by which a man marries the sister of his deceased wife, and the levirate, by which a woman marries the brother of her deceased husband. Replacement marriages in cases of spousal incompatibility also confirm the importance of group alliances.

Many cultures permit plural marriages. The two kinds of polygamy are polygyny and polyandry. The former involves multiple wives; the latter, multiple husbands. Polygyny and polyandry are found in varied social and cultural contexts and occur for many reasons. Polygyny is much more common than is polyandry. There are demographic, economic, and ecological reasons for plural marriage systems.

GLOSSARY

agnates: Members of the same patrilineal descent group.

brideprice: See *progeny price.*

bridewealth: See *progeny price.*

cross cousins: Children of a brother and a sister.

dowry: A marital exchange in which the wife's group provides substantial gifts to the husband's family.

endogamy: Marriage between people of the same social group.

exogamy: Rule requiring people to marry outside their own group.

fraternal polyandry: Marriage of a group of brothers to the same woman or women.

genitor: Biological father of a child.

incest: Sexual relations with a close relative.

latent function: A custom's underlying function, often unperceived by natives.

levirate: Custom by which a widow marries the brother of her deceased husband.

manifest function: The reasons that natives offer for a custom.

marriage: Socially approved relationship between a socially recognized male (the husband) and a socially recognized female (the wife) such that the children born to the wife are accepted as the offspring of both husband and wife.

moiety: One of two descent groups in a given population; usually moieties intermarry.

parallel cousins: Children of two brothers or two sisters.

pater: Socially recognized father of a child; not necessarily the genitor.

plural marriage: See *polygamy*.

polyandry: Variety of plural marriage in which a woman has more than one husband.

polygamy: Any marriage with more than two spouses.

polygyny: Variety of plural marriage in which a man has more than one wife.

primogeniture: Inheritance rule that makes the oldest child (usually the oldest son) the only heir.

progeny price: A gift from the husband and his kin to the wife and her kin before, at, or after marriage; legitimizes children born to the woman as members of the husband's descent group.

serial monogamy: Marriage of a given individual to several spouses, but not at the same time.

sororate: Custom by which a widower marries the sister of the deceased wife.

STUDY QUESTIONS

1. What is marriage and what kinds of rights may be transmitted by it?
2. What explanations have been offered for the universality of the incest taboo? Which do you prefer, and why?
3. What are the respective roles of endogamy and exogamy within the Indian caste system?
4. What were the manifest and latent functions of privileged royal incest?
5. What is bridewealth? What else is it called, and why?
6. What is the difference between sororate and levirate? What do they have in common?
7. What is the difference between polygyny and polyandry?
8. What are some of the reasons for polygyny?
9. What are some of the reasons for polyandry?
10. What general conclusions do you draw from the two chapters on kinship and marriage?

SUGGESTED ADDITIONAL READING

BOHANNAN, P., AND J. MIDDLETON, EDS.
1968   *Marriage, Family, and Residence.* Garden City, NY: Natural History Press. Articles about marriage, incest, exogamy, and family and household organization.

CHAGNON, N.
1992   (orig. 1988) *Yanomamo,* 4th ed. Fort Worth: Harcourt Brace. Latest edition of classic case study of marital alliances and politics in a tribal society—now in the context of genocide and habitat destruction.

COLLIER, J. F., ED.
1988   *Marriage and Inequality in Classless Societies.* Stanford, CA: Stanford University Press. Marriage and issues of gender stratification in bands and tribes.

FOX, R.
1985   *Kinship and Marriage.* New York: Viking Penguin. Well-written survey of kinship and marriage systems and theories about them.

GOODY, J., AND S. T. TAMBIAH
1973   *Bridewealth and Dowry.* Cambridge: Cambridge University Press. Marital exchanges in comparative perspective.

HART, C. W. M., A. R. PILLING, AND J. C. GOODALE
1988   *The Tiwi of North Australia,* 3rd ed. Fort Worth: Harcourt Brace. Latest edition of classic case study of Tiwi marriage arrangements, including polygyny, and social change over sixty years of anthropological study.

LEACH, E.
1985   *Social Anthropology.* New York: Oxford University Press. A well-known British anthropologist who studied the kinship and marriage systems of many peoples wrote this nontechnical survey of social anthropology and the anthropologists who have contributed to it.

LEVINE, N.
1988   *The Dynamics of Polyandry: Kinship, Domesticity, and Population in the Tibetan Border.* Chicago: University of Chicago Press. Case study of fraternal polyandry and household organization in northwestern Nepal.

POTASH, B., ED.
1986   *Widows in African Societies: Choices and Constraints.* Stanford, CA: Stanford University Press. Ten case studies giving widows' perspectives on African marriage systems.

RADCLIFFE-BROWN, A. R., AND D. FORDE, EDS.
1994   *African Systems of Kinship and Marriage.* New York: Columbia University Press. Reissue of a classic work, indispensable to understand kinship, descent, and marriage.

CHAPTER 16

GENDER

GENDER ISSUES AMONG FORAGERS

In the News: Masai Gender Roles

GENDER ISSUES AMONG HORTICULTURALISTS
Reduced Gender Stratification—Matrilineal, Uxorilocal Societies
Reduced Gender Stratification—Matrifocal Societies
Increased Gender Stratification—Patrilineal-Virilocal Societies
Etoro Homosexuality

GENDER ISSUES AMONG AGRICULTURALISTS

Box: Hidden Women, Public Men—Public Women, Hidden Men

GENDER ISSUES AND INDUSTRIALISM
The Feminization of Poverty

WHAT DETERMINES VARIATION IN GENDER ISSUES?

Because anthropologists study biology, society, and culture, they are in a unique position to comment on nature (biological predispositions) and nurture (environment) as determinants of human behavior. Human attitudes, values, and behavior are limited not only by our genetic predispositions—which are often difficult to identify—but also by our experiences during enculturation. Our attributes as adults are determined both by our genes and by our environment during growth and development.

Debate about the effects of nature and nurture proceeds today in scientific and public arenas. **Naturists** assume that some—they differ about how much—human behavior and social organization is biologically determined. **Nurturists, or environmentalists,** do not deny that some universal aspects of human behavior may have a genetic base. However, they find most attempts to link behavior to genes unconvincing. The basic environmentalist assumption is that human evolutionary success rests on flexibility, or the ability to adapt in various ways. Because human adaptation relies so strongly on cultural learning, we can change our behavior more readily than members of other species can.

The nature-nurture debate emerges in the discussion of human sex-gender roles and sexuality. Men and women differ genetically. Women have two X chromosomes, and men have an X and a Y. The father determines a baby's sex because only he has the Y chromosome to transmit. The mother always provides an X chromosome.

The chromosomal difference is expressed in hormonal and physiological contrasts. Humans are sexually dimorphic. **Sexual dimorphism** refers to marked differences in male and female biology besides the contrasts in breasts and genitals. Men and women differ not just in primary (genitalia and reproductive organs) and secondary (breasts, voice, hair distribution) sexual characteristics but in average weight, height, and strength.

Just how far, however, do these genetically and physiologically determined differences go? What effect do they have on the way men and women act and are treated in different cultures? On the environmentalist side, anthropologists have discovered substantial variability in the roles of men and women in different cultures. The anthropological position on sex-gender roles and biology may be stated as follows:

> The biological nature of men and women [should be seen] not as a narrow enclosure limiting the human organism, but rather as a broad base upon which a variety of structures can be built. (Friedl 1975, p. 6)

Although in most cultures men tend to be somewhat more aggressive than women, many of the behavioral and attitudinal differences between the sexes emerge from culture rather than biology. *Sex* differences are biological, but *gender* encompasses all the traits that a culture assigns to and inculcates in males and females. "Gender," in other words, refers to the cultural construction of male and female characteristics (Rosaldo 1980b).

Given the "rich and various constructions of gender" within the realm of cultural diversity, Susan Bourque and Kay Warren (1987) note that the same images of masculinity and femininity do not always apply. Margaret Mead did an early ethnographic study of variation in gender roles. Her book *Sex and Temperament in Three Primitive Societies* (1935/1950) was based on field work in three societies in Papua–New Guinea: Arapesh, Mundugumor, and Tchambuli. The extent of personality variation in men and women in these three societies on the same island amazed Mead. She found that Arapesh men and women both acted as Americans have traditionally expected women to act—in a mild, parental, responsive way. Mundugumor men and women both, in contrast, acted as she believed we expect men to act—fiercely and aggressively. Tchambuli men were "catty," wore curls, and went shopping, but Tchambuli women were energetic and managerial and placed less emphasis on personal adornment than did the men. [Drawing on their recent case study of the Tchambuli, whom they call the Chambri, Errington and Gewertz (1987), while recognizing gender malleability, have disputed the specifics of Mead's account.]

There is a growing field of feminist scholarship within anthropology (di Leonardo, ed. 1991; Nash and Safa 1986; Rosaldo 1980b; Strathern 1988), and in recent years ethnographers have been gathering systematic ethnographic data about gender in many cultural settings (Morgen, ed. 1989; Mukhopadhyay and Higgins 1988). We can see that the gender roles vary with environment, economy, adaptive strategy, and type of political system. Before we examine the cross-cultural data, some definitions are in order.

Gender roles are the tasks and activities that a culture assigns to the sexes. Related to gender roles are **gender stereotypes,** which are oversimplified but strongly held ideas about the characteristics of males and females. **Gender stratification** describes an unequal distribution of rewards (socially valued resources, power, prestige, and personal freedom) between men and women, reflecting their different positions in a social hierarchy (Light, Keller, and Calhoun 1994). According to Ann Stoler (1977), the "economic determinants of female status" include freedom or autonomy (in disposing of one's labor and its fruits) and social power (control over the lives, labor, and produce of others).

In stateless societies, gender stratification is often more obvious in regard to prestige than it is in regard to wealth. In her study of the Ilongots of northern Luzon in the Philippines, Michelle Rosaldo (1980a) described gender differences related to the positive cultural value placed on adventure, travel, and knowledge of the external world. More often than women, Ilongot men, as headhunters, visited distant places. They acquired knowledge of the external world, amassed experiences there, and returned to express their knowledge, adventures, and feelings in public oratory. They received acclaim as a result. Ilongot women had inferior prestige because they lacked external experiences on which to base knowledge and dramatic expression. On the basis of Rosaldo's study and findings in other state-

less societies, Ong (1989) argues that we must distinguish between prestige systems and actual power in a given society. High male prestige may not entail economic or political power held by men over their families.

GENDER ISSUES AMONG FORAGERS

Several studies have shown that economic roles affect gender stratification. In one cross-cultural study Peggy Sanday (1974) found that gender stratification decreased when men and women made roughly equal contributions to subsistence. She found that gender stratification was *greatest* when the women contributed either *much more* or *much less* than the men did.

This finding applied mainly to food producers, not to foragers. In foraging societies gender stratification was most marked when men contributed much *more* to the diet than women did. This was true among the Eskimo, Inuit, and other northern hunters and fishers. Among tropical and semitropical foragers, by contrast, gathering usually supplies more food than hunting and fishing do. Gathering is generally women's work; men usually hunt and fish. With gathering prominent, gender status tends to be more equal than it is when hunting and fishing are the main subsistence activities.

Gender status is also more equal when the do-

Among foragers, gender stratification is most marked when men contribute much more to the diet than women do—as has been true among the Eskimos, Inuit, and other northern hunters and fishers. These Yu'pik men (Russian Eskimos) are butchering a walrus taken from the Bering Sea.

mestic and public spheres aren't sharply separated. (**Domestic** means within or pertaining to the home.) Strong differentiation between the home and the outside world is called the **domestic-public dichotomy** or the *private-public contrast*. The outside world can include politics, trade, warfare, or work. Often when domestic and public spheres are clearly separated, public activities have greater prestige than domestic ones do. This can promote gender stratification, because men are more likely to be active in the public domain than women are. Cross-culturally, women's activities tend to be closer to home than men's are. Thus, another reason hunter-gatherers have less gender stratification than food producers do is that the domestic-public dichotomy is more developed among food producers.

A division of labor linked to gender has been found in all cultures. However, the particular tasks assigned to men and women don't always reflect differences in strength and endurance. Food producers often assign the arduous tasks of carrying water and firewood and pounding grain to women. In 1967 in the Soviet Union women filled 47 percent of the factory positions, including many unmechanized jobs requiring hard physical labor. Most Soviet sanitation workers, physicians, and nurses were women (Martin and Voorhies 1975). Many jobs that men do in some societies are done by women in others, and vice versa.

Certain roles are more sex-linked than others.

Men are the usual hunters and warriors. Given such weapons as spears, knives, and bows, men make better fighters because they are bigger and stronger on the average than are women in the same population (Divale and Harris 1976). The male hunter-fighter role also reflects a tendency toward greater male mobility.

In foraging societies, women are either pregnant or lactating during most of their childbearing period. Late in pregnancy and after childbirth, carrying a baby limits a woman's movements, even her gathering. Given the effects of pregnancy and lactation on mobility, it is rarely feasible for women to be the primary hunters (Friedl 1975). Warfare, which also requires mobility, is not found in most foraging societies, nor is interregional trade well developed. Warfare and trade are two public arenas that contribute to status inequality of males and females among food producers.

The !Kung San illustrate the extent to which the activities and spheres of influence of men and women may overlap among foragers (Draper 1975). Traditional !Kung gender roles were interdependent. During gathering, women discovered information about game animals, which they passed on to the men. Men and women spent about the same amount of time away from the camp, but neither worked more than three days a week. Between one-third and one-half of the band stayed home while the others worked.

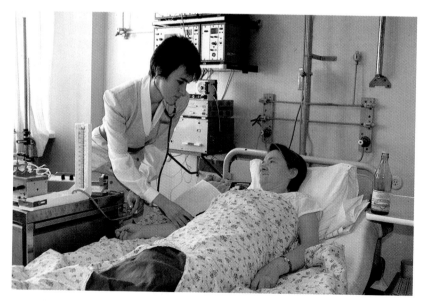

Many jobs that men do in some societies are done by women in others, and vice versa. In the Soviet Union most physicians, nurses, sanitation workers, and about half of all factory workers were women. Here, an endocrinologist examines a patient in a state hospital in Riga, Latvia, formerly a Soviet Baltic state.

IN THE NEWS: MASAI GENDER ROLES

A gender-based division of labor has been found in all cultures, but the tasks assigned by gender don't necessarily reflect differences in strength or endurance. Many food-producing societies, including the patrilineal, polygynous Masai pastoralists described here, assign heavy subsistence work to women, leaving the men free to be warrior-raiders. This article also describes increasing Masai poverty in the Ngorongoro Crater area, where much of their traditional pasture land is now reserved for wild game and ecotourism.

Ngorongoro Conservation Area, Tanzania—Parimitoro Ole Kasiaro, a 35-year-old elder of the Masai tribe, recently married his third wife. Waiting in the wings is a fourth, a 10-year-old girl paid for with cattle by his father to her father before she was born.

With three underfed wives and three scrawny children, Mr. Kasiaro, whose cattle are dying of disease and who often confesses to being hungry himself, knows he cannot afford another wife. But Masai custom, which is paramount among the mud and dung houses here on the edge of the Serengeti plain, dictates that he must in time marry again.

Mr. Kasiaro is proud of his Masai heritage, which anthropologists find remarkable for being so resilient to Western influences. But he admits to being troubled by some aspects of his society, especially its miserable treatment of women.

"Men in this community live as supervisors," he said, surveying a group of women sitting in the dirt. The women were resting after lugging containers of water from a stream as men stood by watching. "They leave the women to do all the everyday activities. It is not unusual to see a woman, even if she is pregnant, looking after cattle, sheep and goats, or taking donkeys to fetch cornmeal from the very distant shops."

Traditionally, Masai women performed the heavy work, leaving men free to be warriors, defending territory and raiding cattle. The warrior days are over, but rather than pitch in with the domestic chores, men typically spend their days drinking alcohol or playing bao, a popular board game. . . .

Mr. Kasiaro led an effort last year to help the women sell Masai jewelry to the tourists who drive past on their way to see the big game around the Ngorongoro Crater or the nearby Serengeti plain. But Mr. Kasiaro discovered that the women could not run a shop and lacked sufficient capital to buy the beads to make the elaborate necklaces the tourists want to buy.

"The men offered no capital for the women," he said. "The women had to sell their own necklaces to start."

After last year's rather poor beginning, Mr. Kasiaro is looking for a way to educate the women in running a small business. He believes that the income from the crafts will give the Masai women a new independence. And he sees another value in the project.

When men have money, he said, they often spend it on homemade liquor. "But when women get money," he continued, "they spend it on cornmeal for their children and helping the families."

Mr. Kasiaro's concern about the status of women has evolved slowly, and comes mainly, he suggested, from his better educational background, travels and reading.

Unlike most of the other men and women in the villages around Ngorongoro, Mr. Kasiaro attended school. As a member of the regional council he travels regularly to the regional capital of Arusha, 80 miles to the east, and has been to Dar-es-Salaam, the national capital, on several occasions. He recently accompanied a group of Masai dancers on a trip to Denmark, the first time he has been out of Africa.

A disproportional division of labor is by no means confined to Masai culture. The World Bank estimates that about 70 percent of the food crops in Africa are cultivated by women. Efforts by international organizations to improve the lot of the African woman have met with meager success, largely because many of the continent's national economies have weakened, putting women in even more vulnerable positions.

Such is the case among the estimated 300,000 Masai in Tanzania, particularly those living around the Ngorongoro Crater, where much of the traditional rangeland for the all-important Masai cattle has been reserved for game and tourists. As a result, the Masai in the area are much poorer and have clung to their traditional ways to a greater degree than the estimated 200,000 Masai in southern Kenya.

Mr. Kasiaro said that the first to be affected by the rising poverty were the women, who must look after the malnourished and often sick children.

Source: Jane Perlez, "Woman's Work Is Never Done (Not by Masai Men)," *The New York Times,* December 2, 1991, p. A4.

The !Kung saw nothing wrong in doing the work of the other gender. Men often gathered food and collected water. A general sharing ethos dictated that men distribute meat and that women share the fruits of gathering. Boys and girls of all ages played together. Fathers took an active role in raising children. Resources were adequate, and competition and aggression were discouraged. Exchangeability and interdependence of roles are adaptive in small groups.

Patricia Draper's field work among the !Kung is especially useful in showing the relationships between economy, gender roles, and stratification because she studied both foragers and a group of former foragers who had become sedentary. Just a few thousand !Kung continue their culture's traditional foraging pattern. Most are now sedentary, living near food producers or ranchers (see Kent 1992; Solway and Lee 1990; Wilmsen 1989).

Draper studied sedentary !Kung at Mahopa, a village where they herded, grew crops, worked for wages, and did a small amount of gathering. Their gender roles were becoming more rigidly defined. A domestic-public dichotomy was developing as men traveled farther than women did. With less gathering, women were confined more to the home. Boys could gain mobility through herding, but girls' movements were more limited. The equal and communal world of the bush was yielding to the social features of sedentary life. A differential ranking of men according to their herds, houses, and sons began to replace sharing. Males came to be seen as the most valuable producers.

If there is some degree of male dominance in every contemporary society, it may be because of changes such as those which have drawn the !Kung into wage work, market sales, and thus the world capitalist economy. A historical interplay between local, national, and international forces influences systems of gender stratification (Ong 1989). In traditional foraging cultures, however, egalitarianism extended to the relations between the sexes. The social spheres, activities, rights, and obligations of men and women overlapped. Foragers' kinship systems tend to be bilateral (calculated equally through males and females) rather than favoring either the mother's side or the father's side. Foragers may live with either the husband's or the wife's kin and often shift between one group and the other.

One last observation about foragers: It is among

them that the public and private spheres are least separate, hierarchy is least marked, aggression and competition are most discouraged, and the rights, activities, and spheres of influence of men and women overlap the most. Our ancestors lived entirely by foraging until 10,000 years ago. If there is any most "natural" form of human society, it is best (although imperfectly—see the box in Chapter 12) represented by foragers. Despite the popular stereotype of the club-wielding caveman dragging his mate by the hair, relative gender equality is a much more likely ancestral pattern.

GENDER ISSUES AMONG HORTICULTURALISTS

Gender roles and stratification among cultivators vary widely, depending on specific features of the economy and social structure. Demonstrating this, Martin and Voorhies (1975) studied a sample of 515 horticultural societies, representing all parts of the world. They looked at several variables, including descent and postmarital residence, the percentage of the diet derived from cultivation, and the productivity of men and women.

Women were found to be the main producers in horticultural societies. In 50 percent of those societies, women did most of the cultivating. In 33 percent, contributions to cultivation by men and women were equal. In only 17 percent did men do most of the work. Women tended to do a bit more cultivating in matrilineal compared with patrilineal societies. They dominated horticulture in 64 percent of the matrilineal societies versus 50 percent of the patrilineal ones.

Reduced Gender Stratification— Matrilineal, Uxorilocal Societies

Cross-cultural variation in gender status is related to rules of descent and postmarital residence (Martin and Voorhies 1975; Friedl 1975). Among horticulturalists with matrilineal descent and **uxorilocality** (residence after marriage with the wife's relatives), female status tends to be high. Matriliny and uxorilocality disperse related males, rather than consolidating them. By contrast, patriliny and **virilocality** (residence after marriage with the husband's kin) keep male relatives together.

Women tend to have high status in matrilineal, uxorilocal societies for several reasons. Descent-group membership, succession to political positions, allocation of land, and overall social identity all come through female links. Among the Minangkabau in Malaysia (Peletz 1988), matriliny gave women sole inheritance of ancestral rice fields. Uxorilocality created solidary clusters of female kin. Minangkabau women had considerable influence beyond the household (Swift 1963). In such matrilineal contexts, women are the basis of the entire social structure. Although public authority may be (or may appear to be) assigned to the men, much of the power and decision making may actually belong to the senior women.

Anthropologists have never discovered a **matriarchy,** a society ruled by women. Still, some matrilineal societies, including the **Iroquois** (Brown 1975), a confederation of tribes in aboriginal New York, show that women's political and ritual influence can rival that of the men.

We saw that among foragers gender status was most equal when there was no sharp separation of male and female activities and of public and domestic spheres. However, gender stratification can also be reduced by roles that remove men from the local community. We now refine our generalizations: It is the sharp contrast between male and female roles *within the local community* that promotes gender stratification. Gender stratification may be reduced when women play prominent local roles, while men pursue activities in a wider, regional system. Iroquois women, for example, played a major subsistence role, while men left home for long periods. As is usual in matrilineal societies, *internal* warfare was uncommon. Iroquois men waged war only on distant groups; this could keep them away for years.

Iroquois men hunted and fished, but women controlled the local economy. Women did some fishing and occasional hunting, but their major productive role was in horticulture. Women owned the land, which they inherited from matrilineal kinswomen. Women controlled the production and distribution of food.

Iroquois women lived with their husbands and children in the family compartments of a communal longhouse. Women born in a longhouse remained there for life. Senior women, or **matrons,** decided which men could join the longhouse as husbands, and they could evict incompatible men. Women therefore controlled alliances between descent groups, an important political job in tribal society.

Iroquois women thus managed production and distribution. Social identity, succession to office and titles, and property all came through the female line, and women were prominent in ritual and politics. Related tribes made up a confederacy, the League of the Iroquois, with chiefs and councils.

A council of male chiefs managed military operations, but chiefly succession was matrilineal. The

Women have high status in matrilineal, uxorilocal societies because descent-group membership, succession to political positions, allocation of land, and overall social identity come through female links. Among these Minangkabau of Negeri Sembilan (Malaysia), matriliny gave women sole inheritance of ancestral rice fields and promoted clusters of female kin.

matrons of each longhouse nominated a man as their representative. If the council rejected their first nominee, the women proposed others until one was accepted. Matrons constantly monitored the chiefs and could impeach them. Women could veto war declarations, withhold provisions for war, and initiate peace efforts. In religion, too, women shared power. Half the tribe's religious practitioners were women, and the matrons helped select the others.

Reduced Gender Stratification— Matrifocal Societies

Nancy Tanner (1974) also found that the combination of male travel and a prominent female economic role reduced gender stratification and promoted high female status. She based this finding on a survey of the **matrifocal** (mother-centered, often with no resident husband-father) organization of certain societies in Indonesia, West Africa, and the Caribbean. Matrifocal societies are not necessarily matrilineal. A few are even patrilineal.

For example, Tanner (1974) found matrifocality among the Igbo of eastern Nigeria, who are patrilineal, virilocal, and polygynous (men have multiple wives). Each wife had her own house, where she lived with her children. Women planted crops next to their houses and traded surpluses. Women's associations ran the local markets, while men did the long-distance trading.

In a case study of the Igbo, Ifi Amadiume (1987) noted that either sex could fill male gender roles. Before Christian influence, successful Igbo women and men used wealth to take titles and acquire wives. Wives freed husbands (male and female) from domestic work and helped them accumulate wealth. Female husbands were not considered masculine but preserved their femininity. Igbo women asserted themselves in women's groups, including those of lineage daughters, lineage wives, and a community-wide women's council led by titled women. The high status and influence of Igbo women rested on the separation of males from local subsistence and on a marketing system that allowed women to leave home and gain prominence in distribution and—through these accomplishments—in politics.

Increased Gender Stratification— Patrilineal-Virilocal Societies

The Igbo are unusual among patrilineal-virilocal societies, many of which have marked gender stratification. Martin and Voorhies (1975) link the decline of matriliny and the spread of the **patrilineal-virilocal complex** (consisting of patrilineality, virilocality, warfare, and male supremacy) to pressure on resources. Faced with scarce resources, patrilineal-virilocal cultivators such as the Yanomami often wage warfare against other villages. This favors vir-

In many parts of Africa, including the Bamenda Highlands of Cameroon (shown here), women are active in commerce. Polygyny may even help the aspiring market woman, who can leave her children with cowives while she pursues a business career.

ilocality and patriliny, customs that keep related men together in the same village, where they make strong allies in battle. Such societies tend to have a sharp domestic-public dichotomy, and men tend to dominate the prestige hierarchy. Men may use their public roles in warfare and trade and their greater prestige to symbolize and reinforce the devaluation or oppression of women.

The patrilineal-virilocal complex characterizes many societies in highland Papua–New Guinea. Women work hard growing and processing subsistence crops, raising and tending pigs (the main domesticated animal and a favorite food), and doing domestic cooking, but they are isolated from the public domain, which men control. Men grow and distribute prestige crops, prepare food for feasts, and arrange marriages. The men even get to trade the pigs and control their use in ritual.

In densely populated areas of the Papua–New Guinea highlands, male-female avoidance is associated with strong pressure on resources (Lindenbaum 1972). Men fear all female contacts, including sex. They think that sexual contact with women will weaken them. Indeed, men see everything female as dangerous and polluting. They segregate themselves in men's houses and hide their precious ritual objects from women. They delay marriage, and some never marry.

By contrast, the sparsely populated areas of Papua–New Guinea, such as recently settled areas, lack taboos on male-female contacts. The image of woman as polluter fades, heterosexual intercourse is valued, men and women live together, and reproductive rates are high.

Etoro Homosexuality

One of the most extreme examples of male-female sexual antagonism in Papua–New Guinea comes from the **Etoro** (Kelly 1976), a group of 400 people who subsist by hunting and horticulture in the Trans-Fly region. The Etoro also illustrate the power of culture in molding human sexuality. The following account applies only to Etoro males and their beliefs. Etoro cultural norms prevented the male anthropologist who studied them from gathering comparable information about female attitudes. Etoro opinions about sexuality are linked to their beliefs about the cycle of birth, physical growth, maturity, old age, and death.

In some parts of Papua–New Guinea, the patrilineal-virilocal complex has extreme social repercussions. Regarding females as dangerous and polluting, men may segregate themselves in men's houses (such as this one, located near the Sepik River), where they hide their precious ritual objects from women.

Etoro men believe that semen is necessary to give life force to a fetus, which is said to be placed within a woman by an ancestral spirit. Because men are believed to have a limited supply of semen, sexuality saps male vitality. The birth of children, nurtured by semen, symbolizes a necessary (and unpleasant) sacrifice that will lead to the husband's eventual death. Heterosexual intercourse, which is required only for reproduction, is discouraged. Women who want too much sex are viewed as witches, hazardous to their husbands' health. Etoro culture permits heterosexual intercourse only about 100 days a year. The rest of the time it is tabooed. Seasonal birth clustering shows that the taboo is respected.

So objectionable is heterosexuality that it is removed from community life. It can occur neither in sleeping quarters nor in the fields. Coitus can happen only in the woods, where it is risky because poisonous snakes, the Etoro say, are attracted by the sounds and smells of sex.

Although coitus is discouraged, homosexual acts are viewed as essential. Etoro believe that boys cannot produce semen on their own. To grow into men and eventually give life force to their children, boys must acquire semen orally from older men. From the age of ten until adulthood, boys are inseminated by older men. No taboos are attached to this. Homosexual activity can go on in the sleeping area or garden. Every three years a group of boys around the age of twenty are formally initiated into manhood. They go to a secluded mountain lodge, where they are visited and inseminated by several older men.

Etoro homosexuality is governed by a code of propriety. Although homosexual relationships between older and younger males are culturally essential, those between boys of the same age are discouraged. A boy who gets semen from other youths is believed to be sapping their life force and stunting their growth. When a boy develops very rapidly, this suggests that he is ingesting semen from other boys. Like a sex-hungry wife, he is shunned as a witch.

Etoro homosexuality rests not on hormones or genes but on cultural traditions. The Etoro represent one extreme of a male-female avoidance pattern that is widespread in Papua–New Guinea and in patrilineal-virilocal societies.

GENDER ISSUES AMONG AGRICULTURALISTS

As horticulture developed into agriculture, women lost their role as primary cultivators. Certain agricultural techniques, particularly plowing, were assigned to men because of their greater average size and strength (Martin and Voorhies 1975). Except when irrigation was used, plowing eliminated the need for constant weeding, an activity usually done by women.

Cross-cultural data illustrate these changes in productive roles. Women were the main workers in 50 percent of the horticultural societies surveyed but in only 15 percent of the agricultural groups. Male subsistence labor dominated 81 percent of the agricultural societies but only 17 percent of the horticultural ones (Martin and Voorhies 1975) (see Table 16.1).

With agriculture, women were cut off from production for the first time in human history. Belief systems started contrasting men's valuable extradomestic labor with women's domestic role, now viewed as inferior. (**Extradomestic** means outside the home; within or pertaining to the public domain.) Changes in kinship and postmarital residence patterns also hurt women. Descent groups and polygyny declined with agriculture, and the nuclear family became more common. Living with her husband and children, a woman was isolated from her kinswomen and cowives. Female sexuality is carefully supervised in agricultural economies; men have easier access to divorce and extramarital sex, reflecting a "double standard."

Still, female status in agricultural societies is not inevitably bleak. Gender stratification is associated with plow agriculture rather than with intensive cultivation per se. Studies of peasant gender roles and stratification in France and Spain (Harding 1975; Reiter 1975), which have plow agriculture, show that people think of the house as the female sphere and the fields as the male domain. However, such a dichotomy is not inevitable, as my own research among Betsileo agriculturalists in Madagascar shows.

Betsileo women play a prominent role in agriculture, contributing a third of the hours invested in

Table 16.1 *Male and Female Contributions to Production in Cultivating Societies*

	Horticulture (Percentage of 104 Societies)	Agriculture (Percentage of 93 Societies)
Women are primary cultivators	50	15
Men are primary cultivators	17	81
Equal contributions to cultivation	33	3

Source: Martin and Voorhies 1975, p. 283.

rice production. They have their customary tasks in the division of labor, but their work is more seasonal than men's is.

No one has much to do during the ceremonial season, between mid-June and mid-September. Men work in the rice fields almost daily the rest of the year. Women's cooperative work occurs during transplanting (mid-September through November) and harvesting (mid-March through early May). Along with other members of the household, women do daily weeding in December and January. After the harvest, all family members work together winnowing the rice and then transporting it to the granary.

If we consider the strenuous daily task of husking rice by pounding (a part of food preparation rather than production per se), women actually contribute slightly more than 50 percent of the labor devoted to producing and preparing rice before cooking.

Not just women's prominent economic role but traditional social organization enhances female status among the Betsileo. Although postmarital residence is mainly virilocal, descent rules permit married women to keep membership in and a strong allegiance to their own descent groups. Kinship is broadly and bilaterally (on both sides—as in contemporary North America) calculated. The Betsileo exemplify Aihwa Ong's (1989) generalization that bilateral (and matrilineal) kinship systems, combined with subsistence economies in which the sexes have complementary roles in food production

and distribution, are characterized by reduced gender stratification. Such societies are common among South Asian peasants (Ong 1989).

The Betsileo woman has obligations to her husband and his kin, but they are also obligated to her and her relatives. Often accompanied by their husbands and children, women pay regular visits to their home villages. The husband and his relatives help the wife's kin in agriculture and attend ceremonials hosted by them. When a woman dies, she is normally buried in her husband's ancestral tomb. However, a delegation from her own village always comes to request that she be buried at home. Women often marry into villages where some of their kinswomen have previously married; thus, even after marriage a woman lives near some of her own relatives.

Betsileo men do not have exclusive control over the means of production. Women can inherit rice fields, but most women, on marrying, relinquish their shares to their brothers. Sometimes a woman and her husband cultivate her field, eventually passing it on to their children.

Traditionally, Betsileo men participate more in politics, but the women also hold political office. Women sell their produce and products in markets, invest in cattle, sponsor ceremonials, and are mentioned during offerings to ancestors. Arranging marriages, an important extradomestic activity, is more women's concern than men's. Sometimes Betsileo women seek their own kinswomen as wives for their sons, reinforcing their own prominence in

Bilateral kinship systems, combined with subsistence economies in which the sexes have complementary roles in food production and distribution, have reduced gender stratification. Such features are common among Asian rice cultivators, such as the Ifugao of the Philippines (shown here).

HIDDEN WOMEN, PUBLIC MEN—PUBLIC WOMEN, HIDDEN MEN

For the past few years, one of Brazil's top sex symbols has been Roberta Close, whom I first saw in a furniture commercial. Roberta, whose looks reminded me of those of the young Natalie Wood, ended her pitch with an admonition to prospective furniture buyers to accept no substitute for the advertised product. "Things," she warned, "are not always what they seem."

Nor was Roberta. This petite and incredibly feminine creature was actually a man. Nevertheless, despite the fact that he—or she (speaking as Brazilians do)—is a man posing as a woman, Roberta has won a secure place in Brazilian mass culture. Her photos decorate magazines. She has been a panelist on a TV variety show and has starred in a stage play in Rio with an actor known for his super-macho image. Roberta even inspired a well-known, and apparently heterosexual, pop singer to make a "video" honoring her. In it she pranced around Rio's Ipanema

Things aren't always what they seem. Roberta Close, a known transvestite (a transsexual as of 1989) who for years has been one of Brazil's top sex symbols, is genetically male.

Beach in a bikini, showing off her ample hips and buttocks.

The video depicted the widespread male appreciation of Roberta's beauty. As confirmation, one heterosexual man told me that he had recently been on the same plane

as Roberta and had been struck by her looks. Another man said he wanted to have sex with her. These comments, it seemed to me, illustrated striking cultural contrasts about gender and sexuality. In Brazil, a Latin American country noted for its *machismo*, heterosexual men do not feel that attraction toward a transvestite blemishes their masculine identities.

Roberta Close exists in relation to a gender-identity scale that jumps from extreme femininity to extreme masculinity, with little in between. Masculinity is stereotyped as active and public, femininity as passive and domestic. The male-female contrast in rights and behavior is much stronger in Brazil than it is in North America. Brazilians confront a more rigidly defined masculine role than North Americans do.

The active-passive dichotomy also provides a stereotypical model for male homosexuality: One man is supposed to be the active, masculine (inserting) partner, whereas the

---

village life and continuing kin-based female solidarity in the village.

The Betsileo illustrate the idea that intensive cultivation does not necessarily entail sharp gender stratification. We can see that gender roles and stratification reflect not just the type of adaptive strategy but also specific environmental variables and cultural attributes. Betsileo women continue to play a significant role in their society's major economic activity, rice production.

Plowing has become prominent in Betsileo agriculture only recently, but irrigation makes weeding, in which women participate, a continued necessity. If new tools and techniques eventually reduce women's roles in transplanting, harvesting, and weeding, gender stratification may develop. In the

meantime, several features of the economy and social organization continue to shield the Betsileo from the gender hierarchies found in many agricultural and virilocal societies.

We have seen that virilocality is usually associated with gender stratification. However, some cultures with these institutions, including the Betsileo and the matrifocal Igbo of eastern Nigeria, offer contrasts to the generalization. The Igbo and Betsileo are not alone in allowing women a role in trade. Many patrilineal, polygynous societies in West Africa also allow women to have careers in commerce. Polygyny may even help an aspiring woman trader, who can leave her children with her cowives while she pursues a business career. She repays them with cash and other forms of assistance.

other is the passive, effeminate one. The latter man is derided as a *bicha* (intestinal worm), but little stigma attaches to the inserter. However, for the Brazilian men who are unhappy with active masculinity or passive effeminacy there is one other choice—active femininity. For Roberta Close and others like her, the cultural demand of ultramasculinity has yielded to a performance of ultrafemininity. These men-women form a third gender in relation to Brazil's more polarized male-female identity scale.

Transvestites such as Roberta are particularly prominent in Rio's annual Carnaval, when an ambience of inversion rules the city. In the culturally accurate words of the American popular novelist Gregory McDonald, who sets one of his books in Brazil at Carnaval time:

Everything goes topsy-turvy.... Men become women; women become men; grown-ups become children; rich people pretend they're poor; poor people, rich; sober people become drunkards;

thieves become generous. Very topsy-turvy. (McDonald 1984, p. 154)

Most notable in this costumed inversion (DaMatta 1991), men dress as women. Carnaval reveals and expresses normally hidden tensions and conflicts as social life is turned upside down. Reality is illuminated through a dramatic presentation of its opposite.

This is the final key to Roberta's cultural meaning. She emerged in a setting in which male-female inversion is part of the year's most popular festival. Transvestites are the pièces de résistance at Rio's Carnaval balls, where they dress as scantily as the real women do. They wear postage-stamp bikinis, sometimes with no tops. Photos of real women and transformed ones vie for space in the magazines. It is often impossible to tell the born women from the hidden men. Roberta Close is a permanent incarnation of Carnaval—a year-round reminder of the spirit of Carnavals past, present, and yet to come.

Roberta emerges from a Latin cul-

ture whose gender roles contrast strongly with those of the United States. From small village to massive city, Brazilian males are public and Brazilian females are private creatures. Streets, beaches, and bars belong to the men. Although bikinis adorn Rio's beaches on weekends and holidays, there are many more men than women there on weekdays. The men revel in their ostentatiously sexual displays. As they sun themselves and play soccer and volleyball, they regularly stroke their genitals to keep them firm. They are living publicly, assertively, and sexually in a world of men.

Brazilian men must work hard at this public image, constantly acting out their culture's definition of masculine behavior. Public life is a play whose strong roles go to men. Roberta Close, of course, is a public figure. Given that Brazilian culture defines the public world as male, we can perhaps better understand now why the nation's number one sex symbol is a man who excels at performing in public as a woman.

GENDER ISSUES AND INDUSTRIALISM

The domestic-public dichotomy, which is developed most fully among patrilineal-virilocal food producers and plow agriculturalists, has also affected gender stratification in industrial societies, including the United States and Canada. However, gender roles have been changing rapidly in North America. The "traditional" idea that "a woman's place is in the home" actually emerged in the United States as industrialism spread after 1900. Earlier, pioneer women in the Midwest and West had been recognized as fully productive workers in farming and home industry. Under industrialism, attitudes about gendered work came to vary with class and region. In early industrial Europe, men, women,

and children had flocked to factories as wage laborers. American slaves of both sexes had done grueling work in cotton fields. With abolition, southern African-American women continued working as field hands and domestics. Poor white women labored in the South's early cotton mills. In the 1890s more than 1 million American women held menial, repetitive, and unskilled factory positions (Margolis 1984; Martin and Voorhies 1975).

After 1900 European immigration produced a male labor force willing to work for wages lower than those of American-born men. Those immigrant men moved into factory jobs that previously had gone to women. As machine tools and mass production further reduced the need for female labor, the notion that women were biologically unfit for factory work began to gain ground (Martin and Voorhies 1975).

Maxine Margolis (1984) has shown how gendered work, attitudes, and beliefs have varied in response to American economic needs. For example, wartime shortages of men have promoted the idea that work outside the home is women's patriotic duty. During the world wars the notion that women are biologically unfit for hard physical labor faded. Inflation and the culture of consumption have also spurred female employment. When prices and/or demand rise, multiple paychecks help maintain family living standards.

The steady increase in female paid employment since World War II also reflects the baby boom and industrial expansion. American culture has traditionally defined clerical work, teaching, and nursing as female occupations. With rapid population growth and business expansion after World War II, the demand for women to fill such jobs grew steadily. Employers also found that they could increase their profits by paying women lower wages than they would have to pay returning male war veterans.

Margolis (1984) contends that changes in the economy lead to changes in attitudes toward and about women. Woman's role in the home is stressed during periods of high unemployment, although if wages fall or inflation occurs simultaneously, female employment may still be accepted. Between 1970 and 1993 the proportion of women in the American workforce increased from 38 to 46 percent, and more than 58 million women now have

paid jobs. Women now fill more than half (53 percent) of all professional jobs (*American Almanac* 1994–1995, pp. 398, 407). Table 16-2 presents figures on the ever-increasing cash employment of American wives and mothers.

The average male full-time wage and salary worker earned $26,728 in 1993, versus $20,520 for the average woman (77 percent of the male rate, up from 65 percent in 1987 and 68 percent in 1989) (*American Almanac* 1994–1995, p. 429). Table 16.3 details employment in the United States in 1992 by gender and job type. Notice that the income gap between women and men was least marked—but still evident—in professional jobs, where women averaged 71 percent of the male income (unchanged between 1989 and 1992). The gap was widest in sales, where women averaged little more than half the male salary.

Today's jobs are not especially demanding in terms of physical labor. With machines to do the heavy work, the smaller average body size and lesser average strength of women are no longer impediments to blue-collar employment. The main reason we don't see more modern-day Rosies working alongside male riveters is that the U.S. workforce itself is abandoning heavy-goods manufacture. In the 1950s two-thirds of American jobs were blue-collar, compared with 16 percent today. The location of those jobs has shifted within the world capitalist economy. Third World countries with cheaper labor produce steel, automobiles, and other heavy goods less expensively than the United States can, but the United States excels at services. The

Table 16.2 *Cash Employment of American Mothers, Wives, and Husbands, 1950–1993**

Year	Percentage of Married Women, Husband Present with Children under 18	Percentage of All Married Women†	Percentage of All Married Men‡
1950	19	N/A	N/A
1960	28	32	89
1970	40	40	86
1975	45	44	83
1980	54	50	81
1985	61	54	79
1993	68	59	77

*Civilian population sixteen years and older.
†Husband present.
‡Wife present.
Source: American Almanac 1994–1995, pp. 398, 402.

Wartime shortages of men have promoted the idea that extradomestic labor is women's patriotic duty. During the world wars the notion that women were biologically unfit for hard physical labor faded. Shown here is World War II's famous Rosie the Riveter.

American mass education system has many inadequacies, but it does train millions of people for service- and information-oriented jobs, from sales clerks to computer operators.

The Feminization of Poverty

Alongside the economic gains of many American women, particularly professionals, stands an opposite extreme: the feminization of poverty. This refers to the increasing proportion of America's poor who are women. More than half of U.S. households with sub-poverty-level incomes (3.6 of 6.9 million families) have female heads. The feminization of poverty accounts for almost all the increase (53 percent) in poverty in the United States since 1970 (Barringer 1989).

Feminine poverty has been a trend in the United States since World War II, but it has accelerated recently. In 1959 the female-headed households accounted for 26 percent of the American poor. That figure has more than doubled. About half the female poor are "in transition," facing an economic crisis caused by the departure, disability, or death of a husband. The other half are more permanently dependent on the welfare system or on friends or relatives living nearby (Schaefer and Lamm 1992). The feminization of poverty and its consequences in regard to living standards and health are widespread even among wage earners. Many American women,

Table 16.3 *Earnings in the United States (1992), by Gender and Job Type for Year-Round Full-Time Workers**

	MEDIAN ANNUAL SALARY		RATIO OF EARNINGS FEMALE/MALE	
	Women	**Men**	**1992**	**1989**
Median earnings	$21,440	$30,358	71	68
By job type:				
Executive/administrative/managerial	$27,495	$42,509	65	61
Professional	$31,261	$44,015	71	71
Sales	$17,924	$31,346	57	54
Service	$12,931	$20,606	63	62

*By occupation of longest job held.
Source: American Almanac 1994–1995, pp. 429, 431.

especially African-American women, work part time for low wages and meager benefits. Fourteen percent of the American population, some 35 million people, had no health insurance in 1991 (Pear 1992).

The fate of less fortunate children in America, whose poverty has increased by 25 percent since 1970, is linked to the feminization of poverty. Almost 40 percent of poor people in the United States are children under age eighteen. More than 25 percent of American children now live with one parent, usually the mother. And almost one-fourth of children under six in the United States live in households whose incomes are below the poverty level. In mother-only homes, 59 percent of the children live in poverty, compared with 13 percent in married-couple households. The poverty figures are 46 percent of children in white (non-Hispanic) mother-only homes, compared with 69 percent for both African Americans and Hispanics (*American Almanac* 1994–1995, p. 476).

WHAT DETERMINES VARIATION IN GENDER ISSUES?

We see that gender roles and stratification have varied widely across cultures and through history. Among many foragers and matrilineal cultivators, there is little gender stratification. Competition for resources leads to warfare and the intensification of production. These conditions favor patriliny and virilocality. To the extent that women lose their productive roles in agricultural and pastoral societies, the domestic-public dichotomy is accentuated and gender stratification is sharpened. With industrialism, attitudes about gender vary in the context of female extradomestic employment. Gender is flexible and varies with cultural, social, political, and economic factors. The variability of gender in time and space suggests that it will continue to change. The biology of the sexes is not a narrow enclosure limiting humans but a broad base upon which a variety of structures can be built (Friedl 1975).

SUMMARY

In recent years anthropologists have gathered systematic ethnographic data about gender in many cultural settings. Gender roles and gender stratification vary with environment, economy, adaptive strategy, level of social complexity, and degree of participation in the world capitalist economy. *Gender roles* are the tasks and activities that a culture assigns to each sex. Related to gender roles are *gender stereotypes*—oversimplified but strongly held ideas about the characteristics of males and females. *Gender stratification* describes an unequal distribution of rewards (socially valued resources, power, prestige, and personal freedom) between men and women, reflecting their different positions in a social hierarchy. In stateless societies, gender stratification is often much more obvious in regard to prestige than it is in regard to wealth or power.

Where gathering is prominent, gender status is more symmetrical than is the case when hunting or fishing dominates the foraging economy. Gender status is more equal when the domestic and public spheres are not sharply separated. Foragers lack two public arenas that contribute to higher male status among food producers: warfare and organized interregional trade. Among foragers, hierarchy is least marked, aggression and competition are most discouraged, and the rights, activities, and spheres of influence of men and women overlap the most.

Gender stratification, which tends to increase as cultivation intensifies, is also linked to descent and postmarital residence. Matrilineal-uxorilocal systems occur in societies where population pressure on strategic resources is minimal and warfare is infrequent. Women's status is high in such societies because descent-group membership, political succession, land allocation, and overall social identity come through female links. Although there are no matriarchies, women in many societies wield power and make decisions. If women play a major subsistence role while men leave home for long periods, sexual equality is favored. Gender stratification is marked when male and female spheres are sharply differentiated within the local community.

Scarcity of resources promotes intervillage warfare, patriliny, and virilocality. The localization of related males is adaptive for military solidarity. Men may use their public roles in war and extradomestic distribution to symbolize and reinforce their oppression of women.

Agriculture intensifies production and reliance on crops. With plow agriculture, gender stratification increases as men assume responsibility for subsistence. With the advent of plow agriculture, women were removed from production for the first time in human history. The distinction between women's domestic work and men's extradomestic "productive" labor reinforced the contrast between men as public and valuable and women as domestic and inferior. The Betsileo illustrate, however, that intensive cultivation per se does not entail a low status for women.

Americans' attitudes toward gender vary with class and region. The attitude that woman's place is in the home emerged with early industrialism. When the need for female labor declines, the idea that women are unfit for many jobs increases. Forces such as war, inflation, falling wages, the baby boom, and employment patterns help account for female cash employment and Americans' attitudes toward it. Alongside the economic gains of many American women, particularly professionals, stands an opposite extreme: the feminization of poverty. The *feminization of poverty*, which refers to the increasing proportion of America's poor who are women, accounts for virtually the entire increase in poverty in the United States since 1970. Sharp differences between the public and private spheres and the gender stratification that such a distinction promotes do not appear to be cultural universals.

GLOSSARY

domestic: Within or pertaining to the home.

domestic-public dichotomy: Contrast between women's role in the home and men's role in public life, with a corresponding social devaluation of women's work and worth.

environmentalists: See *nurturists*.

Etoro: Papua–New Guinea culture in which males are culturally trained to prefer homosexuality.

extradomestic: Outside the home; within or pertaining to the public domain.

gender roles: The tasks and activities that a culture assigns to each sex.

gender stereotypes: Oversimplified but strongly held ideas about the characteristics of males and females.

gender stratification: Unequal distribution of rewards (socially valued resources, power, prestige, and personal freedom) between men and women, reflecting their different positions in a social hierarchy.

Iroquois: Confederation of tribes in aboriginal New York; matrilineal with communal longhouses and a prominent political, religious, and economic role for women.

matriarchy: A society ruled by women; unknown to ethnography.

matrifocal: Mother-centered; often refers to a household with no resident husband-father.

matrons: Senior women, as among the Iroquois.

naturists: Those who argue that human behavior and social organization are biologically determined.

nurturists: Those who relate behavior and social organization to environmental factors. Nurturists focus on variation rather than universals and stress learning and the role of culture in human adaptation.

patrilineal-virilocal complex: An interrelated constellation of patrilineality, virilocality, warfare, and male supremacy.

sexual dimorphism: Marked differences in male and female biology besides the contrasts in breasts and genitals.

uxorilocality: Customary residence with the wife's relatives after marriage.

virilocality: Customary residence with the husband's relatives after marriage.

STUDY QUESTIONS

1. What is the dominant position in anthropology regarding the argument that the destinies of men and women are linked with their respective anatomies and genetic makeups?
2. What is the difference between gender roles, gender stereotypes, and gender stratification?
3. How do gender roles in traditional !Kung society compare with those in U.S. or Canadian society?
4. How does gender stratification differ in societies that are matrilineal and uxorilocal compared with those that are patrilineal and virilocal?
5. How are Etoro sexual practices related to patterns of male-female relations in Papua–New Guinea and in patrilineal-virilocal cultures generally?
6. How does gender stratification differ in agricultural versus horticultural societies?
7. How have gender roles in the United States changed in the twentieth century? What has caused these changes?
8. What determines variation in gender roles, and what does this variation suggest for societies of the future?

SUGGESTED ADDITIONAL READING

BEHAR, R., AND D. A. GORDON, EDS.
  1995 *Women Writing Culture.* Berkeley: University of California Press. Feminist scholars reflect on identity and difference.

BONVILLAN, N.
  1995 *Women and Men: Cultural Constructions of Gender.* Englewood Cliffs, NJ: Prentice-Hall. A cross-cultural study of gender roles and relationships, from bands to industrial societies.

BOSERUP, E.
  1970 *Women's Role in Economic Development.* London: Allen & Unwin. A classic examination of woman's changing role as cultivation intensifies, including plow agriculture and the domestic-public dichotomy.

BOURQUE, S. C., AND K. B. WARREN
  1981 *Women of the Andes: Patriarchy and Social Change in Two Peruvian Villages.* Ann Arbor: University of Michigan Press. Comparison of two communities with respect to traditional and modern gender hierarchies, capitalization, and directions of development.

CARVER, T.
  1995 *Gender Is Not a Synonym for Women.* Boulder, CO: Lynne Reinner. Gender in relation to class, race, ethnicity, sex, and sexuality.

COLLIER, J. F., AND S. J. YANAGISAKO, EDS.
  1987 *Gender and Kinship: Essays toward a Unified Analysis.* Stanford, CA: Stanford University Press. Several essays examine women, men, kinship, and marriage in varied cultural settings.

CONNELL, R. W.
  1995 *Masculinities.* Berkeley: University of California Press. Changing notions of masculinity in the context of a global economy.

DAHLBERG, F., ED.
  1981 *Woman the Gatherer.* New Haven, CT: Yale University Press. Female roles and activities among prehistoric and contemporary foragers.

DI LEONARDO, M., ED.
  1991 *Gender at the Crossroads of Knowledge: Feminist Anthropology in the Postmodern Era.* Berkeley: University of California Press. Up-to-date presentation of issues in feminist anthropology. Twelve essays discuss biological anthropology, primate studies, the global economy, reproductive technologies, race, and gender.

GILMORE, D.
  1990 *Manhood in the Making: Cultural Concepts of Masculinity.* New Haven, CT: Yale University Press. Cross-cultural study of manhood as an achieved status.

GORDON, A. A.
  1996 *Transforming Capitalism and Patriarchy: Gender and Development in Africa.* Boulder, CO: Lynne Reinner. The implications for women of current political and economic reform efforts in Africa.

KIMMEL, M. S., AND M. A. MESSNER, EDS.
  1995 *Men's Lives,* 3rd ed. Needham Heights, MA: Allyn & Bacon. The study of men in society and concepts of masculinity as they vary from culture to culture.

MARGOLIS, M.
  1984 *Mothers and Such: American Views of Women and How They Changed.* Berkeley: University of California Press. The evolution of the female role, women's work, and attitudes about female nature and activities in the United States since its settlement.

MILLER, B. D., ED.
  1993 *Sex and Gender Hierarchies.* New York: Cambridge University Press. A series of articles, including several essays on human gender hierarchies, as well as those of nonhuman primates.

MORGEN, S., ED.
  1989 *Gender and Anthropology: Critical Reviews for Research and Teaching.* Washington, DC: American Anthropological Association. Most up-to-date review of scholarship on gender in many areas of the world and in a biosocial perspective.

MUKHOPADHYAY, C., AND P. HIGGINS
  1988 Anthropological Studies of Women's Status Revisited: 1977–1987. *Annual Review of Anthropology* 17: 461–495. Extensive review of the cross-cultural literature on the subject.

NASH, J., AND H. SAFA, EDS.
  1986 *Women and Change in Latin America.* South Hadley, MA: Bergin and Garvey. Articles by anthropologists on gender, political economy, and social change in Latin America.

NEVID, J. S., AND RATHUS, S. A.
  1995 *Human Sexuality in a World of Diversity,* 2nd ed. Needham Heights, MA: Allyn & Bacon. Multicultural and ethnic perspectives.

NUSSBAUM, M., AND J. GLOVER, EDS.
  1995 *Women, Culture, and Development: A Study of Human Capabilities.* New York: Oxford University Press. Issues of gender justice and female equality worldwide.

REITER, R., ED.
    1975   *Toward an Anthropology of Women*. New York: Monthly Review Press. Classic anthology, with a particular focus on peasant societies.

ROSALDO, M. Z.
    1980   *Knowledge and Passion: Notions of Self and Social Life*. Stanford, CA: Stanford University Press. Role of travel, experience, knowledge, and emotion in the gender hierarchy of a stateless society in the Philippines.

ROSALDO, M. Z., AND L. LAMPHERE, EDS.
    1974   *Woman, Culture, and Society*. Stanford, CA: Stanford University Press. Another classic anthology, covering many areas of the world.

SACHS, C. E.
    1996   *Gendered Fields: Rural Women, Agriculture, and Environment*. Boulder, CO: Westview. How the changing global economy affects rural women.

WARD, M. C.
    1996   *A World Full of Women*. Needham Heights, MA: Allyn & Bacon. A global and comparative approach to the study of women.

CHAPTER 17

RELIGION

ORIGINS, FUNCTIONS, AND EXPRESSIONS OF RELIGION
Animism
Mana and Taboo
Magic and Religion
Anxiety, Control, Solace
The Social Functions of Ritual Acts
Rites of Passage
Totems: Symbols of Society
The Nature of Ritual

ANALYSIS OF MYTH
Structural Analysis
Fairy Tales

Box: Halloween: An American Ritual of Rebellion

In the News: A Japanese Ritual of Rebellion

Secular Rituals

RELIGION AND CULTURE

RELIGION AND CHANGE
Revitalization Movements

RELIGION AND CULTURAL ECOLOGY
The Adaptive Significance of Sacred Cattle in India
The Cultural Ecology of Ceremonial Feasts

The anthropologist Anthony F. C. Wallace has defined **religion** as "belief and ritual concerned with supernatural beings, powers, and forces" (1966, p. 5). Like ethnicity or language, religion may be associated with social divisions within and between societies and nations. Religious behavior and beliefs both unite and divide. Participation in common rites may affirm, and thus maintain, the social solidarity of a religion's adherents. On the other hand, religious differences may be associated with bitter enmity.

In studying religion cross-culturally, anthropologists pay attention not only to the social roles of religion but also to the nature and content of religious acts, actions, events, processes, settings, practitioners, specialists, and organizations. We also consider such verbal manifestations of religious beliefs as prayers, chants, invocations, myths, fables, tales, texts, and statements about ethics, standards, and morality.

The supernatural is the extraordinary realm outside (but believed to touch on) the observable world. It is nonempirical, unverifiable, mysterious, and inexplicable in ordinary terms. Supernatural beings—gods and goddesses, ghosts, and souls—are not of the material world. Nor are supernatural forces, some of which are wielded by beings. Other sacred forces are impersonal; they simply exist. In many societies, however, people believe that they can benefit from, become imbued with, or manipulate supernatural forces.

Religion, as defined here, exists in all human societies. It is a cultural universal. However, we shall see that it isn't always easy to distinguish the supernatural from the natural and that different cultures conceptualize supernatural entities very differently.

ORIGINS, FUNCTIONS, AND EXPRESSIONS OF RELIGION

Any statement about when, where, why, and how religion arose, or any description of its original nature, is pure speculation. Nevertheless, although such speculations are inconclusive, many have revealed important functions and effects of religious behavior. Several theories will be examined now.

Animism

The founder of the anthropology of religion was the Englishman Sir Edward Burnett Tylor (1871/1958). Religion was born, Tylor thought, as people tried to understand conditions and events they could not explain by reference to daily experience. Tylor believed that our ancestors—and contemporary nonindustrial peoples—were particularly intrigued with death, dreaming, and trance. In dreams and trances, people experience a form of suspended animation. On waking, they recall images from the dream world.

Tylor concluded that attempts to explain dreams and trances led early humans to believe that two entities inhabit the body, one active during the day and the other—a double or soul—active during sleep and trance states. Although they never meet, they are vital to each other. When the double permanently leaves the body, the person dies. Death is departure of the soul. From the Latin for soul, *anima,* Tylor named this belief animism.

Tylor proposed that religion evolved through stages, beginning with animism. **Polytheism** (the belief in multiple gods) and then **monotheism** (the belief in a single, all-powerful deity) developed later. Because religion originated to explain things people didn't understand, Tylor thought it would decline as science offered better explanations. To an extent, he was right. We now have scientific explanations for many things that religion once elucidated. Nevertheless, because religion persists, it must do something more than explain the mysterious. It must, and does, have other functions.

Mana and Taboo

There was a competing view to Tylor's theory of **animism** (the belief in souls and other spiritual *beings*) as the first religion. The alternative was that early humans saw the supernatural as a domain of impersonal power, or *force,* that people could control under certain conditions. Such a conception of the supernatural is particularly prominent in Melanesia, the area of the South Pacific that includes Papua–New Guinea and adjacent islands. Melanesians believed in **mana,** a sacred impersonal force existing in the universe. Mana can reside in people, animals, plants, and objects.

Melanesian mana was similar to our notion of luck. Melanesians attributed success to mana, which people could acquire or manipulate in different ways, such as through magic. Objects with mana could change someone's luck. For example, a charm belonging to a successful hunter might transmit the hunter's mana to the next person who held it. A woman might put a rock in her garden, see her yields improve dramatically, and attribute the change to the force contained in the rock.

Beliefs in manalike forces are widespread, although the specifics of the religious doctrines vary. Consider the contrast between mana in Melanesia and Polynesia (the islands included in a triangular area marked by Hawaii to the north, Easter Island to the east, and New Zealand to the southwest). In Melanesia, one could acquire mana by chance, or by working hard to get it. In Polynesia, however, mana was not potentially available to everyone but was attached to political offices. Chiefs and nobles had more mana than ordinary people did.

So charged with mana were the highest chiefs that contact with them was dangerous to the commoners. The mana of chiefs flowed out of their bodies wherever they went. It could infect the ground, making it dangerous for others to walk in the chief's footsteps. It could permeate the containers and utensils chiefs used in eating. Contact between chief and commoners was dangerous because mana could have an effect like an electric shock. Because high chiefs had so much mana, their bodies and possessions were **taboo** (set apart as sacred and off-limits to ordinary people). Contact between a high chief and commoners was forbidden. Because ordinary people couldn't bear as much sacred current as royalty could, when commoners were accidentally exposed, purification rites were necessary.

We see that one function of religion is to explain. The belief in souls explains what happens in sleep, trance, and death. Melanesian mana explains success that people can't understand in ordinary, natural terms. People fail at hunting, warfare, or gardening not because they are lazy, stupid, or inept but because success comes—or doesn't come—from the supernatural world.

The beliefs in spiritual beings (e.g., animism) and supernatural forces (e.g., mana) fit within the definition of religion given at the beginning of this chapter. Most religions include both spirits and impersonal forces. Likewise the supernatural beliefs of contemporary North American people include beings (gods, saints, souls, demons) and forces (charms, talismans, and sacred objects).

Beliefs in mana—a supernatural force or power, which people may manipulate for their own ends—are widespread. Mana can reside in people, animals, plants, and objects, such as the skull held here by a member of the head-hunting Iban tribe of Malaysia.

Magic and Religion

Magic refers to supernatural techniques intended to accomplish specific aims. These techniques include spells, formulas, and incantations used with deities or with impersonal forces. Magicians use *imitative magic* to produce a desired effect by imitating it. If magicians wish to injure or kill someone, they may imitate that effect on an image of the victim. Sticking pins in "voodoo dolls" is an example. With *contagious magic*, whatever is done to an object is believed to affect a person who once had contact with it. Sometimes practitioners of contagious magic use body products from prospective victims—their nails or hair, for example. The spell performed on the body product is believed to reach the person eventually and work the desired result.

We find magic in cultures with diverse religious beliefs. It can be associated with animism, mana, polytheism, and even monotheism. Magic is neither simpler nor more primitive than animism or the belief in mana.

Anxiety, Control, Solace

Religion and magic don't just explain things and help people accomplish goals. They also enter the domain of feelings. In other words, they do not have just explanatory (cognitive) functions but have emotional ones as well. For example, supernatural beliefs and practices can help reduce anxiety. Magical techniques can dispel doubts that arise when outcomes are beyond human control. Similarly, religion helps people face death and endure life crises.

Although all societies have techniques to deal with everyday matters, there are certain aspects of people's lives over which they lack control. When people face uncertainty and danger, according to Malinowski, they turn to magic.

> [H]owever much knowledge and science help man in allowing him to obtain what he wants, they are unable completely to control chance, to eliminate accidents, to foresee the unexpected turn of natural events, or to make human handiwork reliable and adequate to all practical requirements. (1931/1978, p. 39)

Malinowski found that the Trobriand Islanders used magic when sailing, a hazardous activity. He proposed that because people can't control matters such as wind, weather, and the fish supply, they turn to magic. People may call on magic when they come to a gap in the knowledge or powers of practical control yet have to continue in a pursuit (Malinowski 1931/1978).

According to Malinowski, magic is used to establish control, but religion "is born out of . . . the real tragedies of human life" (Malinowski 1931/1978, p. 45). Religion offers emotional comfort, particularly when people face a crisis. Malinowski saw tribal religions as concerned mainly with such crises of life as birth, puberty, marriage, and death.

The Social Functions of Ritual Acts

Magic and religion can reduce anxiety and allay fears. Ironically, rituals and beliefs can also *create* anxiety and a sense of insecurity and danger (Radcliffe-Brown 1962/1965). Anxiety may arise *because* a rite exists. Indeed, participation in a rite may build up a common stress whose reduction, through the completion of the rite, enhances the solidarity of the participants.

Rites of Passage

The traditional vision quests of Native Americans, particularly the Plains Indians, illustrate **rites of passage** (customs associated with the transition from one place or stage of life to another), which are found throughout the world. Among the Plains Indians, to move from boyhood to manhood, a youth temporarily separated from his community. After a period of isolation in the wilderness, often featuring fasting and drug consumption, the young man would see a vision, which would become his guardian spirit. He would then return to his community as an adult.

The rites of passage of contemporary cultures include confirmations, baptisms, bar and bat mitzvahs, and fraternity hazing. Passage rites involve changes in social status, such as from boyhood to manhood and from nonmember to sorority sister. More generally, a rite of passage may mark any change in place, condition, social position, or age.

All rites of passage have three phases: separation, margin, and aggregation. In the first phase, people withdraw from the group and begin moving from one place or status to another. In the third phase, they reenter society, having completed the rite. The *margin* phase is the most interesting. It is the period between states, the limbo during which people have left one place or state but haven't yet entered or joined the next. We call this the liminal phase of the passage rite (Turner 1974).

Liminality always has certain characteristics. Liminal people occupy ambiguous social positions. They exist apart from ordinary distinctions and expectations, living in a time out of time. They are cut off from normal social contacts. A variety of contrasts may demarcate liminality from regular social life. For example, among the Ndembu of Zambia, a chief had to undergo a passage rite before taking of-

Liminal people, like these Mandji girls in Gabon, West Africa, who are temporarily confined to a menstrual hut, exist apart from ordinary distinctions and expectations, living in a time out of time. They are cut off from normal social contacts. A variety of contrasts, such as their body paint, may demarcate liminality from regular social life.

fice. During the liminal period, his past and future positions in society were ignored, even reversed. He was subjected to a variety of insults, orders, and humiliations.

Unlike the vision quest and the Ndembu initiation, which are individual experiences, passage rites are often collective. Several individuals—boys being circumcised, fraternity or sorority initiates, men at military boot camps, football players in summer training camps, women becoming nuns—pass through the rites together as a group. Table 17.1 summarizes the contrasts or oppositions between liminality and normal social life.

Most notable is a social aspect of *collective liminality* called **communitas** (Turner 1969), an intense community spirit, a feeling of great social solidarity, equality, and togetherness. People experiencing liminality together form a community of equals. The social distinctions that have existed before or will exist afterward are temporarily forgotten. Liminal people experience the same treatment and conditions and must act alike. Liminality may be marked ritually and symbolically by *reversals* of ordinary behavior. For example, sexual taboos may be intensified, or conversely, sexual excess may be encouraged.

Liminality is part of every passage rite. Furthermore, in certain societies, it can become a permanent feature of particular groups. This happens most notably in state-organized societies. Religious groups often use liminal characteristics to set them-

selves off from others. Humility, poverty, equality, obedience, sexual abstinence, and silence may be

Table 17.1 *Oppositions between Liminality and Normal Social Life*

Liminality	Normal Social Structure
transition	state
homogeneity	heterogeneity
communitas	structure
equality	inequality
anonymity	names
absence of property	property
absence of status	status
nakedness or uniform dress	dress distinctions
sexual continence or excess	sexuality
minimization of sex distinctions	maximization of sex distinctions
absence of rank	rank
humility	pride
disregard of personal appearance	care for personal appearance
unselfishness	selfishness
total obedience	obedience only to superior rank
sacredness	secularity
sacred instruction	technical knowledge
silence	speech
simplicity	complexity
acceptance of pain and suffering	avoidance of pain and suffering

Source: Adapted from Victor W. Turner, *The Ritual Process.* Copyright © 1969 by Victor W. Turner. By permission of Aldine de Gruyter, New York.

Passage rites are often collective. A group—such as these initiates in Togo or these Marine recruits in South Carolina— passes through the rites as a unit. Such liminal people experience the same treatment and conditions and must act alike. They share communitas, an intense community spirit, a feeling of great social solidarity or togetherness.

conditions of membership in a sect. Liminal features may also signal the sacredness of persons, settings, and events by setting them off as extraordinary—outside normal social space and regular time.

Totems: Symbols of Society

Thus rituals may serve the social function of creating temporary or permanent solidarity between people—forming a social community. We see this also in religious practices known as totemism. Totemism was important in the religions of the Native Australians. *Totems* could be animals, plants, or geographical features. In each tribe, groups of people had particular totems. Members of each totemic group believed themselves to be descendants of their totem. They customarily neither killed nor ate it, but this taboo was lifted once a year, when people assembled for ceremonies dedicated to the totem.

These annual rites were believed to be necessary for the totem's survival and reproduction.

Totemism is a religion that uses nature as a model for society. The totems are usually animals and plants, which are part of nature. People relate to nature through their totemic association with natural species. Because each group has a different totem, social differences mirror natural contrasts. Diversity in the natural order becomes a model for separation in the social order. However, although totemic plants and animals occupy different niches in nature, on another level they are united because they all are part of nature. The unity of the human social order is enhanced by symbolic association with and imitation of the natural order (Durkheim 1912/1961; Radcliffe-Brown 1962/1965; Lévi-Strauss 1963).

One role of religious rites and beliefs is to affirm, and thus maintain, the solidarity of a religion's adherents. ("A family that prays together stays together.") Totems are sacred emblems symbolizing common identity. In totemic rites, people gather together to honor their totem. In so doing, they use ritual to maintain the social oneness that the totem symbolizes.

The Nature of Ritual

Several features distinguish **rituals** from other kinds of behavior (Rappaport 1974). Rituals are formal—stylized, repetitive, and stereotyped. People perform them in special (sacred) places and at set times. Rituals include **liturgical orders**—sequences of words and actions invented prior to the current performance of the ritual in which they occur.

These features link rituals to plays, but there are important differences. Plays have audiences rather than participants. Actors merely *portray* something, but ritual performers—who make up congregations—are *in earnest*. Rituals convey information about the participants and their traditions. Repeated year after year, generation after generation, rituals translate enduring messages, values, and sentiments into action.

Rituals are *social* acts. Inevitably, some participants are more committed than others are to the beliefs that lie behind the rites. However, just by taking part in a joint public act, the performers signal that they accept a common social and moral order, one that transcends their status as individuals.

ANALYSIS OF MYTH

Cross-cultural research has documented a rich variety of ideas about the supernatural, including animism, mana, taboo, and totemism. We have seen that participation in a ritual creates solidarity. Regardless of their particular thoughts and varied degrees of commitment, the participants temporarily submerge their individuality in a community. Like descent, marriage, gender, and the other social forces we have examined, religion can be a powerful molder of social solidarity.

Nevertheless, the anthropological study of religion is not limited to religion's social effects or its expression in rites and ceremonies. Anthropology also studies religious and quasi-religious stories about supernatural entities—the myths and tales of long ago or far away that are retold across the generations in every society.

Myths often include people's own account of their creation, of the beginning of their world and the extraordinary events that affected their ancestors. They may also tell of the continuing exploits and activities of deities or spirits either in an alternative world or as they come into occasional contact with mortals. Myths, legends, and folk tales express cultural beliefs and values. They offer hope, excitement, and escape. They also teach lessons that society wants taught.

Structural Analysis

One way of studying myth is structural analysis, or **structuralism,** developed by Claude Lévi-Strauss, a prolific French anthropologist. Lévi-Straussian structuralism (1967) aims not at *explaining* relations, themes, and connections among aspects of culture but at *discovering* them. It differs in its goals and results from the methods of gathering and interpreting data usually used in the sciences. Because structuralism is as close to the humanities as it is to science, structuralist methods have been used in analyzing literature and art as well as in anthropology.

Myths and folk tales are the (oral) literature of nonliterate societies. Lévi-Strauss used structuralism to analyze the cultural creations of such societies, including their myths. Structuralism rests on Lévi-Strauss's belief that human minds have certain characteristics which originate in features of the *Homo sapiens* brain. These common mental structures lead people everywhere to think similarly regardless of their society or cultural background. Among these universal mental characteristics are the need to classify: to impose order on aspects of nature, on people's relation to nature, and on relations between people.

According to Lévi-Strauss, a universal aspect of classification is opposition, or contrast. Although many phenomena are continuous rather than discrete, the mind, because of its need to impose order, treats them as being more different than they are. Things that are quantitatively rather than qualitatively different are made to seem absolutely dissimilar. Scientific classification is the Western academic outgrowth of the universal need to impose order. One of the most common means of classifying is by using **binary opposition.** Good and evil, white and black, old and young, high and low are oppositions that, according to Lévi-Strauss, reflect the human need to convert differences of degree into differences of kind.

Lévi-Strauss has applied his assumptions about classification and binary opposition to myths and folk tales. He has shown that these narratives have simple building blocks—elementary structures of "mythemes." Examining the myths of different cultures, Lévi-Strauss shows that one tale can be converted into another through a series of simple operations, for example, by doing the following:

1. Converting the positive element of a myth into its negative
2. Reversing the order of the elements
3. Replacing a male hero with a female hero
4. Preserving or repeating certain key elements

Through such operations, two apparently dissimilar myths can be shown to be variations on a common structure, that is, to be transformations of each other. One example is Lévi-Strauss's analysis of "Cinderella" (1967), a widespread tale whose elements vary between neighboring cultures. Through reversals, oppositions, and negations, as the tale is told, retold, diffused, and incorporated within the traditions of successive societies, "Cinderella" becomes "Ash Boy," after a series of contrasts related to the change in hero's gender.

Structuralism has been widely applied to the myths of nonindustrial cultures, but we can also use it to analyze narratives in our own society. Interested students may wish to read the Appendix, which includes several examples—including *Star Wars* and *The Wizard of Oz*—drawn from contemporary popular culture.

Fairy Tales

In his book *The Uses of Enchantment: The Meaning and Importance of Fairy Tales* (1975) the psychologist Bruno Bettelheim drew a useful distinction between two kinds of tale: the tragic myth and the hopeful folk tale. Tragic myths include many Biblical accounts (that of Job, for example) and Greco-Roman myths that confront humans with powerful, capricious, and awesome supernatural entities. Such tales focus on the huge gap between mortals and the supernatural. In contrast, the folk or fairy tales found in many cultures use fantasy to offer hope and to suggest the possibility of growth and self-realization. Bettelheim argues that this message is particularly important for children. The characters in the myths and tales of bands and tribes are not powerful beings but plants, animals, humans, and nature spirits who use intelligence, physical prowess, or cunning to accomplish their ends. State societies retain hopeful tales along with the tragedies.

Bettelheim urges parents to read or tell folk or fairy tales to their children. He chides American parents and librarians for pushing children to read "realistic" and "prosocial" stories, which often are dull, complex, and psychologically empty. Folk or fairy tales, in contrast, allow children to identify with heroes who win out in the end. These stories offer confidence that no matter how bad things seem now, they will improve. They give reassurance that although small and insignificant now, the child will eventually grow up and achieve independence from parents and siblings.

Similar to the way Lévi-Strauss focuses on binary oppositions, Bettelheim analyzes how fairy tales permit children to deal with their ambivalent feelings (love and hate) about their parents and siblings. Fairy tales often split the good and bad aspects of the parent into separate figures of good and evil. Thus, in "Cinderella," the mother is split in two, an evil stepmother and a fairy go(o)dmother. Cinderella's two evil stepsisters disguise hostile and rivalrous feelings toward real siblings. A tale such as "Cinderella" permits the child to deal with hostile feelings toward parents and siblings, since the positive feelings are preserved in the idealized good figure.

HALLOWEEN: AN AMERICAN RITUAL OF REBELLION

Brazil is famous for *Carnaval*, a pre-Lenten festival celebrated the four days before Ash Wednesday. Carnival occurs, but has a limited distribution, in the United States. Here we know it as the Mardi Gras for which New Orleans is famous. Mardi Gras (Fat Tuesday) is part of a Latin tradition that New Orleans, because of its French background, shares with Brazil. France and Italy also have carnival. Nowhere, however, do people invest as much in carnival—in money, costumes, time, and labor—as they do in Rio de Janeiro. There, on the Saturday and Sunday before Mardi Gras, a dozen samba schools, each with thousands of members, take to the streets to compete in costumes, rhythmic dancing, chanting, singing, and overall presentation.

The United States lacks any national celebration that is exactly equivalent to carnival, but we do have Halloween, which is similar in some respects. Even if Americans don't dance in the street on Halloween, children do go out ringing bells and demanding "trick or treat." As they do things they don't do on ordinary nights, they also disguise themselves in costumes, as Brazilians do at carnival.

The common thread in the two events is that they are times of culturally permitted *inversion*—carnival much more strongly and obviously than Halloween (see the box in Chapter 16, "Gender"). In the United States Halloween is the only nationally celebrated occasion that dramatically inverts the normal relationship between children and adults. Halloween is a night of disguises and reversals. Normally, children are at home or in school, taking part in supervised activities. Kids are domesticated and diurnal—active during the day. Halloween per-

Halloween is a kind of ritual of rebellion, which allows subordinates (children) to turn, symbolically at least, on the powerful (adults). Children love to cloak themselves in evil as they enjoy special privileges of naughtiness.

mits them to become—once a year—nocturnal invaders of public space. Furthermore, *they can be bad*. Halloween's symbolism is potent. Children love to cloak themselves in evil as they enjoy the special privileges of naughtiness. Darth Vader and Freddy Krueger are much more popular Halloween figures than are Luke Skywalker and the Smurfs.

Properly enculturated American kids aren't normally let loose on the streets at night. They aren't usually permitted to ask their neighbors for doles. They don't generally walk around the neighborhood dressed as witches, goblins, or vampires. Traditionally, the expectation that children be good little boys and girls has been overlooked on Halloween. "Trick or treat" recalls the days when the children who didn't get treats would pull tricks such as soaping windows, turning over flower boxes, and setting off firecrackers on a grouch's porch.

Halloween is like the "rituals of rebellion" that anthropologists have

described in African societies, times when normal power relations are inverted, when the powerless turn on the powerful, expressing resentments they suppress during the rest of the year. Halloween lets kids meddle with the dark side of the force. Children can command adults to do their bidding and punish the adults if they don't. Halloween behavior inverts the scoldings and spankings that adults inflict on kids. For adults, Halloween is a minor occasion, not even a holiday. For children, however, it's a favorite time, a special night. Kids know what rituals of rebellion are all about.

Halloween is therefore a festival that inverts two oppositions important in American life: the adult-child power balance and expectations about good and evil. Halloween's origin can be traced back 2,000 years to Samhain, the Day of the Dead, the most significant holiday in the Celtic religion (Santino 1983). Given its historical development through pagan rites, church suppression, and beliefs about witches and demons, Halloween continues to turn the distinction between good and bad on its head. Innocent children dress as witches and demons and act out their fantasies of rebellion and destruction. Once during the year, real adult witches are interviewed on talk shows, where they have a chance to describe their beliefs as solemnly as orthodox religious figures do. Puritan morality and the need for proper public behavior are important themes in American society. The rules are in abeyance on Halloween, and normal things are inverted. This is why Halloween, like *Carnaval* in Brazil, persists as a ritual of reversal and rebellion, particularly as an escape valve for the frustrations and resentments that build during enculturation.

IN THE NEWS: A JAPANESE RITUAL OF REBELLION

A ritual of rebellion is an institutionalized way for people to express resentments they usually suppress. The Japanese New Year's Eve ritual described here is like Halloween (see the box in this chapter) and Carnaval (see the box in Chapter 16, "Gender"). It is a formal relief-valve that lets people reverse, temporarily, their ordinary "polite" behavior and vent their frustrations.

Ashikaga, Japan, Jan. 1—The life of a typical Japanese—working endless hours, enduring long commutes on packed trains and adhering to rigid rules of behavior—would drive many Americans to the brink of rage. But Japanese seem to bottle up any anger and maintain their world-famous politeness.

Except just before midnight on New Year's Eve in Ashikaga.

In this city about 50 miles north of Tokyo, people take this one occasion to let it all hang out and say what they really think about the year gone by. In one of the strangest festivals in a country full of festivals, they walk up a dark mountain road to a temple screaming curses into the starry night sky that they would never say directly to their fellow man.

"Once a year, we can get rid of our pent-up frustrations," said Ryoken Numajiri, the head priest of the Saishoji Temple. The temple is the headquarters for the Akutare Matsuri, which might best be translated as the "naughty festival" or perhaps the "festival of abusive language."

This year, of course, there was plenty for the roughly 400 participants to be abusive about, what with a national political scandal, the economy in the dumps and the stock market continuing its three-year slide. This city of 170,000 did not escape the pain, with the nearby electronics and automobile factories reducing overtime hours and part-time jobs. . . .

But other marchers complained about daily life, about too much schoolwork, or poor grades on tests. For some it was just an opportunity to escape from normal social strictures. "Women are not allowed to say such words," said Miyoko Kuwako, a housewife. "But it's O.K. tonight."

The festival, which is the only one of its kind in Japan, originated more than 200 years ago as a relief valve for repressed workers, Mr. Numajiri said. At that time, he said, women were brought in from the surrounding countryside to work in factories making material for kimonos. The work was arduous, and the hours were long. But in return for persevering through the year, their boss would take them to the temple once a year so they could let off steam.

Japanese place a high value on patience and perseverance. Even when they do let loose, Japanese curses are mild by American standards, with a more limited selection of swear words.

Bettleheim contends that it doesn't matter much whether the hero is male or female, because children of both sexes can usually find psychological satisfaction of some sort in a fairy tale. However, traditional male heroes usually slay dragons, giants, or monsters (representing the father) and free princesses from captivity, whereas female characters accomplish something, such as spinning straw into gold or capturing a witch's broomstick, and then return home or establish a home of their own.

Secular Rituals

We must recognize certain problems in the cross-cultural study of religion and in the definition of religion given earlier. The first problem: If we define religion with reference to supernatural beings, powers, and forces, how do we classify ritual-like behavior that occurs in secular contexts? Some anthropologists believe that there are both sacred and secular rituals. Secular rituals include formal, invariant, stereotyped, earnest, repetitive behavior that takes place in nonreligious settings.

A second problem: If the distinction between the ordinary and the supernatural is not consistently made in certain societies, how can we tell what is religion and what is not? The Betsileo of Madagascar, for example, view witches and dead ancestors as real people who play roles in ordinary life. However, their powers are not empirically demonstrable.

A third problem: The kind of behavior considered appropriate for religious occasions varies tremendously from culture to culture. One society may consider drunken frenzy the surest sign of faith, whereas another may inculcate quiet reverence. Who is to say which is "more religious"?

The main word shouted by the festival participants was "bakayaro!" which might be literally translated as "you idiot" but sometimes has the connotation of "God damn it." It is the expletive a Japanese driver might yell out the window when another car suddenly cuts in front of his. It might not seem so bad, but it is one of the closest things here to a four-letter word.

New Year's Eve and New Year's Day are traditionally times when millions of Japanese, some clad in traditional kimonos, flock to Buddhist temples or Shinto shrines. But not in the way they do it in Ashikaga.

At 11 P.M. about 200 people began walking up a mountain road to the Saishoji temple led by a man blowing a shell known as a horagai, which is supposed to fend off bad tidings. Many were carrying lanterns and wearing cardboard hats bearing the picture of Bishamonten, one of the seven gods of fortune in Japanese Buddhism and the god in whose honor Mr. Numajiri's temple was built 1,200 years ago. Another 200 people or so followed in buses.

Cries of "bakayaro!" split the night, the extended final "o" sound trailing off into the sky like a coyote's howl. Occasionally there was a more specific complaint like "My teacher is an idiot!" or "Give me a raise!"

After a 40-minute walk, the crowd stormed up the steps to the temple, which is situated atop a 1,000-foot-high hill. The crowd rang the temple bell, clapped their hands and prayed, and bellowed a few more lusty bakayaro's to exorcise the year gone by.

But at the stroke of 12, the insults turned to cries of "congratulations" and "Happy New Year." Many of the worshipers went inside for another ceremony that is unique to this temple, in which people drink sake that is poured onto their foreheads and drips down their faces. The ceremony is supposed to insure that happiness will flow in the year ahead.

Mr. Numajiri, wearing a billowing green robe, called out the name of each worshiper and read aloud his or her wishes for the new year, which the visitors had conveniently circled on multiple-choice lists handed them at the door.

The person whose name was called knelt on the floor and raised a wide red lacquer bowl to his or her lips. As a big taiko drum was pounded, Mr. Numajiri poured the sake onto the person's forehead, and the sake ran down the nose and into the bowl and was consumed.

After venting their anger over the year past and drinking to the year to come, participants said they felt relieved, ready once again to do battle in the factories and offices and crowded trains of modern Japan.

Source: Andrew Pollack, "A Festival That Permits Japanese to Be Impolite," *The New York Times,* January 2, 1993, p. A4.

RELIGION AND CULTURE

Religion is a cultural universal because it has so many causes, effects, and meanings for the people who take part in it. But religions are parts of particular cultures, and cultural differences show up systematically in religious beliefs, practices, and institutions. Religious forms do not vary randomly from society to society. The religions associated with nation-states and stratified societies differ from those of cultures in which social contrasts and power differentials are less marked.

Considering several cultures, Wallace (1966) identified four types of religion: shamanic, communal, Olympian, and monotheistic. The simplest type is shamanic religion. Unlike priests, **shamans** aren't full-time religious officials but part-time religious figures who mediate between people and supernatural beings and forces. All cultures have medico-magico-religious specialists. *Shaman* is the general term encompassing curers ("witch doctors"), mediums, spiritualists, astrologers, palm readers, and other diviners. Wallace found shamanic religions to be most characteristic of hunting and gathering societies, particularly those found in the northern latitudes, such as the Eskimos and the native peoples of Siberia.

Although they are only part-time specialists, shamans often set themselves off symbolically from ordinary people by assuming a different or ambiguous sex or gender role. (In nation-states, priests, nuns, and vestal virgins do something similar by taking vows of celibacy and chastity.) Transvestism is one way of being sexually ambiguous. Among the Chukchee of Siberia (Bogoras 1904), where coastal populations fished and interior groups hunted,

Hunter, gatherer, and shaman are the world's oldest professions. Shamanic religions are typically found among foragers, such as the San (shown here). This San shaman (left) falls into a trance as he heals.

male shamans copied the dress, speech, hair arrangements, and life styles of women. These shamans took other men as husbands and sex partners and received respect for their supernatural and curative expertise. Female shamans could join a fourth gender, copying men and taking wives.

Among the Crow of the North American Plains, certain ritual duties were reserved for **berdaches,** men who rejected the male role of bison hunter, raider, and warrior and joined a third gender (Lowie 1935). *Berdaches* dressed, spoke, and styled their hair like women and pursued such traditionally female activities as cooking and sewing. The fact that certain key rituals could be done only by *berdaches* indicates their regular and normal place in Crow social life.

Communal religions have, in addition to shamans, community rituals such as harvest cere-

monies and rites of passage. Although communal religions lack *full-time* religious specialists, they believe in several deities (**polytheism**) who control aspects of nature. Although some hunter-gatherers, including Australian totemites, have communal religions, these religions are more typical of farming societies.

Olympian religions, which arose with nation-state organization and marked social stratification, add full-time religious specialists—professional priesthoods. Like the nation-state itself, the priesthood is hierarchically and bureaucratically organized. The term *Olympian* comes from Mount Olympus, home of the classical Greek gods. Olympian religions are polytheistic. They include powerful anthropomorphic gods with specialized functions, for example, gods of love, war, the sea, and death. Olympian **pantheons** (collections of supernatural beings) were prominent in the religions of many nonindustrial nation-states, including the Aztecs of Mexico, several African and Asian kingdoms, and classical Greece and Rome. Wallace's fourth type—**monotheism**—also has priesthoods and notions of divine power, but it views the supernatural differently. In monotheism, all supernatural phenomena are manifestations of, or are under the control of, a single eternal, omniscient, omnipotent, and omnipresent supreme being.

RELIGION AND CHANGE

Revitalization Movements

Religion helps maintain social order, but it can also be an instrument of change, sometimes even of revolution. As a response to conquest or foreign domination, religious leaders often undertake to alter or revitalize a society. We call such movements *nativistic movements* (Linton 1943) or **revitalization movements** (Wallace 1956).

Christianity originated as a revitalization movement. Jesus was one of several prophets who preached new religious doctrines while the Middle East was under Roman rule. It was a time of social unrest, when a foreign power ruled the land. Jesus inspired a new, enduring, and major religion. His contemporaries were not so successful.

The Handsome Lake religion arose around 1800 among the Iroquois of New York State (Wallace

1970*b*). Handsome Lake, the founder of this revitalization movement, was a chief of one of the Iroquois tribes. The Iroquois had suffered because of their support of the British against the American colonials. After the colonial victory and a wave of immigration to their homeland, the Iroquois were dispersed on small reservations. Unable to pursue traditional horticulture and hunting in their homeland, the Iroquois became heavy drinkers and quarreled among themselves.

Handsome Lake was a heavy drinker who started having visions from heavenly messengers. The spirits warned him that unless the Iroquois changed their ways, they would be destroyed. His visions offered a plan for coping with the new order. Witchcraft, quarreling, and drinking would end. The Iroquois would copy European farming techniques, which, unlike traditional Iroquois horticulture, stressed male rather than female labor. Handsome Lake preached that the Iroquois should also abandon their communal longhouses and matrilineal descent groups (large kinship groups based exclusively on genealogical links through females) for more permanent marriages and individual family households. The teachings of Handsome Lake produced a new church and religion, one that still has members in New York and Ontario. This revitalization movement helped the Iroquois adapt to and survive in a modified environment. They eventually gained a reputation among their non-Indian neighbors as sober family farmers.

RELIGION AND CULTURAL ECOLOGY

We have considered religious beliefs, practices, institutions, and personnel in different types of society. Finally we turn to the cultural ecology of religion. How does behavior motivated by beliefs in supernatural beings, powers, and forces help people survive in their material environments? In this section we will see how beliefs and rituals function as part of a group's cultural adaptation to its environment.

The Adaptive Significance of Sacred Cattle in India

The people of India worship zebu cattle, which are protected by the Hindu doctrine of *ahimsa,* a principle of nonviolence that forbids the killing of animals generally. Western economic development experts occasionally (and erroneously) cite the Hindu cattle taboo to illustrate the idea that religious beliefs can stand in the way of rational economic decisions. Hindus seem to be irrationally ignoring a valuable food (beef) because of their cultural or religious traditions. The economic developers also

India's zebu cattle are protected by the doctrine of ahimsa, *a principle of nonviolence that forbids the killing of animals generally. This Hindu doctrine puts the full power of organized religion behind the command not to destroy a valuable resource even in times of extreme need.*

comment that Indians don't know how to raise proper cattle. They point to the scraggly zebus that wander about town and country. Western techniques of animal husbandry grow bigger cattle that produce more beef and milk. Western planners lament that Hindus are set in their ways. Bound by culture and tradition, they refuse to develop rationally.

However, these assumptions are both ethnocentric and wrong. Sacred cattle actually play an important adaptive role in an Indian ecosystem that has evolved over thousands of years (Harris 1974, 1978). Peasants' use of cattle to pull plows and carts is part of the technology of Indian agriculture. Indian peasants have no need for large, hungry cattle of the sort that economic developers, beef marketers, and North American cattle ranchers prefer. Scrawny animals pull plows and carts well enough but don't eat their owners out of house and home. How could peasants with limited land and marginal diets feed supersteers without taking food away from themselves?

Indians use cattle manure to fertilize their fields. Not all the manure is collected, because peasants don't spend much time watching their cattle, which wander and graze at will during certain seasons. In the rainy season, some of the manure that cattle deposit on the hillsides washes down to the fields. In this way, cattle also fertilize the fields indirectly. Furthermore, in a country where fossil fuels are scarce, dry cattle dung, which burns slowly and evenly, is a basic cooking fuel.

Far from being useless, as the development experts contend, sacred cattle are essential to Indian cultural adaptation. Biologically adapted to poor pasture land and a marginal environment, the scraggly zebu provides fertilizer and fuel, is indispensable in farming, and is affordable for peasants. The Hindu doctrine of *ahimsa* puts the full power of organized religion behind the command not to destroy a valuable resource even in times of extreme need.

The Cultural Ecology of Ceremonial Feasts

In previous chapters we saw that feasts hosted by big men and chiefs bring people together from several places and thus forge regional communities and political alliances. We saw that potlatching on the Pacific Coast of North America evened out vari-

ations in local production by distributing resources throughout the region. Potlatching also prevented economic differentiation, because wealth was either destroyed or given away (and thus converted into prestige) rather than being hoarded or reinvested to create additional wealth.

In many tribes, intercommunity feasting is a leveling, redistributive mechanism, helping to even out imbalances in access to strategic resources. Although intercommunity feasting is often done for religious purposes, particularly to fulfill obligations to dead ancestors, this religious behavior has real-world effects that may be more obvious to anthropologists than to natives, as the following case illustrates.

This example comes from my own field work among the Betsileo, who grow rice and use cattle as draft animals. The Betsileo live in dispersed hamlets and villages. Hamlets begin as small settlements with two or three households. Over time many grow into villages. All the settlements have ancestral tombs, which are very important in Betsileo culture. It costs much more to build a tomb than to build a house. It's right to spend more on the tomb, say the Betsileo, because one spends eternity in it. A house is just a temporary home.

The Betsileo may be buried in the same tomb as any one of their eight great-grandparents. When a woman has children, she also earns burial rights in her husband's tomb. Most men belong to their father's descent group, live in his village, and will be buried in his tomb. Nevertheless, Betsileo attend ceremonies at all their ancestral tombs, in all of which they have burial rights.

After the annual rice harvest in April and May comes the ceremonial season, when agricultural work is least taxing. Ceremonies honor the ancestors as the Betsileo open the tombs. Sometimes they simply rewrap corpses and bones in new shrouds. Sometimes, in more elaborate ceremonies, they take the bodies and bones outside, dance with them, wrap them in new cloth, and return them to the tomb. Whenever a tomb is built, bodies and bones are moved in from an older family tomb.

During their ceremonies, the Betsileo kill cattle. They offer a small part of the beef to the ancestors; living people eat the rest. After offering meat to the ancestors, people remove it from the altar and eat it as well. The custom of cattle sacrifice arose at a time when there were no markets and the Betsileo lived in small hamlets. At that time, ceremonial distribution was the Betsileo's only source of beef. It was not feasible to kill and eat an entire animal in a small hamlet, because there were too few people to consume it. Nor could the Betsileo buy meat in markets. They got beef by attending ceremonials in villages where they had kinship, descent, and marriage links.

Betsileo also kill cattle for funerals. Again, some beef is dedicated to the ancestors but eaten by the living. People attend the funerals of neighbors, kin, in-laws, and fictive kin. Because funerals occur throughout the year, the Betsileo eat beef and thus obtain animal protein regularly. However, although people can die at any time, Betsileo deaths cluster in certain seasons—especially November to February, the rainy season. This is a period of food shortages, when much of the rice harvested the previous April has been eaten. Many funerals, occasions on which beef and rice are distributed, occur at precisely the time of year (the preharvest season of food scarcity) when people are hungriest. In Betsileo cultural adaptation, funerals distribute food beyond the local group and to the poorest people, helping them survive the lean season.

Today, settlements are larger and the Betsileo have markets. Ceremonies persist, but there are fewer big feasts than there once were. Naturally,

any discussion of the adaptive functions of Betsileo religion raises the question whether the Betsileo started the ceremonies because they recognized their potential adaptive usefulness. The answer is no, but the question is instructive.

The Betsileo maintain these rituals because they honor, commemorate, or appease ancestors, relatives, fictive kin, in-laws, and neighbors. The tomb ceremonies serve many of the social and psychological functions of religion we have discussed. However, although Betsileo receive invitations to several ceremonies each year, they don't attend them all. What determines the individual's decision to attend? If a distant relative or acquaintance dies when people are eating well, they may decide not to go or to send someone junior in their place. However, if an equally distant relative dies during the season of scarcity, many Betsileo, especially poorer people, opt for a day or two of feasting. Some of my Betsileo friends, usually those with small rice fields, became funeral hoppers during the lean season. They used a series of personal connections to attend every available funeral and ceremony. Betsileo ceremonies do not simply maintain social solidarity. They also play a role in cultural adaptation by regulating access to strategic resources, including the nutrients that people need to resist disease and infection and to survive (Kottak 1980).

SUMMARY

Religion, a cultural universal, consists of belief and behavior concerned with supernatural beings, powers, and forces. Cross-cultural studies have revealed many functions of religion. Tylor focused on religion's explanatory role, suggesting that animism—the belief in souls—is religion's most primitive form. He argued that religion evolved from animism through polytheism to monotheism. As science provided better explanations, Tylor thought that religion would eventually disappear. However, a different view of the supernatural also occurs in nonindustrial societies. This sees the supernatural as a domain of raw, impersonal power or force (called *mana* in Polynesia and Melanesia). People can manipulate and control mana under certain conditions.

When ordinary technical and rational means of doing things fail, people may turn to magic, using it when they lack control over outcomes. Religion offers comfort and psychological security at times of crisis. However, rites can also create anxiety. Rituals are formal, invariant, stylized, earnest acts that require people to subordinate their particular beliefs to a social collectivity. Rites of passage have three stages: separation, liminality or margin, and aggregation. Passage rites can mark any change in social status, age, place, or social condition. Collective rites are often cemented by communitas, a feeling of intense solidarity.

The study of religion also leads anthropologists to the cross-cultural analysis of myths and folk tales. These forms of creative expression reveal native theories about the creation of the world and supernatural entities. Myths express cultural values, offer hope, and teach enculturative lessons. The myths of state-organized societies include cautionary tragedies as well as hopeful tales typical of bands and tribes. Lévi-Strauss, the inventor of the structural analysis of myth, has argued that people universally classify aspects of nature and culture by means of binary opposition. Such opposition makes phenomena that are continuous seem more distinct. Structural analysis aims not to explain but to discover otherwise hidden connections among aspects of culture. This approach links anthropology to the humanities.

Wallace defines four types of religion: shamanic, communal, Olympian, and monotheistic. Each has its characteristic ceremonies and practitioners. Religion helps maintain social order, but it can also promote change. Revitalization movements incorporate old and new beliefs and have helped people adapt to changing environments. Besides their psychological and social functions, religious beliefs and practices play a role in the adaptation of human populations to their environments. The Hindu doctrine of *ahimsa*, which prohibits harm to living things, makes cattle sacred and beef a tabooed food. The taboo's force stops peasants from killing their draft cattle even in times of extreme need. This preserves a vital resource for Indian agriculture. Intercommunity feasting also falls within a cultural ecological framework. Betsileo tomb ceremonies redistribute food and other scarce resources.

GLOSSARY

ahimsa: Hindu doctrine that prohibits harming life, and thus cattle slaughter.

animism: Belief in souls or doubles.

berdaches: Among the Crow Indians, members of a third gender, for whom certain ritual duties were reserved.

binary opposition: Pairs of opposites, such as good-evil and old-young, produced by converting differences of degree into qualitative distinctions; important in structuralism.

communal religions: In Wallace's typology, these religions have, in addition to shamanic cults, communal cults in which people organize community rituals such as harvest ceremonies and rites of passage.

communitas: Intense community spirit, a feeling of great social solidarity, equality, and togetherness; characteristic of people experiencing liminality together.

liminality: The critically important marginal or in-between phase of a rite of passage.

liturgical order: A set sequence of words and actions invented prior to the current performance of the ritual in which it occurs.

magic: Use of supernatural techniques to accomplish specific aims.

mana: Sacred impersonal force in Melanesian and Polynesian religions.

monotheism: Worship of an eternal, omniscient, omnipotent, and omnipresent supreme being.

Olympian religions: In Wallace's typology, develop with state organization; have full-time religious specialists—professional priesthoods.

pantheon: A collection of supernatural beings in a particular religion.

polytheism: Belief in several deities who control aspects of nature.

religion: Belief and ritual concerned with supernatural beings, powers, and forces.

revitalization movements: Movements that occur in times of change, in which religious leaders emerge and undertake to alter or revitalize a society.

rites of passage: Culturally defined activities associated with the transition from one place or stage of life to another.

ritual: Behavior that is formal, stylized, repetitive, and stereotyped, performed earnestly as a social act; rituals are held at set times and places and have liturgical orders.

shaman: A part-time religious practitioner who mediates between ordinary people and supernatural beings and forces.

structuralism: Structural analysis; technique developed by Lévi-Strauss not to explain sociocultural similarities and differences but to uncover themes, relations, and other cross-cultural connections.

taboo: Set apart as sacred and off-limits to ordinary people; prohibition backed by supernatural sanctions.

STUDY QUESTIONS

1. How do anthropologists define religion, and what are the problems with this definition?
2. What are the cognitive (explanatory), psychological (emotional), and social functions of religion?
3. What are rituals, and how do they differ from other acts?
4. What is a rite of passage, and what are its phases?
5. Can you give examples of rites of passage from your own experience or from North American culture in general?
6. What is structural analysis, and how do its aims differ from those of science?

7. Can you suggest an aspect of your culture that might be appropriate for a structural analysis? Sketch such an analysis.
8. What are shamans? How are they similar to and different from priests?

9. How do revitalization movements function as an instrument of social change?
10. What ethnographic example could illustrate how religious beliefs and practices have material consequences or ecological functions?

SUGGESTED ADDITIONAL READING

BETTELHEIM, B.
  1975   *The Uses of Enchantment: The Meaning and Importance of Fairy Tales.* New York: Vintage. Neo-Freudian perspective on fairy tales and myths.
BROWN, K. M.
  1991   *Mama Lola: A Vodou Priestess in Brooklyn.* Berkeley: University of California Press. Ethnographic study of a religious community and its leader.
CHILD, A. B., AND I. L. CHILD
  1993   *Religion and Magic in the Lives of Traditional Peoples.* Englewood Cliffs, NJ: Prentice-Hall. A cross-cultural study.
COMBS-SCHILLING, E.
  1989   *Sacred Performances: Islam, Sexuality, and Sacrifice.* New York: Columbia University Press. Historical ethnography of the Moroccan state, focusing on its use of Islamic concepts and ideals, placed in the context of Islam as a world religion.
HARGROVE, E. C.
  1986   *Religion and Environmental Crisis.* Athens: University of Georgia Press. Religion and ecological issues.
HERDT, G.
  1986   *The Sambia: Ritual and Gender in New Guinea.* Fort Worth: Harcourt Brace. This case study also draws out the cross-cultural implications of ritualized homosexuality from boyhood to marriage.
KEHOE, A. B.
  1989   *The Ghost Dance Religion: Ethnohistory and Revitalization.* Fort Worth: Harcourt Brace. Case studies of various religious events important in Native American history and culture.
KLASS, M.
  1995   *Ordered Universes: Approaches to the Anthropology of Religion.* Boulder, CO: Westview. Wide-ranging overview of key issues in the anthropology of religion.
LEHMANN, A. C., AND J. E. MEYERS, EDS.
  1993   *Magic, Witchcraft, and Religion: An Anthropological Study of the Supernatural,* 3rd ed. Mountain View, CA: Mayfield. A comparative reader covering Western and non-Western cultures.
LESSA, W. A., AND E. Z. VOGT, EDS.
  1978   *Reader in Comparative Religion: An Anthropological Approach,* 4th ed. New York: Harper & Row. Excellent collection of major articles on the origins, functions, and expressions of religion in comparative perspective.
MAIR, L.
  1969   *Witchcraft.* New York: McGraw-Hill. Analysis of the social contexts and functions of witchcraft and witchcraft accusations; relies heavily on African data.
MORRIS, B.
  1987   *Anthropological Studies of Religion: An Introductory Text.* New York: Cambridge University Press. Up-to-date text on religion cross-culturally.
RAPPAPORT, R. A.
  1979   *Ecology, Meaning, and Religion.* Richmond, CA: North Atlantic Books. Various essays on religion in cultural and ecological perspective.
SERED, S. S.
  1996   *Priestess, Mother, Sacred Sister: Religions Dominated by Women.* New York: Oxford University Press. The meaning of religion in women's lives across time and space.
TAYLOR, C.
  1996   *The Black Churches of Brooklyn.* New York: Columbia University Press. The vitality of the church in urban adaptations of African-Americans.
TURNER, V. W.
  1995   (orig. 1969) *The Ritual Process.* Hawthorne, NY: Aldine de Gruyter. Liminality among the Ndembu discussed in a comparative perspective.
WALLACE, A. F. C.
  1966   *Religion: An Anthropological View.* New York: Random House. Survey of anthropological approaches to religion.

CHAPTER 18

PERSONALITY AND WORLDVIEW

THE INDIVIDUAL AND CULTURE

PERSONALITY

EARLY CULTURE AND PERSONALITY RESEARCH
Margaret Mead: Child Training and Gender Roles
Ruth Benedict: Cultures as Individuals
National Character

Box: Varieties of Human Sexuality

CROSS-CULTURAL STUDIES

In The News: Making Room on the Couch for Culture

WORLDVIEW
Peasants and Limited Good
The (Sub)Culture of Poverty
The Protestant Ethic and Capitalism

Culture is both public and individual, both in the world and in people's minds. Anthropologists are interested not only in public and collective behavior but also in how *individuals* think, feel, and act. The individual and culture are linked because human social life is a process in which individuals internalize the meanings of *public* (i.e., cultural) messages. Then, alone and in groups, people influence culture by converting their private understandings into public expressions (D'Andrade 1984). We may study this process by focusing on shared, public aspects of culture or by focusing on individuals. Anthropology and psychology intersect in **psychological anthropology,** the ethnographic and cross-cultural study of differences and similarities in human psychology. Focusing on the individual, psychological anthropology exists because a complete account of cultural process requires both perspectives—private and public.

THE INDIVIDUAL AND CULTURE

One area of psychological anthropology is **cognitive anthropology**—the ethnographic and cross-cultural study of cognition—which includes learning, ways of knowing, and the organization of knowledge, perceptions, and meaning. Cognitive anthropology examines private understanding by analyzing aspects of individual behavior, including speech. (This links it to some areas of linguistic anthropology, including the study of meaning, as discussed in the next chapter.)

Drawing on cognitive science, Naomi Quinn and Claudia Strauss (1989, 1994) propose an approach that explicitly links the individual and culture. They start with the assumption that every culture is both (1) a network of shared understandings and (2) a changing product involving negotiation by its individual members. Quinn and Strauss draw on **schema theory,** which is prominent in modern cognitive science (Casson 1983). According to this theory, the mind builds schemata (the plural of *schema*) to filter new experience and reconstruct past experience, shaping memories to conform to current expectations. Linked to schema theory is **connectionism**—the idea that things that consistently occur together in an individual's experience become strongly associated in that person's mind. A schema develops when a set of linked experiences forms a network of strong mental associations.

Schemata produce simplified versions of experience, so that we remember the typical, or modal, event rather than the unusual one. Remembering typical events, we fill in missing information according to expectations created by strong associations. To describe how a child internalizes associations—develops and uses schemata—Quinn and Strauss use the example of a middle-class American girl born just after World War II. During childhood

As members of a culture repeatedly enact their shared mental schemata in public behavior, the typical pattern is reinforced further in their separate minds. If children learn that family goes with food and wine, they build associations of feelings around kinship, food, and wine. Shown here, the conclusion of a Sunday lunch in France's Loire Valley.

this girl builds up a chain of associations in which mother goes with "food, kitchen, home, indoors, everyday routine. Father goes with basement, garage, office, outdoors, special occasions" (Quinn and Strauss, 1989, pp. 6–7). These associations are strengthened because the girl's experience constantly reinforces them. The tendency to remember the typical rather than the unusual can lead individuals to forget or misremember (mistakenly reconstruct in memory) times when the father cooked or the mother worked in the garage.

Diversity among the world's cultures reflects the fact that babies have malleable neural networks, permitting varied learning paths during enculturation. However, as individuals grow, their schemata harden. They make new experiences fit the established pattern more than they change with new experience. One reason why schemata are shared by people in the same culture is the tendency to rely on modal mental images. Although my experience has differed from yours, if we both have experienced the same broad pattern, our schemata retain it. As we enact our shared schemata in our public behavior, the typical pattern is reinforced further in our separate minds.

Cognition and emotions develop together as part of schema formation. Thus if a child learns that mother goes with food, he or she also builds associations of feelings around motherhood and food.

Schemata explain not only the shared aspect of culture but also its openness to diverse individual interpretations and the possibility of cultural change. To illustrate this, Quinn and Strauss (1989, 1994) add a second middle-class American girl to their example. Both girls may have learned that mother goes with kitchen and father goes with office, but beyond that there may be great differences. One girl may associate her father's arrival home with anticipation; the other, with dread. Individual experiences and feelings give rise to differences in schemata among people who grow up in the same culture.

Society has both unifying and divisive forces. Unique schemata arise from distinct individual experiences, while shared schemata are built up from common experience. In modern nations some schemata are shared by millions because of people's exposure to the mass media. Other schemata are shared by smaller groups—ethnic and regional subcultures, people who accidentally share similar experiences, and experts with the same formal training (such as anthropologists). Schemata are like the *levels of culture* discussed in Chapter 3 in that both are associated with a continuum of shared experience and learning. However, schema theory focuses on the cognitive attributes of the *individuals* who share understandings.

Schema theory leaves room for individual creativity, disagreement, resistance, and change. Peo-

Margaret Mead's controversial book Coming of Age in Samoa *(1928/1961), based on a nine-month study, compared Samoan and American adolescence. Samoan personality and culture have changed since Mead did her field work. These young women are celebrating Flag Day in Pago Pago, American Samoa.*

ple aren't doomed to re-create all the patterns they observed in childhood. New social options can provide fresh models for adult behavior. New experiences can create new associations, and associations may be altered by conscious intervention. In such ways behavior (and culture) can change. Our children's schemata and behavior will be both like and unlike our own.

PERSONALITY

Psychological anthropology is sometimes described as the study of "culture and personality." According to one definition, **personality**

> is a more or less enduring organization of forces within the individual associated with a complex of fairly consistent attitudes, values, and modes of perception which account in part for the individual's consistency of behavior. (Barnouw 1985, p. 10)

The consistency of an individual's personality reveals itself in varied settings—work, rest, play, creative activities, and interaction with others. Thus, we can think of personality as an individual's characteristic ways of thinking and acting.

People have different personalities because, except for identical twins, everyone is genetically unique. Furthermore, from conception on, no two people encounter exactly the same environment. The experiences of childhood and later life combine with genetic predispositions to form the psychological attributes of the adult. However, as we saw in the discussion of schema theory, personality attributes can change as adults encounter new problems, situations, and experiences or through conscious intervention.

Psychologists are correct in assuming that despite cultural diversity, all humans share certain mental traits. These similarities aren't necessarily genetic but may arise from universal or nearly universal experiences—birth itself; stages of physiological development; interaction with parents, siblings, and others; and experiences with light and dark, heat and cold, and wet and dry objects.

Anthropologists only occasionally comment on— usually to question— the existence of psychological universals. Instead, the study of culture and personality pursues anthropology's characteristic interest in diversity by examining psychological data cross-culturally. Psychological anthropologists draw on techniques developed by psychologists to examine personality variation within a society and between societies. Research methods include observing behavior in varied settings, conversing about wide-ranging topics, administering psychological tests, analyzing dreams, and collecting life histories. Because child rearing is crucial in personality formation, anthropologists have investigated this process in many societies. As a result, we can generalize about factors that produce certain personalities.

In modern nations, regional, ethnic, and socioeconomic differences influence child-rearing patterns, individual opportunities, and thus personality formation. In studying relationships between personality and culture, anthropologists must examine (1) personality traits common to all or most members of a society and (2) those associated only with social subdivisions. We also consider personality variation that is *not* typical of either society at large or its subgroups, which we call *deviant* behavior.

EARLY CULTURE AND PERSONALITY RESEARCH

Margaret Mead: Child Training and Gender Roles

Margaret Mead (profiled in Chapter 1) did several studies of culture and personality in the Pacific islands, focusing on childhood and adolescence. Her early book *Coming of Age in Samoa* (1928/1961), based on a nine-month study of Samoan girls, compared Samoan and American adolescence. Mead's hypothesis was that the psychological changes associated with puberty are not biologically based but culturally determined. She described Samoan adolescence as a relatively easy period, lacking the sexual frustrations and stresses characteristic of American adolescence.

Later researchers in other Samoan villages reached different conclusions. A study by Derek Freeman (1983) offers a particularly harsh judgment of Mead's ethnography. Rather than the carefree sexual experimentation Mead described, Freeman found a strict virginity complex. Instead of casual and friendly relations between the sexes, Freeman found male-female hostility. His Samoan boys competed in macho contests that involved sneaking up on girls and raping them with their fingers.

How do other anthropologists evaluate Freeman's findings and his criticisms of Mead? We know that in any culture, customs vary from village to village and decade to decade. Mead and Freeman worked at different times (fifteen years apart) and in different villages. Freeman's Samoans may well have differed from the people Mead observed in 1930. Furthermore, different anthropologists have particular interests, skills, and biases, which affect their interpretations.

Besides their own biases, ethnographers should be aware of variation within any culture they are studying. They must avoid the tendency to imply that a particular village is homogeneous or that it represents the entire culture. Freeman's attack on Mead is merely the most publicized in a series of disagreements between anthropologists who offer contrasting interpretations of a given culture (see also Solway and Lee 1990; Wilmsen 1989). Ethnographers need to be more sensitive to variation within a culture as well as to ways in which their particular interests may influence their field work.

Culture and personality research has been criticized more than most other aspects of ethnography. Long before Freeman's attack, anthropologists (e.g., Harris 1968) had faulted Mead's work for being too impressionistic. Mead relied heavily on her own impressions about the emotions of Samoan girls. Although she did report deviant cases, Mead claimed to focus on the *typical* adolescent experience. However, because she presented little statistical data, the ratio of normal to deviant could not be established. In defending her research, Mead stated that "the student of the more intangible and psychological aspects of human behavior is forced to illuminate rather than demonstrate a thesis" (1928/1961, p. 260). More recent approaches to culture and personality research that are less impressionistic than Mead's are discussed below.

Ruth Benedict: Cultures as Individuals

Like Mead's work, Ruth Benedict's widely read book *Patterns of Culture* (1934/1959) influenced research on culture and personality. Using published sources rather than personal field experiences, Benedict contrasted the cultural orientations of the Kwakiutl of the Northwest Coast of North America and the Zuni of the American Southwest. The Kwakiutl, whose potlatch system was described in Chapter 11, are unusual foragers. They inhabit a rich environment and have tribal or chiefdom rather than band organization. The Zuni, tribal agriculturalists, are one of the Pueblo peoples of the American Southwest.

Benedict proposed that particular cultures are integrated by one or two dominant psychological themes and that entire cultures—here the Zuni and the Kwakiutl—can be labeled by means of their psychological attributes. Thus she called the Kwakiutl *Dionysian* and the Zuni *Apollonian*, from the Greek gods of wine and light, respectively. Benedict portrayed the Dionysian Kwakiutl as striving to escape limitations, achieve excess, and break into another order of experience. Given these goals, they valued drugs and alcohol, fasting, self-torture, and frenzy. In contrast, Benedict's Apollonian Zuni were noncompetitive, gentle, and peace-loving. She found no Dionysian traits (strife, factionalism, painful ceremonies, disruptive psychological states) among the Zuni. They valued a middle-of-the-road existence and distrusted excess.

Benedict's approach was **configurationalism.** In this view, cultures are integrated wholes, configured uniquely so as to be different from all others. She thought that cross-cultural comparison of particular features is less feasible than demonstrating each culture's distinctive patterning. However, later scholars have faulted Benedict for stereotyping cultures, for example, by ignoring cooperative features of Kwakiutl life and strife, suicide, and alcoholism among the Zuni. Unfortunately, Benedict's risky use of individual psychological labels to characterize whole cultures influenced later descriptions of national character.

National Character

Studies of **national character** were popular in the United States from World War II until the early 1950s. These studies were flawed because they used a few informants to generalize about the psychological features of entire nations. Several anthropologists tried to help the American war effort by describing Japanese culture and personality structure (Benedict 1946; Gorer 1943). Because the war pre-

VARIETIES OF HUMAN SEXUALITY

Margaret Mead called attention to the fact that sexual behavior varies from culture to culture. A later, more systematic cross-cultural study (Ford and Beach 1951) found wide variation in attitudes about masturbation, bestiality (sex with animals), and homosexuality. Even in a single culture, such as the United States, attitudes about sex differ with socioeconomic status, region, and rural versus urban residence. However, even in the 1950s, before the "age of sexual permissiveness" (the late 1960s and 1970s) began, research showed that almost all American men (92 percent) and more than half of American women (54 percent) admitted to masturbation. Between 40 and 50 percent of American farm boys had sex with animals. In the famous Kinsey report (Kinsey, Pomeroy, and Martin 1948), 37 percent of the men surveyed admitted having had at least one homosexual experience leading to orgasm. In a later study of 1,200 unmarried women, 26 percent reported homosexual activities.

Attitudes toward homosexuality, masturbation, and bestiality in other cultures differ strikingly, as I find when I contrast the cultures I know best—the United States, urban and rural Brazil, and Madagascar. During my first stay in Arembepe, Brazil, when I was nineteen years old and unmarried, young men told me details of their experience with prostitutes in the city. In Arembepe, a rural community, sex with animals was common. Targets of the male sex drive included cattle, horses, sheep, goats, and turkeys. Arembepe's women were also more open about their sex lives than their North American counterparts were.

Arembepeiros talked about sex so willingly that I wasn't prepared for the silence and avoidance of sexual subjects that I encountered in Madagascar. My wife's and my discreet attempts to get the Betsileo to tell us at least the basics of their culture's sexual practices led nowhere. I did discover from city folk that, as in many non-Western cultures, traditional ceremonies were times of ritual license, when normal taboos lapsed and Betsileo men and women engaged in what Christian missionaries described as "wanton" sexuality. Only during my last week in Madagascar did a young man in the village of Ivato, where I had spent a year, take me aside and offer to write down the words for genitals and sexual intercourse. He could not say these tabooed words, but he wanted me to know them so that my knowledge of Betsileo culture would be as complete as possible.

I have never worked in a culture with institutionalized homosexuality of the sort that exists among several tribes in Papua–New Guinea, such as the Kaluli (Schieffelin 1976) or Sambia (Herdt 1981, 1986). The

vented field work in Japan, American anthropologists had to do "studies of culture at a distance." They interviewed Japanese people in the United States, watched Japanese films, and read books, magazines, and histories. Because their aim was to describe *common* behavior patterns and personality traits, these anthropologists often ignored variation. They assumed that each individual represented groupwide patterns, at least partially. However, these national character researchers never used samples that properly encapsulated the range of variation in a complex nation.

Sigmund Freud's psychoanalytic influence was apparent in national character studies. The most famous example was the purported relationship between Japanese toilet training, said to be severe and early, and a "compulsive" Japanese personality preoccupied with ritual, order, and cleanliness (Benedict 1946; Gorer 1943; LaBarre 1945). Some anthropologists even argued that the compulsion engendered by strict toilet training made the Japanese particularly aggressive in warfare. However, later research showed that modal Japanese were actually *less* preoccupied with toilet training than Americans were.

Many early descriptions of personality and national character contained ethnocentric and personal impressions. Without careful field work, objectivity and cultural relativism faded. (From the perspective of cultural relativism, the values and moral standards of one culture shouldn't be used to evaluate another.) It's difficult to believe that anthropologist Ralph Linton, a contributor to culture and personality research, wrote in a professional report about tribes of Madagascar that

the Betsimisaraka are stupid and lazy, and insolent unless kept in check. . . . The Tsimahety are moderately

Kaluli believe that semen has a magical quality that promotes knowledge and growth. Before traveling into alien territory, boys must eat a mixture of ginger, salt, and semen to enhance their ability to learn a foreign language. At age eleven or twelve, a Kaluli boy forms a homosexual relationship with an older man chosen by his father. (This man cannot be a relative, because that would violate their incest taboo.) The older man has anal intercourse with the boy. The Kaluli cite the boy's peach-fuzz beard, which appears thereafter, as evidence that semen promotes growth. The young Kaluli men also have homosexual intercourse at the hunting lodges, where they spend an extended period learning the lore of the forest and the hunt from older bachelors.

Homosexual activities were absent, rare, or secret in only 37 percent of seventy-six societies for which data were available (Ford and Beach 1951). In the others, various forms of homosexuality were considered normal and acceptable. Sometimes sexual relations between people of the same sex involved transvestism on the part of one of the partners. However, this was not true of homosexuality among the Sudanese Azande, who valued the warrior role (Evans-Pritchard 1970). Prospective warriors—boys aged twelve to twenty—left their families and shared quarters with adult fighting men, who paid bridewealth for, and had sex with, them. During this apprenticeship, the boys performed the domestic duties of women. Upon reaching warrior status, young men took their own boy brides. Later, retiring from the warrior role, Azande men married women. Flexible in their sexual expression, Azande men had no difficulty shifting to heterosexual coitus.

There appears to be greater cross-cultural acceptance of homosexuality than of bestiality or masturbation. Most societies in the Ford and Beach (1951) study discouraged masturbation, and only five allowed human-animal sex. However, these figures measure only the social approval of sexual practices, not their actual frequency. As in our own society, socially disapproved sex acts are more widespread than people admit.

We see nevertheless that flexibility in human sexual expression is an aspect of our primate heritage. Both masturbation and homosexual behavior exist among chimpanzees and other primates (White 1989). The primate sexual potential is molded both by the environment and by reproductive necessity. Heterosexuality is practiced in all human societies—which, after all, must reproduce themselves—but alternatives are also widespread (Davis and Whitten 1987). The sexual component of personality—just how humans express their "natural" sexual urges—is a matter that culture and environment determine and limit.

straightforward and courageous, and are courteous to whites, but indifferent. . . . The Sakalava are by far the bravest of the . . . tribes, and are also fairly intelligent. (1927, pp. 296–297)

If some anthropologists find it difficult to maintain scholarly objectivity during an ethnographic survey, it is much more difficult to provide a balanced description of an enemy nation. This reveals major flaws—impressionism and ethnocentrism—in national character studies, which are rarely done today.

CROSS-CULTURAL STUDIES

In the late 1930s, in a series of seminars at Columbia University, the psychoanalyst Abram Kardiner (1939) developed the idea of **basic personality structure** (fundamental shared personality traits acquired by adapting to a culture). Several anthropologists gave accounts of societies they had studied, which Kardiner interpreted psychoanalytically. Kardiner's theoretical framework is more useful than those of other early culture and personality researchers. He believed that a basic personality structure typifies people in any society. Basic personality exists in the context of cultural institutions—patterned ways of doing things in that society.

Cultural institutions fall into two categories: primary and secondary. *Primary institutions* include kinship, child care, sexuality, and subsistence. In adapting to primary institutions, the individual develops his or her personality. Because the primary patterns are similar throughout the society, many personality traits are shared. These shared traits make up the society's basic personality structure. *Secondary institutions* arise as individuals deal with

Primary institutions, such as kinship, child care, and subsistence, are often combined, as in this scene in rural Eritrea. Because primary patterns are similar throughout the society, many personality traits are also shared. According to Kardiner, these shared traits make up that society's basic personality structure.

the primary ones. Images of the gods, for example, may be modeled on a primary institution, such as children's relationship to their parents. Secondary institutions encompass religion, rituals, and folk tales.

Kardiner's framework also linked personality changes to changes in basic institutions. In this view, an alteration in a primary institution, such as subsistence, changes basic personality structure and secondary institutions. Kardiner compared the Tanala and Betsileo of Madagascar—closely related cultures that differed in types of economy. The

Tanala were horticulturalists; the Betsileo, intensive cultivators of irrigated rice. Kardiner argued that certain Betsileo secondary institutions, such as an emphasis on magic and spirit possession, came from anxieties that the demands of irrigated agriculture produced in their basic personality structure. Kardiner also recognized that the diversity of personality types in a culture increases with that culture's social and political complexity. He identified some of the anxieties associated with social stratification, private property, warfare, and state organization.

Since the 1950s, culture and personality studies have tended to follow a comparative strategy like Kardiner's, using data from several societies rather than one or two. There have been noteworthy attempts to improve data quality, to permit accurate cross-cultural generalization about personality formation. For example, one project (Whiting, ed. 1963) dispatched six teams for a coordinated investigation of child rearing in northern India, Mexico, Okinawa, the Philippines, New England, and East Africa. The teams used a common field guide and research techniques. Focusing on 50 to 100 families in each culture, the teams studied interactions between mothers and young children. They interviewed and observed behavior, paying attention to nurturing, self-reliance, responsibility, achievement orientation, dominance, obedience, aggression, and sociability. The teams rated the societies on the basis of psychological tones of child rearing. For example, mothers in some societies were rated more affectionate than were those in others. Child-rearing patterns were then linked to certain culture traits, such as the presence or absence of warfare.

Also in the 1960s, Walter Goldschmidt (1965) organized a project to investigate cultural, psychological, and ecological variation among four groups in East Africa: the Hehe, Kamba, Pokot, and Sebei. All four had mixed economies. In each group, some communities cultivated, others herded, and some did both. Project researcher Robert Edgerton (1965) gathered psychological information in eight communities, one pastoral and one agricultural for each group. He drew a sample of at least thirty adults of each gender for each community and interviewed a total of 505 people.

To assess the personality differences among the groups, Edgerton (1965) analyzed responses to questions, inkblot plates, and color slides. What

IN THE NEWS: MAKING ROOM ON THE COUCH FOR CULTURE

Just as different cultures inculcate different personality types, they also define and deal in different ways with psychological crises, mental illnesses, and unusual behavior. In an increasingly multicultural society, mental health professionals are paying more attention to the role of cultural variation in identifying, diagnosing, and treating mental "disorders." This article also describes a range of culturally specific syndromes, such as Latin American *susto* (lethargy owing to "soul loss") and Malaysian *amok* (brooding followed by a violent outburst). Although a given behavior (e.g., lethargy) may occur in many cultures, some of them may classify that behavior as problematic and needing immediate treatment, whereas others may ignore it or treat it as a passing phenomenon that will correct itself.

The patient seemed psychotic, complaining in a listless ramble, "My soul is not with me anymore—I can't do anything." Seriously disturbed, she had been taken to a psychiatric hospital by her relatives.

The psychiatrist who interviewed the woman discovered the problem had begun when she got bad news from her native Ecuador: an uncle she was close to had died unexpectedly.

"I realized that her clinical picture fit a syndrome known in Latin American cultures as 'susto,' or loss of the soul," said Dr. Juan Mezzich, a psychiatrist at the Mount Sinai School of Medicine in Manhattan, who treated the woman. "In facing the tragic news, the soul of the patient departs with the dead person, leaving the person soulless. In our psychiatric terms, we would say she was depressed."

Dr. Mezzich is at the forefront of a new movement in psychiatry to recognize the cultural trappings that patients bring with them, and to shape diagnosis and treatment accordingly. In the last five years the movement, which comes at a time when an increasing proportion of psychiatric patients in America come from an array of cultures, has led to a growing stream of books and scholarly articles on cultural influences in mental health. Virtually every professional convention for psychotherapists now offers a workshop on how culture affects psychiatric problems.

Last month *The American Journal of Psychiatry* published guide-

lines for psychiatric evaluation that for the first time explicitly recommended that a patient's cultural or ethnic background be considered, including how the patient understands the symptoms he or she is having.

For example, the woman from Ecuador was at first misdiagnosed as psychotic by another psychiatrist. But Dr. Mezzich, who is from Peru, not only knew about the susto syndrome but also devised a treatment for her that drew upon his understanding of her background.

"Instead of just giving her antidepressants, I tried an approach based on Hispanic culture," he said. "There, for susto, you would expect to have a mourning ritual to help the person assimilate the loss. So, with her family, we organized a sort of wake where everyone talked about the loss of her uncle and what it meant to them."

The wake "was quite powerful for her," Dr. Mezzich said. "She didn't need any antidepressants, and within a few meetings, including two with her family, her symptoms lifted and she was back participating fully in life once again."

The anthropological study of psychiatric disorders like susto has yielded a fascinating list of

kinds of conclusions did he reach? He found the Kamba to have male dominance, fear of poverty, and restrained emotions. The Hehe were aggressive, formal, mistrusting, and secretive. Other personality traits marked the Pokot and the Sebei.

Some similarities correlated with language. The Pokot and Sebei spoke languages of the Kalenjin group, and the Hehe and Kamba spoke Bantu languages. The Kalenjin speakers valued both sons and daughters; the Bantu speakers, just sons. The Bantus worried about sorcery and witchcraft and valued

land over cattle. The Bantu groups respected wealthy people; the Kalenjins, prophets.

Economic contrasts also were found to influence personality. The cultivators consulted sorcerers and made group decisions, whereas the pastoralists were more individualistic. The farmers valued hard work; the herders didn't. The cultivators were more hostile and suspicious, indirect, abstract, and anxious and less able to control their emotions and impulses. The herders, by contrast, were more direct, open, and realistic.

syndromes known only in one or another culture, like the sudden, violent outburst known as "amok" in Malaysia; or "koro," the East Asian term for intense anxiety that one's sexual organs will recede into one's body with fatal consequence. Anthropologists say these are not mere ethnographic curiosities. Rather, they say, the syndromes illustrate a broader point, that notions of mental disorder, if not the disorders themselves, are shaped by culture.

Indeed, some disorders of the mind that are well recognized in some cultures simply have no equivalent in Western psychiatry. One such is "taijin kyofusho," a Japanese malady that loosely translates as "fear of people." The name describes a morbid dread that one will do something that will embarrass other people.

"The syndrome revolves around social shame," said Dr. Arthur Kleinman, a medical anthropologist and psychiatrist at Harvard Medical School. "The closest equivalent Western psychiatric diagnosis is social phobia, but that is an anxiety disorder, a fear that people will criticize you. It's not at all the same thing. Japanese clinicians say this psychological problem simply has no parallel in our own culture or diagnostic system—we don't think of the fear of embarrassing other people as a psychological syndrome."

The stamp of culture on mental disorders extends to America itself, Dr. Kleinman asserts. Although it is difficult to see for those immersed in American culture, he contends that there are psychiatric syndromes unique to Western industrialized societies. "Anorexia nervosa seems as culture-bound to America and similar industrialized cultures as amok is to Malaysia," Dr. Kleinman said.

Dr. Spero Manson, a medical anthropologist in the psychiatry department at the University of Colorado Health Science Center and himself a Chippewa, said: "There is simply no such thing as anorexia among native peoples in North America. The overconcern with body stereotypes aren't relevant in Indian cultures—the grave concern with slenderness is itself seen as absurd. Native people would be very concerned about a person who was willfully wasting away, but you just don't find it, except perhaps among highly acculturated Indians."

Dr. Kleinman says that although exotic disorders exist most mental health workers will not confront them directly, but rather will have to deal with differences in how patients describe or experience universal problems like depression. "You need to understand the idiom of distress—how a person talks about his problem," Dr. Kleinman said.

For Hopi Indians, for example, there are five terms that refer to types of depression. Dr. Manson said the nearest English equivalents were "deep worry," "pouting," "drunken-like craziness," "unhappiness" and "heartbroken."

Most of these categories bear only a surface resemblance to psychiatry's concepts of depression, Dr. Manson says. "The term 'heartbroken' translates also as 'heart is dying' or 'spiritual death'—there's really no match for this in the diagnostic manual," Dr. Manson said.

The most common cause of "heartbreak" is a rupture in a close relationship, such as a child being ignored by its mother or the breakup of a teen-age romance. The typical reactions range from being shocked and perplexed to feeling despair and exhaustion.

"Depending on which of these sicknesses a Hopi patient thinks he is suffering from, some treatments would make better sense than others," Dr. Manson said. "Heartbreak, for example, has mainly physiological manifestations, like disturbed sleep and loss of appetite. Typically it's treated with herbs, so a medication would make sense. But for unhappiness the appropriate treatment for a Hopi would be a combination of psychotherapy and group support.

"Take a psychiatrist aware only of the standard psychiatric approaches," Dr. Manson continued. "In comes a Hopi patient, and the questions asked and treatment approach taken may mesh poorly at best with that patient's understanding of what should happen. The psychiatrist's lens might lead him to call it major depression, but that imposes another way of thinking about it."

Many of the syndromes specific to one culture refer to some kind of brief psychosis, Dr. Mezzich said. "In countries like India and Egypt, for example, about half of psychiatric patients have a temporary psychotic state, typically a well-recognized syndrome in those cultures, that had no matching diagnosis in American psychiatry until the diagnosis of acute, transient psychosis was added last year," he said.

Not only has the diagnostic manual changed to take account of disorders specific to one culture, the training of mental health workers is also changing.

"At San Francisco General Hospital, we offer residents training on units that are focused on different cultural groups," said Dr. Francis Lu, co-director of the Cultural Competence and Diversity Program at the hospital and psychiatrist at the University of California. And, for the first time, the national guidelines for training psychiatry residents this year specify that they be trained in assessing any cultural impact on their patients' problems.

From Amok to Zar: Some Culture-Bound Syndromes

Several patterns of aberrant behavior and troubling experience are recognized mostly in specific localities or societies, and may or may not be linked to an official diagnostic category. Here are some of them:

Problem Name	Where Recognized	Description
Amok	Malaysia; similar patterns elsewhere	Brooding followed by a violent outburst; often precipitated by a slight or insult; seems to be prevalent only among men.
Ataque de nervios ("attack of nerves")	Latin America and Mediterranean	An episode of uncontrollable shouting, crying, trembling, heat in chest rising to the head, verbal or physical aggression.
Bilis, colera, or muina	Many Latin groups	Rage perceived as disturbing bodily balances, causing nervous tension, headache, trembling, screaming, etc.
Boufée delirante	East Africa and Haiti	Sudden outburst of agitated and aggressive behavior, confusion and mental and physical excitement.
Brain fag	West Africa; similar symptoms elsewhere	"Brain tiredness," a mental and physical reaction to the challenges of schooling.
Dhat	India; also in Sri Lanka and China	Severe anxiety and hypochondria associated with discharge of semen and feelings of exhaustion.
Falling out or blacking out	Southern United States and Caribbean	Sudden collapse; eyes remain open but sightless; the victim hears but feels unable to move.
Ghost sickness	American Indian tribes	Preoccupation with death and the dead, with bad dreams, fainting, appetite loss, fear, hallucinations, etc.
Hwa-byung	Korea	Symptoms attributed to suppression of anger, like insomnia, fatigue, panic, fear of death, depression, indigestion, etc.
*Koro	Malaysia; related conditions in East Asia	Sudden intense anxiety that sexual organs will recede into body and cause death; occasional epidemics.
Latah	Malaysia, Indonesia, Japan, Thailand	Hypersensitivity to sudden fright, often with nonsense mimicking of others, trancelike behavior.
Locura	United States and Latin America	Psychosis tied to inherited vulnerability and/or life difficulties; incoherence, agitation, hallucinations, possibly violence.
Mal de ojo ("evil eye")	Mediterranean and elsewhere	Sufferers, mostly children, are believed to be under influence of "evil eye," causing fitful sleep, crying, sickness, fever.
Pibloktoq	Arctic and subarctic Eskimo communities	Extreme excitement, physical and verbal violence for up to thirty minutes, then convulsions and short coma.
*Qi-gong psychotic reaction	China	A short episode of mental symptoms after engaging in Chinese folk practice of qi-gong, or "exercise of vital energy."
Shen-k'uei or shenkui	Taiwan and China	Marked anxiety or panic symptoms with bodily complaints attributed to life-threatening loss of semen.
Sin-byung	Korea	Syndrome of anxiety and bodily complaints followed by dissociation and possession by ancestral spirits.
Spell	Southern United States	A trance in which individuals communicate with deceased relatives or spirits; not perceived as a medical event.
Susto ("fright" or "soul loss")	Latin groups in U.S. and Caribbean	Illness tied to a frightening event that makes the soul leave the body, causing unhappiness and sickness.
*Taijin kyofusho	Japan	An intense fear that the body, its parts or functions displease, embarrass, or are offensive to others.
Zar	North Africa and Middle East	Belief in possession by a spirit, causing shouting, laughing, head banging, etc.; not considered pathological.

*Included in an official diagnostic system.
Adapted from *Diagnostic and Statistical Manual of Mental Disorders*, Fourth Edition (American Psychiatric Association), 1994, Washington D.C. *Source:* Daniel Goleman, "Making Room on the Couch for Culture," *The New York Times*, December 5, 1995, pp. B9, B10.

Unlike earlier, more impressionistic culture and personality studies, this one used statistical data, collected in accordance with objective standards. This made it possible to evaluate the respective contributions of culture, language, history, and economy to personality formation. If personality traits correlate with economic systems in East Africa, do similar associations exist on a worldwide scale? Several anthropologists have answered yes.

WORLDVIEW

Peasants and Limited Good

George Foster (1965), for example, found that a distinctive cognitive orientation, ideology, or **worldview** characterizes "classic" peasant economies—the nonindustrial farming communities within nation-states. (A *worldview* is a culture's characteristic way of perceiving, interpreting, and explaining the world.) Foster cited several ethnographic cases to illustrate this peasant worldview, which he called the **image of limited good**. In this ideology everything is perceived as finite: land, wealth, health, love, friendship, honor, respect, status, power, influence, safety, and security. Viewing everything as scarce, peasants believe that individuals can excel only by taking more than their fair share from a common pool, therefore depriving others.

If someone does manage to increase his or her wealth, there are several possible responses. Peasants accept differential wealth that comes from outside the village and clearly hasn't required dipping into the finite local pool. Thus peasants may prosper from wage work outside or favors from external patrons. Profit also may come from sheer luck (winning a lottery, finding a treasure). In all these cases the community supply of good remains intact.

If, however, wealth comes from local activity, forces of public opinion act as leveling mechanisms. Prosperous people may be forced to sponsor ceremonies, which reduce differential wealth, leaving only prestige, which isn't dangerous. Prosperous peasants may also become targets of gossip, envy, ostracism, and physical violence. Given such community responses, peasants try to hide good fortune. Their dress, homes, and diet remain ordinary. Furthermore, people who have had bad luck and sink below the community norm are also distrusted, for they are thought to be envious of everyone else.

Foster found the image of limited good to be most obvious among Latin American and European peasants. African peasants were less individualistic; their competition and rivalry occurred between descent groups rather than between individuals or families. The image of limited good develops when peasant societies emphasize nuclear family organization but not when corporate descent groups are important. Foster also pointed out that the image of

When the image of limited good operates, peasants try to hide differences in wealth. Their dress, homes, and diet remain ordinary. George Foster found the image of limited good to be most obvious among Latin American and European peasants, such as the couple shown here near Avila, Spain.

limited good is a response to the subordinate position of peasants within a larger society. Often, good really is limited by land-ownership patterns, poor health care, and inadequate government services. Foster suggested—and there is considerable evidence to support him—that when access to wealth, power, and influence is more open, the image of limited good declines.

The (Sub)Culture of Poverty

Anthropologist Oscar Lewis (1959) described another constellation of values, the "subculture of poverty," which he often shortened to "culture of poverty." Economically, the **culture of poverty** is marked by low incomes, unemployment, unskilled occupations, little saving, and frequent pawning. Its social attributes include crowded living quarters, lack of privacy, alcoholism, violence, early sex, informal and unstable marriages, and mother-centered households. Psychologically, Lewis argued, the culture of poverty has a distinctive set of values and feelings. These include marginality, insecurity, fatalism, desperation, aggression, gregariousness, sensuality, adventurousness, spontaneity, impulsiveness, absence of planning, and distrust of government.

Lewis argued that these values and customs marginalize people, limiting their chances for success and social mobility. He was explicit about the conditions that give rise to the culture of poverty: a cash economy, unemployment, low wages, and a certain set of values in the dominant class that stresses wealth and property accumulation and regards poverty as resulting from personal inferiority. According to Lewis, poverty doesn't always produce the culture of poverty. For example, when poor people become class-conscious or active in labor unions, they may escape the culture of poverty—although they may still be poor.

Before he began to study the culture of poverty in Mexico City and San Juan, Puerto Rico, Lewis had done field work in India, where he found poverty but no subculture of poverty. Although Hindu villages were poorer than the slums of Mexico City and San Juan, the caste system gave people a sense of social identity and solidarity that was missing in Latin America. Lewis argued that the culture of poverty developed in the absence of such a feeling of belonging and in the context of bilateral kinship

Anthropologist Oscar Lewis coined the term "culture of poverty"—a controversial concept that has been debated for decades by scholars, politicians, and policy makers. Lewis's culture of poverty is marked by low incomes, unemployment, and unskilled occupations. Its social attributes include crowded living quarters and lack of privacy. Although the culture of poverty first emerged in Europe, Lewis found the best contemporary examples in Latin America, such as Mexico City (shown here).

systems. In areas with corporate descent groups, such as India and Africa, the subculture would not develop, even though poverty might be great. Lewis saw something positive in descent-group organization—the feeling that a corporate body continues to exist while individuals come and go. This feeling offers a sense of past and future even to the desperately poor.

Although the culture of poverty first emerged in Europe, with capitalism, industrialization, and urban migration, Lewis found the best contemporary examples in Latin America. It was less marked in the United States, where the welfare system had eliminated many of its causes. Critics have suggested that the poor really don't have a separate subculture (Valentine 1968; Stack 1975); they are merely unable to live up to dominant norms because of their economic disadvantages. Others have suggested that the poor hold two sets of values simultaneously, one shared with the larger society and the other a response to poverty (Parker and Kleiner 1970). The second value set helps the poor adjust psychologically and thus preserves their mental health. Lewis and his critics agreed that if poverty were totally eradicated, the culture of poverty, with its values and feelings of marginality, would disappear as well.

The Protestant Ethic and Capitalism

Consider now the emergence of a worldview and personality structure—the **Protestant ethic**—valuing hard work, thrift, wealth, and capital accumulation. In *The Protestant Ethic and the Spirit of Capitalism* (1904/1958), the influential social theorist Max Weber argued that capitalism demanded an entrepreneurial personality type, which he linked to the values preached by early Protestant leaders. Weber observed that European Protestants tended to be more successful financially than Catholics were, and he attributed this contrast to values stressed by their religion. Weber characterized Catholics as more concerned with immediate happiness and security, Protestants as more ascetic and future-oriented.

Capitalism required that the attitudes of Catholic peasants be replaced by values more compatible with an industrial economy fueled by capital accumulation. Protestantism offered a worldview that valued profit seeking and work. Early Protestants believed that success on earth is a sign of divine favor. According to some Protestant credos, individuals can gain favor through good works. Other sects stressed predestination, the doctrine that only a few mortals are selected for eternal life and that people cannot change their fates. However, material success, achieved through work, can signal that an individual is one of the elect. Here, hard work was valued because success helped convince individuals of their salvation.

The English Puritan variety of Protestantism stressed physical and mental labor; it discouraged leisure and the enjoyment of life. Waste of time was the deadliest sin because work was a duty demanded by God. The Puritans valued the simplicity of the middle-class home and condemned ostentation as worldly enjoyment. Profits, the fruits of successful labor, could be given to the church or reinvested. However, they could not be hoarded, because excess wealth might lead to temptation. People could increase their profit-making activity as long as they kept in mind the common good and didn't engage in harmful, illegal, greedy, or dishonest activity.

According to Weber, the new attitudes and values associated with the Protestant Reformation helped to promote the growth of modern industrial capitalism. However, residues of the traditional Catholic

Weber linked the rise of capitalism to a "Protestant ethic." Today, however, people of many religions and worldviews, such as this high-flying Hong Kong businessman, are successful capitalists. Furthermore, the old Protestant emphasis on honesty and hard work often has little relationship to modern economic maneuvers.

peasant mentality slowed the pace of change. Early Protestants who produced more than they needed for subsistence—who tried to make a profit—stirred up the mistrust, hatred, and moral indignation of others. Successful innovators were people of strong character who could persevere despite resistance and command the confidence of customers and workers.

Weber also argued that rational business organization entailed removing production from the household, its setting in peasant societies. Protestant doctrines made such a split possible by emphasizing individualism: individuals rather than families would be saved or not. The family was a secondary matter for Weber's Protestants.

Today, of course, people of many religions and worldviews are successful capitalists. Furthermore, the old Protestant emphasis on honesty and hard work often has little relationship to modern economic maneuvers. Still, there is no denying Weber's contention that the individualistic focus of Protestantism was compatible with the severance of ties to land and extended family that the Industrial Revolution demanded.

SUMMARY

Anthropologists are interested in public and collective behavior and in how individuals, think, feel, and act. The individual and culture are linked in a process by which individuals internalize, express, and influence the meanings of public messages. Anthropology and psychology intersect in psychological anthropology. With its focus on the individual, psychological anthropology exists because a complete account of cultural processes requires both perspectives—private and public.

One area of psychological anthropology is cognitive anthropology—the ethnographic and cross-cultural study of cognition (the organization of knowledge, perceptions, and meaning). A culture is both a network of shared understandings and a changing product involving negotiation by its individual members.

According to schema theory, the mind builds schemata to filter new experience and reconstruct past experience. Schemata construct simplified versions of experience; we remember the typical (modal) rather than the unusual. Cognition and emotions develop together as part of people's schemata. As individuals grow, their schemata harden. In a given culture, if people experience the same typical pattern, their schemata retain it. However, individual feelings and experiences give rise to differences in schemata among people who grow up in the same culture. Like the idea of levels of culture, schema theory recognizes a continuum of shared experience and learning.

Culture and personality studies examine the personality types that characterize different cultures. Early students of culture and personality, such as Margaret Mead, were criticized for relying too heavily on personal impressions in gathering field data. Assuming that individuals in a culture would share personality traits, certain anthropologists tried to define basic personality structures and national character. National character studies, which were popular during World War II, were criticized on several grounds, including their impressionistic basis and overemphasis on childhood determinism.

Kardiner proposed that a culture's basic personality structure results from individual adaptation to primary institutions, including family organization and type of economy. The basic personality structure then influences secondary institutions, including religion and ideology. More recent, less impressionistic culture and personality generalizations have emerged from problem-oriented field work that uses more objective techniques to get data on personality formation.

Several studies have suggested or documented correlations between economic systems and personality type or worldview. Foster found an "image of limited good" to be part of the cognitive orientation of "classic" peasant societies. Lewis identified a gregarious, spontaneous, fatalistic, marginalizing subculture of poverty associated with real poverty, capitalism, and bilateral kinship. Weber attributed the emergence of industrial capitalism to asceticism, emphasis on hard and constant work, and profit seeking, all of which he associated with Protestantism.

GLOSSARY

basic personality structure: According to Abram Kardiner, personality traits shared by members of a society; acquired in adapting to a culture's primary institutions.

cognitive anthropology: Area of psychological anthropology; the ethnographic and cross-cultural study of cognition, including learning, ways of knowing, and the organization of knowledge, perceptions, and meaning.

configurationalism: View associated with Ruth Benedict. Cultures are integrated wholes, each uniquely different from all others.

connectionism: Linked to schema theory; the idea that things that consistently occur together in an individual's experience become strongly associated in that person's mind.

culture of poverty: Coined by Oscar Lewis; has economic, social, and psychological characteristics—gregariousness, spontaneity, fatalism, marginality; associated with real poverty, capitalism, and bilateral kinship.

image of limited good: Peasant worldview in which all desired things are considered finite; belief that when one person takes too much, everyone else is deprived.

national character: Personality traits shared by the inhabitants of a nation.

personality: An individual's characteristic ways of thinking and acting and the underlying structure that produces this consistency.

Protestant ethic: Worldview associated with early ascetic Protestantism; values hard and constant work as a sign of salvation; concept developed by Max Weber.

psychological anthropology: Ethnographic and cross-cultural study of differences and similarities in human psychology.

schema theory: Theory that the mind builds schemata (the plural of schema) to filter new experience and reconstruct past experience, shaping memories to conform to current expectations.

worldview: A culture's characteristic way of perceiving, interpreting, and explaining the world.

STUDY QUESTIONS

1. What is psychological anthropology, and why is it necessary?
2. What is cognitive anthropology, and what is its value?
3. What is schema theory, and how does it deal with similarities and differences within cultures?
4. How does schema theory deal with cultural change?
5. What does Derek Freeman's criticism of Margaret Mead teach us about ethnography and psychological anthropology?
6. What were the contributions and shortcomings of the studies of culture and personality by Mead, Benedict, and Kardiner?
7. What were the aims and limitations of national character studies?
8. What kinds of correlations between ecology-economy and personality have been discovered?
9. What is Foster's concept of the image of limited good, and how does it help us understand peasant behavior?
10. What is the culture of poverty, and under what conditions does it emerge and persist?
11. How did Weber relate the Protestant ethic to the development of capitalism?

SUGGESTED ADDITIONAL READING

BARNOUW, V.
   1985   *Culture and Personality*, 4th ed. Belmont, CA: Wadsworth. One of the most readable and complete introductions to the field.
BOCK, P. K.
   1980   *Continuities in Psychological Anthropology*. San Francisco: W. H. Freeman. Overview of psychological anthropology.
BOURGUIGNON, E.
   1979   *Psychological Anthropology: An Introduction to Human Nature and Cultural Differences*. New York: Harcourt Brace Jovanovich. Textbook with a focus on child development and socialization.
BRADY, I., ED.
   1983   Special Section: Speaking in the Name of the Real: Freeman and Mead on Samoa. *American Anthropologist* 85: 908–947. Several anthropologists evaluate Freeman's charges, Mead's work, and the implications of the controversy for psychological anthropology and ethnography.
CARRIER, J.
   1995   *De Los Otros: Intimacy and Homosexuality among Mexican Men. Hidden in the Blood*. New York: Columbia University Press. Male-male sexual relations in Mexico, based on twenty-five years of ethnographic research.
D'ANDRADE, R.
   1995   *The Development of Cognitive Anthropology*. New York: Cambridge University Press. A historical account of the development of cognitive anthropology; how cultural knowledge is organized within and between human minds.

DAVIS, D. L., AND R. G. WHITTEN
   1987   The Cross-Cultural Study of Human Sexuality. *Annual Review of Anthropology* 16: 69–98. Review of recent research.
DESJARLAIS, R., L. EISENBERG, B. GOOD, AND A. KLEINMAN, EDS.
   1995   *World Mental Health: Problems and Priorities in Low-Income Countries*. New York: Oxford University Press. Scholars from more than nineteen countries comment on mental health problems in international, cross-cultural context.
FREEMAN, D.
   1983   *Margaret Mead and Samoa: The Making and Unmaking of an Anthropological Myth*. Cambridge, MA: Harvard University Press. Controversial work criticizing the renowned anthropologist.
FREILICH, M., D. RAYBECK, AND J. SAVISHINSKY
   1991   *Deviance: Anthropological Perspectives*. Westport, CT: Bergin and Garvey. Cross-cultural case studies shed light on the cultural construction of what is "normal" and what isn't.
HATFIELD, E., AND R. L. RAPSON
   1996   *Love and Sex: Cross-Cultural Perspectives*. Needham Heights, MA: Allyn & Bacon. Love, sex, passion, desire—a cross-cultural examination of intimate relationships.
HOLLAND, D., AND N. QUINN, EDS.
   1987   *Cultural Models in Language and Thought*. Cambridge: Cambridge University Press. Cognition through linguistic examples.
JODELET, D.
   1991   *Madness and Social Representations: Living with the Mad in One French Community*. Translated from the French by Gerard Duveen. Berkeley:

University of California Press. Ethnographic study of a French community where the mentally ill have played a prominent role for seventy years; a reconsideration of madness in society.

LEVINE, R. A.
1982   *Culture, Behavior, and Personality: An Introduction to the Comparative Study of Psychosocial Adaptation*, 2nd ed. Chicago: Aldine. Original, sophisticated text of psychological anthropology by an anthropologist-psychoanalyst.

MEAD, M.
1961   (orig. 1928) *Coming of Age in Samoa*. New York: Morrow Quill. Popular report of Mead's first field work, a study of female adolescents in a Polynesian society.

SHWEDER, R. A., AND R. A. LEVINE, EDS.
1984   *Culture Theory: Essays on Mind, Self, and Emotion*. Cambridge: Cambridge University Press. Papers on social and emotional development during childhood.

SHORE, B.
1996   *Culture in Mind: Meaning, Construction, and Cultural Cognition*. New York: Oxford University Press. Culture as expressed in public institutions and as represented in human minds; explores the extent to which humans are similar psychologically, or to which they are different owing to cultural variation.

SPINDLER, G. D., ED.
1978   *The Making of Psychological Anthropology*. Berkeley: University of California Press. Various anthropologists describe their personal experiences in contributing to culture and personality research.

SUAREZ-OROZCO, M. M., AND G. AND L. SPINDLER, EDS.
1994   *The Making of Psychological Anthropology II*. Fort Worth: Harcourt Brace. Several essays focus on psychoanalytic thinking about intrapsychic process and adaptation to the perceived outer world; the volume also views psychological anthropology in the context of anthropology as a whole.

WINZELER, R. L.
1995   *Latah in Southeast Asia: The Ethnography and History of a Culture-Bound Syndrome*. New York: Cambridge University Press. Based on ethnography in Malaysia, an analysis of the social functions of the behavioral syndrome known as *latah*.

LANGUAGE AND COMMUNICATION

THE STRUCTURE OF LANGUAGE
Phonemes and Phones

TRANSFORMATIONAL-GENERATIVE GRAMMAR

LANGUAGE, THOUGHT, AND CULTURE
The Sapir-Whorf Hypothesis
Focal Vocabulary
Meaning

SOCIOLINGUISTICS
Linguistic Diversity in Nation-States

Box: Jocks, Burnouts, and Runts

Gender Speech Contrasts

Stratification and Symbolic Domination

In the News: Japan's Feminine Falsetto Falls
Right Out of Favor

HISTORICAL LINGUISTICS

CYBERSPACE: A NEW REALM OF COMMUNICATION
Inequality in Cyberspace

In the News: Using Modern Technology to
Preserve Linguistic Diversity

Elitism and Gatekeeping
Cyberspace and Social Reality

Language, spoken (*speech*) and written (*writing*—which has existed for about 6,000 years), is the human being's primary means of communication. As was discussed in Chapter 7, the key features of language include cultural transmission, productivity, and displacement. Like culture in general, of which language is a part, language is transmitted through learning, as part of enculturation. Language is based on the arbitrary, learned associations between words and the things they stand for. *Productivity* refers to our ability to produce expressions (words, phrases, and sentences) that are comprehensible to other speakers of the same language. Linguistic *displacement* describes our ability to speak (or write) of things and events that are not present. Monkeys and apes, our nearest relatives, use *call systems* in the wild, but humans don't have to see objects before we make the sounds (say the words) that stand for them. (*Call systems*, remember from Chapter 7, are vocal systems of communication used by nonhuman primates; they consist of a limited number of sounds—*calls*—that are produced only when particular environmental stimuli are encountered.) Human conversations are not bounded by place or by personal experience. Language allows us to discuss the past and future, share our experiences with others, and benefit from their experiences.

Language may be associated with cultural similarities and differences in (or between) societies or nations. The similarities are with speakers of the same language or dialect; the differences are between that group and others.

Anthropologists study language in its social and cultural context. Linguistic anthropology illustrates anthropology's characteristic interest in comparison, variation, and change. Some linguistic anthropologists reconstruct ancient languages by comparing their contemporary descendants and in so doing make discoveries about history. Others make inferences about the universal features of language, linking them to uniformities in the human brain. Still others study linguistic differences to discover the varied worldviews and patterns of thought in a multitude of cultures. Sociolinguists examine dialects and styles in a single language to show how speech reflects social differences (Fasold 1990; Labov 1972*a, b*). Linguistic anthropologists also explore the role of language in colonization, capitalist expansion, state formation, class relations, and political and economic dependence (Geis 1987).

THE STRUCTURE OF LANGUAGE

Until the late 1950s linguists thought that the study of a language should proceed through a sequence of stages of analysis. The first stage was **phonology,** the study of sounds used in speech. Phonological analysis would determine which speech sounds (**phones**) were present and significant in that language. Speech sounds can be recorded using the International Phonetic Alphabet, a series of symbols devised to describe dozens of sounds that occur in different languages. The next stage was **morphology,** the study of the forms in which sounds combine to form **morphemes**—words and their meaningful constituents. Thus, the word *cats* would be analyzed as containing two morphemes—*cat,* the name for a kind of animal, and *-s,* a morpheme indicating plurality. The language's **lexicon** was a dictionary containing all its morphemes and their meanings. The next step was to study **syntax,** the arrangement and order of words in phrases and sentences. This stage-by-stage analysis sometimes created the erroneous impression that phonology, morphology, lexicon, and syntax were unconnected. All this was revolutionized by an approach known as *transformational-generative grammar,* to which we shall return after a brief consideration of phonology.

Phonemes and Phones

No language includes all the sounds designated by the symbols in the International Phonetic Alphabet. Nor is the number of **phonemes**—significant sound contrasts in a given language—infinite. Phonemes lack meaning in themselves, but they are the smallest sound *contrasts* that distinguish meaning. We discover them by comparing **minimal pairs,** words that resemble each other in all but one sound. An example is the minimal pair *pit/bit.* These two words are distinguished by a single sound contrast between /p/ and /b/ (we enclose phonemes in slashes). Thus /p/ and /b/ are phonemes in English. Another example is the different vowel sound of *bit* and *beat* (Figure 19.1). This contrast serves to distinguish these two words and the two phonemes /I/ and /i/ in English.

Standard (American) English (SE), the "region-free" dialect of TV network newscasters, has about thirty-five phonemes—at least eleven vowels and

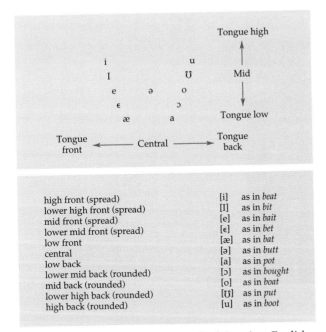

Figure 19.1 *Vowel phonemes in Standard American English shown according to height of tongue and tongue position at front, center, or back of mouth. Phonetic symbols are identified by English words that include them; note that most are minimal pairs. (Adaptation of excerpt and figure 2-1 from* Aspects of Language, *third edition, by Dwight Bolinger and Donald Sears, copyright © 1981 by Harcourt Brace Jovanovich, Inc., reprinted by permission of the publisher.)*

twenty-four consonants. The number of phonemes varies from language to language—from fifteen to sixty, averaging between thirty and forty. The number of phonemes also varies between dialects of a given language. In American English, for example, vowel phonemes vary noticeably from dialect to dialect. Readers should pronounce the words in Figure 19.1, paying attention to (or asking someone else) whether they distinguish each of the vowel sounds. Most Americans don't pronounce them all.

Phonetics is the study of speech sounds in general, what people actually say in various languages. **Phonemics** studies the significant sound contrasts (phonemes) of a *particular* language. In English, /b/ and /v/ are phonemes, occurring in minimal pairs such as *bat* and *vat*. In Spanish, however, the contrast between [b] and [v] doesn't distinguish meaning, and they are therefore not phonemes (we enclose phones that are not phonemic in brackets). Spanish speakers normally use the [b] sound to pronounce words spelled with either *b* or *v*.

In any language a given phoneme extends over a phonetic range. In English the phoneme /p/ ignores the phonetic contrast between the [pʰ] in *pin* and the [p] in *spin*. Most English speakers don't even notice that there is a phonetic difference. [pʰ] is aspirated, so that a puff of air follows the [p]. The [p] in *spin* is not. (To see the difference, light a match, hold it in front of your mouth, and watch the flame as you pronounce the two words.) The contrast between [pʰ] and [p] is phonemic in some languages. That is, there are words whose meaning is distinguished only by the contrast between an aspirated and an unaspirated [p].

Native speakers vary in their pronunciation of certain phonemes. This variation is important in the evolution of language. With no shifts in pronunciation, there can be no linguistic change. The section on sociolinguistics below considers phonetic variation and its relationship to social divisions and the evolution of language.

TRANSFORMATIONAL-GENERATIVE GRAMMAR

Noam Chomsky's influential book *Syntactic Structures* (1957) advocated a new method of linguistic analysis—**transformational-generative grammar.** In Chomsky's view, a language is more than the surface phenomena just discussed (sounds, words, and word order). Beneath the surface features discovered through stage-by-stage analysis of particular languages, all languages share a limited set of organizing principles.

Chomsky views language as a uniquely human possession, qualitatively different from the communication systems of all other animals. Every normal child who grows up in a society develops language easily and automatically. Chomsky thinks that this occurs because the human brain contains a genetically transmitted blueprint, or basic linguistic plan, for building language. He calls this plan a **universal grammar.** When children learn a language, they don't start from scratch, because they already have the outline. As they learn their native language, children experiment with different parts of the blueprint. In so doing, they discover that their language uses some sections but not others. They gradually reject principles used in other languages and accept only the ones in their own.

According to Noam Chomsky the human brain contains a genetically transmitted blueprint, or basic linguistic plan, for building language. As they learn their native language, children experiment with different parts of that blueprint. They gradually reject principles used in other languages and accept only the ones in their own—Japanese in this case.

The fact that children everywhere begin to speak at about the same age buttresses Chomsky's theory that humans are "wired" for language. Furthermore, people master features of language at similar rates. There are universals in language acquisition, such as improper generalizations (*foot, foots; hit, hitted*), which are eventually corrected. Children experiment with linguistic rules, accepting and refining some while rejecting others.

As we learn to speak, we master a specific grammar, a *particular* set of rules—the ones our language has taken from the universal set. These rules let us convert what we want to say into what we do say. People who hear us and speak our language understand our meaning. Our knowledge of the rules enables us to use language creatively, to *generate* an infinite number of sentences according to a finite number of rules. We can produce sentences that no one has ever uttered before, and we can understand other people's original statements.

Chomsky distinguishes between a native speaker's linguistic **competence** (what the speaker must—and does—know about his or her language in order to speak and understand) and **performance** (what the person actually says in social situations). Competence develops during childhood and becomes an unconscious structure. The linguist's job is to discover this structure by looking at deep structures, surface structures, and the transformational rules that link them.

When a speaker wishes to express a thought, a sentence is formed at what Chomsky calls the level of **deep structure** (the mental level) in the speaker's mind. That sentence rises to the **surface structure** (actual speech)—expressed in sound—and passes from speaker to hearer. When a *sentence* (roughly defined as a complete thought) is spoken, the hearer figures out its meaning by translating it back into his or her own deep structure (Figure 19.2).

Figure 19.2 *How a message passes from speaker to hearer according to Chomsky's model. The speaker translates meaning (the semantic component) into sound (the phonological component) through grammar (deep structure, a transformational rule, and a surface-structure sentence). The hearer decodes in reverse order to find meaning.*

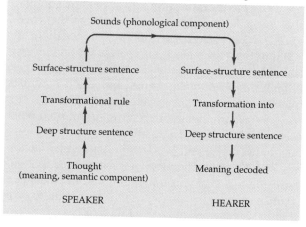

On the surface—the object of traditional linguistics—languages seem more different than they really are. Similarities are more evident at the level of deep structure. Chomsky proposed that by studying the deep structures of many languages, linguists might eventually discover the grammatical building blocks on which all languages are based.

LANGUAGE, THOUGHT, AND CULTURE

According to Chomsky, the human brain contains a limited set of rules for organizing language. The fact that people can learn foreign languages and that words and ideas can be translated from one language into another tends to support Chomsky's position that all humans have similar linguistic abilities and thought processes.

The Sapir-Whorf Hypothesis

Other linguists and anthropologists take a different approach to the relationship between language and thought. Rather than seeking universal linguistic structures as clues to universal mental processes, they believe that different languages produce different ways of thinking. This position is sometimes known as the **Sapir-Whorf hypothesis** after Edward Sapir (1931) and Benjamin Lee Whorf (1956), its prominent early advocates. They argued that languages lead their speakers to think about things in particular ways. For example, the third-person singular pronouns of English (*he, she; him, her; his, hers*) distinguish gender, whereas those of the Palaung, a small tribe in Burma, do not (Burling 1970). Gender exists in English, although a fully developed noun-gender and adjective-agreement system, as in French and other Romance languages (*la belle fille, le beau fils*), does not. The Sapir-Whorf hypothesis therefore might suggest that English speakers can't help paying more attention to differences between males and females than do the Palaung and less than do French or Spanish speakers.

English divides time into past, present, and future. Hopi, a language of the Pueblo region of the Native American Southwest, does not. However, Hopi distinguishes between events that exist or have existed (what we use past and present to dis-

cuss) and those which don't or don't yet (our future events, along with imaginary and hypothetical events). Whorf argued that this difference gives English and Hopi speakers different perceptions of time and reality. Language thus causes differences in thought.

Focal Vocabulary

A lexicon (or vocabulary) is a language's dictionary, its set of names for things, events, and ideas. Lexicon influences perception. Thus, Eskimos have several distinct words for different types of snow that in English are all called *snow*. Most English speakers

A lexicon, or vocabulary, is a language's dictionary, its set of names for things, events, and ideas. Eskimos have several distinct words for different types of snow that in English are all called "snow." Eskimos recognize and think about differences in snow that English speakers do not see because our language provides us with just one word.

never notice the differences between these types of snow and might have trouble seeing them even if someone pointed them out. Eskimos recognize and think about differences in snow that English speakers don't see because our language provides us with just one word.

Similarly, the Nuer of Sudan have an elaborate vocabulary to describe cattle. Eskimos have several words for snow and Nuer have dozens for cattle because of their particular histories, economies, and environments (Eastman 1975; Brown 1958). When the need arises, English speakers can also elaborate their snow and cattle vocabularies. For example, skiers name varieties of snow with words that are missing from the lexicons of Florida retirees. Similarly, the cattle vocabulary of Texas ranchers is much more extensive than that of a salesperson in a New York City department store. Such specialized sets of terms and distinctions that are particularly important to certain groups (those with particular *foci* of experience or activity) are known as **focal vocabulary.**

Vocabulary and lexical distinctions belong to the area of language that changes most readily. New words and distinctions, when needed, appear and spread. For example, who would have "faxed" anything a decade ago? Often-used words tend to be or become simple (*monolexemes*) rather than compound expressions (*rain* versus *tropical storm*) (Brown 1958). Names for items get simpler as they become common and important. A television has become a *TV*, an automobile a *car*, and a videocassette recorder a *VCR*.

Language, culture, and thought are interrelated. However, it would be more accurate to say that changes in culture produce changes in language and thought than the reverse. Consider differences between female and male Americans in regard to the color terms they use (Lakoff 1975). Distinctions implied by such terms as *salmon, rust, peach, beige, teal, mauve, cranberry,* and *dusky orange* aren't in the vocabularies of most American men. However, many of them weren't even in American women's lexicons fifty years ago. These changes reflect changes in American economy, society, and culture. Color terms and distinctions have increased with the growth of the fashion and cosmetic industries. A similar contrast in Americans' lexicons shows up in football, basketball, and hockey vocabularies.

Sports fans, more often males than females, use more terms in reference to and make more elaborate distinctions between the games they watch. Thus cultural contrasts and changes affect lexical distinctions (for instance, *peach* versus *salmon*) within semantic domains (for instance, color terminology). **Semantics** refers to a language's meaning system.

Meaning

Speakers of particular languages use sets of terms to organize, or categorize, their experiences and perceptions. Linguistic terms and contrasts encode (embody) differences in meaning that people perceive. **Ethnoscience,** or **ethnosemantics,** studies such classification systems in various languages. Well-studied ethnosemantic *domains* (sets of related things, perceptions, or concepts named in a language) include kinship terminology and color terminology. When we study such domains, we are examining how those people perceive and distinguish between kin relationships or colors. Other ethnosemantic domains include ethnomedicine—the terminology for the causes, symptoms, and cures of disease (Frake 1961); ethnobotany—native classification of plant life (Conklin 1954; Berlin, Breedlove, and Raven 1974); and ethnoastronomy (Goodenough 1953).

The ways in which people divide up the world—the contrasts they perceive as meaningful or significant—reflect their experiences. Anthropologists have discovered that certain lexical domains and vocabulary items evolve in a determined order. For example, after studying color terminology in more than 100 languages, Berlin and Kay (1969/1992) discovered ten basic color terms: *white, black, red, yellow, blue, green, brown, pink, orange,* and *purple* (they evolved in more or less that order). The number of terms varied with cultural complexity. Representing one extreme were Papua–New Guinea cultivators and Australian hunters and gatherers, who used only two basic terms, which translate as *black* and *white* or *dark* or *light*. At the other end of the continuum were European and Asian languages with all the color terms. Color terminology was most developed in areas with a history of using dyes and artificial coloring.

SOCIOLINGUISTICS

No language is a homogeneous system in which everyone speaks just like everyone else. Linguistic *performance* (what people actually say) is the concern of sociolinguists. The field of **sociolinguistics** investigates relationships between social and linguistic variation, or language in its social context. How do different speakers use a given language? How do linguistic features correlate with social stratification, including class, ethnic, and gender differences (Tannen 1990; Tannen, ed. 1993)? How is language used to express, reinforce, or resist power (Geis 1987)?

Sociolinguists don't deny that people who speak the same language share deep structures and rules which permit mutually intelligible communication. However, sociolinguists focus on features that vary systematically with social position and situation. To study variation, sociolinguists must do field work in order to define, observe, and measure variable aspects of language. Different aspects of variable speech must be quantified. To show that linguistic features correlate with social, economic, and political differences, the social attributes of speakers must also be measured and related to speech (Fasold 1990; Labov 1972*a*).

Variation within a language at a given time is historical change in progress. According to the principle of **linguistic uniformitarianism,** the same forces that have produced large-scale linguistic changes over the centuries, working gradually, are still at work and can be observed in linguistic events taking place today (Labov 1972*b*). Linguistic change doesn't occur in a vacuum but in society. Only when new ways of speaking are associated with social factors can they be imitated, spread, and play a role in linguistic change.

Linguistic Diversity in Nation-States

As an illustration of the linguistic variation encountered in all nation-states, consider the contemporary United States. Ethnic diversity is revealed by the fact that millions of Americans learn first languages other than English. Spanish is the most common. Most of these people eventually become bilinguals, adding English as a second language. In many multilingual (including colonized) nations, people use

Linguistic variation exists in all nation-states. Reflecting ethnic diversity, millions of people in the United States learn first languages other than English. Most of these people eventually add English as a second language. In this Bergen county, New Jersey, classroom English is taught as a second language.

two languages on different occasions—one in the home, for example, and the other on the job or in public.

Whether bilingual or not, we all vary our speech in different contexts; we engage in **style shifts.** In certain parts of Europe, people regularly switch dialects. This phenomenon, known as **diglossia,** applies to "high" and "low" variants of the same language, for example, in German and Flemish (spoken in Belgium). People employ the "high" variant at universities and in writing, professions, and the mass media. They use the "low" variant for ordinary conversation with family members and friends.

Just as social situations influence our speech, so do geographical, cultural, and socioeconomic differences. Many dialects coexist in the United States with Standard (American) English (SE). SE itself is a dialect that differs, say, from "BBC English," which is the preferred dialect in Great Britain. According to the principle of **linguistic relativity,** all dialects are equally effective as systems of communication, which is language's main job. Our tendency to think of particular dialects as cruder or more sophisticated than others is a social rather than a linguistic judgment. We rank certain speech patterns because we recognize that they are used by groups that we also rank. People who say *dese, dem,* and *dere* instead

JOCKS, BURNOUTS, AND RUNTS

Depending on where we live, Americans have certain stereotypes about how people in other regions talk. Some stereotypes, spread by the mass media, are more generalized than others. Most Americans think they can imitate a "southern accent." We also have nationwide stereotypes about speech in New York City (the pronunciation of *coffee*, for example) and Boston ("I pahked the kah in Hahvahd Yahd").

Many Americans also believe that midwesterners don't have accents. This belief stems from the fact that midwestern dialects don't have many stigmatized linguistic variants—speech patterns that people in other regions recognize and look down on, such as *r*lessness and *dem, dese,* and *dere* (instead of *them, these,* and *there*).

Actually, regional patterns influence the way all Americans speak. Midwesterners do have detectable accents. College students from out of state easily recognize that their in-state classmates speak differently. In-state students, however, have difficulty hearing their own speech peculiarities, because they are accustomed to them and view them as normal.

In Detroit-area high schools, sociolinguist Penelope Eckert, as described in her book *Jocks and Burnouts* (1989), studied variation in speech correlated with high school social categories. Eckert's study has revealed links between speech and social status—the high school manifestation of a larger and underlying American social class system. Social variation showed up most clearly in the division of the high school population into two main categories— "jocks" and "burnouts."

Along with teachers, administrators, and parents (particularly "jock parents"), jocks helped maintain the school's formal and traditional social structure. They participated more in athletics, student government, and organized school-based activities. In contrast, burnouts (a social label derived from their tendency to smoke cigarettes) had their main social networks in their neighborhoods. They took school social structure less seriously.

A comparable split exists in many public high schools, although the specific names of the two categories vary from place to place. Jocks have been called "tweeds" or "preppies," and burnouts have been called "freaks," "greasers," "hoods," and "rednecks." This social division correlates with linguistic differences. Many adult speech habits are set when people are teens, as adolescents copy the speech of people they like and admire. Because jocks and burnouts move in different social systems, they come to talk differently. Eckert is still analyzing the specific differences.

The first step in a sociolinguistic study is to find out which speech forms vary. In New York City, the pronunciation of *r* varies systematically with social class and thus can be used in studies of sociolinguistic variation. However, this feature doesn't vary much among midwesterners, most of whom are adamant *r* pronouncers. However, vowel pronunciation does vary considerably among midwesterners and can be used in a sociolinguistic study.

Far from having no accents, midwesterners, even in the same high school, exhibit sociolinguistic variation. Furthermore, dialect differences in Michigan are immediately obvious to people, like myself, who come from other parts of the country. One of the best examples of variable vowel pronunciation is the /e/ phoneme, which occurs in words like *ten, rent, French, section, lecture, effect, best,* and *test.* In southeastern Michigan there are four different ways of pronouncing this phoneme. Speakers of Black English and immigrants from Appalachia often pronounce *ten* as *tin,* just as southerners habitually do. Some Michiganians say *ten,* the correct pronunciation in Standard English. However, two other pronunciations are more common. Instead of *ten,* many Michiganians say *tan,* or *tun* (as though they were using the word *ton,* a unit of weight).

My students often astound me with their pronunciation. One day I met one of my Michigan-raised teaching assistants in the hall. She was deliriously happy. When I asked why, she replied, "I've just had the best suction."

"What?" I said.

"I've just had a wonderful suction," she repeated.

"What?" I still wasn't understanding.

She finally spoke more precisely. "I've just had the best saction." She considered this a clearer pronunciation of the word *section.*

Another TA complimented me, "You luctured to great effuct today." After an exam a student lamented that she hadn't been able to do her "bust on the tust." Once I lectured about uniformity in the fast-food restaurant chains. One of my students had just vacationed in Hawaii, where, she told me, hamburger prices were higher than they were on the mainland. It was, she said, because of the runt. Who, I wondered, was this runt? The very puny owner of Honolulu's McDonald's franchise? Perhaps he advertised on television "Come have a hamburger with the runt." Eventually I figured out that she was talking about the high cost of *rent* on those densely packed islands.

of *these, them,* and *there* communicate perfectly well with anyone who recognizes that the *d* sound systematically replaces the *th* sound in their speech. However, this form of speech has become an indicator of low social rank. We call it, like the use of *ain't,* "uneducated speech." The use of *dem, dese,* and *dere* is one of many phonological differences that Americans recognize and look down on.

Gender Speech Contrasts

Women's speech tends to be more similar to the standard dialect than men's is. Consider the data in Table 19.1, gathered in Detroit. In all social classes, but particularly in the working class, men were more apt to use double negatives (e.g., "I don't want none"). Women are more careful about "uneducated speech." This trend shows up in both the United States and England. Men may adopt working-class speech because they associate it with masculinity. Perhaps women pay more attention to the media, where standard dialects are employed. Also, women may compensate for the socioeconomic barriers they have faced by copying the linguistic norms of upper-status groups.

According to Robin Lakoff (1975), the use of certain types of words and expressions has reflected women's lesser power in American society (see also Coates 1986; Tannen 1990). For example, *Oh dear, Oh fudge,* and *Goodness!* are less forceful than *Hell* and *Damn.* Men's customary use of "forceful" words reflects their traditional public power and presence. Furthermore, men can't normally use certain "women's words" (*adorable, charming, sweet, cute, lovely, divine*) without raising doubts about their masculinity.

Stratification and Symbolic Domination

We use and we evaluate speech—and language changes—in the context of *extralinguistic* forces— social, political, and economic. Mainstream Americans evaluate the speech of low-status groups negatively, calling it "uneducated." This is not because these ways of speaking are bad in themselves but because they have come to symbolize low status. Consider variation in the pronunciation of *r.* In some parts of the United States *r* is regularly pronounced, and in other (*r*less) areas it is not. Originally, American *r*less speech was modeled on the fashionable speech of England. Because of its prestige, *r*lessness was adopted in many areas and continues as the norm around Boston and in the South.

New Yorkers sought prestige by dropping their *r*'s in the nineteenth century, after having pronounced them in the eighteenth. However, contemporary New Yorkers are going back to the eighteenth-century pattern of pronouncing *r*'s. What matters, and what governs linguistic change, is not the reverberation of a strong midwestern *r* but *social* evaluation, whether *r*'s happen to be "in" or "out."

Studies of *r* pronunciation in New York City have clarified the mechanisms of phonological change. William Labov (1972*b*) focused on whether *r* was pronounced after vowels in such words as *car, floor, card,* and *fourth.* To get data on how this linguistic variation correlated with social class, he used a series of rapid encounters with employees in three New York City department stores, each of whose prices and locations attracted a different socioeconomic group. Saks Fifth Avenue (68 encounters) catered to the upper middle class, Macy's (125) attracted middle-class shoppers, and S. Klein's (71) had predominantly lower-middle-class and working-class customers. The class origins of store personnel tended to reflect those of their customers.

Having already determined that a certain department was on the fourth floor, Labov approached ground-floor salespeople and asked where that department was. After the salesperson had answered, "Fourth floor," Labov repeated his "Where?" in order to get a second response. The second reply was more formal and emphatic, the salesperson presumably thinking that Labov hadn't heard or understood the first answer. For each salesperson, therefore, Labov had two samples of /r/ pronunciation in two words.

Table 19.1 *Multiple Negation ("I don't want none") According to Gender and Class (in percentages)*

	Upper Middle Class	Lower Middle Class	Upper Working Class	Lower Working Class
Male	6.3	32.4	40.0	90.1
Female	0.0	1.4	35.6	58.9

Source: From *Sociolinguistics: An Introduction to Language and Society* by Peter Trudgill (London: Pelican Books, 1974, revised edition 1983), p. 85, copyright © Peter Trudgill, 1974, 1983. Reproduced by permission of Penguin Books Ltd.

IN THE NEWS: JAPAN'S FEMININE FALSETTO FALLS RIGHT OUT OF FAVOR

Gender differences in speech may show up in grammar, vocabulary, phonology, or intonation, and they may be accentuated by style shifting in certain social contexts. This article describes the traditional tendency for Japanese women to adopt a very high-pitched voice when speaking in public. However, this linguistic standard of politeness is fading today, as a result of familiarity with gender roles in other cultures and exposure to the mass media (where female announcers now use lower voices).

Smiling beatifically at the restless shoppers, more like a saint than an elevator operator, Hiromi Saito opened her mouth to do her duty.

"I thank you from the bottom of my heart for favoring us by paying an honorable visit to our store," she said in The Voice. "I will stop at the floor your honorable self is kind enough to use, and then I will go to the top floor."

The Voice is as fawning as her demeanor, as sweet as syrup, and as high as a dog whistle. Any higher, and it would shatter the crystal on the seventh floor.

Most Japanese women cannot muster the Mount Fuji-like heights of Miss Saito's voice, but their voices regularly skirt the foothills. For a quick gauge of the status of women in Japan, just cock your ear and listen to Japanese women speak—or squeak.

European women no longer rearrange their bodies with corsets, and Chinese no longer cripple their daughters by binding their feet. But many Japanese women speak well above their natural pitch, especially in formal settings, on the phone or when dealing with customers.

"When slaves talk, they have their slave language," said Fujiko Hara, an interpreter in Tokyo. "Those girls are trained to be robots. With the elevator girls, you don't see a person but a doll."

Yet in a sign that the dolls are coming to life, women's voices in Japan are dropping significantly. Japan still has many squeakers, but a growing number of women speak in natural voices.

"When girls speak in really high voices, I just want to kick them in the head," said Mari Shimakura, a 15-year-old in Tokyo. "It's totally fake and really annoying. It gives me a headache. Mom tells me I speak in too low a voice, and that I should raise it. But I can't change it."

One standard-bearer of the changing times is Miyuki Morita, who was rejected when she first tried to enter broadcasting, as a disk jockey. "They said my voice was too somber, and they wouldn't hire me," Ms. Morita recalled. She eventually found a job with a television station in northern Japan, and she tried to imitate other female journalists who spoke in high voices.

"Then when I saw a video of myself, I saw my face, but it wasn't my voice," she said. "It didn't sound convincing. So I settled back to my voice."

That voice is now among the best known in Japan. Ms. Morita is the evening anchor of NHK News, the most popular television news program in the country.

Other evidence that women's voices are dropping comes from taped announcements on subway platforms in Tokyo. Older recordings are clearly higher pitched than the newer ones.

The pitch of female singers is also falling. Tadahiro Murao, professor of music at Aichi University of Education, has analyzed the frequency of 200 songs dating from the 1950's, and found a clear trend. "From the late 1980's, the pitch of female songs has dropped dramatically," Professor Murao said. "In fact, there was a popular duet last year in which the female vocalist sang the lower part, and the male sang the higher part."

Why have women traditionally spoken in high voices in Japan?

"Your voice in the office and your voice at home are totally different," said Harumi Yamamoto, who works at a computer company in Tokyo. "The point is that when you are with a customer, you want to be polite. If you're being courteous your voice naturally rises."

Almost everyone agrees that high pitch is wrapped up in the Japanese preoccupation with courtesy. In polite conversation in Japan, people routinely denigrate themselves and try to sound unsure even about things they are certain of.

One technique women use to sound tentative, and therefore polite, is to raise their pitch and let their sentences trail off, the way Americans sometimes ask questions.

Labov calculated the percentages of workers who pronounced /r/ at least once during the interview. These were 62 percent at Saks, 51 percent at Macy's, but only 20 percent at S. Klein's. He also found that personnel on upper floors, where he asked "What floor is this?" (and where more expensive items were sold), pronounced r more often than ground-floor salespeople did.

We all engage in style shifting, varying our speech in different social contexts. Language use also varies by gender. Japanese women, such as this department store elevator operator, traditionally adopt a high-pitched voice for public speaking.

"A lower voice sounds too bullying, too aggressive, too manly," said Julie Saito, a reporter at Asahi Shimbun.

Ms. Saito said Japanese men seem attracted by high voices and girlish behavior, which some Japanese women then emulate. The attraction to young girls is known here as the Loli-con—short for Lolita Complex—and it is a Japanese phenomenon, the basis for endless psychoanalyses of the Japanese mind and libido.

"A high voice sounds more cute, more like a girlish image of women," Ms. Saito said. "In the United States I project more confidence, while in Japan I find I act in a more cute way."

Ms. Saito, like many bilingual women, speaks in a higher pitch in Japanese. Indeed, she said that when she returned recently from a visit to the United States, she telephoned her Japanese friends and they said, "Your voice sounds so low."

To be sure, in normal conversation at home or with friends, Japanese women sound normal to an American ear. But listen to the same woman apologizing to her boss on the phone, and her voice may go off the register.

"I have a lot of friends who visit me from Western countries, and although they don't understand Japanese, they told me that they'd noticed that Japanese women

speak in shrill, infantile voices," said Hideki Kasuya, professor of speech science as Utsunomiya University, a male expert on the pitch of women's voices in Japan. "I had felt the same thing myself, and that is why I started my research."

Professor Kasuya has found that female television announcers in the United States speak in a significantly lower pitch than female Japanese announcers. But his latest measurements this year found that the voices of female Japanese announcers had dropped noticeably since his first survey four years ago.

In the meantime, Hiromi Saito and 18 other elevator operators continue to speak in falsetto as they announce the floors at the Mitsukoshi Department Store in the Ginza district here. Miss Saito, as chief of the unit, trains the newcomers to raise their pitch.

"Girls with a lower pitch have a struggle when they come here to work at first," she said. "But after a month or so, you see a transformation. And after three months, they have a completely different voice."

Why do this?

"It may be hard for Americans to understand," said Sayori Iwata, a Mitsukoshi spokeswoman, "but in Japan, it's considered beautiful to sacrifice yourself for the service of others."

Source: Nicholas D. Kristof, "Japan's Feminine Falsetto Falls Right Out of Favor," *The New York Times,* December 13, 1995, pp. A1, A4.

In Labov's study, *r* pronunciation was clearly associated with prestige. Certainly the job interviewers who had hired the salespeople never counted *r*'s before offering employment. However, they did

use speech evaluations to make judgments about how effective certain people would be in selling particular kinds of merchandise. In other words, they practiced sociolinguistic discrimination, using linguistic features in deciding who got certain jobs.

In stratified societies, our speech habits help determine our access to employment and other material resources. Because of this, "proper language" itself becomes a strategic resource—and a path to wealth, prestige, and power (Gal 1989). Illustrating this, many ethnographers have described the importance of verbal skill and oratory in politics (Beeman 1986; Bloch, ed. 1975; Brenneis 1988; Geis 1987). Remember, too, that a "great communicator," Ronald Reagan, dominated American society in the 1980s as a two-term President.

The French anthropologist Pierre Bourdieu views linguistic practices as *symbolic capital* which properly trained people may convert into economic and social capital. The value of a dialect—its standing in a "linguistic market"—depends on the extent to which it provides access to desired positions in the labor market. In turn, this reflects its legitimation by formal institutions—the educational establishment, state, church, and prestige media. In stratified societies, even people who don't use the prestige dialect accept its authority and correctness, its "symbolic domination" (Bourdieu 1982, 1984). Thus, linguistic forms, which lack power in themselves, take on the power of the groups and relationships they symbolize. The education system, however (defending its own worth), denies this, misrepresenting prestige speech as being inherently better. The linguistic in-

Whether it's fair or not, people judge you by the way you talk. In stratified societies, our speech habits help determine our access to employment and other resources. "Proper language" itself becomes a strategic resource, correlated with wealth, prestige, and power. Linguistic stratification may reflect both class and ethnic contrasts. In Guatemala a Spanish-speaking elite couple enjoy a garden breakfast served by an Indian maid.

security of lower-class and minority speakers is a result of this symbolic domination.

HISTORICAL LINGUISTICS

Sociolinguists study contemporary variation in speech—language change in progress. **Historical linguistics** deals with longer-term change. Historical linguists can reconstruct many features of past languages by studying contemporary **daughter languages.** These are languages that descend from the same parent language and that have been changing separately for hundreds or even thousands of years. We call the original language from which they diverge the **protolanguage.** French and Spanish, for example, are daughter languages of Latin, their common protolanguage. Historical linguists also classify languages according to their degree of relationship.

Language changes over time. It evolves—varies, spreads, divides into **subgroups** (languages within a taxonomy of related languages that are most closely related). Dialects of a single parent language become distinct daughter languages, especially if they are isolated from one another. Some of them split, and new "granddaughter" languages develop. If people remain in the ancestral homeland, their speech patterns also change. The evolving speech in the ancestral homeland should be considered a daughter language like the others.

A close relationship between languages doesn't necessarily mean that their speakers are closely related biologically or culturally, because people can adopt new languages. In the equatorial forests of Africa, "pygmy" hunters have discarded their ancestral languages and now speak those of the cultivators who have migrated to the area. Immigrants to the United States spoke many different languages on arrival, but their descendants now speak fluent English.

Knowledge of linguistic relationships is often valuable to anthropologists interested in history, particularly events during the past 5,000 years. Cultural features may (or may not) correlate with the distribution of language families. Groups that speak related languages may (or may not) be more culturally similar to each other than they are to groups whose speech derives from different linguistic ancestors. Of course, cultural similarities aren't limited to speakers of related languages. Even groups whose members speak unrelated languages have contact through trade, intermarriage, and warfare. Ideas and inventions diffuse widely among human groups. Many items of vocabulary in contemporary English come from French. Even without written documentation of France's influence after the Norman Conquest of England in 1066, linguistic evidence in contemporary English would reveal a long period of important firsthand contact with France. Similarly, linguistic evidence may confirm cultural contact and borrowing when written history is lacking. By considering which words have been borrowed, we can also make inferences about the nature of the contact.

CYBERSPACE: A NEW REALM OF COMMUNICATION

The world navigable via computer—cyberspace—is part of a larger high-tech communications environment, which may be called advanced information technology (AIT). A related term, used by Vice President Al Gore, is national information infrastructure (NII), which is better called GII, because it is global in scope. Other elements of this environment include computer hardware and software, modems, advanced telephone systems, cable TV, satellite dishes, faxes, and even radio and TV talk shows, all of which have both integrative and disintegrative functions.

Just as AIT cannot be understood apart from other changes going on in society, it should not be studied just nationally; one of its key features is its international scope. Along with modern transportation systems, AIT plays a key role in connecting people worldwide. It has challenged, or is challenging, the authoritarian governments of the former Soviet Union, Iran, China, Vietnam, Singapore, Malaysia, and Indonesia. AIT undermines authoritarian states by allowing the expression of diverse opinions, including dissident voices.

A developing interdisciplinary field known as science and technology studies (STS) recognizes that science and technology are crucial arenas for creating culture and sociality in today's world (Escobar 1994). AIT has the capacity to both unite and divide because it connects people in both wider and narrower networks. Many of us subscribe to specialized newsgroups, on-line services, and BBSs (bulletin board services). A particular newsgroup unites people from all over the world who share a common interest. Yet because most interests are special, the Internet and related environments also encourage, maintain, reinforce, and strengthen differences.

Some of the groups linked by AIT are transnational. Fax machines and E-mail promote the almost instantaneous global diffusion of fairly complex documents. The thousands of newsgroups on Usenet are read internationally by people with a common interest. Some newsgroups focus on health issues (e.g., alt.support.tinnitus) or politics (alt.politics.clinton). Others focus on nations (e.g., the soc.culture groups such as soc.culture.brazil and soc.culture.singapore). They provide a common forum for scholars and others interested in a particular nation, or for its citizens in various locales. Some newsgroups are support groups for people with a common malady, experience, identity, or TV obsession (e.g., alt.tv.melrose-place). The narrow-focus groups can be quite esoteric (e.g., alt.sex.bestiality.hamster.duct-tape or alt.wesley.crusher.die.die.die). Some newsgroups are commercial and allow the posting of ads. Proper *netiquette,* the evolving set of rules for Internet communication, makes it obligatory to distinguish between commercial and noncommercial forums. Those who post improperly, whether deliberately or unwittingly, subject themselves to a prime Internet sanction—the flame—a series of angry messages from offended group members all over the world.

Narrow-focus groups may be based on work cultures and other affinity groups—homogeneous groups of user-participants (Harvey 1996). They may link members of a single organization in one place, branches of that organization in different places, or similar professionals—for example, ENT (ear, nose, and throat) physicians all over the world.

Transecting groups create direct communication channels between groups that previously had, or otherwise have, trouble communicating—for example, physicians and patients. Transecting groups include health-oriented support groups on the Internet—to which physicians, sufferers, and other "experts" regularly contribute. Other forums focusing on health conditions are available on-line at various sites, including the WorldWide Web and live (real-time) forums.

Inequality in Cyberspace

Although AIT links the world, access to its riches is unequal both among and within nations. The less-

IN THE NEWS: USING MODERN TECHNOLOGY TO PRESERVE LINGUISTIC DIVERSITY

Linguistic diversity is reduced when people abandon their ancestral tongue for a dominant or national language. The anthropologist H. Russell Bernard has been a pioneer in teaching speakers of endangered languages how to write their language using a computer. Bernard's work permits the preservation of languages and cultural memories. Native peoples from Mexico to Cameroon are using their mother tongue to express themselves as individuals and to provide insiders' accounts of different cultures.

Jesús Salinas Pedraza, a rural schoolteacher in the Mexican state of Hidalgo, sat down to a word processor a few years back and produced a monumental book, a 250,000-word description of his own Indian culture written in the Nähñu language. Nothing seems to be left out: folktales and traditional religious beliefs, the practical uses of plants and minerals and the daily flow of life in field and village.

But it is more than the content that makes the book a remarkable publishing event, for Mr. Salinas is neither a professional anthropologist nor a literary stylist. He is, though, the first person to write a book in Nähñu (NYAW-hnyu), the native tongue of several hundred thousand Indians but a previously unwritten language.

Such a use of microcomputers and desktop publishing for languages with no literary tradition is now being encouraged by anthropologists for recording ethnographies from an insider's perspective. They see this as a means of preserving cultural diversity and a wealth of human knowledge. With even greater urgency, linguists are promoting the techniques as a way of saving some of the world's languages from imminent extinction.

Half of the world's 6,000 languages are considered by linguists to be endangered. These are the languages spoken by small societies that are dwindling with the encroachment of larger, more dynamic cultures. Young people feel economic pressure to learn only the language of the dominant culture, and as the older people die, the non-written language vanishes, unlike languages with a history of writing, like Latin.

Dr. H. Russell Bernard, the anthropologist at the University of Florida at Gainesville who taught Mr. Salinas to read and write his native language, said: "Languages have always come and gone. Neither the language of Jesus nor that of Caesar are spoken today. But languages seem to be disappearing faster than ever before."

In 30 years of field studies, Dr. Kenneth Hale, a linguist at the Massachusetts Institute of Technology and a leader in efforts to preserve endangered languages, said he had worked with at least eight that have become extinct and many others that are "seriously imperiled."

Dr. Michael E. Krauss, the director of the Alaska Native Language Center at the University of Alaska in Fairbanks, estimates that 300 of the 900 indigenous languages in the Americas are moribund. That is, they are no longer being spoken by children, and so could disappear in a generation or two. Only two of the 20 native languages in Alaska are still being learned by children.

"Languages no longer being learned as mother-tongue by children are beyond endangerment," Dr. Krauss said. Unless the current course is somehow reversed, he added, these languages "are already doomed to extinction, like species lacking reproductive capacity."

Dr. Krauss asks: "Should we mourn the loss of Eyak or Ubykh any less than the loss of the panda or California condor?"

At a symposium a few years ago in Mexico on "The Politics of Linguistic Revitalization," representatives of Latin American Indians passed a resolution saying, "The loss of a language in the world means the disappearance of the cultural heritage transmitted by it, and the truncation of an alternate route of cultural development for humankind."

In an effort to preserve language diversity in Mexico, Dr. Bernard and Mr. Salinas decided in 1987 on a plan to teach the Indian people to read and write their own language using microcomputers. They established a native literacy center in Oaxaca, Mexico, where others could follow in the footsteps of Mr. Salinas and write books in other Indian languages.

The Oaxaca center goes beyond most bilingual education programs, which concentrate on teaching people to speak and read their native languages. Instead, it operates on the premise that, as Dr. Bernard decided, what most native languages lack is native authors who write books in their own languages.

"Without popular literacy, all but a few endangered languages will soon disappear," Dr. Bernard said. "And when non-written languages disappear, they disappear forever."

Mr. Salinas set the example. He had grown up speaking both Spanish and Nähñu, one of the more widely spoken of the 56 Indian languages in Mexico. The Nähñu Indians are also known as the Otomí, a name they now reject because of its pejorative connotations in Mexican Spanish.

While conducting research in Mexico in the 1970's, Dr. Bernard taught Mr. Salinas to read and write the Nähñu language, using a modified version of an alphabet that had been developed by missionaries. The Summer Institute of Linguistics, a world-wide evangelical Protestant organization based in Dallas, has for decades developed the alphabets for hundreds of Indian languages.

Virtually all indigenous languages now have rudimentary writing systems, including alphabets, a dictionary and some grammar. In Nähñu and many other languages, however, the only book is a Bible translation.

Next Dr. Bernard adapted computer software for writing Nähñu on a word processor and for printing manuscripts and books, which would not have been affordable through traditional publishing. In this way, Mr. Salinas first produced a book of Nähñu folktales and, two years ago, his magnum opus on Nähñu culture. A translation in English, by Dr. Bernard, is entitled, "Native Ethnography: A Mexican Indian Describes His Culture."

There is a long tradition of training people of a remote culture to be what anthropologists call informants. These people would describe the legends and customs and sometimes dictate their autobiographies. But these were usually taped interviews with an anthropologist and not the direct work of an indigenous person.

The Oaxaca project's influence is spreading. Impressed by the work of Mr. Salinas and others, Dr. Norman Whitten, an anthropologist at the University of Illinois, arranged for schoolteachers from Ecuador to visit Oaxaca and learn the techniques.

Now Ecuadorian Indians have begun writing about their cultures in the Quechua and Shwara languages. Others from Bolivia and Peru are learning to use the computers to write their languages, including Quecha, the tongue of the ancient Incas, still spoken by about 12 million Andean Indians.

Anthropologists in Cameroon have introduced the technology in that African country of more than 200 tribal languages. At the end of a two-week training course, Dr. Bernard said, each of the five speakers of the Kom language would turn on the computer in the morning and start typing Kom without hesitation. Anything they could say, they could write.

Dr. Bernard emphasized that these native literacy programs are not intended to discourage people from learning the dominant language of their country as well. "I see nothing useful or charming about remaining monolingual in any Indian language if that results in being shut out of the national economy," he said.

Anthropologists acknowledge that bilingualism can be a sensitive political issue. In places struggling to create a workable nation, the preservation of separate languages can be seen as potentially divisive, setting one group against another.

But anthropologists and leaders of native cultures generally favor bilingualism because it preserves a distinctive culture, which often gives the people more power than if they were completely assimilated. A distinctive language can be a strong force in establishing cultural uniqueness, or ethnicity, which in turn can reinforce a group's claim to a share of power.

Such efforts may be too late for hundreds of languages and dwindling cultures, anthropologists and linguists say, but in time to help preserve some of the cultural heterogeneity of the planet.

Source: John Noble Wilford, "In a Publishing Coup, Books in 'Unwritten' Languages," *The New York Times,* December 31, 1991, pp. B5, 6.

Global linguistic richness is reduced as people abandon their ancestral tongues for dominant and national languages. Computers are being used to help people write, and thus preserve, endangered languages. General U.S. culture poses threats to the language and culture of this Apache woman, shown with her grandchildren in Whiteriver, Arizona.

developed countries (LDCs) have poorer access than do Japan, Western Europe, North America, and Australia–New Zealand. Poverty and technological underdevelopment are key factors limiting access in Africa and many parts of Latin America and Oceania. In Asia, authoritarian governments attempt to devise means of limiting their citizens' access, even as they recognize the economic benefits of connectivity (e.g., instant access to financial information). China, for example, has priced cyberspace connectivity beyond the reach of ordinary people.

Even within a "developed" nation like the United States, socioeconomic, demographic, and cultural factors affect access to and use of cyberspace. Not everyone has been or will be integrated equally. There is privileged access to AIT by class, race, ethnicity, gender, education, profession, age, and family background. Young people tend to be more comfortable with AIT than old people are. Kids who grow up with computers in their homes become familiar with them and are more likely to use them than are the offspring of computerless homes.

Class affects both access to and use of AIT. Families with higher incomes and greater wealth tend to have better access to the range of high-tech items. Members of such families also tend to have and get better educations, and participate more in the information-processing settings and professions in which AIT is used most regularly. There is some evidence that communication via cyberspace can break down barriers between differentially privileged members of a physical community (town or city). Michaelson (1996) describes communication networks linking homeless people using public library computers and middle-class people using computers in homes, jobs, and schools, as well as similar connectivity between children and elderly persons. These communication networks would not have been established without computers.

Still, communication via AIT has not banished class bias, despite several democratizing features of cyberspace communication. Class-based contrasts are reduced, but not eliminated. One equalizing feature of *cyberspeak* (the range of styles and conventions people use when they write messages in cyberspace) is its informality compared to print. Specific communicative and linguistic practices develop in different media. Language is neither as fixed nor as precise as it is in writing for print. Cyberwriters aren't as concerned with typos as are

writers for print. Writing exclusively in capital letters (using the Caps Lock key) is bad form ("shouting"). Lowercase letters are proper, and some people hardly use capital letters at all. Others are more attentive to the canons of print, and this—along with vocabulary and punctuation—is a way in which training and education show up. Class anonymity is not fully possible. Nor, probably, is gender. Using expletives or beginning a message with the salutation "Dude" suggest male identity. Female use of cyberspace sometimes shows some of the sociolinguistic insecurity that has been noted in other contexts (Lakoff 1975; Tannen 1990). From postings I have read I suspect that women are more likely to end their messages with disclaimers, such as "But that's just my opinion," whereas men choose the more emphatic IMHO (in my humble opinion) to express the same sentiment.

Groups with more restricted access to AIT include minorities, the poor, females, old people, and the LDCs. There is some indication that cultural factors affect minority use of AIT—African-Americans may view the computing environment as a "white thing." People with different cultural backgrounds will interpret and use technological artifacts in different ways, but socioeconomic factors also play an important role. Despite the American ideology of equality, and the self-identification of most Americans with the middle class, many disturbing, and lingering, aspects of our culture are based on socioeconomic stratification.

From case studies of economic development in the LDCs—Java's green revolution (see Chapter 22), for example—we know that an initial uneven distribution of resources often becomes the basis for greater inequality as the technological shift progresses. This lesson has an American application. If current class-based trends in access to technology continue, we face results like Java's. The United States has a "persistent and substantial inequality in the access to new technology among both schools and school children. . . . The poorer a school is, the less likely that school is to have any of this new technology" (Tarr-Whelan, quoted by Grassmuck 1985). Math, science, the computer, and information processing are the strategic resources of a high-tech society, just as dams and irrigation canals are for Java's rice farmers. Microcomputers and associated AIT are concentrated in affluent school districts. Unless our schools provide widespread access to

Math, science, computer hardware and software, and information processing are the strategic resources of a high-tech society. The United States has a persistent and substantial inequality in access to new technology among both schools and school children. Shown here are some of the lucky ones— elementary school kids in Cupertino, California.

AIT equipment and training, continuation of the current distribution pattern, based on income and differential tax support, will ensure that we raise a differentially privileged generation of computer whizzes and dolts, the children of richer and poorer Americans, respectively.

If access doesn't start at home it may begin in a public setting, such as a school or library. But in the United States, school and library funding varies markedly among regions, states, cities, towns, and neighborhoods. Access to cyberspace requires not only computers and software but wiring of classrooms and payment of phone charges for connectivity to wider systems. Many schools have computers, but they still lack proper software and the physical means of connecting to the wider, information-rich resources of the Internet and the WorldWide Web.

Elitism and Gatekeeping

In addition to the communication-style differences based on class, elitism affects cyberspace in other ways. All liberating technologies face attempts by elites to seize control, proposals to guide that medium toward prosocial goals (social engineering), and claims to know better than ordinary people do how the system should be used. We may generalize that elites, censors, and others who think they "know best" will attempt to regulate or control

any potentially democratizing medium, from television to cyberspace. David Hess (1995) has noted the history of early and primary use of cyberspace and AIT by the U.S. defense establishment, academics, and corporations. Escobar (1994) speculates that military and profit-oriented applications will continue to dominate cyberspace.

One of the most flagrant manifestations of elitism occurred as 2 million members of America On-Line (AOLers) joined the Internet a few years ago. Traditional users lambasted the novices for their ignorance of proper netiquette. AOLers have not yet managed to shake their stigmatized status as second-class citizens of cyberspace. There is even a newsgroup entitled "alt.aol-sucks."

Even as they challenge elitism and traditional authority, democratizing media still have barriers and gatekeepers. It takes special knowledge, background, and flexibility to hook up with the various communication modes available via AIT, and with constantly changing systems. The elderly are at a disadvantage, although retirees have the time to use cyberspace productively. Older people even have trouble using the array of information-extraction opportunities available via the touch-tone phone. Use of an ATM (automatic teller machine) can be frightening for people with low-tech abilities or poor eyesight. Still, cyberspace could eventually prove to be a social boon for the elderly, who, like other segments of the North American population, are more socially isolated from their families now than they were thirty years ago.

Cyberspace is regulated, then, by people's backgrounds and demographic characteristics. Also, users regulate one another through direct statements, flames, and other devices (e.g., "kill" or "squelch" commands that snip particular links) when someone is seen as abusing the canons of a specific group or of cyberspace generally.

There are more formal gatekeepers, too. Exhibiting a certain distrust of open information, including pornography—especially its availability to children—a 1996 U.S. law expanded government regulation of cyberspace. Other bills would increase regulation to fight crime, terrorism, or "hate speech." Many cyberspace forums are already "moderated," and all systems have *sysops* (systems operators), who play some kind of regulatory role in terms of access, if not of what is said on-line. Still, many real-time on-line forums permit instantaneous, free-for-all, unmoderated conversation. These are much more democratic than, say, radio talk shows, for which gatekeepers screen callers.

Cyberspace and Social Reality

Social scientists are studying ways in which AIT is fostering new social constructions of reality, and computers are changing notions of identity and the self. Virtual worlds—for example, anonymous computer role-playing games (MUDs, or multiple user dimensions)—are ways of extending various selves into forms of cybersocial interactions (Escobar 1994). People make statements about and manipulate their identities when they choose various "handles," their names in cyberspace. If someone engages in on-line communication through multiple channels—for example, a university gateway, a commercial service, and a BBS—he or she may have various handles and identities. The individual must then keep track of those identities for different accounts. In some contexts, people manipulate ("lie about") their ages and genders and create their own cyberfantasies.

Guiding this discussion so far has been the implicit assumption that people use AIT for their own ends—for purposes that make sense to them in the context of their everyday lives, to make those lives a little easier or more interesting. Sometimes, however, use of AIT is imposed. Superiors (e.g., company management) may force subordinates to use AIT, then follow that use closely, perhaps to monitor work performance.

Social scientists are still investigating how the use of cyberspace is related to the use of other media and to participation in face-to-face groups and communities. One unresolved question is how participation in an on-line forum affects participation in face-to-face groups based on the same issue (e.g., alcohol abuse). There is no a priori reason to assume that one form of participation will diminish the other. For example, my research in Brazil (Kottak 1990a) revealed television's role in promoting a general media hunger; the more people watched TV, the more they were likely to use all available media. The number of media-hungry people and information addicts is increasing worldwide; such people will surely be attracted to cyberspace. And the growth of real-life support groups has been correlated with their appearance on various media (print, radio, TV, and in cyberspace).

I do not see that AIT plays an especially novel or important role in promoting the decline of face-to-face communities, which have been declining for other reasons for many years. Long ago, social scientists linked this phenomenon to urbanization. For example, in several books, the anthropologist Robert Redfield (1941) attempted to identify the main contrasts between rural and urban life. He contrasted rural communities, whose social relations are on a face-to-face basis, with cities, where impersonality characterizes many aspects of life.

In many ways, cyberspace replicates New York City. People sleep in different apartments and have little to do with their neighbors. They get up and go to work, where they interact with their coworkers. They get together with family, friends, and people who share their interests—in varied settings.

Social scientists disagree about the effects of cyberspace-based (virtual) communities on face-to-face social life, and more research is needed in this area. Despite certain rather utopian visions of the role of virtual networks in integrating physical communities (Kling 1996), I doubt that AIT will play much of a role in strengthening whole local communities—towns and cities. Rather, I predict that AIT will be used mainly to facilitate communication among affinity groups—relatives, friends, and people with common identities, experiences, or interests, especially work interests. AIT will be used

Social scientists disagree about the actual and potential effects of cyberspace-based (virtual) communities on face-to-face social life. One function of AIT (advanced information technology) is to facilitate communication among affinity groups—relatives, friends, people with common identities, experiences, or interests—such as these groups of World Wide Web browsers at the Cyber Cafe in Soho, Manhattan, New York.

especially for immediate communication within groups of coworkers and members of common organizations. Its main role, however, will be to establish and maintain links among physically dispersed people who have, and will come to have, even more in common.

SUMMARY

Language, the main system humans use to communicate, features productivity and displacement, and is culturally transmitted. Linguistic anthropologists share anthropology's general interest in uniformity and diversity in time and space. Linguistic anthropology examines meaning systems, relationships between language and culture, linguistic universals, sociolinguistics, and linguistic change.

No language includes all the sounds (phones) that the human vocal apparatus can make. Phonology—the study of speech sounds—focuses on sound contrasts (phonemes) that distinguish meaning in a given language. In sociolinguistics, variation among speakers of the same language correlates with social contrasts and exemplifies linguistic change in progress.

In his transformational-generative approach, Chomsky argues for an innate blueprint for building language in the human brain. All people share this genetically determined capacity for language, though not for any particular language. Each language's grammar is a particular set of rules taken from the universal set. Once we master our language's rules, we can generate an infinite number of statements. Surface structures, the object of traditional linguistic study, make languages seem more different than they are. The similarities lie deeper, at the level of deep structure.

There are culturally distinctive as well as universal relationships between language and mental processes. The lexicons and grammars of particular languages can lead speakers to perceive and think in particular ways. Studies of domains such as kinship, color terminologies, and pronouns show that speakers of different languages categorize their experiences differently. However, language does not tightly restrict thought, because cultural changes can produce changes in thought and in language, particularly in surface structure.

Sociolinguistics investigates relationships between social and linguistic variation. It focuses on performance (the actual use of language) rather than competence (rules shared by all speakers of a given language). Sociolinguists do field work with several informants and quantify their observations. Only when features of speech acquire social meaning are they imitated. If they are valued, they will spread.

People vary their speech on different occasions, shifting styles, dialects, and languages, particularly in the modern world system. As linguistic systems, all languages and dialects are equally complex, rule-governed, and effective for communication. However, speech is used, is evaluated, and changes in the context of political, economic, and social forces. The linguistic traits of a low-status group are negatively evaluated (often even by members of that group) not because of their *linguistic* features but because they are associated with and symbolize low *social* status. One dialect, supported by the dominant institutions of the state, exercises symbolic domination over the others.

Historical linguistics is useful for anthropologists interested in historical relationships between populations. Cultural similarities and differences often correlate with linguistic ones. Linguistic clues can suggest past contacts between cultures. Related languages—members of the same language family—descend from an original protolanguage. Relationships between languages don't necessarily mean that there are biological ties between their speakers, because people can learn new languages.

The world navigable via computer—cyberspace—is part of a larger, global, high-tech communications environment, advanced information technology (AIT). One effect of AIT has been to undermine certain authoritarian states by allowing the expression of diverse opinions and dissident voices. AIT can both unite and divide; it connects people in both wider and narrower networks. Narrow-focus groups may be based on work cultures and other affinity groups, or homogeneous groups of user-participants. AIT also creates transecting groups, or direct communication channels between people who otherwise may have trouble communicating—for example, physicians and patients.

Access to AIT is unequal both among and within nations. There is privileged access by class, race, ethnicity, gender, education, profession, age, and family background. Groups with more restricted access to AIT include minorities, the poor, females, old people, and the less-developed countries. Specific communicative and linguistic practices develop in different media. *Netiquette* is the evolving set of rules for Internet communication. Liberating technologies typically face attempts by elites to seize control, as censors and others who think they know best attempt to regulate potentially democratizing media. Although they may challenge elitism and traditional authority, democratizing media still have barriers and gatekeepers. AIT is fostering new social constructions of reality, and computers are changing notions of identity and the self. Social scientists disagree about the effects of cyberspace-based (virtual) communities on face-to-face social life—an area where more research is needed.

GLOSSARY

competence: What native speakers must (and do) know about their language in order to speak and understand it.

daughter languages: Languages developing out of the same parent language; for example, French and Spanish are daughter languages of Latin.

deep structure: In transformational grammar, the mental level; a sentence is formed in the speaker's mind and then interpreted by the hearer.

diglossia: The existence of "high" (formal) and "low" (informal, familial) dialects of a single language, such as German.

ethnoscience: See *ethnosemantics*.

ethnosemantics: The study of lexical (vocabulary) contrasts and classifications in various languages.

focal vocabulary: A set of words and distinctions that are particularly important to certain groups (those with particular foci of experience or activity), such as types of snow to Eskimos or skiers.

grammar: The formal organizing principles that link sound and meaning in a language; the set of abstract rules that makes up a language.

historical linguistics: Subdivision of linguistics that studies languages over time.

language: Human beings' primary means of communication; may be spoken or written; features productivity and displacement and is culturally transmitted.

lexicon: Vocabulary; a dictionary containing all the morphemes in a language and their meanings.

linguistic relativity: Notion that all languages and dialects are equally effective as systems of communication.

linguistic uniformitarianism: Belief that explanations for long-term change in language should be sought in ordinary forces that continue to work today; thus, the forces that have produced linguistic changes over the centuries are observable in linguistic events (variation) taking place today.

minimal pairs: Words that resemble each other in all but one sound; used to discover phonemes.

morpheme: Minimal linguistic form (usually a word) with meaning.

morphology: The study of form; used in linguistics (the study of morphemes and word construction) and for form in general—for example, biomorphology relates to physical form.

performance: What people actually say; the use of speech in social situations.

phone: Any speech sound.

phoneme: Significant sound contrast in a language that serves to distinguish meaning, as in minimal pairs.

phonemics: The study of the sound contrasts (phonemes) of a particular language.

phonetics: The study of speech sounds in general; what people actually say in various languages.

phonology: The study of sounds used in speech.

protolanguage: Language ancestral to several daughter languages.

Sapir-Whorf hypothesis: Theory that different languages produce different ways of thinking.

semantics: A language's meaning system.

sociolinguistics: Study of relationships between social and linguistic variation; study of language (performance) in its social context.

style shifts: Variations in speech in different contexts.

subgroups: Languages within a taxonomy of related languages that are most closely related.

surface structure: In transformational grammar, the message that passes from speaker to hearer; an actual speech event.

syntax: The arrangement and order of words in phrases and sentences.

transformational-generative grammar: Approach associated with Noam Chomsky; views language as a set of abstract rules with deep and surface structures.

transecting groups: Networks created through direct communication channels between groups that previously had, or otherwise have, trouble communicating—e.g., physicians and patients.

universal grammar: According to Chomsky, a genetically transmitted blueprint for language, that is, basic linguistic plan in the human brain.

STUDY QUESTIONS

1. Why is linguistic anthropology a subdiscipline of anthropology? What does it share with the other subdisciplines? How does it link up with cultural anthropology?
2. What is Noam Chomsky's transformational-generative grammar, and how does it relate to the issue of "human nature"?
3. What is the Sapir-Whorf hypothesis, and how does it relate to cultural diversity?
4. What is sociolinguistics, and how does it relate

to the distinction between competence and performance?

5. Several examples of interrelationships between social and linguistic variation have been given. Can you cite comparable sociolinguistic examples from your own experience?

6. How do men and women differ in their use of language?

7. What is historical linguistics, and what are the issues it studies?

8. What is linguistic relativity, and how does it relate to symbolic domination by prestige dialects?

9. What is AIT? How do linguistic, socioeconomic, and cultural factors influence access to, and use of, cyberspace?

10. How is cyberspace used to create social networks and identities?

SUGGESTED ADDITIONAL READING

APPEL, R., AND P. MUYSKEN
    1987   *Language Contact and Bilingualism.* London: Edward Arnold. Issues of linguistic contact.
BARON, D.
    1986   *Grammar and Gender.* New Haven, CT: Yale University Press. Differences in grammatical patterns and strategies of men and women.
BEEMAN, W.
    1986   *Language, Status, and Power in Iran.* Bloomington, IN: Indiana University Press. Informative case study using sociolinguistic analysis to examine issues of speech, performance, and power.
BONVILLAIN, N.
    1993   *Language, Culture, and Communication: The Meaning of Messages.* Englewood Cliffs, NJ: Prentice-Hall. Up-to-date text on language and communication in cultural context.
BURKE, P., AND R. PORTER
    1987   *The Social History of Language.* Cambridge: Cambridge University Press. Language in society through history.
COATES, J.
    1986   *Women, Men, and Language.* London: Longman. Gender differences in language.
COOK-GUMPERZ, J.
    1986   *The Social Construction of Literacy.* Cambridge: Cambridge University Press. Literacy in its social and cultural context.
FASOLD, R. W.
    1990   *The Sociolinguistics of Language.* Oxford: Basil Blackwell. Recent text with up-to-date examples.
GEIS, M. L.
    1987   *The Language of Politics.* New York: Springer-Verlag. Thorough examination of political uses of speech and oratory and the manipulation of language in power relations.
GUMPERZ, J. J.
    1982   *Language and Social Identity.* Cambridge: Cambridge University Press. Well-known sociolinguist discusses language and social identification.
HANKS, W. F.
    1995   *Language and Communicative Practices.* Boulder, CO: Westview. The nature and role of language in communication and society.
HELLER, M.
    1988   *Codeswitching: Anthropological and Sociolinguistic Perspectives.* Berlin: Mouton de Gruyter. Style shifting and diglossia.
HEWITT, R.
    1986   *White Talk, Black Talk.* Cambridge: Cambridge University Press. Black English Vernacular and its relationship to Standard English and white dialects.
KRAMARAE, R., M. SHULZ, AND M. O'BARR, EDS.
    1984   *Language and Power.* Beverly Hills, CA: Sage. Issues of language, politics, and symbolic domination.
LAKOFF, R.
    1975   *Language and Woman's Place.* New York: Harper & Row. Influential nontechnical discussion of how women use and are treated in Standard American English.
MAHER, J. C., AND G. MACDONALD, EDS.
    1995   *Diversity and Language in Japanese Culture.* New York: Columbia University Press. The articles in this volume describe and analyze the often-overlooked ethnic, cultural, and linguistic diversity existing within modern Japan.
MUHLHAUSLER, P.
    1986   *Pidgin and Creole Linguistics.* London: Basil Blackwell. New languages of travel, trade, and colonialism.
ROMAINE, S.
    1994   *Language in Society: An Introduction to Sociolinguistics.* New York: Oxford University Press. An introduction to sociolinguistics.
SALZMANN, Z.
    1993   *Language, Culture, and Society: An Introduction to Linguistic Anthropology.* Boulder, CO: West-

view. The function of language in culture and society.

TANNEN, D.
1990   *You Just Don't Understand: Women and Men in Conversation.* New York: Ballantine. Popular book on gender differences in speech and conversational styles.

TANNEN, D., ED.
1993   *Gender and Conversational Interaction.* New York: Oxford University Press. Twelve papers about conversational interaction illustrate the complexity of the relation between gender and language use.

THOMASON, S. G., AND T. KAUFMAN
1988   *Language Contact, Creolization, and Genetic Linguistics.* Berkeley: University of California Press. Language in the world system.

TRUDGILL, P.
1983   *Sociolinguistics: An Introduction to Language and Society,* rev. ed. Baltimore: Penguin. Readable short introduction to the role and use of language in society.

WOOLARD, K. A.
1989   *Double Talk: Bilingualism and the Politics of Ethnicity in Catalonia.* Stanford, CA: Stanford University Press. Field study of diglossia.

CHAPTER 20

THE WORLD SYSTEM, INDUSTRIALISM, AND STRATIFICATION

THE EMERGENCE OF THE WORLD SYSTEM

INDUSTRIALIZATION
Causes of the Industrial Revolution

STRATIFICATION

Box: The American Periphery

Open and Closed Class Systems

INDUSTRIAL AND NONINDUSTRIAL SOCIETIES IN THE WORLD SYSTEM TODAY
The Effects of Industrialization on the World
 System

Although field work in small communities is anthropology's hallmark, isolated groups are impossible to find today. Truly isolated cultures probably have never existed. For thousands of years, human groups have been in contact with one another. Local societies have always participated in a larger system, which today has global dimensions. We call it the *modern world system*, by which we mean a world in which nations are economically and politically interdependent.

City, nation, and world increasingly invade the local communities. Today, if anthropologists want to study a fairly isolated society, they must journey to the highlands of Papua–New Guinea or the tropical forests of South America. Even in those places they will probably encounter missionaries or prospectors. In contemporary Australia, sheep owned by people who speak English graze where totemic ceremonies once were held. Farther in the outback some descendants of those totemites work in a movie crew making *Crocodile Dundee IV*. A Hilton hotel stands in the capital of faraway Madagascar, and a paved highway now has an exit for Arembepe, the Brazilian fishing village I have been studying since 1962. When and how did the modern world system begin?

The world system and the relations between the countries within that system are shaped by the world capitalist economy. World-system theory can be traced to the French social historian Fernand Braudel. In his three-volume work *Civilization and Capitalism, 15th–18th Century* (1981, 1982, 1984), Braudel argues that society consists of parts assembled into an interrelated system. Societies are subsystems of bigger systems, with the world system as the largest.

THE EMERGENCE OF THE WORLD SYSTEM

As Europeans took to ships, developing a transoceanic trade-oriented economy, people throughout the world entered Europe's sphere of influence. In the fifteenth century Europe established regular contact with Asia, Africa, and eventually the New World (the Caribbean and the Americas). Christopher Columbus's first voyage from Spain to the Bahamas and the Caribbean in 1492 was soon followed by additional voyages. These journeys opened the way for a major exchange of people, resources, diseases, and ideas, as the Old and New Worlds were forever linked (Crosby 1972, 1986; Viola and Margolis 1991). Led by Spain and Portugal, Europeans extracted silver and gold, conquered the natives (taking some as slaves), and colonized their lands.

Previously in Europe as throughout the world, rural people had produced mainly for their own needs, growing their own food and making clothing, furniture, and tools from local products. Pro-

The pace of social change is accelerating within the modern world system, based on international capitalism. This Malaysian woman pumps gasoline produced from Middle Eastern petroleum by a multinational organization (Shell) based in the Netherlands.

duction beyond immediate needs was undertaken to pay taxes and purchase trade items such as salt and iron. As late as 1650 the English diet, like diets in most of the world today, was based on locally grown starches (Mintz 1985). However, in the 200 years that followed, the English became extraordinary consumers of imported goods. One of the earliest and most popular of those goods was sugar (Mintz 1985).

Sugar was originally domesticated in Papua–New Guinea and was first processed in India. Reaching Europe via the Middle East and the eastern Mediterranean, it was carried to the New World by Columbus (Mintz 1985). The climate of Brazil and the Caribbean proved ideal for growing sugarcane, and Europeans built plantations there to supply the growing demand for sugar. This led to the development in the seventeenth century of a plantation economy based on a single cash crop—a system known as monocrop production.

The demand for sugar in a growing international market spurred the development of the transatlantic slave trade and New World plantation economies based on slave labor. By the eighteenth century, an increased English demand for raw cotton let to rapid settlement of what is now the southeastern United States and the emergence there of another slave-based monocrop production system. Like sugar, cotton was a key trade item that fueled the growth of the world system.

Columbus brought sugar to the New World, where it became the basis of a slave-based plantation economy geared toward profit in a growing international market. Sugar continues as an economic mainstay of many Caribbean nations such as Haiti.

The increasing dominance of international trade led to the **capitalist world economy** (Wallerstein 1982), a single world system committed to production for sale or exchange, with the object of maximizing profits rather than supplying domestic needs. **Capital** refers to wealth or resources invested in business, with the intent of producing a profit; the defining attribute of capitalism is economic orientation to the world market for profit.

The key claim of world-system theory is that an identifiable social system extends beyond individual states and nations. That system is formed by a set of economic and political relations that has characterized much of the globe since the sixteenth century, when the Old World established regular contact with the New World.

According to Wallerstein (1982), the nations within the world system occupy three different positions: core, periphery, and semiperiphery. There is a geographic center or **core,** the dominant position in the world system, which consists of the strongest and most powerful nations, with advanced systems of production. In core nations, "the complexity of economic activities and the level of capital accumulation is the greatest" (Thompson 1983, p. 12). Core countries specialize in producing the most "advanced" goods, using the most sophisticated technologies and mechanized means of production. The core produces capital-intensive high-technology goods and exports some of them to the periphery and semiperiphery.

Semiperiphery and **periphery** nations, which roughly correspond to what is usually called the Third World, have less power, wealth, and influence. The semiperiphery is intermediate between the core and the periphery. Contemporary nations of the semiperiphery are industrialized. Like core nations, they export both industrial goods and commodities, but they lack the power and economic dominance of core nations. Thus Brazil, a semiperiphery nation, exports automobiles to Nigeria and auto engines, orange juice extract, and coffee to the United States.

Economic activities in the periphery are less mechanized and use human labor more intensively than do those in the semiperiphery. The periphery produces raw materials and agricultural commodities for export to the core and the semiperiphery. However, in the modern world, industrialization is invading even peripheral nations. The relationship between the core and the periphery is fundamentally exploitative. Trade and other forms of economic relations between core and periphery tend to benefit capitalists in the core at the expense of the periphery (Shannon 1989).

INDUSTRIALIZATION

By the eighteenth century the stage had been set for the **Industrial Revolution**—the historical transformation (in Europe, after 1750) of "traditional" into "modern" societies through industrialization of the economy. Industrialization required capital for investment. The established system of transoceanic trade and commerce supplied this capital from the enormous profits it generated. Wealthy people sought investment opportunities and eventually found them in machines and engines to drive machines. Industrialization increased production in both farming and manufacturing, as capital and scientific innovation fueled invention.

European industrialization developed from (and eventually replaced) the **domestic system** (or home handicraft system) of manufacture. In this system, an organizer-entrepreneur supplied the raw materials to workers in their homes and collected the finished products from them. The entrepreneur, whose sphere of operations might span several villages, owned the materials, paid for the work, and arranged the marketing.

Causes of the Industrial Revolution

The Industrial Revolution began in the cotton products, iron, and pottery trades, whose manufacture could be broken down into simple routine motions that machines could perform. Factories could produce cheap staple goods. Industrialization began in industries that produced *goods that were widely used already*. This illustrates **Romer's rule**—a generalization about evolutionary processes, biological or cultural, originally proposed by the paleontologist Alfred S. Romer (1960). The key is that an innovation that evolves to *maintain* an existing system can play a major role in *changing* that system. Romer used the rule to explain the evolution of land-dwelling vertebrates from fish. The ancestors of land vertebrates were animals that lived in pools of water that dried up seasonally. Fins gradually evolved into legs, not

to permit vertebrates to live full-time on the land but to enable them to get back to the water when particular pools dried up. In other words, an innovation (legs) that proved essential to land life originated to maintain life in the water.

We can apply Romer's rule to many major changes in human life. One example is the transition to food production in the Middle East, discussed in Chapter 10. The "first farmers" did not start cultivating in order to become cultivators but to maintain the basis of their traditional foraging economy. According to this theory, population increase forced foragers into a marginal zone that lacked the bountiful wild fields of wheat and barley of their nearby homeland. They began sowing seeds (cultivating) in the marginal zone in order to create artificial fields like the natural ones in which they once had gathered. The actions of those ancient Middle Easterners had unintended consequences. The process they set in motion led to full-fledged food production, as their descendants eventually developed new varieties of wheat and barley that outyielded the wild forms.

Similarly, the Industrial Revolution led to a dramatic increase in production. When manufacturing moved from home to factory, where machinery replaced handwork, agrarian societies evolved into industrial ones. Industrialization fueled urban growth and created a new kind of city, with factories crowded together in places where coal and labor were cheap.

Revolution is not the right term to describe either food production or industrialism, because both were long-term processes that began in order to maintain rather than to change. Romer's lesson is that evolution (biological or cultural) tends to occur in small increments. Gradually changing systems make adaptations to maintain themselves as they change. The rule also applies to conscious economic changes: People usually want to *change just enough to maintain what they have*. Motives to modify behavior arise within a particular culture and reflect the small concerns and demands of daily life, such as improved crop yields and increased profit (assuming that the profit motive has been established in that culture).

Romer's rule helps us understand why the Industrial Revolution began in England rather than France. The French did not have to transform their domestic manufacturing system, but merely expand it. With a late eighteenth-century population at least twice that of Great Britain, France could simply augment its domestic system of production by drawing in new homes. Thus, the French could increase production *without innovating*—they could enlarge the existing system rather than adopt a new one. However, to meet mounting demand for staples—at home and in the colonies—England had to industrialize.

Britain's population doubled during the eighteenth century (particularly after 1750) and did so again between 1800 and 1850. This demographic explosion fueled consumption, but British entrepreneurs couldn't meet the increased demand with the traditional production methods. This spurred experimentation, innovation, and rapid technological change.

Several factors propelled industrialization. English industrialization drew on national advantages in natural resources. Great Britain was rich in coal and iron ore, and had navigable waterways and easily negotiated coasts. It was a seafaring island-nation located at the crossroads of international trade. These features gave Britain a favored position for importing raw materials and exporting manufactured goods. Another factor in England's industrial growth was the fact that much of its eighteenth-century colonial empire was occupied by English settler families who looked to the mother country as they tried to replicate European civilization in the New World. These colonies bought large quantities of English staples.

It has also been argued that particular cultural values and religion contributed to industrialization. Thus, many members of the emerging English middle class were Protestant nonconformists. Their beliefs and values encouraged industry, thrift, the dissemination of new knowledge, inventiveness, and willingness to accept change (Weber 1904/1958). Weber's ideas about the Protestant ethic and the spirit of capitalism were discussed in Chapter 18.

STRATIFICATION

The social theorists Karl Marx and Max Weber focused on the stratification systems associated with industrialization. The socioeconomic effects of industrialization were mixed. English national income tripled between 1700 and 1815 and increased thirty times more by 1939. Standards of comfort rose, but prosperity was uneven. At first, factory workers got wages higher than those available in the domestic system. Later, owners started recruiting labor in places where living standards were low and labor (including that of women and children) was cheap.

Social ills increased with the growth of factory towns and industrial cities, with conditions like those Charles Dickens described in *Hard Times*. Filth and smoke polluted the nineteenth-century cities. Housing was crowded and unsanitary, with insufficient water and sewage disposal facilities and rising disease and death rates. This was the world of Ebenezer Scrooge, Bob Cratchit, Tiny Tim—and Karl Marx.

From his observations in England and his analysis of nineteenth-century industrial capitalism, Marx (Marx and Engels 1848/1976) saw socioeconomic stratification as a sharp and simple division between two opposed classes: the bourgeoisie (capitalists) and the proletariat (propertyless workers). The bourgeoisie traced its origins to overseas ventures and the world capitalist economy, which had transformed the social structure of northwestern Europe, creating a wealthy commercial class.

Industrialization shifted production from farms and cottages to mills and factories, where mechanical power was available and where workers could be assembled to operate heavy machinery. The **bourgeoisie** were the owners of the factories, mines, large farms, and other means of production. The **working class,** or proletariat, was made up of people who had to sell their labor to survive. With the decline of subsistence production and with the rise of urban migration and the possibility of unemployment, the bourgeoisie came to stand between workers and the means of production.

Industrialization hastened the process of **proletarianization**—the separation of workers from the means of production. The bourgeoisie also came to dominate the means of communication, the schools, and other key institutions. Marx viewed the nation-state as an instrument of oppression and religion as a method of diverting and controlling the masses.

Class consciousness (recognition of collective interests and personal identification with one's economic group) was a vital part of Marx's view of class. He saw bourgeoisie and proletariat as socioeconomic divisions with radically opposed inter-

THE AMERICAN PERIPHERY

In a comparative study of two counties at opposite ends of Tennessee, Thomas Collins (1989) reviews the effects of industrialization on poverty and unemployment. Hill County, with an Appalachian white population, is on the Cumberland Plateau in eastern Tennessee. Delta County, which is predominantly African-American, is 60 miles from Memphis in western Tennessee's lower Mississippi region. Both counties once had economies based on agriculture and timber, but jobs in those sectors declined sharply with the advent of mechanization. Both counties have unemployment rates more than twice that of Tennessee as a whole. More than a third of the people in each county live below the poverty level. Such poverty pockets represent a slice of the world periphery within modern America. Given very restricted job opportunities, the best-educated local youths have migrated to northern cities for three generations.

To increase jobs, local officials and business leaders have tried to attract industries from outside. Their efforts exemplify a more general rural southern strategy, which began during the 1950s, of courting industry by advertising "a good business climate"—which means low rents, cheap utilities, and a nonunion labor pool. However, few firms are attracted to an impoverished and poorly educated work force. All the industries that have come to such areas have very limited market power and a narrow profit margin. Such firms survive by offering low wages and minimal benefits, with frequent layoffs. These industries tend to emphasize traditional female skills such as sewing and mostly attract women.

The garment industry, which is highly mobile, is Hill County's main employer. The knowledge that a garment plant can be moved to another locale very rapidly tends to reduce employee demands. Management can be as arbitrary and authoritarian as it wishes. The un-employment rate and low educational level ensure that many women will accept sewing jobs for a bit more than the minimum wage.

In neither county has new industry brought many jobs for men, who have a higher unemployment rate than do women (as do blacks, compared with whites). Collins found that many men in Hill County had never been permanently employed; they had just done temporary jobs, always for cash.

The effects of industrialization in Delta County have been similar. That county's recruitment efforts have also drawn only marginal industries. The largest is a bicycle seat and toy manufacturer, which employs 60 percent women. Three other large plants, which make clothing and auto seat covers, employ 95 percent women. Egg production was once significant in Delta County but folded when the market for eggs fell in response to rising national concern over the effects of cholesterol.

In both counties the men, ignored

---

ests. Marx viewed classes as powerful collective forces that could mobilize human energies to influence the course of history. Finding strength through common experience, workers would develop organizations to protect their interests and increase their share of industrial profits.

And so they did. During the nineteenth century trade unions and socialist parties emerged to express a rising anticapitalist spirit. The concerns of the English labor movement were to remove young children from factories and limit the hours during which women and children could work. The profile of stratification in industrial core nations gradually took shape. Capitalists controlled production, but labor was organizing to improve wages and working conditions. By 1900 many governments had factory legislation and social-welfare programs. Mass living standards in core nations rose as population grew.

The modern capitalist world system maintains the distinction between those who own the means of production and those who don't. The class division into capitalists and propertyless workers is now worldwide. Nevertheless, modern stratification systems aren't simple and dichotomous. They include (particularly in core and semiperiphery nations) a growing middle class of skilled and professional workers. Gerhard Lenski (1966) argues that social equality tends to increase in advanced industrial societies as the masses acquire and use political power and get economic benefits. In his scheme, the shift of political power to the masses reflects the growth of the middle class, which reduces the polarization between owning and working classes.

by industrialization, maintain an informal economy. They sell and trade used goods through personal networks. They take casual jobs, such as operating farm equipment on a daily or seasonal basis. Collins found that maintaining an automobile was the most important and prestigious contribution these men made to their families. Neither county has public transportation; Hill County even lacks school buses. Families need cars to get women to work and kids to school. Men who keep an old car running longest get special respect.

Reduced opportunities for men to do well at work—to which American culture attributes great importance—lead to a feeling of lowered self-worth, which is expressed in physical violence. The rate of domestic violence in Hill County exceeds the state average. Spousal abuse arises from men's demands to control women's paychecks. (Men regard the cash they earn themselves as their own, to spend on male activities.)

One important difference between the two counties involves unionization. In Delta County, organizers have waged campaigns for unionization. There is just one unionized plant in Delta County now, but recent campaigns in two other factories failed in close votes. Attitudes toward workers' rights in Tennessee correlate with race. Rural southern whites usually don't vote for unions when they have a chance to do so, whereas African-Americans are more likely to challenge management about pay and work rules. Local blacks view their work situation in terms of black against white rather than from a position of working-class solidarity. They are attracted to unions because they see only whites in managerial positions and resent differential advancement of white factory workers. One manager expressed to Collins that "once the work force of a plant becomes more than one-third black, you can expect to have union representation within a year" (Collins 1989, p. 10). Responding to this probability of

unionization, canny core capitalists from Japan don't build plants in the primarily African-American counties of the lower Mississippi. The state's Japanese factories cluster in eastern and central Tennessee.

Poverty pockets of the rural South (and other regions) represent a slice of the world periphery within modern America. Through mechanization, industrialization, and the other changes promoted by larger systems, local people have been deprived of land and jobs. After years of industrial development, a third of the people of Hill and Delta counties remain below the poverty level. Emigration of educated and talented locals continues as the opportunities shrink. Collins concludes that rural poverty won't be reduced by attracting additional peripheral industries because these firms lack the market power to improve wages and benefits. Different development schemes are needed for these counties and the rural South generally.

The proliferation of middle-class occupations creates opportunities for social mobility, and the stratification system grows more complex (Giddens 1973).

Faulting Marx for an overly simple and exclusively economic view of stratification, Weber (1992/1968) defined three dimensions of social stratification: wealth (economic status), power (political status), and prestige (social status). Although, as Weber showed, wealth, power, and prestige are separate components of social ranking, they do tend to be correlated. Weber also believed that social identities based on ethnicity, religion, race, nationality, and other attributes could take priority over class (social identity based on economic status). In addition to class contrasts, the modern world system is cross-cut by status groups, such as ethnic and religious groups and nations (Shannon 1989). Class conflicts tend to occur within nations, and nationalism has prevented global class solidarity, particularly of proletarians.

Although the capitalist class dominates politically in most countries, the leaders of core nations have found it to be in their interest to allow proletarians to organize and make demands. Growing wealth has made it easier for core nations to grant higher wages (Hopkins and Wallerstein 1982). However, the improvement in core workers' living standards wouldn't have occurred without the world system. The added surplus that comes from the periphery allows core capitalists to maintain their profits while satisfying the demands of core workers. In the periphery, wages and living standards are much lower. The current *world stratification system* features a substantial contrast between both capitalists and workers in the core nations and workers on the periphery.

With the expansion of the world capitalist economy, people on the periphery have been removed from the land by large landowners and agribusiness interests. One result is increased poverty, including food shortages. Displaced people can't earn enough to buy the food they can no longer grow. The effects of the world economy can also create peripheral regions within core nations, such as areas of the rural South in the United States (see the box "The American Periphery" in this chapter).

Bangladesh illustrates some of the causes of Third World poverty and food shortages. Climate, soils, and water availability in Bangladesh are favorable for a productive agriculture. Indeed, before the arrival of the British in the eighteenth century, Bangladesh (then called Bengal) had a prosperous local cotton industry. There was some stratification, but peasants had enough land to provide an adequate diet. Land was neither privately owned nor part of the market economy. Under colonialism, the British forced the Bengalis to grow cash crops for export and converted land into a commodity that could be bought and sold.

Increased stratification was a result of colonialism and tighter linkage with the world capitalist economy. The peasantry of Bangladesh gradually lost its land. A study done in 1977 (Bodley 1985) showed that a small group of wealthy people owned most of the land. One-third of the households owned no land at all. Poverty was expressed in food shortages. Many landless people worked as sharecroppers, with landowners claiming at least half the crop. The peasants were underpaid for their crops and overcharged for the commodities they needed. Local landowners (capitalists of the periphery) also monopolized international development aid and even emergency food aid.

Open and Closed Class Systems

Inequalities, which are built into the structure of state organization, tend to persist across the generations. The extent to which they do or don't is a measure of the openness of the stratification system, the ease of social mobility it permits. Within the world capitalist economy, stratification has taken many forms, including caste, slavery, and class systems.

Caste systems are closed, hereditary systems of stratification that are often dictated by religion. Hierarchical social status is ascribed at birth, so that people are locked into their parents' social position. Caste lines are clearly defined, and legal and religious sanctions are applied against those who seek to cross them.

The world's best-known caste system is associated with Hinduism in traditional India, Pakistan, and Sri Lanka. As described by Gargan (1992),

In India's caste system, most untouchables are impoverished and powerless people at the bottom of the caste hierarchy. Untouchables are assigned menial tasks, which include janitorial duties and other "unclean" activities, like piling up cow cakes—cattle dung, used as a cooking fuel.

caste-based stratification remains important in modern India. In a national population of 850 million people, an estimated 5 million adults and 10 million children are bonded laborers. These people live in complete servitude, working to repay real or imagined debts. Most of them are untouchables, impoverished and powerless people at the bottom of the caste hierarchy. Some families have been bonded for generations; people are born into servitude because their parents or grandparents were sold previously. Bonded workers toil unpaid in stone quarries, brick kilns, and rice paddies.

Once indentured, it is difficult to escape. Bonded labor is against Indian law, but it persists despite court rulings and efforts to stop it. Social workers obtain court orders to release bonded workers, but local officials and police often ignore them. Agents for quarries and kilns continue to entice untouchables into bonded labor with deceptive promises. Others enter bondage seeking to repay loans that can never be fully repaid. Thus the caste system, which is described more fully in the chapter on marriage, continues to form a highly restrictive system of social and economic stratification in India.

Another castelike system, **apartheid,** existed until recently in South Africa. In that legally maintained hierarchy, blacks, whites, and Asians had their own separate (and unequal) neighborhoods, schools, laws, and punishments.

In **slavery** people are treated as property. In the Atlantic slave trade millions of human beings were treated as commodities. The plantation systems of the Caribbean, the southeastern United States, and Brazil were based on forced slave labor. Slaves were like proletarians in that they lacked control over the means of production, but proletarians have some control over where they work, how much they work, for whom they work, and what they do with their wages. Slaves, in contrast, have nothing to sell—not even their own labor (Mintz 1985). Slavery is the most extreme and coercive form of legalized inequality.

Vertical mobility is an upward or downward change in a person's social status. A truly **open class system** would facilitate mobility, with individual achievement and personal merit determining social rank. Hierarchical social statuses would be achieved on the basis of people's efforts. Ascribed statuses (family background, ethnicity, gender, religion) would be less important. Open class systems would

Plantation systems in the New World were based on forced slave labor. Proletarians, such as these "white slaves of England," also lacked control over the means of production, but they did have some control over where and for whom they worked.

have blurred class lines and a wide range of status positions.

Compared with nonindustrial states and contemporary peripheral and semiperipheral nations, core industrial nations tend to have more open class systems. Under industrialism, wealth is based to some extent on **income**—earnings from wages and salaries. Economists contrast such a *return on labor* with interest, dividends, and rent, which are *returns on property* or capital.

Even in advanced industrial nations, stratification is more marked in wealth than it is in income. Thus in 1992 the bottom fifth of American households got

4.4 percent of total national income, compared with 44.6 percent for the top fifth (*American Almanac* 1994, p. 470). However, if we consider wealth rather than income, the contrast is much more extreme: One percent of American families hold one-third of the nation's wealth (Light, Keller, and Calhoun 1994).

INDUSTRIAL AND NONINDUSTRIAL SOCIETIES IN THE WORLD SYSTEM TODAY

World-system theory stresses the existence of a global culture. It emphasizes historical contacts and linkages between local people and international forces. The major forces influencing cultural interaction during the past 500 years have been commercial expansion and industrial capitalism (Wolf 1982; Wallerstein 1982). As state formation had done previously, industrialization accelerated local participation in larger networks. According to Bodley (1985), perpetual expansion (whether in population or consumption) is the distinguishing feature of industrial economic systems. Unlike bands and tribes, which are small, self-sufficient, subsistence-based systems, industrial economies are large, highly specialized systems in which local areas don't consume the products they produce and in which market exchanges occur with profit as the primary motive (Bodley 1985).

After 1870 European business began a concerted search for more secure markets in Asia, Africa, and other less-developed areas. This process, which led to European imperialism in Africa, Asia, and Oceania, was aided by improved transportation, which brought huge new areas within easy reach. Europeans also colonized vast areas of previously unsettled or sparsely settled lands in the interior of North and South America and Australia. The new colonies purchased masses of goods from the industrial centers and shipped back wheat, cotton, wool, mutton, beef, and leather. Thus began the second phase of colonialism (the first had been in the New World after Columbus) as European nations competed for colonies between 1875 and 1914, a process that helped cause World War I.

Industrialization spread to many other nations in a process that continues today (Table 20.1). By 1900, the United States had become a core nation within the world system (Figure 20.1). It had overtaken Great Britain in iron, coal, and cotton production. In a few decades (1868–1900), Japan changed from a medieval handicraft country to an industrial one, joining the semiperiphery by 1900 and moving to the core between 1945 and 1970.

Twentieth-century industrialization has added hundreds of new industries and millions of new jobs. Production has increased, often beyond immediate demand, and this has spurred strategies such as advertising to sell everything that industry could churn out. Mass production gave rise to a culture of overconsumption, which valued acquisitiveness and conspicuous consumption. Bodley defines overconsumption as "consumption in a given area that exceeds the rates at which natural resources are produced by natural processes, to such an extent that the long-run stability of the culture involved is threatened" (1985, p. 39). Industrialization entailed a shift from reliance on renewable resources to the use of fossil fuels. Fossil fuel energy, stored over millions of years, is being rapidly depleted to support a previously unknown and probably unsustainable level of consumption (Bodley 1985).

Table 20.1 *Ascent and Decline of Nations within the World System*

Periphery to Semiperiphery	Semiperiphery to Core	Core to Semiperiphery
United States (1800–1860)	United States (1860–1900)	Spain (1620–1700)
Japan (1868–1900)	Japan (1945–1970)	
Taiwan (1949–1980)	Germany (1870–1900)	
S. Korea (1953–1980)		

Source: Reprinted by permission of Westview Press from *An Introduction to the World-System Perspective* by Thomas Richard Shannon. Copyright Westview Press 1989, Boulder, Colorado.

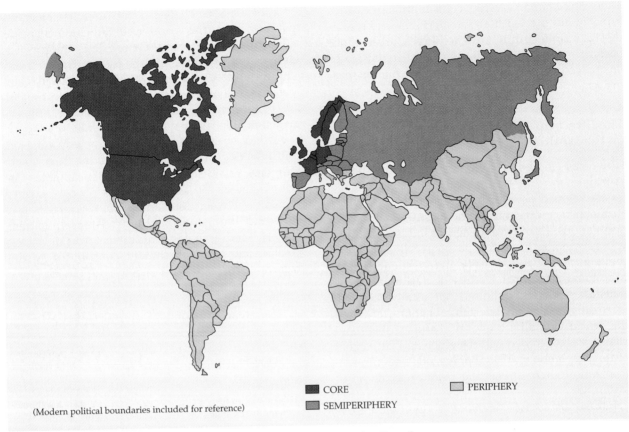

CORE

SEMIPERIPHERY

PERIPHERY

(Modern political boundaries included for reference)

Figure 20.1 *The world system in 1900. (Reprinted by permission of Westview Press from* An Introduction to the World-System Perspective *by Thomas Richard Shannon. Copyright Westview Press 1989, Boulder, Colorado.)*

Manufacturing has been declining in the United States but not internationally. Continuing to place capital above national loyalty, North American (and Western European and Japanese) businesses pursue their search for markets, profits, and cheap labor abroad. These women, employed by a toy factory on the Mexican side of the U.S.–Mexico border, are willing to work for lower wages than American workers would accept. Because capitalists do not freely subordinate their profit-seeking goals to national interests, most countries have erected protective barriers designed to protect their own products from foreign competition.

Table 20.2 compares energy consumption in various types of cultures. Americans are the world's foremost consumers of nonrenewable resources. Since becoming a core nation in 1900, the United States has tripled its per capita energy use while increasing its total energy consumption thirtyfold.

The Effects of Industrialization on the World System

How has industrialization affected the Third World—Latin America, Africa, the Pacific, and the less-developed parts of Asia? One effect is the destruction of indigenous economies, ecologies, and populations. Two centuries ago, as industrialization was developing, 50 million people still lived beyond the periphery in politically independent bands, tribes, and chiefdoms. Occupying vast areas, those nonstate societies, although not totally isolated, were only marginally affected by nation-states and the world capitalist economy. Bands, tribes, and chiefdoms controlled half the globe and 20 percent of its population in 1800 (Bodley, ed. 1988). Industrialization then tipped the balance in favor of states.

Industrialization is "a global process that has destroyed or transformed all previous cultural adaptations and has given humanity the power not only to bring about its own extinction as a species, but also to speed the extinction of many other species and to alter biological and geological processes as well"

(Bodley 1985, p. 4). The negative effects of an expanding industrial world system include genocide, ethnocide, and ecocide. **Genocide** is the physical destruction of ethnic groups by murder, warfare, and introduced diseases. When ethnic groups survive but lose or severely modify their ancestral cultures, we speak of **ethnocide.** The term for the destruction of local ecosystems is **ecocide.**

As industrial states have conquered, annexed, and "developed" nonstates, there has been genocide on a grand scale. Bodley (1988) estimates that an average of 250,000 indigenous people perished annually between 1800 and 1950. Foreign diseases (to which the natives had no resistance), warfare, slavery, land grabbing, and other forms of dispossession and impoverishment contributed to this genocide.

Table 20.2 *Energy Consumption in Various Contexts*

Type of Society	Daily Kilocalories per Person
Bands and tribes	4,000–12,000
Preindustrial states	26,000 (maximum)
Early industrial states	70,000
Americans in 1970	230,000
Americans in 1990	275,000

Source: From John H. Bodley, *Anthropology and Contemporary Human Problems,* 1985. Reprinted by permission of Mayfield Publishing, Mountain View, CA.

The notion of a constant struggle to tame nature is a hallmark of industrialism and promotes increasing exploitation of the earth's finite store of natural resources. Industrialism, seemingly a cultural evolutionary advance, may eventually prove disastrous because of the ecological destruction left in its wake. This 1989 photo illustrates the ecocide that has been caused by gold prospectors—using poisonous mercury—in Brazilian rivers.

Fortunately, many native groups, having been incorporated as ethnic minorities within nation-states, recouped their population. Many indigenous peoples survive and maintain their ethnic identity despite having lost their ancestral cultures to varying degrees (partial ethnocide).

Today's world contains some 200 million people who are members of conquered tribes or of still autonomous tribal nations, of which, however, only a handful survive. Compare this with 75 million people living in perhaps 150,000 independent bands and tribes 10,000 years ago at the dawn of food production (Bodley, ed. 1988). Many descendants of tribespeople live on as culturally distinct colonized peoples, many of whom aspire to autonomy. As the original inhabitants of their territories, they are called **indigenous peoples.** They become *peasants* when their dependency and integration within states are complete and they remain on the land. When they move to urban areas, they are often called **ethnic minorities.** Bodley (1988) argues that indigenous peoples have consistently resisted integration within nation-states because such integration—usually into the impoverished classes—is likely to lead to a decline in their quality of life.

Many contemporary nations are repeating—at an accelerated rate—the process of resource depletion that occurred in Europe and the United States during the Industrial Revolution. Fortunately, however, today's world has some environmental watchdogs that were absent during the first centuries of the Industrial Revolution. Given national and international cooperation and sanctions, the modern world may benefit from the lessons of the past.

Today, native groups are typically classified as "ethnic minorities" or "indigenous peoples" within nation-states. Indigenous peoples have devised various methods to survive and to maintain their ethnic identity. The Kayapó Indians of Brazil are notable for using modern media to record their history and culture and for enlisting outsiders to work with them to ensure their cultural survival.

SUMMARY

Local societies increasingly participate in wider systems—regional, national, and global. Columbus's voyages opened the way for a major and continuing exchange between the Old and New Worlds. The first plantation economies based on a single cash crop (most notably sugar) appeared in the seventeenth century. In the eighteenth century a monocrop economy based on slave labor also emerged in the cotton plantations of the southeastern United States.

The capitalist world economy is based on production for sale, with the goal of maximizing profits. The capitalist world economy has political and economic specialization based on three positions. Core, semiperiphery, and periphery have existed within the world system since the sixteenth century, although the particular countries filling these niches have changed.

The Industrial Revolution—the historical transformation of "traditional" into "modern" societies through industrialization of the economy—began around 1760. Transoceanic trade and commerce supplied capital for industrial investment. Industrialization developed from the domestic system of manufacture and increased production in farming and manufacturing. Industrialization began in industries that produced goods that were widely used already. This illustrates Romer's rule: an innovation that evolves to maintain an existing system can play a major role in changing that system. The Industrial Revolution started in England rather than in France because French industry could grow through expansion of the domestic system. England, with fewer people, had to industrialize.

Marx saw socioeconomic stratification as a sharp and simple division between the bourgeoisie (capitalists) and the proletariat (propertyless workers). Industrialization hastened the separation of workers from the means of production. Class consciousness was a vital part of Marx's view of class. Weber, on the other hand, believed that social solidarity based on ethnicity, religion, race, or nationality could take priority over class.

The modern capitalist world system maintains the distinction between those who own the means of production and those who don't, but the division is now worldwide. Modern stratification systems also include a middle class of skilled and professional workers.

In addition to class contrasts, the modern world system is cross-cut by status groups, of which nations are the most important. Class conflicts tend to occur within nations, and nationalism has prevented global class solidarity. World stratification features a substantial contrast between capitalists and workers in the core nations and workers on the periphery. With the expansion of world capitalism, Third World peoples have been removed from the land by large landowners and agribusiness interests.

The extent to which inequalities persist across the generations is a measure of the openness of the stratification system, the ease of social mobility it permits. Within the world capitalist economy, stratification has taken many forms, including caste, slavery, and class systems. Caste systems are closed, hereditary systems of stratification, often dictated by religion. In slavery, the most extreme and coercive form of legalized inequality, people are treated as property. Core industrial nations tend to have the most open class systems.

The major forces influencing cultural interaction during the past 500 years have been commercial expansion and industrial capitalism. During the first half of the nineteenth century, industrialization spread to Belgium, France, Germany, and the United States. After 1870 businesses began a concerted search for more secure markets. This process led to European imperialism in Africa, Asia, and Oceania. Europeans also colonized vast areas of previously unsettled or sparsely settled lands in the interior of North and South America and Australia.

By 1900 the United States had become a core nation within the world system. Mass production gave rise to a culture of overconsumption, which valued acquisitiveness and conspicuous consumption. Industrialization shifted reliance from renewable resources to fossil fuels. One effect of industrialization is the destruction of indigenous economies, ecologies, and populations. Two centuries ago, 50 million people still lived in politically independent bands, tribes, and chiefdoms, which controlled half the globe and 20 percent of its population. Industrialization tipped the balance in favor of states. The negative effects of the industrial world system include genocide, ethnocide, and ecocide.

GLOSSARY

apartheid: Castelike system in South Africa; blacks, whites, and Asians have separate (and unequal) neighborhoods, schools, laws, and punishments.

bourgeoisie: One of Marx's opposed classes; owners of the means of production (factories, mines, large farms, and other sources of subsistence).

capital: Wealth or resources invested in business, with the intent of producing a profit.

capitalist world economy: The single world system, which emerged in the sixteenth century, committed to production for sale, with the object of maximizing profits rather than supplying domestic needs.

caste system: Closed, hereditary system of stratification, often dictated by religion; hierarchical social status is ascribed at birth, so that people are locked into their parents' social position.

class consciousness: Recognition of collective interests and personal identification with one's economic group (particularly the proletariat); basic to Marx's view of class.

core: Dominant structural position in the world system; consists of the strongest and most powerful states with advanced systems of production.

domestic system (of manufacture): Also known as "home handicraft production"; preindustrial manufacturing system in which organizer-entrepreneurs supplied raw materials to people who worked at home and collected finished products from them.

ecocide: Destruction of local ecosystems.

ethnic minorities: Indigenous peoples who have moved to urban areas.

ethnocide: Process in which ethnic groups survive but lose or severely modify their ancestral cultures.

genocide: Physical destruction of ethnic groups by murder, warfare, and introduced diseases.

income: Earnings from wages and salaries.

indigenous peoples: The original inhabitants of particular territories; often descendants of tribespeople who live on as culturally distinct colonized peoples, many of whom aspire to autonomy.

Industrial Revolution: The historical transformation (in Europe, after 1750) of "traditional" into "modern" societies through industrialization of the economy.

monocrop production: System of production, often on plantations, based on the cultivation of a single cash crop.

open class system: Stratification system that facilitates social mobility, with individual achievement and personal merit determining social rank.

periphery: Weakest structural position in the world system.

proletarianization: Separation of workers from the means of production through industrialism.

Romer's rule: Evolutionary rule stating that an innovation that evolves to maintain an existing system can play a major role in changing that system.

semiperiphery: Structural position in the world system intermediate between core and periphery.

slavery: The most extreme and coercive form of legalized inequality; people are treated as property.

vertical mobility: Upward or downward change in a person's social status.

working class: Or proletariat; those who must sell their labor to survive; the antithesis of the bourgeoisie in Marx's class analysis.

STUDY QUESTIONS

1. What is the world-system perspective, and why is it important in anthropology?
2. What is the capitalist world economy? When did it originate, and what are its features?
3. What is the defining feature of capitalism? Why does capitalism require a world economy?
4. What are core, semiperiphery, and periphery? What is their relationship to world capitalism?
5. What was the Industrial Revolution, and how did it differ from previous life in villages, towns, and cities?
6. Why might the Industrial "Revolution" be better viewed in an evolutionary context?
7. What is Romer's rule, and how does it apply to food production and the Industrial Revolution?
8. Why did the Industrial Revolution begin in England rather than France?
9. How did proletarianization change human work?
10. How did the views of Marx and Weber on stratification differ?
11. What are the differences between open and closed class systems?
12. How is the world stratification system related to structural positions within the world capitalist economy?
13. What have been the major forces influencing cultural interaction during the past 500 years?
14. How does industrialization destroy the indigenous economies, ecologies, and populations?

SUGGESTED ADDITIONAL READING

BRAUDEL, F.
   1973   *Capitalism and Material Life: 1400–1800.* London: Weidenfeld and Nicolson. The role of the masses in the history of capitalism.
   1977   *Afterthoughts on Material Civilization and Capitalism.* Baltimore: Johns Hopkins University Press. Reflections on the history of industrial capitalism.
   1982   *Civilization and Capitalism, 15th–18th Century. Volume II: The Wheels of Commerce.* New York: HarperCollins. On the history of capitalism and the role of trade from precapitalist mercantilism to the present.
   1984   *Civilization and Capitalism, 15th–18th Century. Volume III: The Perspective of the World.* New York: HarperCollins. On the emergence of the world capitalist economy; case histories of European countries and various areas of the rest of the world.
CROSBY, A. W., JR.
   1972   *The Columbian Exchange: Biological and Cultural Consequences of 1492.* Westport, CT: Greenwood Press. Describes how Columbus's voyages opened the way for a major exchange of people, resources, and ideas as the Old and New Worlds were forever joined together.

1986 *Ecological Imperialism: The Biological Expansion of Europe 900–1900.* Cambridge: Cambridge University Press. The spread of diseases, foods, people, and ecological devastation, as the world system took shape.

KEARNEY, M.
1996 *Reconceptualizing the Peasantry: Anthropology in Global Perspective.* Boulder, CO: Westview. The nature of peasant life styles and subsistence patterns within the modern world system.

MINTZ, S.
1985 *Sweetness and Power: The Place of Sugar in Modern History.* New York: Viking Penguin. The place of sugar in the formation of the modern world system.

ROSEBERRY, W.
1988 *Political Economy. Annual Review of Anthropology* 17: 161–185. Reviews works on industrialization, political economy, local and regional social history, and world-system studies.

VIOLA, H. J., AND C. MARGOLIS
1991 *Seeds of Change: Five Hundred Years since Columbus, a Quincentennial Commemoration.* Washington, DC: Smithsonian Institution Press. People, plants, animals, and customs mingle between the Old World and the New—based on a Smithsonian exhibition.

WALLERSTEIN, I.
1974 *The Modern World-System: Capitalist Agriculture and the Origins of the European World-Economy in the Sixteenth Century.* New York: Academic Press. The origins of the capitalist world economy; a classic work.

1980 *The Modern World-System II: Mercantilism and the Consolidation of the European World Economy, 1600–1750.* New York: Academic Press. Further development of the world system and the underpinnings of industrialization.

WILMSEN, E. N., AND P. MCALLISTER, EDS.
1996 *The Politics of Difference: Ethnic Premises in a World of Power.* Chicago: University of Chicago Press. The enhanced importance of nationalism, ethnicity, and identity politics in the modern world system.

WOLF, E. R.
1982 *Europe and the People without History.* Berkeley: University of California Press. An anthropologist examines the effects of European expansion on tribal peoples and sets forth a world-system approach to anthropology.

CHAPTER 21

APPLIED ANTHROPOLOGY

THEORY AND PRACTICE
Applied Anthropology and the Subdisciplines

ANTHROPOLOGY AND EDUCATION

URBAN ANTHROPOLOGY
Urban versus Rural

Urban Poverty and Homelessness

MEDICAL ANTHROPOLOGY

In the News: AIDS and Gender in Africa

Box: Spirit Possession in Malaysian Factories

CAREERS IN ANTHROPOLOGY

Anthropology can reduce ethnocentrism by instilling an appreciation of cultural diversity. This broadening, educational role affects the knowledge, values, and attitudes of people exposed to anthropology. Now we focus on the question: What contributions can anthropology make in identifying and solving problems stirred up by contemporary currents of economic, social, and cultural change, including industrialization and the spread of the world system?

Applied anthropology refers to the application of anthropological data, perspectives, theory, and methods to identify, assess, and solve social problems. There are two important professional groups of applied anthropologists (also called *practicing anthropologists*). The older is the independent Society for Applied Anthropology (SfAA), founded in 1941. The second, the National Association for the Practice of Anthropology (NAPA), was established as a unit of the American Anthropological Association in 1983. (Many people belong to both groups.) Practicing anthropologists work, regularly or occasionally, for nonacademic clients: governments, nongovernmental organizations (NGOs), tribal and ethnic associations, interest groups, businesses, and social-service, medical, and educational agencies. Practicing anthropologists make it their business to apply their specialized knowledge and skills to problem solving.

THEORY AND PRACTICE

One of the applied anthropologist's most valuable research tools is the ethnographic method. Ethnographers study societies firsthand, living with and learning from ordinary people. Ethnographers are participant-observers, taking part in the events they study in order to understand native thought and behavior. Ethnographic techniques guide applied anthropologists in both foreign and domestic settings.

Other "expert" participants in social-change programs may be content to converse with officials, read reports, and copy statistics. However, the applied anthropologist's likely early request is some variant of "take me to your villagers." We know that local people must play an active role in the changes that affect them and that "the people" have information that "the experts" lack.

Anthropological theory—the body of findings and generalizations of the subdisciplines—also guides applied anthropology. Anthropology's holistic perspective—its interest in biology, society, culture, and language—permits the evaluation of many issues that affect people. Anthropology's **systemic perspective** recognizes that changes don't occur in a vacuum. A project or program always has multiple effects, some unforeseen. For example, dozens of economic development projects intended to increase productivity through irrigation have worsened public health by creating waterways where diseases thrive. In an American example of unintended consequences, a program aimed at enhancing teachers' appreciation of cultural differences led to ethnic stereotyping (Kleinfeld 1975). Specifically, Native American students did not welcome teachers' frequent comments about their Indian heritage. The students felt set apart from their classmates and saw this attention to their ethnicity as patronizing and demeaning.

Theory aids practice, and application fuels theory. As we compare social-change policy and projects, our understanding of cause and effect increases. We add new generalizations about culture change to those discovered in traditional and ancient cultures.

Applied Anthropology and the Subdisciplines

Applied anthropologists come from all four subdisciplines. Biological anthropologists work in public health, nutrition, genetic counseling, substance abuse, epidemiology, aging, and mental illness. They apply their knowledge of human anatomy and physiology to the improvement of automobile safety standards and to the design of airplanes and spacecraft. In forensic work, biological anthropologists help police identify skeletal remains. Similarly, forensic archaeologists reconstruct crimes by analyzing physical evidence.

An important role for applied archaeologists has been created by legislation requiring surveys of prehistoric and historic sites threatened by dams, highways, and other projects supported by federal funds. To save as much as possible of the past when actual sites cannot be preserved is the work of **salvage archaeology.** Applied cultural anthropologists sometimes work with the applied archaeologists,

An important role for applied archaeologists has been created by legislation requiring surveys of historic sites. To save as much as possible of the past when actual sites cannot be preserved is the work of salvage archaeology. New York City has yielded one of the largest African-American archaeological sites in the United States.

assessing the human problems generated by the change and determining how they can be reduced.

Cultural anthropologists work with social workers, business people, media researchers, advertising professionals, factory workers, nurses, physicians, gerontologists, mental-health professionals, school personnel, and economic development experts. Linguistic anthropology, particularly sociolinguistics, aids education. Knowledge of linguistic differences is important in an increasingly multicultural society whose populace grows up speaking many languages and dialects. Because linguistic differences may affect children's schoolwork and teachers'

evaluations, many schools of education now require courses in sociolinguistics.

ANTHROPOLOGY AND EDUCATION

Anthropology and education refers to anthropological research in classrooms, homes, and neighborhoods. Some of the most interesting research has been done in classrooms, where anthropologists observe interactions among teachers, students, parents, and visitors. Jules Henry's classic account of the American elementary school classroom (1955) shows how students learn to conform to and compete with their peers. Anthropologists also follow students from classrooms into their homes and neighborhoods, viewing children as total cultural creatures whose enculturation and attitudes toward education belong to a context that includes family and peers.

Sociolinguists and cultural anthropologists work side by side in education research, for example, in a study of Puerto Rican seventh-graders in the urban Midwest (Hill-Burnett 1978). In classrooms, neighborhoods, and homes, anthropologists uncovered some misconceptions by teachers. For example, the teachers had mistakenly assumed that Puerto Rican parents valued education less than did non-Hispanics. However, in-depth interviews revealed that the Puerto Rican parents valued it more.

Researchers also found that certain practices were preventing Hispanics from being adequately educated. For example, the teachers' union and the board of education had agreed to teach "English as a foreign language." However, they had not provided bilingual teachers to work with Spanish-speaking students. The school started assigning all students (including non-Hispanics) with low reading scores and behavior problems to the English-as-a-foreign-language classroom.

This educational disaster brought together a teacher who spoke no Spanish, children who barely spoke English, and a group of English-speaking students with reading and behavior problems. The Spanish speakers were falling behind not just in reading but in all subjects. They could at least have kept up in the other subjects if a Spanish speaker had been teaching them science, social studies, and math until they were ready for English-language instruction in those areas.

URBAN ANTHROPOLOGY

By 2025 the developing countries will account for 85 percent of the world's population, compared with 77 percent in 1992 (Stevens 1992). Solutions to future problems will depend increasingly on understanding non-Western cultural backgrounds. The Southern Hemisphere is steadily increasing its share of world population, and the fastest population growth rates are in Third World cities. The world had only 16 cities with more than a million people in 1900, but there were 276 such cities in 1990. By 2025, 60 percent of the global population will be urban, compared with 37 percent in 1990 (Stevens 1992). Rural migrants usually move to slums, where they live in hovels, without utilities and public sanitation facilities.

If current trends continue, urban population increase and the concentration of people in slums will be accompanied by rising rates of crime and water, air, and noise pollution. These problems will be most severe in the less-developed countries. Almost all (97 percent) of the projected world population increase will occur in developing countries, 34 percent in Africa alone (Lewis 1992). Still, global population growth will also affect the Northern Hemisphere, through international migration.

As social complexity, industrialization, and urbanization spread globally, anthropologists increasingly study these processes and the social problems they create. Urban anthropology, which has theoretical (basic research) and applied dimensions, is the cross-cultural and ethnographic study of global urbanization and life in cities. The United States and Canada have also become popular arenas for urban anthropological research on topics such as ethnicity, poverty, class, and subcultural variations (Mullings, ed. 1987).

Urban versus Rural

Recognizing that a city is a social context that is very different from a tribal or peasant village, an early student of Third World urbanization, the anthropologist Robert Redfield, focused on contrasts between rural and urban life. He contrasted rural communities, whose social relations are on a face-to-face basis, with cities, where impersonality characterizes many aspects of life. Redfield (1941) proposed that urbanization be studied along a rural-urban contin-

uum. He described differences in values and social relations in four sites that spanned such a continuum. In Mexico's Yucatán peninsula, Redfield compared an isolated Maya-speaking Indian community, a rural peasant village, a small provincial city, and a large capital. Several studies in Africa (Little 1971) and Asia were influenced by Redfield's view that cities are centers through which cultural innovations spread to rural and tribal areas.

In any nation, urban and rural represent different social systems. However, cultural diffusion occurs as people, products, and messages move from one to the other. Migrants bring rural practices and beliefs to town and take urban patterns back home.

Most African cities have ethnic associations that link rural and urban social systems. In Kampala, Uganda, shown here, urban members of the Luo tribe are organized by traditional clan ties and rural areas of origin. Luo associations provide economic and moral support, including transportation of destitute people back to the country.

The experiences and social forms of the rural area affect adaptation to city life. For example, principles of tribal organization, including descent, provide migrants to African cities with coping mechanisms that Latin American peasants lack. City folk also develop new institutions to meet specific urban needs (Mitchell 1966).

African urban groups include ethnic associations, occupational groups, social clubs, religious groups, and burial societies. Through membership in these groups, urban Africans have networks of personal support. Ethnic or "tribal" associations, which build a bridge between one social system and another (rural and urban), are common both in West and East Africa (Little 1965; Banton 1957).

The ideology of such associations is that of a gigantic kin group. The members call one another "brother" and "sister." As in an extended family, rich members help their poor relatives. When members fight among themselves, the group acts as judge. A member's improper behavior can lead to expulsion—an unhappy fate for a migrant in an ethnically heterogeneous city.

Modern North American cities also have kin-based ethnic associations. One example comes from Los Angeles, which has the largest Samoan immigrant community (12,000 people) in the United States. Samoans in Los Angeles draw on their traditional system of *matai* (respect for elders) to deal with modern urban problems. For example, in 1992,

a white policeman shot and killed two unarmed Samoan brothers. When a judge dismissed charges against the officer, local leaders used the *matai* system to calm angry youths (who have formed gangs, like other ethnic groups in the Los Angeles area). Clan leaders and elders organized a well-attended community meeting, in which they urged young members to be patient. Los Angeles Samoans aren't just traditionalists; they also use the American judicial system. They brought a civil case against the officer in question and pressed the U.S. Justice Department to initiate a civil-rights case in the matter (Mydans 1992*b*).

Urban Poverty and Homelessness

In 1992, 14.5 percent of the American population (37 million people) lived below the official poverty level (*American Almanac* 1994, p. 476). (The comparable figures were 11.4 percent and 24.5 million people in 1978.) Poverty and homelessness are obvious on the streets of big cities worldwide. For example, millions of rural Brazilians have migrated to burgeoning urban shantytowns (*favelas*). Abandoned children camp in the streets, bathe in fountains, beg, rob, and scavenge like their homeless counterparts in North America.

Homelessness in North America is an extreme form of downward mobility, which may follow job loss, layoffs, or situations in which women and chil-

Kin-modeled, ethnic, and voluntary associations help reduce the stress of urban life on migrants. In the Los Angeles area, youths of many national backgrounds, like these Cambodians, have formed gangs.

Poverty is particularly obvious in big cities throughout the world. Millions of rural Brazilians have settled in burgeoning urban shanty towns (favelas), *such as this one in Rio de Janeiro.*

dren flee from domestic abuse. The causes of homelessness are varied—psychological, economic, and social. They include inability to pay rent, eviction, sale of urban real estate to developers, and mental illness. In New York City many of the urban poor sleep in cardboard cartons and at train stations, on sidewalks and near warm-air gratings. They feed themselves by begging, scavenging, and raiding garbage (particularly that of restaurants) for food. The homeless are the foragers of modern society. They are poorly clad urban nomads, shaggy men and bag ladies who carry their meager possessions with them as they move.

Today's most extreme socioeconomic contrasts within the world capitalist economy are between the richest people in core nations and the poorest people on the periphery. However, as the gap between rich and poor has widened in North America, the social distance between the underclasses of core and periphery has shrunk. The road to Bangladesh passes through Times Square.

MEDICAL ANTHROPOLOGY

Both biological and cultural, both academic and applied, anthropologists work in **medical anthropology.** This growing field considers the sociocultural context and implications of disease and illness. **Disease** refers to an etic or scientifically identified health threat caused by a bacterium, virus, fungus, parasite, or other pathogen. **Illness** is an emic condition of poor health felt by an individual (Inhorn and Brown 1990). Cross-cultural research shows that perceptions of good and bad health, along with health threats and problems, are culturally constructed. Different ethnic groups and cultures recognize different illnesses, symptoms, and causes and have developed different health-care systems and treatment strategies.

Disease also varies among cultures. Traditional and ancient foragers, because of their small numbers, mobility, and relative isolation from other groups, lacked most of the epidemic infectious diseases that affect agrarian and urban societies (Inhorn and Brown 1990; Cohen and Armelagos, eds. 1984). Epidemic diseases like cholera, typhoid, and bubonic plague thrive in dense populations, and thus among farmers and city dwellers. The spread of malaria has been linked to population growth and deforestation associated with food production.

Certain diseases have spread with economic development. **Schistosomiasis** (liver flukes) is probably the fastest-spreading and most dangerous parasitic infection now known (Heyneman 1984). It is propagated by snails that live in ponds, lakes, and waterways, usually ones created by irrigation projects. A study done in a Nile Delta village in Egypt (Farooq 1966) illustrated the role of culture (religion) in the spread of schistosomiasis. The disease

We see that the incidence of particular diseases varies between societies, and cultures interpret and treat illness differently. Standards for sick and healthy bodies are cultural constructions that vary in time and space (Martin 1992). Still, all societies have what George Foster and Barbara Anderson (1978) call "disease-theory systems" to identify, classify, and explain illness. According to Foster and Anderson (1978), there are three basic theories about the causes of illness: personalistic, naturalistic, and emotionalistic. **Personalistic disease theories** (see box "Spirit Possession in Malaysian Factories") blame illness on agents (often malicious),

Homelessness may follow job loss, layoffs, or situations in which women and children flee from domestic abuse. The urban poor sleep in cardboard cartons and at bus and train stations, on sidewalks and near warm-air gratings. This homeless man and woman lived in New York's Tompkins Square Park in 1989.

Certain diseases have spread with economic development. Schistosomiasis (liver flukes) is probably the fastest spreading and most dangerous parasitic infection now known. It is propagated by snails that live in ponds, lakes, and waterways (often ones created by irrigation projects) such as this one in Luxor, Egypt.

was more common among Muslims than among Christians because of an Islamic practice called *wudu*, ritual ablution (bathing) before prayer. In eastern Africa AIDS and other sexually transmitted diseases (STDs) have spread along highways, via encounters between male truckers and female prostitutes. STDs are also spread through prostitution as young men from rural areas seek wage work in cities, labor camps, and mines. When the men return to their natal villages, they infect their wives (Larson 1989; Miller and Rockwell, eds. 1988). Cities have also been prime sites of STD transmission in Europe, Asia, and North and South America.

IN THE NEWS: AIDS AND GENDER IN AFRICA

In Africa AIDS and other sexually transmitted diseases are spreading along highways and rivers, mainly via encounters between male travelers and female prostitutes. AIDS is also spread as men move from rural areas to cities, where they engage in wage work—and casual sex. Later the men infect their wives. Focusing on the increasing threat to women, this article reports on the heterosexual transmission of AIDS in the Third World.

Amsterdam, July 20—Women throughout the world are becoming infected with the virus that causes AIDS about as often as men, and by the year 2000 most new infections will be in women, the World Health Organization's leading official on the disease told an international meeting here today.

Worldwide since Jan. 1, "close to half of the one million newly infected adults have been women," said Dr. Michael H. Merson, who heads W.H.O.'s global program on AIDS. He added that "women's rising infection rates have been accompanied by a corresponding rise in the number of children born to them infected with H.I.V.," the virus that causes AIDS.

Also, millions of infants may escape infection but are destined to become AIDS orphans when their mothers die.

In the first few years after the discovery of AIDS in 1981, gay men in urban areas accounted for about two-thirds of all AIDS cases in adults in the United States, Europe and parts of Latin America. But more recently, that proportion has fallen due to an increasing trend for heterosexual women to become infected through sexual intercourse with infected men.

"The disease is now everywhere, and we want to get home the point that the AIDS epidemic is becoming heterosexual everywhere," Dr. Merson said in an interview.

The growing number of H.I.V.-infected women reflects the surge in the epidemic in third world countries. W.H.O. estimates that from 10 million to 12 million adults and 1 million children have been infected. The overwhelming majority are in Africa and Asia. By the year 2000, W.H.O. estimates, up to 40 million people will be infected. But the Global AIDS Policy Coalition, based at Harvard University, has said the number could reach 110 million.

"The virus is following roads and navigable rivers deeper and deeper into the countryside," Dr. Merson said. "Tomorrow we can expect little difference between urban and rural areas."

To combat AIDS, health workers must find out what has worked in some areas and apply it on a wider basis, Dr. Merson said, echoing remarks made a month ago by Dr. Jonathan Mann, the director of the International AIDS Center at Harvard.

Dr. Merson and others said that women had to be empowered to have more control over their health. Women at the meeting have urged quick licensing of female condoms and greater research efforts to develop germicides that kill H.I.V. and other microbes that are spread by sex while still allowing the option of pregnancy.

The meeting participants, who number more than 11,000, were told of a recent study of women attending a clinic in Rwanda in Africa where one-fourth of those with only one lifetime sex partner had been infected with H.I.V., presumably by their steady partner.

---

such as sorcerers, witches, ghosts, or ancestral spirits. **Naturalistic disease theories** explain illness in impersonal terms. One example is Western medicine or **biomedicine,** which links illness to scientifically demonstrated agents, which bear no personal malice toward their victims. Thus Western medicine attributes illness to organisms (e.g., bacteria, viruses, fungi, or parasites) or toxic materials. Other naturalistic ethnomedical systems blame poor health on unbalanced body fluids. Many Latin cultures classify food, drink, and environmental conditions as "hot" or "cold." People believe their health suffers when they eat or drink hot or cold substances together or under inappropriate conditions.

One shouldn't drink something cold after a hot bath or eat a pineapple (a "cold" fruit) when one is menstruating (a "hot" condition).

Emotionalistic disease theories assume that emotional experiences cause illness. For example, Latin Americans may develop *susto,* an illness caused by anxiety or fright (Bolton 1981; Finkler 1985). Its symptoms (lethargy, vagueness, distraction) are similar to those of "soul loss," a diagnosis of similar symptoms made by people in Madagascar. Modern psychoanalysis also focuses on the role of the emotions in physical and psychological well-being.

All societies have **health-care systems**—beliefs,

Dr. Mann, who is chairman of the international AIDS meeting here, said in an interview that the AIDS epidemic had shown that "male-dominated societies are a threat to public health" because women have less power to protect themselves from disease.

Even though the infection rate for women is increasing, surprising new evidence from studies reported today shows that women do not die of AIDS faster than men, as had been thought, and that there are no gender differences in the occurrence of H.I.V.-related illnesses. The findings came from teams in Atlanta, Chicago, New York City and the National Institutes of Health, a Federal agency in Bethesda, Md., and run counter to studies reported several years ago.

W.H.O. has urged the wider distribution of condoms as well as campaigns to motivate behavioral change as two chief ways to combat the spread of H.I.V. infections.

Population Services International, a nonprofit organization in Washington, said it had been successful in increasing the use of condoms in Zaire in Africa, one of the countries hit hardest by AIDS, through a Madison Avenue technique called social marketing.

Condoms are distributed through pharmacies, grocery stores, bars, restaurants, movie theaters and clinics.

Last August, 3.6 million condoms were sold through that group's program, compared with 300,000 condoms for the entire year of 1988. Richard A. Frank, president of Population Services International, said such condom use had averted an estimated 7,200 cases of H.I.V. infection.

The program has been expanded to include 10 other African countries, and an additional program is targeted at prostitutes in Bombay, India.

Mr. Frank cited United States Census Bureau figures estimating that a 20 percent increase in condom use in the cities of developing countries could reduce the level of H.I.V. infection in those areas in the year 2015 by approximately one-half.

Anke A. Ehrhardt of the New York State Psychiatric Institute and Columbia University criticized the meager data about sexual behavior and changes in such behavior in the United States. She said, "Efforts to assess sexual behavior, design prevention programs, and to rigorously assess their effectiveness have been hampered by a battle between social scientists and representatives of religious and moralizing groups."

She told the participants that prevention messages to women and men needed to be gender-specific. "To make condom use the norm, we must particularly target heterosexual men," she said. "At the same time, women need to be given messages and tools that they can truly control." She said condom use was not a method that women could control.

Dr. Stephen Mills of the San Francisco Department of Health reported findings from a study showing "compelling evidence that Magic Johnson's H.I.V. diagnosis had the profound behavioral effect of motivating men and women to get tested for H.I.V." The effect was most profound among women, Dr. Mills said. He suggested that the influence of publicity about celebrities was underutilized in preventing AIDS.

Source: Lawrence K. Altman, "Women Worldwide Nearing Higher Rate for AIDS than Men," *The New York Times,* July 21, 1992, pp. C1, C3.

customs, specialists, and techniques aimed at ensuring health and preventing, diagnosing, and curing illness. A society's illness-causation theory is important for treatment. When illness has a personalistic cause, shamans and other magicoreligious specialists may be good curers. They draw on varied techniques (occult and practical), which comprise their special expertise. A shaman may cure soul loss by enticing the spirit back into the body. Shamans may ease difficult childbirths by asking spirits to travel up the vagina and guide the baby out (Lévi-Strauss 1967). A shaman may cure a cough by counteracting a curse or removing a substance introduced by a sorcerer.

All cultures have health-care specialists. If there is a "world's oldest profession" besides hunter and gatherer, it is **curer,** or shaman. The curer's role has some universal features (Foster and Anderson 1978). Thus curers emerge through a culturally defined process of selection (parental prodding, inheritance, visions, dream instructions) and training (apprentice shamanship, medical school). Eventually, the curer is certified by older practitioners and acquires a professional image. Patients believe in the skills of the curer, whom they consult and compensate.

We should not lose sight, ethnocentrically, of the difference between **scientific medicine** and West-

SPIRIT POSSESSION IN MALAYSIAN FACTORIES

Successive waves of integration into the world system have washed Malaysia, a former British colony. The Malays have witnessed sea trade, conquest, the influx of British and Chinese capital, and immigration from China and India. For centuries Malaysia has been part of the world system, but the immediate effects of industrialization, including effects on mental health, are recent. The Malaysian government has promoted export-oriented industry to bring rural Malays into the capitalist system. This has been done in response to rural discontent over poverty and landlessness as some 10,000 families per year are pushed off the land. Since 1970 transnational companies have been installing labor-intensive manufacturing operations in rural Malaysia. Between 1970 and 1980 agriculture's contribution to the national labor force fell from 53 to 41 percent as manufacturing jobs proliferated.

The industrialization of Malaysia is part of a global strategy. To escape the mounting labor costs in the core, corporations headquartered in Japan, Western Europe, and the United States have been moving labor-intensive factories to the periphery. Malaysia now has hundreds of Japanese and American subsidiaries, which mainly produce garments, foodstuffs, and electronics components. In electronics plants in rural Malaysia, thousands of young women from peasant families now assemble microchips and microcomponents for transistors and capacitors. Aihwa Ong (1987) did a study of electronics assembly workers in an area where 85 percent of the workers were young unmarried females from nearby villages.

Ong found that factory discipline and social relations contrasted strongly with traditional community life. Previously, agricultural cycles and daily Islamic prayers, rather than production quotas and work shifts, had framed the rural economy and social life. Villagers had planned and done their own work, without bosses. In factories, however, village women had to cope with a rigid work routine and constant supervision by men.

Factory relations of production featured a hierarchy, pay scale, and division of labor based on ethnicity and gender. Japanese men filled top management, while Chinese men were the engineers and production supervisors. The Malay men also worked as supervisors of the factory work force, which consisted of nonunion female semiskilled workers from poor Malay peasant families.

The Japanese firms in rural Malaysia were paternalistic. Managers assured village parents that they would care for their daughters as though they were their own. Unlike the American firms, the Japanese subsidiaries worked hard at maintaining good relations with rural elders. Management gave money for village events, visited workers' home communities, and invited parents to the plant for re-

ern medicine per se (Lieban 1977). Despite advances in pathology, microbiology, biochemistry, surgery, diagnostic technology, and applications, many Western medical procedures have little justification in logic or fact. Overprescription of tranquilizers and drugs, unnecessary surgery, and the impersonality and inequality of the physician-patient relationship are questionable features of Western medical systems.

Still, biomedicine surpasses tribal treatment in many ways. Although medicines like quinine, coca, opium, ephedrine, and rauwolfia were discovered in nonindustrial societies, traditional medicines aren't as effective against bacteria as antibiotics are. Preventive health care has improved during the twentieth century. Today's surgical procedures are safer and more effective than those of traditional societies.

But industrialization has spawned its own health problems. Modern stressors include noise, air and water pollution, poor nutrition, dangerous machinery, impersonal work, isolation, poverty, homelessness, and substance abuse. Health problems in industrial nations are due as much to economic, social, political, and cultural factors as to pathogens. In modern North America, for example, poverty contributes to many illnesses, including arthritis, heart conditions, back problems, and hearing and vision impairment. Poverty is even a factor in the differential spread of infectious diseases.

Medical anthropology, which is based on biological, sociocultural, and cross-cultural research, has

ceptions. In return, village elders accorded high status to the Japanese managers. The elders colluded with the managers to urge young women to accept and stay with factory work.

The discipline, diligence, and obedience that factories value is learned in local schools, where uniforms help prepare girls for the factory dress code. Peasant women wear loose, flowing tunics, sarongs, and sandals, but factory workers must don tight overalls and heavy rubber gloves, in which they feel constrained and controlled.

Assembling electronics components requires precise, concentrated labor. Demanding, exhausting, depleting, and dehumanizing, labor in these factories illustrates the separation of intellectual and manual activity that Marx considered the defining feature of industrial work. One woman said about her bosses, "They exhaust us very much, as if they do not think that we too are human beings" (Ong 1987, p. 202). Nor does factory work bring women a substantial financial reward, given low wages, job uncertainty, and family claims on wages. Young women typically work just a few years. Production quotas, three daily shifts, overtime, and surveillance take their toll in mental and physical exhaustion.

One response to factory discipline and relations of production is spirit possession, which Ong interprets as an unconscious protest against labor discipline and male control of the industrial setting. Sometimes possession takes the form of mass hysteria. The spirits have simultaneously invaded as many as 120 factory workers. Weretigers (the Malay equivalent of the werewolf) arrive to avenge the construction of a factory on aboriginal burial grounds. Disturbed earth and grave spirits swarm on the shop floor. First the women see the spirits; then their bodies are invaded. The women become violent and scream abuses. The vengeful weretigers send the women into sobbing, laughing, and shrieking fits. To deal with possession, factories employ local medicine men, who sacrifice chickens and goats to fend off the spirits. This solution works only some of the time; possession still goes on. Factory women continue to act as vehicles to express the anger of avenging ghosts and their own frustrations.

Ong argues that spirit possession expresses anguish caused by and resistance to capitalist relations of production. However, she also notes that by engaging in this form of rebellion, factory women avoid a direct confrontation with the source of their distress. Ong concludes that spirit possession, while expressing repressed resentment, doesn't do much to modify factory conditions. (Unionization would do more.) Spirit possession may even help maintain the current conditions of inequality and dehumanization by operating as a safety valve for accumulated tensions.

theoretical and applied dimensions. Anthropologists have served as cultural interpreters in public health programs, which must pay attention to native theories about the nature, causes, and treatment of illness. Successful health interventions are not forced on communities; they must fit into local cultures and be accepted by local people. When Western medicine is introduced, people usually retain many of their old methods while also accepting new ones (see Green 1987/1992). Native curers may go on treating certain conditions (like *susto* or spirit possession), whereas M.D.s may deal with others. If both modern and traditional specialists are consulted and the patient is cured, the native curer may get more credit than the physician.

A more personal treatment of illness that emulates the non-Western curer-patient-community relationship could help Western systems. Western medicine tends to draw a rigid line between biological and psychological causation. Non-Western theories usually lack this sharp distinction, recognizing that poor health has intertwined physical, emotional, and social causes. The mind-body opposition is part of Western folk taxonomy, not of science.

CAREERS IN ANTHROPOLOGY

Many college students find anthropology interesting and consider majoring in it. However, their parents or friends may discourage them by asking, "What kind of job are you going to get with an

Western medicine and scientific medicine are not the same thing. Many Western medical procedures have no clear justification, but scientific medicine surpasses tribal health-care systems in several ways. Clinics such as this one bring antibiotics, minor surgery, and preventive medicine to the Masai of Kenya.

anthropology major?" The purpose of this section is to answer that question. The first step in answering "What do you do with an anthropology major?" is to consider the more general question "What do you do with any college major?" The answer is "Not much, without a good bit of effort, thought, and planning." A survey of graduates of the literary college of the University of Michigan showed that few had jobs that were clearly linked to their majors. Medicine, law, and many other professions require advanced degrees. Although many colleges offer bachelor's degrees in engineering, business, accounting, and social work, master's degrees are often needed to get the best jobs in those fields.

A broad college education, and even a major in anthropology, can be an excellent basis for success in many fields. A recent survey of women executives showed that most had not majored in business but in the social sciences or humanities. Only after graduating did they study business, obtaining a master's degree in business administration. These executives felt that the breadth of their college educations had contributed to their success in business careers. Anthropology majors go on to medical, law, and business schools and find success in many professions that often have little explicit connection to anthropology.

Anthropology's breadth provides knowledge and an outlook on the world that are useful in many kinds of work. For example, an anthropology major

combined with a master's degree in business is excellent preparation for work in international business and economic development. However, job seekers must convince employers that they have a special and valuable "skillset."

Breadth is anthropology's hallmark. Anthropologists study people biologically, culturally, socially, and linguistically, in time and space, in developed and underdeveloped nations, in simple and complex settings. Most colleges have anthropology courses that compare cultures and others that focus

Careers in anthropology include work for international development and conservation agencies, including USAID (U.S. Agency for International Development) and WWF (World Wide Fund for Nature). Anthropological training has contributed to this reforestation project in Ecuador.

on particular world areas, such as Latin America, Asia, and Native North America. The knowledge of foreign areas acquired in such courses can be useful in many jobs. Anthropology's comparative outlook, its longstanding Third World focus, and its appreciation of diverse life styles combine to provide an excellent foundation for overseas employment.

Even for work in North America, the focus on culture is valuable. Every day we hear about cultural differences, about social problems whose solutions require a multicultural viewpoint—an ability to recognize and reconcile ethnic differences. Government, schools, and private firms constantly deal with people from different social classes, ethnic groups, and tribal backgrounds. Physicians, attorneys, social workers, police officers, judges, teachers, and students can all do a better job if they understand social differences in a part of the world that is one of the most ethnically diverse in history.

Anthropologists also work to help natives threatened by external systems. As highways and power-supply systems cross tribal boundaries, the "modern" world comes into conflict with historic land claims and traditions. An anthropological study is often considered necessary before permission is granted to extend a public system across native lands.

Knowledge about the traditions and beliefs of subgroups within a nation is important in planning and carrying out programs that affect those subgroups. Attention to social background and cultural categories helps ensure the welfare of affected ethnic groups, communities, and neighborhoods. Experience in planned social changes—whether community organization in North America or economic development overseas—shows that a proper social study should be done before a project begins. When local people want the change and it fits their life style and traditions, it will be more successful, beneficial, and cost-effective. There will be not only a more humane but a more economical solution to a real social problem.

People with anthropology backgrounds are doing well in many fields. Furthermore, even if the job has little or nothing to do with anthropology in a formal or obvious sense, anthropology is always useful when we work with fellow human beings. For most of us, this means every day of our lives.

SUMMARY

Applied anthropology is the application of anthropological data, perspectives, theory, and methods to identify, assess, and solve contemporary social problems. Applied (or practicing) anthropologists work for governments, nongovernmental organizations, tribal, ethnic, and interest groups, businesses, social services, and educational agencies. Applied anthropology draws its practitioners from biological, archaeological, linguistic, and cultural anthropology. Ethnography has become one of applied anthropology's most valuable research tools, along with the comparative, cross-cultural perspective. Holism allows applied anthropologists to perceive the biological, social, cultural, and linguistic dimensions of policy issues. A systemic perspective helps anthropologists recognize that all changes have multiple consequences, some unintended.

Applied anthropology has many domains. The anthropology and education researchers work in classrooms, homes, neighborhoods, and other settings relevant to education. Some of their research leads to policy recommendations.

In the face of globalization and urbanization, both academic and applied anthropologists have turned their attention to migration from rural areas to cities and across national boundaries. Urban anthropology includes the study of life in cities and the process of urbanization that affects people throughout the world. The United States and Canada have become popular arenas for urban anthropological research on topics such as ethnicity, poverty, class, and subcultural variation.

Rural social relations are personal and face to face, but impersonality characterizes many aspects of life in cities. Although urban and rural are different social systems, there is cultural diffusion from one to the other. Rural and tribal social forms affect adjustment to the city. For example, principles of tribal organization, including descent, provide migrants to African cities with adaptive mechanisms.

Medical anthropology unites biological and cultural, theoretical and applied, anthropologists in the cross-cultural study of health problems and conditions, disease, illness, disease theories, and health-care systems. Characteristic diseases reflect diet, population density, economy, and social complexity. The three main native theories of illness are personalistic, naturalistic, and emotionalistic. *Personalistic causes* refer to such agents as witches and sorcerers. In this context, shamans can be effective curers. Western medicine, or biomedicine, is not the same as scientific medicine. The latter has made many advances, particularly in bacterial diseases and surgery.

Broad college education, including anthropology and foreign-area courses, offers excellent background and preparation for many fields. Anthropology's comparative outlook, longstanding Third World focus, and cultural relativism provide an excellent basis for overseas employment. Even for work in North America, a focus on culture is valuable. Anthropological training is useful in dealing with issues that reflect cultural contrasts and problems whose solutions require an ability to recognize and reconcile social or ethnic differences. Anthropologists have worked for and with natives threatened by external sys-tems. Anthropology majors attend medical, law, and business schools and succeed in many fields, some of which have little explicit connection with anthropology.

Experience with social-change programs, whether community organization in North America or economic development abroad, offers a common lesson. If local people want the change and if the change fits their life style and traditions, the change will be more successful, beneficial, and cost-effective.

GLOSSARY

anthropology and education: Anthropological research in classrooms, homes, and neighborhoods, viewing students as total cultural creatures whose enculturation and attitudes toward education belong to a larger context that includes family, peers, and society.

applied anthropology: The application of anthropological data, perspectives, theory, and methods to identify, assess, and solve contemporary social problems.

biomedicine: Western medicine, which attributes illness to scientifically demonstrated agents—biological organisms (e.g., bacteria, viruses, fungi, or parasites) or toxic materials.

curer: Specialized role acquired through a culturally appropriate process of selection, training, certification, and acquisition of a professional image; the curer is consulted by patients, who believe in his or her special powers, and receives some form of special consideration; a cultural universal.

disease: An etic or scientifically identified health threat caused by a bacterium, virus, fungus, parasite, or other pathogen.

emotionalistic disease theories: Theories that assume that illness is caused by intense emotional experiences.

health-care systems: Beliefs, customs, and specialists concerned with ensuring health and preventing and curing illness; a cultural universal.

illness: An emic condition of poor health felt by an individual.

medical anthropology: Unites biological and cultural anthropologists in the study of disease, health problems, health-care systems, and theories about illness in different cultures and ethnic groups.

naturalistic disease theories: Includes scientific medicine; theories that explain illness in impersonal systemic terms.

personalistic disease theories: Theories that attribute illness to sorcerers, witches, ghosts, or ancestral spirits.

salvage archaeology: The branch of applied archaeology aimed at preserving sites threatened by dams, highways, and other projects.

schistosomiasis: Disease caused by liver flukes transmitted by snails inhabiting ponds, lakes, and waterways, often created by irrigation projects.

scientific medicine: As distinguished from Western medicine, a health-care system based on scientific knowledge and procedures, encompassing such fields as pathology, microbiology, biochemistry, surgery, diagnostic technology, and applications.

systemic perspective: View that changes have multiple consequences, some unforeseen.

STUDY QUESTIONS

1. What is applied anthropology? Is it the same as practicing anthropology?
2. What are the main professional groups of applied anthropologists?
3. What is the ethnographic method? What is its relevance for modern society, contemporary problems, and applied anthropology?
4. What is educational anthropology, and what are its applications?
5. What is urban anthropology, and what are its applications?
6. What is medical anthropology, and what are its applications?
7. What is the relevance of anthropological training to employment opportunities in North America and abroad?
8. How has federal legislation concerning historic and prehistoric sites affected anthropologists?

SUGGESTED ADDITIONAL READING

AMICK III, B., S. LEVINE, A. R. TARLOV, AND
D. C. WALSH, EDS.
1995 *Society and Health.* New York: Oxford University Press. Social and cultural determinants of health; frames health policy within a larger social policy context.

ANDERSON, R.
1996 *Magic, Science, and Health: The Aims and Achievements of Medical Anthropology.* Fort Worth: Harcourt Brace. Up-to-date text, focusing on variation associated with race, gender, ethnicity, age, and ableness.

BODLEY, J. H.
1995 *Anthropology and Contemporary Human Problems,* 3rd ed. Mountain View, CA: Mayfield. Environmental, political, social, and economic problems, possible solutions, and prospects for the future of humanity.

BOND, G. C., J. KRENISKE, I. SUSSER, AND J. VINCENT, EDS.
1996 *AIDS in Africa and the Caribbean.* Boulder, CO: Westview. This volume uses detailed ethnographic studies from Africa and the Caribbean to examine AIDS in a global and comparative context.

EDDY, E. M., AND W. L. PARTRIDGE, EDS.
1978 *Applied Anthropology in America.* New York: Columbia University Press. Historical review of applications of anthropological knowledge in the United States.

FERRARO, G. P.
1994 *The Cultural Dimension of International Business,* 2nd ed. Englewood Cliffs, NJ: Prentice-Hall. How the theory and insights of cultural anthropology can influence the conduct of international business.

Human Organization
The quarterly journal of the Society for Applied Anthropology. An excellent source for articles on applied anthropology and development.

JOHNSON, T. J., AND C. F. SARGENT, EDS.
1990 *Medical Anthropology: A Handbook of Theory and Method.* New York: Greenwood Press. Nineteen articles cover theoretical perspectives, medical systems, health issues, methods in medical anthropology, and issues of policy and advocacy.

JOHNSTON, F. E., AND S. LOW
1994 *Children of the Urban Poor: The Sociocultural Environment of Growth, Development, and Malnutrition in Guatemala City.* Boulder, CO: Westview. Biomedical and ethnographic perspectives illuminate stresses on and strategies of the urban poor, with special reference to the effects of poverty on children.

KUNITZ, S. J.
1994 *Disease and Social Diversity: The European Impact on the Health of Non-Europeans.* New York: Oxford University Press. Social, political, and cultural forces that shape the distribution of diseases in human populations.

McELROY, A., AND P. K. TOWNSEND
1996 *Medical Anthropology in Ecological Perspective,* 3rd ed. Boulder, CO: Westview. This established introduction to medical anthropology shows that field's multidisciplinary roots and its relevance to contemporary health problems and issues, including AIDS, nutritional anthropology, and environmental hazards.

MULLINGS, L., ED.
1987 *Cities of the United States: Studies in Urban Anthropology.* New York: Columbia University Press. Includes several case studies and argues for more applied and advocacy research in American cities.

MURPHY, R. F.
1990 *The Body Silent.* New York: W. W. Norton. An anthropologist's personal journey into the world of people with disabilities.

PODOLEFSKY, A., AND P. J. BROWN, EDS.
1994 *Applying Anthropology: An Introductory Reader,* 3rd ed. Mountain View, CA: Mayfield. These articles from the various subfields of anthropology show how anthropologists pose and solve contemporary problems.

RUSHING, W. A.
1995 *The AIDS Epidemic: Social Dimensions of an Infectious Disease.* Boulder, CO: Westview. The sociocultural conditions that have contributed to the spread of AIDS.

SARGENT, C. F., AND C. B. BRETTELL
1996 *Gender and Health: An International Perspective.* Englewood Cliffs, NJ: Prentice-Hall. How culture affects the relation among gender, health-care organization, and health policy.

SPINDLER, G. D., ED.
1982 *Doing the Ethnography of Schooling: Educational Anthropology in Action.* New York: Holt, Rinehart and Winston. Efforts by anthropologists to throw light on the sources of inequality and other problems found in schools.

TAYLOR, A.
1993 *Women Drug Users: An Ethnography of a Female Injecting Community.* New York: Oxford Uni-

versity Press. Ethnographic account of female drug users in Great Britain.

VAN WILLINGEN, J.

1993   *Applied Anthropology: An Introduction,* rev. ed. South Hadley, MA: Bergin and Garvey. Excellent review of the growth of applied anthropology and its links to general anthropology.

1987   *Becoming a Practicing Anthropologist: A Guide to Careers and Training Programs in Applied Anthropology.* NAPA Bulletin 3. Washington, DC: American Anthropological Association/National Association for the Practice of Anthropology. Useful brief guide for students contemplating a career in applied anthropology.

WEAVER, T., GEN. ED.

1973   *To See Ourselves: Anthropology and Modern Social Issues.* Glenview, IL: Scott, Foresman. Classic anthology of articles on the social responsibility of the anthropologist, anthropology and the Third World, race and racism, poverty and culture, education, violence, environment, intervention, and anthropology in the contemporary United States.

WILSON, C.

1995   *Hidden in the Blood: A Personal Investigation of AIDS in the Yucatán.* New York: Columbia University Press. An ethnographer's personal account of the AIDS crisis in Merida, the capital of Mexico's Yucatán.

WULFF, R. M., AND S. J. FISKE, EDS.

1987   *Anthropological Praxis: Translating Knowledge into Action.* Boulder, CO: Westview. Cases illustrating the use of anthropology in solving human problems in various areas.

DEVELOPMENT AND INNOVATION

DEVELOPMENT
The Brazilian Sisal Scheme
The Greening of Java
Equity
The Third World Talks Back
The Code of Ethics

STRATEGIES FOR INNOVATION
Overinnovation
Underdifferentiation
Third World Models and Culturally Appropriate
   Development
Box: Culturally Appropriate Marketing

During the Industrial Revolution, a strong current of thought viewed industrialization as a beneficial process of organic development and progress. Many economists still assume that industrialization increases production and income. They seek to create in Third World ("developing") countries a process like the one that first occurred spontaneously in eighteenth-century Great Britain.

DEVELOPMENT

Economic development plans usually are guided by some kind of **intervention philosophy,** an ideological justification for outsiders to guide native peoples in specific directions. Bodley (1988) argues that the basic belief behind interventions—whether by colonialists, missionaries, governments, or development planners—has been the same for more than 100 years. This belief is that industrialization, modernization, westernization, and individualism are desirable evolutionary advances and that development schemes that promote them will bring long-term benefits to natives. In a more extreme form, intervention philosophy may pit the assumed wisdom of enlightened colonial or other First World planners against the purported conservatism, ignorance, or "obsolescence" of "inferior" natives.

Anthropologists dispute such views. We know that for thousands of years bands and tribes have done "a reasonable job of taking care of themselves" (Bodley, ed. 1988, p. 93). Indeed, because of their low energy needs, they have managed their resources better than we manage our own. Many problems that people face today are due to their position within nation-states and their increasing dependence on the world cash economy.

Sometimes when natives are reluctant to change, it isn't because they have unduly conservative attitudes but because powerful interest groups oppose reform. Many Third World governments are reluctant to tamper with existing socioeconomic conditions in their countries (Manners 1956/1973). The attempt to bring the "green revolution" to Java that is analyzed below illustrates this situation. Resistance by elites to land reform is a reality throughout the Third World. Millions of people in colonies and underdeveloped nations have learned from bitter experience that if they increase their incomes, their taxes and rents also rise.

Conflicts between governments (colonial or postcolonial) and natives often arise when outside interests exploit resources on tribal lands. Driven by deficits and debts, governments seek to wrest as much wealth as possible from the territory they administer. This goal helps explain the worldwide intrusion on indigenous peoples and their local ecosystems by highway construction, mining, hydroelectric projects, ranching, lumbering, agribusiness, and planned colonization (Bodley, ed. 1988).

Studying people at the local level, ethnographers have a unique view of the impact of national and international planning on intended "beneficiaries." Local-level research often reveals inadequacies in the measures that economists use to assess development and a nation's economic health. For example, per capita income and gross national product don't measure the distribution of wealth. Because the first is an average and the second is a total, they may rise as the rich get richer and the poor get poorer.

Today, many government agencies, international groups, and private foundations encourage attention to local-level social factors and the cultural dimension of development. Anthropological expertise is important because social problems can doom the projects to failure. A study of fifty development projects (Lance and McKenna 1975) judged only twenty-one to be successes. Social and cultural incompatibilities had doomed most of the failed projects.

For example, a 1981 anthropological study of a multimillion-dollar development project in Madagascar uncovered several reasons for its failure. The project had been planned and funded by the World Bank in the late 1960s. The planners (no anthropologists among them) anticipated none of the problems that emerged. The project was aimed at draining and irrigating a large plain to increase rice production. Its goal was to raise production through machinery and double cropping—growing two crops annually on the same plot. However, the planners disregarded several things, including the unavailability of spare parts and fuel for the machines. The designers also ignored the fact, well known to anthropologists, that cross-culturally, intensive cultivation is associated with dense populations. If there are no machines to do the work, there have to be

An anthropological study of an irrigated rice project in Madagascar found several reasons for the project's failure. The designers ignored the fact that intensive cultivation is associated with dense populations. If there are no machines to do the work, there have to be people around to do it—like these Betsileo women who are transplanting rice in the traditional manner.

people around to do it. However, population densities in the project area (15 per square kilometer) were much too low to support intensive cultivation without modern machinery.

The planners should have known that labor and machinery for the project were unavailable. Furthermore, many local people were understandably hostile toward the project because it gave their ancestral land away to outsiders. (Unfortunately, this is a common occurrence in development projects.) Many land-grant recipients were members of regional and national elites who used their influence to get fields that were intended for poor farmers. The project also suffered from technical problems. The foreign firm hired to dig the irrigation canals dug them lower than the land they had to irrigate, and so the water couldn't flow up into the fields.

Hundreds of millions of dollars of development funds could have produced greater human benefits if anthropologists had helped plan, supervise, and evaluate the projects. Planners who are familiar with the language and customs of a country can make better forecasts about project success than can those who are not. Accordingly, anthropologists increasingly work in organizations that promote, manage, and assess programs that influence human life in the United States and abroad.

However, ethical dilemmas often confront applied anthropologists (Escobar 1991, 1995). Our respect for cultural diversity is often offended because efforts to extend industry and technology may entail profound cultural changes. Foreign aid doesn't usually go where need and suffering are greatest. It is spent on political, economic, and strategic priorities as national leaders and powerful interest groups perceive them. Planners' interests don't always coincide with the best interests of the local people. Although the aim of most development projects is to enhance the quality of life, living standards often decline in the target area (Bodley, ed. 1988).

The Brazilian Sisal Scheme

A well-studied case in which development harmed the intended beneficiaries occurred in an arid area of Brazil's northeastern interior called the *sertão*. Here development increased dependence on the world economy, ruined the local subsistence economy, and worsened local health and income distribution. Until the 1950s the *sertão*'s economy was based on corn, beans, manioc, and other subsistence crops. The *sertão* was also a grazing region for cattle, sheep, and goats. Most years peasants subsisted on their crops. However, about once every decade a major drought drastically reduced yields and forced people to migrate to the coast to seek jobs. To develop the northeast and dampen the effects of drought, the Brazilian government began encouraging peasants to plant **sisal,** a fibrous plant used to make rope, as a cash crop.

To ready sisal for export, preparation in the field was necessary. Throughout the *sertão* there arose local centers with decorticating machines, devices that strip water and residue from sisal leaf, leaving only the fiber. These machines were expensive. Small-scale farmers couldn't afford them and had to use machines owned by the elite.

Small teams of workers were in charge of decorticating. Two jobs were especially hard, both done by adult men. One was that of disfiberer, the person who fed the sisal leaf into the machine. This was a demanding and dangerous job. The machine exerted a strong pull, making it possible for the disfiberers to get their fingers caught in the press. The other job was that of residue man, who shoveled away the residue that fell under the machine and brought new leaves to the disfiberer.

Anthropologist Daniel Gross (1971a) studied the effects of sisal on the people of the *sertão*. Most sisal growers were people who had converted most of their land to the cash crop, completely abandoning subsistence cultivation. Because sisal takes four years to mature, peasants had to seek wage work, often as members of a decorticating team, until they

could harvest their crop. When they did harvest, they often found that the price of sisal on the world market was less than it had been when they planted the crop. Moreover, once sisal was planted, its strong root system made it almost impossible for the peasants to return to other crops. The land and people of the *sertão* became hooked on sisal.

A nutritionist, Barbara Underwood, collaborated with Gross in studying the new economy's effects on nutrition. For people to subsist, they must consume sufficient calories to replace those they expend in daily activity. Gross calculated the energy expended in two of the jobs on the decorticating team: disfiberer and residue man. The former expended an average of 4,400 calories per day; the latter, 3,600 calories.

Gross then examined the diets of the households headed by each man. The disfiberer earned the equivalent of $3.65 per week, whereas the residue man made less—about $3.25. The disfiberer's household included just himself and his wife. The residue man had a pregnant wife and four children, aged three, five, six, and eight. By spending most of his income on food, the disfiberer was getting at least 7,100 calories a day for himself and his wife. This was ample to supply his daily needs of 4,400 calories. It also left his wife a comfortable 2,700 calories.

However, the residue man's household was less fortunate. With more than 95 percent of his tiny in-

To develop its impoverished northeast and to dampen the effects of drought, the Brazilian government has encouraged peasants to plant sisal, a fibrous plant used to make rope, as a cash crop. In this region, where an estimated 600,000 families now depend on sisal cultivation, a shift from a subsistence economy to a cash economy led neither to a better diet nor to more leisure time for most people.

come going for food, he could provide himself, his wife, and his four children with only 9,400 calories per day. Of this, he consumed 3,600 calories—enough to go on working. His wife ate 2,200 calories. His children, however, suffered nutritionally. Table 22.1 compares the minimum daily requirements for his children with their actual intake.

Long-term malnutrition has results that are reflected in body weight. Table 22.1 shows that the weights of the residue man's malnourished children compared poorly with the standard weights for their ages. The longer malnutrition continues, the greater is the gap between children with poor diets and those with normal diets. The residue man's oldest children had been malnourished longest. They compared least favorably with the standard body weight.

The children of sisal workers were being malnourished to enable their fathers to go on working for wages that were too low to feed them. However, the children of business people and owners of decorticating machines were doing better; malnutrition was much less severe among them. Finally, the nutrition of sisal workers was also worse than that of traditional cultivators in the *sertão*. People who had reached adulthood before sisal cultivation began had more normal weights than did those who grew up after the shift.

This study is important for understanding problems that beset many people today. A shift from a subsistence economy to a cash economy led neither to a better diet nor to more leisure time for most people. The rich merely got richer and the poor got poorer. Badly planned and socially insensitive economic development projects often have such unforeseen consequences.

Table 22.1 *Malnutrition among the Children of a Brazilian Sisal Residue Man*

| Age of Child | CALORIES | | Percentage of Standard Body Weight |
	Minimum Daily Requirement	Actual Daily Allotment	
8 (M)	2,100	1,100	62
6 (F)	1,700	900	70
5 (M)	1,700	900	85
3 (M)	1,300	700	90

Source: Gross and Underwood 1971, p. 733.

The Greening of Java

Like Gross in Brazil, anthropologist Richard Franke (1977) conducted an independent study of discrepancies between goals and results in a scheme to promote social and economic change in Java, Indonesia. Experts and planners of the 1960s and 1970s assumed that as small-scale farmers got modern technology and more productive crop varieties, their lives would improve. The media publicized new, high-yielding varieties of wheat, maize, and rice. These new crops, along with chemical fertilizers, pesticides, and new cultivation techniques, were hailed as the basis of a **green revolution.** This "revolution" was expected to increase the world's food supply and thus improve the diets and living conditions of victims of poverty, particularly in land-scarce, overcrowded regions.

The green revolution was an economic success. It did increase the global food supply. New strains of wheat and rice doubled or tripled farm supplies in many Third World countries (except Sub-Saharan Africa). Thanks to the green revolution, world food prices declined by more than 20 percent during the 1980s (Stevens 1992). But its social effects were not what its advocates had intended, as we learn from Javanese experience.

Java received a genetic cross between rice strains from Taiwan and Indonesia—a high-yielding "miracle" rice known as IR-8. This hybrid could raise the productivity of a given plot by at least half. Governments throughout southern Asia, including Indonesia, encouraged the cultivation of IR-8, along with the use of chemical fertilizers and pesticides.

The Indonesian island of Java, one of the most densely populated places in the world (over 700 people per square kilometer), was a prime target for the green revolution. Java's total crop was insufficient to supply its people with minimal daily requirements of calories (2,150) and protein (55 grams). In 1960 Javanese agriculture supplied 1,950 calories and 38 grams of protein per capita. By 1967 these already inadequate figures had fallen to 1,750 calories and 33 grams. Could miracle rice, by increasing crop yields 50 percent, reverse the trend?

Java shares with many other underdeveloped nations a history of socioeconomic stratification and colonialism. Indigenous contrasts in wealth and power were intensified by Dutch colonialism. Although Indonesia gained political independence

Governments throughout southern Asia, including Indonesia, have encouraged cultivation of new rice varieties and use of chemical fertilizers and pesticides. Shown here are experimental seedlings at Java's Rice Research Center.

from the Netherlands in 1949, internal stratification continued. Today, contrasts between the wealthy (government employees, business people, large landowners) and the poor (small-scale peasants) exist even in small farming communities. Stratification led to problems during Java's green revolution.

In 1963 the University of Indonesia's College of Agriculture launched a program in which students went to live in villages. They worked with peasants in the fields and shared their knowledge of new agricultural techniques while learning from the peasants. The program was a success. Yields in the affected villages increased by half. The program, directed by the Department of Agriculture, was expanded in 1964; nine universities and 400 students joined. These intervention programs succeeded where others had failed because the outside agents recognized that economic development rests not only on technological change but on political change as well. Students could observe firsthand how interest groups resisted attempts by peasants to improve their lot. Once, when local officials stole fertilizer destined for peasant fields, students got it back by threatening in a letter to turn evidence of the crime over to higher-level officials.

The combination of new work patterns and political action was achieving promising results when, in 1965–1966, there was an insurrection against the government. In the eventual military takeover, Indonesia's President Sukarno was ousted and re-

placed by President Suharto. Efforts to increase agricultural production resumed soon after Suharto took control. However, the new government assigned the task to multinational corporations based in Japan, West Germany, and Switzerland rather than to students and peasants. These industrial firms were to supply miracle rice and other high-yielding seeds, fertilizers, and pesticides. Peasants adopting the whole green revolution kit were eligible for loans that would allow them to buy food and other essentials in the lean period just before harvesting.

Java's green revolution soon encountered problems. One pesticide, which had never been tested in Java, killed the fish in the irrigation canals and thus destroyed an important protein resource. One development agency turned out to be a fraud, set up to benefit the military and government officials.

Java's green revolution also encountered problems at the village level because of entrenched interests. Traditionally, peasants had fed their families by taking temporary jobs, or borrowing, from wealthier villagers before the harvest. However, having accepted loans, the peasants were obliged to work for wages lower than those paid on the open market. Low-interest loans would have made peasants less dependent on wealthy villagers, thus depriving local patrons of cheap labor.

Local officials were put in charge of spreading information about how the program worked. Instead they limited peasant participation by withholding information. Wealthy villagers also discouraged peasant participation more subtly: They raised doubts about the effectiveness of the new techniques and about the wisdom of taking government loans when familiar patrons were nearby. Faced with the thought that starvation might follow if innovation failed, peasants were reluctant to take risks—an understandable reaction.

Production increased, but wealthy villagers rather than small-scale farmers reaped the benefits of the green revolution. Just 20 percent of one village's 151 households participated in the program. However, because they were the wealthiest households, headed by people who owned the most land, 40 percent of the land was being cultivated by means of the new system. Some large-scale landowners used their green revolution profits at the peasants' expense. They bought up peasants' small plots and purchased labor-saving machinery, including rice-milling machines and tractors. As a result, the poorest peasants lost both their means of subsistence—land—and local work opportunities. Their only recourse was to move to cities, where a growing pool of unskilled laborers depressed already low wages.

In a complementary view of the green revolution's social effects, Ann Stoler (1977) focused on gender and stratification. She took issue with Esther Boserup's (1970) contention that colonialism and development inevitably hurt Third World women more than men by favoring commercial agriculture and excluding women from it. Stoler found that the green revolution had permitted some women to gain power over other women and men. Javanese women were not a homogeneous group but varied by class. Stoler found that whether the green revolution helped or harmed Javanese women depended on their position in the class structure. The status of landholding women rose as they gained control over more land and the labor of more poor women. The new economy offered wealthier women higher profits, which they used in trading. However, poor women suffered along with poor men as traditional economic opportunities declined. Nevertheless, the poor women fared better than did the poor men, who had no access at all to off-farm work.

Like Gross's analysis of the Brazilian sisal scheme, these studies of the local effects of the green revolution reveal results different from those foreseen by policy makers, planners, and the media. Again we see the unintended and undesirable effects of development programs that ignore traditional social, political, and economic divisions. New technology, no matter how promising, does not inevitably help the intended beneficiaries. It may very well hurt them if vested interests interfere. The Javanese student-peasant projects of the 1960s worked because peasants need not just technology but also political clout. Two ambitious development programs in Brazil and Java, although designed to alleviate poverty, actually increased it. Peasants stopped relying on their own subsistence production and started depending on a more volatile pursuit—cash sale of labor. Agricultural production became profit-oriented, machine-based, and chemical-dependent. Local autonomy diminished as linkages with the world system increased. Production rose, as the rich got richer and poverty increased.

Equity

A common goal, in theory at least, of development policy is to promote equity. **Increased equity** means reduced poverty and a more even distribution of wealth. However, if projects are to increase equity, they must have the support of reform-minded governments. Peasants oppose projects that interfere too much with their basic economic activities. Similarly, wealthy and powerful people resist projects that threaten their vested interests, and their resistance is usually more difficult to combat.

Some types of projects, particularly irrigation schemes, are more likely than others to widen wealth disparities, that is, to have a negative equity impact. An initial uneven distribution of resources (particularly land) often becomes the basis for greater skewing after the project. The social impact of new technology tends to be more severe, contributing negatively to quality of life and to equity, when inputs are channeled to or through the rich, as in Java's green revolution.

Many fisheries projects have also had negative equity results. In Bahia, Brazil (Kottak 1992), sailboat owners (but not nonowners) got loans to buy motors for their boats. To repay the loans, the owners increased the percentage of the catch they took from the men who fished in their boats. Over the

Carelessly-planned fisheries projects may increase social inequality. Brazilian boat owners were given loans to buy motors. To repay the loans, the owners increased the percentage of the catch they took from the men who fished in their boats. Then they used their rising profits to buy larger and more expensive boats (such as those shown here in Buzios, Brazil). The result was stratification—the creation of a stratum of wealthy people within formerly classless communities.

years, they used the rising profits to buy larger and more expensive boats. The result was stratification—the creation of a group of wealthy people within a formerly egalitarian community. These events hampered individual initiative and interfered with further development of the fishing industry. With new boats so expensive, ambitious young men who once would have sought careers in fishing no longer had any way to obtain their own boats. To avoid such results, credit-granting agencies must seek out enterprising young fishers rather than giving loans only to owners and established business people.

The Third World Talks Back

In the postcolonial world, anthropologists from the industrial core nations have paid attention to criticisms leveled against them by Third World colleagues. For example, the late Mexican anthropologist Guillermo Batalla (1966) decried certain "conservative and essentially ethnocentric assumptions" of applied anthropology in Latin America. He criticized the heavy psychological emphasis of many studies. These studies, he argued, focused too much on attitudes and beliefs about health and nutrition and not enough on the material causes of poor health and malnutrition. Another problem he mentioned was the misuse of cultural relativism by certain anthropologists. Batalla faulted those researchers for refusing to interfere in existing social situations because they considered it inappropriate to judge and to promote change.

Batalla also criticized the multiple causation theory, which assumes that any social event has countless small and diverse causes. Such a theory does not perceive major social and economic inequities as targets for attack. Batalla also faulted certain anthropologists who see communities as isolated units, because local-level changes are always accepted or opposed in a larger context. He argued that applied anthropologists should pay more attention to regional, national, and international contexts. Finally, Batalla criticized anthropologists for thinking that diffusion, usually of technical skills and equipment from the First World, is the most significant process involved in change.

Batalla didn't argue that all applied anthropology suffers from these faults. However, his points are generally valid, and many Third World social scientists agree with him. Those scholars have also criticized American anthropology for the links that have existed between some anthropologists and government agencies that don't promote the best interests of the people.

The Code of Ethics

Largely in response to critics like Batalla, in 1971 the American Anthropological Association (AAA) adopted a code of ethics entitled "AAA: Principles of Professional Responsibility." Its preamble suggests that anthropologists should avoid research that can damage either the people studied or the scholarly community. The code covers six areas of professional responsibility.

1. **Responsibility to Those Studied.** Anthropologists' main responsibility is to the people they study. Anthropologists should do all they can to protect their informants' welfare and to respect their dignity and privacy. If interests conflict, these people come first. Their rights and interests must be protected. Specifically, anthropologists should let informants know the aims and anticipated consequences of their research. They should ensure that informants preserve their anonymity in data collection. Informants should not be exploited for personal gain. Anthropologists must anticipate and take steps to avoid damaging effects of the publication of their result. Reflecting the AAA's disapproval of secret research, reports should be available to the public.

2. **Responsibility to the Public.** As scholars who devote their lives to understanding human diversity, anthropologists should speak out about what they know and believe because of their professional expertise. They should contribute to an adequate definition of social reality, upon which public opinion and policy can be based. Anthropologists should also be aware of the limitations of their expertise.

3. **Responsibility to the Discipline.** Anthropologists are responsible for the reputations of their discipline and their colleagues. They should maintain their integrity in the field so that their behavior will not jeopardize future research by others.

4. **Responsibility to Students.** Professors should be fair, candid, and committed to the welfare and academic progress of their students. They should make students aware of ethical problems in research.

5. **Responsibility to Sponsors.** Anthropologists should be honest about their qualifications, capabilities, and aims. They should not accept employment that violates professional ethics. They should retain the right to make their own decisions on ethical issues during research.

6. **Responsibility to One's Own and to Host Governments.** Anthropologists should demand assurance that agreements with governments don't require them to compromise professional responsibilities and ethics in order to pursue their research.

This statement of the principles of professional responsibility was designed to offer guidelines. However, the code also provides for censure of unprofessional conduct. When the actions of one anthropologist jeopardize others or appear unethical, colleagues may examine those actions and take measures that lie within the mandate of the AAA. A committee on ethics is now a permanent part of the AAA.

STRATEGIES FOR INNOVATION

Too many true local needs cry out for a solution to waste money by funding projects that are inappropriate in area A but needed in area B or unnecessary anywhere. Social expertise can sort out the A's and B's and fit the projects accordingly. Projects that put people first by responding to the needs for change they perceive must be identified. After that, social expertise is needed to ensure efficient and socially compatible ways of carrying out the projects.

In a comparative study of sixty-eight development projects from all around the world, I found the **culturally compatible economic development projects** to be twice as successful financially as the incompatible ones (Kottak 1990b, 1991). This finding shows that using anthropological expertise in planning, to ensure cultural compatibility, is cost-effective. To maximize social and economic benefits, projects must (1) be culturally compatible, (2) respond to locally perceived needs, (3) involve people in planning and carrying out the changes that affect them, (4) harness traditional organizations, and

To maximize social and economic benefits, development projects should: (1) be culturally compatible, (2) respond to locally perceived needs for change, (3) harness traditional organizations, and (4) have a proper (and flexible) social design for carrying out the project. This Zambian farm club, which draws on traditional social organization, plants cabbages.

(5) be flexible. Applied anthropologists should not just implement (carry out) development policies; they are as qualified as economists are to make policy.

Overinnovation

In my comparative study, the compatible and successful projects avoided the fallacy of **overinnovation** (too much change). Instead, they (intuitively) applied Romer's rule, which was used in the chapter "The World System, Industrialism, and Stratification," to explain why the Industrial Revolution took place in England. Recall that Romer (1960) developed his rule to explain the evolution of land-dwelling vertebrates from fish. The ancestors of land animals lived in pools of water that dried up seasonally. Fins evolved into legs to enable those animals to get back to water when particular pools dried up. Thus an innovation (legs) that later proved essential to land life originated to maintain life in the water.

Romer's lesson is that an innovation that evolves to *maintain* a system can play a major role in *changing* that system. Evolution occurs in increments. Systems take a series of small steps to maintain themselves, and they gradually change. Romer's rule can be applied to economic development, which, after all, is a process of (planned) socioeconomic evolution. Applying Romer's rule to development, we would expect people to resist projects that require major changes in their daily lives, espe-

cially ones that interfere with subsistence pursuits. People usually want to change just enough to keep what they have. Motives for modifying behavior come from the traditional culture and the small concerns of ordinary life. Peasants' values are not such abstract ones as "learning a better way," "progressing," "increasing technical know-how," "improving efficiency," or "adopting modern techniques." (Those phrases exemplify intervention philosophy.) Instead, their objectives are down-to-earth and specific ones. People want to improve yields in a rice field, amass resources for a ceremony, get a child through school, or pay taxes. The goals and values of subsistence producers differ from those of people who produce for cash, just as they differ from the intervention philosophy of development planners. Different value systems must be considered during planning.

Note that development guided by Romer's rule can even be compatible with social "revolutions" that reallocate land in highly stratified nations. If land reform permits peasants to go on farming their fields and get more of the product, it can be very successful.

Failed projects usually work in opposition to Romer's rule. For example, one South Asian project promoted the cultivation of onions and peppers, expecting this practice to fit into a preexisting labor-intensive system of rice-growing. Cultivation of these cash crops wasn't traditional in the area. It conflicted with existing crop priorities and other interests of farmers. The labor peaks for pepper and

Applying Romer's rule to development, people usually want to change just enough to keep what they have. Motives for modifying behavior come from the traditional culture and the small concerns of ordinary life. For example, understanding that deforestation causes local shortages of firewood and water can lead people to reforest. These people in Rwanda tend tree seedlings, which they will plant as part of a reforestation project.

onion production coincided with those for rice, to which farmers gave priority.

Throughout the world, project problems have arisen from inadequate attention to, and consequent lack of fit with, local culture. Another naive and incompatible project was an overinnovative scheme in Ethiopia. Its major fallacy was to try to convert nomadic herders into sedentary cultivators. It ignored traditional land rights. Outsiders—commercial farmers—were to get much of the herders' territory. The pastoralists were expected to settle down and start farming. This project neglected social and cultural issues. It helped wealthy outsiders instead of the natives. The planners naively expected free-ranging herders to give up a generations-old way of life to work three times harder growing rice and picking cotton.

Underdifferentiation

The fallacy of **underdifferentiation** is the tendency to view "the less-developed countries" as more alike than they are. Development agencies have often ignored cultural diversity (e.g., between Brazil

Project problems often arise from inadequate attention to, and consequent lack of fit with, local culture. In Ethiopia, overinnovative planners wanted to convert nomadic herders into sedentary farmers. The planners naively expected free-ranging herders to give up a generations-old way of life to work three times harder plowing, growing rice, and picking cotton.

and Burundi) and adopted a uniform approach to deal with very different sets of people. Neglecting cultural diversity, many projects also have tried to impose incompatible property notions and social units. Most often, the faulty social design assumes either (1) individualistic productive units that are privately owned by an individual or couple and worked by a nuclear family or (2) cooperatives that are at least partially based on models from the former Eastern bloc and Socialist countries.

Often development aims at generating *individual* cash wealth through exports. This goal contrasts with the tendency of bands and tribes to share resources and to depend on local ecosystems and renewable resources (Bodley, ed. 1988). Development planners commonly emphasize benefits that will accrue to individuals; more concern with the effects on communities is needed (Bodley, ed. 1988).

One example of faulty Euro-American models (the individual and the nuclear family) was a West African project designed for an area where the extended family was the basic social unit. The project succeeded despite its faulty social design because the participants used their traditional extended family networks to attract additional settlers. Eventually, twice as many people as planned benefitted as extended family members flocked to the project area. This case shows that local people are not helpless victims of the world system. Settlers modified the project design that had been imposed on them by using the principles of their traditional society.

The second dubious foreign social model that is common in development strategy is the cooperative. In my comparative study of development projects, new cooperatives fared badly. Cooperatives succeeded only when they harnessed preexisting local-level communal institutions. This is a corollary of a more general rule: Participants' groups are most effective when they are based on traditional social organization or on a socioeconomic similarity among members.

Neither foreign social model—the nuclear family farm or the cooperative—has an unblemished record in development. An alternative is needed: greater use of Third World social models for Third World development. These are traditional social units, such as the clans, lineages, and other extended kinship groups of Africa, Oceania, and many other nations, with their communally held estates and resources. The most humane and productive strategy for change is to base the social design for innovation on traditional social forms in each target area.

Third World Models and Culturally Appropriate Development

Many governments lack a genuine commitment to improving the lives of their citizens. Interference by major powers has also kept governments from enacting needed reforms. In many highly stratified societies, particularly in Latin America, the class structure is very rigid. Movement of individuals into the middle class is difficult. It is equally hard to raise the living standards of the lower class as a whole. These nations have a long history of control of government by powerful interest groups that tend to oppose reform.

In some nations, however, the government acts more as an agent of the people. Madagascar provides an example. As in many areas of Africa, precolonial states had developed in Madagascar before its conquest by the French in 1895. The people of Madagascar, the Malagasy, had been organized into descent groups before the origin of the state. Imerina, the major precolonial state of Madagascar, wove descent groups into its structure, making members of important groups advisers to the king and thus giving them authority in government. Imerina made provisions for the people it ruled. It collected taxes and organized labor for public works projects. In return, it redistributed resources to peasants in need. It also granted them some protection against war and slave raids and allowed them to cultivate their rice fields in peace. The government maintained the water works for rice cultivation. It opened to ambitious peasant boys the chance of becoming, through hard work and study, state bureaucrats.

Throughout the history of Imerina—and continuing in modern Madagascar—there have been strong relationships between the individual, the descent group, and the state. Local Malagasy communities, where residence is based on descent, are more cohesive and homogeneous than are communities in Java or Latin America. Madagascar gained political independence from France in 1960. Although it was still economically dependent on France when I first did research there in 1966–1967, the new government was committed to a form of socialist develop-

Third World models for Third World development include traditional cultural and social units, such as the extended kinship groups of Africa and Oceania. The social design for innovation should be based on existing groups and institutions in each target area. A traditional system of planning and management by temples and priests has been harnessed for culturally appropriate agricultural development in Bali, Indonesia.

ment. Its economic development schemes were increasing the ability of the Malagasy to feed themselves. Government policy emphasized increased production of rice, a subsistence crop, rather than cash crops. Furthermore, local communities, with their traditional cooperative patterns and solidarity based on kinship and descent, were treated as partners in, not obstacles to, the development process.

In a sense, the descent group is preadapted to equitable national development. In Madagascar, members of local descent groups have customarily pooled their resources to educate their ambitious members. Once educated, these men and women gain economically secure positions in the nation. They then share the advantages of their new positions with their kin. For example, they give room and board to rural cousins attending school and help them find jobs.

Malagasy administrations appear generally to have shared a commitment to democratic economic development. Perhaps this is because government officials are of the peasantry or have strong personal ties to it. By contrast, in Latin American countries, the elites and the lower class have different origins and no strong connections through kinship, descent, or marriage.

Furthermore, societies with descent-group organization contradict an assumption that many social scientists and economists seem to make. It is not inevitable that as nations become more tied to the world capitalist economy, native forms of social or-

ganization will break down into nuclear family organization, impersonality, and alienation. Descent groups, with their traditional communalism and corporate solidarity, have important roles to play in economic development.

The use of descent groups in Malagasy rice production exemplifies culturally appropriate innovation. So does a successful Papua–New Guinea resettlement project. Here, participants used their profits just as (in Romer's study) the ancestors of land vertebrates had used their finlike legs. They changed (began producing palm oil for sale) not to forge a brand-new life style but to maintain their ties with home. The settlers constantly revisited their homelands, in which they invested in the social life and ceremonies. This cash crop project fit Oceanian values and customs involving competition for wealth and capital, such as big-man systems. The settlers came from different tribes, but intertribal mingling was already part of local experience. Marriage between people who speak different dialects and languages is common in Papua–New Guinea, as is participation in common religious movements.

Realistic development promotes change but not overinnovation. Many changes are possible if the aim is to preserve local systems while making them work better. Successful projects respect, or at least don't attack, local cultural patterns. Effective development draws on indigenous cultural practices and social structures.

CULTURALLY APPROPRIATE MARKETING

Innovation succeeds best when it is culturally appropriate. This axiom of applied anthropology could guide the international spread not only of development projects, but also of businesses, such as fast food. Each time McDonald's or Burger King expands to a new nation, it must devise a culturally appropriate strategy for fitting into the new setting.

McDonald's has been successful internationally, with more than a quarter of its sales outside the United States. One area where McDonald's is expanding is Brazil, where 30 to 40 million middle-class people, most living in densely packed cities, provide a concentrated market for a fast-food chain. Still, it took McDonald's some time to find the right marketing strategy for Brazil.

In 1980 I visited Brazil after a seven-year absence. One manifestation of Brazil's growing participation in the world economy was the appearance of two McDonald's res-

taurants in Rio de Janeiro. There wasn't much difference between Brazilian and American McDonald's. The restaurants looked alike. The menu was more or less the same, as was the taste of the quarter-pounders. I picked up an artifact, a white paper bag with yellow lettering, exactly like the take-out bags then used in American McDonald's. An advertising device, it carried several messages about how Brazilians could bring McDonald's into their lives. However, it seemed to me that McDonald's Brazilian ad campaign was missing some important points about how fast food should be marketed in a culture that values large, leisurely lunches.

The bag proclaimed, "You're going to enjoy the [McDonald's] difference," and listed several "favorite places where you can enjoy McDonald's products." This list confirmed that the marketing people were trying to adapt to Brazilian middle-class culture, but they were making

some mistakes. "When you go out in the car with the kids" transferred the uniquely developed North American cultural combination of highways, affordable cars, and suburban living to the very different context of urban Brazil. A similar suggestion was "traveling to the country place." Even Brazilians who own country places can't find McDonald's, still confined to the cities, on the road. The ad creator had apparently never attempted to drive up to a fast-food restaurant in a neighborhood that had no parking spaces.

Several other suggestions pointed customers toward the beach, where *cariocas* (Rio natives) do spend much of their leisure time. One could eat McDonald's products "after a dip in the ocean," "at a picnic at the beach," or "watching the surfers." These suggestions ignored the Brazilian custom of consuming cold things, such as beer, soft drinks, ice cream, and ham and cheese sand-

SUMMARY

Development plans are usually guided by some kind of intervention philosophy, an ideological justification for outsiders to direct native peoples toward particular goals. Development is usually justified by the belief that industrialization, modernization, westernization, and individualism are desirable and beneficial evolutionary advances. However, bands and tribes, with their low-energy adaptations, usually manage resources better than industrial states do. Many problems that Third World people face today are due to their positions within nation-states and their increasing dependence on the world cash economy. Conflicts between governments and natives may arise when outsiders claim resources on tribal lands. There has been worldwide intrusion on indigenous peoples and their local ecosystems by roads, mining, hydroelectric projects, ranching, lumbering, agribusiness, and planned colonization.

Increasingly, the government agencies, international

groups, and private foundations are encouraging attention to local-level social factors and the cultural dimension of social change and economic development. Anthropologists work in organizations that promote, manage, and assess programs that affect human life in North America and abroad.

Development projects that replace subsistence pursuits with economies dependent on the unpredictable alternations of the world capitalist economy can be especially damaging. Following a shift from subsistence to cash cropping in Northeastern Brazil, local material conditions worsened. Research on the socioeconomic effects of sisal cultivation reveals some unforeseen consequences (e.g., negative equity) that may accompany development. Similarly, research in Java found that the green revolution was failing because it stressed new technology rather than a combination of technology and peasant political organization. Java's green revolution was increasing poverty

wiches, at the beach. Brazilians don't consider a hot, greasy hamburger proper beach food. They view the sea as "cold" and hamburgers as "hot"; they avoid "hot" foods at the beach.

Also culturally dubious was the suggestion to eat McDonald's hamburgers "lunching at the office." Brazilians prefer their main meal at midday, often eating at a leisurely pace with business associates. Many firms serve ample lunches to their employees. Other workers take advantage of a two-hour lunch break to go home to eat with the spouse and children. Nor did it make sense to suggest that children should eat hamburgers for lunch, since most kids attend school for half-day sessions and have lunch at home. Two other suggestions—"waiting for the bus" and "in the beauty parlor"— did describe common aspects of daily life in a Brazilian city. However, these settings have not proved especially inviting to hamburgers or fish filets.

The homes of Brazilians who can afford McDonald's products have cooks and maids to do many of the things that fast-food restaurants do in the United States. The suggestion that McDonald's products be eaten "while watching your favorite television program" is culturally appropriate, because Brazilians watch TV a lot. However, Brazil's consuming classes can ask the cook to make a snack when hunger strikes. Indeed, much televiewing occurs when the husband gets home from the office.

Most appropriate to the Brazilian life style was the suggestion to enjoy McDonald's "on the cook's day off." Throughout Brazil, Sunday is that day. The Sunday pattern for middle-class families is a trip to the beach, liters of beer, a full midday meal around 3 P.M., and a light evening snack. McDonald's has found its niche in the Sunday evening meal, when families flock to the fast-food restaurant, and it is to this market that its advertising is now appropriately geared.

McDonald's is expanding rapidly in Brazilian cities, and in Brazil as in North America, teenage appetites are fueling the fast-food explosion. As McDonald's outlets appeared in urban neighborhoods, Brazilian teenagers used them for after-school snacks, while families had evening meals there. As an anthropologist could have predicted, the fast-food industry has not revolutionized Brazilian food and meal customs. Rather, McDonald's is succeeding because it has adapted to preexisting Brazilian cultural patterns.

The main contrast with North American customs is that the Brazilian evening meal is lighter. McDonald's now caters to the evening meal rather than to lunch. Once McDonald's realized that more money could be made by fitting in with, rather than trying to Americanize, Brazilian meal habits, it started aiming its advertising at that goal.

rather than ending it, although women were not as hard hit by the new economy as men were. Because so many projects have failed for social and political reasons, development organizations are increasingly using anthropologists in planning, supervision, and evaluation. Modern applied anthropologists keep ethical guidelines in mind as they try to help people facing economic and social changes. The American Anthropological Association (AAA) has issued a statement of professional conduct that lays out the responsibilities of anthropologists to informants, universities, colleagues, students, sponsors, and governments. The AAA has also committed itself to taking action against breaches of professional ethics.

Governments are not equally committed to eradicating poverty and increasing equity. Local interest groups often oppose reform, and resistance by elites is especially hard to combat. Culturally compatible projects tend to be more financially successful than incompatible ones are. This

means that the use of anthropological expertise in development not only promotes more humane changes but is also cost-effective.

Compatible and successful projects avoid the fallacy of overinnovation and apply Romer's rule: An innovation that evolves to maintain a system can play a major role in changing that system. Natives are unlikely to cooperate with projects that require major changes in their daily lives, especially ones that interfere too much with customary subsistence pursuits. People usually want to change just enough to keep what they have. Peasants' motives to change come from their traditional culture and the small concerns of everyday existence. Peasant values are not abstract and long term and thus differ from those of development planners.

The fallacy of underdifferentiation refers to the tendency to see less-developed countries as an undifferentiated group. Neglecting cultural diversity and the local context, many projects impose culturally biased and incompatible property notions and social units on the intended beneficiaries. The most common flawed social models are the nuclear family farm and the cooperative, neither of which has an unblemished record in development. A more promising alternative is to harness Third World social units for purposes of development. These traditional social forms include the clans, lineages, and other extended kinship groups of Africa and Oceania, with their communally held resources. The most productive strategy for change is to base the social design for innovation on traditional social forms in each target area.

GLOSSARY

culturally compatible economic development projects: Projects that harness traditional organizations and locally perceived needs for change and that have a culturally appropriate design and implementation strategy.

equity, increased: A reduction in absolute poverty and a fairer (more even) distribution of wealth.

green revolution: Agricultural development based on chemical fertilizers, pesticides, twentieth-century cultivation techniques, and new crop varieties such as IR-8 ("miracle rice").

intervention philosophy: Guiding principle of colonialism, conquest, missionization, or development; an ideological justification for outsiders to guide native peoples in specific directions.

overinnovation: Characteristic of projects that require major changes in natives' daily lives, especially ones that interfere with customary subsistence pursuits.

sertão: Arid interior of northeastern Brazil; backlands.

sisal: Plant adapted to arid areas; its fiber is used to make rope.

underdifferentiation: Planning fallacy of viewing less-developed countries as an undifferentiated group; ignoring cultural diversity and adopting a uniform approach (often ethnocentric) for very different types of project beneficiaries.

STUDY QUESTIONS

1. What is an intervention philosophy, and how does such a philosophy characterize the goals of economic development?
2. What are equity goals, and what were the equity results of the Brazilian sisal scheme and Java's green revolution?
3. How did the equity results of Java's green revolution differ for men and for women?
4. What were Batalla's criticisms of applied anthropology?
5. How do anthropologists deal with the matter of professional ethics?
6. What are some common reasons for the failure of economic development programs?
7. What does it mean to say that an economic development project is "culturally compatible"? What are the advantages of ensuring that projects are culturally compatible?
8. What is Romer's rule, and how does it apply to development strategy?
9. What are some examples of the fallacy of overinnovation?
10. What is the fallacy of underdifferentiation? What are some possible alternatives to it?
11. How might descent-group organization contribute to economic development?
12. In your opinion, what criteria should be used to evaluate the success of an economic development program?

SUGGESTED ADDITIONAL READING

BARLETT, P. F., ED.
1980 *Agricultural Decision Making: Anthropological Contribution to Rural Development.* New York: Academic Press. How farmers choose what to plant and decide how to plant it in various cultures.

BENNETT, J. W., AND J. R. BOWEN, EDS.
1988 *Production and Autonomy: Anthropological Studies and Critiques of Development.* Monographs in Economic Anthropology, No. 5, Society for Economic Anthropology. New York: University Press of America. Twenty-three articles on

many social aspects of economic development.

BODLEY, J. H.
  1995 *Anthropology and Contemporary Human Problems,* 3rd ed. Mountain View, CA: Mayfield. Overview of major problems of today's industrial world: overconsumption, the environment, resource depletion, hunger, overpopulation, violence, and war.

BODLEY, J. H., ED.
  1988 *Tribal Peoples and Development Issues: A Global Overview.* Mountain View, CA: Mayfield. An overview of case studies, policies, assessments, and recommendations concerning tribal peoples and development.

CERNEA, M., ED.
  1991 *Putting People First: Sociological Variables in Rural Development,* 2nd ed. New York: Oxford University Press (published for the World Bank). First collection of articles by social scientists based on World Bank files and project experiences. Examines development successes and failures and the social and cultural reasons for them.

ESCOBAR, A.
  1995 *Encountering Development: The Making and Unmaking of the Third World.* Princeton, NJ: Princeton University Press. A critique of economic development and development anthropology.

KORTEN, D. C.
  1980 Community Organization and Rural Development: A Learning Process Approach. *Public Administration Review,* September–October, pp. 480–512. People-oriented development strategies as opposed to the "blueprint" approach used by most development agencies.

LANSING, J. S.
  1991 *Priests and Programmers: Technologies of Power in the Engineered Landscape of Bali.* Princeton, NJ: Princeton University Press. The role of a traditional priesthood in managing irrigation and culturally appropriate economic development in Bali, Indonesia.

NUSSBAUM, M., AND J. GLOVER, EDS.
  1995 *Women, Culture, and Development: A Study of Human Capabilities.* New York: Oxford University Press. How to overcome generalized inequities between men and women in the less-developed countries.

ROBERTSON, A. F.
  1995 *The Big Catch: A Practical Introduction to Development.* Boulder, CO: Westview. A case-oriented approach to the role of anthropologists in economic development.

SELIGSON, M. A.
  1984 *The Gap between Rich and Poor: Contending Perspectives on the Political Economy of Development.* Boulder, CO: Westview. Equity issues in development.

WORSLEY, P.
  1984 *The Three Worlds: Culture and World Development.* Chicago: University of Chicago Press. Examines the nature of development processes and critiques existing theories.

CHAPTER 23

CULTURAL EXCHANGE, CREATIVITY, AND SURVIVAL

PEOPLE IN MOTION
Postmodern Moments in the World System
Cultural Contact in Larger Systems

DOMINATION
Development and Environmentalism

Box: Voices of the Rainforest

Religious Domination

RESISTANCE AND SURVIVAL
Weapons of the Weak

In the News: "Things Have Happened to Me as in a Movie"

SYNCRETISMS, BLENDS, AND ACCOMMODATION
Cargo Cults
Cultural Imperialism, Stimulus Diffusion, and Creative Opposition

MAKING AND REMAKING CULTURE
Popular Culture
Indigenizing Popular Culture
A World System of Images
A Transnational Culture of Consumption

THE CONTINUANCE OF DIVERSITY

In a global culture that heralds diversity, the linkages in the modern world system have both enlarged and erased old boundaries and distinctions. Arjun Appadurai (1990, p. 1) characterizes today's world as a "translocal" "interactive system" that is "strikingly new." Whether as refugees, migrants, tourists, pilgrims, proselytizers, laborers, business people, development workers, employees of nongovernmental organizations (NGOs), politicians, soldiers, sports figures, or media-borne images, people travel more than ever.

So important is the transnational migration that many Mexican villagers find "their most important kin and friends are as likely to be living hundreds or thousands of miles away as immediately around them" (Rouse 1991). Most migrants maintain their ties with their native land (phoning, visiting, sending money, watching "ethnic TV"), so that, in a sense, they live multilocally—in different places at once. Dominicans in New York City, for example, have been characterized as living "between two islands"—Manhattan and the Dominican Republic (Grasmuck and Pessar 1991). Many Dominicans—like migrants from other countries—migrate to the United States temporarily, seeking cash to transform their life styles when they return to the Caribbean.

PEOPLE IN MOTION

With so many people "in motion," the unit of anthropological study expands from the local community to the **diaspora**—the offspring of an area who have spread to many lands. Anthropologists increasingly follow descendants of the villages we have studied as they move from rural to urban areas and across national boundaries. For the 1991 annual meeting of the American Anthropological Association in Chicago, the anthropologist Robert Van Kemper organized a session of presentations about long-term ethnographic field work. Kemper's own long-time research focus has been the Mexican village of Tzintzuntzan, which, with his mentor George Foster, Kemper has studied for decades. However, their database now includes not just Tzintzuntzan, but its descendants all over the world (one of whom reached Alaska in 1990). Given the Tzintzuntzan diaspora, Kemper was even able to use some of his time in Chicago to visit people from

With so many contemporary people "in motion" (for example, as transnational migrants), the unit of anthropological study has expanded from the local community to the diaspora—the offspring of an area (e.g., Africa) who have spread to many lands, such as these Afro-Caribbean pub owners in West Broomwich, England.

Tzintzuntzan who had established a colony there. In today's world, as people move, they take their traditions and their anthropologists along with them.

Postmodernity describes our time and situation—today's world in flux, these people on the move who have learned to manage multiple identities depending on place and context. In its most general sense, **postmodern** refers to the blurring and breakdown of established canons (rules or standards), categories, distinctions, and boundaries. The word is taken from **postmodernism**—a style and movement in architecture that succeeded modernism, beginning in the 1970s. Postmodern architecture rejected the rules, geometric order, and austerity of modernism. Modernist buildings were expected to have a clear and functional design. Postmodern design is "messier" and more playful. It draws on a diversity of styles from different times and places—including popular, ethnic, and non-Western cultures. Postmodernism extends "value" well beyond classic, elite, and Western cultural forms. *Postmodern* is now used to describe comparable developments in music, literature, and visual art. From this origin, *postmodernity* describes a world in which traditional standards, contrasts, groups, boundaries, and identities are opening up, reaching out, and breaking down.

Globalization promotes intercultural communication, including travel and migration, which bring people from different cultures into direct contact. The world is more integrated than ever. Yet *disinte-gration* also surrounds us. Nations dissolve (Yugoslavia, Czechoslovakia, the Soviet Union), as do political blocs (the Warsaw Pact nations) and ideologies ("Communism"). The notion of a "Free World" collapses because it existed mainly in opposition to a group of "Captive Nations"—a label that has lost much of its meaning.

Simultaneously new kinds of political and ethnic units are emerging. Ethnicity, "once a genie contained in the bottle of some sort of locality . . . has now become a global force, forever slipping in and through the cracks between states and borders" (Appadurai 1990, p. 15). For example, not only do Native American cultures survive, there is a grow-

ing Panindian identity (Nagel 1996), and an international Pantribal movement as well. Thus in June 1992 the World Conference of Indigenous Peoples met in Rio de Janeiro concurrently with UNCED (the United Nations Conference on the Environment and Development). Along with diplomats, journalists, and environmentalists came 300 representatives of the tribal diversity that survives in the modern world—from Lapland to Mali (Brooke 1992).

Postmodern Moments in the World System

Increasingly anthropologists experience what I call "postmodern moments in the world system." Some of my most vivid ones can be traced back to Ambal-

Not only do Native American cultures survive, but there is a growing Panindian identity and an international Pan-tribal movement as well. In June 1992 the World Conference of Indigenous Peoples met in Rio de Janeiro concurrently with UNCED—the United Nations Conference on the Environment and Development. Along with diplomats, journalists, and environmentalists came 300 representatives of the tribal diversity that survives in the modern world.

avao, Madagascar. In 1966–67 my wife and I rented a house in that town in southern Betsileo country. We spent weekends there when we came in from the rural villages where our field work was based.

By 1966 Madagascar was independent from France, but its towns still had foreigners to remind them of colonialism. Besides us, Ambalavao had at least a dozen world system agents, including an Indian cloth merchant, Chinese grocers, and a few French people. A French consultant was there to help develop the tobacco industry, and two young men in the French equivalent of the Peace Corps were teaching school.

One of them, Noel, served as principal of the junior high school. He lived across the street from a prominent local family (who served as our sponsors in a rural village, their ancestral community, we were studying). Since Noel often spoke disparagingly of the Malagasy, I was surprised to see him courting a young woman from this family. She was Lenore, the sister of Leon, a schoolteacher who became one of my best friends. My wife and I left Ambalavao in December 1967. Noel and the other world system agents stayed on.

Each of my revisits to Madagascar has brought postmodern moments—encounters with people and products on the move, in multilocal and unexpected contexts. After 1967, my next trip to Madagascar came in February 1981. I was doing applied anthropology as a consultant for the World Bank. This work took me to a new area, the Lake Alaotra region, where I was to evaluate the social and cultural reasons for the failure of an expensive irrigation project. Near Alaotra (Madagascar's largest lake), I had no choice but to stay at the Water Lily Hotel. I shared the hotel with a dozen prostitutes, my Malagasy collaborator (a professor of geography), an American World Bank officer, and a Russian technician assigned to this desolate region (instead of Siberia, we joked), perhaps for life. For breakfast I drank Orange Crush (the only bottled drink available) and watched a rat run through the dining room.

During my 1981 stay in Antananarivo, the capital, I was confined each evening to the newly built Hilton hotel by a curfew imposed after a civil insurrection. I shared the hotel with a group of Russian MIG pilots (and their wives), there to teach the Malagasy to defend their island, strategically placed in the Indian Ocean, against imagined enemies.

Later, I went down to Betsileo country to visit Leon, my schoolteacher friend from Ambalavao, who had become a prominent politician. Unfortunately for me, he was in Moscow, participating in a three-month Soviet exchange program.

My next visit to Madagascar was in summer 1990. Again I was doing applied anthropology, this time for the United States Agency for International Development (USAID). My job was to help design a socially sound conservation project, aimed at preserving Madagascar's rich biodiversity. This time a postmodern moment occurred when I met Emily, the twenty-two-year-old daughter of Noel and Lenore, whose courtship I had witnessed in 1967. One of her aunts brought Emily to meet me at my hotel in Antananarivo, where Emily was participating in a program organized by USAID.

Emily was about to visit several cities in the United States, where she planned to study marketing. I met her again just a few months later in Gainesville, Florida, where she was taking a course at Santa Fe Community College. As we lunched in a Mexican restaurant, Emily sold me some woodwork she had brought from Madagascar. She asked my wife and me to help her market other Malagasy crafts. Finally she asked us about her father, whom she had never met. She told us she had sent several letters to France, but Noel had never responded.

Descendants of Ambalavao (and thus of rural Betsileo villages) now live all over the world. Emily, a child of colonialism, has two aunts in France (married to French men) and another in Germany (working as a diplomat). Members of her family, which is not especially wealthy, although regionally prominent, have traveled to Russia, Canada, the United States, France, Germany, and West Africa.

Cultural Contact in Larger Systems

This book has examined many aspects of increasing participation by local cultures in wider systems—regional, national, and global. Since the 1920s anthropologists have been investigating the changes that arise from contact between industrial and nonindustrial societies. Studies of "social change" and "acculturation" are abundant. British and American ethnographers, respectively, have used these terms to describe the same process. *Acculturation* refers to changes that result when groups come into continuous firsthand contact—changes in the cultural patterns of either or both groups (Redfield, Linton, and Herskovits 1936, p. 149).

Acculturation differs from diffusion, or cultural borrowing, which can occur without firsthand contact. For example, most North Americans who eat hot dogs ("frankfurters") have never been to Frankfurt, nor have most North American Sony owners or sushi eaters ever visited Japan. Although *acculturation* can be applied to any case of cultural contact and change, the term has most often described **westernization**—the influence of Western expansion on native cultures. Thus natives who wear store-bought clothes, learn Indo-European languages, and otherwise adopt Western customs are called acculturated.

DOMINATION

Different degrees of destruction, domination, resistance, survival, adaptation, and modification of native cultures may follow interethnic contact. In the most destructive encounters native and subordinate cultures face obliteration. Yet in many modern arenas the contact leads to cultural exchange. Today many non-Western cultures are making important contributions to an emerging world culture.

In cases where contact between the indigenous cultures and more powerful outsiders leads to destruction—a situation most characteristic of colonialist and expansionist eras—a "shock phase" often follows the initial encounter (Bodley, ed. 1988). Traders and settlers may exploit the native people. Such exploitation may increase mortality, disrupt subsistence, fragment kin groups, damage social support systems, and inspire new religious movements (Bodley, ed. 1988). There may be civil repression backed by military force. Such factors may lead to the tribe's cultural collapse (*ethnocide*) or its physical extinction (*genocide*).

More recently, in the development/modernization era, native landscapes and their traditional management systems have been attacked and often destroyed. Outsiders often attempt to remake native landscapes and cultures in their own image. A name for this process—"terraforming"—can be borrowed from science fiction. Anticipating space exploration and planetary colonization, science fiction writers have imagined a policy of **terraforming.** This refers to the use of technology to make other worlds as much like earth (*terra*) as possible—so that earth colonists can feel at home.

By analogy, we can say that dominant nations and cultures have "terraformed" right here on earth. Political and economic colonialists have tried to redesign conquered and dependent lands, peoples, and cultures, imposing their cultural standards on others. The aim of many agricultural development projects, for example, seems to have been to make the world as much like Iowa as possible, complete with mechanized farming and nuclear family ownership—despite the fact that these models may be inappropriate for settings outside the North American heartland.

Development and Environmentalism

Today it is often multinational corporations, usually based in core nations, rather than the governments of those nations, who are changing the nature of Third World economies. However, nations do tend to support the predatory enterprises that seek cheap labor and raw materials in countries outside the core, such as Brazil, where economic development has contributed to ecological devastation.

Simultaneously, environmentalists from core nations increasingly preach ecological morality to the rest of the world. This doesn't play very well in Brazil, whose Amazon is a focus of environmentalist attention. Brazilians complain that northerners talk about global needs and saving the Amazon after having destroyed their own forests for First World economic growth. Akbar Ahmed (1992) finds the non-Western world to be cynical about Western ecological morality, seeing it as yet another imperialist message. "The Chinese have cause to snigger at the Western suggestion that they forgo the convenience of the fridge to save the ozone layer" (Ahmed 1992, p. 120).

In the last chapter we saw that development projects usually fail if they try to replace native forms with culturally alien property concepts and productive units. A strategy that incorporates the native forms is more effective than the fallacies of overinnovation and underdifferentiation. To those fallacies in promoting cultural diffusion, we may add "the fallacy of the noble global." This refers to a modern intervention philosophy that seeks to impose global ecological morality without due attention to cultural variation and autonomy. Countries

VOICES OF THE RAINFOREST

The government of Papua–New Guinea has approved oil exploration by American, British, Australian, and Japanese companies in the rainforest habitat of the Kaluli and other indigenous peoples. The forest degradation that usually accompanies logging, ranching, road building, and drilling endangers plants, animals, peoples, and cultures. Lost along with trees are songs, myths, words, ideas, artifacts, and techniques—the cultural knowledge and practices of rainforest people like the Kaluli, whom the anthropologist and ethnomusicologist Steven Feld has been studying for fifteen years.

Feld teamed up with Mickey Hart of the Grateful Dead in a project designed to promote the cultural survival of the Kaluli through their music. For years Hart has worked to preserve musical diversity through educational funding, concert promotion, and recording, including a successful series called "The World" on the Rykodisc label. *Voices of the Rainforest,* released in that series in April

1991, was the first CD completely devoted to indigenous music from Papua–New Guinea. In one hour it encapsulates twenty-four hours of a day in Kaluli life in Bosavi village. The recording permits a form of cultural survival and diffusion in a high-quality commercial product. Bosavi is presented as a "soundscape" of blended music and natural environmental sounds. Kaluli weave the natural sounds of birds, frogs, rivers, and streams into their texts, melodies, and rhythms. They sing and whistle with birds and waterfalls. They compose instrumental duets with birds and cicadas.

The rock star Sting, known for his support of the Amazon rainforest and the Kayapó Indians, isn't the only media figure working to save endangered habitats, peoples, and cultures. The Kaluli project was launched on Earth Day 1991 at *Star Wars* creator George Lucas's Skywalker Ranch. There Randy Hayes, the Executive Director of the Rainforest Action Network, and musician Mickey Hart spoke about the

linked issues of rainforest destruction and musical survival. Next came a San Francisco benefit dinner for the Bosavi People's Fund. This is the trust established to receive royalties from the Kaluli recording—a financial prong in Steven Feld's strategy to foster Kaluli cultural survival.

Voices of the Rainforest is being marketed as "world music." This term is intended to point up musical diversity, the fact that musics originate from all world regions and all cultures. Our postmodern world recognizes more than one canon (standard for excellence). (As used here, *postmodern* refers to the blurring and breakdown of established canons, categories, distinctions, and boundaries. Postmodernism reaches out to include less formal, precise, and restricted standards—extending "value" well beyond Western and elite culture.) In the postmodern view, "tribal" music joins Western "classical" music as a form of artistic expression worth performing, hearing, and preserving. Hart's series of-

---

and cultures may resist interventionist philosophies aimed at either development or globally oriented environmentalism.

A clash of cultures related to environmental change may occur when *development threatens indigenous peoples and their environments.* Native groups like the Kayapó Indians of Brazil and the Kaluli of Papua–New Guinea (see box) may be threatened by regional, national, and international development plans (such as a dam or commercially driven deforestation) that would *destroy* their homelands.

A second clash of cultures related to environmental change occurs when *external regulation threatens indigenous peoples.* Native groups may be harmed by regional, national, and international environmental plans that seek to *save* their homelands. Sometimes outsiders expect local people to give up many of

their customary economic and cultural activities without clear substitutes, alternatives, or incentives. The traditional approach to conservation has been to restrict access to protected areas, hire park guards, and punish violators.

Problems often arise when external regulation replaces the native system. Like development projects, conservation schemes may ask people to change the way they have been doing things for generations to satisfy planners' goals rather than local goals. In locales as different as Madagascar, Brazil, and the Pacific Northwest of North America people are being asked, told, or forced to change or abandon basic economic activities because to do so is good for "nature" or "the globe." Ironically, well-meaning conservation efforts can be as insensitive as development schemes that promote radical

fers musics of non-Western origin as well as those of ethnically dominated groups of the Western world. Like Paul Simon's recordings *Graceland* and *Rhythm of the Saints*, which draw on African and Brazilian music, a "world music" record series helps blur the boundaries between the exotic and the familiar. The local and the global unite in a transnational popular culture.

Hart's record series aims at preserving "endangered music" against the artistic loss suffered by indigenous peoples. Its intent is to give a "world voice" to people who are being silenced by the dominant world system. In 1993, Hart launched a new series, The Library of Congress Endangered Music Project, which will include digitally remastered field recordings collected by the American Folklife Center. The first of this series, *The Spirit Cries*, concentrates on music from a broad range of cultures in South and Central America and the Caribbean. Proceeds from this project will be used to support the performers and their cultural traditions.

In *Voices of the Rainforest*, Feld and Hart excised all "modern" and "dominant" sounds from their recording. Gone are the world system sounds that Kaluli villagers now hear every day. The recording temporarily silences the "machine voices": the tractor that cuts the grass on the local airstrip, the gas generator, the sawmill, the helicopters, and light planes buzzing to and from the oil-drilling areas. Gone, too, are the village church bells, Bible readings, evangelical prayers and hymns, and the voices of teachers and students at an English-only school.

Initially, Feld anticipated criticism for attempting to create an idealized Kaluli "soundscape" insulated from invasive forces and sounds. Among the Kaluli he expected varied opinions about the value of his project:

It is a soundscape world that some Kaluli care little about, a world that other Kaluli momentarily choose to forget, a world that some Kaluli are increasingly nostalgic and uneasy about, a world that other Kaluli are still living and creating and listening to. It is a sound world that increasingly fewer Kaluli will actively know about and value, but one that increasingly more Kaluli will only hear on cassette and sentimentally wonder about. (Feld 1991, p. 137)

Despite these concerns, Feld was met with an overwhelmingly positive response when he returned to Papua–New Guinea in 1992 armed with a boombox and the recording. The Education Department has put copies of the recording into every high school library. The people of Bosavi also reacted very favorably. Not only did they appreciate the recording, they have also been able to build a much-needed community school with the *Voices of the Rainforest* royalties that have been donated to the Bosavi Peoples Fund.

Source: Based on Steven Feld, "Voices of the Rainforest," *Public Culture* 4(1): 131–140(1991).

changes without involving local people in planning and carrying out the policies that affect them. When people are asked to give up the basis of their livelihood, they usually resist. Like development projects, conservation plans succeed best when they are socially sensitive and guided by a knowledge of local culture, and when they involve the local people in the plans and decisions that affect them.

Religious Domination

Religious proselytizing can promote ethnocide, as native beliefs and practices are replaced by Western ones. Sometimes a religion and associated customs are completely replaced by ideology and behavior more compatible with Western culture. One example is the Handsome Lake religion (as described in the chapter on religion), which led the Iroquois Indians to copy European farming techniques, stressing male rather than female labor. The Iroquois also gave up their communal longhouses and matrilineal descent groups for nuclear family households. The teachings of Handsome Lake led to a new church and religion. This revitalization movement helped the Iroquois survive in a drastically modified environment, but much ethnocide was involved.

Handsome Lake was a native who created a new religion, drawing on Western models. More commonly, missionaries and proselytizers representing the major world religions, especially Christianity and Islam, are the proponents of religious change. Protestant and Catholic missionization continues even in remote corners of the world. Evangelical

Native peoples, such as these Tanala ("Forest people") of eastern Madagascar, may be threatened by development plans that would destroy their homelands. Ironically, native groups may also be harmed by environmental plans that seek to save their homelands. Because environmental preservation depends on local cooperation, conservation schemes must be culturally appropriate.

Protestantism, for example, is advancing in Peru, Brazil, and other parts of Latin America. It challenges a jaded Catholicism that has too few priests and that is sometimes seen mainly as women's religion.

Sometimes the political ideology of a nation-state (for example, "godless communism") is pitted against traditional religion. Officials of the former Soviet empire discouraged Catholicism, Judaism, and Islam. In Central Asia, Soviet dominators destroyed Muslim mosques and discouraged religious practice. On the other hand, governments often use their power to advance a religion, such as Islam in Iran or Sudan. A military government seized power in Sudan in 1989. It immediately launched a cam-

paign to change that country of 25 million people, where one-third are not Muslims, into an Islamic nation.

RESISTANCE AND SURVIVAL

Systems of domination—political, cultural, or religious—always have their more muted aspects along with their public dimensions. In studying apparent cultural domination, or actual political domination, we must pay careful attention to what lies beneath the surface of evident, public, behavior. In public the oppressed may seem to accept their own domination, but they always question it offstage. James Scott (1990) uses **"public transcript"** to describe the open, public interactions between dominators and oppressed—the outer shell of power relations. He uses **"hidden transcript"** to describe the critique of power that goes on offstage, where the power holders can't see it.

In public the oppressed and the elites observe the etiquette of power relations. The dominants act like haughty masters while their subordinates show humility and defer. Antonio Gramsci (1971) developed the concept of **hegemony** for a stratified social order in which subordinates comply with domination by internalizing its values and accepting its "naturalness" (this is the way things were meant to be). According to Pierre Bourdieu (1977, p. 164), every social order tries to make its own arbitrariness (including its oppression) seem natural. All hegemonic ideologies offer explanations about why the existing order is in everyone's interest. Often promises are made (things will get better if you're patient). Gramsci and others use the idea of hegemony to explain why people conform even without coercion, why they knuckle under when they don't really have to.

Hegemony, the internalization of a dominant ideology, is one way to curb resistance. Another way is to let subordinates know they will eventually gain power—as young people usually foresee when they let their elders dominate them. Another way of curbing resistance is to separate or isolate subordinates and supervise them closely. According to Michel Foucault (1979), describing control over prisoners, solitude (as in solitary confinement) is an effective way to induce submission. Subordinates may conclude that the severity of punishment makes open resistance too risky.

Weapons of the Weak

Often, situations that seem to be hegemonic do have active resistance, but it is individual and disguised rather than collective and defiant. Scott (1985) uses Malay peasants, among whom he did field work, to illustrate small-scale acts of resistance—which he calls "weapons of the weak." The Malay peasants used an indirect strategy to resist a corrupt Islamic tithe (religious tax). The goods (usually rice) that peasants had to give went to the provincial capital. In theory, the tithe would come back as charity, but it never did. Peasants didn't resist the tithe by rioting, demonstrating, or protesting. Instead they used a "nibbling" strategy, based on small acts of resistance. For example, they failed to declare their land or lied about the amount they farmed. They underpaid or delivered rice paddy contaminated with water, rocks, or mud, to add weight. Because of this resistance, only 15 percent of what was due was actually paid (Scott 1990, p. 89).

Subordinates also use various strategies to resist *publicly*, but again, usually in disguised form. Discontent may be expressed in public rituals and language, including metaphors, euphemisms, and folk tales. For example, trickster tales (like the Brer Rabbit stories told by slaves in the southern United States) celebrate the wiles of the weak as they triumph over the strong.

Resistance is most likely to be expressed openly when the oppressed are allowed to assemble. The hidden transcript may be publicly revealed on such occasions. People see their dreams and anger shared by others with whom they haven't been in direct contact. The oppressed may draw courage from the crowd, from its visual and emotional impact and its anonymity. Sensing danger, the elites discourage such public gatherings. They try to limit and control holidays, funerals, dances, festivals, and other occasions that might unite the oppressed. Thus in the southern United States gatherings of five or more slaves were forbidden unless a white person was present.

Factors that interfere with community formation—such as geographic, linguistic, and ethnic separation—also work to curb resistance. Consequently, southern U.S. plantation owners sought slaves with diverse cultural and linguistic backgrounds. But such divisive factors can be overcome. Despite the measures used to divide them, the slaves resisted, developing their own popular culture, linguistic codes, and religious vision. The masters taught portions of the Bible that stressed compliance, but the slaves seized on the story of Moses, the promised land, and deliverance. The cornerstone of slave religion became the idea of a reversal in the conditions of whites and blacks. Slaves also resisted directly, through sabotage and flight. In many New World areas slaves managed to establish free communities in the hills and other isolated areas (Price, ed. 1973).

Hidden transcripts tend to be publicly expressed at certain times (festivals and *Carnavals*) and in cer-

Because of its costumed anonymity and its ritual structure (reversal), Carnaval *is an excellent arena for expressing normally suppressed speech. This is vividly symbolized by these Carnaval headdresses in Trinidad.*

IN THE NEWS: "THINGS HAVE HAPPENED TO ME AS IN A MOVIE"

In 1992 Rigoberta Menchú, a 33-year-old Quiché Indian, received the Nobel Peace Prize for her fight on behalf of Indians and human rights in Guatemala. Ms. Menchú has continued her father's leadership role in a grassroots organization, the Committee of Peasant Unity. Her work has also been assisted by a Mexican NGO—a liberal Catholic group called "the Guatemalan Church in Exile." Ms. Menchú's father and brother were tortured (as described in this autobiographical selection) during the ongoing Guatemalan civil war. Most of the 100,000 people believed to have been killed in that war, which has lasted three decades, have been unarmed Indian peasants. Ms. Menchú's father, mother, and brother were eventually killed in separate incidents. Rigoberta Menchú planned to use her $1.2 million prize to campaign for peace in Guatemala and the rights of Indians throughout the hemisphere.

I am a native of the Quiché people of Guatemala. My life has been a long one. Things have happened to me as in a movie. My parents were killed in the repression. I have hardly any relatives living. It has been the lot of many, many Guatemalans.

We were a very poor family. My parents worked cutting cotton, cutting coffee. Two of my brothers died on the plantation. One of them got sick and died. The other died when the landowner ordered cotton sprayed while we were in the field. My brother was poisoned, and we buried him on the plantation.

My father was a catechist, and in Guatemala a catechist is a leader of the community, preaching the Gospel. We began to evolve in the Catholic religion and became catechists.

We grew up—and really you can't say we started fighting only a short time ago, because it has been 22 years since my father fought over the land. The landowners wanted to take away our little bit of land, and so my father fought for it. So he went to speak with the mayors and judges in various parts of Guatemala. For many years, he was tricked because he did not speak Spanish. None of us spoke Spanish. So they made my father travel all over to sign papers, letters, telegrams, which meant that not only he, but the whole community, had to sacrifice to pay the expenses.

My father was imprisoned many times. First, he was accused of causing unrest among the population. When he was in jail, the army kicked us out of our houses.

They burned our clay pots. It was really hard for us to understand this situation. Then my father was sentenced to 18 years in prison, but we were able to work with lawyers to get him released. After a year and two months, he returned home with more courage to go on fighting and angrier because of what had happened.

A short time later, he was tortured by the landowners' bodyguards. Some armed men took him away. We found him lying in the road, about two kilometers from home, barely alive. The priests had come out to take him to the hospital. He had been in the hospital for six months when he heard he was going to be taken out and killed. The landowners had been discussing it loudly. We had to find a private clinic so he would heal.

In 1977, my father was in jail again. The military told us it didn't want us to see him, because he had committed many crimes. From lawyers we learned he was going to be executed. Many union workers, students, peasants and some priests demonstrated. My father was freed, but he was told he was going to be killed anyway for being a Communist.

In 1979, five armed men, their faces covered, kidnapped one of my little brothers. He was 16. Since my father couldn't go out,

---

tain places (for example, markets). Because of its costumed anonymity and its ritual structure (reversal), *Carnaval* is an excellent arena for expressing normally suppressed speech and aggression—antihegemonic discourse. (**Discourse** includes talk, speeches, gestures, and actions.) *Carnavals*, public rituals of reversal, celebrate freedom through immodesty, dancing, gluttony, and sexuality (DaMatta 1991). *Carnaval* may begin as a playful outlet for frustrations built up during the year.

Over time it may evolve into a powerful annual critique of domination and a threat to the established order (Gilmore 1987). (Recognizing that ceremonial license could turn into political defiance, the Spanish dictator Francisco Franco outlawed *Carnaval*.)

In medieval Europe, according to Mikhail Bakhtin (1984), the market was the main place where the dominant ideology was questioned. The anonymity of the crowd and of commerce put peo-

we went with my mother and members of the community to make a complaint to the army, but they said they didn't know anything. We went to City Hall, to all the jails in Guatemala. My mother was very upset. It had taken a lot for my brother to survive, and so it was very hard to accept his disappearance.

At that time the army published a bulletin saying that they had some guerrillas in their custody and that they were going to punish them in public. My mother said: "I hope to God my son is there. I want to know what has happened to him." We walked for one day and almost the whole night to get to the town. Hundreds of soldiers had gathered the people to witness what they were going to do. After a while a truck arrived with 20 people who had been tortured in different ways.

Among them we recognized my brother. We had to calm my mother down, telling her that if she gave herself away she was going to die right there for being family of a guerrilla. We were crying, but almost all the rest of the people were crying also at the sight of the tortured people. The army had pulled my little brother's fingernails out, cut off parts of his ears and other parts of his body, his lips, and he was covered with scars and swollen all over. Among the prisoners was a woman and parts of her breasts and other parts of her body were cut off.

An army captain gave a very long speech, saying that if we got involved with Communism the same things would happen to us. Then he explained the various types of torture they had applied to the prisoners. After three hours, the officer ordered the troops to strip the prisoners and said, "Part of the punishment is still to come." He ordered them tied to some posts. The people didn't know what to do, and my mother was overcome with despair. And none of us knew how we could bear the situation. The officer ordered the prisoners covered with gasoline and they set fire to them, one by one.

Source: Rigoberta Menchú, "Things Have Happened to Me as in a Movie," *The New York Times,* October 17, 1992, p. A25. Adapted from an autobiographical chapter in *You Can't Drown the Fire: Latin American Women Writing in Exile,* Cleis Press, 1989 San Francisco.

Rigoberta Menchú (left), the winner of the 1992 Nobel Peace Prize, is shown here in Mexico City with her friend Rosalina Tuyuc.

ple on an equal footing. The rituals and deference used with lords and clergy didn't apply to the marketplace. Later in Europe the hidden transcript also went public in pubs, taverns, inns, cabarets, beer cellars, and gin mills. These places fostered a popular culture—in games, songs, gambling, blasphemy, and disorder—which was at odds with the official culture. People met in an atmosphere of freedom encouraged by alcohol. Church and state alike condemned these activities as subversive.

SYNCRETISMS, BLENDS, AND ACCOMMODATION

Many new forms of popular expression have emerged from the interplay of local, regional, national, and international cultural forces. **Syncretisms,** for example, are cultural *blends* that emerge from acculturation. One example is the mixture of African, Native American, and Roman Catholic saints and deities in Caribbean vodun, or "voodoo,"

One example of cultural syncretism (blending as a result of contact between cultures) is the mixture of African, Native American, and Roman Catholic saints and deities in Caribbean vodun, or "voodoo," cults. This photo was taken at a Day of the Dead ceremony in Port-au-Prince, Haiti, on October 31, 1993.

cults. This blend is also present in **candomblé,** an "Afro-Brazilian" cult. Another syncretism is the blend of Melanesian and Christian beliefs in cargo cults.

Cargo Cults

Many religious movements (like the Handsome Lake religion discussed earlier) have arisen in response to the spread of colonialism, European domination, and the world capitalist economy. Revitalization movements may emerge when natives have regular contact with industrial societies but are denied their wealth, technology, and living standards. Some such movements attempt to *explain* European domination and wealth and to achieve similar success magically by mimicking European behavior and manipulating symbols of the desired life style. Some of the best-known examples are the syncretic **cargo cults** of Melanesia and Papua–New Guinea, which weave Christian doctrine with aboriginal beliefs. They take their name from their focus on cargo—European goods of the sort natives have seen unloaded from the cargo holds of ships and airplanes.

In one early cult, members believed that the spirits of the dead would arrive in a ship. These ghosts would bring manufactured goods for the natives and would kill all the whites. More recent cults replaced ships with airplanes (Worsley 1959/1985). Many cults have used elements of European culture

as sacred objects. The rationale is that Europeans use these objects, have wealth, and therefore must know the "secret of cargo." By mimicking how Europeans use or treat objects, natives hope also to come upon the secret knowledge needed to gain cargo.

For example, having seen Europeans' reverent treatment of flags and flagpoles, the members of one cult began to worship flagpoles. They believed the flagpoles were sacred towers that could transmit messages between the living and the dead. Other natives built airstrips to entice planes bearing canned goods, portable radios, clothing, wristwatches, and motorcycles. Near the airstrips they made effigies of towers, airplanes, and radios. They talked into the cans in a magical attempt to establish radio contact with the gods.

Some cargo cult prophets proclaimed that success would come through a reversal of European domination and native subjugation. The day was near, they preached, when natives, aided by God, Jesus, or native ancestors, would turn the tables. Native skins would turn white, and those of Europeans would turn brown; Europeans would die or be killed.

As syncretisms, cargo cults blend aboriginal and Christian beliefs. Melanesian myths told of ancestors shedding their skins and changing into powerful beings and of dead people returning to life. Christian missionaries, who had been in Melanesia since the late nineteenth century, also spoke of resurrection. The cults' preoccupation with cargo is related to traditional Melanesian big-man systems. Previously we saw (in Chapter 12) that a Melanesian big man had to be generous. People worked for the big man, helping him amass wealth, but eventually he had to give a feast and give away all that wealth. Because of their experience with big-man systems, Melanesians believed that all wealthy people eventually had to give their wealth away. For decades they had attended Christian missions and worked on plantations. All the while they expected Europeans to return the fruits of their labor as their own big men did. When the Europeans refused to distribute the wealth or even to let natives know the secret of its production and distribution, cargo cults developed.

Like arrogant big men, Europeans would be leveled, by death if necessary. However, natives lacked the physical means of doing what their traditions said they should do. Thwarted by well-armed colonial forces, natives resorted to magical leveling. They called on supernatural beings to intercede, to kill or otherwise deflate the European big men and redistribute their wealth.

Cargo cults are religious responses to the expansion of the world capitalist economy. However, this religious mobilization had political and economic results. Cult participation gave Melanesians a basis for common interests and activities and thus helped pave the way for political parties and economic interest organizations. Previously separated by geography, language, and customs, Melanesians started forming larger groups as members of the same cults and followers of the same prophets. The cargo cults paved the way for political action through which the indigenous peoples eventually regained their autonomy.

Cultural Imperialism, Stimulus Diffusion, and Creative Opposition

Cultural imperialism refers to the rapid spread or advance of one culture at the expense of others, or its imposition on other cultures, which it modifies, replaces, or destroys—usually because of differential economic or political influence. Thus children in the French colonial empire learned French history, language, and culture from standard textbooks also used in France. Tahitians, Malagasy, Vietnamese, and Senegalese learned the French language by reciting from books about "our ancestors the Gauls." Ironically, modern French intellectuals, seemingly forgetting France's colonialist past, are quick to complain about American cultural imperialism. Thus in 1992 French intellectuals protested the opening of Euro Disney as a threat to French (and European) culture. A French minister of culture, Jack Lang, often lamented the extent to which American films and TV programs (purportedly) dominate popular culture in many countries.

The matter isn't as simple as the French intellectuals imagine. People aren't passive victims of cul-

Under French colonialism, native children in places as different as Tahiti, Madagascar, Vietnam, and Senegal learned the French language by reciting from books about "our ancestors the Gauls." More recently, many French citizens have criticized or resisted American "cultural imperialism"— one prominent symbol of which has been Euro Disneyland.

tural imperialism. Contemporary people—often with considerable creativity—constantly revise, rework, resist, and reject the messages they get from external systems.

Some critics worry that modern technology, including the mass media, is killing off traditional cultures by homogenizing products to reach more people. But others see an important role for modern technology in allowing social groups (local cultures) to express themselves and thus in disseminating particular subcultures (Marcus and Fischer 1986, p. 122). Modern radio and TV, for example, constantly bring local happenings (for example, a "chicken festival" in Iowa) to the attention of a larger public. The North American media play a role in stimulating local activities of many sorts. Similarly in Brazil, local practices, celebrations, and performances are changing in the context of outside forces, including the mass media and tourism.

In the town of Arembepe TV coverage has stimulated participation in a traditional annual performance, the *Chegança*. This is a fishermen's dance-play, that reenacts the Portuguese discovery of Brazil. Arembepeiros have traveled to the state capital to perform the *Chegança* before television cameras, for a TV program featuring traditional performances from many rural communities. Here one sees television's role in allowing social groups to express themselves and in disseminating local cultures.

One national Brazilian Sunday-night variety program (*Fantástico*) is especially popular in rural areas because it shows such local events. In several towns along the Amazon River, annual folk ceremonies are now staged more lavishly for TV cameras. In the Amazon town of Parantíns, for example, boatloads of tourists arriving any time of year are shown a videotape of the town's annual Bumba Meu Boi festival. This is a costumed performance mimicking bull-fighting, parts of which have been shown on *Fantástico*. This pattern, in which communities preserve, revive, and intensify the scale of traditional ceremonies to perform for TV and tourists, is expanding.

However, Brazilian television has also played a "top-down" role, by spreading the popularity of national (and international) holidays, like *Carnaval* and Christmas (Kottak 1990a). TV has aided the national spread of *Carnaval* beyond its traditional urban centers, especially Rio de Janeiro. Still, local re-

actions to the nation-wide broadcasting of *Carnaval* and its trappings (elaborate parades, costumes, and frenzied dancing) are not simple or uniform responses to external stimuli. Like syncretisms, these new forms of popular expression are cultural creations that develop from the interplay of local, regional, national, and international forces.

Rather than direct adoption of *Carnaval*, or rote imitation of it, local Brazilians respond in various ways. These reactions include "stimulus diffusion" and "creative opposition." **Stimulus diffusion** describes the process by which a group modifies a custom by adopting images and behavior associated with an external practice, without borrowing the practice itself. We see stimulus diffusion when Brazilians don't take up *Carnaval* itself but modify their local festivities to fit *Carnaval* images. **Creative opposition** occurs when people change their behavior as they consciously and actively avoid or spurn an external image or practice. We see creative opposition when local Brazilians deliberately reject *Carnaval*, sometimes by celebrating traditional local festivals on a previously unimagined scale, sometimes by rejecting certain local practices perceived as similar to the disdained external practice.

In Brazilian towns national *Carnaval* coverage seems more often to inspire stimulus diffusion than direct borrowing through simple imitation. Local groups work hard not on *Carnaval* per se but on incorporating its elements and themes in their own ceremonies. Some of these have grown in scale, in imitation of *Carnaval* celebrations shown on national TV. But local reactions can also be negative, even hostile. One example is Arembepe, where *Carnaval* has never been important, probably because of its calendrical closeness to the main local festival, which is held in February to honor Saint Francis of Assisi. In the past, villagers couldn't afford to celebrate both occasions. Now, not only do the people of Arembepe reject *Carnaval*, they are also increasingly hostile to their own main festival. Arembepeiros resent the fact that Saint Francis has become "an outsiders' event," because it draws thousands of tourists to Arembepe each February. The villagers think that commercial interests and outsiders have appropriated Saint Francis.

In creative opposition, many Arembepeiros now say they like and participate more in the traditional June festivals honoring Saint John, Saint Peter, and Saint Anthony. In the past these were observed on a much smaller scale than was Saint Francis. Arembepeiros celebrate them now with a new vigor and enthusiasm, as they react to outsiders and their celebrations, real and televised.

MAKING AND REMAKING CULTURE

Any media-borne image, such as *Carnaval,* can be considered a **text**—something that is creatively "read," interpreted, and assigned meaning by each person who receives it. *Carnaval* images in Brazil illustrate some ways in which "readers" produce their own meanings from a text. Such meanings may be very different from what the creators of the text imagined. (The reading or meaning that the creators intended—or the one that the elites consider to be the intended or correct meaning—can be called the **hegemonic reading.**)

"Readers" of media messages constantly produce their own meanings. They may resist or creatively oppose the hegemonic meanings of a text, or they may seize on the antihegemonic aspects of a text. We saw this process when American slaves preferred the Biblical story of Moses and deliverance to the hegemonic lessons of obedience that their masters taught.

Popular Culture

In his book *Understanding Popular Culture* (1989), John Fiske views each individual's use of popular culture as a creative act (an original "reading" of a text). (For example, Madonna, the Grateful Dead, or *Star Wars* mean something different to each of their fans.) As Fiske puts it, "the meanings I make from a text are pleasurable when I feel that they are *my* meanings and that they relate to *my* everyday life in a practical, direct way" (1989, p. 57). All of us can creatively "read" magazines, books, music, television, films, celebrities, and other popular culture products.

Individuals also draw on popular culture to express resistance. Through their use of popular culture, people can symbolically resist the unequal power relations they face each day—in the family, at work, and in the classroom. Forms and readings of popular culture (from rap music to sitcoms) can express discontent and resistance by groups that are or feel oppressed.

Indigenizing Popular Culture

To understand culture change, it is important to recognize that meaning is not inherent or imposed but locally manufactured. People assign their own meanings and value to the texts, messages, and products they receive. Those meanings reflect their cultural backgrounds and experiences. When forces from world centers enter new societies, they are **indigenized**—modified to fit the local culture. This is true of cultural forces as different as fast food, music, housing styles, science, terrorism, celebrations,

The notion of cultural imperialism is flawed because it views people as victims rather than as creative agents in their own transformation. Native Australians saw Rambo as a representative of the Third World battling the white officer class. This "reading" of Rambo expressed their hostility toward white paternalism and existing race relations. Shown here, a Rambo poster in Jakarta, Indonesia.

and political ideas and institutions (Appadurai 1990).

The notion of cultural imperialism is flawed because it views people as victims rather than as creative agents in their own transformation. For example, Michaels (1986) found *Rambo* to be a popular movie among aborigines in the deserts of central Australia, who had manufactured their own meanings from the film. Their "reading" was very different from the one imagined by the movie's creators, and by most Americans. The Native Australians saw Rambo as a representative of the Third World battling the white officer class. This reading expressed their negative feelings about white paternalism and existing race relations. The Native Australians also created tribal ties and kin links between Rambo and the prisoners he was rescuing. All this made sense, based on their experience. Native Australians are disproportionately represented in Australian jails, and their most likely liberator would be someone with a personal link to them. These readings of *Rambo* were relevant meanings produced *from* the text, not *by* it (Fiske 1989).

A World System of Images

All cultures express imagination—in dreams, fantasies, songs, myths, and stories. Today, however, more people in many more places imagine "a wider set of 'possible' lives than they ever did before. One important source of this change is the mass media, which present a rich, ever-changing store of possible lives . . ." (Appadurai 1991, p. 197). The United States as a media center has been joined by Canada, Japan, Western Europe, Brazil, Mexico, Nigeria, Egypt, India, and Hong Kong.

Film industries in Hong Kong and Hollywood have worked together to spread images of masculinity and violence across nations. Old martial arts traditions have been reformulated to meet the fantasies of contemporary male youth, especially in Asia. This, in turn, has fueled violence in national and international politics, through a worldwide arms trade (Appadurai 1990).

As print has done for centuries (Anderson 1991), the electronic mass media can also spread, and even create, national and ethnic identities. Like print, television and radio can diffuse the cultures of different countries within their own boundaries, thus enhancing national cultural identity. For example,

millions of Brazilians who were formerly cut off (by geographic isolation or illiteracy) from urban and national events and information now join in a national communication system, thanks to the national TV network called *Globo*. Through television modern Brazilians have a sense of regular participation in national events (Kottak 1990*a*).

Cross-cultural studies of television contradict a belief Americans ethnocentrically hold about televiewing in other countries. This misconception is that American programs inevitably triumph over local products. This doesn't happen when there is appealing local competition. In Brazil, for example, the most popular network (TV Globo) relies heavily on native productions. American imports like *Dallas* and *Dynasty* have drawn small audiences. TV Globo's most popular programs are *telenovelas*, locally made serials that are similar to American soap operas. Globo plays each night to the world's largest and most devoted audience (60 to 80 million viewers throughout the nation). The programs that attract this horde are made by Brazilians, for Brazilians. Thus it is not North American culture but a new pan-Brazilian national culture, which Brazilian TV is propagating. Brazilian productions also compete internationally. They are exported to over 100 countries, spanning Latin America, Europe, Asia, and Africa.

We may generalize that American programming that is culturally alien won't do very well anywhere, when a quality local choice is available. Confirmation comes from many countries. National productions are highly popular in Japan, Mexico, India, Egypt, and Nigeria. In a survey during the mid-1980s, 75 percent of Nigerian viewers preferred local productions. Only 10 percent favored imports, and the remaining 15 percent liked the two options equally. Local productions are successful in Nigeria because "they are filled with everyday moments that audiences can identify with. These shows are locally produced by Nigerians" (Gray 1986). Thirty million people watched one of the most popular series, *The Village Headmaster*, each week. That program brought rural values to the screens of urbanites who had lost touch with their rural roots (Gray 1986).

The electronic mass media also play a key role in preserving ethnic and national identities among people who lead transnational lives. As groups move, they stay linked to each other and to their homeland through the media. Diasporas have enlarged the markets for media and travel services targeted at specific ethnic, national, or religious audiences. For a fee, a PBS station in Fairfax, Virginia, offers more than thirty hours a week to immigrant groups in the D.C. area, to make programs in their own languages. *Somali Television*, for instance, is a half-hour program with about 5,000 Somali viewers, who can see their flag and hear their language on TV each week. Starting the program is a reading from the Koran, with clips of mosques from around the world (thus contributing, too, to a transnational Islamic identity). Formerly, an entertainment segment featured folk dances and Somali music. As Somalia's civil war dragged on, the entertainment segment was replaced in 1992 by images of bony children and parched countryside. *Somali Television* also features obituaries, rallies, and a segment called "Somalia Today," which has interviews with diplomats, immigration lawyers, and travel agents discussing air fares. Guests represent various tribes and subclans. *Somali Television* became a vital link between emigrant Somalis and their homeland. This was particularly true before images of Somalia became widespread on network news in late 1992 and early 1993 (*New York Times*, December 18, 1992).

A Transnational Culture of Consumption

Another key transnational force is finance. Money makers look beyond national boundaries for places to invest. As Appadurai (1991, p. 194) puts it, "money, commodities, and persons unendingly chase each other around the world." Many Latin American communities have lost their autonomy because their residents now depend on cash derived from international labor migration. The United States also relies more on foreign cash. Long dominated by domestic capital, the economy of the United States is increasingly influenced by foreign investment, especially from Britain, Canada, Germany, the Netherlands, and Japan (Rouse 1991). The American economy has also increased its dependence on foreign labor—through both the immigration of laborers and the export of jobs.

Contemporary global culture is driven by flows of people, technology, finance, information, and ideology (Appadurai 1990). Business, technology, and the media have increased the craving for commodities and images throughout the world. This has forced nation-states, including "Iron Curtains," to open to a global culture of consumption. Almost everyone today participates in this culture. Few people have never seen a T-shirt advertising a Western product. Michael Jackson's recordings blast through the streets of Rio de Janeiro, while taxi drivers from Toronto to Madagascar play Brazilian *lambada* tapes. Peasants and tribal people participate in the modern world system not only because they (willingly or unwillingly) work for cash but also because their products and images are appropriated by world capitalism (Root 1996). They are commercialized by others (like the San in the movie *The Gods Must Be Crazy*). And, seizing their own destinies, often helped by outsiders, indigenous peoples also market their own images and products through outlets like the Body Shop and Cultural Survival.

The electronic mass media play a prominent role in today's global culture of consumption. Taxi drivers from Canada to Madagascar play Brazilian lambada *tapes. In 1983 Michael Jackson's* Beat It *blasted through the streets of Rio de Janeiro. A decade later, Michael Jackson films a video in one of Rio's shantytowns.*

David Maybury-Lewis's ten-program 1992 TV series *Millennium (Tribal Wisdom and the Modern World)* was designed to remedy misconceptions about tribal people, to help ensure their autonomy and survival.

Some social commentators see contemporary flows of people, technology, finance, information, and ideology as a cultural imperialist steamroller. This view ignores the selective, synthesizing activity of human beings as they deal with external forces, images, and messages. Anthropological studies show that domination is usually met by resistance and that cultural diffusion is a creative process.

THE CONTINUANCE OF DIVERSITY

Anthropology has a crucial role to play in promoting a more humanistic vision of social change, one that respects the value of cultural diversity. The existence of anthropology is itself a tribute to the continuing need to understand social and cultural similarities and differences. Anthropology teaches us that the adaptive responses of humans can be more flexible than can those of other species because our main adaptive means are sociocultural. However, the cultural forms, institutions, values, and customs of the past always influence subsequent adaptation, producing continued diversity and giving a certain uniqueness to the actions and reactions of different groups.

Let us hope that vigorous cultural differences will continue to prevent what some social scientists see as a bland convergence in the future, so that free and open investigation of human diversity can continue. With our knowledge and our awareness of our professional responsibilities, let us work to keep anthropology, the study of humankind, the most humanistic of all the sciences.

SUMMARY

The linkages in the modern world system have both enlarged and erased old boundaries and distinctions. People travel more than ever, but migrants maintain their ties with home, so that they live multilocally. With so many people "in motion," the unit of anthropological study expands from the local community to the diaspora. *Postmodernity* describes this world in flux, these people on the move who have learned to manage multiple social identities depending on place and context. New kinds of political and ethnic units are emerging as others break down or disappear.

Different degrees of destruction, domination, resistance, survival, adaptation, and modification of native cultures may follow interethnic contact. This may lead to the tribe's cultural collapse (*ethnocide*) or its physical extinction (*genocide*). The native landscape and its traditional management system may be attacked. Outsiders often attempt to remake native landscapes and cultures in their own image, a process called *terraforming*.

Multinational business corporations are a major force in the modern world system. Core nations continue to send predatory enterprises to noncore nations, where multinationals have fueled economic development and ecological devastation. Countries and cultures may resist interventionist philosophies aimed at either development or globally oriented environmentalism.

A clash of cultures related to environmental change may occur when development threatens indigenous peoples and their environments. Another clash may occur when external regulation threatens indigenous peoples. Native groups may be harmed by regional, national, and international environmental plans that seek to *save* their homelands. Like development projects, conservation schemes may ask people to change the way they have been doing things for generations to satisfy planners' goals rather than local goals. When people are asked to give up the basis of their livelihood, they usually resist. Like development plans, the most effective conservation strategies pay attention to the needs and wishes of the people living in the affected area.

Religious proselytizing can promote ethnocide, as native beliefs and practices are replaced by Western ones. Sometimes the political ideology of a nation-state is pitted against traditional religion. Governments often use their power to advance a religion.

Systems of domination have their muted aspects along with their public dimensions. "Public transcript" describes the open, public interactions between dominators and oppressed. "Hidden transcript" describes the critique of power that goes on offstage, where the power holders can't see it. *Hegemony* describes a stratified social order in which subordinates comply with domination by internalizing its values and accepting its "naturalness."

Often, situations that appear hegemonic have active resistance, but it is individual and disguised rather than collective and defiant. Subordinates also use various strategies to resist publicly, but again, usually in disguised form. Discontent may be expressed in public rituals and language. Resistance is most likely to be expressed openly when the oppressed are allowed to assemble.

Many forms of popular expression have emerged from the interplay of local, regional, national, and international cultural forces. *Syncretisms* are cultural blends that emerge from acculturation. *Cargo cults* developed in an acculturative context produced by expansion of the world capitalist economy and colonialism. These cults blend native expectations about tribal big men with magical explanations for the wealth of foreign overlords. Cargo cults have forged people into larger communities that have gained political and economic influence.

Cultural imperialism refers to the rapid spread or advance of one culture at the expense of others, or its imposition on other cultures, which it modifies, replaces, or destroys—usually because of differential economic or political influence. But people aren't passive victims of cultural imperialism. Contemporary people—often with considerable creativity—constantly revise, rework, resist, and reject the messages they get from external systems.

Some critics worry that modern technology, including the mass media, is killing off traditional cultures by homogenizing products to reach more people. But others see an important role for modern technology in allowing local cultures to express themselves. *Stimulus diffusion* describes the process by which a group modifies a custom by adopting images and behavior associated with an external practice, without borrowing the practice itself. *Creative opposition* occurs when people change their behavior as they consciously and actively avoid or spurn an external image or practice.

Any media-borne image can be considered a *text*—something that is creatively "read," interpreted, and assigned meaning by each person who receives it. People may resist or creatively oppose the hegemonic meaning of a text, or they may seize on the antihegemonic aspects of a text. Forms and readings of popular culture can express discontent and resistance by groups that are or feel oppressed. Meaning is not inherent or imposed but locally manufactured. When forces from world centers enter new societies, they are *indigenized*—modified to fit the local culture.

All cultures express imagination, but today, through the mass media, people imagine a wider set of possible lives than they ever did before. The electronic mass media can spread, even create, national and ethnic identities. Like print, television and radio can diffuse the cultures of different countries within their own boundaries, thus enhancing national cultural identity. The electronic mass media also play a key role in preserving ethnic and national identities among people who lead transnational lives.

Contemporary global culture is driven by flows of people, technology, finance, information, and ideology. Transnational finance and labor modify the economic control and the ethnic mix of local life. Business, technology, and the media have increased the craving for commodities and images throughout the world, creating a global culture of consumption. Anthropological studies show that domination is usually met by resistance and that cultural diffusion is a creative process.

GLOSSARY

candomblé: A syncretic "Afro-Brazilian" cult.

cargo cults: Postcolonial, acculturative religious movements, common in Melanesia, that attempt to explain European domination and wealth and to achieve similar success magically by mimicking European behavior.

creative opposition: Process in which people change their behavior as they consciously and actively avoid or spurn an external image or practice.

cultural imperialism: The rapid spread or advance of one culture at the expense of others, or its imposition on other cultures, which it modifies, replaces, or destroys—usually because of differential economic or political influence.

diaspora: The offspring of an area who have spread to many lands.

discourse: Talk, speeches, gestures, and actions.

hegemonic reading (of a "text"): The reading or meaning that the creators intended, or the one the elites consider to be the intended or correct meaning.

hegemony: As used by Antonio Gramsci, a stratified social order in which subordinates comply with domination by internalizing its values and accepting its "naturalness."

hidden transcript: As used by James Scott, the critique of power by the oppressed that goes on offstage—in private—where the power holders can't see it.

indigenized: Modified to fit the local culture.

postmodern: In its most general sense, describes the blurring and breakdown of established canons (rules, standards), categories, distinctions, and boundaries.

postmodernism: A style and movement in architecture that succeeded modernism. Compared with modernism, postmodernism is less geometric, less functional, less austere, more playful, and more willing to include elements from diverse times and cultures; *postmodern* now describes comparable developments in music, literature, and visual art.

postmodernity: Condition of a world in flux, with people on the move, in which established groups, boundaries, identities, contrasts, and standards are reaching out and breaking down.

public transcript: As used by James Scott, the open, public interactions between dominators and oppressed—the outer shell of power relations.

stimulus diffusion: The process by which a group modifies a custom by adopting images and behavior associated with an external practice, without borrowing the practice itself.

syncretisms: Cultural blends, or mixtures, that emerge from acculturation, particularly under colonialism, such as African, Native American, and Roman Catholic saints and deities in Caribbean vodun, or "voodoo," cults.

terraforming: From science fiction, the use of technology to make other worlds as much like earth (*terra*) as possible; applied by analogy to results of political and economic domination on earth.

text: Something that is creatively "read," interpreted, and assigned meaning by each person who receives it; includes any media-borne image, such as *Carnaval*.

westernization: The acculturative influence of Western expansion on native cultures.

STUDY QUESTIONS

1. What does it mean to say that linkages in today's world system have both enlarged and erased old boundaries and distinctions?
2. What does it mean to say that people live multilocally?
3. What is the difference between postmodernity and postmodernism? How has postmodernity affected the units of anthropological study?
4. What are the main forces influencing interaction between cultures?
5. What is the difference between acculturation and diffusion?
6. What is terraforming, and how does it relate to political and economic domination?
7. What are some of the similarities between development and environmentalism as interventionist philosophies?
8. How may external regulation harm indigenous peoples, and what is the best strategy for effective environmentalism?
9. What are some ways in which religious proselytizing has led to forms of ethnocide?
10. What is meant by the hidden and public transcripts in situations of domination?
11. What strategies do the oppressed use to resist publicly, and at what times and places is this usually done?
12. What are some examples of syncretisms?
13. How are cargo cults related both to traditional social structure and to the expansion of the world capitalist economy?
14. What are some of the arguments for and against the interpretation of the mass media as forms of cultural imperialism?
15. What are examples of stimulus diffusion and creative opposition?
16. What is "text," and how does its reading relate to the role of the individual in popular culture?
17. What does it mean to say that there is a new world system of images?
18. What contributions do the media make to national and ethnic identity?
19. What are examples of contemporary global flows of people, technology, finance, information, and ideology?

SUGGESTED ADDITIONAL READING

AHMED, A. S.
    1992   *Postmodernism and Islam: Predicament and Promise.* New York: Routledge. Clear presentation of postmodernism, in relation to the media and to images of Islam.
BALICK, M. J., E. ELISABETSKY, AND S. A. LAIRD
    1995   *Medicinal Resources of the Tropical Forest: Biodi-*

versity and Its Importance to Human Health. New York: Columbia University Press. The medicinal and health implications of deforestation at the local, regional, national, and global levels.
BODLEY, J. H.
    1995   *Anthropology and Contemporary Human Problems,* 3rd ed. Mountain View, CA: Mayfield.

Overview of major problems of today's industrial world: overconsumption, the environment, resource depletion, hunger, overpopulation, violence, and war.

CULTURAL SURVIVAL
1992   *At the Threshold.* Cambridge, MA: Cultural Survival. Originally published as the Spring 1992 issue of *Cultural Survival Quarterly.* Manual for the promotion of the rights of indigenous peoples. Highlights activist successes, gives instructions for affecting policy, working in schools and communities, directly helping native societies, and using the media as a human-rights ally.

DaMATTA, R.
1991   *Carnivals, Rogues, and Heroes: An Interpretation of the Brazilian Dilemma.* Translated from the Portuguese by John Drury. Notre Dame, IN: University of Notre Dame Press. Classic study of Brazilian *Carnaval* in relation to Brazilian national culture.

FELD, S.
1990   *Sound and Sentiment: Birds, Weeping, Poetics, and Song in Kaluli Expression,* 2nd ed. Philadelphia: University of Pennsylvania Press. Ethnographic study of sound as a cultural system among the Kaluli people of Papua–New Guinea.

FISKE, J.
1989   *Understanding Popular Culture.* Boston: Unwin Hyman. The role of the individual in using popular culture, constructing meaning, and resisting everyday power relations.

LUTZ, C., AND J. L. COLLINS
1993   *Reading National Geographic.* Chicago: University of Chicago Press. How the cultural narratives of the magazine are received and interpreted; the relation between images of other peoples, cultures, and life styles and middle-class North American values.

MARCUS, G. E., AND F. R. MYERS, EDS.
1995   *The Traffic in Culture: Refiguring Art and Anthropology.* Berkeley, CA: University of California Press. Art, society, and the marketing of culture in global pespective.

NAGEL, J.
1996   *American Indian Ethnic Renewal: Red Power and the Resurgence of Identity and Culture.* New York: Oxford University Press. The meaning of activism for Native American individual ethnic identification; the role of federal, tribal, and personal politics in the growth of American Indian identity.

PUBLIC CULTURE
Journal published by the University of Chicago. Articles deal with the anthropology of the modern and postmodern world system.

ROOT, D.
1996   *Cannibal Culture: Art, Appropriation, and the Commodification of Difference.* Boulder, CO: Westview. How Western art and commerce classify, co-opt, and commodify "native" experiences, creations, and products.

SCOTT, JAMES C.
1990   *Domination and the Arts of Resistance.* New Haven, CT: Yale University Press. A study of institutionalized forms of domination, such as colonialism, slavery, serfdom, racism, caste, concentration camps, prisons, and old-age homes—and the forms of resistance that oppose them.

APPENDIX

AMERICAN POPULAR CULTURE

ANTHROPOLOGISTS AND AMERICAN CULTURE

FOOTBALL

STAR TREK **AS A SUMMATION OF DOMINANT CULTURAL THEMES**

FANTASY FILMS AS MYTH

DISNEY MYTH AND RITUAL

A Pilgrimage to Walt Disney World
Within the Magic Kingdom

RECOGNIZING RELIGION

RITUALS AT McDONALD'S

ANTHROPOLOGY AND AMERICAN "POP" CULTURE

Although culture is shared, all cultures have divisive as well as unifying forces. Tribes are divided by residence in different villages and membership in different descent groups. Nations, though united by government, are divided by class, region, ethnicity, religion, and political party. Unifying forces in tribal cultures include marriage, trade, and segmentary lineage structure. In any society, of course, a common cultural tradition also provides a basis for uniformity.

Whatever unity the contemporary American culture has doesn't rest on a particularly strong central government. Nor is our national unity based on segmentary lineage structure or marital exchange networks. In fact, many of the commonalities of experience, belief, behavior, and activity that enable us to speak of "contemporary American culture" are relatively new. Like the globalizing forces discussed in Chapter 23 they are founded on and perpetuated by twentieth-century developments, particularly in business, transportation, and the mass media.

ANTHROPOLOGISTS AND AMERICAN CULTURE

When anthropologists study urban ethnic groups or relationships between class and household organization, they focus on variation, a very important topic. When we look at the creative use that each individual makes of popular culture, as we did in Chapter 23, we are also considering variation. However, anthropology traditionally has been concerned as much with uniformity as with variation. "National character" studies of the 1940s and 1950s foreshadowed anthropology's interest in unifying themes in modern nations. Unfortunately, those studies, of such countries as Japan and Russia, focused too much on the psychological characteristics of individuals.

Contemporary anthropologists interested in national culture realize that culture is an attribute of groups. Despite increasing ethnic diversity in the United States, we can still talk about an "American national culture." Through common experiences in their enculturation, especially through the media, most Americans do come to share certain knowledge, beliefs, values, and ways of thinking and acting (as was discussed in Chapter 3, "Culture"). The shared aspects of national culture override differences among individuals, genders, regions, or ethnic groups.

Chapter 23 examined the creative use that individuals and cultures make of introduced cultural forces, including media images. That chapter discussed how, through different "readings" of the same media "text," individuals and cultures constantly make and remake popular culture. Here we take a different approach, focusing on some of the "texts" that have diffused most successfully in a given national culture. Such "texts" spread because they are culturally appropriate and—for various cultural reasons—able to carry some sort of meaning to millions of Americans. Previous chapters have focused on variation and diversity, but this Appendix stresses unifying factors—common experiences, actions, and beliefs in American culture.

Anthropologists *should* study American society and culture. Anthropology, after all, deals with universals, generalities, and uniqueness. A national culture is a particular cultural variant, as interesting as any other. Although survey research is traditionally used to study modern nations, techniques developed to interpret and analyze smaller-scale societies, where sociocultural uniformity is more marked, can also contribute to an understanding of American life.

Native anthropologists are those who study their own cultures—for example, American anthropologists working in the United States, Canadian anthropologists working in Canada, or Nigerians working in Nigeria. Anthropological training and field work abroad provide an anthropologist with a certain degree of detachment and objectivity that most natives lack. However, life experience as a native gives an advantage to anthropologists who wish to study their own cultures. Nevertheless, more than when working abroad, the native anthropologist is both participant and observer, often emotionally and intellectually involved in the events and beliefs being studied. Native anthropologists must be particularly careful to resist their own emic biases (their prejudices as natives). They must strive to be as objective in describing their own cultures as they are in analyzing others.

Natives often see and explain their behavior very differently than anthropologists do. For example, most Americans have probably never considered the possibility that apparently secular, commercial, and recreational institutions such as sports, movies, Walt Disney enterprises, and fast-food restaurants have things in common with religious beliefs, symbols, and behavior. However, these similarities can be demonstrated anthropologically. Anthropology helps us understand ourselves. By studying other cultures, we learn both to appreciate and to question aspects of our own. Furthermore, the same

techniques that anthropologists use in describing and analyzing other cultures can be applied to American culture.

American readers may not find the analyses that follow convincing. In part this is because you are natives, who know much more about your own culture than you do about any other. Also, as we saw in Chapter 23, people in a culture may "read" that culture differently. Furthermore, American culture assigns a high value to differences in individual opinion—and to the belief that one opinion is as good as another. Here I am trying to extract *culture* (widely shared aspects of behavior) from diverse *individual* opinions, actions, and experiences.

The following analyses depart from areas that can be easily quantified, such as demography or economics. We are entering a more impressionistic domain, where cultural analysis sometimes seems more like philosophy or humanities than like science. You will be right in questioning some of the conclusions that follow. Some are surely debatable; some may be wrong. However, if they illustrate how anthropology can be used to shed light on aspects of your own life and experience and to revise and broaden your understanding of your own culture, they will have served a worthwhile function.

A reminder (from Chapter 3, "Culture") about culture, ethnocentrism, and native anthropologists is needed here. For anthropologists, *culture* means much more than refinement, cultivation, education, and appreciation of "classics" and "fine arts"—its popular usage. Curiously, however, when some anthropologists confront their own culture, they forget this. They carry an image of themselves as adventurous and broad-minded specialists in the unusual, the ethnic, and the exotic. Like other academics and intellectuals, they may regard American "pop" culture as trivial and unworthy of serious study. In doing so, they demonstrate ethnocentrism and reveal a bias that comes with being members of an academic-intellectual subculture.

In examining American culture, native anthropologists must be careful to overcome the bias associated with the academic subculture. Although some academics discourage their children from watching television, the fact that TVs outnumber toilets in American households is a significant cultural fact that anthropologists can't afford to ignore. My own research on Michigan college students may be generalizable to other young Americans. They visit Mc-Donald's more often than they visit houses of worship. I found that almost all had seen a Walt Disney movie and had attended rock concerts or football games. If these observations are true of young Americans generally, as I suspect they are, such shared experiences are major features of American enculturation patterns. Certainly any extraterrestrial anthropologist doing field work in the United States would stress them. Within the United States the mass media and the culture of consumption have created major themes in contemporary national culture. These themes merit anthropological study.

From the popular domains of sports, TV, movies, theme parks, and fast food, I have chosen certain very popular "texts." I could have used other texts (for example, blue jeans, baseball, or pizza) to make the same points—that there are powerful shared aspects of contemporary American national culture and that anthropological techniques can be used to interpret them.

FOOTBALL

Football, we say, is only a game, yet it has become a popular spectator sport. On fall Saturdays millions of people travel to and from college football games. Smaller congregations meet in high school stadiums. Millions of Americans watch televised football. Indeed, more than half the adult population of the United States watches the Super Bowl. Because football is of general interest to Americans, it is a unifying cultural institution that merits anthropological attention. Our most popular sports manage to attract people of diverse ethnic backgrounds, regions, religions, political parties, jobs, social statuses, levels of wealth, and genders.

The popularity of football, particularly professional football, depends directly on the mass media, especially television. Is football, with its territorial incursion, hard hitting, and violence—occasionally resulting in injury—popular because Americans are violent people? Are football spectators vicariously realizing their own hostile and aggressive tendencies? Anthropologist W. Arens (1981) discounts this interpretation. He points out that football is a peculiarly American pastime. Although a similar game is played in Canada, it is less popular there. Baseball has become a popular sport in the Caribbean, parts of Latin America, and Japan. Basketball and volleyball are also spreading. However, throughout most of the world, soccer is the most popular sport. Arens argues that if football were a particularly effective channel for expressing aggression, it would have spread (like soccer and baseball) to many other countries, where people have as many aggressive tendencies and hostile feelings as Americans do. Furthermore, he suggests that if a sport's popularity rested simply on a bloodthirsty temperament, boxing, a far bloodier sport, would be America's national pastime. Arens concludes that the explanation for the sport's popularity lies elsewhere, and I agree.

He contends that football is popular because it symbolizes certain key features of American life. In particular, it is characterized by teamwork based on elaborate specialization and division of labor, which are pervasive features of modern life. Susan Montague and Robert Morais (1981) take the analysis a step further. They argue that Americans appreciate football because it presents a miniaturized and simplified version of modern organizations. People have trouble understanding organizational bureaucracies, whether in business, universities, or government. Football, the anthropologists argue, helps us understand how decisions are made and rewards are allocated in organizations.

Montague and Morais link football's values, particularly teamwork, to those associated with business. Like corporate workers, the ideal players are diligent and dedicated to the team. Within corporations, however, decision making is complicated, and workers aren't always rewarded for their dedication and good job performance. Decisions are simpler and rewards are more consistent in football, these anthropologists contend, and this helps explain its popularity. Even if we can't figure out how Citibank and IBM run, any fan can become an expert on football's rules, teams, scores, statistics, and patterns of play. Even more important, football suggests that the values stressed by business really do pay off. Teams whose members work hardest, show the most spirit, and best develop and coordinate their talents can be expected to win more often than other teams do.

STAR TREK AS A SUMMATION OF DOMINANT CULTURAL THEMES*

Star Trek, a familiar, powerful, and enduring force in American popular culture, can be used to illustrate the idea that popular media content often is derived from prominent values expressed in many other domains of culture. Americans first encountered the Starship *Enterprise* on NBC in 1966. *Star Trek* was shown in prime time for just three seasons. However, the series not only survives but thrives today in syndication, reruns, books, cassettes, and theatrical films. Revived as a regular weekly series with an entirely new cast in 1987, *Star Trek: The Next Generation* became the third most popular syndicated program in the United States (after *Wheel of Fortune* and *Jeopardy*). *Deep Space Nine* and *Voyager* have been somewhat less popular successors in the *Star Trek* family.

What does the enduring mass appeal of *Star Trek* tell us about American culture? I believe the answer to be this: *Star Trek* is a transformation of a fundamental American origin myth. The same myth shows up in the image and celebration of Thanksgiving, a distinctively American holiday. Thanksgiving sets the myth in the past, and *Star Trek* sets it in the future.

When they encounter the word *myth,* most Americans probably think of stories about Greek, Roman, or Norse gods and heroes. However, all societies have myths. Their central characters need not be unreal, superhuman, or physically immortal. Such tales may be rooted in actual historical events.

> The popular notion that a "myth" is . . . "untrue"—indeed that its untruth is its defining characteristic—is not only naive but shows misunderstanding of its very nature. Its "scientific truth" or otherwise is irrelevant. A myth is a statement about society and man's place in it and the surrounding universe. (Middleton, ed. 1967, p. x)

Myths are hallowed stories that express fundamental cultural values. They are widely and recurrently told among, and have special meaning to, people who grow up in a particular culture. Myths may be set in the past, present, or future or in "fan-tasyland." Whether set in "real time" or fictional time, myths are always at least partly fictionalized.

The myths of contemporary America are drawn from a variety of sources, including such popular-culture fantasies as *Star Wars, The Wizard of Oz* (see below), and *Star Trek.* Our myths also include real people, particularly national ancestors, whose lives have been reinterpreted and endowed with special meaning over the generations. The media, schools, churches, communities, and parents teach the national origin myths to American children. The story of Thanksgiving, for example, continues to be important. It recounts the origin of a national holiday celebrated by Protestants, Catholics, and Jews. All those denominations share a belief in the Old Testament God, and they find it appropriate to thank God for their blessings.

Again and again Americans have heard idealized retellings of that epochal early harvest. We have learned how Indians taught the Pilgrims to farm in the New World. Grateful Pilgrims then invited the Indians to share their first Thanksgiving. Native American and European labor, techniques, and customs thus blended in that initial biethnic celebration. Annually reenacting the origin myth, the American public schools commemorate "the first Thanksgiving" as children dress up as Pilgrims, Indians, and pumpkins.

More rapidly and pervasively as the mass media grow, each generation of Americans writes its own revisionist history. Our culture constantly reinterprets the origin, nature, and meaning of national holidays. The collective consciousness of contemporary Americans includes TV-saturated memories of "the first Thanksgiving" and "the first Christmas." Our mass culture has instilled the widely shared images of a *Peanuts*-peopled Pilgrim-and-Indian "love-in."

We also conjure up a fictionalized Nativity with Mary, Joseph, Jesus, manger animals, shepherds, three eastern kings, a little drummer boy, and, in some versions, Rudolph the Red-Nosed Reindeer. Note that the interpretation of the Nativity that American culture perpetuates is yet another variation on the same dominant myth. We remember the Nativity as a Thanksgiving involving interethnic contacts (e.g., the three kings) and gift giving. It is set in Bethlehem rather than Massachusetts.

We impose our present on the past as we reinterpret quasi-historic and actual events. For the future

---

*This section is adapted from *Prime-Time Society: An Anthropological Analysis of Television and Culture* by Conrad Phillip Kottak. © 1990 by Wadsworth, Inc. Used by permission of the publisher.

we do it in our science-fiction and fantasy creations. *Star Trek* places in the future what the Thanksgiving story locates in the past—*the myth of the assimilationist, incorporating, melting-pot society.* The myth says that America is distinctive not just because it is assimilationist but because it is *founded* on unity in diversity. (Our *origin* is unity in diversity. After all, we call ourselves "the United States.") Thanksgiving and *Star Trek* illustrate the credo that unity through diversity is essential for survival (whether of a harsh winter or of the perils of outer space). Americans survive by sharing the fruits of specialization.

Star Trek proclaims that the sacred principles that validate American society, because they lie at its foundation, will endure across the generations and even the centuries. The Starship *Enterprise* crew is a melting pot. Captain James Tiberius Kirk is symbolic of real history. His clearest historical prototype is Captain James Cook, whose ship, the *Endeavor,* also sought out new life and civilizations. Kirk's infrequently mentioned middle name, from the Roman general and eventual emperor, links the captain to the earth's imperial history. Kirk is also symbolic of the original Anglo-American. He runs the *Enterprise* (America is founded on free enterprise), just as the laws, values, and institutions derived from England continue to run the United States.

McCoy's Irish (or at least Gaelic) name represents the next wave, the established immigrant. Sulu is the successfully assimilated Asian-American. The African-American female character Uhura, "whose name means freedom," indicates that blacks will become full partners with all other Americans. However, Uhura was the only major female character in the original crew. Female extradomestic employment was less characteristic of American society in 1966 than it is now.

One of *Star Trek*'s constant messages is that strangers, even enemies, can become friends. Less obviously, this message is about cultural imperialism, the assumed irresistibility of American culture and institutions. Soviet nationals (Chekhov) could be seduced and captured by an expansive American culture. Spock, although from Vulcan, is half human, with human qualities. We learn, therefore, that our assimilationist values will eventually not just rule the earth but extend to other planets as well. By "the next generation," Klingons, even more alien

than Vulcans, and personified by Bridge Officer Worf, have joined the melting pot.

Even God is harnessed to serve American culture, in the person of Scotty. His role is that of the ancient Greek *deus ex machina.* He is a stage controller who "beams" people up and down, back and forth, from earth to the heavens. Scotty, who keeps society going, is also a servant-employee who does his engineering for management—illustrating loyalty and technical skill.

The Next Generation contains many analogues of the original characters. Several "partial people" are single-character personifications of particular human qualities represented in more complex form by the original *Star Trek* crew members. Kirk, Spock, and McCoy have all been split into multiple characters. Captain Jean-Luc Picard has the intellectual and managerial attributes of James T. Kirk. With his English accent and French name, Picard, like Kirk, draws his legitimacy from symbolic association with historic Western European empires. First Officer Riker replaces Kirk as a romantic man of action.

Spock, an alien (strange ears) who represents science, reason, and intellect, has been split in two. One half is Worf, a Klingon bridge officer whose cranial protuberances are analogous to Spock's ears. The other is Data, an android whose brain contains the sum of human knowledge. Two female characters, an empath and the ship's doctor, have replaced Dr. McCoy as the repository of healing, emotion, and feeling.

Mirroring contemporary American culture, *The Next Generation* features prominent black, female, and physically handicapped characters. An African-American actor plays the Klingon Mr. Worf. Another, LeVar Burton, appears as Geordi La Forge. Although blind, Geordi manages, through a vision-enhancing visor, to see things that other people cannot. His mechanical vision expresses the characteristic American faith in technology. So does the android, Data.

During its first year, *The Next Generation* had three prominent female characters. One was the ship's doctor, a working professional with a teenage son. Another was an empath, the ultimate "helping professional." The third was the ship's security officer.

America is more specialized, differentiated, and professional than it was in the sixties. The greater role specificity and diversity of *Next Generation* characters reflect this. Nevertheless, both series convey the central *Star Trek* message, one that dominates the culture that created them: Americans are diverse. Individual qualities, talents, and specialties divide us. However, we make our livings and survive as members of cohesive, efficient groups. We explore and advance as members of a crew, a team, an enterprise, or, most generally, a society. Our nation is founded on and endures through assimilation—effective subordination of individual differences within a smoothly functioning multiethnic team. The team is American culture. It worked in the past. It works today. It will go on working across the generations. Orderly and progressive democracy based on mutual respect is best. Inevitably, American culture will triumph over all others—by convincing and assimilating rather than conquering them. Unity in diversity guarantees human survival, and for this we should be thankful.

FANTASY FILMS AS MYTH

Techniques that anthropologists use to analyze myths can be extended to two fantasy films that most students have seen. *The Wizard of Oz* has been telecast annually for decades. *Star Wars* is one of the most popular films of all time. Both are familiar and significant cultural products with obvious mythic qualities. The contributions of the French structuralist anthropologist Claude Lévi-Strauss and the neo-Freudian psychoanalyst Bruno Bettelheim (as discussed in the religion chapter) permit the following analysis of visual fairy tales that contemporary Americans know well. I will show that *Star Wars* is a systematic structural transformation of *The Wizard of Oz*. I cannot say how many of the resemblances were conscious and how many merely express a collective unconscious that *Star Wars* writer and director George Lucas shares with other Americans through common enculturation.

The Wizard of Oz and *Star Wars* both begin in arid country, the first in Kansas and the second on the desert planet Tatooine (Table A.1). *Star Wars* changes *The Wizard*'s female hero into a boy, Luke Skywalker. Fairy tale heroes usually have short, common first names and second names that describe their origin or activity. Thus Luke, who travels aboard spaceships, is a Skywalker, while Dorothy Gale is swept off to Oz by a cyclone (a gale of wind). Dorothy leaves home with her dog, Toto,

who is pursued by and has managed to escape from a woman who in Oz becomes the Wicked Witch of the West. Luke follows his "Two-Two" (R2D2), who is fleeing Darth Vader, the witch's structural equivalent.

Dorothy and Luke each live with an uncle and an aunt. However, because of the gender change of the hero, the primary relationship is reversed and inverted. Thus Dorothy's relationship with her aunt is primary, warm, and loving, whereas Luke's relationship with his uncle, though primary, is strained and distant. Aunt and uncle are in the tales for the same reason. They represent home (the nuclear family of orientation), which children (according to American culture norms) must eventually leave to make it on their own. As Bettelheim (1975) points out, fairy tales often disguise parents as uncle and aunt, and this establishes social distance. The child can deal with the hero's separation (in *The Wizard of Oz*) or the aunt's and uncle's death (in *Star Wars*) more easily than with the death of or separation from real parents. Furthermore, this permits the child's strong feelings toward his or her real parents to be represented in different, more central characters, such as the Wicked Witch of the West and Darth Vader.

Both films focus on the child's relationship with the parent of the same sex, dividing that parent into three parts. In *The Wizard*, the mother is split into two parts bad and one part good. They are the Wicked Witch of the East, dead at the beginning of the movie; the Wicked Witch of the West, dead at the end; and Glinda, the good mother, who survives. The first *Star Wars* films reversed the proportion of good and bad, giving Luke a good father (his own), the Jedi knight who is proclaimed dead at the film's beginning. There is another good father, Ben Kenobi, who is ambiguously dead when the movie ends. Third is a father figure of total evil, Darth Vader. As the good-mother third survives *The Wizard of Oz*, the bad-father third lives on after *Star Wars*, to strike back in the sequel.

The child's relationship with the parent of the opposite sex is also represented in the two films. Dorothy's father figure is the Wizard of Oz, an initially terrifying figure who later is proved to be a fake. Bettelheim notes that the typical fairy tale father is disguised as a monster or giant or else (when preserved as a human) is weak, distant, or ineffective. Children wonder why Cinderella's father lets

Table A.1 Star Wars *as a Structural Transformation of* The Wizard of Oz

Star Wars	*The Wizard of Oz*
Male hero (Luke Skywalker)	Female hero (Dorothy Gale)
Arid Tatooine	Arid Kansas

Luke follows R2D2:
    R2D2 flees Vader
	Dorothy follows Toto:
	    Toto flees witch

Luke lives with uncle and aunt:
    Primary relationship with uncle (same sex as hero)
    Strained, distant relationship with uncle
	Dorothy lives with uncle and aunt:
	    Primary relationship with aunt (same sex as hero)
	    Warm, close relationship with aunt

Tripartite division of same-sex parent:
    2 parts good, 1 part bad father
    Good father dead at beginning
    Good father dead (?) at end
    Bad father survives
	Tripartite division of same-sex parent:
	    2 parts bad, 1 part good mother
	    Bad mother dead at beginning
	    Bad mother dead at end
	    Good mother survives

Relationship with parent of opposite sex (Princess Leia Organa):
    Princess is unwilling captive
    Needle
    Princess is freed
	Relationship with parent of opposite sex (Wizard of Oz):
	    Wizard makes impossible demands
	    Broomstick
	    Wizard turns out to be sham

Trio of companions:
    Han Solo, C3PO, Chewbacca
	Trio of companions:
	    Scarecrow, Tin Woodman, Cowardly Lion

Minor characters:
    Jawas
    Sand People
    Stormtroopers
	Minor characters:
	    Munchkins
	    Apple Trees
	    Flying Monkeys

Settings:
    Death Star
    Verdant Tikal (rebel base)
	Settings:
	    Witch's castle
	    Emerald City

Conclusion:
    Luke uses magic to accomplish goal (destroy Death Star)
	Conclusion:
	    Dorothy uses magic to accomplish goal (return to Kansas)

her be treated badly by her stepmother and stepsisters, why the father of Hansel and Gretel does not throw out his new wife instead of his children, and why Snow White's father doesn't tell the queen she's narcissistic. Dorothy counts on the wizard to save her but finds that he makes seemingly impossible demands and in the end is just an ordinary man. She succeeds on her own, no longer relying on a father who offers no more than she herself possesses.

In *Star Wars* (although not in the later films in the trilogy), Luke's mother figure is Princess Leia Organa. Bettelheim notes that boys commonly fantasize their mothers to be unwilling captives of their fathers, and fairy tales often disguise mothers as princesses whose freedom the boy-hero must obtain. In graphic Freudian imagery, Darth Vader threatens Princess Leia with a needle the size of the witch's broomstick. By the end of the film, Luke has freed Leia and defeated Vader.

There are other striking parallels in the structure of the two films. Fairy tale heroes are often accompanied on their adventures by secondary characters who personify the virtues needed in a successful quest. Dorothy takes along wisdom (the Scarecrow), love (the Tin Woodman), and courage (the Lion). *Star Wars* includes a structurally equivalent trio—Han Solo, C3PO, and Chewbacca—but their association with particular qualities is not as precise. The minor characters are also structurally parallel: Munchkins and Jawas, Apple Trees and Sand People, Flying Monkeys and Stormtroopers. And compare settings—the witch's castle and the Death Star, the Emerald City and the rebel base. The endings are also parallel. Luke accomplishes his objective on his own, using the Force (Oceanian mana, magical power). Dorothy's aim is to return to Kansas. She does that by tapping her shoes together and drawing on the Force in her ruby slippers.

All successful cultural products blend old and new, drawing on familiar themes. They rearrange them in novel ways and thus win a lasting place in the imaginations of the culture that creates or accepts them. *Star Wars* successfully used old cultural themes in novel ways, and it drew on *the* American fairy tale, one that had been available in book form since the turn of the century.

DISNEY MYTH AND RITUAL

Just as anthropological techniques developed to analyze myths also fit fantasy films, anthropology can show how an ostensibly secular activity, a visit to Walt Disney World, takes on some of the attributes of a religious pilgrimage. The North American Disney "shrines"—Disneyland in California and Walt Disney World in Florida—owe their success not just to the amusement they offer but to years of preprogramming that have influenced Americans for over half a century. Disney's creations—films, television programs, a cable TV channel, cartoons, comics, toys, and amusement parks—have been important forces in American enculturation. I will examine the Disney mythology and then look at what happens during a visit to Walt Disney World. We shall see that certain observations about religion also apply to this quasi-religious dimension of contemporary American culture.

Walt Disney, who died in 1966, was a highly successful businessman whose commercial empire was built on movies, television programs, and amusement parks. Disney products have cultural as well as commercial significance. Specifically, exposure to Disney creations (just as to *Star Wars* and *The Wizard of Oz*) has been part of Americans' common enculturation, particularly since 1937, when *Snow White and the Seven Dwarfs*, Disney's first full-length cartoon, was released. Disney products, transmitted through the mass media, provide a set of quasi-mythological symbols. Diffused worldwide, they have affected enculturation in many nations. Particularly important are the images of childhood fantasy, the cartoon characters—unusual humans and humanlike animals—that continue to be part of the mythology of American childhood.

Disney mythology shows similarities with myths of other cultures and can be analyzed in the same terms. In myths, binary oppositions (polar contrasts) are often resolved by mediating figures, entities that somehow link opposites. Consider the binary opposition between nature and culture, which is a concern of people everywhere. We know scientifically that many differences between humans and other animals are differences of degree rather than kind. However, religions and myths, for thousands of years and throughout the world, have been concerned with demonstrating just the opposite—that people stand apart from nature, that humans are unique. The opposition between people and nature has been symbolized by major attributes of culture, such as speech ("In the beginning was the word"), technology (Prometheus stole fire from the gods), thought (the soul), and knowledge (the Fall of Adam and Eve). Human knowledge of good and evil is opposed to animal innocence.

Myths often use mediating figures to resolve oppositions. Animals, for example, are given human abilities, thus bridging the opposition between culture and nature. In Genesis, a humanlike animal (a bipedal, talking, lying snake) brings culture and nature closer together. In the beginning, Adam and Eve are innocent parts of nature, yet they are unique because of their creation in God's image. The snake encourages Original Sin, which keeps humans unique, but in a far less exalted way. The punishment for eating forbidden fruit is a destiny of physical labor, a struggle with nature. That humans are a part of nature while also being different from other animals is explained by the serpent-mediator's role in the Fall. The fall of humanity is paralleled in the fall of the serpent—from culture-bearing creature to belly-crawling animal.

According to Lévi-Strauss (1967), myths often resolve an apparent contradiction. Mediating figures and events may resolve such oppositions as culture versus nature by showing that just as mythical animals can have human abilities and thus be cultural, people, while different from nature, are also part of nature. People are like animals in many ways, dependent on natural resources and participants in natural systems.

Disney creations address the culture-nature opposition. Disney conferred human attributes on his animated (from *anima*, Latin for "soul") characters. These qualities include talking, laughing, tricking, bumbling, lying, singing, making friends, and participating in family life. In most of his movies, the animals—and witches, dwarfs, fairies, mermaids, and other not-quite-human characters—deny the opposition of culture and nature by having more human qualities than the stereotypically perfect heroes and heroines do.

In *Cinderella*, for example, the nature-culture opposition is inverted (turned over, reversed). Mice—natural (undomesticated) animals that are ordinarily considered pests—are endowed with speech and other cultural attributes and become Cinderella's loyal friends. The cat, ordinarily a part of culture (domesticated), becomes a dark creature of evil who almost blocks Cinderella's transformation from domestic servant into princess. The reversal of the normal opposition—that is, cat-culture-good versus mouse-nature-bad—shows how Disney characterization overcomes the opposition between culture and nature. Similarly, just as natural animals in Disney films are depicted as cultural creatures, people are often represented as being closer to nature than they normally are. In several Disney films human actors are used to portray close relationships between children and undomesticated animals such as raccoons, foxes, bears, and wolves. Disney's choice of Kipling's *The Jungle Book* as the subject matter for a cartoon and, more recently, a live-action feature also illustrates this second means of dealing with the nature-culture opposition.

A Pilgrimage to Walt Disney World

With Disney as creator and myth maker for so many Americans, his shrines could hardly fail. In many cultures, religion focuses on sacred sites. Infertile women in Madagascar seek fecundity by spilling the blood of a rooster in front of phallic stones. Australian totems are associated with holy sites where, in mythology, totemic beings first emerged from the ground. Sacred groves provide symbolic unity for dispersed clans among the Jie of Uganda (Gulliver 1965/1974). A visit to Mecca (*haj*) is an obligation of Islam. Pilgrims seek miraculous cures at shrines such as Lourdes and Fátima, which are associated with Roman Catholicism. In the arid *sertão* of northeastern Brazil, thousands of pilgrims journey each August 6 to fulfill their vows to a wooden statue in a cave—Bom Jesus de Lapa. Similarly, but virtually every day of the year, thousands of American families travel long distances and invest significant amounts of money to experience Disneyland and Walt Disney World.

A conversation with anthropologist Alexander Moore, then of the University of Florida, first prompted me to think of Walt Disney World as analogous to religious pilgrimage centers. The behavior of the millions of Americans who visit it is comparable to that of religious pilgrims. Moore pointed out that like other shrines, Walt Disney World has an inner, sacred center and an outer, more secular domain. At Walt Disney World, appropriately enough, the inner, sacred area is known as "the Magic Kingdom."

Motels, restaurants, and campgrounds dot the approach to Disney World, becoming increasingly concentrated near the park. You enter Walt Disney World on "World Drive." You can choose between the Magic Kingdom or turnoffs to Epcot Center and the MGM Theme Park. The following analysis applies only to the Magic Kingdom. A sign on World Drive instructs you to turn to a specified radio station. A recording played continuously throughout the day gives information about where and how to park and how to proceed on the journey to the Magic Kingdom. It also promotes new Magic Kingdom activities and special attractions, such as "America on Parade" and "Senior American Days."

Travelers enter the mammoth parking lot by driving through a structure like a turnpike toll booth. As they pay the parking fee, they receive a brochure describing attractions both inside and outside the central area. (Campgrounds, lakes, islands, and an "international shopping village" are in the park's outlying areas.) Sections of the parking lot have totemlike designations—Minnie, Goofy, Pluto, and Chip 'n' Dale—each with several numbered rows. Uniformed attendants direct motorists to parking places. They make sure that cars park within the marked spaces and that every space is filled in order. As visitors emerge from their cars, they are directed to open-air trainlike buses called trams. Lest they forget where their cars are parked, they are told as they board the tram to "remember" Minnie, Pluto, or whichever mythological figure has become the temporary guardian of their vehicle. Many travelers spend the first minute of the tram ride reciting "Minnie 30, Minnie 30," memorizing the automobile's row number. Leaving the tram, visitors hurry to booths where they purchase entrance to the Magic Kingdom and its attractions ("adventures"). They then pass through turnstiles behind the ticket sales booths and prepare to be transported, by "express" monorail or ferryboat, to the Magic Kingdom itself.

Because the approach to the central area occurs in gradual stages, the division of Walt Disney World into outer, secular space and inner, sacred space is not clear-cut. Moving concentrically inward, the zones become gradually rather than abruptly more sacred. Even after one passes the parking lot and turnstiles, a zone that is still secular, with hotels, beaches, and boating areas, comes before the Magic Kingdom. This is the obviously more ordinary part of Walt Disney World, where visitors can check into hotels and eat in restaurants that recall similar places throughout the United States. The "Polynesian" architecture and decor of one of the hotel complexes aren't unusual for Sun Belt condominium communities. Nor do the white beaches, paddle boats, and water sports visible in this peripheral area suggest anything other than a typical vacationland. Although visitors have the option of taking a "local" monorail to one of the hotels, most pilgrims board the express monorail directly to the Magic Kingdom. The alternative to this futuristic mode of transportation is a more sedate ferryboat.

On the express monorail, which bridges the opposition between the secular areas and the Magic Kingdom, similarities between Disney pilgrims and participants in rites of passage are especially obvious. (Rites of passage may be transitions in space, age, or social status.) Disney pilgrims who ride the express monorail exhibit, as one might expect in a transition from secular to sacred space (a magic kingdom), many of the attributes associated with liminal states, as discussed in the chapter on religion." Like liminal periods in other passage rites, aboard the monorail all prohibitions that apply everywhere else in Disney World are intensified. In the secular areas and in the Magic Kingdom itself people may smoke and eat, and in the secular areas they can consume alcohol and go shoeless, but all these things are taboo on the monorail. Like ritual passengers, monorail riders temporarily relinquish control over their destinies. Herded like cattle into the monorail, passengers move out of ordinary space and into a time out of time in which social distinctions disappear and everyone is reduced to a common level. As the monorail departs, a disembodied voice prepares the pilgrims for what is to come, enculturating them in the lore and standards of Walt Disney World.

Symbols of rebirth at the end of liminality are typical of liminal periods. Rebirth symbolism is an aspect of the monorail ride. As the monorail speeds through the Contemporary Resort Hotel, travelers facing forward observe and pass through an enormous tiled mural that covers an entire wall. Just before the monorail reaches the hotel, but much more clearly after it emerges, travelers see Walt Disney World's primary symbol—Cinderella's castle. The sudden emergence from the mural into full view of the Magic Kingdom is a simulation of rebirth.

Within the Magic Kingdom

Once the monorail pulls into the Magic Kingdom station, the transition is complete. Passengers are on their own. Attendants, so prominent at the other end of the line, are conspicuously absent. Walking down a ramp, travelers pass through another turnstile; a transit building where lockers, phones, rest rooms, strollers, and wheelchairs are available; and a circular open area. Soon they are in the Magic Kingdom, walking down "Main Street, U.S.A."

The Magic Kingdom itself invites comparison with shrines and rites. Pilgrims agree implicitly to constitute a temporary community, to spend a few hours or days observing the same rules, sharing experiences, and behaving alike. They share a common social status as pilgrims, waiting for hours in line and partaking in the same "adventures." Several anthropologists have argued that the major social function of rituals is to reaffirm, and thus to maintain, solidarity among members of a congregation. Victor Turner (1974) suggested that certain rituals among the Ndembu of Zambia serve a mnemonic function (they make people remember). Women's belief that they can be made ill by the spirits of their deceased matrilineal kinswomen leads them to take part in rites that remind them of their ancestors.

Similar observations can be made about Walt Disney World. Frontierland, Liberty Square, Main Street, U.S.A., Tomorrowland, Fantasyland, and Mickey's Birthdayland—the major sections of the Magic Kingdom—make us remember departed presidents (our national ancestors) and American history. They also juxtapose and link together the past, present, and future; childhood and adulthood; the real and the unreal. Many of the adventures, or rides, particularly the roller coasters, can be compared to anxiety-producing rites. Anxiety is dispelled when the pilgrims realize that they have survived simulated speeds of 90 miles an hour.

Detaching oneself from American culture, one might ask how a visitor from Madagascar would view Disney World adventures, particularly those based on fantasy. In Madagascar, as in many nonindustrial societies, witches are actual people—part of reality rather than fantasy. Peasants in Brazil and elsewhere believe in witches, werewolves, and nefarious creatures of the night. A villager from Madagascar would find it hard to understand why Americans voluntarily take rides designed to produce uncertainty and fright.

Yet the structure and attractions of the Magic Kingdom also relate to higher levels of sanctity. They represent, recall, and reaffirm not only Walt Disney's creative acts but the values of American society at large. In Liberty Square's Hall of Presidents, pilgrims silently and reverently view moving, talking lifelike dummies. Like Tanzanian rites, the Magic Kingdom makes us remember not just presidents and history but characters in children's literature such as Tom Sawyer. And, of course, we meet the cartoon characters who, in the person of costumed humans, walk around the Magic Kingdom, posing for photographs with children.

The juxtaposition of past, present, future, and fantasy symbolizes eternity. It argues that our nation, our people, our technological expertise, our beliefs, myths, and values will endure. Dress codes for employees reaffirm the stereotype of the clean-cut American. Disney propaganda uses Walt Disney World itself to illustrate what American creativity joined with technical know-how can accomplish. Students in American history are told how our ancestors carved a new land out of wilderness. Similarly, Walt Disney is presented as a mythic figure, creator of cosmos out of chaos—a structured world from the undeveloped chaos of Florida's central interior.

A few other links between Walt Disney World and religious and quasi-religious symbols and shrines should be examined. Disney World's most potent symbol is Cinderella's castle, complete with a moat where pilgrims throw coins and make wishes. On my first visit I was surprised to discover that the castle has a largely symbolic function as a trademark or logo for Walt Disney World. The castle has little utilitarian value. A few shops on the ground floor were open to the public, but the rest of the building was off limits. In interpreting Cinderella's castle, I recalled a lecture given in 1976 by British anthropologist Sir Edmund Leach. In describing the ritual surrounding his dubbing as a knight, Leach noted that Queen Elizabeth stood in front of the British throne and did not, in accordance with our stereotype of monarchs, sit on it. Leach surmised that the primary value of the throne is to represent, to make concrete, something enduring but abstract—the British sovereign's right to rule. Similarly, the most important thing about Cinderella's castle is its symbolism. It offers concrete testimony to the eternal aspects of Disney creations.

RECOGNIZING RELIGION

Some anthropologists think that rituals are distinguished from other behavior by special emotions, nonutilitarian intentions, and supernatural entities. However, other anthropologists define ritual more broadly. Writing about football, W. Arens (1981) pointed out that behavior can simultaneously have sacred and secular aspects. On one level, football is "simply a sport"; on another, it is a public ritual. Similarly, Walt Disney World, an amusement park, is on one level a mundane, secular place, but on another it assumes some of the attributes of a sacred place.

In the context of comparative religion, this isn't surprising. The French sociologist/anthropologist Émile Durkheim (1912/1961) pointed out long ago that almost everything from the sublime to the ridiculous has in some societies been treated as sacred. The distinction between sacred and profane doesn't depend on the intrinsic qualities of the sacred symbol. In Australian totemism, for example, sacred beings include such humble creatures as ducks, frogs, rabbits, and grubs, whose inherent qualities could hardly have given rise to the religious sentiment they inspire. If frogs and grubs can be elevated to a sacred level, why not Disney creations?

Many Americans believe that recreation and religion are separate domains. From my field work in Brazil and Madagascar and my reading about other societies, I believe that this separation is both ethnocentric and false. Madagascar's tomb-centered ceremonies are times when the living and the dead are joyously reunited, when people get drunk, gorge themselves, and enjoy sexual license. Perhaps the gray, sober, ascetic, and moralistic aspects of many religious events in the United States, in taking the "fun" out of religion, force us to find our religion in fun. Many Americans seek in such apparently secular contexts as amusement parks, rock concerts, and sporting events what other people find in religious rites, beliefs, and ceremonies.

Standing back from the native explanations provided by my culture, I perceive Walt Disney not merely as a commercial figure and view his amusement parks not simply as recreational domains. There is a deeper level of attachment between Americans and Disney creations. The implication is not that this constitutes a religion, although there are parallels with passage rites and religious pilgrimages. There is no doubt, however, that Disney, his parks, and his creations do constitute powerful enculturative forces in the contemporary United States.

RITUALS AT McDONALD'S

Each day, on the average, a new McDonald's restaurant opens somewhere in the world. The number of McDonald's outlets today far surpasses the total number of all fast-food restaurants in the United States in 1945. McDonald's has grown from a single hamburger stand in San Bernardino, California, into today's international web of thousands of outlets. Have factors less obvious to American natives than relatively low cost, fast service, and taste contributed to McDonald's success? Could it be that natives—in consuming the products and propaganda of McDonald's—are not just eating but experiencing something comparable in certain respects to participation in religious rituals? To answer this question we must briefly review the nature of ritual.

Rituals, we know from the chapter on religion, are formal—stylized, repetitive, and stereotyped. They are performed in special places at set times. Rituals include liturgical orders—set sequences of words and actions laid down by someone other than the current performers. Rituals also convey information about participants and their cultural traditions. Performed year after year, generation after generation, rituals translate messages, values, and sentiments into action. Rituals are social acts. Inevitably, some participants are more strongly committed than others are to the beliefs on which the rituals are founded. However, just by taking part in a joint public act, people signal that they accept an order that transcends their status as mere individuals.

For many years, like millions of other Americans, I have occasionally eaten at McDonald's. Eventually I began to notice certain ritual-like aspects of Americans' behavior at these fast-food restaurants. Tell your fellow Americans that going to McDonald's is similar in some ways to going to church and their bias as natives will reveal itself in laughter, denial, or questions about your sanity. Just as football is a game, *Star Wars* a movie, and Walt Disney World an amusement park, McDonald's, for natives, is just a place to eat. However, an analysis of what natives do at McDonald's will reveal a very high degree of formal, uniform behavior by staff members and customers alike. It is particularly interesting that this invariance in word and deed has developed without any theological doctrine. McDonald's ritual aspect is founded on twentieth-century technology, particularly automobiles, television, work away from home, and the short lunch break. It is striking nevertheless that one commercial organization should be so much more successful than other businesses, the schools, the military, and even many religions in producing behavioral invariance. Factors other than lost cost, fast service, and the taste of the food—all of which are approximated by other chains—have contributed to our acceptance of McDonald's and adherence to its rules.

Remarkably, when Americans travel abroad, even in countries noted for good food, many visit the local McDonald's outlet. The same factors that lead us to frequent McDonald's at home are responsible. Because Americans are thoroughly familiar with how to eat and more or less what they will pay at McDonald's, in its outlets overseas they have a home away from home. In Paris, whose people aren't known for making tourists, particularly Americans, feel at home, McDonald's offers sanctuary. It is, after all, an American institution, where natives, programmed by years of prior experience, can feel completely at home. Given its international spread, McDonald's is no longer merely an American institution—a fact that McDonald's advertising has not ignored. A TV commercial linked to the 1996 Olympics (of which McDonald's was an "official sponsor") portrayed an Asian athlete finding sanctuary from an alien American culture at a Mc-

Donald's restaurant in Atlanta. For her, the ad proclaimed, McDonald's was home-culture turf.

This devotion to McDonald's rests in part on uniformities associated with its outlets: food, setting, architecture, ambience, acts, and utterances. The McDonald's symbol, the golden arches, is an almost universal landmark, as familiar to Americans as Mickey Mouse, Mr. Rogers, and the flag. A McDonald's near my university (recently closed) was a brick structure whose stained-glass windows had golden arches as their central theme. Sunlight flooded in through a skylight that was like the clerestory of a church.

Americans enter a McDonald's restaurant for an ordinary, secular act—eating. However, the surroundings tell us that we are somehow apart from the variability of the world outside. We know what we are going to see, what we are going to say, and what will be said to us. We know what we will eat, how it will taste, and how much it will cost. Behind the counter, agents wear similar attire. Permissible utterances by customer and worker are written above the counter. Throughout the United States, with only minor variation, the menu is in the same place, contains the same items, and has the same prices. The food, again with only minor regional variation, is prepared according to plan and varies little in taste. Obviously, customers are limited to what they can choose. Less obviously, they are limited in what they can say. Each item has its appropriate designation: "large fry," "quarter pounder with cheese." The novice who innocently asks, "What kind of hamburgers do you have?" or "What's a Big Mac?" is out of place.

Other ritual phrases are uttered by the person behind the counter. After the customer has completed an order, if no potatoes are requested, the agent ritually asks, "Any fries?" Once food is presented and picked up, the agent conventionally says, "Have a nice day." (McDonald's has surely played a strong role in the diffusion of this cliché into every corner of contemporary American life.) Nonverbal behavior is also programmed. As customers request food, agents look back to see if the desired sandwich item is available. If not, they tell you, "That'll be a few minutes," and prepare your drink. After this a proper agent will take the order of the next customer in line. McDonald's lore and customs are even taught at a "seminary" called Hamburger University in Illinois. Managers who attend the program pass on what they learn to the people who work in their restaurants.

It isn't simply the formality and regularity of behavior at McDonald's but its total ambience that invites comparison with sacred places. Like the Disney organization, McDonald's image makers stress clean living and draw on an order of values—"traditional American values"—that transcends McDonald's itself. Agents submit to dress codes. Kitchens, grills, and counters sparkle. Understandably, as the world's number-one fast-food chain, McDonald's has also evoked hostility. In 1975 the Ann Arbor campus McDonald's was the scene of a ritual rebellion—desecration by the Radical Vegetarian League, which held a "puke-in." Standing on the second-story balcony just below the clerestory, a dozen vegetarians gorged themselves on mustard and water and vomited down on the customer waiting area. McDonald's, defiled, lost many customers that day.

The formality and invariance of behavior in a demarcated setting suggest analogies between McDonald's and rituals. Furthermore, as in a ritual, participation in McDonald's occurs at specified times. In American culture our daily food consumption is supposed to occur as three meals: breakfast, lunch, and dinner. Americans who have traveled abroad are aware that cultures differ in which meal they emphasize. In many countries, the midday meal is primary. Americans are away from home at lunchtime because of their jobs and usually take less than an hour for lunch. They view dinner as the main meal. Lunch is a lighter meal symbolized by the sandwich. McDonald's provides relatively hot and fresh sandwiches and a variety of subsidiary fare that many American palates can tolerate.

The ritual of eating at McDonald's is confined to ordinary, everyday life. Eating at McDonald's and religious feasts are in complementary distribution in American life. That is, when one occurs, the other doesn't. Most Americans would consider it inappropriate to eat at a fast-food restaurant on Christmas, Thanksgiving, Easter, or Passover. Our culture regards these as family days, occasions when relatives and close friends get together. However, although Americans neglect McDonald's on holidays, television reminds us that McDonald's still endures, that it will welcome us back once our holiday is over. The television presence of McDonald's is particularly obvious on such occasions—whether through a float in the Macy's Thanksgiving Day parade or through sponsorship of special programs, particularly "family entertainment."

Although Burger King, Wendy's, and Arby's compete with McDonald's for the fast-food business, none rivals McDonald's success. The explanation may lie in the particularly skillful ways in which McDonald's advertising plays up the features just discussed. Its commercials are varied to appeal to different audiences. On Saturday morning television, with its steady stream of cartoons, McDonald's is a ubiquitous sponsor. The commercials for children's shows usually differ from the ones adults see in the evening and on sports programs. Children are reminded of McDonald's through fantasy characters, headed by clown Ronald McDonald. Children can meet "McDonaldland" characters again at outlets. Their pictures appear on cookie boxes and plastic cups. Children also have a chance to meet Ronald McDonald as actors scatter visits throughout the country. One can even rent a Ronald for a birthday party.

Adult advertising has different but equally effective themes. Breakfast at McDonald's has been promoted by a fresh-faced, sincere, happy, clean-cut young woman. Healthy, clean-living Americans gambol on ski slopes or in mountain pastures. The single theme, however, that for years has run through the commercials is personalism. McDonald's, the commercials drone on, is something other than a fast-food restaurant. It's a warm, friendly place where you are graciously welcomed and feel at home, where your children won't get into trouble. McDonald's commercials tell you that you aren't simply an anonymous face in an amorphous crowd. You find respite from a hectic and impersonal society, the break you deserve. Your individuality and dignity are respected at McDonald's.

McDonald's advertising tries to deemphasize the fact that the chain is a commercial organization. One jingle proclaimed "You, you're the one; we're fixin' breakfast for ya"—not "We're making millions off ya." Commercials make McDonald's seem like a charitable organization by stressing its program of community good works. "Family" television entertainment such as the film *The Sound of Music* is "brought to you by McDonald's." McDonald's commercials regularly tell us that it supports and works to maintain the values of American family life.

As with the Disney organization, the argument here is not that McDonald's has become a religion. Rather, I am suggesting that specific ways in which Americans participate in McDonald's bear analogies to religious systems involving myth, symbol, and ritual. Just as in rituals, participation in McDonald's requires temporary subordination of individual differences in a social and cultural collectivity. In a land of ethnic, social, economic, and religious diversity, we demonstrate that we share something with millions of other Americans. Furthermore, as in rituals, participation in McDonald's is linked to a cultural system that transcends the chain itself. By eating there, we say something about ourselves as Americans, about our acceptance of certain collective values and ways of living. By returning to McDonald's, we affirm that certain values and life styles, developed through the collective experience of Americans before us, will continue.

ANTHROPOLOGY AND AMERICAN "POP" CULTURE

The examples considered in this Appendix are shared cultural forms that have appeared and spread rapidly during the twentieth century because of major changes in the material conditions of American life—particularly work organization, communication, and transportation. Most contemporary Americans deem at least one automobile a necessity. Televisions outnumber toilets in American households. Through the mass media, institutions such as sports, movies, TV shows, amusement parks, and fast-food restaurants have become powerful elements of American national culture. They provide a framework of common expectations, experiences, and behavior overriding differences in region, class, formal religious affiliation, political sentiments, gender, ethnic group, and place of residence. Although some of us may not like these changes, it's difficult to deny their significance.

The rise of these institutions is linked not just to the mass media but also to decreasing participation in traditional religion and the weakening of ties based on kinship, marriage, and community within industrial society. Neither a single church, nor a strong central government, nor segmentary lineage organization unites most Americans. Unification through the mass media and consumption opens a new chapter in the exploration of cultural diversity.

These dimensions of contemporary culture are dismissed as passing, trivial, or "pop" by some. However, because millions of people share them, they deserve and are receiving scholarly attention. Such studies help fulfill the promise that by studying anthropology, we can learn more about ourselves. Americans can view themselves not just as members of a varied and complex nation but also as a population united by distinctive shared symbols, customs, and experiences. American culture takes its place within the realm of cultural diversity. That, after all, is the subject matter of anthropology.

BIBLIOGRAPHY

ABELMANN, N., AND J. LIE
  1995 *Blue Dreams: Korean Americans and the Los Angeles Riots.* Cambridge, MA: Harvard University Press.
ADAMS, R. M.
  1981 *Heartland of Cities.* Chicago: Aldine.
AGAR, M. H.
  1980 *The Professional Stranger: An Informal Introduction to Ethnography.* New York: Academic Press.
AHMED, A. S.
  1992 *Postmodernism and Islam: Predicament and Promise.* New York: Routledge.
AKAZAWA, T.
  1980 *The Japanese Paleolithic: A Techno-Typological Study.* Tokyo: Rippo Shobo.
AKAZAWA, T., AND C. M. AIKENS, EDS.
  1986 *Prehistoric Hunter-Gatherers in Japan: New Research Methods.* Tokyo: University of Tokyo Press.
ALBERT, B.
  1989 Yanomami "Violence": Inclusive Fitness or Ethnographer's Representation? *Current Anthropology* 30: 637–640.
AMADIUME, I.
  1987 *Male Daughters, Female Husbands.* Atlantic Highlands, NJ: Zed.
AMERICAN ALMANAC 1994–1995
  1994 *Statistical Abstract of the United States,* 114th ed. Austin, TX: Reference Press.
AMERICAN ANTHROPOLOGICAL ASSOCIATION
       AAA Guide: A Guide to Departments, a Directory of Members. (Formerly *Guide to Departments of Anthropology.*) Published annually by the American Anthropological Association, Washington, DC.

       Anthropology Newsletter. Published 9 times annually by the American Anthropological Association, Washington, DC.

       General Anthropology: Bulletin of the Council for General Anthropology.
AMICK III, B., S. LEVINE, A. R. TARLOV, AND D. C. WALSH, EDS.
  1995 *Society and Health.* New York: Oxford University Press.
ANDERSON, B.
  1991 *Imagined Communities: Reflections on the Origin and Spread of Nationalism,* rev. ed. London: Verso.
ANDERSON, R.
  1996 *Magic, Science, and Health: The Aims and Achievements of Medical Anthropology.* Fort Worth: Harcourt Brace.
ANN ARBOR NEWS
  1989 Population Control Key to World Hunger, Economist Says. September 10, p. C1.
AOKI, M. Y., AND M. B. DARDESS, EDS.
  1981 *As the Japanese See It: Past and Present.* Honolulu: University Press of Hawaii.
APPADURAI, A.
  1990 Disjuncture and Difference in the Global Cultural Economy. *Public Culture* 2(2):1–24.
  1991 Global Ethnoscapes: Notes and Queries for a Transnational Anthropology. In *Recapturing Anthropology: Working in the Present,*

ed. R. G. Fox, pp. 191–210. Santa Fe: School of American Research Advanced Seminar Series.

APPEL, R., AND P. MUYSKEN
1987   *Language Contact and Bilingualism.* London: Edward Arnold.

APPELL, G. N.
1978   *Ethical Dilemmas in Anthropological Inquiry: A Case Book.* Waltham, MA: Crossroads Press.

APPIAH, K. A.
1990   Racisms. In *Anatomy of Racism,* ed. David Theo Goldberg, pp. 3–17. Minneapolis: University of Minnesota Press.

ARENS, W.
1981   Professional Football: An American Symbol and Ritual. In *The American Dimension: Cultural Myths and Social Realities,* 2nd ed., eds. W. Arens and S. P. Montague, pp. 1–10. Sherman Oaks, CA: Alfred.

ARENS, W., AND S. P. MONTAGUE
1981   *The American Dimension: Cultural Myths and Social Realities,* 2nd ed. Sherman Oaks, CA: Alfred.

ARNOLD, B., AND B. GIBSON, EDS.
1995   *Celtic Chiefdom, Celtic State.* New York: Cambridge University Press.

ASHMORE, W., AND R. SHARER
1995   *Discovering Our Past: A Brief Introduction to Archaeology,* 2nd ed. Mountain View, CA: Mayfield.

BAILEY, R. C.
1990   *The Behavioral Ecology of Efe Pygmy Men in the Ituri Forest, Zaire.* Ann Arbor, MI: Anthropological Papers, Museum of Anthropology, University of Michigan, no. 86.

BAILEY, R. C., G. HEAD, M. JENIKE, B. OWEN, R. RECHTMAN, AND E. ZECHENTER
1989   Hunting and Gathering in Tropical Rain Forests: Is It Possible? *American Anthropologist* 91: 59–82.

BAKER, P. T.
1978   *The Biology of High Altitude Peoples.* New York: Cambridge University Press.

BAKER, P. T., AND J. S. WEINER, EDS.
1966   *The Biology of Human Adaptability.* Oxford: Oxford University Press.

BAKHTIN, M.
1984   *Rabelais and His World.* Translated by Helen Iswolsky. Bloomington: Indiana University Press.

BALICK, M. J., E. ELISABETSKY, AND S. A. LAIRD
1995   *Medicinal Resources of the Tropical Forest: Biodiversity and Its Importance to Human Health.* New York: Columbia University Press.

BANTON, M.
1957   *West African City. A Study in Tribal Life in Freetown.* London: Oxford University Press.

BARASH, D. P.
1982   *Sociobiology and Behavior,* 2nd ed. Amsterdam: Elsevier.

BARLETT, P. F., ED.
1980   *Agricultural Decision Making: Anthropological Contribution to Rural Development.* New York: Academic Press.

BARNARD, A.
1979   Kalahari Settlement Patterns. In *Social and Ecological Systems,* eds. P. Burnham and R. Ellen, pp. 131–144. New York: Academic Press.

BARNOUW, V.
1985   *Culture and Personality,* 4th ed. Belmont, CA: Wadsworth.

BARON, D.
1986   *Grammar and Gender.* New Haven: Yale University Press.

BARRINGER, F.
1989   32 Million Lived in Poverty in '88, a Figure Unchanged. *The New York Times,* October 19, p. 18.
1992   New Census Data Show More Children Living in Poverty. *The New York Times.* May 29, pp. A1, A12, A13.

BARRY, H., M. K. BACON, AND I. L. CHILD
1959   Relation of Child Training to Subsistence Economy. *American Anthropologist* 61: 51–63.

BARTH, F.
1968   (orig. 1958). Ecologic Relations of Ethnic Groups in Swat, North Pakistan. In *Man in Adaptation: The Cultural Present,* ed. Yehudi Cohen, pp. 324–331. Chicago: Aldine.
1969   *Ethnic Groups and Boundaries: The Social Organization of Cultural Difference.* London: Allyn and Unwin.

BAR-YOSEF, O.
1987   Pleistocene Connections between Africa and Southwest Asia: An Archaeological Perspective. *African Archaeological Review* 5: 29–38.

BATALLA, G. B.
1966   Conservative Thought in Applied Anthropology: A Critique. *Human Organization* 25: 89–92.

BEEMAN, W.
1986   *Language, Status, and Power in Iran.* Bloomington: Indiana University Press.

BEHAR, R., AND D. A. GORDON, EDS.
1995   *Women Writing Culture.* Berkeley: University of California Press.

BELL, W.
1981 Neocolonialism. In *Encyclopedia of Sociology*, p. 193. Guilford, CT: DPG Publishing.

BENEDICT, B.
1970 Pluralism and Stratification. In *Essays in Comparative Social Stratification*, eds. L. Plotnicov and A. Tuden, pp. 29–41. Pittsburgh: University of Pittsburgh Press.

BENEDICT, R.
1946 *The Chrysanthemum and the Sword*. Boston: Houghton Mifflin.
1959 (orig. 1934). *Patterns of Culture*. New York: New American Library.

BENNETT, J. W.
1969 *Northern Plainsmen: Adaptive Strategy and Agrarian Life*. Chicago: Aldine.

BENNETT, J. W., AND J. R. BOWEN, EDS.
1988 *Production and Autonomy: Anthropological Studies and Critiques of Development*. Monographs in Economic Anthropology, no. 5, Society for Economic Anthropology. New York: University Press of America.

BERLIN, B. D., E. BREEDLOVE, AND P. H. RAVEN
1974 *Principles of Tzeltal Plant Classification: An Introduction to the Botanical Ethnography of a Mayan-Speaking People of Highland Chiapas*. New York: Academic Press.

BERLIN, B. D., AND P. KAY
1969 *Basic Color Terms: Their Universality and Evolution*. Berkeley: University of California Press.
1992 *Basic Color Terms: Their Universality and Evolution*, 2nd ed. Berkeley: University of California Press.

BERNARD, H. R.
1994 *Research Methods in Anthropology, Qualitative and Quantitative Approaches*, 2nd ed. Thousand Oaks, CA: Sage.

BERREMAN, G. D.
1962 Pahari Polyandry: A Comparison. *American Anthropologist* 64: 60–75.
1975 Himalayan Polyandry and the Domestic Cycle. *American Ethnologist* 2: 127–138.

BETTELHEIM, B.
1975 *The Uses of Enchantment: The Meaning and Importance of Fairy Tales*. New York: Vintage.

BINFORD, L. R.
1968 Post-Pleistocene Adaptations. In *New Perspectives in Archeology*, ed. S. R. Binford and L. R. Binford, pp. 313–341. Chicago: Aldine.

BINFORD, L. R., AND S. R. BINFORD
1979 Stone Tools and Human Behavior. In *Human Ancestors, Readings from Scientific American*, eds. G. L. Isaac and R. E. F. Leakey, pp. 92–101. San Francisco: W. H. Freeman.

BIRD-DAVID, N.
1992 Beyond "The Original Affluent Society": A Culturalist Reformulation. *Current Anthropology* 33(1): 25–47.

BIRDSELL, J. B.
1981 *Human Evolution: An Introduction to the New Physical Anthropology*, 3rd ed. Boston: HarperCollins.

BLANTON, R. E., S. A. KOWALEWSKI, G. M. FEINMAN, AND L. M. FINSTEN, EDS.
1993 *Ancient Mesoamerica: A Comparison of Change in Three Regions*, 2nd ed. New York: Cambridge University Press.

BLOCH, M., ED.
1975 *Political Language and Oratory in Traditional Societies*. London: Academic.

BOAS, F.
1966 (orig. 1940). *Race, Language, and Culture*. New York: Free Press.

BOAZ, N. T.
1993 *Quarry: Closing In on the Missing Link*. New York: Free Press.

BOCK, P. K.
1980 *Continuities in Psychological Anthropology*. San Francisco: W. H. Freeman.

BODLEY, J. H.
1985 *Anthropology and Contemporary Human Problems*, 2nd ed. Mountain View, CA: Mayfield.
1995 *Anthropology and Contemporary Human Problems*, 3rd ed. Mountain View, CA: Mayfield.

BODLEY, J. H., ED.
1988 *Tribal Peoples and Development Issues: A Global Overview*. Mountain View, CA: Mayfield.

BOGORAS, W.
1904 The Chukchee. In *The Jesup North Pacific Expedition*, ed. F. Boas. New York: Memoir of the American Museum of Natural History.

BOGUCKI, P. I.
1988 *Forest Farmers and Stockherders: Early Agriculture and Its Consequences in North-Central Europe*. New York: Cambridge University Press.

BOHANNAN, P.
1955 Some Principles of Exchange and Investment among the Tiv. *American Anthropologist* 57: 60–70.
1995 *How Culture Works*. New York: Free Press.

BOHANNAN, P., AND J. MIDDLETON, EDS.
1968 *Marriage, Family, and Residence*. Garden City, NY: Natural History Press.

BOLTON, R.
1981 Susto, Hostility, and Hypoglycemia. *Ethnology* 20(4): 227–258.

BOND, G. C., J. KRENISKE, I. SUSSER, AND J. VINCENT, EDS.
1996 *AIDS in Africa and the Caribbean.* Boulder, CO: Westview.

BONVILLAN, N.
1993 *Language, Culture, and Communication: The Meaning of Messages.* Englewood Cliffs, NJ: Prentice-Hall.
1995 *Women and Men: Cultural Consequences of Gender.* Englewood Cliffs, NJ: Prentice-Hall.

BOSERUP, E.
1965 *The Conditions of Agricultural Growth.* Chicago: Aldine.
1970 *Women's Role in Economic Development.* London: Allen and Unwin.

BOURDIEU, P.
1977 *Outline of a Theory of Practice.* Translated by Richard Nice. Cambridge: Cambridge University Press.
1982 *Ce Que Parler Veut Dire.* Paris: Fayard.
1984 *Distinction: A Social Critique of the Judgment of Taste.* Translated by R. Nice. Cambridge, MA: Harvard University Press.

BOURGUIGNON, E.
1979 *Psychological Anthropology: An Introduction to Human Nature and Cultural Differences.* New York: Harcourt Brace Jovanovich.

BOURQUE, S. C., AND K. B. WARREN
1981 *Women of the Andes: Patriarchy and Social Change in Two Peruvian Villages.* Ann Arbor: University of Michigan Press.
1987 Technology, Gender and Development. *Daedalus* 116(4): 173–197.

BOWER, J., AND D. LUBELL, EDS.
1988 *Prehistoric Cultures and Environments in the Late Quaternary of Africa.* Cambridge Monographs in African Archaeology, 26. Oxford, England: B.A.R.

BRACE, C. L.
1964 A Nonracial Approach towards the Understanding of Human Diversity. In *The Concept of Race,* ed. A. Montagu, pp. 103–152. New York: Free Press.
1995 *The Stages of Human Evolution,* 5th ed. Englewood Cliffs, NJ: Prentice-Hall.

BRACE, C. L., AND F. B. LIVINGSTONE
1971 On Creeping Jensenism. In *Race and Intelligence,* eds. C. L. Brace, G. R. Gamble, and J. T. Bond, pp. 64–75. Anthropological Studies, no. 8. Washington, DC: American Anthropological Association.

BRADLEY, C., C. MOORE, M. BURTON, AND D. WHITE
1990 A Cross-Cultural Historical Analysis of Subsistence Change. *American Anthropologist* 92(2): 447–457.

BRADY, I., ED.
1983 Special Section: Speaking in the Name of the Real: Freeman and Mead on Samoa. *American Anthropologist* 85: 908–947.

BRAIDWOOD, R. J.
1975 *Prehistoric Men,* 8th ed. Glenview, IL: Scott, Foresman.

BRAUDEL, F.
1973 *Capitalism and Material Life: 1400–1800.* Translated by M. Kochan. London: Weidenfeld and Nicolson.
1981 *Civilization and Capitalism, 15th–18th Century, Volume I: The Structure of Everyday Life: The Limits.* Translated by S. Reynolds. New York: Harper & Row.
1982 *Civilization and Capitalism, 15th–18th Century, Volume II: The Wheels of Commerce.* New York: HarperCollins.
1984 *Civilization and Capitalism, 15th–18th Century, Volume III: The Perspective of the World.* New York: HarperCollins.

BRENNEIS, D.
1988 Language and Disputing. *Annual Review of Anthropology* 17: 221–237.

BRIM, J. A., AND D. H. SPAIN
1974 *Research Design in Anthropology.* New York: Harcourt Brace Jovanovich.

BROGGER, J.
1992 *Nazaré: Women and Men in a Prebureaucratic Portuguese Fishing Village.* Fort Worth: Harcourt Brace.

BRONFENBRENNER, U.
1975 Nature with Nurture: A Reinterpretation of the Evidence. In *Race and IQ,* ed. A. Montagu, pp. 114–144. New York: Oxford University Press.

BROOKE, J.
1992 Rio's New Day in Sun Leaves Laplander Limp. *The New York Times,* June 1, p. A7.

BROWN, D.
1991 *Human Universals.* New York: McGraw-Hill.

BROWN, J. K.
1975 Iroquois Women: An Ethnohistoric Note. In *Toward an Anthropology of Women,* ed. R. Reiter, pp. 235–251. New York: Monthly Review Press.

BROWN, K. M.
1991 *Mama Lola: A Vodou Priestess in Brooklyn.* Berkeley: University of California Press.

BROWN, R. W.
1958 *Words and Things.* Glencoe, IL: Free Press.

BRUMFIEL, E. M.
1980 Specialization, Market Exchange, and the Aztec State: A View from Huexotla. *Current Anthropology* 21(4): 459–478.

BRYANT, B., AND P. MOHAI
    1991   Race, Class, and Environmental Quality in the Detroit Area. In *Environmental Racism: Issues and Dilemmas,* eds. Bryant and Mohai. Ann Arbor: University of Michigan Office of Minority Affairs.

BUCHLER, I. R., AND H. A. SELBY
    1968   *Kinship and Social Organization: An Introduction to Theory and Method.* New York: Macmillan.

BURKE, P., AND R. PORTER
    1987   *The Social History of Language.* Cambridge: Cambridge University Press.

BURLING, R.
    1970   *Man's Many Voices: Language in Its Cultural Context.* New York: Harcourt Brace Jovanovich.

BURNS, J. F.
    1992a   Bosnian Strife Cuts Old Bridges of Trust. *The New York Times,* May 22, pp. A1, A6.
    1992b   A Serb, Fighting Serbs, Defends Sarajevo. *The New York Times,* July 12, Section 4, p. E3.

BURTON, F. D., AND M. EATON
    1995a   *The Multimedia Guide to Non-Human Primates.* Englewood Cliffs, NJ: Prentice-Hall. A CD-ROM combining photos, illustrations, video, sound, and text—presenting over 200 species of nonhuman primates.
    1995b   *The Guide to Non-Human Primates.* Englewood Cliffs, NJ: Prentice-Hall. The print version of the above.

CAMPBELL, B. G., AND J. D. LOY
    1996   *Humankind Emerging.* New York: Harper-Collins.

CANN, R. L., M. STONEKING, AND A. C. WILSON
    1987   Mitochondrial DNA and Human Evolution. *Nature* 325: 31–36.

CARNEIRO, R. L.
    1956   Slash-and-Burn Agriculture: A Closer Look at Its Implications for Settlement Patterns. In *Men and Cultures,* Selected Papers of the Fifth International Congress of Anthropological and Ethnological Sciences, pp. 229–234. Philadelphia: University of Pennsylvania Press.
    1968   (orig. 1961). Slash-and-Burn Cultivation among the Kuikuru and Its Implications for Cultural Development in the Amazon Basin. In *Man in Adaptation: The Cultural Present,* ed. Y. A. Cohen, pp. 131–145. Chicago: Aldine.
    1970   A Theory of the Origin of the State. *Science* 69: 733–738.

CARRIER, J.
    1995   *De Los Otros: Intimacy and Homosexuality among Mexican Men: Hidden in the Blood.* New York: Columbia University Press.

CARTER, J.
    1988   Freed from Keepers and Cages, Chimps Come of Age on Baboon Island. *Smithsonian,* June, pp. 36–48.

CARVER, T.
    1995   *Gender Is Not a Synonym for Women.* Boulder, CO: Lynne Reinner.

CASSON, R.
    1983   Schemata in Cognitive Anthropology. *Annual Review of Anthropology* 12: 429–462.

CAVALLI-SFORZA, L. L.
    1977   *Elements of Human Genetics,* 2nd ed. Menlo Park, CA: W. A. Benjamin.

CERNEA, M., ED.
    1991   *Putting People First: Sociological Variables in Rural Development,* 2nd ed. New York: Oxford University Press (published for The World Bank).

CHAGNON, N.
    1992   (orig. 1983). *Yanomamo: The Fierce People,* 4th ed. New York: Harcourt Brace.

CHAGNON, N. A., AND W. IRONS, EDS.
    1979   *Evolutionary Biology and Human Social Behavior: An Anthropological Perspective.* North Scituate, MA: Duxbury.

CHAMPION, T., AND C. GAMBLE, EDS.
    1984   *Prehistoric Europe.* New York: Academic Press.

CHANG, K. C.
    1977   *The Archaeology of Ancient China.* New Haven: Yale University Press.

CHATTY, D.
    1996   *Mobile Pastoralists: Development Planning and Social Change in Oman.* New York: Columbia University Press.

CHENEY, D. L., AND R. M. SEYFARTH
    1990   In the Minds of Monkeys: What Do They Know and How Do They Know It? *Natural History,* September, pp. 38–46.

CHENEY, D. L., R. M. SEYFARTH, B. B. SMUTS, AND R. W. WRANGHAM
    1987   The Study of Primate Societies. In *Primate Societies,* eds. B. B. Smuts, D. L. Cheney, R. M. Seyfarth, R. W. Wrangham, and T. T. Struhsaker, pp. 1–8. Chicago: University of Chicago Press.

CHILD, A. B., AND I. L. CHILD
    1993   *Religion and Magic in the Lives of Traditional Peoples.* Englewood Cliffs, NJ: Prentice-Hall.

CHOMSKY, N.
    1957   *Syntactic Structures.* The Hague: Mouton.

CIOCHON, R. L.
    1983   Hominoid Cladistics and the Ancestry of Modern Apes and Humans. In *New Interpretations of Ape and Human Ancestry,* eds. R. L. Ciochon and R. S. Corruccini, pp. 783–843. New York: Plenum.

CLAMMER, J., ED.
1976 *The New Economic Anthropology.* New York: St. Martin's.

CLARK, J. D., AND S. A. BRANDT
1984 *From Hunters to Farmers: The Causes and Consequences of Food Production in Africa.* Berkeley: University of California Press.

CLIFFORD, J.
1982 *Person and Myth: Maurice Leenhardt in the Melanesian World.* Berkeley: University of California Press.

1988 *The Predicament of Culture: Twentieth-Century Ethnography, Literature, and Art.* Cambridge: Harvard University Press.

CLIFTON, J. A.
1970 *Applied Anthropology: Readings in the Uses of the Science of Man.* Boston: Houghton Mifflin.

COATES, J.
1986 *Women, Men, and Language.* London: Longman.

COE, M. D., AND K. FLANNERY
1964 Microenvironments and Mesoamerican Prehistory. *Science* 143: 650–654.

COHEN, M. N., AND G. J. ARMELAGOS, EDS.
1984 *Paleopathology at the Origins of Agriculture.* New York: Academic Press.

COHEN, ROGER
1995 Serbs Shift Opens a Chance for Peace, a U.S. Envoy Says. *The New York Times,* September 1, pp. A1, A6.

COHEN, RONALD
1967 *The Kanuri of Bornu.* New York: Harcourt Brace Jovanovich.

COHEN, R., AND E. R. SERVICE, EDS.
1978 *Origins of the State: The Anthropology of Political Evolution.* Philadelphia: Institute for the Study of Human Issues.

COHEN, Y.
1974a *Man in Adaptation: The Cultural Present,* 2nd ed. Chicago: Aldine.

1974b Culture as Adaptation. In *Man in Adaptation: The Cultural Present,* 2nd ed., ed. Y. A. Cohen, pp. 45–68. Chicago: Aldine.

COLE, S.
1975 *Leakey's Luck: The Life of Louis Bazett Leakey, 1903–1972.* New York: Harcourt Brace Jovanovich.

COLLIER, J. F., ED.
1988 *Marriage and Inequality in Classless Societies.* Stanford: Stanford University Press.

COLLIER, J. F., AND S. J. YANAGISAKO, EDS.
1987 *Gender and Kinship: Essays toward a Unified Analysis.* Stanford, CA: Stanford University Press.

COLLINS, T. W.
1989 Rural Economic Development in Two Tennessee Counties: A Racial Dimension. Paper presented at the annual meetings of the American Anthropological Association, Washington, DC.

COLSON, E., AND T. SCUDDER
1975 New Economic Relationships between the Gwembe Valley and the Line of Rail. In *Town and Country in Central and Eastern Africa,* ed. David Parkin, pp. 190–210. London: Oxford University Press.

1988 *For Prayer and Profit: The Ritual, Economic, and Social Importance of Beer in Gwembe District, Zambia, 1950–1982.* Stanford, CA: Stanford University Press.

COMAROFF, J.
1982 Dialectical Systems, History and Anthropology: Units of Study and Questions of Theory. *Journal of Southern African Studies* 8: 143–172.

COMBS-SCHILLING, E.
1989 *Sacred Performances: Islam, Sexuality, and Sacrifice.* New York: Columbia University Press.

CONKLIN, H. C.
1954 *The Relation of Hanunóo Culture to the Plant World.* Unpublished Ph.D. dissertation, Yale University.

CONNAH, G.
1987 *African Civilizations.* New York: Cambridge University Press.

CONNELL, R. W.
1995 *Masculinities.* Berkeley: University of California Press.

CONNOR, W.
1972 Nation-Building or Nation Destroying. *World Politics* 24(3): 319–355.

COOK-GUMPERZ, J.
1986 *The Social Construction of Literacy.* Cambridge: Cambridge University Press.

COOPER, F., AND A. L. STOLER
1989 Introduction, Tensions of Empire: Colonial Control and Visions of Rule. *American Ethnologist* 16: 609–621.

CRICK, F. H. C.
1968 (orig. 1962). The Genetic Code. In *The Molecular Basis of Life: An Introduction to Molecular Biology, Readings from Scientific American,* pp. 198–205. San Francisco: W. H. Freeman.

CROSBY, A. W., JR.
1972 *The Columbian Exchange: Biological and Cultural Consequences of 1492.* Westport, CT: Greenwood Press.

1986 *Ecological Imperialism: The Biological Expansion of Europe 900–1900.* Cambridge: Cambridge University Press.

CULTURAL SURVIVAL
1992 *At the Threshold.* Cambridge, MA: Cultural Survival. Originally Spring 1992 issue of *Cultural Survival Quarterly.*

CULTURAL SURVIVAL QUARTERLY
Quarterly journal. Cambridge, MA: Cultural Survival.

DAHLBERG, F., ED.
1981 *Woman the Gatherer.* New Haven: Yale University Press.

DALTON, G., ED.
1967 *Tribal and Peasant Economies.* Garden City, NY: Natural History Press.

DAMATTA, R.
1991 *Carnivals, Rogues, and Heroes: An Interpretation of the Brazilian Dilemma.* Translated from the Portuguese by John Drury. Notre Dame, IN: University of Notre Dame Press.

D'ANDRADE, R.
1984 Cultural Meaning Systems. In *Culture Theory: Essays on Mind, Self, and Emotion,* eds. R. A. Shweder and R. A. Levine, pp. 88–119. Cambridge: Cambridge University Press.
1995 *The Development of Cognitive Anthropology.* New York: Cambridge University Press.

DARWIN, C.
1958 (orig. 1859). *On the Origin of Species.* New York: Dutton.

DARWIN, E.
1796 (orig. 1794). *Zoonomia, Or the Laws of Organic Life,* 2nd ed. London: J. Johnson.

DAS, V.
1995 *Critical Events: An Anthropological Perspective on Contemporary India.* New York: Oxford University Press.

DAVIS, D. L., AND R. G. WHITTEN
1987 The Cross-Cultural Study of Human Sexuality. *Annual Review of Anthropology* 16: 69–98.

DEGLER, C.
1970 *Neither Black nor White: Slavery and Race Relations in Brazil and the United States.* New York: Macmillan.

DELAMONT, S.
1995 *Appetites and Identities: An Introduction to the Social Anthropology of Western Europe.* London: Routledge.

DELSON, E., ED.
1985 *Ancestors: The Hard Evidence.* New York: Alan R. Liss.

DELUMLEY, H.
1976 (orig. 1969). A Paleolithic Camp at Nice. In *Avenues to Antiquity, Readings from Scientific American,* ed. B. M. Fagan, pp. 36–44. San Francisco: W. H. Freeman.

DENTAN, R. K.
1979 *The Semai: A Nonviolent People of Malaya.* Fieldwork edition. New York: Harcourt Brace.

DESJARLAIS, R., L. EISENBERG, B. GOOD, AND A. KLEINMAN, EDS.
1995 *World Mental Health: Problems and Priorities in Low-Income Countries.* New York: Oxford University Press.

DESPRES, L., ED.
1975 *Ethnicity and Resource Competition.* The Hague: Mouton.

DE VOS, G. A., AND H. WAGATSUMA
1966 *Japan's Invisible Race: Caste in Culture and Personality.* Berkeley: University of California Press.

DE VOS, G. A., W. O. WETHERALL, AND K. STEARMAN
1983 *Japan's Minorities: Burakumin, Koreans, Ainu and Okinawans.* Report no. 3. London: Minority Rights Group.

DIAMOND, J.
1989 Blood, Genes, and Malaria. *Natural History,* February, pp. 8–18.
1990 A Pox upon Our Genes. *Natural History,* February, pp. 26–30.

DI LEONARDO, M., ED.
1991 *Gender at the Crossroads of Knowledge: Feminist Anthropology in the Postmodern Era.* Berkeley: University of California Press.

DIVALE, W. T., AND M. HARRIS
1976 Population, Warfare, and the Male Supremacist Complex. *American Anthropologist* 78: 521–538.

DOBZHANSKY, T., F. J. AYALA, G. L. STEBBINS, AND J. W. VALENTINE
1977 *Evolution.* San Francisco: W. H. Freeman.

DRAPER, P.
1975 !Kung Women: Contrasts in Sexual Egalitarianism in Foraging and Sedentary Contexts. In *Toward an Anthropology of Women,* ed. R. Reiter, pp. 77–109. New York: Monthly Review Press.

DRENNAN, R. D., AND C. A. URIBE, EDS.
1987 *Chiefdoms in the Americas.* Landon, MD: University Press of America.

DURKHEIM, E.
1951 (orig. 1897). *Suicide: A Study in Sociology.* Glencoe, IL: Free Press.
1961 (orig. 1912). *The Elementary Forms of the Religious Life.* New York: Collier Books.

DWYER, K.
1982 *Moroccan Dialogues: Anthropology in Question.* Baltimore: Johns Hopkins University Press.

EAGLETON, T.
1983 *Literary Theory: An Introduction.* Minneapolis: University of Minnesota Press.

EARLE, T.

1987 Chiefdoms in Archaeological and Ethnohistorical Perspective. *Annual Review of Anthropology* 16: 279–308.

1991 *Chiefdoms: Power, Economy, and Ideology*. New York: Cambridge University Press.

EASTMAN, C. M.

1975 *Aspects of Language and Culture*. San Francisco: Chandler and Sharp.

ECKERT, P.

1989 *Jocks and Burnouts: Social Categories and Identity in the High School*. New York: Teachers College Press, Columbia University.

EDER, J.

1987 *On the Road to Tribal Extinction: Depopulation, Deculturation, and Adaptive Well-Being among the Batak of the Philippines*. Berkeley: University of California Press.

EDDY, E. M., AND W. L. PARTRIDGE, EDS.

1978 *Applied Anthropology in America*. New York: Columbia University Press.

EDGERTON, R.

1965 "Cultural" versus "Ecological" Factors in the Expression of Values, Attitudes and Personality Characteristics. *American Anthropologist* 67: 442–447.

EISELEY, L.

1961 *Darwin's Century*. Garden City, NY: Doubleday, Anchor Books.

ELDREDGE, N.

1985 *Time Frames: The Rethinking of Darwinian Evolution and the Theory of Punctuated Equilibria*. New York: Simon & Schuster.

ERLANGER, S.

1992 An Islamic Awakening in Central Asian Lands. *The New York Times*, June 9, pp. A1, A7.

ERRINGTON, F., AND D. GEWERTZ

1987 *Cultural Alternatives and a Feminist Anthropology: An Analysis of Culturally Constructed Gender Interests in Papua New Guinea*. New York: Cambridge University Press.

ESCOBAR, A.

1991 Anthropology and the Development Encounter: The Making and Marketing of Development Anthropology. *American Ethnologist* 18: 658–682.

1994 Welcome to Cyberia: Notes on the Anthropology of Cyberculture. *Current Anthropology* 35(3): 211–231.

1995 *Encountering Development: The Making and Unmaking of the Third World*. Princeton, NJ: Princeton University Press.

EVANS-PRITCHARD, E. E.

1940 *The Nuer: A Description of the Modes of Livelihood and Political Institutions of a Nilotic People*. Oxford: Clarendon Press.

1970 Sexual Inversion among the Azande. *American Anthropologist* 72: 1428–1433.

FAGAN, B. M.

1987 *The Great Journey: The Peopling of Ancient America*. London: Thames and Hudson.

1994 *Archeology: A Brief Introduction*, 5th ed. New York: HarperCollins.

1996 *World Prehistory: A Brief Introduction*, 3rd ed. New York: HarperCollins.

FAROOQ, M.

1966 Importance of Determining Transmission Sites in Planning Bilharziasis Control: Field Observations from the Egypt-49 Project Area. *American Journal of Epidemiology* 83: 603–612.

FASOLD, R. W.

1990 *The Sociolinguistics of Language*. Oxford: Basil Blackwell.

FEDIGAN, L. M.

1982 *Primate Paradigms: Sex Roles and Social Bonds*. Montreal: Eden Press.

FELD, S.

1991 Voices of the Rainforest. *Public Culture* 4(1): 131–140.

FENLASON, L.

1990 Wolpoff Questions "Eve's" Origin Date, Says It Ignores Contradictory Fossil Data. *University Record* (University of Michigan, Ann Arbor) 45(21): 12.

FERGUSON, R. B., AND N. L. WHITEHEAD

1991 *War in the Tribal Zone: Expanding States and Indigenous Warfare*. Santa Fe: School of American Research Press.

FERRARO, G. P.

1994 *The Cultural Dimension of International Business*, 2nd ed. Englewood Cliffs, NJ: Prentice-Hall.

FINKLER, K.

1985 *Spiritualist Healers in Mexico: Successes and Failures of Alternative Therapeutics*. South Hadley, MA: Bergin and Garvey.

FISHER, A.

1988a The More Things Change. *MOSAIC* 19(1): 22–33.

1988b On the Emergence of Humanness. *MOSAIC* 19(1): 34–45.

FISKE, J.

1989 *Understanding Popular Culture*. Boston: Unwin Hyman.

FLANNERY, K. V.

1969 Origins and Ecological Effects of Early Domestication in Iran and the Near East. In *The

Domestication and Exploitation of Plants and Animals, eds. P. J. Ucko and G. W. Dimbleby, pp. 73–100. Chicago: Aldine.

1972   The Cultural Evolution of Civilizations. *Annual Review of Ecology and Systematics* 3: 399–426.

1973   The Origins of Agriculture: *Annual Review of Anthropology* 2: 271–310.

FLANNERY, K. V., ED.
1986   *Guila Naquitz: Archaic Foraging and Early Agriculture in Oaxaca, Mexico.* Orlando: Academic Press.

FLANNERY, K. V., J. MARCUS, AND R. G. REYNOLDS
1989   *The Flocks of the Wamani: A Study of Llama Herders on the Punas of Ayacucho, Peru.* San Diego: Academic Press.

FORD, C. S., AND F. A. BEACH
1951   *Patterns of Sexual Behavior.* New York: Harper Torchbooks.

FORMAN, SHEPARD, ED.
1994   *Diagnosing America: Anthropology and Public Engagement.* Ann Arbor: University of Michigan Press.

FOSSEY, D.
1981   The Imperiled Mountain Gorilla. *National Geographic* 159: 501–523.

1983   *Gorillas in the Mist.* Boston: Houghton Mifflin.

FOSTER, G. M.
1965   Peasant Society and the Image of Limited Good. *American Anthropologist* 67: 293–315.

FOSTER, G. M., AND B. G. ANDERSON
1978   *Medical Anthropology.* New York: McGraw-Hill.

FOUCAULT, M.
1979   *Discipline and Punish: The Birth of the Prison.* Translated by Alan Sheridan. New York: Vintage Books, University Press.

FOUTS, R. S., D. H. FOUTS, AND T. E. VAN CANTFORT
1989   The Infant Loulis Learns Signs from Cross-Fostered Chimpanzees. In *Teaching Sign Language to Chimpanzees,* eds. R. A. Gardner, B. T. Gardner, and T. E. Van Cantfort, pp. 280–292. Albany: State University of New York Press.

FOX, J. W.
1987   *Maya Postclassic State Formation.* Cambridge: Cambridge University Press.

FOX, R.
1985   *Kinship and Marriage.* New York: Viking Penguin.

FOX, R. G., ED.
1990   *Nationalist Ideologies and the Production of National Cultures.* American Ethnological Society Monograph Series, no. 2. Washington, DC: American Anthropological Association.

FRAKE, C. O.
1961   The Diagnosis of Disease among the Subanun of Mindanao. *American Anthropologist* 63: 113–132.

FRANKE, R.
1977   Miracle Seeds and Shattered Dreams in Java. In *Readings in Anthropology,* pp. 197–201. Guilford, CT: Dushkin.

FREEMAN, D.
1983   *Margaret Mead and Samoa: The Making and Unmaking of an Anthropological Myth.* Cambridge, MA: Harvard University Press.

FREILICH, M., D. RAYBECK, AND J. SAVISHINSKY
1991   *Deviance: Anthropological Perspectives.* Westport, CT: Bergin and Garvey.

FRENCH, H. W.
1992   Unending Exodus from the Caribbean, with the U.S. a Constant Magnet. *The New York Times,* May 6, pp. A1, A8.

FREUD, S.
1950   (orig. 1918). *Totem and Taboo.* Translated by J. Strachey. New York: W. W. Norton.

FRICKE, T.
1994   *Himalayan Households: Tamang Demography and Domestic Processes,* 2nd ed. New York: Columbia University Press.

FRIED, M. H.
1960   On the Evolution of Social Stratification and the State. In *Culture in History,* ed. S. Diamond, pp. 713–731. New York: Columbia University Press.

1967   *The Evolution of Political Society: An Essay in Political Anthropology.* New York: McGraw-Hill.

FRIEDL, E.
1975   *Women and Men: An Anthropologist's View.* New York: Harcourt Brace Jovanovich.

FRIEDMAN, J.
1994   *Cultural Identity and Global Process.* Thousand Oaks, CA: Sage.

FRIEDMAN, J., AND M. J. ROWLANDS, EDS.
1978   *The Evolution of Social Systems.* Pittsburgh: University of Pittsburgh Press.

FRISANCHO, A. R.
1975   Functional Adaptation to High Altitude Hypoxia. *Science* 187: 313–319.

1993   *Human Adaptation and Accommodation.* Ann Arbor: University of Michigan Press.

FUTUYMA, D. J.
1983   *Science on Trial.* New York: Pantheon.

GAL, S.
1989   Language and Political Economy. *Annual Review of Anthropology* 18: 345–367.

GARBARINO, M. S., AND R. F. SASSO
1994   *Native American Heritage,* 3rd ed. Prospect Heights, IL: Waveland.

GARDNER, R. A., B. T. GARDNER, AND T. E. VAN
CANTFORT, EDS.
  1989 *Teaching Sign Language to Chimpanzees.* Albany: State University of New York Press.
GARGAN, E. A.
  1992 A Single-Minded Man Battles to Free Slaves. *The New York Times,* June 4, p. A7.
GEERTZ, C.
  1973 *The Interpretation of Cultures.* New York: Basic Books.
  1983 *Local Knowledge.* New York: Basic Books.
  1995 *After the Fact: Two Countries, Four Decades, One Anthropologist.* Cambridge, MA: Harvard University Press.
GEIS, M. L.
  1987 *The Language of Politics.* New York: Springer-Verlag.
GELLNER, E.
  1983 *Nations and Nationalism.* Ithaca, NY: Cornell University Press.
GIBBS, N.
  1989 How America Has Run Out of Time. *Time,* April 24, pp. 59–67.
GIDDENS, A.
  1973 *The Class Structure of the Advanced Societies.* New York: Cambridge University Press.
GILMORE, D.
  1987 *Aggression and Community: Paradoxes of Andalusian Culture.* New Haven: Yale University Press.
  1991 *Manhood in the Making: Cultural Concepts of Masculinity.* New Haven: Yale University Press.
GLICK-SCHILLER, N., AND G. FOURON
  1990 "Everywhere We Go, We Are in Danger": Ti Manno and the Emergence of Haitian Transnational Identity. *American Ethnologist* 17(2): 327–347.
GOLDBERG, D. T., ED.
  1990 *Anatomy of Racism.* Minneapolis: University of Minnesota Press.
GOLDSCHMIDT, W.
  1965 Theory and Strategy in the Study of Cultural Adaptability. *American Anthropologist* 67: 402–407.
GOODALL, J.
  1968a A Preliminary Report on Expressive Movements and Communication in Gombe Stream Chimpanzees. In *Primates: Studies in Adaptation and Variability,* ed. P. C. Jay, pp. 313–374. New York: Harcourt Brace Jovanovich.
  1968b The Behavior of Free Living Chimpanzees in the Gombe Stream Reserve. *Animal Behavior Monographs* 1: 161–311.
  1986 *The Chimpanzees of Gombe: Patterns of Behavior.* Cambridge, MA: Belknap Press, Harvard University Press.
  1988 *In the Shadow of Man,* rev. ed. Boston: Houghton Mifflin.
GOODENOUGH, W. H.
  1953 *Native Astronomy in the Central Carolines.* Philadelphia: University of Pennsylvania Press.
GOODMAN, J., P. E. LOVEJOY, AND A. SHERRATT
  1995 *Consuming Habits: Drugs in History and Anthropology.* London: Routledge.
GOODMAN, M., M. L. BABA, AND L. L. DARGA
  1983 The Bearings of Molecular Data on the Cladograms and Times of Divergence of Hominoid Lineages. In *New Interpretations of Ape and Human Ancestry,* eds. R. L. Ciochon and R. S. Corruccini, pp. 67–87. New York: Plenum.
GOODY, J.
  1977 *Production and Reproduction: A Comparative Study of the Domestic Domain.* New York: Cambridge University Press.
GOODY, J., AND S. T. TAMBIAH
  1973 *Bridewealth and Dowry.* Cambridge: Cambridge University Press.
GORDON, A. A.
  1996 *Transforming Capitalism and Patriarchy: Gender and Development in Africa.* Boulder, CO: Lynne Reinner.
GORER, G.
  1943 Themes in Japanese Culture. *Transactions of the New York Academy of Sciences* (Series II) 5: 106–124.
GORMAN, C. F.
  1969 Hoabinhian: A Pebble-Tool Complex with Early Plant Associations in Southeast Asia. *Science* 163: 671–673.
GRABURN, N., ED.
  1971 *Readings in Kinship and Social Structure.* New York: Harper & Row.
GRAMSCI, A.
  1971 *Selections from the Prison Notebooks.* Edited and translated by Quenten Hoare and Geoffrey Nowell Smith. London: Wishart.
GRASMUCK, S., AND P. PESSAR
  1991 *Between Two Islands: Dominican International Migration.* Berkeley: University of California Press.
GRASSMUCK, K.
  1985 Local Educators Join Push for "a Computer in Every Classroom." *The Ann Arbor News,* February 10, p. A11. (Quotes testimony of Linda Tarr-Whelan of the National Education Association to the House Committee on Science, Research and Technology.)

GRAY, J.
1986 With a Few Exceptions, Television in Africa Fails to Educate and Enlighten. *Ann Arbor News*, December 8.

GRAY, J. P.
1985 *Primate Sociobiology.* New Haven: HRAF Press.

GREAVES, T. C.
1995 Problems Facing Anthropologists: Cultural Rights and Ethnography. *General Anthropology* 1(2): 1, 3–6.

GREEN, E. C.
1992 (orig. 1987). The Integration of Modern and Traditional Health Sectors in Swaziland. In *Applying Anthropology*, eds. A. Podolefsky and P. J. Brown, pp. 246–251. Mountain View, CA: Mayfield.

GROSS, D.
1971a The Great Sisal Scheme. *Natural History*, March, pp. 49–55.

GROSS, D., AND B. UNDERWOOD
1971 Technological Change and Caloric Costs: Sisal Agriculture in Northeastern Brazil. *American Anthropologist* 73: 725–740.

GULLIVER, P. H.
1974 (orig. 1965). The Jie of Uganda. In *Man in Adaptation: The Cultural Present*, 2nd ed., ed. Y. A. Cohen, pp. 323–345.

GUMPERZ, J. J.
1982 *Language and Social Identity.* Cambridge: Cambridge University Press.

GUTHRIE, S.
1995 *Faces in the Clouds: A New Theory of Religion.* New York: Oxford University Press.

HALL, E. T.
1990 *Understanding Cultural Differences.* Yarmouth, ME: Intercultural Press.
1992 *An Anthropology of Everyday Life: An Autobiography.* New York: Doubleday.

HAMBURG, D. A., AND E. R. McCOWN, EDS.
1979 *The Great Apes.* Menlo Park, CA: Benjamin Cummings.

HAMILTON, M. B.
1995 *The Sociology of Religion: Theoretical and Comparative Perspectives.* London: Routledge.

HANKS, W. F.
1995 *Language and Communicative Practices.* Boulder, CO: Westview.

HARCOURT, A. H., D. FOSSEY, AND J. SABATER-PI
1981 Demography of *Gorilla gorilla. Journal of Zoology* 195: 215–233.

HARDING, S.
1975 Women and Words in a Spanish Village. In *Toward an Anthropology of Women*, ed. R. Reiter, pp. 283–308. New York: Monthly Review Press.

HARGROVE, E. C.
1986 *Religion and Environmental Crisis.* Athens, GA: University of Georgia Press.

HARLAN, J. R., AND D. ZOHARY
1966 Distribution of Wild Wheats and Barley. *Science* 153: 1074–1080.

HARRIS, M.
1964 *Patterns of Race in the Americas.* New York: Walker.
1968 *The Rise of Anthropological Theory.* New York: Crowell.
1970 Referential Ambiguity in the Calculus of Brazilian Racial Identity. *Southwestern Journal of Anthropology* 26(1): 1–14.
1974 *Cows, Pigs, Wars, and Witches: The Riddles of Culture.* New York: Random House.
1978 *Cannibals and Kings.* New York: Vintage.
1989 *Our Kind: Who We Are, Where We Came from, Where We Are Going.* New York: Harper & Row.

HARRIS, M., AND C. P. KOTTAK
1963 The Structural Significance of Brazilian Racial Categories. *Sociologia* 25: 203–209.

HARRIS, N. M., AND G. HILLMAN
1989 *Foraging and Farming: The Evolution of Plant Exploitation.* London: Unwin Hyman.

HARRISON, G. G., W. L. RATHJE, AND W. W. HUGHES
1994 Food Waste Behavior in an Urban Population. In *Applying Anthropology: An Introductory Reader*, 3rd ed., eds. A. Podolefsky and P. J. Brown, pp. 107–112. Mountain View, CA: Mayfield.

HART, C. W. M., A. R. PILLING, AND J. C. GOODALE
1988 *The Tiwi of North Australia*, 3rd ed. Fort Worth: Harcourt Brace.

HARTL, D.
1983 *Human Genetics.* New York: Harper & Row.
1989 *Principles of Population Genetics*, 2nd ed. Sunderland, MA: Sinaeur.

HARVEY, K.
1996 Online for the Ancestors: The Importance of Anthropological Sensibility in Information Superhighway Design. *Social Science Computing Review* 14(1): 65–68.

HATFIELD, E., AND R. L. RAPSON
1996 *Love and Sex: Cross-Cultural Perspectives.* Needham Heights, MA: Allyn & Bacon.

HAUSFATER, G., AND S. HRDY, EDS.
1984 *Infanticide: Comparative and Evolutionary Perspectives.* Hawthorne, NY: Aldine.

HAWKES, K., J. O'CONNELL, AND K. HILL
1982 Why Hunters Gather: Optimal Foraging and the Aché of Eastern Paraguay. *American Ethnologist* 9: 379–398.

HAYDEN, B.
1981 Subsistence and Ecological Adaptations of Modern Hunter/Gatherers. In *Omnivorous Primates: Gathering and Hunting in Human Evolution,* eds. R. S. Harding and G. Teleki, pp. 344–421. New York: Columbia University Press.

HEADLAND, T. N., ED.
1992 *The Tasaday Controversy: Assessing the Evidence.* Washington, DC: American Anthropological Association.

HEADLAND, T. N., AND L. A. REID
1989 Hunter-Gatherers and Their Neighbors from Prehistory to the Present. *Current Anthropology* 30: 43–66.

HEATH, D. B., ED.
1995 *International Handbook on Alcohol and Culture.* Westport, CT: Greenwood Press.

HEIDER, K. G.
1988 The Rashomon Effect: When Ethnographers Disagree. *American Anthropologist* 90: 73–81.
1991 *Grand Valley Dani: Peaceful Warriors,* 2nd ed. Fort Worth: Harcourt Brace.

HELLER, M.
1988 *Codeswitching: Anthropological and Sociolinguistic Perspectives.* Berlin: Mouton deGruyter.

HENRY, D. O.
1989 *From Foraging to Agriculture: The Levant at the End of the Ice Age.* Philadelphia: University of Pennsylvania Press.

HENRY, J.
1955 Docility, or Giving Teacher What She Wants. *Journal of Social Issues* 2: 33–41.

HERDT, G.
1981 *Guardians of the Flutes.* New York: McGraw-Hill.
1986 *The Sambia: Ritual and Gender in New Guinea.* Fort Worth: Harcourt Brace.

HERRNSTEIN, R. J.
1971 I.Q. *Atlantic* 228(3): 43–64.

HERRNSTEIN, R. J., AND C. MURRAY
1994 *The Bell Curve: Intelligence and Class Structure in American Life.* New York: Free Press.

HESS, D. J.
1995 A Democratic Research Agenda in the Social Studies of the National Information Infrastructure. Paper prepared for the National Science Foundation Workshop on Culture, Society, and Advanced Information Technology. Washington, DC: May 31–June 1, 1995.

HESS, D. J., AND R. A. DAMATTA, EDS.
1995 *The Brazilian Puzzle: Culture on the Borderlands of the Western World.* New York: Columbia University Press.

HEWITT, R.
1986 *White Talk, Black Talk.* Cambridge: Cambridge University Press.

HEYERDAHL, T.
1971 *The Ra Expeditions.* Translated by P. Crampton. Garden City, NY: Doubleday.

HEYNEMAN, D.
1984 Development and Disease: A Dual Dilemma. *Journal of Parasitology* 70: 3–17.

HILL, C. E., ED.
1986 *Current Health Policy Issues and Alternatives: An Applied Social Science Perspective.* Southern Anthropological Society Proceedings. Athens, GA: University of Georgia Press.

HILL, J. H.
1978 Apes and Language. *Annual Review of Anthropology* 7: 89–112.

HILL, K., H. KAPLAN, K. HAWKES, AND A. HURTADO
1987 Foraging Decisions among Aché Hunter-Gatherers: New Data and Implications for Optimal Foraging Models. *Ethology and Sociobiology* 8: 1–36.

HILL-BURNETT, J.
1978 Developing Anthropological Knowledge through Application. In *Applied Anthropology in America,* eds. E. M. Eddy and W. L. Partridge, pp. 112–128. New York: Columbia University Press.

HINDE, R. A.
1983 *Primate Social Relationships: An Integrated Approach.* Sunderland, MA: Sinaeur.

HOBHOUSE, L. T.
1915 *Morals in Evolution,* rev. ed. New York: Holt.

HOBSBAWM, E. J.
1992 *Nations and Nationalism since 1780: Programme, Myth, Reality,* 2nd ed. New York: Cambridge University Press.

HOEBEL, E. A.
1954 *The Law of Primitive Man.* Cambridge, MA: Harvard University Press.
1968 (orig. 1954). The Eskimo: Rudimentary Law in a Primitive Anarchy. In *Studies in Social and Cultural Anthropology,* ed. J. Middleton, pp. 93–127. New York: Crowell.

HOLE, F., K. V. FLANNERY, AND J. A. NEELY
1969 *The Prehistory and Human Ecology of the Deh Luran Plain.* Memoir no. 1. Ann Arbor: University of Michigan Museum of Anthropology.

HOLLAND, D., AND N. QUINN, EDS.
1987 *Cultural Models in Language and Thought.* Cambridge: Cambridge University Press.

HOLLOWAY, R. L.
1975 (orig. 1974). The Casts of Fossil Hominid Brains. In *Biological Anthropology, Readings*

from Scientific American, ed. S. H. Katz, pp. 69–78. San Francisco: W. H. Freeman.

HOLMES, L. D.
1987 *Quest for the Real Samoa: The Mead/Freeman Controversy and Beyond.* South Hadley, MA: Bergin and Garvey.

HOPKINS, T., AND I. WALLERSTEIN
1982 Patterns of Development of the Modern World System. In *World System Analysis: Theory and Methodology,* by T. Hopkins, I. Wallerstein, R. Bach, C. Chase-Dunn, and R. Mukherjee, pp. 121–141. Thousand Oaks, CA: Sage.

HOSTETLER, J., AND G. E. HUNTINGTON
1992 *Amish Children: Education in the Family,* 2nd ed. Fort Worth: Harcourt Brace.

1996 *The Hutterites in North America,* 3rd ed. Fort Worth: Harcourt Brace.

HOWELLS, W. W.
1976 Explaining Modern Man: Evolutionists versus Migrationists. *Journal of Human Evolution* 5: 477–496.

HUMAN ORGANIZATION
Quarterly journal. Oklahoma City: Society for Applied Anthropology.

INGOLD, T., D. RICHES, AND J. WOODBURN
1991 *Hunters and Gatherers.* New York: Berg (St. Martin's).

INHORN, M. C., AND P. J. BROWN
1990 The Anthropology of Infectious Disease. *Annual Review of Anthropology* 19: 89–117.

IRVING, W. N.
1985 Context and Chronology of Early Man in the Americas. *Annual Review of Anthropology* 14: 529–555.

ISAAC, G. L.
1972 Early Phases of Human Behavior: Models in Lower Paleolithic Archaeology. In *Models in Archaeology,* ed. D. L. Clarke, pp. 167–199. London: Methuen.

1978 Food Sharing and Human Evolution: Archaeological Evidence from the Plio-Pleistocene of East Africa. *Journal of Anthropological Research* 34: 311–325.

JACOBY, R., AND N. GLAUBERMAN, EDS.
1995 *The Bell Curve Debate: History, Documents, Opinions.* New York: Free Press.

JAMESON, F.
1984 Postmodernism, or the Cultural Logic of Late Capitalism. *New Left Review* 146: 53–93.

1988 *The Ideologies of Theory: Essays 1971–1986.* Minneapolis: University of Minnesota Press.

JANSON, C. H.
1986 Capuchin Counterpoint: Divergent Mating and Feeding Habits Distinguish Two Closely Related Monkey Species of the Peruvian Forest. *Natural History* 95: 44–52.

JENSEN, A.
1969 How Much Can We Boost I.Q. and Scholastic Achievement? *Harvard Educational Review* 29: 1–123.

JODELET, D.
1991 *Madness and Social Representations: Living with the Mad in One French Community.* Translated from the French by Gerard Duveen. Berkeley: University of California Press.

JOHANSON, D. C., AND M. EDEY
1981 *Lucy: The Origins of Humankind.* New York: Simon & Schuster.

JOHANSON, D. C., AND T. D. WHITE
1979 A Systematic Assessment of Early African Hominids. *Science* 203: 321–330.

JOHNSON, A. W.
1978 *Quantification in Cultural Anthropology: An Introduction to Research Design.* Stanford, CA: Stanford University Press.

JOHNSON, A. W., AND T. EARLE, EDS.
1987 *The Evolution of Human Societies: From Foraging Group to Agrarian State.* Stanford, CA: Stanford University Press.

JOHNSON, T. J., AND C. F. SARGENT, EDS.
1990 *Medical Anthropology: A Handbook of Theory and Method.* New York: Greenwood.

JOHNSTON, F. E., AND S. LOW
1994 *Children of the Urban Poor: The Sociocultural Environment of Growth, Development, and Malnutrition in Guatemala City.* Boulder, CO: Westview.

JOLLY, A.
1985 *The Evolution of Primate Behavior,* 2nd ed. New York: Macmillan.

JOLLY, C. J., AND F. PLOG
1986 *Physical Anthropology and Archaeology,* 4th ed. New York: McGraw-Hill.

JOLLY, C. J., AND R. WHITE
1995 *Physical Anthropology and Archaeology,* 5th ed. New York: McGraw-Hill.

JONES, G., AND R. KRAUTZ
1981 *The Transition to Statehood in the New World.* Cambridge: Cambridge University Press.

KAN, S.
1986 The 19th-Century Tlingit Potlatch: A New Perspective. *American Ethnologist* 13: 191–212.

1989 *Symbolic Immortality: the Tlingit Potlatch of the Nineteenth Century.* Washington, DC: Smithsonian Institution Press.

KAPLAN, R. D.
1994 The Coming Anarchy: How Scarcity, Crime, Overpopulation, and Disease Are Rapidly De-

stroying the Social Fabric of Our Planet. *Atlantic Monthly,* February, pp. 44–76.

KARDINER, A., ED.
1939 *The Individual and His Society.* New York: Columbia University Press.

KEARNEY, M.
1996 *Reconceptualizing the Peasantry: Anthropology in Global Perspective.* Boulder, CO: Westview.

KEHOE, A. B.
1989 *The Ghost Dance Religion: Ethnohistory and Revitalization.* Fort Worth: Harcourt Brace.

KEISER, L.
1991 *Friend by Day, Enemy by Night: Organized Vengeance in a Kohistani Community.* Fort Worth: Harcourt Brace.

KELLY, R. C.
1976 Witchcraft and Sexual Relations: An Exploration in the Social and Semantic Implications of the Structure of Belief. In *Man and Woman in the New Guinea Highlands,* eds. P. Brown and G. Buchbinder, pp. 36–53. Special Publication, no. 8. Washington, DC: American Anthropological Association.

KENNEDY, R. G.
1994 *Hidden Cities: The Discovery and Loss of Ancient North American Civilization.* New York: Free Press.

KENT, S.
1992 The Current Forager Controversy: Real Versus Ideal Views of Hunter-Gatherers. *Man* 27: 45–70.

KENT, S., AND H. VIERICH
1989 The Myth of Ecological Determinism: Anticipated Mobility and Site Organization of Space. In *Farmers as Hunters: The Implications of Sedentism,* ed. S. Kent, pp. 96–130. New York: Cambridge University Press.

KIMMEL, M. S., AND M. A. MESSNER, EDS.
1995 *Men's Lives,* 3rd ed. Needham Heights, MA: Allyn & Bacon.

KING, B. J., ED.
1994 *The Information Continuum: Evolution of Social Information Transfer in Monkeys, Apes, and Hominids.* Santa Fe: School of American Research Press.

KINSEY, A. C., W. B. POMEROY, AND C. E. MARTIN
1948 *Sexual Behavior in the Human Male.* Philadelphia: W. B. Saunders.

KIRSCH, P. V.
1984 *The Evolution of the Polynesian Chiefdoms.* Cambridge: Cambridge University Press.

KLASS, M.
1995 *Ordered Universes: Approaches to the Anthropology of Religion.* Boulder, CO: Westview.

KLEINFELD, J.
1975 Positive Stereotyping: The Cultural Relativist in the Classroom. *Human Organization* 34: 269–274.

KLEYMEYER, C. D., ED.
1994 *Cultural Expression and Grassroots Development: Cases from Latin America and the Caribbean.* Boulder, CO: Lynne Rienner.

KLINEBERG, O.
1951 Race and Psychology: In *The Race Question in Modern Science.* Paris: UNESCO.

KLING, R.
1996 Synergies and Competition between Life in Cyberspace and Face-to-Face Communities. *Social Science Computing Review* 14(1): 50–54.

KLUCKHOHN, C.
1994 *Mirror for Man: A Survey of Human Behavior and Social Attitudes.* Greenwich, CT: Fawcett.

KLUGE, A. G.
1983 Cladistics and the Classification of the Great Apes. In *New Interpretations of Ape and Human Ancestry,* eds. R. L. Ciochon and R. S. Corruccini, pp. 151–177. New York: Plenum.

KORTEN, D. C.
1980 Community Organization and Rural Development: A Learning Process Approach. *Public Administration Review,* September–October, pp. 480–512.

KOTTAK, C. P.
1980 *The Past in the Present: History, Ecology, and Social Organization in Highland Madagascar.* Ann Arbor: University of Michigan Press.

1990a *Prime-Time Society: An Anthropological Analysis of Television and Culture.* Belmont, CA: Wadsworth.

1990b Culture and Economic Development. *American Anthropologist* 92(3): 723–731.

1991 When People Don't Come First: Some Lessons from Completed Projects. In *Putting People First: Sociological Variables in Rural Development,* 2nd. ed., ed. M. Cernea, pp. 429–464. New York: Oxford University Press.

1992 *Assault on Paradise: Social Change in a Brazilian Village,* 2nd ed. New York: McGraw-Hill.

KRAMARAE, R., M. SHULZ, AND M. O'BARR, EDS.
1984 *Language and Power.* Thousand Oaks, CA: Sage.

KRETCHMER, N.
1975 (orig. 1972). Lactose and Lactase. In *Biological Anthropology, Readings from Scientific American,* ed. S. H. Katz, pp. 310–318. San Francisco: W. H. Freeman.

KROEBER, A. L., AND C. KLUCKHOHN
1963 *Culture: A Critical Review of Concepts and Definitions.* New York: Vintage.

KUNITZ, S. J.
   1994   *Disease and Social Diversity: The European Impact on the Health of Non-Europeans.* New York: Oxford University Press.

LABARRE, W.
   1945   Some Observations of Character Structure in the Orient: The Japanese. *Psychiatry* 8: 326–342.

LABOV, W.
   1972a   *Language in the Inner City: Studies in the Black English Vernacular.* Philadelphia: University of Pennsylvania Press.

   1972b   *Sociolinguistic Patterns.* Philadelphia: University of Pennsylvania Press.

LAGUERRE, M.
   1984   *American Odyssey: Haitians in New York.* Ithaca, NY: Cornell University Press.

LAKOFF, R.
   1975   *Language and Woman's Place.* New York: Harper & Row.

LAMBERG-KARLOVSKY, C. C., AND J. A. SABLOFF
   1995   *Ancient Civilizations: The Near East and Mesoamerica.* Prospect Heights, IL: Waveland.

LANCE, L. M., AND E. E. MCKENNA
   1975   Analysis of Cases Pertaining to the Impact of Western Technology on the Non-Western World. *Human Organization* 34: 87–94.

LANSING, J. S.
   1991   *Priests and Programmers: Technologies of Power in the Engineered Landscape of Bali.* Princeton, NJ: Princeton University Press.

LARSON, A.
   1989   Social Context of Human Immunodeficiency Virus Transmission in Africa: Historical and Cultural Bases of East and Central African Sexual Relations. *Review of Infectious Diseases* 11: 716–731.

LEACH, E. R.
   1955   Polyandry, Inheritance and the Definition of Marriage. *Man* 55: 182–186.

   1961   *Rethinking Anthropology.* London: Athlone Press.

   1985   *Social Anthropology.* New York: Oxford University Press.

LEAKEY, R. E., M. G. LEAKEY, AND A. C. WALKER
   1988   Morphology of *Afropithecus turkanensis* from Kenya. *American Journal of Physical Anthropology* 76: 289–307.

LECLAIR, E. E., AND H. K. SCHNEIDER, EDS.
   1968   (orig. 1961). *Economic Anthropology: Readings in Theory and Analysis.* New York: Holt, Rinehart and Winston.

LEE, R. B.
   1974   (orig. 1968). What Hunters Do for a Living, or, How to Make Out on Scarce Resources. In *Man in Adaptation: The Cultural Present,* 2nd ed., ed. Y. A. Cohen, pp. 87–100. Chicago: Aldine.

   1979   *The !Kung San: Men, Women, and Work in a Foraging Society.* New York: Cambridge University Press.

   1984   *The Dobe !Kung.* Fort Worth: Harcourt Brace.

LEE, R. B., AND I. DEVORE, EDS.
   1977   *Kalahari Hunter-Gatherers: Studies of the !Kung San and Their Neighbors.* Cambridge, MA: Harvard University Press.

LEHMANN, A. C., AND J. E. MYERS, EDS.
   1993   *Magic, Witchcraft, and Religion: An Anthropological Study of the Supernatural,* 3rd ed. Mountain View, CA: Mayfield.

LENSKI, G.
   1966   *Power and Privilege: A Theory of Social Stratification.* New York: McGraw-Hill.

LESSA, W. A., AND E. Z. VOGT, EDS.
   1978   *Reader in Comparative Religion: An Anthropological Approach,* 4th ed. New York: Harper & Row.

LEVINE, N.
   1988   *The Dynamics of Polyandry: Kinship, Domesticity, and Population on the Tibetan Border.* Chicago: University of Chicago Press.

LEVINE, R. A.
   1982   *Culture, Behavior, and Personality: An Introduction to the Comparative Study of Psychosocial Adaptation,* 2nd ed. Chicago: Aldine.

LEVINE, R. A., ED.
   1974   *Culture and Personality: Contemporary Readings.* Chicago: Aldine.

LÉVI-STRAUSS, C.
   1963   *Totemism.* Translated by R. Needham. Boston: Beacon Press.

   1967   *Structural Anthropology.* New York: Doubleday.

   1969   (orig. 1949). *The Elementary Structures of Kinship.* Boston: Beacon Press.

LEWIS, H. S.
   1989   *After the Eagles Landed: The Yemenites of Israel.* Boulder, CO: Westview.

LEWIS, O.
   1959   *Five Families.* New York: Basic Books.

LEWIS, P.
   1992   U.N. Sees a Crisis in Overpopulation. *The New York Times,* April 30, p. A6.

LIEBAN, R. W.
   1977   The Field of Medical Anthropology. In *Culture, Disease, and Healing: Studies in Medical Anthropology,* ed. D. Landy, pp. 13–31. New York: Macmillan.

LIGHT, D., S. KELLER, AND C. CALHOUN
   1994   *Sociology,* 6th ed. New York: McGraw-Hill.

LINDEN, E.
1986 *Silent Partners: The Legacy of the Ape Language Experiments.* New York: Times Books.

LINDENBAUM, S.
1972 Sorcerers, Ghosts, and Polluting Women: An Analysis of Religious Belief and Population Control. *Ethnology* 11: 241–253.

LINTON, R.
1927 Report on Work of Field Museum Expedition in Madagascar. *American Anthropologist* 29: 292–307.

LITTLE, K.
1971 Some Aspects of African Urbanization South of the Sahara. McCaleb Modules in Anthropology. Reading, MA: Addison-Wesley.

LIVINGSTONE, F. B.
1958 Anthropological Implications of Sickle Cell Gene Distribution in West Africa. *American Anthropologist* 60: 533–562.

1969 Gene Frequency Clines of the β Hemoglobin Locus in Various Human Populations and Their Similarities by Models Involving Differential Selection. *Human Biology* 41: 223–236.

LIZOT, J.
1985 *Tales of the Yanomami: Daily Life in the Venezuelan Forest.* New York: Cambridge University Press.

LOOMIS, W. F.
1967 Skin-Pigmented Regulation of Vitamin-D Biosynthesis in Man. *Science* 157: 501–506.

LOWIE, R. H.
1935 *The Crow Indians.* New York: Farrar and Rinehart.

1961 (orig. 1920). *Primitive Society.* New York: Harper & Brothers.

LUTZ, C., AND J. L. COLLINS
1993 *Reading National Geographic.* Chicago: University of Chicago Press.

LYELL, C.
1969 (orig. 1830–33). *Principles of Geology.* New York: Johnson.

MACKINNON, J.
1974 *In Search of the Red Ape.* New York: Ballantine.

MAHER, J. C., AND G. MACDONALD, EDS.
1995 *Diversity and Language in Japanese Culture.* New York: Columbia University Press.

MAIR, L.
1969 *Witchcraft.* New York: McGraw-Hill.

MALINOWSKI, B.
1927 *Sex and Repression in Savage Society.* London and New York: International Library of Psychology, Philosophy and Scientific Method.

1961 (orig. 1922). *Argonauts of the Western Pacific.* New York: Dutton.

1978 (orig. 1931). The Role of Magic and Religion. In *Reader in Comparative Religion: An Anthropological Approach,* 4th ed., eds. W. A. Lessa and E. Z. Vogt, pp. 37–46. New York: Harper & Row.

MALKKI, LIISA H.
1995 *Purity and Exile: Violence, Memory, and National Cosmology among Hutu Refugees in Tanzania.* Chicago: University of Chicago Press.

MANN, A.
1975 *Paleodemographic Aspects of the South African Australopithecines.* Publications in Anthropology, no. 1. Philadelphia: University of Pennsylvania.

MANNERS, R.
1973 (orig. 1956). Functionalism, Realpolitik and Anthropology in Underdeveloped Areas. *America Indigena* 16. Also in *To See Ourselves: Anthropology and Modern Social Issues,* gen. ed. T. Weaver, pp. 113–126. Glenview, IL: Scott, Foresman.

MARCUS, G. E., AND D. CUSHMAN
1982 Ethnographies as Texts. *Annual Review of Anthropology* 11: 25–69.

MARCUS, G. E., AND M. M. J. FISCHER
1986 *Anthropology as Cultural Critique: An Experimental Moment in the Human Sciences.* Chicago: University of Chicago Press.

MARCUS, G. E., AND F. R. MYERS, EDS.
1995 *The Traffic in Culture: Redefining Art and Anthropology.* Berkeley: University of California Press.

MARGOLIS, M.
1984 *Mothers and Such: American Views of Women and How They Changed.* Berkeley: University of California Press.

1994 *Little Brazil: An Ethnography of Brazilian Immigrants in New York City.* Princeton, NJ: Princeton University Press.

MARKS, J.
1995 *Human Biodiversity: Genes, Race, and History.* New York: Aldine de Gruyter.

MARSHACK, A.
1972 *Roots of Civilization.* New York: McGraw-Hill.

MARTIN, E.
1987 *The Woman in the Body: A Cultural Analysis of Reproduction.* Boston: Beacon Press.

MARTIN, J.
1992 *Cultures in Organizations: Three Perspectives.* New York: Oxford University Press.

MARTIN, K., AND B. VOORHIES
1975 *Female of the Species.* New York: Columbia University Press.

MARTIN, P., AND E. MIDGLEY
1994 Immigration to the United States: Journey to an Uncertain Destination. *Population Bulletin* 49(3): 1–47.

MARX, K., AND F. ENGELS
  1976   (orig. 1848). *Communist Manifesto*. New York: Pantheon.

MAYR, E.
  1970   *Population, Species, and Evolution*. Cambridge, MA: Harvard University Press.

McCASKIE, T. C.
  1995   *State and Society in Pre-Colonial Asante*. New York: Cambridge University Press.

McDONALD, G.
  1984   *Carioca Fletch*. New York: Warner Books.

McELROY, A., AND P. K. TOWNSEND
  1996   *Medical Anthropology in Ecological Perspective*, 3rd ed. Boulder, CO: Westview.

McGRAW, T. K., ED.
  1986   *America versus Japan*. Boston: Harvard Business School Press.

McKUSICK, V.
  1966   *Mendelian Inheritance in Man*. Baltimore: Johns Hopkins University Press.
  1990   *Mendelian Inheritance in Man: Catalogs of Autosomal Dominant, Autosomal Recessive, and X-Linked Phenotypes*, 9th ed. Baltimore: Johns Hopkins University Press.

MEAD, M.
  1950   (orig. 1935). *Sex and Temperament in Three Primitive Societies*. New York: New American Library.
  1961   (orig. 1928). *Coming of Age in Samoa*. New York: Morrow Quill.

MEADOW, R., ED.
  1991   *Harappa Excavations 1986–1990: A Multidisciplinary Approach to Third Millennium Urbanism*. Monographs in World Archeology, no. 3. Madison, WI: Prehistory Press.

MICHAELS, E.
  1986   Aboriginal Content. Paper presented at the meeting of the Australian Screen Studies Association, December, Sydney.

MICHAELSON, K.
  1996   Information, Community, and Access. *Social Science Computing Review* 14(1): 57–59

MIDDLETON, J.
  1967   Introduction. In *Myth and Cosmos: Readings in Mythology and Symbolism*, ed. John Middleton, pp. ix–xi. Garden City, NY: Natural History Press.
  1993   *The Lugbara of Uganda*, 2nd ed. Fort Worth: Harcourt Brace.

MIDDLETON, J., ED.
  1967   *Gods and Rituals*. Garden City, NY: Natural History Press.

MILES, H. L.
  1983   Apes and Language: The Search for Commu-

nicative Competence. In *Language in Primates*, eds. J. de Luce and H. T. Wilder, pp. 43–62. New York: Springer Verlag.

MILLER, B. D., ED.
  1993   *Sex and Gender Hierarchies*. New York: Cambridge University Press.

MILLER, N., AND R. C. ROCKWELL, EDS.
  1988   *AIDS in Africa: The Social and Policy Impact*. Lewiston: Edwin Mellen.

MINTZ, S.
  1985   *Sweetness and Power: The Place of Sugar in Modern History*. New York: Viking Penguin.

MITCHELL, J. C.
  1966   Theoretical Orientations in African Urban Studies. In *The Social Anthropology of Complex Societies*, ed. M. Banton, pp. 37–68. London: Tavistock.

MOERMAN, M.
  1965   Ethnic Identification in a Complex Civilization: Who Are the Lue? *American Anthropologist* 67(5 Part I): 1215–1230.

MONTAGU, A.
  1975   *The Nature of Human Aggression*. New York: Oxford University Press.

MONTAGU, A., ED.
  1975   *Race and IQ*. New York: Oxford University Press.

MONTAGUE, S., AND R. MORAIS
  1981   Football Games and Rock Concerts: The Ritual Enactment. In *The American Dimension: Cultural Myths and Social Realities*, 2nd ed., eds. W. Arens and S. B. Montague, pp. 33–52. Sherman Oaks, CA: Alfred.

MOORE, A. D.
  1985   The Development of Neolithic Societies in the Near East. *Advances in World Archaeology*. 4: 1–69.

MOORE, S. F.
  1986   *Social Facts and Fabrications*. Cambridge: Cambridge University Press.

MORAN, E. F.
  1982   *Human Adaptability: An Introduction to Ecological Anthropology*. Boulder, CO: Westview.

MORGAN, L. H.
  1963   (orig. 1877). *Ancient Society*. Cleveland: World Publishing.

MORGEN, S., ED.
  1989   *Gender and Anthropology: Critical Reviews for Research and Teaching*. Washington, DC: American Anthropological Association.

MORRIS, B.
  1987   *Anthropological Studies of Religion: An Introductory Text*. New York: Cambridge University Press.

Mowat, F.
1987 *Woman in the Mists: The Story of Dian Fossey and the Mountain Gorillas of Africa.* New York: Warner Books.

Muhlhausler, P.
1986 *Pidgin and Creole Linguistics.* London: Basil Blackwell.

Mukhopadhyay, C., and P. Higgins
1988 Anthropological Studies of Women's Status Revisited: 1977–1987. *Annual Review of Anthropology* 17: 461–495.

Mullings, L., ed.
1987 *Cities of the United States: Studies in Urban Anthropology.* New York: Columbia University Press.

Murdock, G. P.
1934 *Our Primitive Contemporaries.* New York: Macmillan.
1957 World Ethnographic Sample. *American Anthropologist* 59: 664–687.

Murphy, R. F.
1990 *The Body Silent.* New York: W. W. Norton.

Murphy, R. F., and L. Kasdan
1959 The Structure of Parallel Cousin Marriage. *American Anthropologist* 61: 17–29.

Mydans, S.
1992a Criticism Grows over Aliens Seized during Riots. *The New York Times,* May 29, p. A8.
1992b Judge Dismisses Case in Shooting by Officer. *The New York Times,* June 4, p. A8.

Nagel, J.
1996 *American Indian Ethnic Renewal: Red Power and the Resurgence of Identity and Culture.* New York: Oxford University Press.

Napier, J. R., and P. H. Napier
1985 *The Natural History of Primates.* Cambridge, MA: MIT Press.

Nash, D.
1993 *A Little Anthropology,* 2nd ed. Englewood Cliffs, NJ: Prentice-Hall.

Nash, J., and H. Safa, eds.
1986 *Women and Change in Latin America.* South Hadley, MA: Bergin and Garvey.

National Association for the Practice of Anthropology
1991 *NAPA Directory of Practicing Anthropologists.* Washington, DC: American Anthropological Association.

Nelson, H., and R. Jurmain
1991 *Introduction to Physical Anthropology,* 5th ed. St. Paul, MN: West.

Netting, R. M. C., R. R. Wilk, and E. J. Arnould, eds.
1984 *Households: Comparative and Historical Studies of the Domestic Group.* Berkeley, CA: University of California Press.

Nevid, J. S., and Rathus, S. A.
1995 *Human Sexuality in a World of Diversity,* 2nd ed. Needham Heights, MA: Allyn & Bacon.

New York Times
1990 Tropical Diseases on March, Hitting 1 in 10. March 28, p. A3.
1992 Alexandria Journal: TV Program for Somalis Is a Rare Unifying Force. December 1992.
1992 Married with Children: The Waning Icon. August 23, p. E2.

Newman, M.
1992 Riots Bring Attention to Growing Hispanic Presence in South-Central Area. *The New York Times,* May 11, p. A10.

Nielsson, G. P.
1985 States and Nation-Groups: A Global Taxonomy. In *New Nationalisms of the Developed World,* eds. E. A. Tiryakian and R. Rogowski, pp. 27–56. Boston: Allen and Unwin.

Nussbaum, M., and J. Glover, eds.
1995 *Women, Culture, and Development: A Study of Human Capabilities.* New York: Oxford University Press.

Oakley, K. P.
1976 *Man the Tool-Maker,* 6th ed. Chicago: University of Chicago Press.

Ong, A.
1987 *Spirits of Resistance and Capitalist Discipline: Factory Women in Malaysia.* Albany: State University of New York Press.
1989 Center, Periphery, and Hierarchy: Gender in Southeast Asia. In *Gender and Anthropology: Critical Reviews for Research and Teaching,* ed. S. Morgen, pp. 294–312. Washington, DC: American Anthropological Association.

Ong, A., and M. G. Peletz, eds.
1995 *Bewitching Women, Pious Men: Gender and Body Politics in Southeast Asia.* Berkeley: University of California Press.

Otterbein, K. F.
1968 (orig. 1963). Marquesan Polyandry. In *Marriage, Family and Residence,* eds. P. Bohannan and J. Middleton, pp. 287–296. Garden City, NY: Natural History Press.

Park, M. A.
1996 *Biological Anthropology.* Mountain View, CA: Mayfield.

Parker, S., and R. Kleiner
1970 The Culture of Poverty: An Adjustive Dimension. *American Anthropologist* 72: 516–527.

Parsons, J. R.
1974 The Development of a Prehistoric Complex Society: A Regional Perspective from the Valley of Mexico. *Journal of Field Archaeology* 1: 81–108.

1976   The Role of Chinampa Agriculture in the Food Supply of Aztec Tenochtitlan. In *Cultural Change and Continuity: Essays in Honor of James Bennett Griffin*, ed. C. E. Cleland, pp. 233–262. New York: Academic Press.

PATTERSON, F.
1978   Conversations with a Gorilla. *National Geographic*, October, pp. 438–465.

PATTERSON, T. C.
1993   *Archaeology: The Historical Development of Civilizations*, 2nd ed. Englewood Cliffs, NJ: Prentice-Hall.

PAUL, R.
1989   Psychoanalytic Anthropology. *Annual Review of Anthropology* 18: 177–202.

PEAR, R.
1992   Ranks of U.S. Poor Reach 35.7 Million, the Most since '64. *The New York Times*, September 3, pp. A1, A12.

PELETZ, M.
1988   *A Share of the Harvest: Kinship, Property, and Social History among the Malays of Rembau*. Berkeley: University of California Press.

PELTO, P.
1973   *The Snowmobile Revolution: Technology and Social Change in the Arctic*. Menlo Park, CA: Cummings.

PELTO, P. J., AND G. H. PELTO
1978   *Anthropological Research: The Structure of Inquiry*, 2nd ed. New York: Cambridge University Press.

PFEIFFER, J.
1985   *The Emergence of Humankind*, 4th ed. New York: HarperCollins.

PHILLIPSON, D. W.
1993   *African Archaeology*, 2nd ed. New York: Cambridge University Press.

PIDDOCKE, S.
1969   The Potlatch System of the Southern Kwakiutl: A New Perspective. In *Environment and Cultural Behavior*, ed. A. P. Vayda, pp. 130–156. Garden City, NY: Natural History Press.

PLATTNER, S., ED.
1989   *Economic Anthropology*. Stanford, CA: Stanford University Press.

PODOLEFSKY, A.
1992   *Simbu Law: Conflict Management in the New Guinea Highlands*. Fort Worth: Harcourt Brace.

PODOLEFSKY, A., AND P. J. BROWN, EDS.
1992   *Applying Anthropology: An Introductory Reader*, 2nd ed. Mountain View, CA: Mayfield.
1994   *Applying Anthropology: An Introductory Reader*, 3rd ed. Mountain View, CA: Mayfield.

POLANYI, K.
1968   *Primitive, Archaic and Modern Economies: Essays of Karl Polanyi*. Edited by G. Dalton. Garden City, NY: Anchor Books.

POSPISIL, L.
1963   *The Kapauku Papuans of West New Guinea*. New York: Harcourt Brace Jovanovich.

POTASH, B., ED.
1986   *Widows in African Societies: Choices and Constraints*. Stanford, CA: Stanford University Press.

PRICE, R., ED.
1973   *Maroon Societies*. New York: Anchor Press, Doubleday.

QUIATT, D., AND V. REYNOLDS
1995   *Primate Behavior: Information, Social Knowledge, and the Evolution of Culture*. New York: Cambridge University Press.

QUINN, N., AND C. STRAUSS
1989   A Cognitive Cultural Anthropology. Paper presented at the Invited Session "Assessing Developments in Anthropology," American Anthropological Association 88th Annual Meeting, November 15–19, 1989, Washington, DC.
1994   A Cognitive Cultural Anthropology. In *Assessing Cultural Anthropology*, ed. R. Borofsky. New York: McGraw-Hill.

RADCLIFFE-BROWN, A. R.
1965   (orig. 1962). *Structure and Function in Primitive Society*. New York: Free Press.

RADCLIFFE-BROWN, A. R., AND D. FORDE, EDS.
1994   *African Systems of Kinship and Marriage*. New York: Columbia University Press.

RAK, Y.
1986   The Neandertal: A New Look at an Old Face. *Journal of Human Evolution* 15(3): 151–164.

RAPPAPORT, R. A.
1974   Obvious Aspects of Ritual. *Cambridge Anthropology* 2: 2–60.
1979   *Ecology, Meaning, and Religion*. Richmond, CA: North Atlantic Books.

READ-MARTIN, C. E., AND D. W. READ
1975   Australopithecine Scavenging and Human Evolution: An Approach from Faunal Analysis. *Current Anthropology* 16: 359–368.

READE, J.
1991   *Mesopotamia*. Cambridge, MA: Harvard University Press.

REDFIELD, R.
1941   *The Folk Culture of Yucatan*. Chicago: University of Chicago Press.

REDFIELD, R., R. LINTON, AND M. HERSKOVITS
1936   Memorandum on the Study of Acculturation. *American Anthropologist* 38: 149–152.

REITER, R.
1975 Men and Women in the South of France: Public and Private Domains. In *Toward an Anthropology of Women*, ed. R. Reiter, pp. 252–282. New York: Monthly Review Press.

REYNOLDS, V.
1971 *The Apes.* New York: Harper Colophon.

RICHARDS, P.
1973 The Tropical Rain Forest. *Scientific American* 229(6): 58–67.

Ricoeur, P.
1971 The Model of the Text: Meaningful Action Considered as a Text. *Social Research* 38: 529–562.

ROBERTS, D. F.
1953 Body Weight, Race and Climate. *American Journal of Physical Anthropology* 11: 533–558.

ROBERTS, S.
1979 *Order and Dispute: An Introduction to Legal Anthropology.* New York: Penguin Books.

ROBERTSON, A. F.
1995 *The Big Catch: A Practical Introduction to Development.* Boulder, CO: Westview.

ROBERTSON, J.
1992 Koreans in Japan. Paper presented at the University of Michigan Department of Anthropology, Martin Luther King Jr. Day Panel, January 1992. Ann Arbor: University of Michigan Department of Anthropology (unpublished).

RODSETH, L., R. W. WRANGHAM, A. M. HARRIGAN, AND B. SMUTS
1991 The Human Community as a Primate Society. *Current Anthropology* 32: 221–254.

ROMAINE, S.
1994 *Language in Society: An Introduction to Sociolinguistics.* New York: Oxford University Press.

ROMER, A. S.
1960 *Man and the Vertebrates,* 3rd ed., Vol. 1. Harmondsworth, England: Penguin.

ROOT, D.
1996 *Cannibal Culture: Art, Appropriation, and the Commodification of Difference.* Boulder, CO: Westview.

ROSALDO, M. Z.
1980a *Knowledge and Passion: Notions of Self and Social Life.* Stanford, CA: Stanford University Press.
1980b The Use and Abuse of Anthropology: Reflections on Feminism and Cross-Cultural Understanding. *Signs* 5(3): 389–417.

ROSEBERRY, W.
1988 Political Economy. *Annual Review of Anthropology* 17: 161–185.

ROUSE, R.
1991 Mexican Migration and the Social Space of Postmodernism. *Diaspora* 1(1): 8–23.

ROYAL ANTHROPOLOGICAL INSTITUTE
1951 *Notes and Queries on Anthropology,* 6th ed. London: Routledge and Kegan Paul.

RUSHING, W. A.
1995 *The AIDS Epidemic: Social Dimension of an Infectious Disease.* Boulder, CO: Westview.

RYAN, S.
1990 *Ethnic Conflict and International Relations.* Brookfield, MA: Dartmouth.
1995 *Ethnic Conflict and International Relations,* 2nd ed. Brookfield, MA: Dartmouth.

SACHS, C. E.
1996 *Gendered Fields: Rural Women, Agriculture, and Environment.* Boulder, CO: Westview.

SADE, D.
1972 A Longitudinal Study of Social Behavior of Rhesus Monkeys. In *The Functional and Evolutionary Biology of Primates,* ed. R. Tuttle, pp. 378–398. Chicago: University of Chicago Press.

SAGGS, H.
1989 *Civilization before Greece and Rome.* New Haven: Yale University Press.

SAHLINS, M. D.
1961 The Segmentary Lineage: An Organization of Predatory Expansion. *American Anthropologist* 63: 322–345.
1968 *Tribesmen.* Englewood Cliffs, NJ: Prentice-Hall.
1972 *Stone Age Economics.* Chicago: Aldine.

SAITOTI, T. O.
1988 *The Worlds of a Maasai Warrior: An Autobiography.* Berkeley: University of California Press.

SALZMAN, P. C.
1974 Political Organization among Nomadic Peoples. In *Man in Adaptation: The Cultural Present,* 2nd ed., ed. Y. A. Cohen, pp. 267–284. Chicago: Aldine.

SALZMANN, Z.
1993 *Language, Culture, and Society: An Introduction to Linguistic Anthropology.* Boulder, CO: Westview.

SANDAY, P. R.
1974 Female Status in the Public Domain. In *Woman, Culture, and Society,* ed. M. Z. Rosaldo and L. Lamphere, pp. 189–206. Stanford, CA: Stanford University Press.

SANDERS, W. T., J. R. PARSONS, AND R. S. SANTLEY
1979 *The Basin of Mexico: Ecological Processes in the Evolution of a Civilization.* New York: Academic Press.

SANKOFF, G.
1980 *The Social Life of Language.* Philadelphia: University of Pennsylvania Press.

SANTINO, J.
1983 Night of the Wandering Souls. *Natural History* 92(10): 42.

SAPIR, E.
1931 Conceptual Categories in Primitive Languages. *Science* 74: 578–584.

SARGENT, C. F., AND C. B. BRETTELL
1996 *Gender and Health: An International Perspective.* Englewood Cliffs, NJ: Prentice-Hall.

SCHAEFER, R.
1989 *Sociology,* 3rd ed. New York: McGraw-Hill.

SCHAEFER, R., AND R. P. LAMM
1992 *Sociology,* 4th ed. New York: McGraw-Hill.

SCHALLER, G.
1963 *The Mountain Gorilla: Ecology and Behavior.* Chicago: University of Chicago Press.

SCHEPER-HUGHES, N.
1987 Culture, Scarcity, and Maternal Thinking: Mother Love and Child Death in Northeast Brazil. In *Child Survival,* ed. N. Scheper-Hughes, pp. 187–208. Boston: D. Reidel.
1992 *Death without Weeping: The Violence of Everyday Life in Brazil.* Berkeley: University of California Press.

SCHIEFFELIN, E.
1976 *The Sorrow of the Lonely and the Burning of the Dancers.* New York: St. Martin's.

SCOTT, J. C.
1985 *Weapons of the Weak.* New Haven: Yale University Press.
1990 *Domination and the Arts of Resistance.* New Haven: Yale University Press.

SCUDDER, T., AND E. COLSON
1980 *Secondary Education and the Formation of an Elite: The Impact of Education on Gwembe District, Zambia.* London: Academic Press.

SCUDDER, T., AND J. HABARAD
1991 Local Responses to Involuntary Relocation and Development in the Zambian Portion of the Middle Zambezi Valley. In *Migrants in Agricultural Development,* ed. J. A. Mollett, pp. 178–205. New York: New York University Press.

SEBEOK, T. A., AND J. UMIKER-SEBEOK, EDS.
1980 *Speaking of Apes: A Critical Anthropology of Two-Way Communication with Man.* New York: Plenum.

SELIGSON, M. A.
1984 *The Gap between Rich and Poor: Contending Perspectives on the Political Economy of Development.* Boulder, CO: Westview.

SERED, S. S.
1996 *Priestess, Mother, Sacred Sister: Religions Dominated by Women.* New York: Oxford University Press.

SERVICE, E. R.
1962 *Primitive Social Organization: An Evolutionary Perspective.* New York: McGraw-Hill.
1966 *The Hunters.* Englewood Cliffs, NJ: Prentice-Hall.
1975 *Origins of the State and Civilization: The Process of Cultural Evolution.* New York: W. W. Norton.

SHABECOFF, P.
1989a Ivory Imports Banned to Aid Elephant. *The New York Times,* June 7, p. 15.
1989b New Lobby Is Helping Wildlife of Africa. *The New York Times,* June 9, p. 14.

SHANKLIN, E.
1995 *Anthropology and Race.* Belmont, CA: Wadsworth.

SHANNON, T. R.
1989 *An Introduction to the World-System Perspective.* Boulder, CO: Westview.

SHIGERU, K.
1994 *Our Land Was a Forest: An Ainu Memoir.* Boulder, CO: Westview.

SHORE, B.
1996 *Culture in Mind: Meaning, Construction, and Cultural Cognition.* New York: Oxford University Press.

SHOSTAK, M.
1981 *Nisa: The Life and Words of a !Kung Woman.* Cambridge, MA: Harvard University Press.

SHREEVE, J.
1992 The Dating Game: How Old Is the Human Race? *Discover* 13(9): 76–83.

SHWEDER, R., AND H. LEVINE, EDS.
1984 *Culture Theory: Essays on Mind, Self, and Emotion.* Cambridge: Cambridge University Press.

SIBLEY, C. G., AND J. E. AHLQUIST
1984 The Phylogeny of the Hominoid Primates, as Indicated by DNA-DNA Hybridization. *Journal of Molecular Evolution* 20: 2–15.

SIGNO, A.
1994 *Economics of the Family.* New York: Oxford University Press.

SILBERBAUER, G.
1981 *Hunter and Habitat in the Central Kalahari Desert.* New York: Cambridge University Press.

SIMONS, A.
1995 *Networks of Dissolution: Somalia Undone.* Boulder, CO: Westview.

SLADE, M.
1984 Displaying Affection in Public, *The New York Times,* December 17, p. B14.

SMALL, M., ED.
1984 *Female Primates: Studies by Women Primatologists.* New York: Alan R. Liss.

SMITH, C. A.
1990 The Militarization of Civil Society in Guatemala: Economic Reorganization as a Continuation of War. *Latin American Perspectives* 17: 8–41.

SMITH, M. G.
1965 *The Plural Society in the British West Indies.* Berkeley: University of California Press.

SMUTS, B. B.
1985 *Sex and Friendship in Baboons.* New York: Aldine.

SOLHEIM, W. G., II.
1976 (orig. 1972). An Earlier Agricultural Revolution. In *Avenues to Antiquity, Readings from Scientific American,* ed. B. M. Fagan, pp. 160–168. San Francisco: W. H. Freeman.

SOLWAY, J., AND R. LEE
1990 Foragers, Genuine and Spurious: Situating the Kalahari San in History (with CA treatment). *Current Anthropology* 31(2): 109–146.

SONNEVILLE-BORDES, D. DE
1963 Upper Paleolithic Cultures in Western Europe. *Science* 142: 347–355.

SPINDLER, G. D., ED.
1978 *The Making of Psychological Anthropology.* Berkeley: University of California Press.
1982 *Doing the Ethnography of Schooling: Educational Anthropology in Action.* New York: Holt, Rinehart and Winston.

SPONSEL, L. E., AND T. GREGOR, EDS.
1994 *The Anthropology of Peace and Nonviolence.* Boulder, CO: Lynne Reinner.

SPRADLEY, J. P.
1979 *The Ethnographic Interview.* New York: Harcourt Brace Jovanovich.

STACEY, J.
1990 *Brave New Families: Stories of Domestic Upheaval in Late Twentieth Century America.* New York: Basic Books.

STACK, C. B.
1975 *All Our Kin: Strategies for Survival in a Black Community.* New York: Harper Torchbooks.

STATISTICAL ABSTRACT OF THE UNITED STATES
1991 111th ed. Washington, DC: U.S. Bureau of the Census, U.S. Government Printing Office.

STAUB, S.
1989 *Yemenis in New York City: The Folklore of Ethnicity.* Philadelphia: Balch Institute Press.

STEPHENS, S., ED.
1996 *Children and the Politics of Culture.* Princeton, NJ: Princeton University Press.

STEPONAITIS, V.
1986 Prehistoric Archaeology in the Southeastern United States. *Annual Review of Anthropology* 15: 363–404.

STEVENS, W. K.
1992 Humanity Confronts Its Handiwork: An Altered Planet. *The New York Times,* May 5, pp. B5–B7.

STEVENSON, R. F.
1968 *Population and Political Systems in Tropical Africa.* New York: Columbia University Press.

STEWARD, J. H.
1955 *Theory of Culture Change.* Urbana: University of Illinois Press.

STOLER, A.
1977 Class Structure and Female Autonomy in Rural Java. *Signs* 3: 74–89.

STRATHERN, M.
1988 *The Gender of the Gift: Problems with Women and Problems with Society in Melanesia.* Berkeley: University of California Press.

SUAREZ-OROZCO, M. M., AND G. AND L. SPINDLER, EDS.
1994 *The Making of Psychological Anthropology II.* Fort Worth: Harcourt Brace.

SUSMAN, R. L.
1987 Pygmy Chimpanzees and Common Chimpanzees: Models for the Behavioral Ecology of the Earliest Hominids. In *The Evolution of Human Behavior: Primate Models,* ed. W. G. Kinzey, pp. 72–86. Albany: State University of New York Press.

SWIFT, M.
1963 Men and Women in Malay Society. In *Women in the New Asia,* ed. B. Ward, pp. 268–286. Paris: UNESCO.

TAGUE, R. G., AND C. O. LOVEJOY
1986 The Obstetric Pelvis of A. L. 288-1 (Lucy). *Journal of Human Evolution* 15: 237–255.

TAINTER, J.
1987 *The Collapse of Complex Societies.* New York: Cambridge University Press.

TANAKA, J.
1980 *The San Hunter-Gatherers of the Kalahari.* Tokyo: University of Tokyo Press.

TANNEN, D.
1990 *You Just Don't Understand: Women and Men in Conversation.* New York: Ballantine.

TANNEN, D., ED.
1993 *Gender and Conversational Interaction.* New York: Oxford University Press.

TANNER, N.
1974 Matrifocality in Indonesia and Africa and among Black Americans. In *Women, Culture, and Society,* eds. M. Z. Rosaldo and L. Lamphere, pp. 127–156. Stanford, CA: Stanford University Press.

TATTERSALL, I.
1995 *The Fossil Trail: How We Know What We Think*

We Know about Human Evolution. New York: Oxford University Press.

TAYLOR, A.
1993   *Women Drug Users: An Ethnography of a Female Injecting Community.* New York: Oxford University Press.

TAYLOR, C.
1996   *The Black Churches of Brooklyn.* New York: Columbia University Press.

TELEKI, G.
1973   *The Predatory Behavior of Wild Chimpanzees.* Lewisburg, PA: Bucknell University Press.

TERRACE, H. S.
1979   *Nim.* New York: Knopf.

THOMASON, S. G., AND T. KAUFMAN
1988   *Language Contact, Creolization and Genetic Linguistics.* Berkeley: University of California Press.

THOMSON, A., AND L. H. D. BUXTON
1923   Man's Nasal Index in Relation to Certain Climatic Conditions. *Journal of the Royal Anthropological Institute* 53: 92–112.

THOMPSON, W.
1983   Introduction: World System with and without the Hyphen. In *Contending Approaches to World System Analysis,* ed. W. Thompson, pp. 7–26. Thousand Oaks, CA: Sage.

TRIGGER, B. G.
1995   *Early Civilizations: Ancient Egypt in Context.* New York: Columbia University Press.

TRUDGILL, P.
1983   *Sociolinguistics: An Introduction to Language and Society,* rev. ed. Baltimore: Penguin.

TURNBULL, C.
1965   *Wayward Servants: The Two Worlds of the African Pygmies.* Garden City, NY: Natural History Press.

TURNER, V. W.
1969   *The Ritual Process: Structure and Antistructure.* Chicago: Aldine de Gruyter.
1995   *The Ritual Process: Structure and Antistructure,* reprint. Hawthorne, NY: Aldine de Gruyter.

TYLOR, E. B.
1889   On a Method of Investigating the Development of Institutions: Applied to Laws of Marriage and Descent. *Journal of the Royal Anthropological Institute* 18: 245–269.
1958   (orig. 1871). *Primitive Culture.* New York: Harper Torchbooks.

UCKO, P. J., AND G. W. DIMBLEBY, EDS.
1969   *The Domestication and Exploitation of Plants and Animals.* Chicago: Aldine.

VALENTINE, C.
1968   *Culture and Poverty.* Chicago: University of Chicago Press.

VALLADAS, H., J. L. REYSS, J. L. JORON, G. VALLADAS, O. BAR-JOSEPH, AND B. VANDERMEERSCH
1988   Thermoluminescence Dating of Mousterian "Proto-Cro-Magnon" Remains from Israel and the Origin of Modern Man. *Nature* 331: 614–616.

VAN CANTFORT, T. E., AND J. B. RIMPAU
1982   Sign Language Studies with Children and Chimpanzees. *Sign Language Studies* 34: 15–72.

VAN SCHAIK, C. P., AND J. A. R. A. M. VAN HOOFF
1983   On the Ultimate Causes of Primate Social Systems. *Behaviour* 85: 91–117.

VAN WILLINGEN, J.
1987   *Becoming a Practicing Anthropologist: A Guide to Careers and Training Programs in Applied Anthropology.* NAPA Bulletin 3. Washington, DC: American Anthropological Association/National Association for the Practice of Anthropology.
1993   *Applied Anthropology: An Introduction,* 2nd ed. South Hadley, MA: Bergin and Garvey.

VAYDA, A. P.
1968   (orig. 1961). Economic Systems in Ecological Perspective: The Case of the Northwest Coast. In *Readings in Anthropology,* 2nd ed., Vol. 2, ed. M. H. Fried, pp. 172–178. New York: Crowell.

VINCENT, J.
1990   *Anthropology and Politics: Visions, Traditions, and Trends.* Tucson: University of Arizona Press.

VIOLA, H. J., AND C. MARGOLIS
1991   *Seeds of Change: Five Hundred Years since Columbus, a Quincentennial Commemoration.* Washington, DC: Smithsonian Institution Press.

WAGLEY, C. W.
1968   (orig. 1959). The Concept of Social Race in the Americas. In *The Latin American Tradition,* ed. C. Wagley, pp. 155–174. New York: Columbia University Press.

WAGNER, R.
1981   *The Invention of Culture,* rev. ed. Chicago: University of Chicago Press.

WALLACE, A. F. C.
1956   Revitalization Movements. *American Anthropologist* 58: 264–281.
1966   *Religion: An Anthropological View.* New York: McGraw-Hill.
1970   *The Death and Rebirth of the Seneca.* New York: Knopf.

WALLERSTEIN, I.
1974   *The Modern World-System: Capitalist Agriculture and the Origins of the European World-Economy in the Sixteenth Century.* New York: Academic Press.

1980 *The Modern World System II: Mercantilism and the Consolidation of the European World-Economy, 1600–1750.* New York: Academic Press.

1982 The Rise and Future Demise of the World Capitalist System: Concepts for Comparative Analysis. In *Introduction to the Sociology of "Developing Societies,"* eds. H. Alavi and T. Shanin, pp. 29–53. New York: Monthly Review Press.

WALLMAN, S., ED.
1977 *Perceptions of Development.* New York: Cambridge University Press.

WARD, M. C.
1996 *A World Full of Women.* Needham Heights, MA: Allyn & Bacon.

WASHBURN, S. L., AND R. MOORE
1980 *Ape into Human: A Study of Human Evolution,* 2nd ed. Boston: Little, Brown.

WATSON, J. D.
1970 *Molecular Biology of the Gene.* New York: Benjamin.

WATSON, P.
1972 Can Racial Discrimination Affect IQ? In *Race and Intelligence; The Fallacies behind the Race-IQ Controversy,* eds. K. Richardson and D. Spears, pp. 56–67. Baltimore: Penguin.

WEAVER, T., GEN. ED.
1973 *To See Ourselves: Anthropology and Modern Social Issues.* Glenview, IL: Scott, Foresman.

WEBER, M.
1958 (orig. 1904). *The Protestant Ethic and the Spirit of Capitalism.* New York: Scribner's.

1968 (orig. 1922). *Economy and Society.* Translated by E. Fischoff et al. New York: Bedminster Press.

WEBSTER'S NEW WORLD ENCYCLOPEDIA
1993 College Edition. Englewood Cliffs, NJ: Prentice-Hall.

WEISS, M. L., AND A. E. MANN
1990 *Human Biology and Behavior: An Anthropological Perspective,* 5th ed. Glenview, IL: Scott, Foresman.

WENKE, R.
1990 *Patterns in Prehistory: Humankind's First Three Million Years,* 3rd ed. New York: Oxford University Press.

WESTERMARCK, E.
1894 *The History of Human Marriage.* London: Macmillan.

WHITE, L. A.
1959 *The Evolution of Culture: The Development of Civilization to the Fall of Rome.* New York: McGraw-Hill.

WHITING, B. E., ED.
1963 *Six Cultures: Studies of Child Rearing.* New York: Wiley.

WHORF, B. L.
1956 A Linguistic Consideration of Thinking in Primitive Communities. In *Language, Thought, and Reality: Selected Writings of Benjamin Lee Whorf,* ed. J. B. Carroll, pp. 65–86. Cambridge, MA: MIT Press.

WILK, R. R.
1996 *Economies and Cultures: An Introduction to Economic Anthropology.* Boulder, CO: Westview.

WILLIAMS, B.
1989 A Class Act: Anthropology and the Race to Nation across Ethnic Terrain. *Annual Review of Anthropology* 18: 401–444.

WILMSEN, E.
1989 *Land Filled with Flies: A Political Economy of the Kalahari.* Chicago: University of Chicago Press.

WILMSEN, E. N., AND P. McALLISTER, EDS.
1996 *The Politics of Difference: Ethnic Premises in a World of Power.* Chicago: University of Chicago Press.

WILSON, C.
1995 *Hidden in the Blood: A Personal Investigation of AIDS in the Yucatan.* New York: Columbia University Press.

WINSLOW, J. H., AND A. MEYER
1983 The Perpetrator at Piltdown. *Science 83,* September, pp. 33–43.

WINZELER, R. L.
1995 *Latah in Southeast Asia: The Ethnography and History of a Culture-Bound Syndrome.* New York: Cambridge University Press.

WITTFOGEL, K. A.
1957 *Oriental Despotism: A Comparative Study of Total Power.* New Haven: Yale University Press.

WOLF, E. R.
1966 *Peasants.* Englewood Cliffs, NJ: Prentice-Hall.
1982 *Europe and the People without History.* Berkeley: University of California Press.

WOLPOFF, M. H.
1980 *Paleoanthropology.* New York: McGraw-Hill.
1995 *Paleoanthropology,* 2nd ed. New York: McGraw-Hill.

WOOLARD, K. A.
1989 *Double Talk: Bilingualism and the Politics of Ethnicity in Catalonia.* Stanford, CA: Stanford University Press.

WORLD ALMANAC & BOOK OF FACTS
Published annually. New York: Newspaper Enterprise Association.

WORLD HEALTH ORGANIZATION
1995 *World Health Report.* Geneva: World Health Organization.

WORSLEY, P.
  1984   *The Three Worlds: Culture and World Development.* Chicago: University of Chicago Press.
  1985   (orig. 1959). Cargo Cults. In *Readings in Anthropology 85/86.* Guilford, CT: Dushkin.

WRANGHAM, R.
  1980   An Ecological Model of Female-Bonded Primate Groups. *Behavior* 75: 262–300.
  1987   The Significance of African Apes for Reconstructing Human Social Evolution. In *The Evolution of Human Behavior: Primate Models,* ed. W. G. Kinzey, pp. 51–71. Albany: State University of New York Press.

WRIGHT, H. T., AND G. A. JOHNSON
  1975   Population, Exchange, and Early State Formation in Southwestern Iran. *American Anthropologist* 77: 267–289.

WRIGHT, S., ED.
  1994   *Anthropology of Organizations.* London: Routledge.

WULFF, R. M., AND S. J. FISKE, EDS.
  1987   *Anthropological Praxis: Translating Knowledge into Action.* Boulder, CO: Westview.

YETMAN, N., ED.
  1991   *Majority and Minority: The Dynamics of Race and Ethnicity in American Life,* 5th ed. Boston: Allyn & Bacon.

YOUNG, W. C.
  1996   *The Rashaayada Bedouin: Arab Pastoralists of Eastern Sudan.* Fort Worth: Harcourt Brace.

INTERNET RESOURCES

Selected Reference Sites in Anthropology from the World Wide Web

Due to the temporary nature of some websites and their continually changing structure and content, we cannot guarantee that the information listed here will always be available.

Part One: General Interest in Anthropology

1. ANTHROPOLOGY RESOURCES ON THE INTERNET
http://www.nitehawk.com/alleycat/anth-faq.html
This site lists discussion groups, World Wide Web Servers, Electronic Journals, and other sources of information in anthropology on the Internet.

2. ANTHROPOLOGY COMMUNICATIONS ON-LINE
http://pegasus.acs.ttu.edu/~wurlr/anthro.html
The subject of this site includes information on finding anthropological films, communicating through print and electronic media, and finding anthropologists themselves.

3. HUBS
http://www.cs.su.oz.au/rkwok/hubs.html
A short but interesting list of links to websites in archaeology and anthropology, including sites on Australia, South America, and Africa.

4. CLASSICS AND MEDITERRANEAN ARCHAEOLOGY HOME PAGE
http://rome.classics.lsa.umich.edu/welcome.html
This very complete site includes a searchable database of a large list of texts, projects, web documents, museums, atlases, and geographic information on archaeology. Also includes preliminary reports from field projects around the world.

5. INSTITUTE OF SOCIAL AND CULTURAL ANTHROPOLOGY
http://www.rsl.ox.ac.uk/isca/index.html

From Oxford University, this website covers anthropological resources in social and cultural studies such as the European Association of Social Anthropologists, the *Journal of Political Ecology*, and the *Journal of Buddhist Ethics*.

6. HUMANITIES HUB
http://www.gu.edu.au/gwis/hub/hub.anthro.html
A nice list of links including anthropology course material, pictorial database of archaeological figurines from Israel, and library resources on-line. Searchable database. Also covers documentary and educational films.

7. EINET GALAXY, ANTHROPOLOGY
http://www.einet.net/galaxy/Social-Sciences/Anthropology.html
A complete list of resources, directories, periodicals, academic organizations, nonprofit organizations, and collections in anthropology.

8. THE BUBL INFORMATION SERVICE
http://bubl.bath.ac.uk/BUBL/Anthropology.html
Includes links to collections of African studies, behavioral sciences, ecolab, International Council on Monuments and Sites, and the World Health Organization.

9. ANTHRONET
http://darwin.clas.virginia.edu/~dew7e/anthronet/
A nice collection of information, including material on biological, linguistic, and sociocultural anthropologists, museum sites, journals, funding sources, and other information.

10. ANTHAP, APPLIED ANTHROPOLOGY COMPUTER NETWORK
http://www.oakland.edu/~dow/anthap.htm
Covers information on applied anthropology, including the National Association for the Practice of Anthropology video, discussion channels, and activities and programs of the American Anthropological Association.

11. COMMERCIAL SOFTWARE IN ANTHROPOLOGY
http://wings.buffalo.edu/academic/department/anthropology/documents/software
The home page was developed as a list of commercial software available in archaeology and anthropology.

12. DIRECT ACCESS TO WEB ANTHROPOLOGY RESOURCES
http://wings.buffalo.edu/academic/department/anthropology/web_sites
On-line databases, interesting places to visit, educational resources, associations, documentaries, and other websites are listed.

13. INTO THE WORLD OF ANTHROPOLOGY
http://www.ed.uiuc.edu/students/b-sklar/basic387.html
A rich database of information on physical anthropology, cultural anthropology, linguistic anthropology and archaeology, with a "Now You Be an Anthropologist" section.

14. ANTHROPOLOGY AND ARCHAEOLOGY
http://galaxy.einet.net/GJ/anthropology.html
Covers links to the Polynesian Voyaging Society, the Hellenic Civilization website, and social anthropology sites around the world.

15. NATIONAL MUSEUM OF NATURAL HISTORY, SMITHSONIAN INSTITUTION
http://nmnhwww.si.edu/departments/anthro.html
Links to the Human Studies Film Archives of the museum of over 7 million feet of historic and contemporary film and video images of human cultures around the world.

16. ANTHROPOLOGY ON THE INTERNET
http://www.umanitoba.ca/anthropology/aaa-revue.html
A hypertext review of general scholarly uses of the Internet in anthropology.

17. ANTHROPOLOGICAL FORUM
http://www.arts.uwa.edu.au/AnthropWWW/Forum.htm
The *Anthropological Forum* is an international journal of Social and Cultural Anthropology and Comparative Sociology.

18. ANTHROPOLOGY AND ARCHAEOLOGY
http://www.sil.org/anthro/anthro.html
Links to Ancient Near East resources, Native American Sites, and the Virtual Library in Anthropology.

19. ANTHROPOLOGY
http://www.esrc.bris.ac.uk/Subjects/anthro.html
This site includes links to Black Studies Gopher, Chicano-LatinoNet, JewishNet, and the National Indian Policy Center.

20. ANTHROPOLOGY ON THE INTERNET
http://dizzy.library.arizona.edu/users/jlcox/first.html
Another collection of good starting points for research in cultural anthropology, archaeology, and linguistics. Covers journals, institutes, museums, and miscellaneous sites.

21. AGAINST THE GRAIN: CULTURAL ANTHROPOLOGY
http://worldweb.net/~beriss/
An interesting collection on cultural criticism and anthropology-related information, particularly concerning Europe and the Caribbean.

22. CLEARINGHOUSE: HUMANITIES
http://www.lib.umich.edu/chouse/inter/135.html
The websites cover over 100 links to user groups, discussion forums, and other sites in anthropology, cross-cultural studies, and archaeology.

23. ANTHROPOLOGY
http://www.usc.edu/dept/v-lib/anthropology.html
An excellent list of specialized fields in anthropology.

24. JOURNAL OF CULTURAL ANTHROPOLOGY
http://www.pitzer.edu/cultanth/
Editor's statement, table of contents, guidelines for submission, etc.

Part Two: Selected Sites Related to Chapters of Kottak: *Anthropology: The Exploration of Human Diversity*, 7th Ed.

Chapter One

1. SIGMUND FREUD
http://www.austria-info.at/personen/freud/index.html

2. DER PHOTOGRAPHS
http://www.xensei.com/users/docued/pics/
This site includes a very nice collection of pho-

tographs from a wide variety of anthropologists, including Margaret Mead.

Chapter Two

1. AUSTRALIAN INSTITUTE OF ABORIGINAL STUDIES
http://ccombs.anu.edu.au/SpecialProj/ASEDA/ASEDA.html
Good example of data organization and field methods.

2. GENEALOGY
http://execpc.com/~dboals/geneo.html
Includes many links for doing genealogical research of many ethnic groups.

Chapter Three

1. EXPLORING ANCIENT WORLD CULTURES
http://www.evansville.edu/~wcweb/wc101

2. GERMANIC LANGUAGE AND CULTURE SITES
http://ukanaix.cc.ukans.edu/~eickwort/cv/hrd_main.html
Covers Germanic, Nordic, Celtic and Pagan cultures.

3. THE LATINO PERSPECTIVE
http://www.epix.net/~syntonic/

Chapter Four

1. ETHNICITY, RACISM, AND THE MEDIA
http://www.brad.ac.uk/bradinfo/research/eram.html

2. YUGOSLAV RESOURCES ON THE INTERNET
http://www.cdsp.neu.edu/info/students/marko/resources.html

3. THE FORMER SOVIET BLOC
http://www.primenet.com/~tevans/newamerican/091895n2.html

Chapter Five

1. BELL CURVE (WITH REVIEWS)
http://www.mosaic.co.za/gavan/Upstream/Issues/bell-curve/

2. BELL CURVE (INTERVIEW WITH AUTHOR)
http://www.skeptic.com/03.2.miele-murray-interview.html

Chapter Six

1. DARWIN'S IDEAS
http://web.mit.edu/lking/www/projects/darwin.html#el

2. CATASTROPHISM
http://pubweb.acns.nwu.edu/~pib/catastro.htm

3. GENETIC ALGORITHMS ARCHIVE
http://www.aic.nrl.navy.mil/galist/

4. BIOLOGY OF AIDS: CRITICAL SCIENTIFIC QUESTIONS
http://www.bocklabs.wisc.edu/duni/aidsquestions.html

5. GENETICS AND THE HUMAN GENOME PROJECT: WHERE SCIENTIFIC AND PUBLIC CULTURES MEET
http://www-leland.stanford.edu/~luce

Chapter Seven

1. PRIMATE GALLERY
http://www.fhcrc.org/~ialwww/PrimateGallery/PrimateGallery.html

2. PRIMATE INFO NET
http://uakari.primate.wisc.edu:70/1/pin
List of resources on primates, including veterinarians, animal welfare, International Directory of Primatologists, and endangered primates.

Chapter Eight

1. PALEONTOLOGY
http://ucmp1.berkeley.edu/FAQ/faq.html
A list of frequently asked questions and their answers about paleontology and fossils, including lists of other servers dealing with paleontology.

2. SCIENCE
http://www.vicnet.net.au/vicnet/science.html
Website sponsored by the Archaeology and Anthropology Society of Victoria, includes resources for teachers.

Chapter Nine

1. W. H. CALVIN'S THE ASCENT OF THE MIND
http://weber.u.washington.edu/~wcalvin/bk5.html

2. VALCAMONICA ROCK ART
http://www.geocities.com/Tokyo/2384/

Chapter Ten

1. PREHISTORIC FOOD PRODUCTION IN MID-CONTINENTAL UNITED STATES
http://spirit.lib.uconn.edu/ArchNet/Topical/Botan/mid-cont.htm
Selected bibliography on early horticulture.

2. NEOLITHIC MOSAIC ON THE NORTH EUROPEAN PLAIN
http://www.princeton.edu/~bogucki/mosaic/html
Covers the introduction of agriculture and farming communities to Europe in 5000–3500 B.C.

3. THE AKKADIAN LANGUAGE
http://www.sron.ruu.nl/~jheise/akkadian/index.html
Website devoted to the cuneiform writing system of ancient Middle East.

4. ASSYRO-BABYLONIAN MYTHOLOGY
http://pubpages.unh.edu/~cbsiren/assyrbabl-faq.html
Overview and history of Mesopotamia, including mythology.

Chapter Eleven

1. FORAGING
http://www.lclark.edu/~wstone/stuff/forager.html
A modern-day forager explains his philosophy.

2. INDONESIA: ENVIRONMENT AND DEVELOPMENT
http://www.worldbank.org/html/ea3dr/welcome.html
Study of the challenges of growing populations, industrialization, and pollution on the environment.

3. SOCIETY OF ECONOMIC ANTHROPOLOGY
http://www.lawrence.edu/~peregrip/seahome.html
Covers issues of diversity and change in the economic systems of the world.

Chapter Twelve

1. THE INDIAN TRIBES
http://www.cs.umu.se/~dphln/wildwest/tribes.html

2. HAVASUPAI TRIBES
http://www.nbs.nau.edu/Tribes/Havasupai/

Chapter Thirteen

1. STONEHENGE ASSOCIATION
http://www.stonehenge-association.co.uk/stonehenge/
Photographs and information about Stonehenge.

2. PAPUA NEW GUINEA
http://www.odci.gov/cia/publications/95fact/pp.html
Statistics, map, and data about Papua New Guinea.

Chapter Fourteen

1. YAHOO SOCIETY AND CULTURE: FAMILIES
http://www.yahoo.com/Society_and_Culture/Families/

2. YAHOO SOCIETY AND CULTURE: GENDER ISSUES: FATHERING
http://www.yahoo.com/Society_and_Culture/Gender_Issues/Men/Fathering/

3. YAHOO SOCIETY AND CULTURE: GENDER ISSUES: MOTHERING
http://www.yahoo.com/Society_and_Culture/Gender_Issues/Women/Mothering/

Chapter Fifteen

1. MARRIAGE AND DIVORCE RATES
http://www.ed.gov/pubs/YouthIndicators/indtab05.html

2. THE POLYGAMY HEADQUARTERS
http://members.aol.com/lanove/

3. THE DIVORCE PAGE
http://www.primenet.com/~dean/

4. ADVICE TO WOMEN ABOUT SINGLE MOTHERHOOD
http://www.parentsplace.com/readroom/smc/advice.html

Chapter Sixteen

1. WOMEN'S WAY
http://www.omix.com/womensway/

2. MEN'S ISSUES PAGES
http://www.vix.com/pub/men/index.html

Chapter Seventeen

1. MYTHS AND LEGENDS
http://pubpages.unh.edu/~cbsiren/myth.html
Very nice complete list of a wide-range of ethnic myths and legends.

2. YAHOO SOCIETY AND CULTURE: RELIGION
http://www.yahoo.com/Society_and_Culture/Religion/

Chapter Eighteen

1. MAX WEBER
http://www.elibrary.com/
Collier's Encyclopedia description of Weber and his work.

Chapter Nineteen

1. NOAM CHOMSKY
http://www.elibrary.com/
Interview with Chomsky, and review of film *Manufacturing Consent* portraying Chomsky's ideas.

2. META INDEX OF LINGUISTICS, NATURAL LANGUAGES, AND COMPUTATIONAL LINGUISTICS RESOURCES
http://www.lcl.cmu.edu/manning/linguistics.html
Guide to linguistic resources on the Web.

Chapter Twenty

1. KARL MARX
http://www.idbsu.edu/surveyrc/Staff/jaynes/marxism/marx.html
Biography, letters, speeches, and information about Karl Marx.

2. INDUSTRIAL REVOLUTION
http://www.england-info.com/pages/history.html
Thorough and interesting report on England in the 1700s, and the impact of the Industrial Revolution.

Chapter Twenty-One

1. WELFARE AND FAMILIES
http://epn.org/idea/welfare.html
Covers the national debate over welfare reform.

2. HOW THE PIE IS SLICED: AMERICA'S GROWING CONCENTRATION OF WEALTH
http://epn.org.prospect/22/22wolf.html

Chapter Twenty-Two

1. MADAGASCAR PAGE
http://www.sas.upenn.edu/African_Studies/Country_Specific/Madagascar.html
Map, information, and Internet resources on Madagascar.

Chapter Twenty-Three and Appendix

1. RAINFOREST ACTION NETWORK
http://www.ran.org/ran
Complete information about rainforest destruction and campaigns to save the forests.

2. WALT DISNEY WORLD
http://206.232.42.10/vacation.html
Official Walt Disney website.

ACKNOWLEDGMENTS

PHOTO CREDITS

Chapter 1
1   Grant Faint/The Image Bank
5   Jerald T. Milanich
6   Robert Phillips/The Image Bank
7   Lowell Georgia/Photo Researchers
9   Melville B. Grosvenor/National Geographic Society Image Collection
10 Irven De Vore/Anthro-Photo
11 Sean Sprague/Impact Visuals
13 UPI/Bettmann Newsphotos
15 Malcolm S. Kirk/Peter Arnold

Chapter 2
19 David Gillison/Peter Arnold
22 Yoram Kahana/Peter Arnold
23 *Left*, Thomas L. Kelly/from "Millennium: Tribal Wisdom and the Modern World" © Biniman Productions Limited; *Right*, H. Uible/Photo Researchers
25 Owen Franken/Stock, Boston
28 Bob Kalman/The Image Works
30 P. F. Bentley/Time Magazine, Time Warner
31 R. Lord/The Image Works

Chapter 3
35 Steve Dunwell/The Image Bank
38 *Top*, Charles Gupton/Tony Stone Images; *Bottom*, Robert Azzi/Woodfin Camp & Associates
40 *Top*, H. Armstrong Roberts; *Bottom*, Ralf-Finn Hestoft/Saba

42 Owen Franken/Stock, Boston
44 *Top*, Noboru Komine/Photo Researchers; *Bottom*, Bob Daemmrich/The Image Works

Chapter 4
49 Susan May Tell/Saba
51 Magnum
53 Magnum
54 Stephanie Maze/Woodfin Camp & Associates
57 McNamara-Zamur/Gamma Liaison
58 Tibor Bognar/The Stock Market
61 Giboux/Gamma Liaison
63 *Top*, Noel Guidu/Gamma Liaison; *Bottom*, Diego Goldberg/Sygma

Chapter 5
69 Sebastiao Barbosa/The Image Bank
70 Jeff Isaac Greenberg/Photo Researchers
72 Donna Binder/Impact Visuals
74 P. J. Griffiths/Magnum
77 Terry Madison/The Image Bank
78 Claude Coivault, from "Millennium: Tribal Wisdom and the Modern World" © Biniman Productions Limited
81 *Top*, Jan Spieczny/Peter Arnold; *Bottom*, David Vance/The Image Bank
82 Xinhua/Gamma Liaison
84 Morton Beebe/The Image Bank

Chapter 6
89 Peter Menzel
91 Noah's Ark by Edward Hicks, 1846, $26\frac{1}{2} \times 30\frac{1}{2}$, Oil

on canvas, Philadelphia Museum of Art, Bequest of Lisa Norris Elkins

95   Alexander Tsiaras/Science Source/Photo Researchers
97   Merrim/Monkmeyer Press
99   Michael Abbey/Photo Researchers
102   Vivian Moos/The Stock Market
104   Peter Menzel
107   *Left,* Robert Caputo/Stock, Boston; *Right,* Clyde H. Smith/Peter Arnold

Chapter 7
113   John Cancalogi/Peter Arnold
114   *Left,* David Agee/Anthro-Photo; *Right,* UPI/ Bettmann
117   Evelyn Gallardo/Peter Arnold
120   Michael Nichols/Magnum
123   Peter Veit/DRK
126   Moore/Anthro-Photo
128   *Left,* Paul Fusco/Magnum; *Right,* Michael Nichols/ Magnum
132   Michael K. Nichols/National Geographic Society Image Collection
135   Gregory G. Dimijian, M.D./Photo Researchers

Chapter 8
141   Africapix/Peter Arnold
143   Tim Davis/Photo Researchers
147   Anna Nosten/Gamma Liaison
149   Morton Beebe/The Image Bank
150   John Reader/Science Photo Library/Photo Researchers
156   John Reader/Science Photo Library/Photo Researchers
159   *Top,* Des Bartlett/Photo Researchers; *Bottom,* Alan Walker, Johns Hopkins University/National Museums of Kenya, Kalakol Account

Chapter 9
167   Jean-Marie Chauvet/Sygma
171   Neg. no. 315466. Courtesy of the American Museum of Natural History. Photo by Charles H. Coles
173   *Left,* Kenneth Garrett/National Geographic Society Image Sales; *Right,* Kenneth Garrett/National Geographic Society Image Sales
174   Musée de l'Homme, Paris
175   Kenneth Garrett/National Geographic Society Image Sales
182   *Left,* David R. Austen/Stock, Boston; *Right,* Gordon Cahan/Photo Researchers
184   Jean-Marie Chauvet/Sygma

Chapter 10
191   Stuart Franklin/Magnum

197   Hinterleitner/Gamma Liaison
198   George Chan/Photo Researchers
200   Mike Yamashita/Woodfin Camp & Associates
201   Earth Sciences
204   Martha Cooper/Peter Arnold
206   Schalkwijk/Art Resource, NY
210   Jacques Jangoux/Peter Arnold

Chapter 11
215   Fred Mayer/Magnum
216   Steve McCurry/Magnum
219   Irene Lengui/Photo Researchers
220   Victor Englebert
221   Paul Chesley/Tony Stone Images
224   *Top,* Victor Englebert; *Bottom,* Bill Gillette/Stock, Boston
225   Michael Salas/The Image Bank
229   John Eastcott/Yva Momatiuk/Woodfin Camp & Associates
230   American Museum of Natural History

Chapter 12
237   Fred Mayer/Magnum
239   George Holton/Photo Researchers
240   Jason Lauré/Woodfin Camp & Associates
245   Burt Glinn/Magnum
248   Roland & Sabrina/Woodfin Camp & Associates
250   The Image Works
251   Douglas Kirkland/The Image Bank
252   Mike Schneps/The Image Bank

Chapter 13
257   Lisl Dennis/The Image Bank
258   Louis H. Jawitz/The Image Bank
259   Diane Lowe/Stock, Boston
260   R. H. Beck Courtesy Department Library Services, American Museum of Natural History
262   Magubane/Gamma Liaison
266   Kenneth Murray/Photo Researchers
267   John Chiasson/Gamma Liaison
269   Christopher Morris/Saba
270   Paul Lowe/Magnum
271   Miguel Rio Branco/Magnum
273   Ripoll/Association Kutubu/Gamma Liaison

Chapter 14
279   Joel Gordon
282   Eastcott/Momatiuk/Woodfin Camp & Associates
283   *Top,* Terry Madison/The Image Bank; *Bottom,* Terry E. Eiler/Stock, Boston
286   *Top,* Bob Daemmrich/Stock, Boston; *Bottom,* The Memory Shop
289   *Top,* Emil Muench/Photo Researchers; *Bottom,* John Eastcott/Yva Momatiuk/Stock, Boston

Chapter 15
297 Donna DeCesare/Impact Visuals
298 Donna Binder/Impact Visuals
300 C. S. Perkins/Magnum
302 Courtesy Dr. Victor A. McKusick, The Johns Hopkins Hospital
304 Mike Yamashita/Woodfin Camp & Associates
306 Cary Wolinski/Stock, Boston
307 Gerard Rancinan/Sygma
309 Frank Fournier/Contact Press Images
310 Emil Muench/Photo Researchers
311 Thomas Kelly

Chapter 16
315 Steve McCurry/Magnum
317 Francois Gohier/Photo Researchers
318 Jeff Isaac Greenberg/Photo Researchers
321 Michael Peletz, Hamilton, NY
322 Wendy Stone/Gamma Liaison
323 George Holton/Photo Researchers
325 Martha Cooper/Peter Arnold
326 AMIGA TV TUDO Magazine, Rio de Janeiero, Brazil, 1/26/90
329 1943 The Curtis Publishing Company

Chapter 17
335 Abbas/Magnum
337 David Alan Harvey/Woodfin Camp & Associates
339 Bruno Barbey/Magnum
340 *Top,* Thierry Secretan Cosmos/Woodfin Camp & Associates; *Bottom,* Michael Minardi/Peter Arnold
343 Susan McCartney/Photo Researchers
346 Anthro-Photo
347 Michele Burgess/The Stock Market

Chapter 18
353 Paul Lau/Gamma Liaison
354 Peter Menzel
355 John Lewis Stage/The Image Bank
360 Dan Connell/Impact Visuals
364 Joseph Nettis/Photo Researchers
365 Stephanie Maze/Woodfin Camp & Associates
366 Lincoln Potter/Gamma Liaison

Chapter 19
371 Robbi Newman/The Image Bank
374 Bruno Barbey/Magnum
375 David Hiser/The Image Bank
377 Jeff Isaac Greenberg/Photo Researchers
381 Charles Gupton/Stock, Boston
382 James Nachtwey/Magnum

385 Lawrence Migdale/Stock, Boston
387 James Wilson/Woodfin Camp & Associates
388 Stacy Rosenstock/Impact Visuals

Chapter 20
393 Chuck O'Rear/Westlight
394 Paul Van Riel/Black Star
395 Les Stone/Sygma
400 Dilip Mehta/Woodfin Camp & Associates
401 Picture Collection, New York Public Library
403 Keith Dannemiller/Saba
404 Michael Nichols/Magnum
405 Miguel Rio Branco/Magnum

Chapter 21
409 C. S. Perkins/Magnum
411 John Giordano/Saba
412 Robert Caputo/Stock, Boston
413 Alon Reininger/Woodfin Camp & Associates
414 Peter Frey/The Image Bank
415 *Top,* Gabe Kirchheimer/Impact Visuals; *Bottom,* Erich Lessing/Magnum
420 *Top,* Yoram Kahana/Peter Arnold; *Bottom,* Steve Maines/Stock, Boston

Chapter 22
425 Peter Frey/The Image Bank
427 Alexander Low/Woodfin Camp & Associates
428 Ricardo Funari/Impact Visuals
430 Andrea Brizzi/The Stock Market
432 Dag Sundberg/The Image Bank
434 Marc & Evelyn Bernheim/Woodfin Camp & Associates
435 *Top,* Sean Sprague/Impact Visuals; *Bottom,* John Moss/Photo Researchers
437 Dr. Steven Lansing

Chapter 23
443 John Eastcott/Yva Momatiuk/Photo Researchers
444 Peter Marlow/Magnum
445 Ricardo Funari/Impact Visuals
450 M. Gunther/Bios/Peter Arnold
451 Rob Crandall/Stock, Boston
453 Gary Payne/Gamma Liaison
454 Haviv/Saba
455 Buu/Deville/Turpin/Gamma Liaison
457 Michael Nichols/Magnum
459 Jornal do Brasil/Magnum

ILLUSTRATION AND TEXT CREDITS

379:   From *Sociolinguistics: An Introduction to Language and Society* by Peter Trudgill (London: Pelican Books, 1974, revised edition 1983), p. 85, copyright © Peter Trudgill, 1974, 1983. Reproduced by permission of Penguin Books Ltd.

381:   From Nicolas D. Kristoff, "Japan's Feminine Falsetto Falls Right Out of Favor," *The New York Times*, December 13, 1995, pp. A1 and A4. Copyright © 1995 by The New York Times Company. Reprinted by permission.

385:   From John Noble Wilford, "In a Publishing Coup, Books in 'Unwritten' Languages," *The New York Times*, December 31, 1991, p. B5. Copyright © 1991 by The New York Times Company. Reprinted by permission.

402, 403:   From *An Introduction to the World-System Perspective* by T. R. Shannon. Copyright © 1989 by WestviewPress. Reprinted by permission of WestviewPress.

404:   From John H. Bodley, *Anthropology and Contemporary Human Problems*, 1985. Reprinted by permission of Mayfield Publishing.

416–417:   From Lawrence K. Altman, "Women Worldwide Nearing Higher Rate for AIDS than Men," *The New York Times*, July 21, 1992, pp. C1 and C3. Copyright © 1992 by The New York Times Company. Reprinted by permission.

429:   From D. Gross and B. Underwood, "Technological Change and Calorie Costs." Reproduced by permission of the American Anthropological Association from *American Anthropologist* 73:3, June 1971. Not for further reproduction.

452–453:   Rigoberta Menchu, "Things Have Happened to Me as in a Movie," *The New York Times*, October 17, 1992, A25. Adapted from an autobiographical chapter in *You Can't Drown the Fire: Latin American Women Writing in Exile*, Cleis Press, 1989.

468–470:   Adapted from *Prime-Time Society: An Anthropological Analysis of Television and Culture* by Conrad Phillip Kottak. © 1990 by Wadsworth, Inc. Used by permission of the publisher.

INDEXES

AUTHOR INDEX

Ahmed, A. S., 447
Altman, L. K., 416-417
Amadiume, I., 298, 322
American Almanac, 55, 281, 284-285, 328-330, 402, 413
American Anthropological Association, 245, 433
Anderson, B., 52-53, 56, 458
Anderson, B. G., 415, 417
Ann Arbor News, 285
Anthropology Newsletter, 245
Aoki, M. Y., 73
Appadurai, A., 444-445, 458-459
Appiah, K. A., 73
Arens, W., 467, 475
Armelagos, G. J., 414

Bailey, R. C., 25, 217, 242
Bakhtin, M., 452
Banton, M., 413
Barnaby, F., 263
Barnard, A., 218
Barnouw, V., 356
Barringer, F., 70, 329
Barth, F., 54, 57
Batalla, G. B., 432-433
Bateson, M. C., 13
Beach, F. A., 358-359
Beeman, W., 382
Benedict, R., 357-358
Bennett, J. W., 3, 8, 41
Berlin, B. D., 376
Bernard, H. R., 31
Berreman, G. D., 310-311
Bettelheim, B., 342, 470-471
Bird-David, N., 229
Bloch, M., 382
Blum, H. F., 79
Boas, F., 6, 12, 45, 78
Bodley, J. H., 400, 402, 404-405, 426-427, 436, 447
Bogoras, W., 345
Bolinger, D., 373
Bolton, R., 416
Boserup, E., 431
Bourdieu, P., 261, 382, 450
Bourque, S. C., 316
Braudel, F., 394
Breedlove, E., 376
Brenneis, D., 382
Bronfenbrenner, U., 84
Brooke, J., 445
Brown, J. K., 321
Brown, P. J., 7, 414
Brown, R. W., 376

Brumfiel, E. M., 267
Bryant, B., 60
Burling, R., 375
Burns, J. F., 57
Calhoun, C., 50, 317, 402
Carneiro, R. L., 219, 258, 265-267
Casson, R., 3, 54
Chagnon, N., 225, 243-244, 299
Chomsky, N., 373-375, 389
Clifford, J., 14, 26
Coates, J., 379
Cohen, M. N., 414
Cohen, Roger, 57
Cohen, Ronald, 309
Cohen, Y., 216-217, 231
Collins, T. W., 398-399
Colson, E., 25-27
Conklin, H. C., 376
Connor, W., 52
Cooper, F., 15
Crick, F. H. C., 94
Crosby A. W., Jr., 394
Cultural Survival Quarterly 244
Cushman, D., 26

Dalton, G., 228
DaMatta, R., 327, 452
D'Andrade, R., 41, 354
Dardess, M. B., 73
Darwin, C., 79,
Davis, D. L., 359
De Vos, G. A., 73-74
Degler, C., 76
Dentan, R. K., 229
DeVore, I., 217
di Leonardo, M., 316
Diagnostic and Statistical Manual of Mental Disorders (DSM-IV), 363
Divale, W. T., 318
Draper, P., 318, 320
Durkheim, E., 20, 341, 475
Dwyer, K., 27

Eagleton, T., 52
Earle, T., 258 259, 260, 263
Eastman, C. M., 376
Eckert, P., 378
Edgerton, R., 360-361
Engels, F., 397
Erlanger, S., 64
Errington, F., 316
Escobar, A., 383, 387-388, 427
Evans-Pritchard, E. E., 246-247, 359

Farooq, M., 414

Fasold, R. W., 372, 377
Feld, S., 448-449
Finkler, K., 416
Fischer, M. M. J., 3, 13-14, 27, 456
Fiske, J., 457-458
Ford, C. S., 358-359
Foster, G. M., 61-62, 364, 367, 415, 417
Foucault, M., 450
Frake, C. O., 376
Franke, R., 429
Freeman, D., 12, 356
Freud, S., 13, 14-15
Fricke, T., 28
Fried, M. ff., 238, 261
Friedl, E., 316, 318, 320, 330

Gal, S., 382
Gargan, E. A., 400
Geertz, C., 12, 14, 26, 36
Geis, M.L., 372, 377, 382
Gewertz, D., 316
Giddens, A., 399
Gilmore, D., 452
Glauberman, N., 81
Goldschmidt, W., 360
Goleman, D., 304-306, 361-363
Goodale, J. C., 309
Goodenough, W. H., 376
Gorer, G., 358
Gramsci, A., 450
Grasmuck, S., 58, 444
Grassmuck, K., 386
Gray, J., 458
Greaves, T. C., 272-273
Green, E. C., 419
Gross, D., 428-429, 431
Gulliver, P. H., 473

Habarad, J., 27
Harding, S., 324
Harrigan, A. M., 301
Harris, M., 70, 75-76, 229, 318, 348, 357
Harrison, G. G., 7
Hart, C. W. M., 309
Harvey, K., 383
Hawkes, K., 217, 242
Head, G., 217, 242
Headland, T. N., 242-243
Henry, J., 411
Herdt, G., 358
Herrnstein, R. J., 81-82
Herskovits, M., 45, 447
Hess, D. J., 387
Heyneman, D., 414
Higgins, P., 316

Hill, K., 217, 242
Hill-Burnett, J., 411
Hobhouse, L. T., 301
Hoebel, E. A., 239, 240
Hopkins, T., 399
Hughes, W. W., 7
Hurtado, A., 217, 242

Inhorn, M. C., 414

Jacoby, R., 81
Jameson, F., 14
Jenicke, M., 217, 242
Jensen, A., 81-82
Johnson, A. W., 25, 258

Kan, S., 230
Kaplan, H., 217, 242
Kaplan, R. D., 267, 269-271
Kardiner.A.,359-360, 367
Kasdan, L. 248
Kay, P., 376
Keller, S., 30, 317, 402
Kelly, R. C., 323
Kent, S., 216, 218, 229, 243, 320
Kinsey, A. C., 358
Kleiner, R., 365
Kleinfeld, J., 41 0
Klimek, D. E., 39
Klineberg, O., 83
Kling, R., 388
Kluckhohn, C., 11
Kottak, C. P., 4-5, 70, 75, 219, 227,
    261, 285, 388, 431, 433, 456,
    458, 468-470
Kristof, N. D., 380-381

LaBarre, W., 358
Labov, W., 372, 377, 379
Laguerre, M,, 58
Lakoff, R., 376, 379, 386
Lamm, R. P., 261, 329
Lance, L. M., 426
Larson, A., 415
Leach, E. R., 298, 300
Lee, R. B., 217, 229, 242-243, 320, 357
Lenski, G., 398
Levine, N., 311
Levi-Strauss, C., 302, 341-342, 349, 417,
    472
Lewis, O., 67, 365
Lewis, P., 412
Lie, J., 60
Lieban, R. W., 418
Light, D., 50, 317, 402
Lindenbaum, S., 323
Linton, R., 4,5, 346, 358-359, 447
Little, K,, 412-413
Loomis, W. F., 79
Lowie, R. H., 301,346

Mackintosh, C., 72
Malinowski, B., 13-15, 21, 26, 29, 338
Manners, R., 426
Marcus, G. E., 3, 13-14, 26-27, 456
Margolis, C., 394
Margolis, M., 58, 327-328
Martin, C. E., 358
Martin, J., 415
Martin, K., 318, 320, 322, 324, 327-328
Martin, P., 55
Marx, K., 397
McDonald, G., 327
McKenna, E. E., 426
Mead, M., 12-13, 14, 316, 355-357
Menchu', R., 452-453
Michaels, E, 458
Michaelson, K., 386
Midgley, E., 55
Miller, N., 415
Mintz, S., 395, 401
Mitchell, J. C., 413
Moerman, M., 51
Mohai, P., 60
Montague, S., 467
Morais, R., 467
Morgan, L. H, 302
Morgen, S., 316
Mukhopadhyay, C., 316
Mullings, L., 412
Murdock, G. P., 241-242
Murphy, R. F., 248
Murray, C., 81-82
Mydans, S., 70, 413

Nagel, J., 445
Nash, f., 316
New York Times
304-306, 319, 344-345, 361 -363,
380-381, 384-385, 416-417, 432-453, 459
Newman, M., 60
Nielsson, G. P., 52

O'Connell, J., 217, 242
Ong, A., 317, 320, 325, 418-419
Owen, B., 217, 242

Parker, S., 365
Paul, R., 15
Pear, R., 330
Peletz, M., 321
Pelto, P., 217
Perlez, J., 319
Pessar, P., 58, 444
Piddocke, S., 230
Pilling, A. R., 309
Podolefsky, A., 7
Polanyi, K., 228
Pollack, A., 344-345
Pomeroy, W. B., 358

Pospisil, L., 245
Potash, B., 308
Price, R., 451
Pryce, J., 72
Public Culture, 448-449

Quinn, N., 354, 355

Radcliffe-Brown, A. R., 338, 341
Rappaport, R, A., 341
Rathje, W. L., 7
Raven, P. H., 376
Rechtman, R., 217, 242
Redfield, R., 45, 388, 412, 447
Reid, L. A., 242
Reiter, R., 324
Ricoeur, P., 14
Robertson, J., 73, 75
Rockwell, R. C., 415
Rodseth, L., 301
Romer, A. S., 396, 434, 437
Root, D., 459
Rosaldo, M. Z., 316-317
Rouse, R., 444, 459
Royal Anthropological Institute, 298
Ryan, S., 50, 59-60, 62

Safa, H., 316
Sahlins, M. D., 228, 246-247
Salzman, P. C., 252
Sanday, P. R., 317
Santino, J., 343
Sapir, E., 375
Schaefer, R., 261, 329
Schieffelin, E., 338
Scott, J. C., 450-451
Scudder, T., 25-27
Sears, D., 373
Service, E. R., 228, 238, 240
Shannon, T. R., 396, 399, 402-403
Shostak, M., 27
Silberbauer, G., 242
Slade, M., 39
Smuts, B. B., 301
Solway, J., 217, 243, 320, 357
Stack, C. B., 284-285, 365
Statistical Abstract of the United States,
    285
Stearman, K., 73-74
Stevens, W. K., 412, 429
Stevenson, R. F., 266
Steward, J., 45
Stoler, A. L., 15, 431
Strathern, M., 316
Strauss, C., 354-355
Swift, M., 321

Tanaka, J., 242
Tannen, D., 377, 379, 386
Tanner, N., 322

Thompson, W., 395
Toner, R., 60
Trudgill, P., 379
Turnbull, C., 217
Turner, V. W., 338-339, 474
Tylor, E. B., 36, 302

Underwood, B., 428-429
University of Michigan, 59

Valentine, C., 365
Vayda, A. P., 231
Vierich, H., 243
Viola, H. J., 394
Voorhies, B., 318, 320, 322, 324,
    327-328

Wagatsuma, II., *73*
Wagley, C. W., 71
Wallace, A. F. C., 336, 345-347, 350
Wallace, A. R., 79
Wallerstein, I., 395, 399, 402
Warren, K. B., 316
Watson, P., 83
Weber, M., 14, 61, 261, 274, 366, 397,
    399
Webster's New World Encyclopedia 11
Westermarck, E., 301
Wetherall, W. O., 73 74
White, L. A., 36-37, 302
Whiting, B. E., 360
Whitten, R. G., 359
Whorf, B. L., 375
Wilford, J. N, 384-385
Williams, B., 58, 70
Williams, B. J., 80
Wilmsen E,, 242, 320, 357
Winslow, J. H., 145
Wittfogel, K. A., 264
Wolf, E. R., 221, 223, 226, 402
World Almanac & Book of Facts, 287
Worsley, P., 454
Wrangham, R. W., 301

Yetman, N., 70

Zechenter, F., 217,242

SUBJECT INDEX

AAA (American Anthropological Association), 410, 433, 439, 444
Abraço 39
Academic subculture, biases in, 466-467
Acculturation, 446-447
  as mechanism of cultural change, 45
Aché culture (Paraguay), 217, 242
Achieved status(es), 50, 401
Acquired immunodeficiency syndrome (*see* AIDS)
Active-passive dichotomy, homosexuality and, 326-327
Actor-oriented research (*see* Emic research strategies)
Adaptation:
  biological [*see* Biological (physiological) adaptation]
  cultural (*see* Cultural adaptation)
  kinds of, 2-3
Adaptive behavior, 41
Adaptive strategies, 216, 231-232
  Betsileo religion as, 349
  of foraging societies, 223
  potlatching, 230-231
Administrative subdivision, state control by, 262
Adultery, disputes over, 240, 247
Advanced information technology (AIT), 383,389
  social reality and, 388-389
  unequal access to, 383, 386-387
Affinals, 290
Affinity groups, cyberspace and, 388-389
Africa:
  apartheid in South Africa, 59, 81,401
  East Africa:
    crime in, 271
    cross-cultural comparison in, 360-361
    Efe culture, 10, 217
    Kalahari Desert, 217
    spread of AIDS in, 415-417
  Sub-Saharan (*see* Sub-Saharan Africa)
  [*see also* San (bushmen)]
African-Americans:
  classification as, 71
  effects of industrialization on, 398-399
  feminization of poverty and, 329-331
  Los Angeles riots and, 60-61
  performance on intelligence tests, 84

sports activities of, 83
use of AIT, 386
Age:
  access to cyberspace and, 386-387
  plural marriage and, 309
Age grades, age sets and, 251
Age sets, 249, 251
  among Masai, 250-251
Age-based division of labor, 223
Age-based social distinctions among foragers, 218
Aggregation phase in rites of passage, 338
Agnates, 300-301
Agribusiness, 400
Agricultural development projects:
  Brazilian sisal scheme, 427-429
  exploitation of indigenous cultures and, 447
  green revolution in Java, 429-431
  rice production, 426-427
Agricultural societies:
  gender roles in, 324-326, 330-331
  gender stratification in, 330-331
  hydraulic economies, 264-265
  population density and, 221
Agriculturalism, peasants, 228
  Agriculture, 219-221, 232
  animal domestication, 219-220
  costs and benefits of, 220-221
  difference from horticulture, 221-222
  domesticated animals, 219-220
  irrigation (see Irrigation)
  as mechanism of cultural change, 45
  terracing, 220-221
Ahimsa(Hindu doctrine),347 348,350
AIDS (acquired immunodeficiency syndrome):
  heterosexual transmission, 416-417
  HIV infection, 416
  spread in eastern Africa, 415-417
AIT (*see* Advanced information technology)
Akutare Matsuri (festival of abusive language), 344-345
Alienation in industrial economies, 225-226
Amazon as global resource, 273
Ambalavo (Madagascar), 446-447
Ambilineal descent, 288, 291-292
Ambilocality, 292
America On-Line (AOL), 387
American Anthropological Association (AAA), 410, 444

"Principles of Professional Responsibility," 433, 439
American Folklife Center, 449
American Journal of Psychiatry, 361
American Museum of Natural History 12-13
American Sign Language (Ameslan), 127-128
Amok (Malaysia), 361, 363
Animal domestication, 216
  by agriculturalists, 219-220
  by pastoralists, 222
Animism, 336
Anorexia nervosa, cultural aspects of, 362
Anthropological expertise, 426
Anthropology, 1-16
  adaptation, variation, and change, 2-3
  applied (*see* Applied anthropology)
  archaeological, 3, 7 8,15
  biological (physical), 3, 8-9, 410
  careers in, 419-421
  cognitive, 354-355, 367
  cultural, 5-7
  economics and, 13-14
  education and, 411
  experimental, 26-27
  feminist, 3~16
  forensic, 10
  general, 3-5
  history and, 15-16
  humanities and, 14
  interpretive, 26
  linguistic (*see* Linguistic anthropology)
  medical, 10, 414 419, 421
  political science and, 13-14
  popular culture and (*see* Popular culture)
  psychology and, 14-15
  relation to other fields, 11-16
  sociology and, 12-13
  systemic perspective of, 410
  treatment of ethnocentrism and cultural relativism, 42-43
  urban (*see* Urban anthropology)
Anti-Basque campaign (Spain), 62
Antihegemonic discourse, suppression of, 452
Anxiety, ritual and, 338
AOL (America On-Line), 387
Apartheid, 59, 81, 401
Apical ancestor, 242
"Apollonian" culture (Zuni), 357

Applied anthropology, 5,10-11, 409-422
    careers in, 419-421
    education and 411
    medical anthropology, 10, 414-419, 421
    theory and practice of, 410-411
    urban anthropology (see Urban
        anthropology)
Arabs, segmentary lineage organization
    of, 248
Arapesh culture (Papua-New Guinea),
    12, 316
Arby's, 478
Archaeological anthropology, 3, 7-8, 16
Archaic states, 258
Arembepe culture (Brazil), 4-5, 21, 29-30,
    394
    Chegança, 456
    racial labels among, 7,5, 76
    sexuality in, 358
Argonauts of the Western Pacific
    (Malinowski), 29
Artifacts, 7
Ascribed status(es), 50-51, 75, 401
    racial descent as, 76
Asia: (See also specific countries)
Assault on Paradise: Social Change in a
    Brazilian Village, (Kottak), 9
Assimilation,,53 54,64-65
    forced, 62, 65
Attitudinal discrimination, 59-60, 65
Aunts, 281
Australian aborigines:
    arranged marriages among, 305
    foraging, 216-217
    language of, 376
    racial classification of, 77-78
    reactions to "Rambo", 457-458
    totemism of, 473, 475
Authority, 238, 253
Azande culture (Sudan), 359

Bahia (Brazil) fisheries project, 431-432
Bailey, Robert, 10
Balanced reciprocity, 228-229, 232
    in industrial societies, 230
Bali (Indonesia), culturally appropriate
    development in, 437
Bands, 217-218
    descent-group organization in, 241-243
    foragers, 232, 239-241
    nuclear families and, 286
    political systems of
    (see Political systems)
    Shoshone band organization, 288
    territory rights in, 224
Bangladesh, poverty of, 400
Bantu, 242
Baseball, 467
Basic personality structure, 359
Basseri tribe (Iran), 252, 254
Bateson, Gregory, 13
"BBC English," 377
Bell Curve, The (Herrnstein & Murray),
    81-82
Bengal (Bangladesh), 400
Berdache (Crow Indians), 346
Bernard, H. Russell, 384- 385

Bestiality, 338, 359
Betsileo culture (Madagascar), 21, 24, 360
    animal domestication of, 219-220
    concept of scarcity in, 227
    gender roles in, 324-326, 330-331
    gender-based division of labor in, 223
    intercommunity feasting among,
        348-350
    irrigation of crops by, 220
    marriage and funeral rituals,
        348-350,475-476
    polygyny among, 310
    sexuality in, 358
    supernatural in, 344
    terracing of fields by, 220
Bettelheim, Bruno, 470 471
Biases:
    in academic subculture, 466-467
    class bias in cyberspace, 386
    cultural biases in intelligence tests,
        83-84
    emic biases in research, 466
    explanations for incest taboo, 301
Bicha, 326-327
Bifurcate collateral kinship terminology,
    292-293
Bifurcate merging kinship terminology,
    290, 293
"Big man," 241, 245-246, 253, 435
"Big Wife," 310
Bilateral kinship calculation, 281
Bilateral kinship systems, 325
Bilingualism, 385
    educational practices and, 411
    performance on intelligence tests, 82
Binary opposition, in myth, 342, 472
Biological anthropology, 3, 8-9, 410
Biological kin types, 280
Biological paternity 298
Biological (physiological) adaptation, 2
    environmental stress and, 41
Biological plasticity:
    study of, 8
Biological urges, cultural expression of, 37
Biologically based universals, 43
Biology, race and, 77-80
Biomedicine, 416
Biopsychological equality 43
Bison hunting, 249, 251
Blackberry Winter (Mead), 13
Blended families, 285
Blood feuds:
    among Eskimos, 240, 253
    leopard-skin man and, 247-248
Blue collar employment, women in,
    328-329
Body Shop (retail business), 459
Bom Jesus de Lapa (shrine), 473
Bonded labor, in India, 401
Bosavi People's Fund, 448,449
Bosnia-Herzegovina, 56-57
Bourgeoisie, 397,406
Brady Bunch, The:
    as blended family, 285-286, 287
    influence of television and, 287
Braun, Carol Moseley, 40
Brazil, 358
    Amazon as global resource, 273

Arembepe culture
    (see Arembepe culture)
    assimilation in, 53-54
    attitudes toward touching and affection,
        38-39
    Carnaval, 327, 343
    complaints about ecological morality,
        447
    culturally appropriate marketing in, 438
    effect of mass media in, 456-457, 458
    favelas (shantytowns) in, 413-414, 459
    gold rush in (1987-1991), 244-245
    Kayapó Indians, 405, 448
    kin attachments in, 285-286
    male-female contrast in, 326-327
    slavery in, 75-76,401
    social race in, 75-77, 85
    sports and cultural standards in, 82-83
    television in, 456, 458
    views of fantasy, 475
    Yanomami culture (see Yanomami
        culture)
Brazilian sisal scheme, 427-429
Brideprice, 306
Bridewealth, 306-308, 312
Buganda (Uganda), 261
    polygyny in, 310
Bumba Meu Boi festival, 456
Burakumin, stigmatization of, 73-75,
Burbank, Victoria, 305
Burger King, 438, 478
Burma, Palaung culture, 375
Burton, LeVar, 469
Burundi, 268
    Hutu-Tutsi war in, 270-271
Bushmen (see !Kung San; San)

Call systems, 372
Cameroon, language preservation in, 385
Canada:
    changing gender roles in, 327-329
    investments in United States, 459
    measures of social complexity in, 28
    multiculturalism in, 55, 58
    nuclear family in, 281
    Quebec independence movement, 269
    subcultures in, 41-42
    urban anthropology in, 412
Candomblé cult, 22-23,454
Capital, 395
    returns on capital, 401
Capitalism, Protestant ethic and, 366
Capitalist economy:
    religious responses to, 454-455
    world economy, 395
Capoid race, 78
Careers in anthropology, 419-421
Cargo cults, 454-455, 461
Caribbean:
    slavery in, 401
    vodun ("voodoo") in, 453-454
Cariocas, 438
Carnaval:
    in Brazil, 327,343
    expression of hidden transcripts,
        451-452
    mass media and, 456-457

outlawed in Spain by Franco, 452
Cash crops, 434-435, 438-439
Cash economy, long-term disadvantages
  of, 429
Cassava (manioc), 221
Caste systems, 303, 312, 400-401
  social identity and, 365
Cattle:
  sacred cattle of India, 347-348
  sacrifice during ceremonial season,
    348-349
Celtic religion, 343
Census(es):
  data gathering for, 21-22
  state control of population and, 261
  United States Census Bureau, 417
Central storage:
  in redistribution, 228
Ceremonial feasts:
  cultural ecology of, 348-349
  marriages, 44
  (See also Funerals)
Ceremonial funds, 226
Ceremonial season, in Betsileo culture,
  348 349
Chambri (Tchambuli) culture (Papua-New
  Guinea), 316
Chechnya, cultural colonialism in, 63-64
Chegança, 456
Chicanos (Mexican-Americans), 51
Chiefdoms, 238, 274
  "big man" in, 241,245-246,253,455
  political and economic systems in,
    258-259
  potlatching and, 229
  social status in, 259-260
  status systems in, 260-261
  (See also Redistribution)
Chiefly redistribution, 259-260
Child rearing:
  cross-cultural studies of, 356, 360
  parental role in enculturation, 39-40
Chomsky, Noam, 373-375, 389
Christianity, as revitalization movement,
  346
Christmas, as American myth, 468
Chukchee culture (Siberia), shamans of,
  345-346
Cinderella:
  culture-nature opposition in, 342,
    470-471
  structural analysis of, 342, 470-471
Cinderella's Castle, symbolism of, 475
Citizenship, in Japan, 74
Civilization, 3
Civilization and Capitalism, 15th-18th
  Century (Braudel), 394
Clans, 241-243
  as pantribal modalities, 248
  stipulated descent in, 242
  tribal social organization and, 288
Class,
  middle class, 398
  speech patterns and, 379-382
  working class (proletariat), 397, 406
Class bias in cyberspace, 386
Class consciousness, 397-398
Class division, 397-398

Class systems, open and closed, 400-402
Classical economic theory, 226
Close, Roberta, 326-327
Closed class systems, 400-402
Code of ethics (AAA), 433, 439
Cognitive anthropology, 354,367
  enculturation and, 354-356
Cold War, end of, 269-270
Collateral households, 283
Collateral relatives, 290
Collective liminality, 339
Collor, Fernando, 245
Colonialism, 62, 65
  British colonial empire, 397
  cultural, 63-64
  domination and, 447
  effects on Bangladesh, 400
  French 455
  imagined communities and, 53
  in Java, 429-430
  Portuguese, 76
  second phase of, 402
  in Soviet Union, 62-64
Colonization, indigenous peoples and, 405
Columbus, Christopher, 394-395,402,405
Coming of Age in Samoa (Mead), 12, 355,
  356-357
Committee of Peasant Unity (Guatemala),
  452
Communal religion, 345-346,350
Communication:
  cyberspace (see Cyberspace)
  intercultural, 444-445
  (See also Language)
Communitas, 339
Communities:
  effects of development on, 436
  studies of, 30, 32
Comparative economics, 14
Competitive exclusion, 163
Complex societies:
  anthropological research in, 29-32
  subcultures in, 41-42
  (See also Urban anthropology)
Condoms, spread of AIDS and, 416-417
Configurationalism, 357
Connectionism, 354
Conservation of resources, 3
Conservation plans, socially sensitive,
  448-449
Contagious magic, 337-338
Contrast, in analysis of myth, 342, 472
Control mechanism, culture as, 36
Convergence, 14
Cook, James, 469
Cooperatives, 436
Core nations, 395, 402, 406
Core values, 40
Correlations, 217
Courts, 262
Cousins, 281
Covenant on Civil and Political Rights,
  272-273
Covenant on Economic, Social and Cultural
  Rights, 272-273
Craft specialization, 225
Creation, myth and, 341
Creative opposition, 456,461

Crime, state handling of, 262
Croatia, 56-57
Croats, "ethnic cleansing" policy against,
  56-57
Crocodile Dundee, 394
Cross cousins, 299
Cross-cultural comparison, 6
Cross-cultural studies:
  of child rearing, 356- 360
  on health, 414
  of personality, 359-361, 364
  of psychological data, 356
Crow Indians, 346
Cuban-Americans, 51
Cultivation, 218-222, 232
  agriculture (see Agriculture)
  cash crops, 434-435, 438-439
  cultivation continuum, 221-222
  horticulture (see Horticultural societies;
    Horticulture)
  intensification of, 222, 426-427
  slash-and-burn, 219
Cultivation continuum, 221 222
Cults:
  Candomblé, 22-23, 454
  cargo cults, 454-455, 461
  vodun ("voodoo"), 453-454
  (See also Religion)
Cultural adaptation, 2-3
  polyandry as, 311-312
"Cultural adaptive kits," 41
Cultural anthropology, 3, 5-7,16, 411
  salvage archaeology and, 410-411
  sociology and, 12-13
  ties to other disciplines, 12
Cultural blends (syncretisms), 453-457,
  461
"Cultural capital" (see Prestige)
Cultural change, 45, 46
  changes in language and, 376
Cultural colonialism, 63-64
Cultural context:
  of incest taboo, 301
  individual psychology and, 15, 361-363
Cultural convergence, 45
Cultural diffusion:
  television and, 458
  urbanization and, 412
Cultural diversity:
  American "pop" culture and (see Popular
    culture)
  ignored by development agencies,
    435-436
  respect for, 460
Cultural ecology, 8
  religion and, 347-349
    ceremonial feasts, 348-349
    sacred cattle, 347-348
Cultural exchange, 443-461
Cultural imperialism, 455-457,461
  as flawed notion, 458
  Star Trek and, 469
Cultural institutions, primary and
  secondary, 359-360
Cultural learning, 236
Cultural relativism:
  ethnocentrism and, 42-43
  misuse of, 432

Cultural rights, as challenge to states, 272
Cultural similarities, language and, 382 383
Cultural Survival (retail business), 459
Cultural transformations, 8
Cultural values, *Star Trek* and, 468
Culturally appropriate development, 436-437
Culturally appropriate marketing, 438-439
Culturally compatible economic development, 433, 439
Culturally permitted inversion:
    Akutare Matsuri, 344-345
    Halloween, 343
    liminality, 339
Culture(s), 2
    aspects of, 43-46
    changes in,45-46, 376
    collapse of mass culture, 268-269, 275
    components of, 36-43, 46
    domination of native cultures, 447-450, 460
    effect of mass media on, 269, 456-457, 461
    environmental changes and, 447-449, 460
    generality of, 37, 43-45
    health issues and, 414
    indigenizing, 457-458, 461
    individualism in American culture, 39,466
    language and, 375-376
        focal vocabulary, 375-376
        meaning and, 376
        Sapir-Whorf hypothesis, 375
    mass media and, 269, 458-459, 461
    meaning and, 376
    mechanisms of change in, 45-46
    native cultures, domination of, 447-450, 460
    personality and, 14, 361-365
    popular culture (*see* Popular culture)
    religion and (*see* Religion)
    remaking, transnational migration and, 457-461
    similarities in, 382-383
    (*See also* Subcultures)
Culture of consumption, 459-460
    mass media and, 267-268
Culture of poverty, 365-366
Culture shock, example of, 4-5
Culture-bound mental disorders, 361-363
Culture-nature opposition, in Disney creations, 472-473
Curer (shaman), 239, 345-346, 417
Cyberspace, 383, 386-389
    America On-Line (AOL), 387
    elitism and gatekeeping in, 387-388
    government regulation and, 387
    inequality in, 383, 386-387
    social reality and, 388-389
    virtual communities, 388-389
    World Wide Web, 383,387
    [*See also* Advanced information technology (AIT); Communication]
Cyberspeak, 386

Dallas, 458
Dance expeditions (intervillage contacts), 246
Dances with Wolves, 249
Dani culture (Papua-New Guinea), 220
Darwin, Charles, 4, 8, 79
Data collection, methods of, 12
Daughter languages, 382
Davis, Susan, 306
Day of the Dead ceremony (Haiti), 454
Day of the Dead (Samhain), 343
De facto discrimination, 59
    in Japan, 74
De jure discrimination, 59
Deep structures of language, 374-375, 377
Deforestation: effects of, 11
Demonstrated descent (lineages), 242
Descent:
    ambilineal, 288, 291-292
    demonstrated (lineages), 242
    incest taboo and, 299
    matrilineal descent, 241, 282-283
    patrilineal, 241
    racial descent as ascribed status, 76
    rule of, 71
    stipulated descent in clans, 242
    (*See also* Descent groups; Family; Kinship; Marriage)
Descent groups, 225, 253, 293
    exogamy in, 241
    incorporation into government structure, 436-437
    local descent group, 243
    moiety organization in, 299
    permanence of, 281-282
    preadaptation to equitable development, 437
    segmentary lineage organization in, 246
    social organization of, 288
    in tribes, 288
Descent-group organization:
    of kin-based bands, 241-243
    social identity and, 365
Descriptive linguistics, 9
Deus ex machina, 469
Development, 426-433
    AAA code of ethics and, 433
    Brazilian sisal scheme, 427-429
    criticism by Third World, 432
    culturally appropriate, 436-437
    equity and, 431-432
    greening of Java, 429-431
    UNCED, 445
    USAID, 420, 446
    (*See also* Agricultural development projects; Economic development)
Development agencies, 435-436
"Development community 272
Deviant behavior, 356
Dialogic ethnographies, 27
Diaspora, 444
Dickens, Charles, 397
Differential access to resources, 260
Differential population growth, 55
Diffusion:
    cultural generalities and, 44
    as mechanism of cultural change, 45-46
    transmission of culture through, 41

Diglossia, 377
Dinkins, David, 59
"Dionysian" culture (Kwakiutl), 357
Direct diffusion, 45
Discrimination:
    in Japan, 73-75, 85
    prejudice and, 59-60, 65
Disease(s), 414
    effects on Yanomami society, 244-245
    industrialization and, 404
    irrigation and, 410
    population reduction and, 230-231
    sexually transmitted, 415
    study of, *10*
    (*See also* AIDS; specific diseases*)
Disease-theory systems, 415-416
Disney, Walt, 472-473, 475
Disney myth and ritual, 472-475
Display of affection, attitudes toward, 38-39
Disputes, mediation of, 244, 247-248, 253
Distribution (*see* Exchange)
Divorce:
    conflict over, 247
    in North America, 308
Dobe !Kung San, 217, 243
Domestic sphere, 317-318
Domestic system of manufacture, 396
Domestic violence, unemployment and, 399
Domestic-public dichotomy, 317-318, 327
Dominant groups, innate inferiority and, 80-81
Domination of native cultures:
    development and environmentalism as, 447-449, 460
    religious domination, 449-450
    resistance to, 450-453
Dowry, 306, 307
Durable alliances, marriage and, 308
Dynasty, 458

East Africa (*see* Africa)
Earth Day 448
Ecocide, 404
Ecological diversity, state formation and, 264, 275
Ecological interdependence, plural societies and, 54
Ecological morality, 447
Ecological niches, 54, 57
Ecology, 8
Economic anthropologists, 226, 232
Economic determinants of female status, 317
Economic development:
    applied anthropology and, 10
    culturally compatible, 433, 439
    elites and, 427
    ethical dilemmas in, 427
    individual wealth and, 436
    intervention philosophy and, 426, 438
Economic systems:
    in chiefdoms, 258-259
    maximization and, 226,228
    motivation in, 226
    perpetual expansion in, 402
Economic typology, 238, 253

Economics:
    anthropology and, 13-14
    perspective of, 6
Economy(ies):
    capitalist, 395, 454-455
    changes in women's roles and, 328
    correlation with social life, 217-218
    defined, 223
    disadvantages of cash economy, 429
    hydraulic agricultural economies,
        264, 275
    industrial, 225-226
    influence on personality 361, 364, 367
    influence on worldview, 364-367
    nonindustrial, 223, 286, 288
    pastoral, 222-223, 252-253
    plantation economies, 395, 409
    social life and, 217-218
    trade-oriented, 394
    (See also Subsistence economy)
Ecosystem, 8
Education, migration and, 58
Efe culture (Zaire), 10, 217
Egalitarian societies, tribal
    horticulturalists, 241, 243
Ego, 280
Egypt:
    Nilotes (Upper Nile region), 78, 246
    schistosomiasis in Nile Delta, 414-415
Ehrhardt, Anke A., 417
Eisenhower, Dwight David, 269
Elites:
    benefits of states for, 263-264
    economic development projects and, 427
    profit from Java's green revolution, 431
    public gatherings discouraged by 451
Elitism in cyberspace, 387-388
Elizabeth II, Queen of England, 475
E-mail, 383
Emic research strategies, 20, 24, 32
Emotional functions of religion, 338
Emotionalistic disease theories, 416
Employment:
    blue-collar, 328-329
    effect on nuclear family, 283
    female, 328
    overseas, in anthropology, 421-422
Enculturation, 14
    cognitive anthropology and, 354-356
    defined, 36
Endeavor, 469
Endogamy, 302-303
    caste and, 303
    Old Order Amish, 302
    royal incest, 303
Energy consumption, 402, 404
Enforcement, by states, 263, 274
England:
    colonial empire of, 397
    as core nation, 402
    foreign investment in U.S., 459
    Industrial Revolution in, 396-397
    Norman Conquest, influence on
        language, 383
    population growth in, 397
English labor movement, 398
Environment:
    intelligence tests and, 82-85

Environmental changes:
    clash of cultures and, 447-449, 460
    racial classification and, 78
Environmental circumscription, state
    formation and, 265-266
Environmental Protection Agency, 10
Environmental racism, 60
Environmental stresses, adaptation to, 41,
Environmentalism, 316
    effect on indigenous cultures, 447
Epcot Center, 473
Epidemic diseases, 414
Equity, development and, 431-432
Eskimos (Inuit):
    foraging, 217
    gender stratification among, 317
    social relationships among, 239-240,
        253
    trade partners, 239
    vocabulary of, 375-376
Ethical dilemmas in economic
    development, 427
Ethnic associations, 55
    urbanization and, 412-413
"Ethnic cleansing," 56-57
Ethnic conflict, 59-64
    examples of, 60-62
    oppression and, 62-64
    prejudice and discrimination, 59-60
Ethnic expulsion policy, 62
Ethnic groups, 50-51
    dominant, 63, 65
    health issues of, 414
    race and (see Race)
Ethnic identity, television and, 458-459
Ethnic minorities, 405
"Ethnic revival," 59
Ethnic stereotyping, 410
Ethnic tolerance, 52-59
    assimilation and, 53-54
    multiculturalism and, 54-59
    plural societies, 54
Ethnic units, emerging, 445
Ethnicity, 50-51, 64
    of Haitian immigrants, 58-59
    mental disorders and, 361-363
    status shifting and, 51
    (See also Race; Social race)
Ethnobotany 376
Ethnocentrism, 410
    assumptions of applied anthropology,
        432
    cultural relativism and, 42-43
    in national character studies, 357-359,
        367
Ethnocide, 62, 65, 404-405, 447, 460
Ethnographic method, 410, 421
Ethnographic present, 27
Ethnographic realism, 26
Ethnography, 4, 6
    ethnographic techniques, 20-27, 32
        emic and etic strategies, 24
        genealogical method, 23
        interviewing, 21-23
        life histories, 20, 24, 32
        longitudinal research, 25-27
        observation, 20-21, 36
        problem-oriented, 24-29

well-informed informants, 22, 24, 28,
    228
evolution of, 26-27
influence on social policy 10-11
as research strategy, 20
study of kinship calculation, 280-281
traditional, 12-13
Ethnology, 6-7
Ethnology (journal), 304-306
Ethnomedicine, 376
    commercial value of, 273
Ethnomusicology, 448-449
Ethnopictures, 6
Ethnoscience, 376
Etlinosemantic domains, 376
Ethnosemantics, 376
Etic research strategies, 20, 24, 32
Etoro culture (Papua-New Guinea),
    homosexuality in, 323-324
Eurasians, hypodescent rule and, 72
Euro Disneyland, cultural imperialism
    and, 455
Europe:
    image of limited good in, 364-365
    (See also Specific countries)
Evangelical Protestantism, 449-450
Evolution, 4,16,
Excavation, 8
Exchange, 228-230
    coexistence of principles, 230
    market principle in, 228
    reciprocity, 228-230, 232
    redistribution (see Redistribution)
Exchange systems, 232
Exogamous lineages within castes, 303
Exogamy, 43, 299
    adaptive advantage of, 302
    in descent groups, 241
Expanded family households, 283-284
Experimental anthropology, 26-27
Extended family, 283
External regulation, indigenous peoples
    threatened by, 448-449
Extradomestic labor, 324

Face-to-face groups, cyberspace and, 388
Factories (see Manufacture)
Factors; of production, 223 -225
Factory work in Malaysia, 418-419
"Fallacy of the noble global," 447
Family
    expanded households:
        Native American, 283
        poverty and, 283-284, 293
    extended families, 283
    nonnuclear arrangements, 284-286
    nuclear (see Nuclear family)
    state intervention in, 262-263
    (See also Descent; Kinship; Marriage)
Family enterprise, 61
Family of orientation, 282
Family of procreation, 282
Family solidarity 61
Fantastico (Brazilian TV), 456
Fantasy, uses of, 342
Fantasy films as myth, 470-472
Father Knows Best, 287

Fatima (shrine), 473
Favelas (shantytowns), 413-414, 459
Fax machines, 383
Feld, Steven, 448-449
Female infanticide, 311
Females:
  attitudes toward, 40
  economic determinants of status, 317
  male-female avoidance and hostility,
    323-324, 356-357
  male-female contrast in Brazil, 326-327
  paid employment of, 328
  upper-status speech and, 379
  (See also Gender; Males)
Feminist anthropology, 316
Feminization of poverty, 329-331
"Festival of abusive language" (Japan),
  344-345
Festivals, mass media and, 456-457
Fictive kinship, in bands, 218
Field methods, 19-32
  in complex societies, 29-32
    new procedures, 31
    urban anthropology (see Urban
      anthropology)
  ethnography (see Ethnography)
  survey research, 27-29, 32
Field notes, 20
Film industry, 458
  effects of television and, 458-459
  fantasy films, 470-472
  nuclear family and, 470
  (See also specific films)
Finance as transnational force, 459-460
First cousin, 281
First World, 62
Fiscal systems, of states, 263-264, 274
Fischer, Edward, 304
Fisheries projects, social impact of,
  431-432
Flagpole worship, 454
Fleisher, Michael, 271
Flexible marriage systems, 311
Focal vocabulary, 375-376
Food production, 3
  environmental obstacles to, 217
  increased regulatory demands and,
    238-239
  local, 394 395
  population density and, 238
  in Third World countries, 429-431
  (See also Agriculture; Cultivation;
    Foraging; Horticulture; Pastoralism;
    specific foods)
Food shortages in Bangladesh, 400
Football, as popular culture, 467, 476
Foraging, 3, 216 218
  adaptive strategies in, 223
  correlates of, 217-218
  potlatching and, 229
  (See also Bands; Foraging societies)
Foraging societies, 232
  Ache culture (Paraguay), 217, 242
  egalitarian, 218
  gender roles in, 317-318, 320, 330
  gender stratification in, 330
  gender-based division of labor in, 218
  generalized reciprocity among, 229

generational terminology in, 292
  nuclear family in, 239, 286, 288, 293
  sedentisim and, 239, 243
  stereotypes of, 243
  (See also Bands)
Force, state formation by, 264-265
Forced assimilation, 62, 65
Forced diffusion, 45
Foreign investment, 459-460
Forensic anthropology 10
Forensic archaeologists, 410
Formal rationality, 14
Fortune, Reo, 13
Fossil fuels, overconsumption of, 402, 404
Foster, George, 444
Fourth World, 62
France, 436
  colonialism of, 455
  cultural imperialism and, 455-456
  domestic manufacturing system,
    396-397
  Norman Conquest, 383
Franco, Francisco, 452
  anti-Basque campaign, 62
Franke, Richard A., 417
Fraternal polyandry, 298, 311
Freud, Sigmund, 13-15, 358
Functional explanations of kinship
  terminology, 292
Functionalist ethnographies, 26
Funerals, 44
  Betsileo rituals, 44, 348-350, 475-476
  cattle sacrifice for, 349

Garbology, 7, 10
Garment industry, in American South,
  398-399
Gatekeeping, in cyberspace, 387-388
Gathering (see Foraging)
Gender:
  age sets and, 249-251, 254
  effects of Java's green revolution, 431
  identity in cyberspace, 386, 388
  prominence of female characters in
    Star Trek, 469
  speech contrasts and, 379
  status in chiefdoms and, 260
  (See also Females; Males)
Gender differences, cultural nature of, 4
Gender roles, 315-331
  in agricultural societies, 324-326,
    330-331
  in Betsileo culture, 324-326, 330-331
  cross-cultural variation, 330
  in fairy tales, 344
  feminization of poverty, 329-331
  in foraging societies, 317-318, 320, 330
  in horticultural societies, 320-324
  in industrial societies, 327-330
  interchangeable, 322, 326
  Masai culture and, 319
  in North America, 327-329
  transsexuality, 326-327
  warfare and, 322-323
Gender stereotypes, 317, 330
Gender stratification, 317, 330

Gender-based division of labor:
  among Eskimos, 239-240
  among foragers, 218
  in nonindustrial societies, 223-225
  universality of, 318
Genealogical method of research, 20, 23,
  32
Genealogical relationships, 280
General anthropology, 3 5
Generality of culture, 37, 43-45
Generalized reciprocity, 228-229, 232
Generational kinship terminology,
  290-293
Generosity (see Redistribution)
Genetic adaptation, 2
Genetics
  endogamy and abnormal offspring, 302
  incest taboo and, 301
  study of human genetics, 8-9
Genitor, 298
Genocide, 60, 447, 460
  industrialization and, 404
Geographic mobility:
  male gender roles and, 318
  in Mbuti culture, 218
  nuclear family and, 288
  polyandry as cultural adaptation to,
    311-312
  state control of population and, 262
Geography, linguistic variation and, 9, 379
Germany:
  foreign investment in U.S., 459
GII (global information infrastructure), 383
Global AIDS Policy Coalition, 416-417
Global culture, in world-system theory, 402
Global information infrastructure (GII), 383
Global resources, 273
Globalization:
  challenges to states, 267-268
  intercultural communication and,
    444-445
  as mechanism of cultural change, 45
Globo (Brazilian TV network), 458
Gods Must Be Crazy, The, 243, 459
Gore, Al, 383
Government:
  as agent of people, 436-437
  decline of, 274-275
  failure to maintain law and order,
    270-271
  incorporation of descent groups into,
    436-437
  regulation of cyberspace, 387
  weakening control of mass media, 268
Graceland (Simon), 449
Grammar, 374
Grandparents, 281
  child care by, 282
Grass-roots organizations (GROs), 272
Grateful Dead, 448, 457
"Grave goods," 240
Great Britain (see England)
Great Plains:
  bison hunting, 249, 250
  pantribal societies in, 249-250
Green revolution (Java), 386, 426, 429-431
GROs (grass-roots organizations), 272

Groups:
    affinity groups, effect of cyberspace on, 388-389
    culture as attribute of, 465
    dominant, innate inferiority and, 80-81
    enculturation in, 38-39
    majority and minority groups, 50-51
    nonkin groups, 248-251
    religious groups, 339-340
    transacting, 383
    transnational, 383
    (*See also* Descent groups; Ethnic groups; Kin groups)
Growing Up in New Guinea (Mead), 12-13
Guatemala, human rights movement in, 452-453
"Guatemalan Church in Exile," 452
Gwembe research project (Zambia), 25-27

Haitian immigrants, ethnicity and, 58-59
Haj (pilgrimage to Mecca), 473
Hale, Kenneth, 384
Halloween, 343
Hamburger University, 477
Handsome Lake, 347, 449
Handsome Lake religion, 346-347, 449, 454
Hara, Fujiko, 380
Hard Times (Dickens), 397
Hart, Mickey, 448-449
Hawaii, royal incest in, 303
Hayes, Randy, 448
Health-care specialists, 417
Health-care systems, 416-417
Hegemonic reading, 457
Hegemony, domination and, 450, 460
Hehe culture (East Africa), 360, 361
Heterosexuality, 416-417
Hidden transcripts, 450
    public expression of, 451-452
"High" language variant, 377
Hinduism:
    caste system and, 400-401
    doctrine of *ahimsa*, 347-348, 350
    sacred cattle of India, 347-348
Hispanics:
    effect of educational practices on, 411
    racial classification of, 70
    status shifting and, 51
Historic sites, archaeological survey of, 410-411
Historical explanation of kinship terminology, 292
Historical linguistics, 9, 382-383, 389
History:
    anthropology and, 15-16
    mass media and revisionist history, 468
Hitler, Adolf, 56
HIV infection, 416
    (*See also* AIDS)
Holism, 2, 11-12
Home handicraft system, 396
Homelessness, in North America, 413-414
Hominids, 2
    evolution of:
        exogamy and, 43
        study of, 8

Homosexual marriages, 298
Homosexuality:
    in Etoro culture, 323-324
    institutionalized, 358-359
    stereotypical model in Brazil, 326-327
Hong Kong, film industry in, 458
Hopi culture (American Southwest), time distinctions in language, 375
Horses, 249
Horticultural societies:
    balanced reciprocity in, 229
    egalitarian, 241, 243
    gender roles in:
        Etoro homosexuality, 323-324
        matrifocal societies, 322
        matrilineal, uxorilocal societies, 320-322
        patrilineal-virilocal societies, 322-323
    gender-based division of labor in, 223
Horticulturalism (*see* Horticultural societies)
Horticulture, 218, 219, 232
    difference from agriculture, 221-222
Human biological plasticity, 8
Human genetics (*see* Genetics)
Human rights movements:
    as challenge to states, 272-273, 275
    in Guatemala, 452-453
Humanities, 11
    anthropology and, 14
Humans:
    study of growth and development, 8
Hunting:
    animal domestication and, 222
    territory and, 224
Hunting and gathering (*see* Foraging)
Hydraulic agricultural economies, state formation and, 264, 275
Hypervitaminosis D, 80
Hypodescent, 71-72
    in Japan, 73
    labeling and, 76
    rule of, 71-72, 85

Ideal culture, 41
Ideal types, 258
Identity politics, 267
Ifugao culture (Philippines), 220
Igbo culture (Nigeria), 322, 326
Il-khan of Qashqai, 252-253
Illness, 414, 421
Ilongot culture (Philippines), 317
Il-rah concept, 252
Image of limited good, 364-365
Imagined communities, 52, 64
Imitative magic, 337
Immediate physiological adaptation, 2
Immigration:
    ethnic associations in Samoan community, 413
    ethnicity of Haitian immigrants, 58-59
    family enterprises and, 61
    Los Angeles riots and, 60-61
    multiculturalism and, 55
    (*See also* Migration; Transnational migration)

Impersonality in industrial economies, 225-226
Imported goods, 395
Incas:
    preservation of Quechua language, 385
    state formation and, 266
Incest taboo, 43, 300-301, 312
    explanations for, 301-302
        adaptive advantage, 302
        biological degradation, 302
        genetic or cultural bias, 301
    unilateral descent rule and, 299
    (*See also* Taboo(s))
Income, vertical mobility and, 401
Increased equity 431-432
Independent invention, 45
India:
    bonded labor in, 401
    caste system in, 303, 312, 400-401
    colonialism in, 62
    Nayar culture, 44, 282-283
Indigenized popular culture, 457-458, 461
Indigenous peoples:
    effect of environmentalism on, 447
    industrialization and, 405
    marketing by, 459
    threatened by external regulation, 448-449
    world conference of, 445
Indirect diffusion, 45
Individual situational learning, 36
Individual wealth, economic development and, 436
Individualism, in American culture, 39, 466
Indonesia:
    ethnic tolerance in, 52-53
Industrial Revolution, 396, 405-406
    causes of, 396-397
    resource depletion and, 405
Industrial societies:
    alienation and impersonality of, 225-226
    feminization of poverty in, 329-331
    gender roles in, 327-330
    kin attachments in, 285, 293
Industrialism, 3
Industrialization:
    effects of, 404-405
    health problems and, 418
    in peripheral nations, 395-396
    perpetual expansion of, 402
    world system and, 396-397
Infanticide:
    among Eskimos, 240
    covert, of females, 311
Infectious diseases [*see* Disease(s)]
Infertility, plural marriage and, 308
Informants (*see* Well-informed informants)
Innate inferiority, dominant groups and, 80-81
Innovation, 433-437
    culturally appropriate development and, 436-437
    culturally appropriate marketing, 438-439
    overinnovation, 434-435, 439, 447
    Romer's rule and, 396, 406, 434
    underdifferentiation and, 435-436, 439

Institutional breakdown, decline of state and, 268, 275
Institutional discrimination, 60, 65
Intellectual differences, cultural nature of, 4-5
Intellectual property rights (IPR), 273
Intelligence, stratification and, 80-85
Intelligence tests, 81-85
  cultural biases in, 83-84
  nonverbal, 83
Intercommunity feasting:
  Betsileo culture (Madagascar), 348-350
  cultural ecology of, 348-349
Internal diversity, collapse of nation-states and, 269
International AIDS Center, 416
International culture, 41
International Phonetic Alphabet, 372
Internet, 268
Interpretive anthropology, 26
Intervention philosophy, 426, 438
Intervention programs, 430-431
Interview schedules, 20-23, 32, 227
Interviews, 20-23, 32
"Intrinsic racism," 73
Inuit (see Eskimos)
IPR (intellectual property rights), 273
Iran, pastoral nomadic tribes of, 252-253
Iroquois Indians (New York):
  gender roles in, 321-322
  Handsome Lake religion of, 346-347,449, 454
Irrigation:
  agriculture and, 220, 264
  disease and, 410
  to increase rice production, 426-427
  population growth and, 264
  (See also Agriculture; Cultivation; Horticulture; specific crops)
Irrigation schemes, social impact of, 431
Isabel, Princess of Brazil, 75
Islam, 63-64
  Islamic fundamentalism, 57
  "kitchen Islam," 63
  mass media and, 267
Iwata, Sayori, 381

Jackson, Michael, 459
Jankowiak, William, 304, 305
Japan,399
  "festival of abusive language," 344-345
  foreign investment in U.S., 459
  industrialization of, 402
  linguistic standards of politeness, 380-381
  overseas factories of, 418-419
  social race in, 72-75
  studies of national character, 357-358
Jati, 303
Jansenism, 81-82
Jeopardy, 468
Jesus,346
Jews, segmentary lineage organization of, 248
Jie culture (Uganda), 473
Jocks and Burnouts (Eckert), 378
Johnson, Earvin ("Magic"), 417

Judges, 262
Judiciary, in states, 262-263, 274
Jungle Book, The (Kipling), 473

Kalahari Desert (Africa), 217
  [See also !Kung San; San (Bushmen)]
Kaluli culture (Papua-New Guinea):
  institutionalized homosexuality in, 358-359
  Voices of the Rainforest project, 448-449
Kamba culture (East Africa), 360-361
Kapauku culture (Indonesia), 245-246
Kasuya, Kideki, 381
Kayapó Indians (Brazil), 405,448
Kemper, R. V., 444
Kenya, 31
Khan, 252
Killing, 240
Kin groups, 281-282
  arranged marriages and, 305
  ethnic associations as, 413
  nuclear family, 44-45
Kin terms, 280-281
Kin-based groups, 238
  descent group organization of bands, 241-243
  ethnic associations, 413
  societies, 23
Kin-based modes of production, 223, 232
King, Rodney, 60
Kinship, 279-293
  differential access to resources and, 260
  kin groups (see Kin groups)
  kinship calculation, 280-281
  kinship terminology (see Kinship terminology)
  nuclear family and (see Nuclear family)
  social status in chiefdoms and, 259
  tribal social organization (see, Tribes)
  (See also Descent; Descent groups; Family Marriage)
Kinship calculation, 280-281
Kinship links:
  in bands, 218
  food production and, 225
Kinship system, in Nayar culture, 282-283
Kinship terminology, 288-292,293
  bifurcate collateral, 292
  bifurcate merging, 290
  generational, 290-292
  lineal terminology, 290
  parental generation, 289-292
  relevance of, 292
Kipling, Rudyard, 473
Kleinman, Arthur, 362
Koreans:
  in Japan, 74-75,
  Los Angeles riots and, 60-61
Koro (East Asia), 362-363
Kottak, Conrad, 4-5
Krauss, Michael E., 384
Ku Klux Klan, 59
Kuikuru culture (South America), 219
!Kung San, 217
  Dobe !Kung San, 217, 243
  gender roles among, 318, 320
  generalized reciprocity among, 229

romantic love and, 304-305
  territory rights among, 224
Kutse San, 243
Kuwako, Miyoko, 344
Kwakiutl culture (North Pacific Coast):
  as "Dionysian" culture, 357
  potlatching among, 230-231

Labor:
  human labor in peripheral nations, 395-396
  marital rights to labor of spouse, 298
  as means of production, 225
Labor intensity, cultivation and, 222
Lakher culture (Southeast Asia), 300-301
Lambada tapes, 459
Lang, Jack, 455
Language(s):
  of Australian aborigines, 376
  culture and thought, 375-376
    focal vocabulary, 375-376
    meaning and, 376
    Sapir-Whorf hypothesis, 375
  endangered, 384
  gender in, 375
  historical linguistics, 382-383, 389
  Japanese "festival of abusive language," 344-345
  kinship calculation and, 280-281
  learning, 21
  linguistic diversity, 384-385
  Nähñu language, 384-385
  national languages, 53
  personality and, 361
  pidgin, 45
  productivity in, 372
  protolanguage, 382
  role in national consciousness, 52
  Serbo-Croatian, 56
  sociolinguistics, 377-382, 389, 411
    gender contrasts, 379-381
    linguistic diversity, 377, 379, 384-385
    social categories and, 378-379, 380-381
    symbolic domination, 379-382
  structure of, 372-373, 389
  study of, 9
  subcultures and, 41-42
  symbolism in, 37
  transformational-generative grammar, 373-375, 389
  universals in acquisition of, 374
  (See also Communication)
Language preservation, 385
Latent function of customs, 303
Latin America:
  ethnocentric assumptions in, 432
  image of limited good in, 364-365
  subculture of poverty in, 365-366
  (See also specific countries)
Law and order, failure to maintain, 270-271
Law of supply and demand, 228
Lawlessness, decline of state and, 268
LDCs (less-developed countries), 272, 383, 386, 412

Leach, Edmund, 475
Leakey, Louis S. B., 9
Leakey, Mary, 9,
Leakey, Richard, 9,
Learning:
    cultural, 2, 14, 36, 354-356
    of language, 21
    situational, 36
    (See also Enculturation)
Leave It to Beaver, 285, 287
Legal paternity, marriage and, 298
Leopard-skin man, 247-248
Less-developed countries (LDCs), 62,272
    access to cyberspace and, 383, 386
    population growth in, 412
Leveling mechanisms, 61-62
Levirate, 308, 312
Lévi-Strauss, Claude, 470
Lexicon, 372, 375-376
Library of Congress Endangered Music
    Project, The, 449
Life histories, 20, 24, 32
Life-cycle changes, ethnic identity and, 50
Liminality, 338-340,474
Limited good, 364-365
Lineages, 241-243, 246-247
    clans and, 288
    demonstrated descent, 242
    exogamous, within castes, 303
    segmentary lineage organization,
        246-248, 253
Lineal kinship terminology, 290, 293
Lineal relatives, 290
Lingua franca, 53
Linguistic anthropology, 3, 9, 11
    cognitive anthropology and, 354
    cyberspace and, 389
    education and, 411
    structure of language, 372
Linguistic competence, 374
Linguistic displacement, 372
Linguistic diversity, preservation of,
    384-385
Linguistic performance, 374, 377
Linguistic relativity, 377, 379
Linguistic uniformitarianism, 377
Linkages, 6
Linking principles, 239
Literacy
    native literacy programs, 385
    popular literacy, 384
Liturgical orders, 341
Liturgies, 21
Local descent group, 243
Local-level research, prior to development,
    426
Long-distance trade, state formation and,
    264, 275
Longitudinal studies 20, 25-27, 32
Long-term physiological adaptation, 2
Los Angeles riots, 60-61, 70
Lourdes, 473
Lovers' Day (Brazil), 39
"Low" language variant, 377
Lu, Francis, 362
Lucas, George, 448, 470

Machismo, 326

Mackintosh, Cameron, 72
Madagascar:
    Ambalavo, 446-447
    anthropological study of development in,
        426-427
    Betsileo culture (see Betsileo culture)
    crime in, 271
    descent groups in government structure,
        436-437
    Merina culture, 310
    Mikea culture, 242
    shrines in, 473
    social strata in, 261
    state formation in, 271-272
    Tanala culture, 360
    views of fantasy, 475
Madonna, 457
Magic, 337-338, 349
Magic Kingdom, 473-475
Maize
    slash-and-burn cultivation, 219
Major lineages, 246-247
Majority groups, 51
Maladaptive behavior, 41
Malaysia:
    anti-taxation strategy, 451
    spirit possession in, 418-419
Male-female avoidance and hostility,
    323-324,356-357
Male-female contrast, 326-327
Males:
    gender roles and geographic mobility,
        318
    working-class speech and, 379
    (See also Females; Gender)
Malinowski, Bronislaw, 14-15, 26, 29
Malnutrition, 428-429
Mana, 303, 336-337, 349,471
Manifest function of customs, 303
Manioc (cassava), 221
Mann, Jonathan, 416-417
Manson, Spero, 362
Manufacture:
    domestic system of, 396-397
    factories:
        in Malaysia, 418-419
        overseas factories of Japan, 418-419
        transition to, 396
    (See also Industrialization; Production)
Manus culture (Admiralty Islands), 13
Mardi Gras, 343
Margin phase, in rites of passage, 338-340
Marginalization, culture of poverty and,
    365
Market principle, 228, 230, 232
Market women:
    benefits of polygyny for, 322, 326
    Igbo culture (Nigeria), 322, 326
    nonsexual marriages and, 298
Marketing:
    culturally appropriate, 438-439
    by indigenous peoples, 459
    state control of markets, 263
    (See also Trade)
Marketplace, hidden transcripts and,
    452-453
Marriage, 297-312
    arranged marriages, 305-306

endogamy and, 302-303, 312
    caste systems, 303
    royal incest, 303
exogamy and, 299-301, 312
explanations for incest taboo, 301-302
homosexual marriages, 298
plural marriages (see Plural marriage)
race and, 73
romantic love and, 304-306
in tribal societies, 303, 306-308, 312
    bridewealth and, 306-308
    durable alliances and, 308
    (See also Descent; Family; Kinship)
Marriage ceremonies, 44
Marriage links:
    in bands, 218
    food production and, 225
Marx, Karl, 397,406, 419
Masai culture (Kenya; Tanzania):
    gender roles in, 319
    pantribal modalities of, 250-251
Mass culture, collapse of, 268-269, 275
Mass hysteria, 419
Mass media, 275
    changing household organization and,
        284-285
    culture and, 269, 458-459, 461
    culture of consumption and, 267-268
    development of schemata and, 355
    effect on traditional cultures, 456-457,
        461
    effects in Brazil, 456-457
    festivals and, 456-457
    film industry (see Film industry)
    influence on collapse of mass culture,
        269
    revisionist history and, 468
    role in transnational identity formation,
        267-268
    television (see Television)
    unification through, 478
    weakening government control of, 268
Masturbation, 358, 359
Matriarchy, 321
Matrifocal societies, 322
Matrilateral skewing, 281
Matrilineal descent, 241
    in Nayar culture, 282, 283
Matrilineal moieties, 299
Matrilineal societies:
    bifurcate merging kinship terminology
        in, 290
    sororate in, 308
    status and roles of women, 320-322
    strict matrilineality, 300-301
Matrons, 321
Maximal lineages, 246-247
Maximization, 232
    alternative ends, 226, 228
Maybury-Lewis, David, 23,460
Mbuti culture (Zaire), 217
    mobility of bands, 218
    silent barter among, 230
McDonald's:
    culturally appropriate marketing,
        438-439
    place in popular culture, 476-478
Mead, Margaret, 12-13, 355-357,367

Meaning:
  components of, 374
  culture and, 376
Mecca, pilgrimage to *(haj),* 473
Mediation:
  by leopard-skin man, 247-248
  by village head, 244
Medical anthropology, 10, 414-419, 421
Melanesia:
  cargo cults, 454-455
  mana in, 336-337, 349
Melanin, 79
Melting pot, *Star Trek* as, 469
Menchú, Rigoberta, 452-453
Mende culture (Sierra Leone), 251
Menstrual hut, 339
Merina culture (Madagascar), 310
Merson, Michael H., 416
Mesopotamian civilization
  formation of states in, 258, 266, 274
Mexico:
  birds as "North American" resource, 273
  urbanization and, 412
Mezzich, Juan, 361
MGM Theme Park, 473
Middle class, 398
Middle East:
  early food production in (*see* Food
    production)
  transition to food production in, 396
  (*See also specific countries*)
Migration, 52
  multiculturalism and, 58
  transnational (*see* Transnational
    migration)
  from Tzintzuntzan (Mexico), 444
  (*See also* Immigration)
Mikea culture (Madagascar), 242
Military organization of states, 263
*Millennium (Tribal Wisdom and the Modern
  World),* 460
Mills, Stephen, 417
Minagkabau culture (Malaysia), 321
Minimal lineages, 246-247
Minimal pairs, 372
Minor lineages, 246-247
Minority groups, 50-51
Miss Saigon, 72
Mobility:
  geographic (*see* Geographic mobility)
  vertical mobility, income and, 401
Mode of production, 223
Modern world system (*see* World system)
Moiety organization, 299
Monographs, 29
Monolexemes, 376
Monotheism, 336, 345-346, 350
Monument building, 263
Moore, Alexander, 473
Moribund languages, 384
Morita, Miyuki, 380
Mormons, polygyny among, 309
Morphemes, 372
Morphology, 372
Motivation, in economic systems, 226
Mpakafo (Malagasy vampire), 227
MUDs (multiple user dimensions), 388

Multicultural viewpoint in
  anthropology, 421
Multiculturalism:
  ethnic identity and, 54-59, 65
  shortcomings of, 60-61
Multilingual nations, 377
Multinational corporations (MNCs):
  "green revolution kits," 430
  predatory enterprises of, 447, 460
Multiple causation theory, criticism of, 432
Multiple user dimensions (MUDs), 388
Multivariate theory of state formation,
  265-266
Mundugumor culture (Papua-New
  Guinea),12, 316
Murao, Tadahiro, 380
Muslim identity, mass media and, 267
Myth:
  analysis of, 341-344
    fairy tales, 342, 344
    structural analysis, 341-342
    visual fairy tales, 470-472
  fantasy films as, 470-472
  Star Trek as, 468

NAFTA (North American Free Trade
  Agreement), 273
Nähñu language, 384-385
Nakasone, Japanese Prime Minister, 72-73
Namesakes, 218, 239
NAPA (National Association for the Practice
  of Anthropology), 410
Narayan, Kirin, 305
Narrow-focus groups, in cyberspace, 383
Nation, 52, 64
National Association for the Practice of
  Anthropology (NAPA), 410
National character, studies of, 357-359,
  367, 465
National culture, 41
National identity, preservation of, 458-459
National information infrastructure (NII),
  383
National Institutes of Health, 417
National languages, 53
Nationalities, 52, 64
Nation-states, 3, 52, 64
  development of cultivation and, 222
  foraging in, 216-217
  (*See also* States)
Native Americans:
  animal domestication by, 222
  classification as, 71
  ethnic stereotyping, 410
  expanded family households of, 283
  Handsome Lake religion,
    346-347, 449, 454
  pantribal movement, 445
  performance on intelligence tests, 83-84
  potlatching among, 230-232
  racial classification of, 77
  Shoshone band organization, 288
  (*See also* Plains Indians; *specific tribes*)
Native anthropologists, 466
Native literacy programs, 385
Native taxonomy, 288, 293
Nativistic movements, 346-347

Natural resources, industrialization and,
  397
Natural selection, 79
Naturalistic disease theories, 416
Nature, imposition of culture on, 37
Nature-nurture debate, 316
Naturists, 316
Navajo, pastoral economy of, 222
Nayar culture (India), kinship system of,
  44, 282-283
Ndembu culture (Zambia):
  liminality in, 338-339
  mnemonic function of ritual, 474
Negative reciprocity, 228-230, 232
Négritude, 53
Neocolonialism, of NGOS, 272
Neolocality, 283, 286
  in tribes, 288
Nepal, polyandry in, 311
Netherlands, investment in U.S., 459
Netiquette, 383, 389
New Guinea (*see* Papua-New Guinea)
New World:
  contact with Old World, 394-395
  state formation in, 258
New World Order, end of Cold War and,
  270
Newsgroups, in cyberspace, 383
NGOs (nongovernmental organizations), 26,
  272-273,275
"Nibbling" strategy against domination, 451
Nigeria, 246-248, 253, 322, 326
NII (national information infrastructure),
  383
Nile Delta, schistosomiasis in, 414-415
Nilotes (Upper Nile region), 78
Nilotic populations, 246
Nirvana, Brady Bunch and, 287
Nobel Peace Prize, 452-453
Nomadism, 222-223, 252-253, 435
Nongovernmental organizations (NGOs),
  26, 272-273, 275
Nonindustrial societies:
  concept of scarcity in, 227
  kin attachments in, 285, 293
  marriage in, 306
  negative reciprocity in, 229-230
  production in, 223-225
  rent funds in, 226, 228
  in world system, 402-405
Nonkin groups, 248-251
Nonnuclear family arrangements,
  284-286
Nonsexual marriages, 298
Nonverbal behavior, ritual in, 477
Nonverbal intelligence tests, 83
Norman Conquest, 383
North America:
  attitudes toward touching and affection,
    38-39
  changing gender roles in, 327-329
  divorce in, 308
  effect of mass media in, 456
  family arrangements in, 281, 284-286
  global resources and, 273
  homelessness in, 413-414
  kinship and descent in, 284-286, 293
  political organization in, 238

serial monogamy in, 308
(See also Canada; United States)
North American Free Trade Agreement
(NAFTA), 273
Nuclear family 282-288, 293
in agricultural societies, 324
among foragers, 286,288
in Canada, 281
cultural generality of, 44-45
in foraging societies, 239, 286, 288
as kin group, 44-45
in Nayar culture (India), 44
non nuclear arrangements and, 284-286
in North America, 281, 284-286
social influences on, 282-284
symbolized on film, 470
in United States, 281
Nuer culture (Sudan):
nonsexual marriages in, 298
segmentary lineage organization in,
246-248, 253
vocabulary of, 376
Numajiri, Ryoken, 344-345
Nurturists, 316

Oaxaca (see Valley of Oaxaca)
Oaxaca project for linguistic preservation,
385
Observation, 20-21, 32
transmission of culture by, 36
Observer-oriented research, 20, 24, 32
Occupational specialization, caste systems
and, 303
Oedipus complex, 14-15
Old Order Amish (Pennsylvania), 302
Old World:
contact with New World, 394-395
state formation in, 258
Olduvai Gorge (Tanzania), 9
Olympian religion, 345-346, 350
Olympic Games, 476-477
Open class system, 401
Oppression, ethnic conflict and, 62-64
Osteology, 8
Overconsumption, 402, 404
Overinnovation, 434-435, 439, 447
Overseas employment, anthropology and,
421-422
Ozzie and Harriet, 284-285, 287

Paharis (South Asia), 310-311
Pakistan:
caste system in, 400-401
plural societies in, 54
Palaung culture (Burma), 375
Paleoanthropology, 8
Paleoecology, 8
Palestine, colonialism in, 62
Pantheons, 346
Pantribal modalities, 248-251, 254
Papua-New Guinea, 12, 358-359
Arapesh culture, 12,316
cargo cults, 454-455
culturally appropriate resettlement
project in, 437
Dani culture, 220

Etoro culture, homosexuality in,
323-324
isolated societies in, 394
Kaluli culture, 358-359, 448-449
lack of state formation in, 266
language in, 376
male-female avoidance in, 323-324
Mundugumor culture, 12,316
Sambia culture, 358
state formation lacking in, 266
sugar production in, 395
Tchambuli culture, 12, 316
Voices of the Rainforest project,448 449
Parallel cousins, 299
Parantíns (Brazil), 456
Parental generation, kinship terminology
for, 289-292
Parents:
portrayal in visual fairy tales, 470-471
role in enculturation of children, 39-40
Participant observation, 13, 20-21, 32
Particularity of culture, 37
Pastoral nomadism, 222, 223
attempted conversion to cultivation, 435
tribes of Iran, 252-253
Pastoralism, 222-223, 232
descent groups and, 225
gender-based division of labor in, 223
pastoral economies, 222-223, 252-253
social organization, 251-253
of tribes, 241
Pater, 298
Patrikin, 300-301
Patrilineal descent, 241
Patrilineal moieties, 299
Patrilineal societies:
bifurcate merging kinship terminology
in, 290
distribution of bridewealth in, 307
gender roles in, 322-323
sororate in, 308
strict patrilineality, 300
Patrilineal-virilocal complex, 322-323
Patterns, in culture, 40
Patterns of Culture (Benedict), 357
Peasant communities, leveling mechanisms
in, 61-62
Peasants, 228, 405
effects of Java's green revolution on,
430-431
image of limited good, 364-365
Pelé, 83
Periphery, 395
in American South, 398-399
peripheral nations, 395
Permanent land use, cultivation and, 222
Permanent political regulation, in
chiefdoms, 259
Perpetual expansion, 402
Persian Gulf War, 267
Personal diaries, 20-21
Personal relationships:
in nonstates, 262
as social building blocks, 239
Personal space, 38-39
Personalitic disease theory, 415-416
Personality, 354, 356, 367
cross-cultural studies of, 359-361, 364

cross-cultural studies of differences,
360-361
culture and, 14
culture and psychiatry, 361-363
early research, 356-359, 367
by Margaret Mead, 356-357, 367
by Ruth Benedict, 357
studies of national character, 357-359,
367, 465
enculturation of traits, 40
individual and culture, 354-356
of village head, 244
Personality, concept of, 240-241
Peru: (See also Incas)
Pesticides, adverse effects of, 430
Philippines, 220, 242-243, 317
Phipps, Susie Guillory, 71
Phonemes, 372-373
Phonemics, 373
Phones, 372
Phonetics, 373
Phonological component of meaning, 374
Phonology, 372
Physical (biological) anthropology, 308
309, 410
Pidgin, 45
Plains Indians:
bison hunting by, 249, 250
pantribal societies, 249-250
vision quests of, 338
(See also Native Americans; specific
tribes)
Plantation economies, 395, 405
Plotnicov, Leonard, 304, 305
Plural marriage, 298, 308, 312
polyandry, 308, 310-312
romantic love and, 305
Plural societies, 54, 65
Pokot culture (East Africa), 360, 361
Political action, hypodescent rule and, 72
Political change, ethnic identity and, 50
Political organization:
"big man" and, 241, 245-246, 253, 455
development of, 274-275
in North America, 238
of pastoralists, 251-253
regional, 245-246
Political science:
anthropology and, 13-14
perspective of, 6
Political systems of chiefdoms, 258-259
Political systems of bands and tribes,
237-254
foraging bands, 239 241
pastoralists, 251-253
tribal cultivators, 241-251
types and trends in, 238-239
(See also Bands; Chiefdoms;
Government; Tribes)
Political units, emerging, 445
Political upheavals, imagined communities
and, 52
Politics, importance of verbal skill in, 382
Polity, 238
Polyandry, 308, 310-312
Polygamy 308
Polygyny, 308-310
benefits to market women, 322, 326

Polynesia, 77
    chiefdoms in, 258-259
    social status in, 259-260
    mana in, 337, 349
Polytheism, 336
    Olympian religions, 345-346, 350
Popular culture (U.S.), 38, 457, 461,
    465-479
    anthropology and, 465-467, 478-479
    Disney myth and ritual, 472-475
    fantasy films as myth, 470-472
    football, 467, 476
    religion and, 475-476
    rituals at McDonald's, 476-478
    Star Trek, 468-470
Popular literacy, 384
Population(s):
    controlled by states, 261-262, 274
    differential growth of, 55
    infectious diseases and, 230-231
    Nilotic, 246
    prehistoric, 8
    study of, 8
    regulation by infanticide, 240
Population density:
    of agricultural societies, 221
    food production and, 238
    intensive cultivation and, 426-427
    nutrition and, 429
Population growth:
    differential, multiculturalism and, 55
    in England, 397
    irrigation and, 264
    in less-developed countries, 412
    state formation and, 265-266, 275
    urban anthropology and, 412
Population Services International, 417
Poro secret society, 251
Portuguese colonization of Brazil, 76
Postmodern, 444
"Postmodern moments in world system,"
    445-446
Postmodernism, 444, 448
Postmodernity, 444, 460
Potassium/argon technique, 145, 163
Potlatching, 230-232
    cultural ecology of, 348
Potsherds, 8
Pottery, 225
Poverty:
    in Bangladesh, 400
    correlation with skin color, 75-76
    expanded family households and,
        283-284, 293
    feminization of, 329-331
    homelessness and, 413-414
    industrialization and, 398-399
    marginalization and, 365
    subculture of, in Latin America,
        365-366
Power, 238,261
    social stratification and, 399
Practicing anthropologists (*see* Applied
    anthropology)
Predictor variables, 28, 31
Prehistoric populations, study of, 8
Prehistory, 7
Prejudice, discrimination and, 59-60, 65

Prestige, 240, 261
    converting wealth into, 246
    potlatching and, 230-231
    social stratification and, 399
Primary cultural institutions, 359
Primates, 9
    study of, 8,
Primatology, 9
Primitive Culture (Tylor), 36
Private ownership, 201, 240-241
Private voluntary organizations (PVOs), 272
Private-public contrast, 317-318
Problem-oriented research, 20, 24-25, 32
Production, 223-226
    in industrial societies, 225-226
    means of, 223-225
        labor, technology and
            specialization, 225
        territory, 224-225
    in nonindustrial societies, 223-225
        organization of, 223
    (*See also* Industrialization; Manufacture)
Productivity, in language, 372
Profit motive, 226
Progeny price, 307
Proletarianization, 397
Proletariat, 397, 406
Pronunciation:
    regional variation in, 378
    variations in, 373
"Proper language," 382
Property rights, marriage and, 298
Proselytizing, ethnocide and, 449, 460
Prostitution, race and, 74
Protestant ethic, capitalism and, 366
Protestant Ethic and the Spirit of Capitalism,
    The (Weber), 366
Protestant Reformation, 366
Protolanguage, 382
Pryce, Jonathan, 72
Psychiatry, culturally specific syndromes,
    361-363
Psychological anthropology, 12,14-16, 41,
    354,367
    (*See also* Personality)
Public gatherings, discouraged
    by elites, 451
Public sphere, 317-318
"Public transcript," 450
Puerto Ricans, 51
Puritans, capitalism and, 366
PVOs (private voluntary organizations), 272
Pygmies (Zaire), 242
    language changes, 382

Qashqai tribe (Iran), 252-254
Quebec, independence movement in, 269
Quechua (Inca) language, preservation of,
    385
Quechua language, preservation of, 385
Questionnaires, 22
Quiché Indians (Guatemala), 452-453

Race, 51, 69-85
    as discredited concept in biology, 77-80
    skin color and, 79-80

social race, 71-76
    stratification and intelligence, 80-85
    unionization and, 399
    (*See also* Ethnicity; Social race)
Racial classification, 70-71
    as discredited concept, 77-80
    by phenotype, 75-77
Racial differences by opposition, 73
Racism, 51
Radical Vegetarian League, 477
Rainforest Action Network, 448
Rambo, 457-458
Random samples, 28-29
Rapport, in ethnography, 22, 29
Rathje, William, 7
Rational allocation of resources, 14, 226
"Readers' of text, 457, 461, 465
Real culture, 41
Reciprocity, 228-230, 232
    in industrial societies, 230
Redistribution, 232
    central storage and, 228
    chiefly redistribution, 259-260
    exchange,228
    in industrial societies, 230
    through taxation by states, 263
Reflexive ethnography, 27
Refugees, 62
Regional political organization, "big man" in
    241, 245-246, 253, 455
Regional subcultures, schemata of, 355
Religion, 335-350
    analysis of myth, 341-344, 349-350
        fairy tales, 342, 344
        secular rituals, 344
        structural analysis, 341-342
        visual fairy tales, 470-472
    authority of leaders and, 259, 263
    cultural ecology and, 347-349
        ceremonial feasts, 348-349
        sacred cattle of India, 347-348
    culture and, 345-346, 350
    decreasing participation in, 478
    diffusion of, 41
    "ethnic cleansing" policies and, 57
    as instrument of social change, 346-347
    origins of, 336-341, 349
        animism, 336
        emotional functions, 338
        magic, 337-338,349
        mana and taboo, 336-337, 349
        nature of ritual and, 341
        rites of passage, 338-340
        social functions of ritual, 338
        totemism, 340-341
    political ideology and, 450
    popular culture and, 475-476
    as public ritual, 475-476
    responses to capitalist economy,
        454-455
    subcultures and, 41-42
    symbolism of, 37
    (*See also* Cults; Myth; Ritual; *specific*
        cults and religions)
Religious domination, 449-450
Rent funds, 226, 228
Replacement funds, 226

Research:
　biases in, 466
　in complex societies
　　(see Complex societies)
　emic and etic strategies, 20, 24, 32
　ethnographic (see Ethnography)
　field methods, 27-29,32
　genealogical method of, 20, 23, 32
　local-level, 426
　longitudinal, 25-27
　problem-oriented research, 20, 24-25,
　　32
　statistical analysis of, 29, 31
　survey research (see Survey research)
Research studies, 8-9
　of child rearing, 356, 360
　community studies, 30, 32
　cross-cultural (see Cross-cultural
　　studies)
　Gwembe project (Zambia), 25-27
　of kinship calculation, 280-281
　longitudinal studies, 20, 32
　national character studies, 357-359,
　　367
　of personality (see Personality)
　twin studies on impact of environment,
　　84
Resettlement, state control of population
　and, 262
Residential segregation, 73, 75
Resistance strategies:
　disguised, 451-453, 461
　popular culture and, 457
Resources:
　concentration of, 265-266
　conservation of, 3
　depletion of, Industrial Revolution and,
　　405
　differential access to, 260
　global, 273
　industrialization and, 397, 405
　management by Third World peoples,
　　426
　rational allocation of, 14, 226
Respondents, 28
Return on labor, 401
Returns on capital, 401
Reversals of behavior:
　Halloween, 343
　Japanese "festival of abusive language,"
　　344-345
　liminality and, 339
Revisionist history, Mass media and, 468
Revitalization movements, 346-347, 449
Rhythm of the Saints (Simon), 449
Rice:
　cultivation of, 201-202, 223-224
　development project for production,
　　426-427
　"miracle strain" ~IR-8,429
Rickets, 79
Rites of passage, 338-340, 474
　collective, 340
Ritual:
　nature of, 341, 349
　particularity of, 43-44
　in popular culture, 476-478
　religion as, 475-476

social functions of, 341, 474
Roman Catholicism:
　capitalism and, 366
　Protestantism and, 449-450
Romantic love, marriage and, 304-306
Romanticized timelessness, 27
Romer's rule, 396, 406, 434
Ronald McDonald, 478
Rosie the Riveter 328-329
Ross, Elizabeth, 10
Royal incest, 303, 312
Rule of descent, 71
Rule of hypodescent, 71-72, 85
Rural economic decline, migration and, 58
Rwanda, 268
　Hutu-Tutsi war in, 270-271

Sacred cattle (India), 347-348
Saito, Hiromi, 380, 381
Saito, Julie, 381
Salinas Pedraza, Jesús, 384-385
Salish culture (North Pacific Coast),
　230-231
Salvage archaeology, 410-411
Salvage ethnography, 26
Sambia culture (Papua-New Guinea), 358
Samhain (Day of the Dead), 343
Samoa, 12,13
　ethnic associations of Samoan
　　immigrants, 413
　Freeman's research in, 356-357
　Mead's research in, 355-357
Samples, 28,29
San (bushmen), 78, 217, 459
　bands of, 217-218
　Dobe !Kung San, 217, 243
　namesake system of, 218, 239
　socioeconomic system of, 242-243
　(See also !Kung San)
Sapir, Edward, 375
Sapir-Whorf hypothesis, 375
SATs (Scholastic Achievement Tests), 82
Scarcity, concept of, 227
Schema theory, 354-356, 367
Schemata, 354-355, 367
Schistosomiasis, 414-415
Scholastic Achievement Tests (SATs), 82
Science, 11
Science and technology studies (STS), 383
Scientific medicine, 417-418
SE [Standard (American) English],
　372-373, 377
Sebei culture (East Africa), 360-361
Second World, 62
Secondary cultural institutions, 359-360
Secret societies, 251
Sectorial fallowing, 221
Secular rituals, 344
Sedentism,
　alteration in gender roles and, 320
　foraging and, 239, 243
　potlatching and, 229
　unsuccessful conversion to, 435
Segmental appeal, promotion by mass
　media, 269

Segmentary lineage organization (SLO),
　246-248, 253
Segregation, 59
　residential, 73, 75
Semai culture (Malaysia), 229
Semantic component of meaning, 374
Semantics, 376
Semiperipheral nations, 395
Separation phase, in rites of passage, 338
Serial monogamy, in North America, 308
Sertão (Brazil):
　pilgrimages in, 473
　sisal scheme in, 427-429
*Sex and Temperament in Three Primitive
　Societies* (Mead), 12, 316
Sex ratios:
　plural marriage and, 309
　polyandry and, 310-311
Sexual dimorphism, 316
Sexual monopoly, marriage as, 298
Sexual orientation, hypodescent and, 71-72
Sexuality:
　in Arembepe and Betsileo cultures, 358
　cultural molding of, 323-324
　effect of Mead's work on study of, 13
　heterosexuality, AIDS and, 416-417
　transsexuality, 326-327
　varieties of, 358-359
Sexually transmitted diseases (STDs), 415
SfAA (Society for Applied Anthropology),
　410
Shamanic religion, 345-346, 350
Shamans (curers), 239, 345-346, 417
Shantytowns *(favelas),* 413-414, 459
Shifting cultivation, 219
Shimakura, Mari, 380
"Shouting" in cyberspace, 386
Shrines, pilgrimage to, 473-474
Shwara language, preservation of, 385
Silent barter (trade), 230
Simon, Paul, 449
Single-parent households, 281, 284, 286
　feminization of poverty and, 330
Sisal scheme (Brazil), 427-429
Sisal workers, inadequate nutrition of,
　428-429
Situational negotiation of social identity, 51
Skin color:
　explanation of, 79-80, 85
　racial classification and, 77-78
Slash-and-burn cultivation, 219
Slave religion, 451
Slavery:
　in Brazil, 75 76, 401
　community formation and, 451
Slavs (Muslim), "ethnic cleansing" policy
　against, 56-57
SLO (segmentary lineage organization),
　246-248, 253
Slovenia, 56
Snow White and the Seven Dwarfs, 472
Snyder, Jimmy ("the Greek"), 83
Soap operas, 458
Soccer, 467
Social acceptance, leveling mechanisms
　and, 61-62
Social aspect of ritual, 341, 474

Social change, religion as instrument of, 346-347
Social class (*see* Caste systems; Class; Social stratification)
Social complexity, measures of, 8
Social construction, kin terms as, 280-281
Social funds, 226
Social identity, situational negotiation of, 51
Social ills, industrialization and, 397
Social indicators, 28, 31
Social life, economy and, 217-218
Social paternity, 298
Social race, 71-76
    differences by opposition, 72-75
    hypodescent rule, 71 72
    phenotype and, 75-77
    (*See also* Ethnicity; Race)
Social reality, cyberspace and, 388-389
Social situational learning, 36
Social stratification, 261
    dimensions of, 274, 399
    effects of Java's green revolution, 431
    (*See also* Caste systems; Class)
Social systems:
    change in structure or form of, 16
    in world-system theory, 395
Social universals, 43
Socially significant relationships, 298
Society(ies), 2
    agricultural (*see* Agricultural societies)
    complex (*see* Complex societies)
    egalitarian, 241, 243
    foragers (*see* Foraging societies)
    horticultural (*see* Horticultural societies)
    industrial (*see* Industrial societies)
    isolated, 394
    kin-based, 23
    matrifocal, 322
    matrilineal (*see* Matrilineal societies)
    nonindustrial (*see* Nonindustrial societies)
    pantribal, 249-250
    patrilineal (*see* Patrilineal societies)
    plural, 54, 65
    tribal (*see* Tribes)
Society for Applied Anthropology (SfAA), 410
Sociocultural anthropology (*see* Cultural anthropology)
Socioeconomic stratification:
    in chiefdoms, 260
    in Java, 429-430
Sociolinguistic variation, 378
Sociolinguistics, 372, 377-382, 389, 411
    gender contrasts, 379-381
    linguistic diversity, 377, 379
    social categories and, 378-381
    symbolic domination, 379-382
Sociolinguists, 9
Sociology, cultural anthropology and, 12-13
Sociopolitical organization, regulation of interrelations and, 238
Sociopolitical typology, 238, 253
Sodalities, 249
Somali Television, 459
Song battles, 240

Sororate, 308, 312
"Soul loss" *(susto)*, 361, 363, 416, 419
Sound of Music, The, 478
"Soundscape," 449
South Africa:
    apartheid in, 59, 81, 401
South America:
    isolated societies in, 394
    (*See also specific countries*)
Southeast Asia:
    Lakher culture, 300-301
    (*See also specific countries*)
Soviet Union:
    colonialism in, 62-64
    gender-based division of labor in, 318
Spain:
    anti-Basque campaign in, 62
    Carnival outlawed by Franco, 452
Special-interest audiences, 269
Specialization:
    as means of production, 225
    in nonindustrial societies, 232
Spirit Cries, The (Hart), 449
Spiritual beings, beliefs in, 337
Sports:
    cultural standards and, 82-83
    football as popular culture, 467, 476
Sri Lanka, caste system in, 400-401
Standard (American) English (SE), 372-373, 377
Stanford, Craig 13,
Star Trek, as popular culture, 468-470
Star Wars, 342, 448, 457, 468, 472, 476
    compared *to Wizard of Oz,* 470-472
Starship Enterprise, 468
State formation:
    lacking in Papua-New Guinea, 266
    in Madagascar, 271-272
    in Mesopotamia, 258, 266, 274
    multivariate theory of, 265-266, 274
    in Old World, 258
    in Western Hemisphere, 258, 274
States, 3, 52, 64, 238
    challenges to, 266-274
        collapse of mass culture, 268-269
        decline of government, 274-275
        globalization and media, 267-268
        nongovernmental organizations, 272
        rights movements, 272-273
        world disorder, 269-272
    development of cultivation and, 222
    origin of, 264-266
        ecological diversity and, 264, 275
        formation by force, 264-265
        hydraulic agriculture and, 264, 275
        long-distance trade and, 264, 275
        multivariate theory of, 265-266
        socioeconomic stratification in, 261
    specialized functions in, 261-264
        enforcement systems, 263, 274
        fiscal systems, 263-264, 274
        judicial systems, 262-263, 274
        population control, 261-262, 274
    status systems in, 260-261
    territorial basis of, 267
Statistical analysis of research, 29, 31
Status(es), 50-51
    achieved, 50,401

    ascribed, 50-51, 75-76, 401
    in chiefdoms, 259-261
    economic, 261
    ethnicity and status shifting, 51
    females economic determinants of, 317
    in matrilineal societies, 320-322
    speech patterns and, 379
    stratum endogamy and, 260
    (*See also* Class; Social stratification; Wealth)
Status shifting, 51
STDs (sexually transmitted diseases), 41
Stereotypes:
    in configurationalism, 357
    of foraging societies, 243
    gender stereotypes, 317, 330
    of homosexuality in Brazil, 326- 327
    in Japan, 73
    in language, 378
    of Native Americans, 410
    prejudice and, 59
Stimulus diffusion, 456, 461
Sting, 448
Stipulated descent (clans), 242
Stonehenge, 258
Stratification systems, open and closed, 400-402, 406
Stratified societies, 81
Stratum, 261
Stratum endogamy, status and, 260
Structuralism, 341-342
STS (science and technology studies), 383
Student-peasant agricultural projects, 430-431
Style shifts in language, 377
Subaltern, 268
Subculture of poverty, 365-366
Subcultures, 41-42, 46
    academic subculture, 466-467
    in ethnic groups, 50
    regional, schemata of, 355
Subgroups, in language, 382
Subordinate stratum, 261
Sub-Saharan Africa:
    food production in, 429
    Subsistence economy:
        goals and values of, 434
        reduced gender stratification and, 325
        shift to cash economy and, 427-429, 438-439
Subsistence funds, 226
Substantive rationality, 14
Sudan, 246-248, 253, 298, 359, 376
Sugar, trade in, 395
Suharto (President of Indonesia), 430
Sukarno (President of Indonesia), 430
Summer Institute of Linguistics, 385
Sumptuary goods, 263-264
Super Bowl, 467
Supernatural, 336
Supernatural forces, beliefs in, 337
Superordinate stratum, 261
Surface structure of language, 374
Survey research, 27-28
    ethnography and, 29, 32
    statistical analysis of, 29, 31
    use in modern context, 466

Susto, 361, 363, 416, 419
Symbiosis, in pastoralism, 222
Symbolic capital, language as, 382
Symbolic domination, in sociolinguistics, 379-382
Symbolic thought, dependence of culture on, 36-37
Symbolism:
    in Disney myth and ritual, 473-475
    in football, 467
    in language, 37
    in *Star Trek,* 468-470
    in visual fairy tales, 470-472
Symbols, 36-37, 46
Syncretisms, 453-457, 461
    cargo cults, 454-455, 461
    cultural imperialism, 455-457, 461
Syntactic Structures (Chomsky), 373
Syntax, 372
Sysops, 387
Systemic perspective of anthropology, 410

Taboos:
    incest taboo (*see* Incest taboo)
    mana and, 336-337, 349
    racism and, 73
Taijin kyofusho (Japan), 362-363
Tajikistan, cultural colonialism in, 63-64
Tanala culture (Madagascar), 360
Tanzania, 319
    crime in, 271
    Olduvai Gorge (*see* Olduvai Gorge)
Tasaday culture (Philippines), 242-243
Taxation, by states, 263
Taxonomy
    native taxonomy, 288, 293
Tchambuli culture (Papua-New Guinea), 12, 316
Teamwork, on *Star Trek,* 470
Technology:
    AIT [*see* Advanced information technology (AIT)]
    as means of production, 225
    unequal access in United States, 386-387
Teeth (*see* Dentition)
Telenovelas, 458
Television:
    effect on traditional cultures, 456-457
    "family" programming, 478
    influence on American mass culture, 287, 388
    as source of cultural change, 458-459
    (*See also* Film industry; Mass media)
Terracing, 220, 221
"Terraforming," 447, 460
Terrestrial primates:
    (*See also* Arboreal primates; Primates; *specific species*)
Territorial basis of states, 267
Territory food production and, 224-225
Text, 457,461, 465
Thanksgiving, 477-478
    as American myth, 468 469
Theft, 240
Third World, 62, 395, 406
    criticism of development, 432

culturally appropriate development in, 436
development in (*see* Development)
    economy of, 447
    effect of MNCs on, 447
    effects of industrialization on, 404-405
    increasing food production, 429-431
    resource management in, 426
    urbanization and, 412-413
Tiv culture (Nigeria), 246-248, 253
Tonowi, 245
Totemism, 340-341
Totems, 242,340, 473, 475
Trade:
    Eskimo trade partners, 239
    long-distance, state formation and, 264, 275
    silent barter, 230
    state control of, 263
    in sugar, 395
    transoceanic, 394
    (*See also* Marketing)
Trade unions, 398
Trade-oriented economy, 394
Transecting groups, 383
Transformational-generative grammar, 372-375, 389
Transformism (*see* Evolution)
Transhumance, in pastoral economies, 222-223
Transnational groups, linked by AIT, 383
Transnational identity, television's role in, 459
Transnational migration:
    continuance of diversity, 460
    domination, 447-450, 460
        development and environmentalism, 447-449
        religious domination, 449-450
    postmodernity 444-447,460
        cultural contact, 446-447
        postmodern moments, 445-446
    remaking culture, 457-460
        culture of consumption, 459-460
        indigenizing culture, 457-458
        mass media and, 458-459
        popular culture, 457, 461
    resistance and survival, 450-453, 460-461
        human rights struggle in Guatemala, 452-453
        weapons of the weak, 451-453
    syncretism, 453-457,461
        cargo cults, 454-455, 461
        cultural imperialism and, 455-457, 461
    (*See also* Immigration; Migration)
Transnationalism, 267
Transoceanic trade, 394
Transsexuality, 326-327
Transvestism, 326-327
    in shamans, 345-346
Tribes (tribal societies), 238
    ambilineal descent in, 288
    Basseri tribe (Iran), 252, 254
    "big man" as leader, 241, 245-246, 253, 455

descent-group organization, 241-243, 288
horticultural or pastoral economy of, 241
lineages and clans in, 288
marriage in, 303, 306-308
neolocality in, 288
nomadic tribes, 252-253, 254
pastoralism of, 241
Qashqai tribe (Iran), 252-254
segmentary lineage organization of, 246-248
social linkages in, 248-251
social organization of, 288
unilocality in, 288
village head of, 243-244
village raiding by, 244 245
(*See also* Bands; Chiefdoms; Government)
Tripartite racial classification, 77
Trobriand Islands, 13
    islanders' belief in magic, 338
    Malinowski's work in, 14-15,29
Tropics, 79
Tuyuc, Rosalina, 433
Twin studies, on impact of environment, 84
Tylor, Edward Burnett, 336, 349
Tzintzuntzan (Mexico), migration from, 444

Uganda, Jie culture, 473
UN Charter, 272-273
UNCED (United Nations Conference on the Environment and Development), 445
Uncle, 281
Underdifferentiation, 435-436, 439, 447
Understanding Popular Culture (Fiske), 457
Underwood, Barbara, 428
Unequal rights, 262
Unilateral descent rule, incest taboo and, 299
Unilineal descent, 241
Unilocal rules of postmarital residence, 288-289
Unionization, 398-399
United Nations, 272-273
United Nations Conference on the Environment and Development (UNCED), 445
United States:
    changing gender roles in, 327-329
    collapse of mass culture in, 268-269, 275
    cotton production in, 395
    film industry in, 458-459, 470-472
    foreign investment in, 459
    Halloween in, 343
    hypodescent in, 71-72
    importance of multiculturalism in, 55, 58
    independence movement in Quebec and, 269
    kin attachments in, 285-286
    measures of social complexity in, 28
    Native Americans (*see* Native Americans; Plains Indians; *specific tribes*)
    nuclear family in, 281

pop culture in (see Popular culture)
slavery in, 401
subcultures in, 41-42
unequal access to technology in, 386-387
urban anthropology in (see Urban anthropology)
variations in pronunciation, 378-382
United States Census Bureau, 417
Universal Declaration of Human Rights, 272-273
Universal grammar, 373
Universality of culture, 43
Untouchables, 400
Upright bipedalism (see Bipedal locomotion)
Urban anthropology, 30-31, 412-414, 421
poverty and homelessness, 413-414
urban versus rural areas, 412-413
Urbanization:
cultural diffusion and, 412
face-to-face groups and, 388
Third World and, 412-413
U.S. Agency for International Development (USAID), 420,446
Usenet, 383
Uses of Enchantment: The Meaning and Importance of Fairy Tales (Bettelheim), 342
Uxorilocality, 288, 290
gender stratification and, 320-322

Valentine's Day, 39
Value systems:
culture of poverty and, 365
of subsistence producers, 434
Variables, 28
Variation, anthropological focus on, 464
Varna, 303
Vertical mobility, 401
Village head, 243-244
Village Headmaster, The (Nigeria), 458
Virilocality, 288-290
gender stratification and, 320-322
Virtual communities, effect on face-to-face groups, 388-389
Virtual worlds, 388
Vision quests, of Plains Indians, 338
Vitamin D, skin color and, 79-80
Vocabulary, 375-376
Voices of the Rainforest (Hart/Feld), 448-449
Voodoo (vodun), 453-454

Wallace, Alfred Russell, 79,
Walt Disney World, 472-475
Warfare:
among Yanomami, 322-323
Hutu-Tutsi war in Rwanda, 270-271
imagined communities and, 52
state formation and, 265-266, 275
Warrior associations, 249
Warsaw Pact nations (Second World), 62
Wealth (economic status), 261
access to cyberspace and, 386
of "big man" 245

individual, economic development and, 436
stratification and, 399, 401-402
Weber, Max, 397, 406
Well-informed informants, 20, 24, 28, 32, 227
finding, 22
Wendy's, 478
Western Hemisphere, formation of states in, 258, 274
Western medicine, 417-419
Westernization, 447
Wheel of fortune, 468
Whitten, Norman, 385
WHO (World Health Organization), 416
Whorf, Benjamin Lee, 375
Wife stealing, disputes over, 240
Wizard of Oz, the, 342, 468, 472
compared to Star Wars, 470-472
Women (see Females)
Wood, Natalie, 326
Working class (proletariat), 397, 406
World Bank, 426,447
World Conference of Indigenous Peoples, 445
World Health Organization (WHO), 416
"World music," 448
World stratification system, 399-400
World system, 3, 393-406
emergence of, 394-396
industrial and nonindustrial societies in, 402-405
industrialization and, 396-397
stratification and, 397-402
World Wide Fund for Nature (WWF), 420
World-system perspective, 6
World-system theory, global culture in, 402
Worldview, 364-366
limited good, 364-365
Protestant ethic and capitalism, 366
subculture of poverty, 365-366
World Wide Web, 383, 387
Wudu (ritual ablution), schistosomiasis and, 415
WWF (World Wide Fund for Nature), 420

Yamamoto, Harumi, 380
Yanomami culture (Brazil; Venezuela):
marriage to cross cousins in, 299-300
specialization in, 225
village head of, 243-244, 253
village raiding and, 244-245
warfare among, 322- 323
Yugoslavia (former), 56-57

Zaire:
distribution of condoms in, 417
Efe culture in, 10, 217
Zambia, Gwembe research project, 25-27
Zuni culture (American Southwest), 357